PERSONNEL: The Human Problems of Management

GEORGE STRAUSS

Professor of Business Administration, School of Business Administration, and Associate Director, Institute of Industrial Relations, University of California, Berkeley

LEONARD R. SAYLES

Professor of Business Administration, Graduate School of Business, Columbia University

Prentice-Hall, Inc., Englewood Cliffs, New Jersey

PERSONNEL

The Human Problems of Management

Second Edition

To Our Fathers: Frank Strauss, and in Memory of Robert Sayles

PERSONNEL: The Human Problems of Management

Second Edition

George Strauss and Leonard R. Sayles

Design by John J. Dunleavy

C

Current printing (last digit):
11 10 9 8 7 6 5

PRENTICE-HALL INTERNATIONAL, INC., *London*
PRENTICE-HALL OF AUSTRALIA, PTY., LTD., *Sydney*
PRENTICE-HALL OF CANADA, LTD., *Toronto*
PRENTICE-HALL OF INDIA PVT. LTD., *New Delhi*
PRENTICE-HALL OF JAPAN, INC., *Tokyo*

Many schools of business, recognizing that every manager must cope directly with human problems and not simply pass them along to the staff personnel department, have integrated human-relations/personnel courses into their core curriculum. This book is addressed to the student of business who wants to equip himself to deal effectively with the human problems of the business organization. Although we focus our attention on the business institution, instructors of courses in the closely allied fields of public, educational, and hospital personnel administration will find that much of the content is also relevant to their particular needs.

Traditionally, personnel texts have emphasized description: "This is what companies do or don't do. This is the easy way of handling people." Or else personnel problems have been treated as a series of clinical cases: Each problem is unique and must be solved by a rational analysis of all the facts that are peculiar to it. Personnel problems also have been regarded as falling within the province of one or another of various specialties: industrial sociology, industrial engineering and management, industrial relations, or social psychology.

We believe that this subject is broader than any of these approaches would suggest. The manager needs analytical techniques that go beyond the transitory practices of specific companies at specific moments in their history. Otherwise he is limited to the rote application of techniques that may be wholly irrelevant to the wide range of problems with which he will be faced in the course of his career. Or, if he limits himself exclusively to clinical procedures, he will fail to develop the managerial scope and flexibility that derive from the ability to fashion valid generalizations.

We have tried to avoid choosing sides among competing approaches. In order to make informed decisions on the human problems of the organization, the manager needs knowledge about individual motivation and behavior in small groups and large organizations, about the impact of technology, about union-management relationships, about the techniques of industrial engineering, and about the skills of face-to-face supervision. He must also have insight into the way in which large organizations function, and into their problems of structure and efficiency. Only then, we believe, can he make a realistic, rational approach to such specific areas of personnel policy as selection, wage and salary administration, and training.

Consequently, what we have tried to say in the chapters ahead does not fit neatly into such categories as "theoretical" or "applied." In one sense this book is "theoretical": We have sought to examine the contributions of the behavioral sciences in the context of management's human-relations problems. But in another sense it is "applied": We have sought, for example, to present specific techniques for evaluating jobs and performance, for conducting time studies, and for establishing safety programs.

Our objective in writing this book has been to suggest a systematic, unified approach to the personnel problems of the business organization. The answers we provide are not simple "do this" or "do that" propositions. In fact, in many areas we cannot even suggest answers; we can only try to frame the "good questions." We do, however, try to suggest a rewarding approach and an analytical framework; we leave for the real-life situation the weighing of variables and risks that must inevitably precede any final decision.

We are also aware that many of our generalizations have very serious limitations. Given the incomplete, imperfect state of our present knowledge, the human problems of organization are not easily or certainly solved. The reader should not mistake the seeming finality of the printed word for incontrovertible truth, for there are many contradictory studies and observations in this field. We hope that the student will not permit the semblance of conviction on our part to dull his own critical judgments and his motivation to think through important problems for himself.

The second edition endeavors to take into account behavioral and organizational research completed during the past half dozen years. For example, our views concerning styles of supervision and leadership patterns have shifted somewhat, given the new work that has been done in this field. There is more emphasis on personnel problems involving technical, professional, and managerial personnel, reflecting the increasing importance of the "white collar" segment in contemporary organizations. We have also endeavored to treat more systematically the function and role of Personnel in the organization.

At the end of most of the chapters, we have placed case problems designed to highlight and dramatize the complex relationships explored in the chapters themselves. We have tried to present representative problems faced by administrators in a variety of organizations. The reader is asked to draw upon both theory and application in solving actual problems taken from our research and teaching files. Each case problem invites the reader to consider the administrative decisions that must be made, the evidence needed as the basis for these decisions, and the analytical framework within which the administrator may act.

We have made frequent cross references to alert the reader to interrelationships among the chapters. And yet each chapter has been written as an independent unit and may be dealt with as such. Instructors will find that they can tailor the sequence and number of chapters assigned to suit the requirements and length of their specific courses.

Business education has been criticized for lack of analytical content, for dullness and "thinness," for failure to come to grips with essential problems, and for normative assumptions. In the last chapter of this book we address ourselves directly to some of the criticisms that have been aimed at the "human-relations movement." We sincerely hope that this book will contribute in some measure to the development of business courses that will excite and challenge the serious student.

Over the years many teachers and colleagues have contributed to this book. When we were graduate students at MIT in the late 1940's, our interests and ideas in this field were influenced by the late Douglas McGregor and by Charles Myers and Paul Pigors; at Cornell, William F. Whyte was a colleague, teacher, and friend. The second edition benefited from the assistance of Professors Arthur Butler, Vaughn Blankenship, and John Drotning of the University of Buffalo; Professors Ivar Berg, Margaret Chandler, and Fred Goldner of Columbia; Professors Lyman Porter and Raymond Miles of the University of California at Berkeley; and Professor Richard Miller of the University of Wisconsin. Mr. Donald B. Miller of IBM and Mr. Joseph Carney of American Metal Climax have added many ideas. Our secretaries, the Misses Janet Gehl and Joyce Phelan, are especially thanked.

George Strauss and Leonard Sayles

Contents

vii

INDIVIDUALS, JOBS, AND GROUPS

Studying the human problems of organizations can be exciting but frustrating too. As with so many problems in behavioral science, one often feels the need to know everything before one can know something. Human organizations are organic in the sense that the various parts are interdependent. For example, you can't understand why an engineer complains about the work he receives from the model shop without knowing something about his needs (and those of his counterpart in the other department), the structure and policies of the larger organization, small group norms, how various supervisors behave, and many other things.

But one has to begin some place to build knowledge and understanding. We think that it is easier to start with some of the building blocks of the organization—individuals, jobs, and groups—and then look at the complex interrelationships involved in administration.

Individuals place a variety of demands on their work; in fact, the workplace is one of the most important institutions for providing human satisfactions. What motivates people? Do individuals differ in the relative importance they place on various needs and how stable are these demands? These are some of the questions which Chapter 1 ("The Meaning of Work") endeavors to answer by mustering relevant research findings.

But individual demands or needs are just one side of the equation. Different kinds of jobs provide more or less of various human satisfactions. In other words, management ought to be able to predict the impact of technological decisions on human reactions to work. Chapter 2 ("Technology and Job Satisfaction: Blue-Collar Work") contrasts the effect of craft, machine-tending, and assembly-line work.

These three categories include the more traditional types of manual jobs. Automation and the growing importance of administrative, professional, and service work introduce quite distinctive new job patterns. The reactions of employees to these developments are examined in Chapter 3 ("Technology and Job Satisfaction: Automation and White-Collar Work").

Motivation and on-the-job behavior are influenced profoundly by still another factor: group identifications. In a sense, every organization gets fractionated over time into a number of smaller groups because people need the close, more personal associations these groups provide in contrast to the effects of the more impersonal, larger institutions. In turn, these informal groups come to modify both individual needs and objectives, the character of the job and the organization. The dynamics of small group elaborations are analyzed in Chapter 4 ("Work Groups and Informal Organization").

Another type of group which has an impact on the larger organization is the labor union, which is, of course, a much more formal, complex entity than the work group. Not every firm has union relations, but because of their crucial importance to the human problems of management and their pervasive influence, it would be unrealistic to endeavor to understand the functioning of organizations without some knowledge of union structure and behavior. Chapter 5 ("Unions and Labor Relations") only endeavors to introduce the subject; you must depend on other sources for a more complete treatment of this technical problem.

The Meaning of Work

It's hard to imagine the changes in human life that have come about in western civilization over the past century and a half. For thousands of years the material conditions of our existence (the way food, clothing, and shelter were produced) remained relatively unchanged. And then, since 1800, at an ever faster pace, we have had steam engines, cotton gins, locomotives, the telegraph, automobiles, airplanes, radio, atomic energy, and space explorations. Our way of life has changed unbelievably—but perhaps in no area has the change been greater than in the way men earn their living.

Let us look for a moment at the "industrial relations" of yesteryear—for only by examining the past can we bring into focus the problems of today. Back in 1800, 90 per cent of the American people lived on farms, and the percentage was not much lower in Europe. Although there were large plantations in some sections of the country, most men owned and worked their own farms, receiving aid at harvest time when neighbor helped neighbor. The family was the basic economic unit. Father worked in the fields. Mother processed the food (in a way housewives rarely do in this age of supermarkets), cooked the meals, spun the wool, made the clothes, and did the household chores. Brother and sister were assigned simple tasks almost as soon as they could walk. Labor relations and family relations were the same.

Economically, the farm was almost self-sufficient. Of course, with a cash crop the farmer might buy an ax, a flintlock, gunpowder, and such luxuries as dishes, sugar, shoes, and books (though luxuries could be either fashioned at home or done without). If the crop was poor, life was less comfortable, but few people worried about unemployment.

A man was his own boss. No one could tell him when to plant or harvest, or could give him a written warning if he started work three minutes late. True, nature and the weather might prove more tyrannical than any foreman, but what a man produced was his own. His motivation was clear: If he was lazy, his own family suffered.

Furthermore (in contrast to what prevails in many jobs today) his efforts brought tangible fruit. Looking at his growing fields, he could say with real

3

satisfaction, "Look what *I* have created." He, his family, his life, and his job were all tied together in a rich oneness that many look back on with nostalgia. (Few farmers today, however, would give up the benefits of tractors or electricity, nor would their wives long enjoy dipping candles and spinning wool. The earlier farmer's hours were long and his frustrations many. The continuing exodus from farm to city over the last century indicates that, for all its disadvantages, many prefer our urban civilization to the simple country life.)

Even in earlier days, in the city perhaps the farmer had a younger brother, a journeyman wagon-maker. He was a wage-earner, not his own boss. And yet, how different the meaning of his job was to him than to his great-great-grandson who tightens bolts on the final line of Chevy No. 3! In the first place, he knew he would not be a journeyman for long. If he saved his money, he might expect to set himself up in business within a few years.

Relations between himself and his boss were simple and easy—at times almost like the relations between father and son. The older man taught the younger what he knew and together they performed the same job. The work was creative and satisfying. Building a wagon required skill, and when the job was finished the worker could see what he had done. He could be proud of his craftsmanship and sure of his place in the world.

Such was the way some men earned their living not so many years ago—even though our picture is admittedly somewhat idyllic. After all, a slave on a plantation or a peasant in Europe was often just a working beast, and few wage-earners had the sense of skill enjoyed by our journeyman wagon-maker. In fact, it may well be "that in modern society there is a far greater scope for skill and craftsmanship than in any previous society, and that far more people are in a position to use such skills." [1]

THE IMPACT OF THE INDUSTRIAL REVOLUTION

The last century and a half has brought a dramatic revolution, not only in what we make, but in how we make it. The industrial revolution has been a revolution not only in technology but also in human relations. As technology grew more and more complex, people became more dependent on one another and the problems of working together became more troublesome. Today the typical American is no longer his own boss; he is not a farmer, but a city dweller. Furthermore, the industrial revolution has brought major changes in what it means to be an employee.

Specialization

The journeyman wagon-maker did a whole job from beginning to end. But one of the distinguishing marks of the industrial revolution is specialization.

---

[1] J. A. C. Brown, *The Social Psychology of Industry* (Baltimore: Pelican, 1954), p. 207. See also Robert Blauner, "Work Satisfaction and Industrial Trends in Modern Society," Walter Galenson and S. M. Lipset, eds., *Labor and Trade Unionism* (New York: Wiley, 1960).

Here is Adam Smith's famous description of the changes that were taking place in pinmaking almost two centuries ago, at the dawn of the industrial revolution in England:

> A workman not educated to this business . . . could scarce, perhaps, with utmost industry, make one pin a day, and certainly not make twenty. But in the way in which this business is now carried on, not only the whole work is a peculiar trade, but it is divided into a number of branches, of which the greater part are likewise peculiar trades. One man draws out the wire, another straightens it, a third cuts it, a fourth points it, a fifth grinds it at the top for receiving the head; to make the head requires two or three distinct operations; to put it on is a peculiar business. . . . I have seen a small manufactory of this sort where ten men only were employed and where some of them consequently performed two or three distinct operations. But though they were very poor, and therefore but indifferently accommodated with the necessary machinery, they could, when they exerted themselves, make upwards of forty-eight thousand pins in a day.[2]

Economically, specialization has brought great advantages. But it has brought many disadvantages as well: boredom and the loss of a sense of individual importance, of accomplishment, of pride in work. How much satisfaction can a man obtain from spending his entire day pointing pins?

Further, workers feel that they are shackled to work processes they have had no hand in developing. The Industrial Engineering Department frequently determines every detail of the job, depriving the individual of any chance to show initiative or originality. Specialization has sharpened the dividing line between workers and management.

Specialization has also developed within management. Instead of a single owner-manager with complete control over the plant, or a foreman with complete control over his department, we have staff departments such as engineering, production scheduling, purchasing, and personnel. No man performs more than a small part of the whole job; no man has significant control over what he does. A dozen staff agencies may be involved in making a simple decision, and the worker is at the very bottom: "Everybody gets consulted but me. I just carry out their orders."

Opportunity To Get Ahead

To make the industrial revolution possible, elaborate machinery was necessary—and machinery requires money. The journeyman craftsman needed little more than his own tools to set himself up in business, but the man on the automobile assembly line cannot hope to compete with General Motors. Unless he wants to operate a small store or a gas station, the modern worker has far less chance to be his own boss than did his great-grandfather.

Even after the average man's chance to become an *independent* industrialist had vanished, the avenue of promotion within a company remained wide open for many years. Fifty years ago an able and ambitious man might conceivably

---

2 *The Wealth of Nations* (New York: Modern Library, 1937), p. 4.

work himself up from sweeper to president. Today, as our technology and business life become more and more complicated, opportunities for the noncollege man become increasingly limited. Sociologists call this phenomenon *blocked mobility*. A man can still get ahead through hard work, but unless he is a college graduate it is a much more arduous task than it used to be.

**Increasing Size
of Business Organization**

The industrial revolution has made business organizations larger and the boss more remote. The journeyman wagon-maker had no trouble talking to his boss; communication was easy. Today, however, a man may spend his lifetime in a steel mill and never talk to the plant manager, let alone the president.

The owner of a wagon shop could easily supervise all phases of manufacture. In a business like AT&T, supervision and coordination require the services of thousands of executives. All this leads to the process of bureaucratization, the making of rules that restrict individual discretion even to the point where top executives find themselves tied down.

Constant Change

In the simple society of the early 1800's, changes were rare. Behavior was governed by tradition: There was no need to tell a man what to do—all he had to do was follow the patterns laid down by his ancestors.

Modern industry is subject to constant change. The very fact of change creates two types of problem: (1) Less can be left to routine; careful planning, deliberate orders, and elaborate communications are essential. Since personal experience and tradition are less valued, there is a correspondingly greater need for rules and regulations. (2) People normally resist change, particularly when it is imposed upon them. Consequently the problems of motivating people to work together have grown more complex.

In short, the industrial revolution has done wonders to make life easier for all of us, but at a serious cost in terms of the rewards and enjoyments that individuals derive from their jobs.

The rest of this chapter will be concerned with three questions: What sorts of needs are satisfied through work? How can these needs be ranked in relative importance? And how important as a source of satisfaction is one's *job*, compared with other means of satisfaction available in life? [3]

NEEDS SATISFIED BY WORKING

Although the authors recognize that all attempts to categorize needs are somewhat artificial, in this book we shall speak of three forms of need satisfaction:

---

[3] We are indebted to our teacher, the late Douglas McGregor, for many of the concepts discussed in this chapter.

1. *Physical and security needs.* These relate to the satisfaction of bodily functions, such as hunger, thirst, shelter, and the like, as well as the need to be secure in the enjoyment of these.

2. *Social needs.* Since human beings are dependent on each other, there are some needs which can be satisfied only when the individual is helped or recognized by other people.

3. *Egoistic needs.* These relate to man's desire to be independent, to do things on his own and to sense accomplishment.

Another way of categorizing needs is in terms of the means by which they are satisfied. Some forms of satisfaction are enjoyed *off the job*—for example, a man spends his pay check after work and away from the job. Other needs are satisfied through having a happy, satisfying work environment *around the job.* A third form of satisfaction can be obtained only through the process of working and so can be called intrinsic or *through-the-job* satisfaction. As we shall see in later chapters (Chapter 6 in particular), this three-way distinction is critical for the motivation of employees. When management emphasizes off-the-job satisfactions, it assumes, in effect, that work is a punishment which employees endure in exchange for rewards to be enjoyed after work. Managers who stress around-the-job satisfactions seek to make the work environment a pleasant one, but do not provide direct, positive motivation for men to work harder. To the extent that through-the-job satisfactions are provided, employees work hard; the harder they work the greater their satisfaction.

As will be seen, both sets of categories—types of needs and ways in which needs are satisfied—overlap a bit and many needs can be placed in more than one category. Nor is there any hard-and-fast relationship between the sets of categories. To a considerable extent, however, physical needs are satisfied off the job, social needs are satisfied through personal contacts around the job, whereas egoistic needs are chiefly satisfied through the job. There are, of course, many exceptions to this "rule." For example, safe working conditions satisfy an important physical need, yet they are enjoyed on the job; status is a social need, yet the status derived from holding an important position is enjoyed away from work as much as on the job; praise is another social need, yet praise from one's boss is often best obtained through doing one's job well; a salesman may satisfy his social needs through his work—the more sales he makes, the greater his opportunity to meet people.

With the above warnings in mind, let us now look at the various forms of need satisfaction obtained from work, starting with physical and security needs.

PRIMARILY PHYSICAL AND SECURITY NEEDS

Money

Ask a man why he works and chances are he will tell you, "to make money." Certainly the need to earn a living is the most powerful single reason why people work, though, as we shall see, nonmonetary incentives are also important.

Money satisfies all types of needs. Its principal use may be to provide the physical necessities of life as well as security; however, social status in our society depends largely on the size of one's earnings; and earning a good income provides many people with an egoistic sense of accomplishment.

The first demand most people make of a job, then, is that it provide them with enough to enjoy a "proper" standard of living. But what we accept as "proper" tends to rise over time. Today we consider a house substandard if it lacks running water or central heating; this was not so a hundred years ago. To many people today, an automobile and a TV set are among the essentials of life. Moreover, our concept of the proper standard of living depends a good bit on what our neighbors have. If the man next door buys a shiny new Buick, our five-year-old Chevy becomes less adequate.

This tremendous interest in material goods is not a natural characteristic of man but a special trait of our own culture. Many other societies ascribe far less importance to material goods than to holiness, wisdom, and physical and military power. The individual's place in society may be determined purely by who his ancestors were; displays of wealth may be regarded as poor taste. Among certain tribes competitiveness is socially tabu; when the missionaries taught these people how to run races, they insisted that every race must end in a dead heat.

Even in our own culture, money is ordinarily more important to the salesman than to the teacher or the minister. Some men refuse a promotion with a higher salary simply because it involves "too much responsibility." And there are people without much "get up and go" who are satisfied to live on a subsistence level and to spend the rest of their time fishing or building model airplanes.

Although, in the larger community, income may be only a rough measure of status, within a plant it measures very precisely the importance of a job. Even the difference of a penny in hourly rates may assume great significance. If one job pays $2.62 an hour and another $2.63, workers feel (a) that the $2.63 job is more important, or (b) that the $2.62 job should be more highly paid.

Who is more important, the plumber or the electrician? If the plumber gets a 20-cent raise, the electrician wants the same—otherwise he feels he is suffering a cut. The National War Labor Board perhaps only slightly exaggerated when it said: "There is no single factor in the entire field of labor relations which does more to break down morale, create individual dissatisfaction, encourage absenteeism, increase labor turnover, and hamper production than obviously unjust inequalities in the wage rates paid to the same individuals in the same labor group within the same plant."

Security

Job security is a fundamental human need; for many people it is more important than either pay or advancement. The forces driving toward unionism, the most serious problems of superior-subordinate relations, the fears surrounding changing technology—all revolve around the need for security.

It is not enough for a man to have his physical needs satisfied from day to day; he wants to make sure they will continue to be satisfied in the future. In some cases, seniority offers the unskilled worker a sense of security akin to that of the farmer who owns his property or the craftsman who possesses special skills. In recent years, however, automation and other economic changes have brought unemployment to many who once thought their jobs secure. Older men, members of minority groups, and those with limited education or outmoded skills find it extremely hard to find steady work again. As a consequence, losing a job can be a catastrophe, both physically and psychologically. No wonder workers' desires to hold on to their "property rights" to their jobs have led to labor-management disputes over working rules and featherbedding, particularly in industries with declining employment.

Illness and old age provide similar threats to security. Understandably, many companies and unions now seek to provide employees with "total" or "employment-to-grave" security against all forms of income interruption.

Advancement

The urge to advance, "to get ahead," is particularly strong in America. In many other societies a man is born to a rigidly defined class and follows his father's occupation without question; bootblack or king, he fullfills as best he can "the station to which God has called him."

Deep in the heart of every "true" American lies the Horatio Alger dream of unlimited occupational mobility, the belief that every man, no matter how humble his birth, can rise to the highest positions in the land. Indeed, our fondest stories concern men like Abe Lincoln who through honesty and hard work make their way from log cabin to White House.

Children are taught that any virtuous man can work his way to the top. "Your future is strictly up to you,"[4] said a National Association of Manufacturers pamphlet in 1951. "Your opportunities will be limited only by your vision of what your future may become, your abilities and how you use them, your character and your determination." At one time it was believed that poverty was largely due to moral weakness, that failure was the fault, not of the system, but of personal character.

Historians and sociologists are finding increasing evidence that the "sweeper-to-president" phenomenon has always been something of a myth.[5] Even a century ago opportunities to get ahead were considerably limited. Yet for a long

---

[4] *Your Future and What You Make of It*, fourth of the "You and Industry Series" (New York: National Association of Manufacturers, 1951), p. 3, as quoted in Ely Chinoy, *The American Automobile Worker and the American Dream* (New York: Doubleday, 1955), pp. 9-10.

[5] Seymour Martin Lipset and Reinhard Bendix, *Social Mobility and Industrial Society* (Berkeley: University of California Press, 1960).

time this myth of unlimited opportunities for "upward mobility" was generally believed and provided hopes for millions. Today this dream may be fading.[6] True, a child born in the 1960's has as good a chance to advance in social status as did his grandfather. But once a man reaches the age of 25 without having gone to college, his chances for advancement in the old-fashioned sense are limited. Such men may still want to get ahead, but they must redefine what they mean by getting ahead in terms that are realistically related to their actual opportunities.

A generalization of this sort, however, is much too broad, and needs careful qualification. In fact, as we shall discuss in future chapters, the very meaning of advancement differs substantially from one segment of the population to another: whether more security, more responsible jobs, higher incomes, greater status, or recognition from one's colleagues. The measure chosen depends in part on the kind of work one does.

PRIMARILY SOCIAL NEEDS

Man is a social animal. He craves *friendship*, is unhappy when left alone for too long, and often associates with his fellows just because he is hungry for companionship. Particularly for employees who have an unsatisfactory home life, the job provides a large part of their social-need satisfaction.

It is social banter that makes many jobs bearable. If there is nothing more constructive to talk about, small issues can be magnified and boredom can be relieved through circulating rumors. In the informal social life of the plant, too, many a worker has a chance to demonstrate skill and initiative. And even the work itself may be socially rewarding for some employees, such as telephone operators and salesclerks who gain great satisfaction from talking to customers.

The job frequently satisfies other social needs besides the need for friendship. Belonging to a clique provides employees with a sense of *identification* and belonging, and they insist on forming "informal groups" even in the face of management opposition. When they are unable to achieve such identification, the job becomes less desirable. Indeed, there is evidence that workers who belong to small, integrated work groups have higher morale than those who work either alone or among large masses of employees with whom they have few social ties. One study explains why steelworkers are more satisfied with their job than automobile assembly-line workers partly on the grounds that steelworkers typically work in small teams; in contrast, on an assembly line a worker can talk only to the two men flanking him, thus making cohesive social groups difficult to form.[7]

Merely working together, *teamwork*, helps to build morale. Most people like *helping others*. Also, when we need it, we like to be *helped* by others.

---

[6] Chinoy, *op. cit.*; Bennett M. Berger, *Working Class Suburb* (Berkeley: University of California Press, 1960), p. 88.

[7] Charles R. Walker, *Steeltown* (New York: Harper & Row, 1950); Charles R. Walker and Robert H. Guest, *Man on the Assembly Line* (New York: Harper & Row, 1952).

Another set of social needs develops out of the subordinate's relationship to his supervisor. Naturally the subordinate wants *to be treated fairly:* He wants a fair hearing when he thinks his supervisor has made a wrong decision, and he wants the right to appeal over the supervisor's head. Most people like *praise* when they do something well (though sometimes praise from a fellow worker is more meaningful than praise from management). The average worker also expects acceptance from his supervisor—that is, understanding and consideration when he makes a mistake. Finally, he wants to *know where he stands.*

Regardless of whether he is doing badly or well, the typical worker wants some *attention* from his boss. Individuals differ in the amount of attention they desire, however, for some want to be left strictly alone and others constantly run to the boss for reassurance. The supervisor must adjust his supervisory practices accordingly (and yet avoid charges of favoritism). But we shall have more to say about this later on.

PRIMARILY EGOISTIC NEEDS

Accomplishment

"The trouble with this work is that I don't have any feeling of accomplishment. I'm just nobody, doing nothing, getting nowhere. I'm just a cog, so small I'd never be missed." So one worker explained his dislike for his job, even though it was one of the highest-paying jobs in the plant.

One of man's strongest needs is the need for a sense of accomplishment, for the feeling that he is getting something done, that his work is of importance. The work "accomplishment" is rather nebulous, however, for it means many things to different people. Let us examine some of the dimensions of this term.

Importance of the work. Work that seems pointless is bound to lead to frustration. One of the most unpleasant forms of punishment used by the military is to have men dig holes and then fill them in again. Compare this with the rich reward that people who perform even menial tasks in a hospital get from "helping people."

Two English researchers, in a study of a candy factory, once found that the greatest dissatisfaction centered in a small work group whose job consisted of unwrapping defective chocolates as part of a salvage operation.[8] The workers felt that their job was far less constructive than that of the other operators. Telephone supervisors report that production and morale are always higher during an emergency. As one said, "It's amazing. An operator may be a low producer and a disciplinary problem, often tardy and absent, but come a blizzard when the highways are closed, she will walk long distances to come to work."

The satisfied worker takes pride in the product he makes: "I get a big kick

---

[8] S. Wyatt and J. N. Langdon, *Fatigue and Boredom in Repetitive Work,* Industrial Health Research Council, Report No. 77 (London: H. M. Stationery Office, 1938).

every time I see it in the store," he may say, or "Our widgets are made to the finest tolerance in the industry." The various forms that this sense of accomplishment may take are suggested by the following quotations: [9]

> *Responsibility for the welfare of others:* "I am very proud of my job because I examine the mine to make sure it is safe. I save a lot of lives by taking chances for them."—*Miner.*
>
> *Service to others:* "There is a lot of satisfaction out of putting something on a man you know looks well on him, and that he is going to get a lot of compliments and he's going to be pleased and all that."—*Salesclerk.*
>
> *Satisfaction in product:* "When you are selling sterling silver, you've got something to talk about and you talk about it truthfully. It's something that turns into an heirloom—never wears out."—*Salesclerk.*

The elevator operator, the janitor, and the groundskeeper—all *want* to feel that their job is important, and good supervision can do much to enhance their sense of accomplishment and their feeling of self-respect, as we shall see in later chapters.

Studies suggest that there is a close correlation between an occupation's prestige and the satisfaction people get from working at it. "Jobs that have high prestige will tend to be valued for their status rewards even when 'objective' aspects of the work are undesirable; similarly low-status jobs will tend to be undervalued and disliked." [10] Low-status work is considered unimportant. "The best way to improve the job may often be, in fact, to change what the outside public thinks about it and its doers." [11]

How the work fits into the whole.   During World War II, the morale in a small plant was very low and turnover was high. Most of the employees were women who spent their days producing a small metal part that had no obvious importance. The women had no idea what it was used for, nor would management tell them. Then one day they were taken by bus to a nearby aircraft plant where they were shown that the part was an important component of the tail assembly of the B-29. For a while at least, production and morale soared.

For a soldier, one of the most important causes of low morale is the feeling that he, as an individual, is unimportant. Since secrecy must be maintained during a military campaign, the soldier, ignorant of the significance of his activities, concludes that they are pointless. Officers may claim that "there is a reason for everything you do in the Army," but enlisted men can't help but be skeptical.

Similarly, in modern industry it is often extremely difficult for the worker "to see his place in the scheme of things, to appreciate his contributions to the total process. Too often the individual job is like the isolated pieces of a jigsaw puzzle. And because there are so many 'pieces,' those at the work level gener-

---

[9] Eugene A. Friedmann and Robert J. Havighurst, *The Meaning of Work and Retirement* (Chicago: University of Chicago Press, 1954), pp. 77, 110, 119.

[10] Robert Blauner, *Alienation and Freedom* (Chicago: University of Chicago Press, 1964), p. 63.

[11] Whiting Williams, *The Mainsprings of Man* (New York: Scribner's, 1925), p. 63.

ally have only the haziest notion of the total pattern. . . . In a real sense, therefore, the job loses its meaning for the worker—the meaning that is in all terms except the pay envelope." [12]

Skill.   All of us enjoy the sense of creativity that springs from doing something well, from being "on top" of our job. The housewife is proud of her cleanliness or her shortbread, the safe-cracker of his sensitive fingers, the professor of his brilliant lecture or his searching questions.

We also like to imagine that our job requires unusual skill, and as a consequence we tend to exaggerate its importance. When describing his job, a worker often stresses its difficulty, complexity, and the length of time required to learn it. Every machine seems to have special quirks in the eyes of its operator.[13] Every trade has its tricks which require skill, ingenuity, and expertise. Even the janitor feels he has developed a number of special techniques (knowing that Executive A likes his desk dusted, but that Executive B never wants his desk touched) that raise him above the level of unskilled labor. "The bricklayer as a rule is more than a workman. He is a craftsman," says the Bricklayers' Union journal.[14] "His work endures and stands the gaff of years . . . I have worked with a certain bricklayer who takes great pride in telling you one of his ancestors used to take his son to Buckingham Palace and point out some of the stately arches which he himself had built. . . . When a bricklayer has finished with a day's work there is something real to compensate for it. He can go home feeling that he has created something that will last longer than he will."

Employees resent any implication that they can be easily replaced by untrained workers. Partly, of course, such an implication threatens their job security. But there is more to it than that: If anybody can do your job, what can you say that you have accomplished in your working life? What more significant sign of utter failure? True, many workers feel that they contribute nothing to their job that a completely untrained man could not contribute, but they are dismally discouraged by this realization. As individuals, they feel they are accomplishing nothing.

This sense of frustration helps explain the popularity of do-it-yourself projects, many of which involve no economic saving for the home craftsman but do provide a sense of skill and creativity. A worker may come home tired from the factory or office and "rest" by working hard in his basement or garden.

For the skilled craftsman the feeling of skill is particularly important; he resents anything that threatens it. Many companies have discovered that it is harder to get employees to lower their standards of quality than to raise them. When management decides that customers will accept lower quality, and that

---

[12] James C. Worthy, *Some Observations on Frederick W. Taylor and the Scientific Management Movement,* paper delivered before the Society for Applied Anthropology, Columbia University, New York City, April 9, 1954.

[13] See Nancy Morse, *Satisfactions With White Collar Jobs* (Ann Arbor: Institute for Social Research, University of Michigan, 1953).

[14] *The Bricklayer, Mason and Plasterer,* Vol. 30 (May 1927), p. 134.

looser tolerances can be maintained, skilled workers stubbornly resist the consequent reduction in skill required. They take real pride in their job and have no desire to make it less difficult. Looser standards mean less sense of accomplishment.

It is for this reason that many companies are plagued by running battles between engineers and top management. The engineers insist on close tolerances and top quality; they try to delay a new model from being put into production until all the "bugs" have been eliminated. Top management regards this desire for perfection as financially ruinous.

Progress and completion. If an employee is to have a feeling of achievement, he must have some way of measuring his progress. Everyone wants to know "How am I doing?" People like "feedback" even when there is no reward or penalty attached to failure or success. Thus, when a man idly throws a piece of paper at a wastepaper basket, he is interested in whether it goes in (even if he doesn't have to clean up afterward). Only if he can set up some goal and know that he has reached it can he feel this sense of achievement. Many routine jobs are considered boring and monotonous precisely because they give the worker no way to check his progress.

Productiveness. Perhaps all that we have been saying adds up to one point: most people have a genuine desire to be productive, to keep busy.[15] Certainly our observations cast doubt on the common assumption that most workers prefer to "goldbrick" than to work. In fact, it is harder to look busy than to work. Time passes more quickly when a worker is absorbed in what he is doing than when he is trying to avoid work. In our society, a healthy individual feels lost without some sort of job or hobby. Normally, expending mental and physical energy is a pleasant, not a painful, experience.

But if all this is true, how can we explain why people often do loaf on the job and go to extraordinary extremes to avoid work? Usually such behavior is a sign of dissatisfaction with the job, with supervision, or with the company as a whole. Workers who feel that they have been treated unfairly direct their energies to beating the system and show high skill in doing as little work as possible. This response, however, is a sure sign that the organization is beset by severe problems.

The sense of productivity and accomplishment is particularly important to executives. One study, which made extensive use of psychological tests, reported:

> They conceive themselves as hard working and achieving people who must accomplish in order to be happy. . . . They obtain continual stimulation from the

---

[15] One astute student suggests that once people have started to work they have a virtual compulsion to keep on going, an urge that he calls "traction." W. Baldamus, *Efficiency and Work* (London: Tavistock Publications, 1961).

pleasure of immediate accomplishment. They feel the necessity to move continually upwards and to accumulate the rewards from increasing accomplishments.[16]

Autonomy

"You know, it's a funny thing. I work all day at the plant and then I come home and what do I do? I work some more—I mean in the shop in the basement. I love to do things with my hands. Funny, that's what I do at work—only it's different.

"You see at work I don't have any freedom. That's the difference. The company tells me when to start working, when I get time to go to the john, when I get my lunch and how long (I get .7 hours—that's 42 minutes for anyone who isn't an engineer). They tell me how fast to work and exactly what motions to make. About the only thing I'm free to do is to think how damn lousy the job is.

"Now, at home I'm my own boss—and believe me, that's a wonderful feeling."

—Autoworker.

Most people like being their own boss. Yet in modern industry only a few employees really have this feeling. The process of specialization has deprived the individual worker of his freedom to plan and organize his own job and has transferred initiative and responsibility to management. As Frederick Taylor, father of the scientific management movement, once put it, "Each man must learn how to give up his own particular way of doing things, adapt his methods to the many new standards, and grow accustomed to receiving and obeying directions covering details, large and small, which in the past have been left to his individual judgment."[17] The effect of this approach has been to strip many jobs of every opportunity for spontaneity and creativity.

Sometimes the tall stories told by workers are indicative of their hidden desires to do things in their own way. For instance, there is the tale of the assembly-line workers who fixed their cars so that when you stepped on the accelerator the windshield wiper started flapping and the horn blew "honkhonk." Then there is the story about the skilled glass blower who for years had been making glass rabbits with straight ears. One day he decided to let the ears droop. "I thought it might be a nice change," he told an amazed management.

Initiative and imagination are essential to any sense of autonomy; yet too often management fails to use the creative abilities of employees. As a consequence, they display their initiative and imagination in forms of which management disapproves, such as sabotage, union activity, and horseplay. Often the creative individual is considered a troublemaker.[18]

We must not paint too black a picture, however, for on many jobs workers

---

[16] William E. Henry, "The Business Executive: A Study in the Psychodynamics of a Social Role," *The American Journal of Sociology*, Vol. 54, No. 4 (January 1949), p. 287.

[17] Frederick W. Taylor, *Shop Management* (New York: Harper, 1919), p. 113.

[18] Some observers report that the trend toward conformity is causing the same thing to happen on the management level. W. H. Whyte, Jr., *The Organization Man* (New York: Simon and Schuster, 1956).

do have a good deal of freedom. We have all seen janitors who really felt they were kings of all they surveyed—and behaved accordingly. Skilled workers, guards, inspectors, and many production workers frequently have this same feeling of independence.

How a man feels depends on both the type of work he does and how he is supervised. Mineworkers, truckdrivers, and railroaders all have above-average job satisfaction, which has been explained by "the absense of close supervision" and the fact that "the contact between employees and supervision is so much less than in factory work." [19] Of course, no one can be boss of everything, but within limits an employee can feel that he is his own boss. This is particularly true if he can feel that what he does is determined by the objective requirements of the situation rather than by human orders. (From an objective point of view, the substation operator in a public utility has almost no freedom; he must constantly make adjustments to meet the changing demands for power. Yet he feels quite independent, since he gets his orders from dials rather than from people.)

Many jobs demand such a high degree of teamwork that the individual worker is deprived of all opportunity to make decisions by himself. But in a situation like this it is often practicable to have the decisions made by the group as a whole. *Participation* in decision-making by the group is the equivalent of autonomy for the individual.

Knowledge

The desire for knowledge is a basic impulse in human beings. People like to know not only "what" is happening to them but "why." They want both to understand the present and to predict the future. Arbitrariness, caprice, and unexpected events all make it hard for us to fashion an orderly, reasonable explanation of the events that shape our lives. To be at the mercy of people and forces that we can neither understand nor control is a serious threat to our sense of security. Take, for example, the unrest that prevails in a shop after a familiar, well-known supervisor is replaced by a new man with unknown preferences, attitudes, and idiosyncrasies.

People want to know about things that are directly important to them, and also about those that are not. Satisfying idle curiosity is a way of spending one's time. The village busybody and the bored receptionist have nothing better to do than to pry into other people's business. The desire for information is so strong that if the truth is not available, appropriate substitutes will be fashioned.

The quest for knowledge has more constructive elements as well. Many people find that learning gives them a sense of achievement. Being an expert on something—whether it is baseball, trout flies, the fine points of one's job, or the ramifications of union politics—gives the individual a sense of uniqueness and progress.

---

[19] Blauner, *op. cit.*, p. 348.

Obviously, all the previously mentioned needs are important, but which is most important? Which can be used most effectively to motivate employees to work for organizational objectives?

This question has been the subject of extensive research.[20] The answer has been found to vary with the individual concerned, his job, the general economic climate, and a host of other factors. Several generalizations seem to be at least partly valid, however, as we shall discuss below.

Needs Hierarchy

According to one hypothesis,[21] human needs can be ordered into a hierarchy, with physical needs being the "lowest" and most basic, followed, in ascending order, by security, social, egoistic, and self-actualization [22] needs. In this hierarchy, a higher, less basic need does not provide motivation unless all lower, more basic needs are satisfied; but once a lower-level need is satisfied, it no longer motivates.

Thus, once physical needs for food, clothing, and shelter are reasonably well satisfied, individuals become relatively more concerned with other needs. First, they seek to satisfy their safety or security needs for protection against danger, threats, and deprivation. (As we have seen, physical and safety needs are usually satisfied through pay, seniority, fringe benefits, and the like.) When the standard of living rises so that security is assured, then social needs take first priority, followed by egoistic needs. Finally, according to this hypothesis, only when most of the less pressing needs are satisfied will individuals turn to the ultimate form of accomplishment, self-actualization, which has been described as "the desire to become ... everything that one is capable of becoming," to make the very most of one's potentialities.[23]

The message for management in this theory is that as long as employees' lower-order needs are unsatisfied, it will be difficult to motivate them with those of a higher order. But once those lower needs *are* reasonably well satisfied, management will have to shift its emphasis to the higher needs if it is to provide continued motivation.

This point is nicely illustrated by two studies of job satisfaction. In an investigation in Nashua, New Hampshire, workers were asked why they wanted to

---

[20] For one comprehensive survey, see Fredrick Herzberg, Bernard Mausner, R. Peterson, and Dora Capwell, *Job Attitudes: A Review of Research and Opinion* (Pittsburgh: Psychological Service of Pittsburgh, 1957).

[21] This hypothesis has been developed at length by A. H. Maslow, *Motivation and Personality* (New York: Harper & Row, 1954), chapters 6-8.

[22] In our discussion of needs in the previous section we have not included self-actualization as a separate need largely because we find it difficult to distinguish this need from such egoistic needs as accomplishment.

[23] A. H. Maslow, "A Theory of Human Motivation," *Psychological Review*, Vol. 50 (July 1943), p. 372.

17

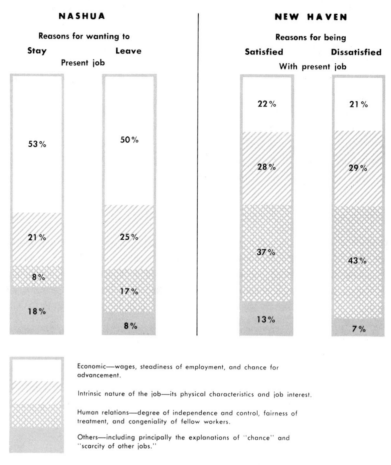

NASHUA

Reasons for wanting to

Stay   Leave

Present job

NEW HAVEN

Reasons for being

Satisfied   Dissatisfied

With present job

53%   50%

22%   21%

28%   29%

21%   25%

37%   43%

8%

18%   17%

8%

13%   7%

Economic—wages, steadiness of employment, and chance for advancement.

Intrinsic nature of the job—its physical characteristics and job interest.

Human relations—degree of independence and control, fairness of treatment, and congeniality of fellow workers.

Others—including principally the explanations of "chance" and "scarcity of other jobs."

Relative importance of various reasons for job satisfaction (or dissatisfaction) as reported by two studies.

stay on their present job and were requested to list any reasons why they might like to leave it.[24] In a similar study in New Haven, Connecticut, workers were asked to give the reasons why they were satisfied or dissatisfied with their present work.[25] Notice in the chart that the relative importance of the various needs was the same whether the workers were responding in terms of staying or quitting, or in terms of being satisfied or dissatisfied. But between the groups there was a significant difference. In Nashua, half the workers emphasized economic reasons; in New Haven, only about one-quarter of them did. Why such a difference?

The answer can be found in the economic conditions existing in the two communities when the studies were made. New Haven was enjoying a period of full employment when jobs were plentiful and minimum economic needs

[24] Charles A. Myers and George P. Shultz, *The Dynamics of a Labor Market* (Englewood Cliffs, N.J.: Prentice-Hall, 1951), pp. 130-131.

[25] Lloyd G. Reynolds and Joseph Shister, *Job Horizons* (New York: Harper & Row, 1949).

were being met. Consequently, social and psychological factors gained importance. In Nashua there was substantial unemployment, created by the closing
of a large textile plant. In effect, the men here were saying, "Better a bad job
than no job at all."

> The attractiveness of any one job factor (such as wages) . . . , is a conse-
> quence of the extent to which other job satisfactions or expectations are being
> fulfilled at the time. When a worker enjoys a steady job paying good wages, he
> is understandably more concerned about the treatment he gets from his super-
> visors, the degree of independence and control he has on the job, and whether
> the job is interesting. But when he loses his high-paid job he is more concerned
> about regaining steady, well-paid employment.[26]

The needs-hierarchy hypothesis has been subjected to a good deal of criticism. The two most telling points are the following:

1. People seem to differ greatly in the extent to which a need must be satisfied before they are willing to move on to a higher level. Furthermore, for some
people egoistic needs may be more basic than social ones. A scientist's physical
needs, for example, may be very easily satisfied, his social needs may be minimal, and his consuming passion for research may involve egoistic and self-
actualizing needs. By forcing the facts, one might say that the scientist conforms
to the needs hierarchy, but doing so does not help us understand his behavior.

2. As we have seen, the various categories of need overlap, and a given need
may be fitted into more than one category. Money is perhaps the most important
single source of need satisfaction; yet depending on the circumstances, it may
satisfy any of the needs listed.

For all these reasons, it is very hard to put the hypothesis in operational form
and to test whether or not it is true. Yet, despite its limitations it does present
some useful insights into human behavior. Other factors must also be considered, however.

Opportunities for satisfaction. People strive to satisfy needs only to the
extent that there is a reasonable chance of success. Needs that are already being
satisfied or that are impossible to satisfy do not seem important. For example,
when a group of hospital doctors were asked what they wanted most from their
jobs, they mentioned prestige and advancement.[27] What about their sense of
accomplishment in curing the sick? That was taken for granted. In general, the
motivations reported were more self-centered than idealistic. Hospital maids,
on the other hand, emphasized the satisfactions they derived from helping
people. Why? The maid's job in itself has little prestige—but she does work for
the hospital and that does have prestige. Cleaning rooms requires little skill,
but the maid derives a feeling of accomplishment from her work because it

---

[20] Myers and Shultz, *op. cit.*, pp. 132-133.

[27] We are indebted to Temple Burling, Edith Lentz, and Robert Wilson, who permitted
us to read the interview notes collected in a study published as *The Give and Take in Hospitals* (New York: Putnam, 1956).

obviously helps the patients. The important point, then, is what needs workers feel they can satisfy in the present situation, not what they might want in a totally different situation.

Substitution of one need for another.   To some extent, people will give up one source of need satisfaction for another. Once job security is obtained, workers will accept loss of social and egoistic satisfaction only in return for a significant increase in pay.[28] Conversely, many will accept lower wages in return for a more desirable job. As one worker put it:

> "Sure this job doesn't pay much. But nobody pushes you and you are your own boss. I could get more in the mills, but I would hate myself for doing it: push, push, and bosses. Life is too short. I like the guys here."

Role of money.   Management is sometimes deceived by workers' demands for money, because money has many meanings in terms of need satisfaction. If we looked solely at union demands on management and at the overt causes of strikes, we might well conclude that workers were interested in money alone. Yet, as we have seen, this is not the whole picture.

There are two reasons for this overemphasis. In the first place, workers may regard higher earnings as a partial compensation for the lack of other forms of need satisfaction. Second, money has a symbolic value. Money earnings are tangible; psychic earnings are not. If one is going to gripe, one seizes on something tangible to gripe about. Dissatisfaction with the job in general is often semiconscious and hard to put into words. If workers went to the boss demanding that he provide them with more interesting work, they would feel pretty foolish; but a demand for an increase of 10 cents an hour can be put in writing.

From the union's point of view, of course, the size of the pay check is a measure of the union's strength and the officers' bargaining skill. Wage improvements can be obtained for everyone at one fell swoop around the bargaining table, but the union can improve human relations only piece-meal through the grievance procedure.

Relationship among needs.   The types of satisfactions emphasized by various occupational groups will vary, depending on what opportunities for satisfaction are available to them, what they have come to expect, and which needs have already been satisfied.[29] Attitude surveys suggest that unskilled blue-collar workers, who have relatively little chance for autonomy or advancement, give relatively strong emphasis to job security and physical working conditions. Craft workers emphasize the *kind* of work they do, while white-collar workers are more likely to mention autonomy and the nature of their job. Service work-

---

[28] The overwhelming majority of employees in an automotive assembly plant indicated that they liked their pay but disliked the job as such. They took the job only for the extra income. Walker and Guest, *op. cit.*, p. 143.

[29] See, for example, Elizabeth L. Lyman, "Occupational Differences in the Value Attached to Work," *American Journal of Sociology*, Vol. 55, No. 2 (September 1955), pp. 138-144;

ers stress the social satisfactions derived from the people they work with and meet. Accountants have relatively less opportunity for being creative on their jobs than do engineers, whereas engineers, in many cases, are concerned with looking well in the eyes of their colleagues. Thus, we should not be surprised that one study shows engineers to be relatively more concerned with achievement, and accountants with advancement.[30] Along the same lines, another finds that "managers mention salary much more frequently than do professsionals . . . who stress the content of the job itself." [31] In a government laboratory, "junior investigators," who had college degrees, were relatively more interested in egoistic, on-the-job satisfactions than were laboratory technicians, who did slightly less skilled work and did not have degrees.[32] Interestingly, the junior investigators gave relatively little emphasis to advancement unless they had been denied promotion; then advancement became a primary goal for them. Finally, we have a study of executives which indicates that although executives at all levels are relatively well satisfied with their job security, lower-level executives are considerably more dissatisfied with their opportunities for autonomy and creativity than are those further up the ladder.[33]

HOW IMPORTANT IS JOB SATISFACTION?

How important is it for any individual to have satisfying work? This question can be divided into two parts: (1) What does dissatisfying work do to the individual? And (2) what does it do to organizational efficiency and productivity? We shall deal briefly with the first question here. The second question will be discussed in later chapters, particularly Chapter 6.

The question of what role work plays in human life is a concern not only of management. It is a psychological, philosophical, moral, and even theological question, one about which scholars have debated endlessly. There is no clear answer, but let us state some of the issues in terms of a debate.[34]

The Case for Work
Being Very Important

One group argues that mature human beings require high levels of egoistic and self-actualizing need-satisfaction from their jobs. The process of growing

---

✓ Nancy Morse and Robert S. Weiss, "The Function and Meanings of Work and the Job," *American Sociological Review*, Vol. 20, No. 2 (April 1955), pp. 191-198; Blauner, *op. cit.*

[30] Fredrick Herzberg, Bernard Mausner, and Barbara Snyderman, *The Motivation to Work* (New York: Wiley, 1959).

[31] Morse and Weiss, *op. cit.*, p. 197.

[32] Stephen T. Boggs, "The Value of Laboratory Workers," *Human Organization*, Vol. 22, No. 3 (Fall 1963), pp. 207-215.

[33] Lyman W. Porter, *Organizational Patterns of Managerial Job Attitudes* (New York: American Foundation for Management Research, 1964).

[34] For a more complete statement of the debate, see George Strauss, "Notes on Power Equalization," in Harold Leavitt, ed., *The Social Science of Organizations* (Englewood Cliffs, N.J.: Prentice-Hall, 1963), pp. 45-57.

up involves accepting more and more challenge and autonomy and becoming more independent. Those who do not have these opportunities (in particular those who are unable to express themselves meaningfully through work) never reach psychological maturity.[35] Since the average man spends nearly a third of his waking hours on the job, if that job does not provide challenge and autonomy he may suffer real frustration, with results that are costly both to himself and his employer. Thus, the fact that many individuals have boring, meaningless jobs may lead to severe social problems.

Indeed, the very act of working satisfies basic human needs. In a survey of work attitudes, a highly affirmative response was given by all occupations and brackets polled. Eighty per cent of those employees questioned in the survey replied that they would continue to work even if they "inherited enough money to live comfortably without working." [36] "Working gives them a feeling of being tied into the larger society, of having something to do, of having a purpose in life." [37] The existence of the Peace Corps suggests that many seek meaning in their work and, indeed, through their work may seek a meaning in life.

The importance of work in modern life is indicated by the impact of unemployment and retirement on persons who have been active and productive for decades.[38] Unless the retired employee can find some other kind of work (a hobby, for instance), the psychological effects of idleness may be extremely upsetting. All of us have heard comments of this sort: "After Dad was pensioned off he just fell apart. He didn't know what to do with himself." Unemployment can be even more demoralizing.

Recent evidence suggests that workers on unskilled (and presumably boring) jobs are significantly more likely to suffer from personality disturbances (as measured by interviews) and psychosomatic illnesses (as measured by dispensary visits) than are skilled workers.[39] Individuals who move from unskilled to skilled work tend to become better adjusted after the move, and vice versa.

In addition, as we shall discuss in later chapters, low morale and poor motivation may lead to inefficiency and low productivity. In sum, so the argument runs, the existence of unrewarding jobs creates an unhealthy situation, which

---

[35] For a classical statement, see Chris Argyris, *Personality and Organization* (New York: Harper & Row, 1957). A later extension of this work is Chris Argyris, *Integrating the Individual and the Organization* (New York: Wiley, 1964).

[36] Morse and Weiss, *op. cit.*, p. 192 and p. 197. Interestingly, a substantial proportion (though not a majority) of middle-class employees mentioned "interest in work" and "accomplishment" as reasons for wanting to keep on working; by contrast blue-collar workers emphasized the importance of "keeping occupied."

[37] *Ibid.*, p. 191.

[38] W. Wight Bakke, *Citizens Without Work* (New Haven: Yale University Press, 1940); Eugene A. Friedmann and Robert J. Havighurst, *The Meaning of Work and Retirement* (Chicago: University of Chicago Press, 1954).

[39] Arthur Kornhauser and Otto M. Reid, *Mental Health of the Industrial Worker: A Detroit Study* (New York: Wiley, 1965); John R. P. French, Robert L. Kahn, and Floyd Mann, eds., "Work, Health and Satisfaction," *Journal of Social Issues*, Vol. 18, No. 3 (July 1962).

is harmful to the individual, to the organization which employs him, and to society generally.

The Case for Job Satisfaction
Not Being Important

The opposing argument is that many people adjust easily to dull work. They center life away from the job, expect relatively few satisfactions from it, and so are not disappointed when it offers them little in the way of challenge or sense of creativity.[40] Indeed, some suggest that many people would not want a high level of challenge and autonomy on the job, even were it available. Possibly such individuals are immature, but their immaturity is due far more to family environment than to the job; they have learned to be dependent in childhood, and are unlikely to change this pattern in later life. (See Chapters 6 and 7.)

It is claimed that most of the evidence designed to show the importance of need satisfaction is misleading, showing in fact that in our culture people want *some* sort of job (and preferably one with high status) but not that the job itself must provide higher orders of satisfaction.

According to some studies, retirement in itself does not bring on the rapid deterioration of physical and mental health as was once supposed; health tends to improve after retirement.[41] Further, evidence on the impact of unskilled work on mental health is still incomplete. Apparently, not everyone suffers equally from unskilled work, and some adjust more easily than others. And it is not clear whether mental ill health results from the intrinsic nature of unskilled work or from the fact that such work pays poorly and has low status both off and on the job.[42] Insofar as mental disturbances are caused by economic and social pressures at home, higher wages may be a better solution than improved satisfaction on the job.

Attitude surveys suggest that most people expect relatively little from work, and so adjust rather easily—though professionals and executives, whose work

---

[40] Lower-class people "tend to accept the unpleasantness of work in order to bring home a pay check. Work is not enjoyable nor is it supposed to be." Argyris, *Integrating the Individual and the Organization*, p. 79.

[41] W. E. Thompson and G. F. Streib, "Situational Determinants: Health and Economic Deprivation in Retirement," *Journal of Social Issues*, Vol. 14, No. 2 (April 1958), pp. 18-34.

[42] In fact, a hasty glance at the research in this field [for example, see Stanislov V. Kasl and John R. P. French, "The Effects of Occupational Status on Physical and Mental Health," *Journal of Social Issues*, Vol. 18, No. 3 (July 1962), pp. 67-89; and Victor H. Vroom and Norman R. F. Maier, "Industrial Social Psychology," in Paul Farnsworth, ed., *Annual Review of Psychology* (Palo Alto: Annual Reviews, 1960)] makes it abundantly clear that unskilled workers are not the only ones to suffer from poor mental health. Depending on which study one looks at or what mental health index is used, one can conclude that executives, clerical personnel, salespeople, and lower-level supervisors *all* suffer from below-average mental health. The evidence makes one sympathize with the old Quaker who said, "All the world is queer except me and thee, and sometimes I suspect thee."

is more satisfying, find such adjustment easier than do factory workers.[43] Thus, a typical poll, taken by *Fortune* in 1957, indicated that even among factory workers 54 per cent found their jobs interesting (compared to 94 per cent among professionals and executives and 72 per cent among salaried employees).[44] On the other hand, other studies suggest that the proportion of those who would choose the same kind of work if they were beginning their career again varied from 91 per cent among mathematicians and 82 per cent among journalists to 52 per cent among skilled printers and 16 per cent among unskilled autoworkers. In other words, workers in general seem to have adjusted to their present jobs, though many would prefer other kinds of work, were it available.

Ideally, it would be better if everyone could lead a fully satisfying life, both on and off the job. Possibly job satisfaction would be greater were we to return to the idyllic preindustrial conditions pictured at the beginning of this chapter —if, for example, cars were made on a handcraft basis rather than on an assembly line. But the cost of doing so would be the abandonment of our modern technological efficiency and a substantial reduction in our standard of living. Few would be willing to pay this price. Or so the argument runs.

Work and Leisure

Perhaps the issues will seem less confused if we step back and examine them from both a historical and a cultural viewpoint. Remember that our present attitude toward work is culturally based. Work has not always been so important as it is today, nor is it likely to be so important in the future. In centuries past, particularly when civilization was flourishing in Greece and Rome, work did not occupy an exalted position. In fact, those of higher social status did not expect to work, for work was primarily restricted to slaves and to free citizens who lacked independent resources.

During the Protestant Reformation, work took on many religious connotations. Work was clearly a duty, a duty to fulfill one's predestined "calling." It was also regarded as an ordained punishment for the sins of man. To fail to work was immoral. Our present feeling about the idle—that they are somehow not behaving morally—is a reflection of this religious emphasis. To maintain respect in our society, rich men must work.

Today, attitudes toward work differ greatly among occupational groups. For

---

[43] The discussion which follows is adapted from Robert Blauner, "Work Satisfaction and Industrial Trends in Modern Society," Walter Galenson and S. M. Lipset, eds., *Labor and Trade Unionism* (New York: Wiley, 1960).

[44] Another major study concludes, "The distribution of alienation and freedom in the typical score card [of the typical workers] is probably consonant with the values and aspirations of the blue-collar labor force today." Blauner, *Alienation and Freedom*, p. 183. Another study suggests, however, that since white-collar workers start out with much higher levels of expectations than do blue-collar workers, white-collar workers end up feeling more frustrated. G. Gurin *et al.*, *Americans View Their Mental Health* (New York: Basic Books, 1960).

some, "work has now become the main business of life" [45] and the chief function of recreation is to recuperate to do more work. Certainly many professionals and executives feel this way. Indeed, some corporations seem to feel that their executives should behave as "Organization Men" twenty-four hours a day. But the central focus of other people's lives is not the job (which is merely a "way of getting a living") but the home or community. Such people find a large measure of challenge, creativity, and autonomy in raising a family, pursuing a hobby, or taking part in community affairs. An eminent sociologist concluded: [46]

> Work, for probably a majority of workers, and even extending into management, may represent an institutional setting that is not the central life interest of the participants. The consequence of this is that while participating in work a general attitude of apathy and indifference prevails. . . . Thus the industrial worker does not feel imposed upon by the tyranny of organizations, company or union.

Further, in many occupations people spend less time on the job today than in the past. A half-century ago the six-day week (for, in some instances, ten to twelve hours a day) was the rule, and vacations and holidays were far from common. Today few people work more than five days a week, and the average worker has at least a two-week vacation and perhaps eight paid holidays a year. Not far over the horizon is the 30-hour, four-day week (already the New York City electricians' contract calls for a 25-hour week), while the Steelworkers' union may be establishing a new trend through negotiating a 13-week "sabbatical" for its members every five years.[47] In addition, our life span grows longer while the retirement age tends to come earlier. All these influences are eroding the key position held by work in our daily lives.

A recent study which summarizes trends throughout the world predicts that work in the future will become increasingly routine and provide fewer and fewer opportunities for creativity and discretion.[48] On the other hand, as working hours grow shorter, there will be a new "bohemianism" off the job as people seek self-expression away from work.

> Leisure will be the happy hunting ground of the independent spirit . . . The new slavery to technology may bring a new dedication to diversity and individualism off the job.[49]

---

[45] Charles R. Walker, *Modern Technology and Civilization* (New York: McGraw-Hill, 1962), p. 439.

[46] Robert Dubin, "Industrial Relations Research and the Discipline of Sociology," *Proceedings of the 11th Annual Meeting* (Madison: Industrial Relations Research Association, 1959).

[47] On the other hand, there are large numbers of moonlighters who seem to prefer work and its monetary rewards to leisure.

[48] Clark Kerr, John T. Dunlop, Frederick H. Harbison, and Charles A. Myers, *Industrialism and Industrial Man* (New York: Oxford, 1964).

[49] *Ibid.*, pp. 237-238.

From such predictions, some conclude that perhaps the best use of our resources is to accelerate automation, shorten the work week as fast as possible, forget about on-the-job satisfactions, and concentrate our energies on making leisure more meaningful.

Others argue that it is impossible to compartmentalize work and leisure activities and that expanded leisure activities will never substitute for what is missing on the job. Indeed, it is suggested that work routines spill over into leisure routines, and that those who have routine jobs tend to engage in passive, routine types of recreation.[50]

Nevertheless, the line between work and nonwork activities is drawn much sharper today than it ever was in the past. Prior to large-scale commuting, people lived and played with the same people they worked with, and a whole series of ceremonies and other social activities tended to integrate work, family, and community life into a seamless web. In those days, people felt little need to "get away" from work (and, of course, less opportunity to do so). Today, since work and play occupy separate spheres in our lives, we feel under pressure to decide which is most important.

Summary of the Argument

JOB SATISFACTION IMPORTANT	JOB SATISFACTION UNIMPORTANT
1. People want self-actualization.	Some people prefer unchallenging work.
2. Those who don't obtain job satisfaction never reach psychological maturity.	Individual personality becomes fixed before people start working. Work is not to blame.
3. Those who fail to obtain job satisfaction become frustrated.	Most people have relatively low levels of aspiration for job satisfaction and expect only routine work.
4. The job is central to man's life.	This is a professor's value. Many people focus their lives on family and community.
5. Those without work are unhappy. People want to work even when they don't have to.	Even though there are social pressures to have *a* job, this does not mean the job must be challenging, etc.
6. Lack of challenging work leads to low mental health.	Poor mental health may be due to low income or low status of routine jobs. Anyway, research findings are not conclusive.
7. Work and leisure patterns spill into each other. Those with uncreative jobs engage in uncreative recreation.	A new bohemianism off the job will make up for increasing boredom at work.
8. Lack of job satisfaction and alienation from work lead to lower morale, lower productivity, and an unhealthy society.	We can provide challenging work for everybody only at the cost of eliminating our mass production technology and high standard of living—and society is unwilling to pay this price.

---

[50] Eric Fromm, *The Sane Society* (New York: Holt, Rinehart and Winston, 1955), p. 136.

Management can do its job only through motivating people to work for management's objectives. But it is impossible to understand motivation without considering what people want and expect from their jobs.

Since people spend about a third of their waking hours at work, it is not surprising that they should expect work to satisfy many sorts of needs—physical, social and egoistic—and that, further, these needs may be satisfied in a wide variety of ways—off the job, around the job, and through the job. Though there is some evidence that these needs can be ranked in a hierarchy, it is fairly clear that the various forms of need satisfaction can be substituted for each other.

There is considerable debate about the importance of satisfaction enjoyed on the job, as opposed to satisfactions derived elsewhere in life. Professors (and they are the ones who do most of the writing in this field) in general place high value on autonomy, creativity, and the quest for maximum self-development. As much as any other group in society, their existence is work-oriented; for them creative achievement is an end in itself and requires no further justification. As a consequence, they are inclined to equate true happiness with interesting work and assume that everyone should be as work-involved as professors are. Perhaps those professors who give such a major role for job satisfaction are right—but the case is not black-and-white.

As for the present authors, we hold a middle-of-the-road position. A man's work is one of the most important (if not the most important) activities in his life. Those who do not have satisfying jobs rarely have fully satisfying lives. As we shall discuss in future chapters, dissatisfying work can lead in many (but not all) circumstances to lower production and friction on the job, so that it may be in management's economic interest to reduce such dissatisfaction. But even where this is not true, management has a certain degree of social responsibility (as we shall discuss in our concluding chapter) to provide work opportunities which are psychologically meaningful. Regardless, we must bear in mind that work is not man's only objective, nor is work satisfaction the sole objective of management.

A safe conclusion is that people differ not only in the importance they assign to work but also, as we shall discuss in Chapters 2 and 3, that jobs differ themselves in the types of satisfactions they offer.

ENGINEERING CONSTRUCTION COMPANY

This company designs and supervises the erection of chemical and petroleum processing plants. It employs a large number of engineers with college degrees, most of whom work in the Field Division or the Drafting Division.

The approximately 1000 engineers in the Field Division supervise the erection of plants throughout the world. As of 1956 (the date of this case), new college graduates received $425 a month. After five years they might reasonably expect $800 a month; after 20 years, $1500. However, few reach these higher salaries. By the end of two years over half have either quit or been discharged. Top management engages in frequent purges, weeding out those it thinks are incompetent. Fierce competition is encouraged for the top jobs. Men are often transferred from one part of the country to another with as little as one week's notice, a policy that creates particular hardships for children who must be constantly uprooted from school. Working conditions on the job are usually poor, with wind, rain, heat, and cold being common.

The Drafting Division contains approximately 500 graduate engineers. Prior to 1935, when the company was much smaller, high school graduates were hired to do drafting, but during the depression, men with college diplomas could be obtained for very little money and the policy of hiring them was started. Pay starts at $2.90 an hour and reaches $3.85 after two years, the highest drafting pay in the city. No one has been laid off for lack of work since the early depression days and discharges for incompetence are rare. There is one section head for every 20 men (salary $8500). Promotions to this job are normally obtained through seniority.

The drafting work on a single project may take as long as two years to complete, and prior to 1950 each project was given to a small group of men who would work on it from beginning to end. Beginning in 1950, substantial changes were made in organization. Individual offices were eliminated and all operations were placed in one large, well-lighted, air-conditioned room. Each man was given a specialty such as heating or wiring, and work now proceeds from one department to another on an assembly-line basis.

In both divisions liberal vacations, sick leave, and a retirement plan are provided. As yet neither division is unionized.

1. List separately for each division the needs which are and are not satisfied.
2. In which division will the engineers be easiest to unionize?
3. What recommendations would you make to management to improve morale and motivation in each division?

Technology and Job Satisfaction:
Blue-Collar Work

The previous chapter explored what employees want from work and the meaning they give to work. This chapter and the next look at the other side of the coin: the impact of differences in work on employee need satisfaction. Many managers and students err in assuming that, even if individuals differ in their preferences, one job is basically like another or that the only important distinctions are those between managerial and nonmanagerial jobs. In this chapter we shall see first that the technology, or work method, selected by management has an overriding effect on the types of satisfactions and dissatisfactions which employees derive from their jobs. And second, we shall describe the techniques by which employees, given the limits that are set by the methods of production, adapt jobs to make them more compatible to their needs. Management ought to understand both processes.[1]

Here we shall deal just with "blue-collar" jobs, those involving manual work, saving the so-called "white-collar" jobs and automation for Chapter 3. We shall contrast two kinds of blue-collar work: (1) craft work (skilled tradesmen) and (2) machine-tending and assembly line (mass-production jobs)—though, of course, most types of work do not fall neatly within one of these categories. For the sake of exposition, we shall compare the extremes and consider how craft and mass production jobs differ in:

1. Interest, variety, and the opportunities for moving around and changing pace.
2. Opportunities to derive a sense of accomplishment (in both psychological and economic terms), of autonomy, and identification with the work.
3. Job pressures and relations with management.
4. Social relations.

These categories, which are related to the physical, egotistic, and social satisfaction discussed in Chapter 1, will become clearer as we observe various examples of men at work.

---

[1] Some of our analysis is derived from Robert Blauner, *Alienation and Freedom* (Chicago: University of Chicago Press, 1964).

Craft work has a long history. The term craft work applies to certain tasks that resist mechanization and that require long and arduous training of their practitioners. Craftsmen still predominate in such industries as entertainment, transportation, construction, and printing, to name a few.

Interest, Variety, and Movement

The craftsman's job provides abundant variety. Unexpected problems constantly crop up, the solutions to which cannot be programed by management. "Traditional skill thus involves the frequent use of judgment and initiative, aspects of a job which give the worker a feeling of control over his environment." [2]

In addition, unlike most factory workers, craftsmen generally move around a good deal, both to perform widely dispersed jobs and to obtain tools, instructions, materials, or assistance. This ease of movement gives a sense of freedom and diversity (also enjoyed by a salesman or a landscape gardener, both of whom prize their mobility). And since the employee is not "tied" to a machine or an assembly line, he can set his own pace. When he must figure out a difficult job problem, he can muse and putter for a time, taking breaks as he sees fit. On the other hand, when the work is going well he can accomplish a great deal quickly, whereby he gains both a little spare time and a sense of competence.

Accomplishment, Autonomy, and Identification

The craftsman has a rich sense of accomplishment; what he has done, he has done for the most part on his own. The machinist can see the model he has built; the plumber can point to his operating sanitary system. Each can be proud not only of his day-to-day work, but also of what he has made of himself. Most skilled jobs require lengthy training. In addition, in most craft work "age-grading," as the anthropologists call it, prevails. That is, an employee gains greater status and recognition with age.

> Because his experience and knowledge accumulates, the old printer at the end of his career maintains his usefulness and is often the most respected man in the shop, unlike the old automobile worker, who may skid to the lowest job in the plant hierarchy.[3]

This sense of accomplishment is enhanced by community recognition. Whereas many factory jobs have no real identity outside the plant, such skills

---

[2] *Ibid.*, p. 43.
[3] *Ibid.*, p. 53.

as those of electrician, machinist, and printer are widely recognized as skilled work and thereby accorded a certain status. The extent of craft identification shows itself in stronger loyalty to (and pride in) the trade than to any single employer, especially in industries where work is unstable and employees move from employer to employer.

A craftsman's ego-satisfaction has been well expressed by a toolmaker:

> "As a tool and die maker, I feel that I have ability that the average man don't have. I can look at almost anything even in this room, tell you how it was made, and if I had to turn around and make the dies to duplicate it, I believe I could. I think it's got all other skill trades beat a hundred miles. In the apprenticeship training—you had to spend 9000 hours in the shop, 9000 hours to become a journeyman tool and die maker, and when you get a job say like on a big molding die, where you've already put say four or five hundred dollars in it, just one slip and it's wrecked, so you got to stop and think. Got to make sure you know what you're doing, and you don't want nobody bothering you when you're doing it. You got to be in good frame of mind, and I believe that when . . . you get the job done, why, you gotta pat yourself on the back. . . ." [4]

Job Pressures and Relations
to Management

There is a counterbalance to work autonomy—responsibility. Since a craftsman works on his own in a relatively unprogramed fashion, he can be held responsible for mistakes—from leaky plumbing to a wrecked train! Much anxiety can be generated by a job: ". . . where you've already put say four or five hundred dollars in it [meaning hours of labor], just one slip and it's wrecked . . ." Of course, the ability to take pressures is a source of pride.

Management can have trouble in supervising craftsmen. Such men feel they know how their job should be done and are therefore reluctant to accept very much direction. They resist being rushed or taking short cuts that violate their conception of correct method. This resistance to close supervision is often reinforced by strong craft unions that have their own work rules (which management is pressured to accept).

This arrangement reverses the traditional situation in which management imposes its rules on the worker. However, well-trained craftsmen who identify with their craft may require less supervision. They are used to accepting responsibility and being held accountable.

Their independence is furthered by management's recognition that craft skills are scarce and that craftsmen cannot easily be replaced by a more compliant employee. Knowing and controlling the work, the methods, the pace, and the tools, the employee is not likely to feel dominated by management.

In short, craftsmen generally feel secure. Their only serious fears arise from

---

[4] Eli Ginzberg and Hyman Berman, *The American Worker In The Twentieth Century* (New York: The Free Press of Glencoe, 1963).

economic instabilities and the threats of massive technological change which will render their skills obsolete (for example, computers that will do typesetting or automated machine tools).

Social Relations

Though craftsmen typically work alone or with a single helper, they identify with fellow employees who share the same training and job experiences. If you visit a construction site during work breaks, you will see clusters of men from a single craft swapping stories of job problems met and conquered and sharing "tricks of the trade." Off-the-job social groups often consist of men who share a common trade. Where the craft involves unusual working hours (as with many newspaper printers or theatrical entertainers) almost all off-the-job friends may be fellow craftsmen (who share the same work schedules). These social groupings reinforce craft identification and are a significant source of job satisfaction. At the same time, the minimal need for interaction on the job, the relative autonomy of the craftsman, also makes it easier to get along with one's fellow workers.

Summary

One study of the craftsman's world concludes:

> When work provides opportunities for control, meaning, and self expression, it becomes an end itself, rather than simply a means to live. . . . Work for craft printers is a source of involvement and commitment. . . . It is almost the expression of an inner need rather than the grudging payment of a debt imposed by external sources.[5]

MACHINE-TENDING AND ASSEMBLING

Many blue-collar workers are machine-tenders or assemblers. Machine-tenders watch and facilitate the operation of semi-automatic equipment; assemblers combine parts by hand or with small tools. Assemblers are often tied together by a moving belt; each takes the partly completed work of the preceding worker as it comes to him on the line, attaches additional parts, and replaces the unit on the line for passage to the next work station.

The way these jobs are now performed has been influenced by the scientific-management movement, best typified by the recommendations of its chief proponent, Frederick Taylor. Taylor believed in: (1) high specialization—breaking down jobs into very small parts, and (2) specifying in advance exactly how the job should be done—in a sense separating the physical work from the thinking. Taylor also favored payment by results or piece work. As Taylor himself put it:

---

[5] Blauner, *op. cit.*, p. 53 and p. 56.

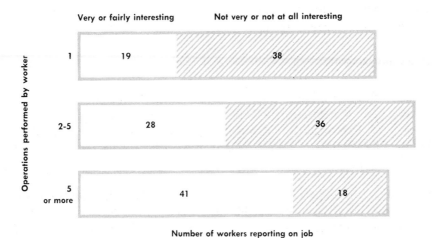

	Very or fairly interesting	Not very or not at all interesting

Operations performed by worker

1   19   38

2-5   28   36

5 or more   41   18

Number of workers reporting on job

Correlation between job interest and job complexity on an automobile assembly line.

> Each man must learn how to give up his own particular way of doing things, adapt his methods to the many new standards, and grow accustomed to receiving and obeying directions covering details, large and small, which in the past have been left to his individual judgment.[6]

This is what is now called "programing," and it is the primary characteristic of *mass-production* technology.

We shall talk about the impact of specialization on organizational structure later. Now we want to see what effect the Taylor movement and accompanying mass-production mechanization had on employee attitudes toward their jobs.

Interest, Variety, and Movement

Machine-tending and assembly jobs provide little opportunity for initiative, ingenuity, and variability. By means of engineering studies, management carefully predetermines the exact motions and pace for each employee. This procedure insures that the work will be done quickly in a uniform, predictable fashion, and precisely coordinated with other jobs. The employee is confined to a fixed work station and is expected to leave it only with permission. What effects will such restrictions have on a man's attitude toward his job?

Short job cycle. An important determinant of job satisfaction is the length of the job cycle: how long it takes to perform a job operation before having to start it all over again. For a college professor the work cycle may be a semester; for a skilled craftsman, if may be several days or weeks. But for the man on a machine or assembly line the work cycle may last less than a minute. At the

---

[6] Frederick W. Taylor, *Shop Management* (New York: Harper, 1919), p. 113.

extreme, he may be simply tightening one or two bolts. Then he has to repeat the same cycle over and over again, with a deadening lack of variety.

> "The job gets so sickening—day in and day out plugging in ignition wires. I get through with one motor, turn around, and there's another staring me in the face. It is sickening." [7]

On jobs of this sort all mental challenge has been eliminated, and in most cases only a few muscles are involved. Life seems one endless procession of bolts to tighten. A study of the automobile assembly line found a high correlation between the number of operations a worker's job called for and his level of interest in his job.[8] See diagram on page 33.

Inability to control pace.   Although some of these jobs allow an employee to stop and start machines, most give him little control over the work pace. For instance, in a textile factory the employee may tend dozens of machines which function automatically. He moves from one to another as they require attention: the mending of a break in the yarn, a maladjustment, the need for new supplies, and so on. His pace is a function of the number and type of machines he has been assigned and the frequency with which his particular skills are required, all of which depend on the engineering of the job—over which he has no control.

Research indicates that workers grow less fatigued and enjoy their work more when they can work at their own rhythm,[9] avoiding abrupt movements and jerky stops and starts. Everyone has a natural tempo at which he works best. Some will be quite happy on a job on which they work relatively fast; others find it impossible to maintain a fast pace.

Most people also like to vary their work rhythm; they may work fast for a while, and then slow down gradually as the day wears on. This variety in pace helps to reduce both fatigue and boredom on the job. The assembly line, however, makes no provision for the preference of individual workers. It sets the pace for him and never lets him change it. Thus the machine may be a worse autocrat than any foreman.

Fortunately, on most mass-production jobs workers do have a slight opportunity to vary their pace through "building a bank" or "getting into a hole." On some jobs a worker can hurry up a bit and build up a reserve or "bank" of completed work and then take a break for a few seconds while the work slides by. By pushing 15 seconds ahead and then falling 15 seconds "in a hole," an energetic worker can earn himself a 30-second break.

Limited attention required.   Another factor affecting the degree of satisfaction a worker derives from his work is the amount of attention it requires. A doctor enjoys his work because his job is constantly new and challenging and

---

[7] Charles R. Walker and Robert Guest, *The Man on the Assembly Line* (Cambridge: Harvard University Press, 1952), p. 55.

[8] *Ibid.*, p. 54.

[9] Georges Friedmann, *Industrial Society* (New York: The Free Press of Glencoe, 1955), p. 159.

absorbs all his attention. Jobs like this are said to require *depth attention*. At the other extreme are the so-called *no-attention jobs*, which are so routine that the worker's mind is free to wander at will. Dishwashing is an example of such work; so, too, is driving over a straight highway with little traffic. Your mind is a thousand miles away, although subconsciously you are still watching the road.

The least-satisfying of all are jobs that require *surface attention*. Here the worker is obliged to perform a routine, unchallenging chore but at the same time to remain relatively alert. ". . . The mind, though not wholly absorbed by work, cannot free itself entirely from it." [10] Examples of this sort of work are watching control gauges, inspecting parts, grading exam papers, or adding up columns of figures. These jobs do not provide the challenge, interest, and sense of autonomy provided by depth-attention jobs; nor do they permit the employee to daydream as he can on a no-attention job.

These classifications, of course, are simply points on a continuum, for there are relatively few cases of, say, a purely no-attention job. Further, the attention demanded by a particular job depends largely on the abilities of the individual employee. A very bright employee may find that a job requires only surface attention, while a less able employee may find that the same job requires depth attention. (The implications for employee selection are obvious.)

Similarly, the amount of attention required varies with the worker's experience. Learning a new job always requires depth attention; then for a while only surface attention is needed; and finally, the job may require almost no attention. When you first learn to drive a car, driving demands depth attention. Later you show surface attention. Only when the routine aspects of driving are purely automatic can you be called a good driver. Yet, even for a good driver, maneuvering into a tight parking space calls for depth attention.

As a worker gains experience on a job, a semiconscious monitor seems to take over to sound the alarm when trouble develops. As one girl described her job: "I used to give full attention to the machine. However, now I can tell what is wrong by the sound."

Accomplishment, Autonomy, and Advancement

Inadequate sense of accomplishment. "This job is endless. It just goes on and on. You don't feel that you are getting anywhere."

We all feel that we are accomplishing something when we can break our work down into units that can be completed successively. If we have two assignments to complete, we breathe a sigh of relief as soon as we finish one. When we are driving a long distance, we break the trip down into sections and feel great satisfaction as we pass by each check point.

Mass-production work characteristically fails to provide this sense of completion, or even a feeling of progress toward a goal. Each employee does only

---

[10] Friedmann, *op. cit.*, p. 146.

a small, specialized part of the total job. Rarely does he have a chance to look at the finished product and say, "Mine, all mine."

Automobile-assembly-line workers often comment that they would like to do the whole job from beginning to end.[11] Work on the assembly line has been compared with work in a steel tube mill as follows:

> On the assembly line, only a small fraction of the "product" is ever seen or handled by most workers. In the tube mill, the whole product, from billet to finished product, as it moves through a series of machines, is worked on by everyone and can be followed by the eye of the members of the crew. Workers frequently go to the cooling and inspection tables to look over for their own satisfaction the job which they have just done.[12]

Excessive specialization deprives the worker of any real sense of skill. Work that has been so subdivided and simplified that it takes almost no time to learn provides little challenge or interest. The worker has no sense of doing a whole job—he sees only part of the total process—and thus his contribution seems negligible and unimportant. Workers who exercise skill take pride in their achievement, but a man who has learned his job in a few hours knows that he can be replaced by almost anyone who happens along. This is one explanation of the tendency of mass-production workers to exaggerate the complexity of their jobs: It is just too humiliating for them to admit how simple their work actually is.

Walker and Guest found a great deal of dissatisfaction among workers who had a genuine desire to do "quality" work but who were prevented from doing so.[13]

> "I try to do quality work, but I'm too rushed. This keeps me from getting pleasure from the work. They say 'haste makes waste,' and they're getting plenty of both."

Lack of autonomy. Specialization assumes that some people will do the thinking and others the work. As Henry Ford put it, "The average worker, I am sorry to say, wants a job on which he does not have to put forth much physical energy—above all, he wants a job on which he does not have to think." [14] But this approach to what the "average worker" wants has been criticized as destructive of morale and wasteful of human abilities:

> Scientific management has failed to utilize properly the greatest resource at its command: the complex and multiple capacities of people. On the contrary . . . it has deliberately sought to utilize as narrow a band of personality and as narrow a range of ability as ingenuity could devise. The process has been fantastically wasteful for industry and society.[15]

---

[11] Walker and Guest, *op. cit.*, pp. 154-155.

[12] Charles R. Walker, "Work Methods, Working Conditions, and Morale," in Arthur Kornhauser, Robert Dubin, and Arthur Ross, eds., *Industrial Conflict* (New York: McGraw-Hill, 1954), pp. 353-354.

[13] Walker and Guest, *op. cit.*, p. 55.

[14] Henry Ford, *My Life and Work* (New York: Doubleday, 1922), p. 22.

[15] James C. Worthy, "Some Observations on Frederick W. Taylor and the Scientific Management Movement," Address given to the Society for Applied Anthropology, New York, April 19, 1954.

It should be noted, however, and we shall return to this point later, that workers differ in their desire to exercise skill and autonomy. Some have no desire for creative challenge on the job—they are happy enough to daydream. Others are deeply disturbed because their work provides so little interest and meaning.

Little opportunity for advancement. One of the significant dissatisfactions associated with most factory jobs is the inability to advance. For one thing there are few promotional steps open; most jobs in the factory require almost the same skill level and provide almost the same pay. Thus, the semiskilled factory worker has to satisfy the need for a sense of advancement very differently from the craftsman.

> The worker learns to set bounds to occupational ambitions. If in his early years he had any illusions about a rapid rise to independence and wealth, these hopes soon wither before the realities of industrial employment. He learns to limit his aspirations to modest and attainable objectives: a change from a second shift, from hourly rated work to incentive work, from a job in labor grade "7" to labor grade "8," or even to another job in the same labor grade which is more desirable for one reason or another. Beyond this most workers have little expectance of going.[16]

Many younger men start to work on an unskilled job expecting that it will be only temporary; they hope to earn a little money and perhaps buy a car, but one day they expect to go to college or start a business of their own. As they get caught up in marriage, family, and mortgages, however, their dreams begin to fade away.[17] Gradually they come to accept their limitations.

In theory, most companies give outstanding workers an opportunity to rise to the top. Yet the technical requirements of modern industry mean that many supervisory jobs can be handled only by men who have had special training. Increasingly, the highest job to which a production worker can aspire is a "factory clerical" position such as expediter or clerk, a position that carries with it slightly higher pay and status, and slightly more freedom from supervision.

It is hard for management today to determine who among the rank and file does have promise and ability, for many jobs offer the worker little chance to display initiative. The docile, submissive worker may be regarded as the good worker. The man with ideas is restless and the union is often more likely than management to give him a chance to express himself. (There is some tendency, however, for management to consider active union members as potential foremen.)

At the same time the unions have done much to reduce the chances of a man to forge ahead on the basis of individual ability. They have emphasized seniority rather than merit, and management has tended to go along with their em-

---

[16] Lloyd G. Reynolds and Joseph Shister, *Job Horizons* (New York: Harper and Row, 1949), p. 89.

[17] For a discussion of these dying hopes, see Ely Chinoy, *The Automobile Worker and the American Dream* (New York: Doubleday, 1955), pp. 9-10.

phasis. In addition, pay grades have been compressed in many companies so that the range between the top- and bottom-paid jobs among unskilled and semiskilled workers is quite narrow. Skilled jobs, such as that of tool and die maker, are often filled through an apprenticeship program, and few men are accepted for such training after 30. Once a man reaches this age, his chances of rising out of the semiskilled class are slight.

✓   *Advancement redefined.*   Some opportunities for upward mobility are, of course, still open to the average worker, but these are somewhat limited (most, but not all, involve seeking off-the-job satisfactions).

1. He can establish a small business, such as a bar, a gas station, or repair service. A substantial minority have made this attempt and failed—though not all fail—and many more dream, with various degrees of seriousness, of going into business for themselves. A great many carry on small business ventures after work as a side line which gives them extra income and a chance to express themselves in a manner they cannot enjoy on the regular job. (This practice is called "moonlighting.")

2. If he is still young, he can go to college or school at night, in the hope of being able to move ahead after graduation.

3. If he realizes that he cannot advance on his own, he may transfer his aspirations to his children. Many factory workers make great financial sacrifices in order to send their children through college.

4. Over the years he may come to regard seniority as a way of getting ahead. After all, unions emphasize seniority as a determinant in layoffs and promotions, and management concurs, with such symbols as long-service pins and testimonial dinners.

5. For some workers, the union provides a chance to "get ahead." Although there are few full-time union jobs with regular salaries, there are many part-time posts, such as steward or executive board member. Negotiating with management, handling grievances, and dealing with day-to-day union business offer many opportunities for creative expression and personal satisfaction.

6. Many workers feel they are advancing when they move to a job that may not be better-paying but that seems "better" in the sense that the work is cleaner, the pace is slower, or the location is away from the assembly line.

7. Finally, if the individual cannot advance by himself, the group to which he belongs may be able to advance the interests of its members. So long as his union can win him a 10-cent hourly wage increase each year, he feels that he has tangible evidence of progress.

8. Many workers interpret "getting ahead" in terms of security and material possessions. As one man put it, "If you've got security, if you've got something to fall back on, you're getting ahead." [18] They measure success not in terms of what they do, but in terms of what they own—a bigger car or a new TV set.

---

[18] Chinoy, *op. cit.*, p. 126.

**Job Pressures and Relations
to Management**

The factory employee has a carefully engineered quota of parts to finish or the requirement that he keep up with the line. Because his job is relatively simple and his methods and output readily observable, he is easy to supervise closely. Management exerts constant pressure to maintain a regular pace and thus maintain productivity. But what of the employee's view?

> *Assembler:* You're always behind. When you get too far behind, you get in a hole.... All hell breaks loose.... The foreman gets sore and they have to rush in a relief man to bail you out.[19]

New employees, particularly, who find themselves falling behind, become anxious about their ability to keep up with the line or make the quota. Being replaceable they worry about being discharged, especially when there is no union or when as new employees they are on a *trial period*. Gradually, though, most develop those patterns of skill and coordination which enable them to meet the engineered standards.

Some workers even prefer machine-paced jobs or assembly lines. At least the "line" controls them impersonally; it keeps the foreman from breathing down their necks. Further, it eliminates the need to pay attention to how fast they are working and thus makes it possible for them to daydream. In effect, the machine sets a rhythm which their body seems to accept.

Unlike craft jobs in which the worker maintains considerable autonomy, most machine and assembly-line work tends to pit workers against managers.[20] As we have suggested, it is tempting to supervise closely since both work methods and output are easy to observe. In mass-production factories, management is constantly trying to reduce labor costs and increase productivity by upping work standards and improving methods, thus forcing the employee to adopt new working procedures and perhaps to change his tempo. Although many engineering changes do *not* require additional physical effort on the part of the worker (in fact, they frequently reduce physical effort), the employee views the increasing output and the necessary changes in his work methods as burdensome and threatening.

Low-skilled employees often fear technological changes that will require them to relearn a job and to struggle to regain adequate quickness. Other anxieties are aroused by the fear that new machines may mean fewer jobs and fewer workers.

Not only are job pressures maximized, but mass-production employees, in

---

[19] Ginzberg *et. al., op. cit.,* pp. 283-284.

[20] A large-scale survey of British companies shows clearly that both labor relations and human relations are least amicable in the type of technology we are now discussing. Joan Woodward, *Management and Technology* (London: HMSO, Department of Scientific and Industrial Research, 1960), p. 18.

contrast to skilled craftsmen, tend to have rather formal relations with management, being unlikely to have any contact with anyone above their immediate supervisor. The status gap between workers and managers tends to be great since such employees, as we have seen, rarely become managers or have significant careers in the firm. Thus, they tend to see the world very differently from their managers who do have career possibilities, and whose success depends on their ability to maintain productivity levels among reluctant employees.

Social Relations

The physical confinement of many factory jobs reduces the opportunity for social relations. In industrial plants employees socialize on the basis of physical proximity rather than occupational status. Congenial on-the-job relationships are important as a means of both reducing boredom and expressing one's total personality since the job requires such a small segment of the individual's mental and physical abilities. Yet, feeling little identification with their occupation, workers are relatively unlikely to make friendships on the job which carry over after work. In fact, most are anxious to get away from every aspect of the job at quitting time.

Social games provide a form of diversion. Gambling of various sorts is common in many factories, from flipping coins to see who pays for coffee, to World Series pools, to bookmaking, and numbers games. Horseplay (mock fighting, high jinks, and brawling) combines social activity and a chance to release aggression. (Accidents often result.)

These on-the-job social activities have become extremely important to workers in mass-production industries. Two astute observers have remarked,

> "Workers seem to want to buy leisure inside rather than outside the plant. ... They may, like many of us in business and professional strata, prefer to complain at home of their hard day's work while secretly profiting from its trivialities." [21]

Adjusting to Mass-Production Work

Aside from elaborating social relations, how do employees adjust to mass-production work? Many learn to ignore the job through daydreaming or to modify the job by various "games at work." Others take more decisive action, either leaving or sabotaging the work.

Daydreaming. Daydreaming is a common means of escaping from the boredom of a no-attention job. As one observer notes, "The revolt against work is widespread and takes manifold forms in the United States. First and foremost it appears in the constant evasion of thought about work, the obsessive reveries

---

[21] David Riesman and Warner Bloomberg, Jr., "Work and Leisure: Fusion or Polarity," in Conrad Arensberg, *et. al., Research in Industrial Human Relations* (New York: Harper & Row, 1957), pp. 72-73.

while on the job." [22] An employee told us: "If I thought about the job all the time I'd go nuts. I think about vacation and going hunting. You don't even know you are working."

The sort of daydream in which workers indulge varies with the individual and the situation.[23] The man who is unhappy with his job and bitter over life in general is likely to brood over his miserable lot. If the work group as a whole is dissatisfied with the job and with the group's relationship with management, the workers tend to dream up grievances and engage in so called "obsessive thinking."

Yet in one study made by the authors, casual observation suggested that workers who daydreamed worked at a more constant pace than those who did not.[24] Most of the complaints about being machine-paced and "tied to the line" came from those who reported they did not daydream on the job.

Who adjusts to monotonous work?   Almost all workers regard a job that requires surface attention from them as boring, mentally exhausting, and undesirable.[25] (This is true even if the same work might require depth attention or no attention from someone else.) But there are some workers who can adjust moderately well to monotonous, no-attention jobs. These workers seem to have little need to derive satisfaction from the job itself and spend their working days in daydreaming.

Whether or not a worker succeeds in adjusting to monotonous work depends in part on his level of aspiration and the importance of the job to his over-all goals. Men as a whole seem less satisfied than women with monotonous work. Single women seem less satisfied than married women, who often spend their work hours thinking about family activities. Among men, the most contented are oldsters approaching retirement, boys awaiting induction into the armed services, and farmers who take a job to supplement their income.

For many people the desire to do an interesting, worthwhile job, and to have a voice in determining how they do their work, is so compelling that they experience acute frustration when that desire is blocked.

Making a game out of work.   In spite of the obvious inefficiency of the practice, some people like to mow their lawns in fancy figure eights. Making a game out of work, as with other "around-the-job" satisfactions, provides variety, gives the worker a chance to show his creativity, and supplies goals to work toward.

On jobs that are not tightly machine-paced, the worker may experiment with various speeds and set himself various output goals. Workers on piece work are

[22] Daniel Bell, "Work in the Life of an American," in William Haber, *et. al.,* eds., *Manpower in the United States* (New York: Harper & Row, 1948), p. 15.

[23] See S. Wyatt and J. N. Langdon, *Fatigue and Boredom in Repetitive Industrial Work,* Industrial Health Research Board, Report 77 (London: HMSO, 1937), p. 10.

[24] See also Wyatt and Langdon, *op. cit.,* p. 35.

[25] Possibly some workers with serious emotional problems may prefer surface-attention work which keeps them from thinking about these problems.

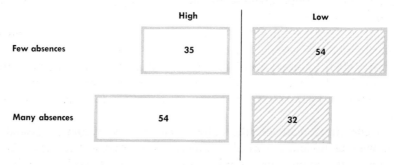

Extent of mass-production characteristics

	High	Low
Few absences	35	54
Many absences	54	32

Absenteeism related to mass-production characteristics of job (175 workers). High and low mass-production characteristics are measured in terms of the job's (1) degree of repetitiveness, (2) degree of mechanical pacing, (3) skill, as measured by learning time, (4) frequency as to break in job routine, (5) frequency of social interaction, and (6) size of interacting group. Charles R. Walker and Robert Guest, The Man on the Assembly Line (Cambridge: Harvard University Press, 1952), p. 120.

particularly likely to set goals for themselves (sometimes called "bogies") and to engage in elaborate calculations to make sure that they produce neither more nor less than the bogey.[26] Although the primary purpose of these calculations is to avoid overproduction that might lead to a cut in the piece rate, they also provide a satisfying diversion from the monotony of work.

Fantasy is another form of game-playing. A female assembly-line worker who had wanted to be a nurse said, "These (pieces) are always getting in trouble. They are sort of helpless, like sick people." Another woman commented, "This job is like cooking. It's something to do with your hands. It keeps you busy."

Modifying the job. Workers can sometimes reduce the monotony of their jobs by introducing variations in their work that are unplanned by management. They may exchange work, modify parts of the job, and avoid others altogether. They drag out set-ups, find excuses to pick up parts more frequently than necessary, and perhaps let the machine break down in order to create a slight change in pace.

Absenteeism and turnover. Another means of adjusting to unpleasant work is to avoid it as much as possible. In practice this leads to absenteeism,

---

[26] (This practice is called "making out.") For an excellent discussion, see Donald Roy, "Work Satisfactions and Social Rewards in Quota Achievement," *American Sociological Review*, Vol. 18, No. 5 (October 1953).

frequent visits to the dispensary, excessive time spent in the washroom, feigned illness, and even quitting. Some have argued that employees may unconsciously seek an accident.

Walker and Guest found correlations between short absences and the "mass-production characteristics" of jobs on the assembly line. Absenteeism was highest on the jobs that required the least skill, were most repetitive, gave workers the least chance to express themselves, and so forth.[27] See diagram page 42.

Antimanagment activities. In a sense, antimanagement activities are an overt reaction to the frustration of mass-production work. Active union participation, for example, provides an opportunity to release aggression and to enjoy a sense of skill and accomplishment that is denied on the job. Similarly, sabotage and wildcat strikes enable a demoralized work group to let off steam.[28] In Detroit, for instance, after long periods of overtime work on boring assembly-line jobs, employees appear pleased with the prospect of a strike!

Summary: Job Satisfactions in Traditional Factory Work

Management pays a price for the work simplification, routinization, and ease of supervision inherent in mass-production work. The cost is largely in terms of apathy and boredom as positive satisfactions are engineered out of jobs. Being confined physically and limited socially to contacting his own immediate supervisor, the factory worker sees very little of the total organization and even less of the total product being manufactured. It is hardly surprising that there is frequently little pride in work or identification with the job. However, employees have put back some of the satisfactions they require by informal modifications of work methods (such as games and trading-off of jobs) and by concerted group activities (these will be detailed further in Chapter 4). Further, many employees have low levels of aspiration which are consistent with the initiative required on these jobs and others have redefined the meaning of advancement to compensate for the absence of significant careers.

Perhaps the most serious problem associated with these jobs is the high frequency of worker-management conflict over technological change and the question of what is a fair day's work. As we have seen, these conflicts are greatest where job pressures are greatest.

---

[27] Another careful research effort showed much the same thing: Absenteeism is higher on the less complex, less demanding jobs: Arthur Turner and Paul Lawrence, *Industrial Jobs and the Worker* (Boston: Division of Research, Harvard Business School, 1965), pp. 35-48. However, still another study indicates that repetitive work has no relationship to turnover: Maurice D. Kilbridge, "Turnover, Absenteeism, and Transfer Rates as Indicators of Employee Dissatisfaction with Repetitive Work," *Industrial and Labor Relations Review*, Vol. 15, No. 1 (October 1961), pp. 21-32.

[28] Leonard Sayles, "Wildcat Strikes," *Harvard Business Review*, Vol. 32, No. 6 (November 1954), pp. 42-52.

Since mass-production jobs are among the most common industrial jobs and represent the most serious problems in human relations, it is worth considering what steps management can take to ameliorate the situation.

Traditionally, technological decisions are made purely on the basis of mechanical efficiency and short-run labor costs. The heritage from scientific management is that employees with simple jobs can be trained and controlled easily. But a heavy price is paid in terms of utter indifference to work, extending from escapist daydreaming to purposeful sabotage.

Job Enlargement

Specialization in mass production has been pushed to the point where the smallest possible band of a worker's ability is being utilized. Already efforts are being made to reverse this process, and with some success.[29] To accomplish this reversal, the engineering factors involved in each individual job must be carefully analyzed. Perhaps the assembly lines can be shortened so that there will be more lines and fewer workers on each line. Instead of assigning one man to each job, a group of men can be assigned to a group of jobs and then allowed to decide for themselves how to organize the work. Such changes permit more social contacts and greater control over the work process. Some companies have experimented with letting machine operators do their own set-ups (formerly done by skilled maintenance personnel) and their own quality control, and sometimes several jobs are combined into one, thus increasing employee responsibility.

> A recent example at the Polaroid Corp. involved operators and assistant operators who worked on a major film assembly machine. They felt that their work was repetitive, that they were in effect "chained to the machine." They also resented being told by the inspection and quality control departments when the film they produced did not meet quality standards.
>
> The solution to relieving their frustrations was to change the operation so that they are now responsible for their own quality. In addition to feeding and controlling the flow of materials through the machine, they take photographs and make graphs to determine quality. It's possible for them to determine immediately if anything is not operating properly and take the necessary corrective action. . . .
>
> Results have been impressive—as operators have taken more interest in the quality of their work, costs per roll of film have gone down and quality yields have gone up. It's also been possible to eliminate several inspecting jobs and transfer the inspectors to more challenging jobs in the company.[30]

---

[29] For an excellent résumé of the literature in this area, see Chris Argyris, *Integrating the Individual and the Organization* (New York: Wiley, 1964).

[30] "Job Enlargement and Job Rotation," *Personnel Management Bulletin,* Report No. 157 (May 15, 1962), p. 1.

Care must be exercised, however, not to convert a job which has become automatic (and that allows daydreaming and unlimited socializing) into one that makes employees tense. Many employees have not only grown used to a no-attention job, but they may actually prefer it to one which requires additional learning, surface attention, and responsibilities.[31]

Job Rotation and Alternation

Some companies are seeking to reduce boredom through systematically moving workers from one job to another. This practice provides variety, lets the employee see more of the total operation, and gives workers a chance to learn additional skills. The company also benefits, since the workers become able to perform a number of different jobs in the event of an emergency.

Yet in one situation we studied, some of the workers objected to being rotated from job to job and jolted out of their routine. They looked upon their job almost as a piece of personal property; being an "expert" on one particular type of work gave them a feeling of status and importance that they lost when they were moved around.

In general, those who opposed job rotation worked on no-attention jobs and enjoyed daydreaming. Being shifted from spot to spot converted these no-attention jobs to surface-attention jobs and made reverie more difficult. On the other hand, workers whose regular job prevented them from daydreaming endorsed rotation as a relief from monotony.

Change of pace. Anything that will give the worker a chance to change his pace when he wishes will make him feel less like a robot and more like a human being—and will lend variety to his work.[32] Further, if workers are permitted to change their pace they can build "banks" and thus obtain visible evidence of accomplishment.

Scheduled rest periods. Extensive research on the impact of rest periods indicates that they may increase both morale and productivity. Scheduled rest periods bring many advantages:

1. They counteract physical fatigue.
2. They provide variety and relieve monotony.
3. They are something to look forward to—getting a break gives a sense of achievement.
4. They provide opportunities for social contacts.

---

[31] *Cf.* Maurice Kilbridge, "Do Workers Prefer Larger Jobs?" *Personnel*, Vol. 37, No. 5 (September 1960), p. 45.

[32] One of the most insistent demands of the United Automobile Workers has been for the right to control the speed of the assembly line. This and safety are the two areas about which the union has the right to strike at any time. For two experiments in which workers substantially increased their output when given control over their work pace, see John R. P. French, "Field Experiments: Changing Group Productivity," in James G. Miller, ed., *Experiments in Social Psychology* (New York: McGraw-Hill, 1950), p. 86; and William F. Whyte *et. al.*, *Money and Motivation* (New York: Harper and Row, 1955), Chapter 10.

Even where there are no formal rest periods, technology permitting, every worker takes a break once in a while, perhaps just by slowing down a bit, or going to the washroom or the coffee machine. If management tries to forbid this practice, workers will still "bootleg" breaks into the work schedule, although the value of the breaks in reducing fatigue will be impaired. Management must recognize that many of the rest periods workers take are minor goals that they set for themselves and rewards they give themselves for making certain quotas, rather than just the result of a desire to get away from work.

Scheduled rest periods seem to reduce the incidence of unscheduled ones. But on the other hand, as we have seen, many jobs fall into natural work units, and the natural time to take a break is at the end of a unit. Indeed, a few moments of relaxation at this point accentuate the feeling of accomplishment. Rest pauses scheduled for the whole department may tend to destroy these natural units, interrupt the work, and reduce the pulling power of the job. Further, when management *tells* workers when to rest, they have less feeling of autonomy than if they were to make the decision for themselves.

Giving a Feeling of Accomplishment

There are many ways in which management can give employees a feeling of accomplishment, though few are appropriate to every situation.

Greater autonomy. Possibly the single effective way of increasing job satisfaction is to give workers more freedom to do their work in their own way— or, if that is impossible, to let the work group as a whole make this decision or at least be consulted when decisions are made. Since this whole area is closely related to the supervisor-worker relationship, however, we shall postpone detailed discussion of it to a later chapter.

Setting goals. In order to satisfy the natural desire for specific assignments, and in order to provide definite goals toward which to work, some companies permit workers to leave early (without loss of income) when they have finished their job. Other plants set daily production quotas which are announced to the entire work force. When these quotas are "accepted" as being "fair," they may well provide motivation for higher production. In a sense, working to achieve a quota makes a game out of the work. On the other hand, employees may regard quotas as a form of management pressure. They will work hard for goals that they have set for themselves, but strongly oppose "unfair" goals set by management.

In any case, psychologists tell us that goals are much more effective (1) if they are realistic, if there is a reasonable chance of attaining them, and (2) if they can be achieved in the relatively near future. Finishing a chapter in an hour is a far more compelling goal than reading a whole book in an evening.

Breaking the work down into meaningful units. Earlier we pointed out that most people get a sense of accomplishment from completing a whole job. But just what constitutes a "whole job" and precisely what is meant by "completion" are matters that can be manipulated by management. By breaking the work down into units or batches, management can give the employee a feeling of completion every time he finishes one batch. The desire to finish a unit has a strong "pulling power" and also enhances the worker's efficiency.

Work units that are too large should be broken down and those that are too small should be lumped together. How large is the optimal unit? One study suggests that it should last for an hour or an hour and a half, depending on the situation.[33]

Maier reports an ingenious example of how the boring work of telephone maintenance in the central office was broken down into smaller units: [34]

> There is no challenge of diagnosing trouble, and the job is very confining since a man can work for hours within the space of a few feet. There is never a real experience of progress. When the job is finished the worker starts all over again.
>
> In one office the frames on which the men worked were subdivided by means of chalk lines. . . . Each block required between one and a half and two hours to complete. The worker made his choice of . . . unit. . . . The benefits of this pattern of work were immediately apparent. . . . Once a man selected a block he worked until it was finished.
>
> Every time a man completed a unit he took a smoke or a stretch. Even lunch and quitting time found no untagged units. The men liked the plan and the supervisors reported that complaining decreased and the trouble with meeting work schedules was eliminated.

Avoiding interruption of natural units. A man who is engrossed in his work resents being disturbed and wastes a good bit of time trying to pick up his work again. Secretaries object to being asked to do something else when they are in the middle of a letter. It is almost a matter of simple courtesy to say, "When you get a break for a minute, could you do this?"

Similarly, workers object to starting a new job just before quitting time, although if they are behind schedule on an existing job they will spurt to finish it up. There is often trouble between shifts when one shift leaves unfinished work for the next shift to complete.

Other forms of goals. On some jobs the worker tends one or more machines and can see no visible accumulation of product. Here management may be able to provide other forms of goals, such as producing x amount per shift, reducing the time required for repairs by a given percentage, or avoiding breakdowns for an entire shift. Or management may change the form of goal altogether.

---

[33] D. Cox and K. M. D. Sharpe, "Research on the Unit of Work," *Occupational Psychology*, Vol. 25, No. 2 (April 1951), pp. 90-108.

[34] *Op. cit.*, p. 489.

One of the most interesting human relations studies arising out of World War II related to the Royal Air Force. Fighter pilots at a certain air base were growing discouraged because an almost perpetual fog kept them from contacting enemy bombers. Their discouragement was reflected in careless flying and high accident rates. When the pilots accepted as a goal the conquering of the weather, which became their new enemy, morale was substantially raised and accidents declined. Thus their need for accomplishment was no longer frustrated.[35]

Providing information on progress.   Even where production has nothing to do with incentive earnings or opportunities for promotion, employees like to know how they are doing.

In a plant that manufactured a large number of small items at high speed, management installed counters on each of the lines, just for supervisory purposes. Soon the employees were spending so much time sneaking a look that additional counters were installed at each work place. Informal competition developed both between lines and between shifts on the same line. Then the foreman brought in a blackboard and chalk and the men began posting their records. (*Question:* What might have happened had management deliberately tried to foster competition?)

An aircraft manufacturer posts bar graphs showing the length of time actually taken to complete various components of the plane as compared to the time planned.[36] A telephone company uses indices of efficiency, particularly among its white-collar employees.[37]

Building career lines.   Management can promote a sense of progress and commitment to the organization by fitting jobs together into promotional ladders. As we have seen, mass-production work typically provides "no place to go," and this lack of opportunity discourages those employees who may be most worth promoting.

Selection.   A good deal of attention is already devoted to endeavoring to preselect those employees whose psychological dispositions are likely to be consistent with the available job satisfactions. More research, however, needs to be done in this area.

Stressing the importance of the job.   If the job becomes too specialized, the worker loses his feeling for the relationship between his work and the overall process. He would like to feel both (1) that he plays a significant part in the work process as a whole, and (2) that the process itself is important.

---

[35] See T. T. Paterson, *Morale in War and Work* (London: Max Parish, 1955).

[36] John Walsh and Max Shousen, "Scoreboards Boost Production," *Supervisory Management,* Vol. 1, No. 5 (May 1956), p. 4.

[37] Of course, such indices may be regarded as a method of exerting pressure. Or they may encourage quantity at the expense of quality. We shall discuss some of these factors later. See Peter M. Blau, *The Dynamics of Industrial Bureaucracy* (Chicago: University of Chicago Press, 1955), Chapter 3.

Many companies take new employees on a trip through the plant to show them how the work they will be doing fits into the total picture. During World War II war heroes were invited to visit war plants, and demonstrations were staged to dramatize what happened when a part misfunctioned. In indoctrinating new employees the telephone company impresses on them the importance of their jobs in saving lives and in helping people in trouble.

Providing Social Satisfactions

On jobs that lack other satisfactions, provisions for social relationships often produce very favorable reactions. Partitions can help identify a social group in what would otherwise be a huge amorphous department. Employees who work in isolation or among strangers (for example, draftsmen who are "farmed out" on a daily basis to engineering departments) can be given a home base by allowing fellow employees who share the same occupational status to get together first thing in the morning or at the end of the shift. Where this is impossible, shared relief time or group meetings may help.

Physical Context of Work

We have been concerned largely with the psychological and social setting of work, and the reactions of employees to this context. But there is also a physical context. Some craft jobs have to be performed in dangerous settings (consider the iron-workers who erect the superstructure of skyscrapers). Many factories (say, smelters) are hot and dirty! Some operations involving chemicals have acrid fumes; textile plants tend to be hot and damp (in part because thread doesn't break easily with high humidity). There are still many jobs which are physically exhausting on the auto assembly lines in Detroit. Many workmen have to be on their feet a good deal; cranemen sit in one place for long, fatiguing hours; and some generator assemblers have to crouch. We could extend this list, but it should be obvious that there are substantial sources of dissatisfaction to be found in the physical conditions under which jobs are performed.

Employees do like clean, comfortably cooled, light and airy workplaces in which they can sit and walk at will and where physical fatigue is at a minimum. Most managers know this, but some jobs are difficult to adapt to these rather universal desires.

Some observers who would argue that certain employees gain satisfaction from doing heavy—even dangerous—work under difficult circumstances. Their sense of "maleness" is enhanced and they poke fun at other men doing "women's" work.

Music. In recent years many companies have begun to play recorded music during work hours. Brisk marches are recommended for certain times of the day, more soothing melodies for others. Claims have been made that music leads to higher production and that some types of music (marches, for instance) have a more beneficial effect than others. Other studies show that although the effects on production are negligible, workers generally enjoy listening to the music, provided it isn't too loud or incessant. Obviously the effect of music varies from one industrial situation to another.[38]

Shorter hours. How long should the work-day be? During World War II the British discovered that a shorter work-day sometimes led to higher production. After the shock of the Dunkirk disaster, the work-week of British factory workers was increased from an average of 56 hours to 69.5 hours. After an initial spurt, production started to fall off until at last it was 12 per cent lower than it had been before the change in hours. Then, when the shorter work-week was restored, production increased to a higher point than ever before. In one case when the work-day was reduced from 12 to 10 hours shop accidents dropped 70 per cent—indicating that fatigue may also create serious safety problems.

CONCLUSION

We are not surprised to find the enormous contrast in job satisfactions derived from craft as compared to mass-production work. What really are more interesting and useful to recall are the various dimensions of these jobs which elicited strong employee reaction. Although most typical industrial jobs will tend to be an admixture of craft and machine operation, one will be able to assess the contribution of many of the following elements to employee reactions.

Interest, Variety, and Movement

Intrinsic variability of the work, length of job cycle, and repetitiveness
Depth-, surface-, or no-attention requirement
Opportunity to develop own work methods, to vary pace and rhythm, to move around and utilize different body muscles, to take breaks
Ability to adjust job requirements to personality

Accomplishment, Autonomy, and Identification

Opportunity to exercise discretion, initiative, and self-expression
Duration and intensity of training required
Availability of a career line, sense of progress in status and earnings
Degree to which work results appear to depend on personal ability and skill
Commitment to and identification with some end result or total process
Sense of completion, of being responsible for a finished product or service
Identification with a recognized and prestigious occupational group

---

[38] A comprehensive review of research on the effects of music is provided by Richard S. Urhbock, "Music on the Job: Its Influence on Morale and Production," *Personnel Psychology*, Vol. 14, No. 1 (Spring 1961), pp. 9-38.

Job Pressures and Relations to Management

    Tightness of work standards, type of pressure exercised by supervision

    Variability of work load through the day

    Potential cost of failure

    Personal vulnerability, the degree to which mistakes can be "assigned" to individuals

    Interpersonal pressures for improved performance from peers

    Ability to contact more than one level of management

    Apparent congruity between interests of managers and employees

    Job security—ease of replacement by others, relative importance of labor costs to total costs

Social Relations

    Required by work process itself

    Available within the work environment

    Impact of hours of work on community social relations

Physical Conditions of Work

    Heat, noise, temperature, humidity, and odors

    Posture imposed, effort required

    Relative cleanliness and attractiveness of work setting

    Length of work-day and work-week

Often the alert manager can relate his observations of employee behavior and the sentiments they express to these various job factors. He is thus in a better position to interpret the underlying source of satisfaction or dissatisfaction. At times, as we have seen, the manager can go one step farther. He can make modifications at the margin of the job, so to speak, by changing the length of the cycle, the opportunity for social relationships, and so on. In a few cases the manager may actually be able to influence the over-all character of the job, whether it tends to fit toward the craft or toward the mass-production end of the continuum.

PROBLEM 1

THE HEADLINER GROUP [39]

    The headliner group is located in the Passenger Trim Department; it is their job to place the fabric covering on the inside of the car roof, stretch it to a fit, smooth out the wrinkles, and glue it into place. Though the job might, at first observation, seem to be rather simple, it is actually something of an art, for far more skill is required to handle the pliable fabric than is needed in working with unyielding metal, the major component of an automobile. To train a man to do the work with any degree of proficiency requires at least a week of constant instruction. For this reason, it is difficult to replace a headliner on short notice and few are trained to do the job.

---

[39] We are indebted to a former student, James T. Bennett, for this case.

The seven men who filled the job were not unaware of this modest skill requirement. They considered themselves superior to most of the assemblers who worked with metal parts, although their job, too, was highly repetitious. They also felt free to complain about anything and everything: heating, lighting, ventilation, the tools with which they worked, and supervisory prejudice.

Although each man performed the same job, the group did not actually work together on a car. Each installed the headliner on every seventh automobile. A worker would get into a unit, remain in it until he finished the work, and then go to the seventh unit back and repeat the cycle. Therefore, the work of a given man was not dependent on the work of any other. The amount of effort required might vary, however. For example, a station wagon would require more work, for it has more interior to be covered by the headliner than a two-door automobile. Similarly, a two-door requires less work than a four-door. Although attempts were made to keep the proportion of each type of unit produced constant during each hour, it was indeed rare when no variation occurred. Difficulties in scheduling, errors, and problems in other departments made the maintenance of a constant "mix" almost impossible. Since these variations had an impact on the work time of the headliners, they were quick to seize on the smallest fluctuations, pressure the foreman for relief, and threaten the foreman with union action.

The major bone of contention of the workers was the time standard imposed on them. It was consistently argued that the job could not be time studied and that there was no "standard time" for the work. The group complained that there were too many variables to consider and even went so far as to aver that changes in the weather (humidity) would have noticeable changes on the material with which they worked. It was claimed that judgment was required for every unit was a little different. Resentment was also strong against their rate of pay. Although they were well-paid and within a few cents of the highest-paid jobs in the plant, the workers believed that their jobs required more effort than that of the door-fitters, the best-paid group. Because their work necessitated that they climb into the automobile, perform the operation with their hands above their heads, and remain stooped over in the unit until the headliner was installed, they contended that the task was the most tiring in the plant. It was also protested that not enough allowance was given for fatigue and contingencies, and that an extra worker should be trained and placed in the group to assist. Although the headliners had complained about the job and the work load, it was possible for them to give each other an extra break during some part of the day. While six men kept up the work, one could leave the job and go for a cup of coffee and a cigarette.

Since the foreman had to get the work from these men to maintain production, he had to have their cooperation. Checks were made on the cost which each foreman's area incurred as well as the quality of his production. Data were recorded daily on these two control items and were given to the foreman, the general foreman, and the department superintendent. Costs and quality were the determinants of the foreman's bonus and directly affected his chances for promotion.

If the foreman placed new pressure on the group to speed up, the quality would drop, the workers would slowly fall further behind, and the utility man would be required to help the men catch up, thus diverting him from his regular duties of relieving others and disrupting the whole relief schedule. Complaints were sure to arise from the others when this occurred.

1. If you were instructing a new foreman in this department, what are the things you would tell him about the "headliners?"

2. What do you know about technology and job satisfaction that would be useful in managing such a group?

3. Do "gripes" and pressure provide any satisfaction? How?

DIRTY BOTTLES

The Milwaukee Brewing Company has been plagued with trouble among its *bottle inspectors*, whose job is to check each bottle carefully to make sure that it is absolutely clean as it leaves the bottle-washing machine. Though there have been many attempts to develop mechanical inspecting devices, none of these has worked with 100 per cent accuracy. As a consequence, each bottle must be visually inspected as it passes by the inspector on a conveyor belt. Although this job is highly paid, it is hard to find men to take it and many quit after working on a few months.

1. What seems to be the basic problem here?

2. What suggestions can you make for solving it?

CANDY WRAPPERS

All candy made by the Quality Candy Company is wrapped by hand. Candy is brought to each wrapper by chute. She wraps each piece and then drops it into another chute which leads to packers in another room.

Each girl handles a different kind of candy and their work locations are isolated from each other.

1. How will the girls react to this sort of work?

2. What can be done to increase their morale and output?

Technology and Job Satisfaction: Automation and White-Collar Work

Two occupational trends have received a great deal of attention in the 1960's. One is the onrush of automation in manufacturing, the other is the growing importance of nonfactory jobs, of service industry, and white-collar work. Both have important implications for job satisfaction and give us a more well-rounded view of the world of work and its impact on the employee. Since it most directly affects what has been described in the previous chapter, let us look first at the jobs created by automation.

AUTOMATION AND CONTINUOUS-PROCESS TECHNOLOGY

Perhaps a definition of automation is in order since the term has come into such widespread use. Although there is no single definition, most authors stress the following components: (1) use of high-speed computers for data processing or control, (2) use of "closed-loop feedback" techniques to facilitate self-control by machines themselves, (3) mechanization of transfer operations, (4) increased use of multiple-purpose equipment, and (5) the combination of jobs and work units in larger self-contained processes.[1]

Detroit Automation

Much "automation" leaves the intrinsic characteristics of jobs unchanged. Workers merely operate more productive machinery that positions the work, checks its accuracy, and transports materials from stage to stage automatically. But the operator continues to be a machine-tender, and a sharp status line continues to separate him from the engineers who install and maintain the

[1] James Bright, *Automation and Management* (Boston: Harvard Business School, Division of Research, 1958); Floyd Mann and L. Richard Hoffman, *Automation and the Worker* (New York: Holt, Rinehart and Winston, 1960), p. 3; Charles R. Walker, *Toward the Automatic Factory* (New Haven, Conn.: Yale University Press, 1957).

equipment and the managers who supervise it. For the most part, this is what is called "Detroit Automation." Jobs may be somewhat less physically demanding, but there is also more pressure associated with the complicated, expensive and potentially very vulnerable processing techniques.[2] Should something go wrong, a great deal of production is lost. As a consequence, supervision may be even closer than before the changes.

Continuous-Process Technology

Something close to true automation does, however, exist today in some plants in the chemical and petroleum industries and in electrical power generation and steel manufacturing. Automation of this sort is most easily adapted to industries in which the product can flow continuously (particularly as a liquid or gas) from entering raw material to finished product through a number of interlinked stages. Continuous steel strip mills and electrical generating plants, where fuel or water power is used to make steam or is applied directly to power turbines, approximate the continuous flows of a chemical plant. In all such factories an employee spends much of his time monitoring gauges and control instruments, and his major work activities come only during breakdowns, and start-up and change-over periods.

Such work contrasts sharply with that of craftsmen and machine operators. As we have seen, a craftsman utilizes manual, motor, perceptual and conceptual skills. He manipulates materials, his own body, and ideas. Engineers have eliminated the conceptual and perceptual element from the job of the semi-skilled machine-tender and the assembly-line worker, though they must still develop some manual dexterity and motor skill, but far less than the craftsmen. Automated employees, however, need few physical skills, but they are expected to use their "heads." [3]

TYPE OF WORKER	SKILLS REQUIRED			
Craftsman	Manual	Motor	Conceptual	Perceptual
Machine-tender and assembly-line worker	Manual	Motor		
Automation worker			Conceptual	Perceptual

Interest, Variety, and Movement

Most jobs in continuous-process plants require an irregular combination of surface attention and depth attention. The *job cycle* is a relatively long one. Dials have to be checked and adjustments made when readings are "off

---

[2] *Cf.* William Faunce, "Automation in the Automobile Industry," *American Sociological Review*, Vol. 23, No. 4 (August 1958), pp. 401-407.

[3] The table is adapted from Joan Woodward, *Industrial Organization: Theory and Practice* (London: Oxford University Press, 1965), pp. 63-64.

standard." In one case in a chemical plant, 50 different instruments are monitored every two hours.[4]

The pace of work is uneven, but in part it can be adjusted to the comfort, convenience, and natural "rhythms" of the employees. Although the checking operations must be periodic, they need not be done precisely on time:

> "Sometimes when it's close to the time for 2 o'clock readings, we might have soup on the stove. You can eat the soup first and do the work later or take the readings at 1:45 and then eat your soup." [5]

In utility generating stations and in some parts of a refinery, the operators may be confined to a control room. In a chemical plant, however, they must take lengthy walks through widely dispersed equipment.

Aside from monitoring operations, the other part of automated jobs consists of handling unexpected breakdowns (and sometimes assisting in regular starting-up and shutting-down activities). In this phase depth attention is called for, and time is of utmost importance. Because of the enormous costs involved in idle equipment, management expects everyone to pitch in energetically when there is trouble. But if there are going to be sufficient personnel available for such emergencies, when things are going smooth, there is of necessity going to be a good deal of idle time.

Unlike a typical mass-production plant where a breakdown is a welcome relief, here a stoppage is a sign of failure. It is also a period of excitement, even drama. The unexpected breaks up the monotony. Locating, diagnosing, and fixing troubles can be absorbing, even though breakdowns also call for very hard work.

Accomplishment, Autonomy, and Identification

"Continuous-processing technology may serve to reverse the historic trend toward the greater division of labor and specialization." [6] It is this involvement in a tangible, complete activity (refining oil, producing electric power) that produces job interest and the satisfaction which grows out of meaningful activity. Employees feel *responsible* for keeping highly expensive technology going. Rather than concentrate on a small, essentially meaningless task, the employee develops a sense of commitment to the total process. Thus, he gains the satisfaction of knowing that in some measure he contributes to an observable, finished product:

> The worker's role changes from providing skills to accepting responsibility ... the very definition of responsibility as a job requirement involves a mean-

---

[4] Robert Blauner, *Alienation and Freedom* (Chicago: University of Chicago Press, 1964), p. 134.

[5] *Ibid.*, p. 138.

[6] *Ibid.*, p. 143.

ingful connection between the worker's own function and the goals of entire enterprise.[7]

In contrast to the mass-production factory, there are not endless, impersonal rows of people repeating small tasks. Instead, relatively few men patrol and control a vast array of massive equipment, or they oversee a control room which is like a command post. Here employees accept some of the functions that supervisors exercise in other technologies.

Their sense of growth and development and importance is further enhanced by the career ladders that develop naturally. A refinery still or a production unit in a chemical plant is handled by a small crew which is differentiated in skill and experience; the lowest-ranking employee is usually called a helper and the top-skilled person can be a head operator stillman or crew chief. Because of the close interdependence of their jobs and the need to be familiar with a variety of complex tasks, new employees are brought in as part of general labor gangs and progress through a series of jobs as their experience increases and they evidence willingness to accept responsibility. Each successive job enables them to get a broader view of operations.

And here management, far more than in craft or mass-production industries, is willing to invest in continuing training. Hence, most employees experience a sense of steady progress in status and earnings. Highly important by-products are, for the employee, substantial job security and, for management, a work-force showing unusually high identification with the company.

The top skilled crew-chief positions involve enormous responsibility and challenge in these industries. As an example, let us look at the chief melter in a newly computerized oxygen-furnace steel plant. Premixed, preweighted ingredients are transported to a huge pressure cooker (the furnace's converter), which heats them for about an hour and is then tapped. Here is a description of the work of the employee who handles the operation, Mr. Peral:

> Mr. Peral directs operations with the computer from a control room several feet from the vessel. He is in touch with his eight men through a loudspeaker system. . . . To make a batch of steel, called a heat, Mr. Peral first has his computer figure out the ingredients, based on orders for specific grades of steel. Then the vessel is tilted to the "charging" side. The press of a button sets off 75 to 80 tons of scrap—. . . . How does Mr. Peral know when it's time to tap? "You've got to know your end points," he says. "You notice how the carbon flame above the vessel is dying? It's about ready." . . . Mr. Peral orders the vessel tilted again toward the charging side. Protected by a metal shield, two of his assistants insert a long pole called a thermocouple into the vessel. . . . If the mixture is not hot enough, the vessel is turned upright again and heated some more."[8]

Here, as elsewhere, machines do not completely displace employees; a number of critical jobs can still be performed more effectively by human beings.

[7] *Ibid.*
[8] *The New York Times,* March 18, 1965, p. 43 and p. 50.

The psychological satisfactions associated with these jobs has been high-lighted by a recent study of an automated electricity-generating plant:

> It would appear that company managements through their design engineers are now in a position to restore to our working population some of the pride and satisfaction that stems from performing interesting and challenging jobs. Rather than making men adjuncts to machines, automation seems to be capable of utilizing workers as human beings with a capacity for intellectual under-standing.[9]

Job Pressures
and Relations to Management

Under automation the speed-up that occurs during breakdowns or change-over periods is not resented as efforts by management to get more work done. Here the employees can see for themselves when hard work is required and the supervisor doesn't have to push them. Also, as we have seen, the technical leadership in these situations often is provided by the top-ranking member of the crew, the chief operator. Since he works right alongside the other members of the gang and shares their values and difficulties, his demands are likely to be interpreted as reasonable.[10]

Mistakes can be terribly expensive, so employees cannot be rushed or ex-cessively pressured by management. Although a craft worker can redo poor-quality work and an assembler's mistakes can be remedied by a repairman farther down the line, an error by a continuous-process employee may cost thousands of dollars before it can be rectified. Checking and repairing involve mental processes which cannot be coordinated by stop watch.

In many circumstances, management is pleased when employees are not working hard—this indicates that things are going well. If the employees work wisely and effectively, there are few or no breakdowns. Under these conditions both employee relaxation and company product are maximized!

There are other reasons why management seldom appears oppressive to employees under this type of technology. Since at least the top-ranking workers are highly experienced and well informed, their opinions are often sought out by supervisors and by engineers. Particularly when pilot-plant operations are conducted, employees are likely to have contact with levels of management above their immediate supervisor and with staff engineers. Thus, in a modern continuous-process steel mill, there is less status distinction between skilled hourly workers and management and more personal relationships than are found in an automobile assembly plant, where relationships are highly formal and primarily limited to order-giving by the immediate manager.[11]

---

[9] Mann and Hoffman, *op. cit.*, pp. 205-206.

[10] One article suggests that leadership exercised by working, "inside" leaders was char-acteristic of man's earliest work groups: F. L. W. Richardson, "Managing Man's Animal Nature," *Pittsburgh Business Review*, Vol. 34, No. 11 (December 1964), p. 4.

[11] *Cf.* Joan Woodward, *Management and Technology* (London: HMSO, 1960).

Since labor costs make up a much smaller percentage of total costs in automated plants than in nonautomated plants, management can provide more generous wages and fringe benefits. More important, since these plants are designed to operate with a minimum of employees, nearly all of whom are required no matter what the scale of operations, employees are less expendable during periods of recession. Furthermore, management as we have noted has a major investment in the career training of its workforce. The employees sense that they are not dealt with as a "variable cost," something that can be let go if business activity declines. Instead, they see themselves as having careers that will last their working life.[12]

Hours of Work

Many automated jobs require shift work and this is a source of dissatisfaction. To get maximum use of expensive equipment, it must be used round-the-clock. And, chemical plants and utilities operate day and night because their processes can't be turned "on" and "off" except at great cost.

Though a few employees like shift work, because it enables them to make alternative use of the daytime, most find that late hours interfere with normal family and social life. Many firms rotate shifts. This procedure avoids charges of discrimination and prevents jockeying for favorable schedules, but it requires employees to get used to constantly changing sleeping and waking hours, not an easy thing to do as anyone knows who has flown across a number of time zones.[13]

Social Relations

Most employees in automated industries work in teams. On some chemical operations there may be only two or three employees per shift; on others ten or so. The employees work closely together and must develop the ability to coordinate their efforts and help each other. In turn, close social relations develop on the team which may carry over into the community.

Whereas social-group boundaries are often ambiguous and vague in traditional industrial plants, they are more clear-cut here. Where hundreds of employees do similar operations under one roof or where an assembly line snakes for a mile or two past thousands working side by side, it is difficult for employees to identify with a specific group of fellow workers. The limited number of employees under automation and their specific relationship to a

---

[12] Of course, this assumes that the employee exhibits reasonable energy and learning ability. In recent years some oil refineries have had to cope with what they termed "obsolete" employees, often through early retirement.

[13] For a more complete treatment of the total subject of working hours see Clyde Dankert, Floyd Mann, and Herbert Northrop, eds., *Hours of Work* (New York: Harper and Row, 1965).

given process serves to unite a social group which has the same boundaries as the work unit.[14]

We should not exaggerate the beneficial effects of automation on social relations, however. Some automated plants have only a small number of employees, widely dispersed, who rarely see each other. Isolated locations plus noise may make difficult all but limited conversation.

Summary: Automation and Job Satisfaction

It would be a mistake to assume that all job-satisfaction problems are solved by the introduction of continuous-process automation. For there is substantial monotony associated with watching and waiting. Future research will likely emphasize the psychological reactions to this *surface-attention problem* since many military (for instance, missile bases and space ships) as well as civilian activities require "dial-watching" tasks to be performed over long periods of time.

> Automation often requires a very high-level person for one hour a week and somebody who is capable of doing nothing for the other 39 hours. . . . You are going to have trouble keeping people from getting a kind of "turnpike fatigue" running one of these machines.[15]

In addition employees are likely to feel substantial anxiety about making costly errors.

More than balancing these dissatisfactions, however, are the through-the-job satisfactions derived from the relatively long work cycles, flexible work rhythms, and the opportunities to work as a team in emergencies. In fact, the entire relationship between management and workers is improved over what obtained in traditional manufacturing: There is more two-way communication and mutual understanding. People handle problems as they arise and there is little need for management to impose quotas and work standards. Employees can see themselves progressing over time on a career through a series of graded job steps. Relatively small numbers and management's investment in training give a sense of individualism which contrasts sharply with the impersonality of the traditional sprawling factory.

True automation is really the opposite of Taylorism and scientific management's mass-production methods. The former involves looking at work processes as a whole and giving employees a broader view and wider responsibilities. Mechanization and mass production foster a piecemeal approach: speeding up a machine here, eliminating an arm motion there, saving an

---

[14] In Chapter 16 we shall see that many work frictions are caused by work environments in which the social group contains other members than the work group which must coordinate itself.

[15] P. L. Cook, Jr., "Social and Economic Effects of Automation," *Twenty First Annual Midwest Conference on Industrial Relations* (Chicago: Graduate School of Business, University of Chicago, 1955), p. 10.

operation some place else. It is hardly any wonder that employee reactions to these widely different technologies vary so dramatically.

A Note: Unskilled Work
and Floating Labor

Automation is having one of its most profound effects in helping to eliminate some of those jobs that used to be filled by completely unskilled, often temporary, employees. Jobs such as those of yard gangs, sweepers, and loaders used to be reserved for "floating labor" who move endlessly from job to job and sometime from region to region. Lacking education, or handicapped by membership in a minority group, they are disqualified from the better jobs. Experience has "taught" them that they have little chance to get ahead, that there is no point even in trying. Just to hold on to what they have is hard enough. When they find a job they work until they get enough to meet their minimum needs, and when they are unemployed their friends support them. Immediate pleasures are their only goal. They show little "drive" or "ambition."

> [Indeed,] only when one knows where his next week's or next month's shelter will come from, can he and his children afford to go in for long-term education and training, the endless search for opportunities, and the tedious apple polishing that the attainment of higher skills and occupational status requires.[16]

Since security and economic advancement mean little to these workers, they look for jobs that provide independence and a feeling of being one's own boss. They may not amount to much by middle-class standards, but they retain the freedom of telling off the boss and quitting their job whenever they want to.[17] Thus, in terms of commitment they represent the antithesis of the employee attitudes that can be fostered by continuous-process automation and its career lines.

WHITE-COLLAR WORK

Economists have observed the following trend as industrialization proceeds. Primary industry (mines and farms) requires a decreasing proportion of the labor force as secondary industry (manufacturing) becomes more important. In its turn, tertiary industry (services) becomes increasingly significant. With increasing incomes, people want and can afford to pay for more services. And service industries (banks, hospitals, stores, and so on) tend to provide a high proportion of white-collar jobs. Even in our factories, the ratios of managers, engineers, clerks, and technicians (all white-collar workers)

---

[16] Allison Davis, "The Motivation of Underprivileged Workers," in William F. Whyte, ed., *Industry and Society* (New York: McGraw-Hill, 1946), p. 89.

[17] See Richard Centers, "Motivation Aspects of Occupational Stratification," *Journal of Social Psychology*, Vol. 28 (November 1948), pp. 187-217.

to production workers grow as more sophisticated technologies are utilized and as more attention is paid to research, design, marketing, finance, and other nonmanufacturing activities.

White vs. Blue Collar

Prestige advantages. In almost every country white-collar carries more prestige than blue-collar. In fact, some developing nations have great difficulty improving their productivity because the educated citizens all want to work in offices (as bank or government employees, lawyers, accountants, and so on) and not in factories. The reasons for the difference in status are not difficult to identify.

The names alone suggest an important difference. Blue-collar workers presumably get their hands and clothes soiled while working; the others can wear spotless white shirts. White-collar jobs are thought to have individuality in contrast to the mass character of factory work, to be "middle class" as distinct from "working class"! They are also "closer," both physically and psychologically, to management, and it is assumed that promotions come easier and salaries are higher in office work than in the plant. For many people whose fathers worked on farms, in mines, or factories, just getting a white-collar job is a major step forward. Finally, the traditional difference in prestige between

Projected Employment Growth for the Next Decade by Occupation *

PERCENTAGE OF LABOR FORCE, 1970 **	OCCUPATION	PROJECTED GROWTH				
		Decline	*No Change*	*Less Than Average*	*Average*	*More Than Average*
14	Service workers (*e.g.*, hairdressers, hospital attendants)					X
23	{ Clerical workers { Sales workers				X	X
24	Professional and technical (*e.g.*, engineers) Managers and proprietors				X	X
13	Craftsmen				X	
17	Operatives: semiskilled workers			X		
5	Laborers (nonfarm)		X			
5	Farm workers	X				

* U.S. Department of Labor, *Manpower Report of the President* (March 1963), Table 28.
** U.S. Department of Labor, *Manpower Report of the President* (March 1965), Page 54.

these two types of jobs reflects assumed differences in the relative difficulty and complexity of brain work as against manual work.

Some have said that white-collar "psychology can be understood as the psychology of prestige striving." [18] Managers have to learn that very substantial ego and social rewards are derived from what may appear to be unimportant differences between jobs. For example, a job title like "staff assistant" may provide a sense of advancement to an employee who was doing the same work when it was called "chief clerk."

Exaggerated differences. But it should be noted that the differences between blue- and white-collar work are declining. At least some factory work is as clean as office work, some much cleaner (for instance, the spotless, temperature-controlled manufacturing facilities where delicate instruments are made and tested). Some factory jobs (like the previously described chief melter in a steel mill) have a larger component of "brain work" than do most routine clerical office jobs. And there is some long-run tendency for the pay differential between blue- and white-collar work to disappear.

White-collar factories. The almost complete disappearance of differences between white- and blue-collar work can be observed in what could best be described as a "white-collar" factory. On a single work floor, there might be an acre of desks and work tables stretching as far as the eye can see. Minutely described, mechanized short-cycle jobs, requiring such "tools" as card punchers or typewriters, are being performed by clerical personnel, all of whom receive very similar wages.

Identification with management has been much reduced on such jobs. Promotions to the supervisory level tend to be reserved for college graduates who come into special training programs that bypass the great majority of lower-skilled office jobs. As a consequence, many white-collar workers substitute the goals of security and prestige for personal advancement.[19]

Of course, the introduction of computers is changing the office scene. Whether or not computers have increased or decreased the number of low-skilled, routine jobs is still being debated. Most modern, "automated" offices are really at a very primitive stage of automation; indeed, the stage is very like mass-production work. Employees who punch data onto computer cards or who place the magnetic ink numerals on the bottom of bank checks are doing finely divided, highly circumscribed, short-cycle jobs. To be sure, there are additional programmers, console operators, and maintenance personnel required, whose jobs are more interesting.[20]

---

[18] C. Wright Mills, *White Collar* (New York: Oxford University Press, 1953), Chapter 4.

[19] Roland J. Pellagrini and Charles H. Coates, "Executives and Supervisors: Contrasting Definitions of Career Success," *Administration Science Quarterly*, Vol. 1, No. 4 (March 1957), pp. 506-512.

[20] For a good review of the impact of mechanization on office jobs see Floyd C. Mann, "Psychological and Organizational Impacts," in John T. Dunlop, ed., *Automation and Technological Change* (Englewood Cliffs, N.J.: Prentice-Hall, 1962).

Thus, we find the reactions of many white-collar workers to their jobs very similar to those described in the previous chapter. Here below, for example, is a self-description provided by an office worker in a large insurance company:

> "As an operator I had to complete 720 units in 4 hours with no more than 11 errors. This quota was often very difficult to meet, especially on nights when the packs were of more than average difficulty. The job was extremely boring.
>
> "Each pack usually contained 180 policyholders' account cards. About 150 of these had to be billed on 'short forms.' There were two types of short forms—a #1 form and #4 form. The number of each type that was billed was recorded on a digital index on the machine. Usually, each pack had about the same number of each of the two types, and I played games of 'basketball' with each pack with the #1's vs. the #4's. Usually the scores were quite close, and on a couple of occasions the game went into overtime—that is, was continued in the next pack. Punching in the seven numbers that made up the policyholder's account number was my way of 'dribbling the ball down the floor,' and pushing in the button that rang up the total was 'the ball going through the basket.'"

Thus, workers in white-collar factories make a game of routine work just as do machine-tenders in factories.

Distinctive "white-collar" jobs. While differences in prestige and the physical characteristics of the work may have been exaggerated, there are white-collar jobs which provide distinctive satisfactions because of their unique properties. These are the jobs which embody major elements of:

1. Human-relations activity
2. Intellectual effort
3. Managerial responsibility

To be sure some positions require all three, but we shall treat them separately. In addition, we shall see that there is an important trend toward professionalization in white-collar work which has profound implications for the supervision of these types of employees.

Where Work Is Human Relations

The social satisfactions which blue-collar workers are able to obtain are enjoyed for the most part *around* the job; for receptionists, salesmen, waitresses, and others in similar jobs, satisfactory social relations are the essence of their work. Thus, these employees enjoy the opportunity to gain social satisfaction *through* work, but, as a consequence they are subject to much potential frustration when these relations become pressureful.

In these human-relations occupations, employees are often required to fit into closely timed relationships with other employees, many of whom may be under great stress just at the time they are asked for their cooperation. This problem can be most easily observed in restaurants where the waiter feels under great pressure to serve his customers quickly and thus earn more tips.

Waiters struggle with bus boys to get their tables cleared and set up quickly to be ready for the next customer. The waiter also may compete with other waiters to get scarce silverware or particular food items in short supply. Conflicts also occur between waiters and personnel in the serving pantry, kitchen and the bar.

Obviously, the need to cooperate under pressure can provide human-relations conflicts where personalities are poorly matched. Many individuals break down under such severe interactional strain: the constant bickering and the need to accommodate to others. For them the relative peace and quiet of a factory job, where "if you do your job no one bothers you," may be far more appealing. Other employees thrive on the hectic pace and the demands of fellow employees and customers alike; for them, interaction under pressure is highly satisfying and only the idleness associated with a slow day or slow season is painful.

A case example: retail selling. Retail selling is typically a fast-paced, unprogramed, demanding occupation and the pressures often exceed those in production work. As in any activity involving a customer, who is not a member of the organization, we find the need to adjust quickly to the whims and fancies of the person who is spending his money and expects *service*.

An example of the human-relations pressures and satisfactions of retailing is provided by the following description of a women's high-fashion specialty store.

> Markhams has three branches in a large midwestern city.[21] It deals in very expensive clothes and has a wealthy clientele. The downtown store is managed by Miss Stoler and her assistant, Sylvia. Frances, Ruth, and Betty are all salesgirls, working on commission.
>
> Whenever Mrs. von Jones and her daughter appear in the store, everyone jumps to attention; they are very good customers. One afternoon, Frances saw them first, greeted them, and used the intercom to call Ruth since they enjoyed having Ruth serve them.
>
> At one point Ruth said to Betty, who now had a customer, too, "Betty, run to the [other] stockroom and get me that size 14." Betty answered that she couldn't right now, she was busy. Ruth, obviously irritated, turned to Sylvia with her request. Sylvia complied.
>
> Ruth soon exhausted the stock of suitable dresses to show Mrs. von Jones. She slipped out to take the back elevator to the Receiving Room, and, peering through the wiremesh security wall, spied several expensive pieces just being unpacked. Upon asking, she was informed that they were destined for a branch store, and would not be ready for transportation until late in the day. She returned in a few minutes with Sylvia, pointed to them, and said, "See, those are the ones." Sylvia, declaring that Miss Stoler had OK'd their removal from the Receiving Room, picked several items for Mrs. von Jones from the rack for the East Side branch, obtained the cost of the dresses from the Receiving Agent, and told Ruth what the price on each would be. Together they went back up the freight elevator.

21 We are indebted to our former student, Mr. M. D. Strickler, for this description.

Ruth used the phone to call to the main floor for some things to be sent up for the daughter. The floor manager promised help, but, since all her girls were busy, she was obliged to take some things up herself. Ruth called the shoe department, described what had been sold thus far, and told the department head to "get up here now, before she leaves. Your customer will wait." Next Ruth went to get an additional fitter, and became quite angry when the Cashier told her, "Your saleslip isn't completed, and I can't process these charges until you get Mrs. von Jones' signature." Ruth took them back to the floor to get her customer's signature.

Miss Stoler began "closing the sale" with both the von Joneses for several garments, and since they wished to take two items with them, had them packed at the Cashier's desk. The Cashier called to the Credit Department for the OK, and was informed to "hold everything." It seemed that the account was 90 days overdue, in a large sum. When Ruth discovered the garments weren't being packed, she called the Credit Department, and demanded that it be OK'd at once. "She's in a hurry and she'll be mad. Besides, she always pays."

[Note particularly the large number of diverse, unpredictable, and stressful contacts handled by Ruth in response to her customer's demands. In turn, many people in the store must adjust their behavior to meet Ruth's job requirements.]

Where Work Is Mental Effort

An increasing number of jobs demand intellectual rather than physical effort. Copywriters, laboratory personnel, engineers, and programers all require creative talents that cannot be programed. Satisfactions on these jobs stem from the ability to do challenging work and find solutions to unique problems. Almost all involve depth attention and a highly variable work pace. As a talented designer explained:

> "When ideas come easily and I feel myself making progress, I can work up to 24 hours at a stretch. I often forget meals and don't really know whether it is night or day out or the weekend. Then there are long periods—maybe weeks— in which I can't seem to get anything done. I am always looking for an excuse for a break. If anyone comes near my office I start talking with them and am always going out for food."

When the work is going badly, deadlines are approaching, or an obstacle can't be overcome, tremendous internal tensions are generated. Even slight inconveniences or frictions cause blow-ups:

> The three programers responsible for finishing the work were a month behind; they could not debug what had been written so far. Worse, the computer was always "over them"; it was perfection and it taunted them by finding even the slightest mistake they made. One night when a supervisor came into the machine room and simply asked, "How are things going?" one of the programers flew into a rage.

Often such employees are restless, constantly seeking new assignments even though they might learn more on their present work or will have more to contribute where they have built up a backlog of experience. Endlessly, they try out new methods—even when the old ones have worked and might be quicker to adapt.

Such people usually have an enormous sense of possessiveness. The drawing or copy or program being worked on is "theirs." Although this attitude brings forth extraordinary effort, it can also make it difficult for such people to accept aid, ideas, and advice from others or to modify their work so that it better fits into the work of others.[22] Many take these jobs so that they can work almost alone, with minimum requirements for supervision or coordination.

In this type of work credit for successes and failures is easy to assign. Completion of a difficult assignment leads to elation, even euphoria. Failure leads to depression.

The nature of their work means that these persons frequently know much more about their subject than does their supervisor.

> "When one of my people gets stuck on a problem, I know I can't provide them with technical assistance. A supervisor fools himself who thinks he can. They're prima donnas. Many of those guys have received so much praise that you have to handle them with kid gloves. So the only way I can help them is to get them to step back a little from what they are doing, by asking the right questions. Often they have just been so intensely immersed in the work that they have missed some little point. Once you get them to take a different tack or step back they find their own mistake quickly enough."

Managerial Jobs

Although the jobs of no two managers are exactly alike, certain characteristics sharply distinguish managerial from nonmanagerial jobs.

Let's look at a typical series of activities constituting a few hours in the life of a manager:

> When Henry came in at 9 A.M. there were already six telephone messages on his desk. He first called back the Employment Office and told them it was all right to hire two temporary secretaries to fill in for vacations. . . . Then he called one of the supervisors in the plant and told him to hold back on the Pickney Order because a parts shortage had turned up yesterday that would delay final assembly work. As his secretary came in to indicate that one of the more nervous expediters was outside waiting to see him, he waved to her their standard signal which meant he was too busy to see anybody. Then he called up Engineering and told them in no uncertain terms that no matter what happened they had to get those drawings done by the afternoon. He ignored the other calls.
>
> As a breather he began glancing at his mail which his secretary had arrayed on the right-hand side of his desk. He soon had picked up a dictating machine to answer those deserving quick attention; several others he handed to the secretary to answer with a "pleasant 'no.'"
>
> To get ready for a meeting with the head of the Division he used a slide rule to work up some figures on comparative costs of contracting-out and doing internally several maintenance jobs. Then he telephoned the Art Department to have the figures placed on large charts for display at the meeting. (He was

---

[22] In such organizations one often hears: NIH, meaning "not invented here," as an explanation of why an idea is rejected.

anxious to make a good impression, since the man responsible for his next pro-motion was going to be there.)

He remembered that at 9:30 he was scheduled to interview a new engineer and he walked out to escort him into his office. It took 20 minutes to learn something of his background and personality.

Next, another supervisor came in to request that the cost accounting depart-ment redo last month's "variance analysis" since he was sure that his groups costs were stated incorrectly. Henry spent ten minutes looking over the figures with the man before agreeing to have them checked. And in the next few minutes, he took a call from a vending-machine company that wanted to install some equipment in the cafeteria, agreed to meet with a union grievance com-mittee at the end of the week, and told an employee that he could not change his vacation date since others were already scheduled.[23]

Within the short space of an hour this executive had been in contact with ten people, engaged in a variety of different types of activity extended from mathematical and mental tactical calculations to interviewing, negotiating, and order-giving. Although he had to respond to other people, the how and when he responded and how he scheduled his day were largely up to him. The unpredictable and ever-changing nature of his job required constant alertness. In that dizzy array of contacts and activities, there was a great deal of challenge and the requirement for real depth attention. For many managers this pace is maintained through a ten- or twelve- (not an eight-) hour day and there is no time to daydream or seek social relationships for their own sake. And yet managers get the same pleasure from the "fielding" of the ever-changing variety of problems that a baseball player gets from a championship game.

Accompanying this pressure are numerous satisfactions derived from having the status of a manager. It is not just the secretary who comes when the buzzer is pressed, but the large number of people whom he can call and who will give him a respectful hearing and who are dependent on him. And, of course, there are his immediate subordinates who accept him as their leader.

Particularly at higher levels of the organization, the manager derives enor-mous satisfaction from power, knowing he can influence critical decisions and may control the expenditure of tens or hundreds of thousands of dollars. And indeed the success or failure of new ventures may well be dependent on his personal acumen and decision-making skill.

In addition, managerial work pays well. In our society, salary is an index of success, a measure of accomplishment. For the executive, salary is the score card that tells him how far and how fast he has moved ahead. What he does with money is less important than the mere fact of earning it.

There is a price to be paid for these satisfactions: heavy responsibilities and anxieties. Mistakes are easy to make, in part because the manager has to please other people, particularly those above him in the organization. Further, the

---

[23] For more extended descriptions of managerial life, see Leonard Sayles, *Managerial Behavior* (New York: McGraw-Hill, 1964); and Walter Guzzardi, Jr., *The Young Exec-utives* (New York: New American Library, 1966).

success of his activities depends upon many people he does not directly control (for instance, the staff departments within the company). Since so much of his job involves decision-making and human-relations skills, the evaluation of which tends to be subjective, most managers feel themselves especially vulnerable to criticism, even to severe penalties (such as demotion) for making decisions which higher management does not like. Further, there is fierce rivalry for promotion at managerial levels—by fair means and foul.[24] Still, most managers thrive on competition.

Unfortunately, successful executives are seldom aware of how different their jobs are from those of nonmanagerial subordinates.

> "These workers don't want to give a fair day's work; they're always looking for a chance to get out of work, to talk or loaf or fool around. They don't want to take responsibility and show what they can do, even though it could lead to a promotion or a raise sometime."

What this manager is forgetting is that these other employees cannot obtain the same intrinsic satisfactions he obtains. They cannot see the same rewards for themselves in the future nor can they get so involved in and committed to the future of the company. Neither participating in the key decisions nor able to see their impact, they view the company as something separate from themselves. For many managers, in contrast, the success of the organization and their own success are inextricably interwoven. And this identification in itself is enormously gratifying.

PROFESSIONALS

An increasing number of employees in jobs requiring high orders of mental ability conceive of themselves as professionals. By this we mean that they identify more with their field of competence than they do with any specific employer. Primarily they seek job opportunities which will enlarge their knowledge and broaden their skills. The same high expectations may increasingly be characteristic of managers who jump with alacrity from company to company to find opportunities to gain a greater sense of fulfillment by dealing with more challenging assignments.

Of course, at least some of these rising aspirations and feelings of independence stem from an extended period of high employment and affluence, at least for those with scarce expertise. The very opposite of the assembly-line worker, who feels himself expendable with every slight shift in demand or technological change, is the professional. Just a few years ago an advance-degree "egg head" on the payroll was considered pure overhead and a luxury. Now such professionals are often working at the core of the business. Many

---

[24] There is a vast literature on besting one's rivals in this intra-management competition. For example: Chester Burger, *Survival in the Executive Jungle* (New York: Macmillan, 1964).

employers make no secret of their growing dependence on "knowledge workers," who constitute an ever larger proportion of the typical payroll.

Status and Professional Autonomy

Most of us tend to think of professionalism as being a characteristic of those very few occupational groups to which society has accorded the highest status: doctors, lawyers, ministers, professors, and the like. Their high status gives them special benefits. Most importantly they do not have to accept many orders; their expert skill makes them immune to pressures from others. They have great autonomy. Further, they expect that when they ask someone else for assistance, it will be forthcoming immediately and without question. (When a doctor makes a request, the nurse typically jumps to serve.)

A profession has an integrated and distinctive body of knowledge which only its members can lay claim to mastering. There is a long, carefully supervised learning period for neophytes; only those who can pass a difficult series of tests are admitted to full-fledged membership. They, in turn, are committed to a lifetime career in their specialty. Also, professionals subscribe to high ethical standards (such as the doctor's Hippocratic Oath) to serve the interests of the broader society rather than selfish goals. These standards are enforced by the professional group itself, which typically has special review and disciplinary procedures to evaluate questionable behavior on the part of its members. Further, professionals expect to be supervised, if at all, by a peer, someone with comparable technical training.

Dual Loyalty
and Sources of Conflict

Professionals have their own standards of what constitutes advancement. To be sure, they are interested in higher incomes and status titles (though they sometimes deny this). Still, many professionals place less value on salary than on other satisfactions. For example, many chemists would not give up a challenging assignment in an organization that had prestige in the profession (say, a highly regarded Foundation-sponsored laboratory) for a higher paying job with an organization that lacked these attributes.

Professionals seek recognition primarily from their fellow professionals. Thus, they are tied to a criterion of excellence that exists outside the organization for which they work. In a way they have a dual loyalty. This dual loyalty may both help and hinder the administration. A man's feeling of professional pride may motivate him to work harder and to maintain higher standards than he would otherwise.

On the other hand, conflict arises when a man is more interested in winning recognition from his professional colleagues than from the organization for which he works. For example, the medical profession has a tendency to look down on physicians who take administrative jobs in hospitals, and for this reason highly qualified men may refuse such assignments. Similarly, engineers, scientists, and professors sometimes turn down promotions that require administrative work which may interfere with their research.[25]

Engineers and scientists with professional orientations may resent work assignments that do not offer challenge and the opportunity to make some kind of break-through. They may prefer seeking new solutions to "tried and true" old methods, preferring basic research to applied research. They can resent accepting orders from supervisors who do not have comparable professional training and find standard rules of conduct within the organization needlessly confining and nothing more than "bureaucratic red tape." [26] As one manager described them: "They are bright, belligerent, and independent."

The New Professionals

Many groups are striving to professionalize themselves and thus join the ranks (and get the privileges) of the older established professions.[27] For example, security analysts, hospital administrators, purchasing agents, programers, and industrial engineers are attempting to establish standards that will set themselves apart from, and hopefully, above individuals claiming some competence in these fields but who lack formal preparation or adequate experience. Understandably, these staff specialists, whose claim to authority is based on formal professional training, often come into conflict with line managers whose knowledge and skill derive primarily from long years of on-the-job experience, intuition, and good common sense.

At times, the claim to the title of "professional" may be a tactic in an inter-group struggle. Managers whose promotions have been blocked or who see themselves losing influence may take refuge in professionalism as a source of job satisfaction.

In some cases management may even encourage individuals who, for one reason or another, are unlikely to raise their organizational status through the normal route of promotions to conceive of themselves as professionals. As professionals, it is hoped, they will be more interested in technical expertise than increased managerial responsibility.[28]

---

[25] Further, the fact that a man is a good scientist or engineer does not necessarily make him a good administrator. In promoting such a person, management may gain a poor administrator and lose a good professional.

[26] *Cf.* Simon Marcson, *The Scientist in American Industry* (Princeton, N.J.: Princeton University, Industrial Relations Section, 1960); and Charles Orth, Joseph Bailey, and Francis Wolek, *Administering Research and Development* (Homewood, Ill.: Irwin, 1964).

[27] For studies of professionalism, see A. M. Carr Saunders and P. S. Wilson, *The Professions* (Oxford: Clarendon Press, 1933); Everett C. Hughes, *Men and Their Work* (New York: The Free Press of Glencoe, 1958); William Kornhauser, *Scientists in Industry* (Berkeley: University of California Press, 1962); George Strauss, "Professionalism and Occupational Associations," *Industrial Relations*, Vol. 2, No. 3 (May 1963), pp. 7-31; and Harold Wilensky, "The Professionalism of Everyone?" *American Journal of Sociology*, Vol. 70, No. 2 (September 1964), pp. 137-158.

[28] Fred Goldner and Richard Ritti, "Professionalization As Career Mobility" (Unpublished Manuscript, 1965).

The Organization
vs. the Professional

It would be a mistake to exaggerate, however, the restlessness of the typical professional working in industry. Many possess scarce, respected skills to which both fellow employees and management are deferential. They often receive special treatment, and their requests for services and assistance are honored before the requests of less prestigious employees. The modern organization provides a wealth of interesting assignments, and many people feel that "real-life" problems, where stakes are great, are much more exciting than problems in a cloistered academic atmosphere. The professional's goals of increased knowledge and skill and the solution of difficult problems are often company goals as well. Thus, the professional may see little conflict between his needs and the company's needs. For professionals, relationships with like-trained supervisors are usually informal, approaching relations between colleagues, and thus more satisfying than those enjoyed by other occupational groups.

CONCLUSION

With the exception of "white-collar factories" we have noted that newer technologies do hold forth the promise of significantly greater through-the-job satisfactions than many of the more traditional jobs associated with manufacturing. In truly automated factories (what we have called process production) as well as in many of the growing white-collar occupations, employees obtain very real ego rewards, derived from identification with the work and opportunities for autonomy, advancement, and a sense of accomplishment. In addition, social relations are a part, not an escape from, the work.

But as we have seen in our discussion of professionalization, these opportunities are more than matched by the rising aspirations of job holders. An increasing number of employees identify more strongly with their occupation than with any employer.

Thus, specialization does not inevitably lead to routine, monotony, and job insecurity. Modern industry calls for specialized persons as well as specialized jobs. The former, both highly trained and self-confident, bear little resemblance to the employees conceived by Taylor and his scientific management.

PROBLEM 1

THE NEW WAITER

When I first came to work as a waiter for the Krautter Restaurant, I was sure I would not stay for very long; there seemed to be so much animosity.

Waiters were supposed to get "set ups" for their table (silver and glassware) from the pantry, but by mid-evening there were always shortages. Many waiters would take more than they needed in order to be sure they would not run out, and some would go into the kitchen to get things directly from the dishwashers, although this was against the rules. Many times there were arguments over hoarding of silver, and the dishwashers frequently chased waiters out of their area of the kitchen.

Busboys cleared tables, but I soon learned that one had to add something extra to the normal share of the tips received by the busboys if one expected to get fast service. Similarly, when customers asked for a special item (for instance, very rare beef) and the restaurant was busy, it was difficult to get the serving chefs to oblige. If you asked twice for something, they took this as an insult to their skill or intelligence, and giving something back to them could cause a mighty uproar. They seemed to have a real "chip on their shoulders."

I noticed that most of the old timers had "paired off" so that one waiter could ask his "buddy" for help when he fell behind. As a newcomer, however, I had difficulty getting anyone to cooperate with me. The result was that I often could not provide the service that customers expected and they would get upset and complain. Often this meant a very low tip and in some cases no tip at all, which is the worst insult a waiter can receive. However, at times I had the feeling that the hostess was sending people to my tables who had a reputation for being poor tippers. This, too, hurt my feelings.

All this was very puzzling to me. Waiting on table had looked so easy. I liked people and was willing to work hard, but this job was much more difficult than I had anticipated.

1. Which of the human-relations problems described here are typical of all service-industry jobs and which represent poor management?
2. What are the potential positive sources of need satisfaction that this new waiter is not describing and that may become more important when his "initiation" period is over.

PROBLEM 2

THE LIFE OF THE PROGRAMER [29]

The Western Insurance Company, a large casualty insurance writer, had more than 5,000 employees. Several years ago it had established a separate computerized data-processing section. The center of activity in this department was the computer itself along with the programing group which developed new computer programs to handle the company's payroll, premium and policyholder records, billings, and so forth. In addition, the department stored computer tapes which contained great quantities of data that were relevant to these activities of the firm.

Unlike most of the clerical personnel in the company, programers did not have to punch a time clock, could take their lunch hour whenever they desired, and had no set coffee breaks. In total, there were about 25 in the group, most of them quite young. Almost all had college degrees, although a few were still attending evening classes. Even so, the programers had also been extensively trained by the company for their specialized work and continued to attend regular company training programs as new techniques and problems were introduced into their division.

---

[29] This description was written by one of the programers at Western Insurance.

The supervisor seemed to have the full confidence of the employees since he himself was an expert in their field. The more skilled and experienced programers were often sought out by the supervisor and other members of management for their advice on highly technical problems. Programing was the type of work in which some of the more routine tasks could be assigned to the youngest, least experienced workers (for example, the coding).

There was actually a good deal of work tension in the group. Although schedules could not be precisely set for the completion of a new program, because of all the uncertainties involved, the company was often in a hurry to finish the program so that data could be processed. Thus, there were pressures to meet deadlines. Further, large programs were divided up among a number of programers, and the work of each individual depended on that of his fellows. The computer itself was a source of tension because it demanded perfect work; and discrepancies or mistakes in logic would show up every time.

As a result, the successful testing of an important program was cause for general celebration throughout the group. Furthermore, a good deal of joking and light-heartedness was utilized to lessen the tension when one or more programers were having difficulties. There was an enormous sense of unity in the group since each man could understand exactly the problem another was facing and the tensions he was working under.

As we have seen the department was physically separate from the rest of the organization. While most of the company worked, particularly in the summer, under sweltering conditions, the programers, because of the needs of the computer, worked in refreshing air-conditioning.

Whereas most employees regarded Western Insurance as "a job," the programers thought of themselves as being specialists. They realized that their task was highly important to over-all company operations, and they had a sense of both responsibility and dedication. They were proud of the fact that they had successfully and jointly overcome a number of difficult schedules to develop the crucial programs that were the underpinning of the company's data-processing operations. This was a highly prestigious and strategic accomplishment. They felt the company could not operate without them.

Although pressure was often high and the work difficult, the constant impersonal push associated with factory work was lacking. And although there were set procedures underlying programing, much was left to the programer's skill, judgment, and discretion. There were no unalterable time tables or precisely defined methods that could be laid out for each project. The coordination came out of the closely timed human-relations patterns that the employees evolved as a means of working together.

Many of the programers often voluntarily remained overtime to complete a project; some worked right through a weekend when they were behind or felt that the work was going especially well. Some of the enthusiasm, of course, stemmed from having been instrumental in the establishment of an important new division and getting in, so to speak, "on the ground floor."

Recognition in the group was bestowed on the basis of ability and accomplishment—and a newcomer soon knew where every programer stood in terms of his ability. High-status programers got the desks enclosed by partitions, had both an "out" and an "in" mail basket on their desks, and enjoyed the privilege of keeping their graphic tools rather than having to return them to a central pool.

1. List each of the elements in the job of the programer that appears to contribute to high motivation. Which may change for the worse?
2. How unique or distinctively related to programing are these and which might be found in most white-collar jobs?

3. Which suggest possible job modifications that management can make in other types of technology to achieve comparable motivational effects?

EN ROUTE [30]

Each newspaper delivery driver was required to make two trips each day with a jumper assigned to his truck as he left the paper's main garage. The stops were outlined on a sheet of paper along with the amount to be delivered at each stop. Drivers knew the time allotment for all routes and would never come back to the plant before that time allotment expired.

One of the most attractive aspects of working as a jumper or a driver was that usually at least six hours of the eight-hour day were spent away from the plant and immediate supervision. Invariably, the men would "pull the route" the quickest way, taking advantage of all short cuts, rearranging the list, and accepting help in unloading from the waiting newsboys. Some did so just to prove that they knew routes better than the men who assigned them.

They would finish unloading all papers and then proceed to a place where the truck could be effectively hidden away from the prying eyes of an occasional newspaper executive who might happen by. The driver and jumper would then pass at their leisure an hour or more in a bar, poolroom, or lunchroom, until it was time to return to the plant.

If you worked as a manager in this newspaper, are there changes you would make in these jobs? Justify your "yes" or "no" answer.

---

[30] We are indebted to a former student, Donald C. Waite III, for this case.

Work Groups and Informal Organization

We have seen that social needs are among the most powerful and compelling on-the-job motivations. The people who make up organizations behave as members of groups, and their membership helps shape their work behavior and attitudes toward the organization and the job. Groups may exercise far stronger control over their members than does management. Since management can achieve its ends only through working with people, it must also work through groups. But before considering the problems of supervising groups, we must first understand why groups develop and how they function.

WHY GROUPS ARE FORMED

Companionship

Psychologists may argue about whether man is born with the need for society or acquires it early in life; yet the need for relationships with other people is one of the strongest and most constant of human drives.

As we have discovered, many jobs call forth only a small fraction of a person's total abilities. To management he may be just another unit of labor or a time-clock number; to his friends on the job he is an individual. To these colleagues an employee can be himself and express his true feelings.

Research indicates employees who have no opportunity for close social contact find their work unsatisfying, and this lack of satisfaction often reflects itself in low production and high turnover and absenteeism. Many years ago Elton Mayo observed that employees in a textile plant who worked at isolated jobs were highly dissatisfied and consistently failed to meet production standards. Staggered rest periods helped a little. But when the company permitted these workers to take rest periods *as a group*, production and satisfaction both increased.[1] Another company, where the girls worked in small, isolated booths, had the same experience. When management put glass partitions between the

---

[1] Elton Mayo, *The Human Problems of an Industrial Civilization* (Boston: Graduate School of Business Administration, Harvard University, 1946), pp. 42-52. It should be

booths, the rate of turnover and the number of grievances both dropped sharply. Similarly, researchers in hospitals have discovered that maids feel uncomfortable when they work only in the company of high-status personnel (doctors, nurses, etc.) with whom they cannot associate with ease. Several hospitals have found that when three or four maids are grouped together as a team, turnover falls and a much better job is done.[2]

Identification

The difference may be subtle—but people want more than just to have friends, they want to *belong*. One can sense that he is part of a larger organization only by indirection, but the shared experiences of one's immediate colleagues are among the most meaningful and potent sources of job satisfaction.

> Extensive studies during World War II indicated that soldiers' willingness to show bravery and make sacrifices was correlated not with loyalty to country or understanding of the war issues, but with loyalty to the immediate group. In other words, men committed acts of heroism that were motivated largely by the desire not to let their buddies down.[3]
>
> Having learned this lesson, the army abandoned its system of bringing individual replacements into combat units and instead began rotating units as a whole.
>
> During the same war the rapidly growing West Coast aircraft industry was troubled by extremely high turnover. No sooner was a worker partially trained than he quit. Research indicates that this pattern was associated with the absence of stable work groups. Since new employees never became part of a stable group, they developed no loyalty to the group and either quit or asked for a transfer at the slightest dissatisfaction.[4]

Other studies indicate that smaller groups tend to enjoy higher morale. Employees working in large departments where everybody does the same job find it hard to form stable social groupings and often have low morale. Many companies with large secretarial pools are putting up waist-high barriers on the office floor to encourage the development of social groups and team spirit.

Understanding from Friends

The daily work routine is rich in opportunities for frustrations and tension. Whether we are harassed by an overbearing customer, an obstreperous type-

---

noted that other factors were introduced that contributed to the improved morale and productivity. The work was broken up into self-contained tasks, and the rest periods themselves helped combat fatigue and monotony.

[2] Temple Burling, Edith Lentz, and Robert Wilson, *The Give and Take in Hospitals* (New York: Putnam, 1956), pp. 181-192.

[3] E. A. Shils, "Primary Groups in the American Army," in R. K. Merton and P. F. Lazarsfeld, eds., *Continuities in Social Research: Studies in the Scope and Method of the American Soldier* (New York: The Free Press of Glencoe, 1950), pp. 16-39.

[4] Elton Mayo and George F. F. Lombard, *Teamwork and Labor Turnover in Aircraft Industry of Southern California* (Boston: Graduate School of Business Administration, Harvard University, 1944).

writer, or a picayune inspector, we all seek a sympathetic ear, preferably from someone who has had similar experiences and can thus share and understand our troubles. Organizations that lack this outlet sometimes rely on the clumsy and expensive system of employee counseling, in which outsiders "hear out" employee troubles.

Guide to Acceptable Behavior

Whenever we are thrown into a new social situation, we are uncertain about how we are expected to behave. Our work days are filled with ambiguous situations. How much time should I take for a coffee break? Is it all right to talk to fellow employees while the boss is in the room? Must all copy be shown to the advertising manager? Even where there are established rules, one question remains: Is everybody expected to live by the letter of the law? Most employees don't want to violate the generally accepted "rules of the game"; at the same time they don't want to conform to restrictive rules that everyone else ignores. They want to know the "right" thing to do. The group fills an important need by providing all its members with a kind of "guide to correct behavior"—correct not in terms of any written policies, but in terms of what is actually acceptable.

Opportunities for Initiative and Creativity

Many jobs which appear superficially dull and routine are made more interesting by the individual ingenuity and spontaneity encouraged and protected by the group. Although it may appear to the casual observer that management has defined a rigid series of job requirements, work groups provide a setting which spurs the individual to modify the job situation more to his own liking:

> Extra work breaks can be obtained because employees spell one another. Unpleasant tasks assigned to one man can be rotated or shared by group agreement.

> Clever techniques for "beating" a difficult incentive formula can be worked out with the collusion of fellow group members.

The key point here is that all of these new activities take initiative and energy. Thus, on jobs which appear to require little of either, an outlet can be found in the informal modifications of the environment that are sanctioned by the group.[5]

---

[5] A good over-all description of this process is Ivar Berg's "Some Unlikely Sources of Initiative and Creativity," in Leonard Sayles, ed., *Individualism and Big Business* (New York: McGraw-Hill, 1964), pp. 35-46.

Help in Solving Work Problems

A new sales clerk may not be sure about how to handle a complicated problem of returning some merchandise. A lab technician may be hesitant about asking his boss to repeat instructions, yet he is afraid that he may ruin the experiment unless he receives additional information. In each case the employee turns to his fellow workers for assistance, often preferring this source of help.[6]

The group's solution to a problem may differ from what management expects, and it may even be more efficient. Red tape is eliminated; shortcuts are evolved; informal channels of communication are established to cut across department boundaries. By the same token, work groups may also engage in featherbedding and work-restriction.

Certain jobs can be done by isolated workers, but working as a group often results in higher individual motivation and a faster work pace. Some groups observe regular rituals (such as a coffee break when a given task is done) which serve to emphasize the group nature of the task.[7] Even schools are experimenting successfully with teaming students together rather than allowing each pupil to work alone or wait his turn to recite. Team members provide mutual help which increases the rate of learning.

Obviously, in most cases management must take the responsibility of making specific work assignments, but there are work situations in which a cohesive group can do a better job of fitting individual personalities to the work process and making expedient job assignment changes as new problems arise. The manager's decisions, since they must encompass a longer time period, are often less flexible and timely than the group's.

Where the technology imposes extreme interdependence, and precise and instant coordination is required, for example in military fighting crews, the organization depends on the group to control and specify the individual's contribution to the total effort.[8]

Protection for the Membership

Groups help protect their members from outside pressures. As we shall discuss later on, groups often resist management demands for additional out-

---

[6] A study of government employees found that they consistently preferred getting assistance from fellow employees to going to the manager, and this ability to provide aid was a source of substantial prestige for the giver. Peter Blau, *Dynamics of Bureaucracy* (Chicago: University of Chicago Press, 1955).

[7] For example, see Donald F. Roy, " 'Banana Time': Job Satisfaction and Informal Interaction," *Human Organization*, Vol. 18, No. 4 (Winter 1959-1960), pp. 158-168.

[8] It has been suggested that turnover of membership in an airline crew can increase the safety hazard since almost instantaneous collaboration is required in emergencies. Such collaboration can only result from working together as a team for a long time. Team members have to be trained as a group as well; it is less useful to train them as individual performers. William Karraker, "Teamwork and Safety in Flight," *Human Organization*, Vol. 17, No. 3 (Fall 1958), pp. 3-8.

put, longer work hours, and higher quality. Most dynamic organizations have a tendency to introduce changes in work methods and routines at a faster rate than the individual can adjust to them. The pace at which these changes are introduced can be materially altered by a determined work group.

Without a sense of group allegiance, individual workers may behave in ways that will injure their fellow workers. The work group often disciplines members who try to earn the supervisor's favor by "squealing" on fellow employees or by turning out too much work, or who fail to help their fellow workers on the job.

> A market-analysis office was required to prepare reports for top management. As time passed, the men made these reports increasingly elaborate, using colored graphs, photographic reproductions, and ever-more detailed data. Some of this window-dressing had real value, but most of it was designed to catch the boss' attention. At last, the men realized that they were spending tremendous amounts of uncompensated overtime in their efforts to outdo one another. Finally, they got together and agreed on standards to limit their competitive efforts.

In some groups the members actually agree on the level of output each will put forth so that no one member will out-perform the others.

The most common target of group power is the immediate manager. Most managers are quick to recognize that although they have the authority to make a wide range of decisions, to make certain decisions would be downright foolhardy (see Chapter 8). The members of the group can express their displeasure by cutting down their work pace, sabotaging the work (discreetly, of course, so that blame will be hard to place), or making their boss look inept to his own superiors.

HOW WORK GROUPS ARE FORMED

When an engineer designs the plans and technology for a new factory, and when an architect designs the office layout, they are also designing the social relations that will prevail within the organization. Management determines where men will work and what opportunities they will have to contact each other during the day. It also determines rates of pay, conditions of work, and the various symbols that are associated with each job. Given these basic elements, a sophisticated observer can predict the social relations that will exist within the organization long before the first employee enters the building.[9]

In telling men where and how they are to work, management is also telling them with whom they will come into contact. Normally, individuals develop friendships with the people they see most often. In fact, employees who have

---

[9] For two such predictive studies, see A. Zaleznik, C. R. Christensen, and F. J. Roethlisberger, *The Motivation, Productivity and Satisfaction of Workers: A Prediction Study* (Boston: Graduate School of Business Administration, Harvard University, 1958); and Leonard Sayles, *Behavior of Industrial Work Groups* (New York: Wiley, 1958).

the greatest opportunities to make contacts on the job make the largest number of friends and are in the best position to become leaders of the group.

> A study of a housing project for married students indicated that friendship patterns were determined by apartment locations. Most families made a majority of their friends within their own building and especially on their own floor. Furthermore, those whose apartments were located on the ground floor nearest the building entrance had the best chance of becoming social leaders. Those who were physically isolated in end units were also most socially isolated and least liked.[10]

Multiple Group-Memberships

Rarely do participants in an organization belong to just one group. Take Adam Kopka, a mechanical engineer in the W Company. He has one group of friends whom he works with on a development project: two electrical engineers, a technician, and a chemist. In addition, he is identified with all those who report to Alex Fisher, the manager of the Special Projects Department, which includes two other project groups. He also feels close to other mechanical engineers who are scattered through the laboratory. His lunch group and after-hours bowling associates may include still other people. Now each of these groups has a different membership, although there may be a great deal of overlapping. For some purposes one group is the most important to Adam; for others, another. The mere fact that he belongs to several groups, however, may subject him to considerable stress when their respective interests come into conflict.

Suppose, for instance, that the mechanical engineers grow concerned that their jobs and point of view are assuming less significance in the laboratory. The engineers agree among themselves to exert greater pressure for higher mechanical-engineering standards in their design work. As long as Adam is in the company of his fellow mechanical engineers, he feels this is a fine decision. Back in his project group, however, he may find that this is a minority position and he is under pressure to emphasize other project goals. Now he feels under cross pressures; he can't be loyal to both groups.

The Group Becomes an Organization

Employees form friendship groups based on their contacts and common interests—and these groups arise out of the life of the organization. Once these groups have been established, however, they develop a life of their own that is almost completely separate from the work process from which it arose. This is a dynamic, self-generating process. Brought together by the formal organization, employees interact with one another. Increasing interaction builds favor-

---

[10] See Leon Festinger, Stanley Schachter, and Kurt Back, *Social Pressures in Informal Groups* (New York: Harper, 1950).

able sentiments toward fellow group-members. In turn, these sentiments become the foundation for an increased variety of activities, many not specified by the job descriptions: special lunch arrangements, trading of job duties, fights with those outside the group, gambling on paycheck numbers. And these increased opportunities for interaction build stronger bonds of identification.[11] Then the group becomes something more than a mere collection of people. It develops a customary way of doing things—a set of stable characteristics that are hard to change. It becomes an *organization* in itself.

Suboptimization: Group Goals

From the point of view of management, what are the major characteristics of these new suborganizations? So far, we have just illustrated that they perform a psychological function for the individual: providing support and permissiveness. Most importantly, the group sets goals for itself that become important motivators for the individual.

In the large organization, everyone—manager and nonmanager—is supposed to be working toward the same objectives. But individuals are likely to put their own need satisfactions ahead of these goals. In addition, groupings of individuals set goals for themselves and these goals take precedence over the total organization's objectives. Here is one example:

> The installation of a new computer in the Y Corporation was delayed two years by an interdepartmental struggle over who would control this new equipment. The Finance group claimed that it should be under their jurisdiction but Production and Sales both wanted a new "Computation and Programing" department to be created. Finance felt it would lose prestige if a separate department was created while Production and Sales believed that the new computer would not be as helpful to them if it was placed in an existing department. Thus, a very costly piece of equipment was wasted for two years, from the point of view of the total organization, because of these special interest groupings.

In a sense, then, the organization pays some price in divisiveness for the help of the group in attaching and holding the individual. This has come to be called the *suboptimization* problem, where small group objectives tend to conflict with or take precedence over the larger organization's goals. Members are motivated primarily by small group goals, not by large organization goals. (For more examples see Chapter 16.)

INTERNAL STRUCTURE OF GROUPS

To perpetuate themselves, to move in the direction of accomplishing their goals, and to provide the protection and support their membership needs, work

---

[11] The best theoretical description of this process is George Homans, *The Human Group* (New York: Harcourt, Brace and World, 1950), pp. 48-155.

groups require an internal structure. "Structure" here means a set of unique characteristics that determine the members' relationships to one another and to supervision, the standards of conduct that are approved and enforced by the group, its system of rewards and punishments, and its system of communication.

All these aspects of group life are in balance with one another, or, as the social scientist would say, they are in equilibrium: (1) They are all interrelated, (2) a change in any one of them has an immediate effect on all the others, and (3) the members strongly resist changes in any part of this interrelated system. What, specifically, are these characteristics that dictate the internal organization of the group?

Leadership

Every group has informal leaders—individuals who have a special sort of status which results in their being followed by other members of the group. The informal leader is a very different sort of leader from the supervisor appointed by management. The formally appointed leader is followed because directly or indirectly he has the power to discharge those who refuse to obey his orders. The informal leader has no such power. Why, then, is he followed?

He is followed because the members learn that the group will not provide them with the benefits they seek unless they have some established leadership. Someone has to take the initiative in getting people to recognize that there is a common problem to be solved. The leader circulates through the group to urge a united front against a new threat from management, or to devise punishment for an uncooperative fellow member. In the process of developing consensus on what needs to be done, a successful leader is careful to sound out the members and to smooth over internal differences of opinion by personal persuasion and suggested compromises. He also serves as the group's representative in contacting the supervisor, or the union, or other work groups.

In summary, the leader performs vital functions that contribute to the group's ability to survive in its environment:

1. He initiates action.
2. He facilitates a consensus.
3. He provides a link or liaison with the outside world: managers, other work groups, the union.

Most observers have a tendency to refer to *the* informal leader, as though a single leader could be identified in every group. Actually, unless the group is very small, the functions we have described are usually shared by several active individuals who together comprise the leadership of the group. Although the supervisor is most aware of the employee who contacts him as the group's representative, he must recognize that within the group, in less obvious positions, there may be other equally influential leaders adept in the use of human-relations skill as well as members who seek leadership but are rejected by the group.[12] The manager needs to be aware of these differences among the more active members of any group to be in a position to influence the group. Often, as we shall see later, it is easier to accomplish change by dealing with the group through its leaders than by attempting to persuade or order individuals to change.

Many studies have been conducted to determine the personality traits that characterize the effective group leader, but none of these studies has been altogether successful. It appears that each group requires a type of leadership suited to its own particular needs. These studies do suggest one important generalization, however: The group leader must live up to the group's idealized conception of what a group member should be. In the study of the bank-wiring room at the Western Electric Company, the informal leader of the group was described as follows:

> He was a key member of the superior clique and . . . one of the two men whose output conformed most closely and consistently to the accepted idea of a proper day's work. . . . In every way, indeed, he embodied the norms the group had adopted as its own. He never broke a rate, "chiseled," "squealed," or took a superior tone. . . .[13]

Some members of a group may aspire to a position of leadership without ever winning group acceptance. Outsiders may assume that these men are more influential than they actually are, when they are particularly active in contacting others. It is important to distinguish between the two types of leader, since the false leader rarely represents the true feelings of the group he pretends to lead.[14]

Group Standards of Behavior

The urge to conform to group standards pervades most social life. Teen-age boys must be careful not to act too differently if they want to be accepted by the gang. Adolescent girls must dress like the other girls in their crowd, even if their parents object. There are group standards in industry as well. Some of these standards exist for the sole purpose of making life more enjoyable for the group members: The accounts receivable department always goes out together for lunch; the maintenance gang spends its breaks playing gin rummy. If you don't do these things—you don't *belong.*

Other customs serve to make the job easier or to heighten the quality of workmanship. Waiters agree among themselves to share all tips equally and to help one another serve and clear tables during rush hours; if a college

---

[12] In fact some studies suggest that every stable group has at least two leaders, a task leader whose function it is to drive the group toward its goal, and a human-relations leader who keeps the group from falling apart.

[13] Homans, *op. cit.*, pp. 147-149.

[14] A good description of these leaders can be found in T. T. Paterson, *Glasgow Limited: A Case-Study in Industrial War and Peace* (Cambridge: Cambridge University Press, 1960), p. 171.

professor has to miss a class, his colleagues will try to stand in for him; retail clerks "spell" one another so that all the counters will be covered while one clerk is taking a break. All these customs reflect the expectations of group members with respect to one another's behavior.

Probably the most important group standards are those that protect the members of the group against real or imagined outside dangers, particularly from upper management. Production workers may agree on a level of output and exert pressure on those who deviate from it—especially on those who produce more than the accepted "bogey." "Eager beavers" in the classroom are frequently reminded that "C" is the "gentleman's grade." Group standards of good workmanship and high quality often make management's task easier; for the group, by taking "troublemakers" in hand, reduces the need 'for management to impose discipline.

Thus, from management's point of view, the pressure to conform to group standards may be most desirable. A standard that a worker can be five minutes late also means that the group will prevent him from abusing this privilege.

> A group of white-collar employees was frequently given the afternoon off when the ball team played a home game. Without any prompting from management, the employees agreed among themselves to come in an hour early to compensate for the short days. Employees who were unenthusiastic about this informal change in the schedule were pressured into conforming, and management gained the extra work time.

Larger groups, particularly in professional pursuits, often maintain ethical standards designed to further the goals of the over-all membership. A study of hospitals, for example, noted that the high level of teaching competence maintained by the senior medical staff, and the high quality of patient care maintained by the junior staff members, could be largely explained in terms of the allegiance felt by both groups to standards of professional conduct.[15] Many a professional, whether he is an attorney, an accountant, or a scientist, undoubtedly is tempted to take short cuts that would save him time and money, and he may be absolutely certain that these short cuts would go undetected. And yet the standards that he has "internalized" during years of training and association with a professional group hold him to certain fixed patterns of behavior. (For other examples see Chapter 3.)

Even work groups performing menial occupations often adopt a "code" that contribute to the organization. One such self-imposed standard that has been observed is the effort to "save the people in the next higher position above from their own mistakes." [16] This code also serves a psychological function for the group: It gives them a sense of greater power and skill and importance than they might otherwise enjoy. On the other hand such standards may make it harder for management. For example, they may be a handicap to an en-

---

[15] Burling, Lentz, and Wilson, *op. cit.*, pp. 79-80.

[16] Everett Hughes, *Men and Their Work* (New York: The Free Press of Glencoe, 1958), p. 46.

gineering administrator who finds it difficult to dissuade his staff from "gold-plating" their work, setting higher-quality standards than are necessary.

It would be a mistake, of course, to assume that all group standards are consistent with the objectives of the larger organization. We have stressed the positive aspects because so much of the literature only emphasizes the negative results of the group effort. But many times groups do urge their members to produce less than they might otherwise accomplish, do try to reject new assignments because they do not approve of the work, and do even coalesce in opposing a new supervisor.

Group Attitudes and Values

In addition to group standards of behavior there are also group standards of attitude or values. People who work closely together naturally adopt common points of view that everyone is expected to share: "Ours is a good job (or a bad one)." "Most people don't realize how difficult our job really is." "Inspection is trying to make our job rough." "You've got to be a college man to make supervisor."

Many of these standards of attitude are without factual basis, of course. They are simply myths that have risen from the group's fears or wishes. Yet the group's acceptance of them *is* a fact—a fact that management must take into account.

> Some years ago, the job of heater in a steel crew was dangerous and difficult. Primarily a hand operation, it required great skill to lift large bars of metal into the furnace via a pulley system. The intense heat made the job even more unpleasant. Now the worst part of the job is handled by automatic equipment, and the operator works some distance away from the furnace. But heaters still feel that their job deserves special financial consideration. Fellow workers support them in this claim, even though it means that more difficult jobs are paid less.

As we have said, the individual becomes wedded to the group as a result of constant association and socializing. Members begin to think and act alike, not only in order to enjoy the fruits of group membership, but because the very process of living together reinforces certain feelings and attitudes in the mind of each member. These attitudes may have existed only weakly before, if at all. Before going to work in XYZ Company, for instance, a recently graduated chemical engineer considered himself only moderately well-trained and useful. After working in a research group composed entirely of chemical engineers, however, he decided that chemical engineers are the most skilled and valuable group in the laboratory. Through constant interaction with a group, certain predispositions are reinforced, or even distorted, in the minds of the members. Further, the goals of the group gradually become as important to each member's feeling of accomplishment as his own individual needs. Once the group has become truly established, the individual members come to identify themselves with its successes and failures.

Pressures to Conform

Why is it that most people are so anxious to conform to group standards? In the first place, as members of the group, they look at things from the group point of view; they tend to identify with the group and, since it helps meet their needs, they accept its goals. Even those who have misgivings about the validity of the standards go along anyway, because they want to be well regarded by their fellows. Finally, the group has effective means of punishing those who insist on doing things their own way.

Ostracism is one of the most effective forms of group punishment for deviant behavior. A member who overproduces, who fails to share important information, or who is officious may find himself isolated from his fellow workers. In extreme cases, no one will talk to him or even acknowledge his presence. In less extreme cases, the deviant may be excluded from ordinary social activities, such as getting the morning coffee, or may be greeted coldly when he reports for work. When he has trouble, no one will come to his aid. Or his connection with the "grapevine" may be rudely cut off. Over a period of time the work situation can become intolerable for the victim.

Sometimes the group resorts to more direct techniques. Someone may "accidentally" let management know about some of the deviant's mistakes. Fellow workers may be slow in giving him the parts or the information he needs. His equipment or desk may be "adjusted" while he is away. In the bank-wiring-room study, one of the inspectors failed to live up to certain group norms. The other workers flooded his inspection station with work so that he could not possibly keep up with it, and they "adjusted" his testing equipment so that it failed to work properly.[17]

The punishments devised to enforce group standards are sometimes highly ingenious. In one office, supervision was lenient in permitting employees to arrive late for work. When one man began to abuse this privilege by arriving very late every day, the group was afraid that management would start to crack down on tardiness. Whenever this employee came in late, his fellow workers applauded him warmly. This gesture served to emphasize their displeasure, and, it was hoped, would encourage management to deal with him on an individual basis.

It would be a mistake to assume that all group members conform. Not only do groups differ in their cohesiveness, in the "hold" they have over their membership, but individuals differ in their response to group pressures. Interesting experiments have been designed to assess the susceptibility of given individuals to group pressure. At one extreme are those who will deny what their own sense organs tell them to be consistent with group opinions. At the other end of the spectrum are those who are unshakable in their own beliefs,

---

[17] Roethlisberger and Dickson, *op. cit.*, p. 487.

even in highly ambiguous situations when the group provides useful information that should cause them to modify their attitudes.[18]

Status Systems

Just as soon as a loose aggregation of individuals develops into a genuine group, subtle status differences begin to arise. Roughly defined, status is a measure of a person's prestige within the group. It is an index to how important he is, to his position in the "pecking order."

Status is generated by group interaction. It provides a sense of security, and failure to have one's status recognized generates insecurity. Think of the senior who is mistaken for a sophomore, or the professor who is introduced as a student. Moreover, status provides a reassuring guide to the members of the group in their contacts with one another. A man with high status expects and receives greater deference than a man with lower status.

How is status determined? What criteria do groups use in assigning higher standing to Mr. A than to Mr. B? Some status decisions are based on the attitudes and behavior of management; others are entirely the product of the informal organization of the group.

Status often depends on *job title*. Obviously a superintendent is more important than a general foreman and a general foreman outranks a foreman. Engineers outrank technicians, secretaries are "above" stenographers. In almost every organization the job titles are subtly graded according to levels of status, and the status of each individual depends in part on the job he holds.

Pay, of course, is one of the most important determinants of the status according to each job. Higher pay means higher status, and even a difference of a few cents per hour may have a significant effect on a job's status. The new manager may find this bewildering and unreasonable.

> Take the case of the checkers and the loaders in one newly unionized plant. The checkers received $1.70 an hour, the loaders $1.60. The checkers insisted that since keeping records involved greater responsibility and required a high-school education, they should receive a pay increase of at least 30 cents. The loaders felt that since their job required considerable skill and physical effort, they should be paid as much as the checkers. The union succeeded in getting 20 cents for the checkers, but won 30 cents for the loaders—and the checkers were more unhappy than ever.

Understandably, many companies encourage their employees to keep their pay scale secret.

How one is paid also helps to determine status. Some companies have monthly, semi-monthly, and weekly payrolls. Being a salaried man on the monthly payroll may be less convenient, but it carries much more prestige than getting a weekly *wage* (which may be computed on an hourly rather

---

[18] *Cf.* Solomon Asch, "Effects of Group Pressure upon the Modification and Distortion of Judgements," in E. Maccoby, T. Newcomb, and E. Hartley, eds., *Readings in Social Psychology* (New York: Holt, Rinehart and Winston, 1958), pp. 174-183.

than an annual basis). Sometimes, unskilled casual workers receive their pay by the day.

Work schedules are also a useful index. The hourly-paid man comes in at 7:30, the office clerks at 8:30, and the executives dribble in from 9:00 on—but the executives often work late at night. The freedom to choose one's hours, or being excused from punching the time-clock, is a mark of distinction. (Henry Ford once made all his executives punch the time-clock—thus lowering even further what was already rock-bottom morale.)

In which company lunchroom can you eat? Are tables reserved for you? Can you leave the building for morning coffee? Do you receive a daily copy of the *Wall Street Journal?* The allocation of these *special privileges* follows status lines.

Then there's the question of *where one works.* In the field or in the home office? In the new building where the important operations occur—or over in the "boneyard"? Working near the end of the production line carries more status than working near the beginning—for the finished product is more valuable and the job more responsible. In some offices, the closer a man works to the big boss the more status he enjoys. To be able to say "I work on the fourteenth floor" may be the pinnacle of prestige.

Among the job factors that affect status are: cleanliness, freedom from supervision, amount of training and skill required, and opportunity for promotion. A study of the restaurant industry revealed substantial differences in the status enjoyed by employees who worked with various vegetables:

> At the top were luxury or decorative items such as parsley, chives and celery. At the top of the regular vegetables were green beans. Next came spinach and carrots. Next to the bottom were sweet and white potatoes, and onions were considered the most undesirable of all. . . .
>
> Comments of the workers showed that they valued highly in vegetables lack of odor, crispness, and cleanness in handling, whereas the vegetable that had an odor and that stained the hands or was sloppy to handle was held in low esteem. The low standing of potato peeling is too well known to require comment, but here at least the workers said they preferred potatoes to onions because they did not smell or stain the hands. . . .[19]

Most jobs carry with them certain *symbols* that bestow varying degrees of status. In the army, shoulder insignia denotes officer rank. Paratroop boots, berets, or wings indicate that enlisted men belong to elite outfits (and for this reason, during World War II, many men wore them without authorization).

In industry, too, there are countless widely recognized symbols. Take clothing, for example. Executives (and often, office people) wear coats. Foremen wear white shirts. Hourly-paid workers wear work clothes. The chef's hat and the machinist's apron are more specialized symbols of prestige.[20]

---

[19] William F. Whyte, *Human Relations in the Restaurant Industry* (New York: McGraw-Hill, 1948), p. 36.

[20] Abraham Zaleznik, *Worker Satisfaction and Development* (Boston: Graduate School of Business Administration, Division of Research, Harvard University, 1956), p. 21.

Even though there was no plant rule, in one company only the higher-paid machinists wore white coats, the rest had white aprons. One lower-paid man wore a coat for a week—but social pressure forced him to discard it.

Some time ago, one of the authors conducted a series of interviews in a plant. Wanting to make it clear that he was primarily interested in studying the union and the work force—and that he was not connected with management—he was careful to wear T-shirts whenever he was in the plant. One day he made the mistake of coming in with a regular shirt and tie. Several workers asked, "What's wrong—sold out to management?"

Among executives, the *type of office* a man has bears strongly on the amount of status he enjoys. Does he have his own office? How large is it? Does he have his own secretary? Does she have a separate office? What type of desk does he have? Does he have a phone? Or, even better, *two* phones? As one carpet company puts it, "A title on the door rates a Bigelow on the floor." [21]

Status depends on *who one is* as well as what one does—that is, on the attributes or characteristics that the employee brings with him from his community and home. The boss' son has status in the plant regardless of what he does—and so does the captain of the plant baseball team. Among the qualities that confer status are education, age, seniority, sex, and ethnic background. Typically in business women are ranked below men. Unfortunately, in our society Negroes are often accorded lower status just because of the color of their skin. The same holds true in some places of Mexicans, Indians, and Asiatics. Other ethnic groups are also arranged according to a regular status hierarchy, with Anglo-Saxons usually at the top and people of southern European background near the bottom. The relative positions on this status ladder may vary from one community to another (for instance: in some places Poles may rank higher than Italians; in other places the reverse may be true), but in every case there is some kind of ranking, together with a struggle among groups to pull themselves up the ladder and others down.

Individual behavior also seems to have some influence on status. People with pleasant personalities, specialized skills, or leadership traits ordinarily enjoy high status, as do individuals who conform closely to the behavioral standards of the group. The man who just doesn't know "how to behave" is likely to lose status—either in an exclusive club or on the factory floor.

It would be a mistake to conceive of status as merely a complication added by the members of an organization. Status systems facilitate the operation of any organization by:

1. Providing ego rewards and social satisfactions to people. As we have seen in Chapter 1, individuals will work hard and make sacrifices to obtain greater prestige.

2. Status provides some security and predictability (and answers at work) by helping people know where they and others "stand."

---

[21] For a sensitive discussion of executive status problems, see J. P. Marquand's novel, *Point of No Return* (Boston: Little, Brown, 1949).

3. Status makes contacts, particularly between relative strangers, easier. Insofar as the relative status of each is known, individuals know who should defer or accommodate to whom. Symbols of status (such as insignia) can provide quick and unquestioning response to request.

> Our colleague Dr. Ivar Berg has told us of the very progressive mental hospital that endeavored to function by eliminating all outward distinctions in dress between patients and staff. The result was chaos; important identifications could not be made, particularly when bizarre behavior was being manifested. In violation of the formal rules of the hospital, the staff began carrying their keys in easy-to-observe places on their person so that they could distinguish patients from fellow staff members.

Status Inconsistency and Ambiguities

Thus there are several different indicators of status—title, pay, type of work performed, symbols, and others. In a sense, each of these is a thermometer which measures a different aspect of status. So long as all these status "thermometers" give approximately the same readings, status is not likely to cause trouble in the organization. But when they read differently, when the various indicators of status give inconsistent or ambiguous measures, personnel unrest and dissatisfaction occur.

For example, more prestigious group members occupy the more prestigious jobs. The longer-service, better-educated employee in a restaurant kitchen would resent being assigned to onion-peeling, particularly if junior employees were chopping greens and celery. The violation of a group standard would produce a disturbing status inconsistency. The same problem prevails when an employee is promoted to a department manager's job but is not given the type of office usually assigned to men of that rank. The university is not immune to these problems. In university towns, the assistant professor who moves into a section of the community normally regarded as the preserve of full professors is considered "strange" or aggressive.

Often a supervisor is unaware of the subtle distinctions drawn by the group among various jobs, work locations, and types of equipment. Seemingly innocent changes in job assignment or work location may precipitate ill feeling and resentment.[22]

---

[22] Professor George Homans of Harvard University has developed what he calls a "theory of distributive justice": First, there are certain elements that a member brings to his job from his past or puts into his work on the job. Examples are age, seniority, sex, ethnicity, responsibility, and education. Homans calls these "investments." Second, there are other status factors the worker expects to get out of his job. Examples are the material rewards (pay, etc.), the interest of the job, and status itself, the prestige accorded him by his fellows. These Homans called "rewards" or "returns."

According to Homans, when the "investments" of an individual member or of one subgroup are higher than those of another, *distributive justice* requires that their "rewards" should be higher, too. When "distributive justice" does not prevail—*i.e.*, when investment is not equal to reward—Homans predicts there will be trouble on the job. (Zaleznik, Christensen, and Roethlisberger, *op. cit.*, pp. 53-56.)

The metal-drawing department had four kinds of machines. Though work on each machine paid the same wages, there were noticeable differences in ease of operation. From the group point of view, it was a promotion to move to a Z machine and a demotion to move to an X machine. This attitude made it much harder for management to transfer men as production needs dictated and led to many grievances, particularly when management tried to move informal leaders to "lower-ranking" jobs.

Thus, the group's conception of what is right and fair is of critical importance in understanding employee reactions to the work situation. We would anticipate that "status anxiety" would show itself where there was status inconsistency. An employee with a prestigious family background and education working on a low-status job would be uncomfortable and likely to demonstrate aggression. The engineer without a college degree working with colleagues who all have a degree would be less sure of himself and might interpret a critical comment by his supervisor as being much stronger than it was intended. Thus, "status anxiety" can mean hypersensitivity, a condition which explains many problems of communications and morale in organizations.

Ambiguous situations in which the status position of an individual or group has not been clearly established can be troublesome. Often periods of organization change provide such situations. Take this example:

> The bookkeeping-clerical operations of a large bank always occupied a status position beneath that of the "front office" groups that dealt with the public (for example, in handling loans and deposits). With the addition of expensive, powerful computers the "back room" operations took on added importance. In fact, some of the key computer and systems specialists had to be paid higher salaries than the loan officers and other "front office" personnel.
>
> When these computer people began requesting some of the special perquisites that had been enjoyed in the past only by the high-status officers (such as executive dining room privileges), there was resentment in the latter group. It took several years for top management in the computer area to attain accepted high status.

In a sense, group relations are characterized by a "culture lag": Status relationships do not keep up with technological and organizational changes. In another company a group of highly trained mechanical engineers could not attract the respect of production supervision because the engineers filled jobs (now expanded) that in the past had been filled by low-status clerical personnel.

Newly created groups (for instance, a special task force or a new department) obviously suffer status anxieties, which are demonstrated through aggressive reaching out for recognition and symbols of prestige (such as office space). Once such groups are established and have been relatively successful in gaining recognition, they are not easily disbanded, even though their original function may have been served. The members of the group, through the process of having fought together for status, now identify with the future of the group. Thus, many committees continue to meet and work groups to function when their work no longer contributes to the objectives of the organization.

Cases like the bank example confront management with a dilemma. Management argues that each group should be treated "equally," but if status distinctions are ignored, this policy is bound to generate trouble. The manager's problem is complicated by the fact that "underdog" departments may be struggling to get ahead and raise their relative status in the organizational community.

Competition for improvements in working conditions and benefits appear to be most frequent among groups that are more than halfway up the status ladder. Their position is somewhat ambiguous; they are almost the best, but not quite. Members of these groups seem to be carrying a chip on their shoulders. They seize on real or imagined slights that they can protest through the grievance procedure, and never miss a chance to put pressure on both union and management. They are always looking for ways to improve their position: making the job a little easier, loosening the incentive standard, or perhaps eliminating some of the less desirable operations. Their special sensitivity marks them off as sources of danger for both union and management, who must treat them with extra care if turmoil is to be avoided. We will go into this problem in more detail in the next chapter.

However, a note of caution must be added. Status systems can be too static for dynamic organizations and thus cannot or should not always be observed. For example, employees whom the group ranks low in status may well be equipped to handle more responsible jobs. And undue emphasis on status may hinder communications between superior and subordinate.[23] (This problem will be discussed further in Chapter 8.)

GROUP COHESION

Just as the work groups are internally differentiated, so there are also significant differences *among* groups. One of the most important is the degree of unity or cohesion within the group. All the elements of group behavior that we have mentioned are influenced by this factor.[24] The more united the group, the greater the likelihood that all members will conform strictly to group standards (in part as a result of heightened pressures to conform) and the greater the likelihood that a small leadership core will represent without challenge the feelings of all members. By definition, cohesive groups are internally consistent in their measures of status and are more likely to act in unison when their expectations are violated, either by management, by one of their own members, or even by another group.

---

23 *Cf.* Louis Barnes, *Organizational Systems and Engineering Groups* (Boston: Harvard University Graduate School of Business, Division of Research, 1960).

24 For two excellent discussions of cohesion, see Dorwin Cartwright and Alvin Zander, eds., *Group Dynamics: Research and Theory* (New York: Harper & Row, 1953), pp. 73-91; and Stanley Seashore, *Group Cohesiveness in the Industrial Work Group* (Ann Arbor: Survey Research Center, University of Michigan, 1954).

New employees may find it difficult to get accepted by highly cohesive groups, and this can create problems for management endeavoring to fill a vacancy. There may be a "trial period"—not unlike a fraternity initiation—in which the newcomer has to prove himself. He must show that he is willing to live up to the norms of the group, that he has an acceptable personality, and that he accepts his status within the group. Exclusiveness can come as an unpleasant shock to the unprepared employee.

For management, it isn't enough simply to recognize that such differences among groups exist. It also wants to be able to predict the conditions that will produce either united or disunited groups. From our own research and that of others, the following factors emerge as some of the determinants of group cohesion.

Status of the group. Other things equal, people are more likely to feel loyalty toward a high-status group than towards a low-status group. Social climbers, for example, are more careful to conform to the norms of the group to which they aspire than to the norms of a group from which they want to escape. Indeed, there is a kind of circular process at work here: A high-status group elicits greater loyalty from its members, which in turn makes the group even stronger and more likely to gain increased status.

What determines the status of a group? All the factors noted above as determining individual status contribute, though interrelations between these factors become quite complex at the group level. For example, when we asked some employees in a public utility to compare their importance relative to that of other groups in the same organization, among the factors they mentioned were these:

1. The company has recognized the difficulty and responsibility associated with our jobs by establishing a special test which new employees must pass before they can do our type of work.
2. Because of the difficulty and dangerous nature of our jobs, no one else can touch our work—although in an emergency we can fill in on other jobs.
3. Our job is a good training ground for high responsibility. Over the years a number of our men have gone on to top management posts.
4. Our office used to be located in company headquarters. Now we are in an isolated building where no one goes unless he has to.
5. Before the company made any major decision our old boss used to be consulted. He was a very important man. Our present boss isn't thought of too highly and doesn't carry much weight in company affairs.

In effect, these employees were listing a number of status criteria: the intrinsic nature of the work, their level of responsibility, their opportunities for promotion, the boss' standing, and even their physical location. Several organization changes (noted in factors 4 and 5) had recently led to a substantial reduction in the status of this group. As a result, the members took less interest in informal company activities and even in the union, and they showed less satisfaction in being identified with the department.

Similarly, employees working at the very bottom of the organization's promotional ladder seldom develop a strong attachment to their work groups.[25] In fact, they sometimes regard themselves as only temporary members of their group.

Size. Small departments are more closely knit than large ones. Loyalty, as we have seen, is a product of constant, face-to-face contacts. Naturally it is easier to have close relationships with all the members of a small group than with all the members of a large one.

Homogeneity. Groups whose members have different interests and backgrounds are often less effective in promoting their own interests than groups whose members are more homogeneous. When, for example, people with sharp differences in rates of pay and job duties work near one another, the resulting informal group is seldom cohesive. This lack of homogeneity may reflect itself in the formation of competing subgroups or cliques, and conflict between these cliques may become so intense that any area of common interest is almost obliterated.

However, cohesiveness can be destroyed in groups composed of people doing similar work who are in competition with one another. A group consisting of store clerks competing actively for scarce customers and merchandise or of vice presidents competing for promotion and the attention of the chief executive would hardly be likely to have much solidarity. In fact, where the likelihood of interpersonal conflict is high, one finds that social groups tend to consist of people working for different bosses and doing different kinds of work.[26]

Communications. Groups in which the members can communicate easily with one another are more likely to be cohesive. Internal group unity can be thwarted in noisy steel mills or along assembly lines.[27] Even scattered groups, like maintenance crews, may become tightly knit if the technology of work requires or permits them to interact frequently with one another. We have observed one highly cohesive group whose members never saw each other on the job and yet were sufficiently cohesive to dominate the union and win substantial wage increases: These were electrical utility substation operators whose jobs required them to communicate by phone. Indeed, one of the determinants of group cohesion is the speed with which rumors or other messages can be transmitted through the group, for rumors contribute to the feeling of common identity.

---

[25] Howard Vollmer, *Employee Rights and The Employment Relationship* (Berkeley: University of California Press, 1960).

[26] *Cf.* Edward L. Gross, "Social Integration and Control of Competition," *American Journal of Sociology,* Vol. 67, No. 3 (Nov. 1961), pp. 270-283.

[27] Charles R. Walker, Robert Guest, and Arthur N. Turner, *Foreman on the Assembly Line* (Cambridge: Harvard University Press, 1956), pp. 131 ff.

Isolation from other groups. Physical isolation from other groups of workers tends to build cohesiveness. Employees on night shifts find it difficult to make nonwork friends. Miners among others have demonstrated in countless lengthy strikes that they will stick together more stubbornly than workers who are more socially integrated with the rest of the community.[28]

Where there is no sharp line between one group and another, cohesion is difficult to achieve. For example, on the assembly line, B may interact with A on his left and C on his right, while D may interact with C on his left and with E on his right. Thus, a chain of interactions develops but little group solidarity.[29]

Supervisory practices. The customary behavior of the supervisor has a direct influence on the degree of cohesion that exists within a group. By fostering competition, and by constantly comparing one employee with another, he may make close relations impossible. On the other hand, he can build solidarity by rewarding cooperative behavior. Among members of management, where there is often sharp competition for promotion and recognition, there is less cohesion than among hourly-paid employees who look to the union for protection against management and have much less expectation of promotion.

Outside pressure. Group members draw together when they are threatened by a common danger. A group of employees may forget their personal differences and close ranks against a new supervisor who is regarded as a threat to the group. The speed with which long-standing feuds are healed under pressure from a common enemy is sometimes wondrous to behold.

What happens when the pressure is removed? Group solidarity may diminish somewhat, but the cooperative patterns that arose during the time of crisis may well persist. Thus, the supervisor who inadvertently produces a strong anticompany clique may find that it survives long after the original grievances have been eliminated.

> In order to introduce a new incentive program, a large manufacturing company hired several new time-study men. As the program got under way, the men met intense opposition from the older industrial engineers, who felt the new program would endanger their relationships with their subordinates, and among the employees themselves who feared that the new program would mean "tighter" work standards. As the hostility mounted, the time-study men drew closer together. Then management capitulated to a strike called to protest the new standards, and the whole program suddenly collapsed. Some of the men in the defunct time-study department were offered other jobs in the organization; still others were helped to find jobs in the adjacent area. Even though the members now work in widely scattered locations, the group continues to meet regularly for dinner and a "chat about old times." Welded together by the pressure they shared, they became a closely knit group.

---

[28] Clark Kerr and Abraham Siegel, "The Interindustry Propensity to Strike—An International Comparison," Arthur Kornhauser, Robert Dubin, and Arthur Ross, eds., *Industrial Conflict* (New York: McGraw-Hill, 1954), pp. 191-193.

[29] Zaleznik *et al., op. cit.,* pp. 120-121.

Changes in accustomed ways of doing things and sudden cancellations of prerogatives may also draw employees together. Management opposition to their new solidarity may serve only to strengthen the group.

Success. A group is likely to be stronger and more cohesive if it has engaged successfully in cooperative action in the past. This is the familiar circular pattern: Cohesive groups are more successful and successful groups are more cohesive. Success, however, is largely a matter of luck and depends on many other factors; for example, whether the group occupies a strategic position in the flow of work.

If a small group discovers that it can cripple a plant by refusing to work, it can use this leverage to win special concessions in the future. Once the group loses this strategic advantage, however, it may fall apart.

> The machine polishers had a reputation for winning grievances and exercising control over the union. A new invention caused the company to cut down on the number of machine polishers employed. The company also failed to loosen up what the polishers felt was an outmoded incentive plan.
> Members of the group began to blame their informal leaders for what had happened. With the recognition of failure came an unwillingness to stick to-gether any longer. Workers began to squabble with one another, particularly over who should have priority to certain jobs. Personal recriminations followed and gradually the men began to request transfers to other departments.

Naturally, when members find that their own group is not successful in pro-tecting them or winning benefits for them, they are unlikely to abide con-sistently by group standards. In fact, members may begin to seek other affilia-tions that offer more security and status. This defection further weakens the group, and it becomes less and less successful.

CONCLUSION

In this chapter we have sought to analyze one important component of every organization: the aggregations of employees we have called groups. Although the boundary lines that determine group membership are affected by management's job assignments and supervisory practices, each group de-velops a momentum of its own. As a result, there is a constant elaboration of informal organization which does not appear on any chart or plan of the company's operations.

People seek membership in existing groups and form new groups for a wide variety of reasons. But at the bottom there always seems to be a search for satisfactions that are not provided directly by the job or by the supervisor —satisfactions such as companionship and protection.

Informal groups have a life of their own; they have customary ways of doing things and of looking at things; they have their own leaders and a minutely defined status hierarchy. These are the stable, enduring components of group life. In other words, informal organization is a *reality* that management can ignore only at its own peril.

Management sometimes tries to evade this reality by emphasizing the organization as a whole, even to the point of trying to break up what it regards as destructive cliques. Yet loyalty to the face-to-face group, to one's fellow workers, is much stronger than loyalty to the larger entity. Indeed, management can develop over-all loyalty only by encouraging teamwork and informal relations. The group may exercise far stronger control over its members than does management itself.

Other managements seek to by-pass the group by telling supervisors they should concentrate on dealing with each employee as an individual. It is certainly true that the supervisor must spend much of his time dealing with the personal needs and idiosyncrasies of his subordinates, yet he is completely missing the realities of the situation if he fails to see that the group is something more than the sum of the individuals concerned.

A good supervisor must understand the social organization with which he works, just as he must be familiar with tools, materials, and technological processes. If he is to avoid making unwitting mistakes, he must know the status structure of the group, its informal leaders, its standards and values. This knowledge will strengthen his tools of leadership immeasurably.

Does this mean that management must *accept* group standards as they are—for example, that it should do nothing to overcome a thoroughly unacceptable "bogey"? No, we think not. In later chapters we shall discuss ways in which management can work through the informal organization instead of fighting it.

First, however, we shall examine an organization that often grows out of the informal organization and exercises strong influence over it: the union.

PROBLEM 1

THE FRUSTRATED SALESMEN [30]

Over the years, salesmen in the ABC Company had developed the habit of perusing office records. Management was anxious to discourage this practice for fear that a salesman who had become intimately familiar with company costs and customers might go over to a competitor. The problem was intensified when new offices were constructed separating the salesmen's quarters from those occupied by the office staff. The salesmen were now expected to request necessary information from the office staff over a four-foot counter, and were never to enter the new premises. Here is the way one observer described the salesmen's determination to preserve the practice of looking at the records:

> "At first the salesmen would try to think of every conceivable way to 'break the barrier.' It became a matter of pride to see if they could enter the office and walk around. They said they had to speak to the accountant, to consult with the president, to check an order with a clerk, to pick up some clean towels—almost any excuse."

---

[30] We are grateful to a former student, J. J. Nerenberg, for the outline of this case.

Management reacted by making the rules against infiltration even more rigid. All salesmen were absolutely forbidden to enter the office except for exceptional reasons. This time the reaction was even more severe. The salesmen began to complain about every sort of petty detail in the office. Their favorite complaint was that the switchboard operator was not giving them all their messages. Next they began to find all sorts of fault with their new quarters. The ceiling tile was installed improperly, the phones were on the wrong side of the desk, the lighting was inadequate, the floor was not cleaned regularly. Fights broke out between the salesmen and the sales manager, and the salesmen began to make aggressive remarks about the office force. They became more clannish and self-conscious.

1. Basically, the changes management introduced were modest ones, and they did not "hurt" the salesmen. Why, then, were they exhibiting such aggressive behavior?
2. What group factors were affected by the change?
3. To what extent were these predictable reactions and of what value would such predictions be to supervision?

PROBLEM 2

THE "OLD GIRLS" [31]

Every summer, the Children's and Infants' Department of Hackett's Department Store had been plagued by friction between the regular full-time clerks and the temporary summer replacements.

The regular clerks had developed close social ties in the years they had spent together. They had a common ethnic background and all but two were unmarried or widowed. Whenever possible, they took their coffee and lunch breaks together and often saw each other after work. Further, the department had frequent slack periods when the clerks could sit around and talk together.

The replacements were drawn either from a "flying squad" of full-time employees who were assigned to different departments as need dictated, or from young high-school girls who took the jobs for the summer. Both groups were extremely unhappy at being sent to the Children's Department, and two of the high-schoolers asked for transfers after a short stay. The reasons became quickly evident. The independent work-structure evolved by the regulars had resulted in a department pattern which violated the store rulebook. There was, for example, a definite "pecking order" governing who could take coffee breaks when, and there were frequent unexplained disappearances and early preparations for departure at closing time. The regulars made little effort to assist or advise the newcomers, and criticized them constantly behind their backs. There were seldom more than two part-time girls in the department at any one time, and since they were unlikely to have known each other before, there was little opportunity for them to develop any relationship.

The major difficulties occurred in the area of commission sales. Although the full-timers had an unspoken agreement not to "push hard" for sales achievements, they bitterly resented any commission earned by replacements. They argued that as senior workers they deserved the lion's share of the commission income. The part-timers didn't need it as much as they did, nor had they worked to build up the department. Furthermore, the full-timers thought of themselves as embodying all the sales know-how in the department; the part-timers "didn't

---

[31] We are indebted to a former student, Eben W. Keyes, II, for this case.

know how to sell." Catastrophe occurred when one of the part-timers made a substantial sale and "sabotaged" the commission of one of the regulars. The high-school girl came to the assistant buyer in tears; she had sold a crib when the full-timer in her area was absent from the department, and had been roundly berated for making the sale! She was told that she did not understand the merchandise, and that the other clerk could have made a larger, more profitable sale.

The part-timers were naturally anxious to build up a good sales record. They were motivated to do a good, capable job—either with a view to winning permanent employment, or, in the case of the "flying squad," to convince management that they were worthy of promotion.

As a result, the "old girls" gave either misleading or incorrect information about merchandise or department policies to the part-timers, in order to slow them down and make their job performance less impressive. When a replacement turned to a full-timer for help while serving a customer, the full-timer would frequently take over and consummate the sale. Part-timers were often sent to the stockroom for more goods or were asked to rearrange displays. The full-timers were directing their energies into undermining the part-timers instead of into trying to improve their own sales records.

1. How do you explain the behavior of the full-time clerks in this department?
2. Was management gaining any compensating advantages from the increased cohesiveness of the full-timers?
3. Is it realistic or typical to find employees doing average or below-average work and still viewing themselves as top-notch salesmen, as in this case?
4. What would you do if you were the buyer (department head) in this case?

PROBLEM 3

NEW AGAINST OLD [32]

The old "standard" spinning machines in a large manufacturing plant were operated chiefly by high-seniority men paid on an hourly rate. For nine years the company had been experimenting with new machines that were faster and easier to run. During the experimental period, the machines had been operated by younger men with low seniority. After a two-year tryout, these operators had been put on incentive rates.

To obtain the union's approval, management granted a "loose" rate (one on which it is easy to obtain high earnings). The union readily accepted, believing that unless the long-run productivity of this particular department was improved, the company would move its operation to another plant.

The old spinners, however, who were politically powerful in the union, resented the incentive system. They feared that it would set a precedent for working too fast and perhaps even reduce the amount of work available to them. Eventually this could mean fewer jobs.

Even before the incentive plan was accepted, the men on the old spinners derided the younger men as "damn fools for working themselves to death." In turn, the younger men were resentful of the old spinners' "creamy jobs" and were upset that the seniority system forced them to take what was then less desirable work, with little chance of obtaining jobs on the old machines.

---

[32] This case is adapted from the authors' earlier book, *The Local Union* (New York: Harper & Row), pp. 43-58. The case may be more meaningful after you read Chapter 5.

After the incentive plan was put into effect, the men began to compare their paychecks in neighborhood bars. It became obvious that the younger men, on incentive, were earning a great deal more than the older spinners on their hourly rate. Since the two types of machine were located right next to each other, the old spinners were able to watch the ever-increasing production on the other line. With growing anxiety, they saw the differential in earnings grow larger and larger.

Some of the high-seniority spinners considered these jobs as rightfully theirs:

"Why should some young guy that has been in the plant less than a year be taking home 30 dollars more a week than guys like us that have been here more than 15 years? We'll be the laughing stock of the plant."

The two lines had never been friendly, but now they began to exchange angry threats. An informed leader among the top-seniority spinners told the "youngsters":

"You guys better save what you are earning because you're not going to be on these jobs very long. We're coming over to take them. They're ours because we're the oldest men in the department."

His counterpart in the young spinner group answered:

"Don't start anything because if you try to bump us [use the seniority provisions of the contract to take their jobs] we're going to fix those jobs so no one wants them.

"We took these jobs when no one else wanted them. We stuck to them through a two-year trial period when everyone else was laughing at us, and you fellows have no right to come over and bump us off."

Three of the more vocal old-timers submitted a formal grievance to their steward outlining their right to the new job and demanding that the union do something about the threat of the youngsters to use production increases to "ruin the new job."

In the meantime, the incentive workers made good their threat to accelerate production, hoping thereby to discourage the older men from any further interest in the job. Their logic was this: if they worked very hard, management would expect much more production than the older men, who had been "spoiled" by their hourly rates, would be willing to put out.

The older men responded by calling a departmental meeting, as authorized by the union constitution. The younger men boycotted the meeting but learned of the results the next day. They, too, submitted a formal grievance in writing, enunciating their claims to the incentive jobs.

1. Analyze the sources of this conflict in terms of the type of group factors involved.
2. Assess the likelihood that struggles *between* employee groups will be an important personnel problem in most organizations.
3. Where these intergroup problems exist, to what extent is management also a participant? Why?

Unions and Labor Relations

Over 17 million Americans belong to unions. This simple fact has profound implications for management. Although we cannot treat union-management relations in depth in this chapter, we will consider why employees join or don't join unions, how unions function within the organization, and what their impact on management is. First, however, let us note that labor relations do *not* represent as distinct a problem in relationships for the organization as we might first assume.

WHY UNION PROBLEMS ARE NOT UNIQUE

Occupational Associations Are Common

As described in Chapter 4, when employees work together and share common experiences they tend to develop into a group and to acquire goals of their own which may differ sharply from the goals of the total enterprise. Most times these groups never go beyond the stage of informal organization (with informal leaders and unwritten objectives). Sometimes, however, where there is a great deal of common occupational identification, employees form occupational associations. There are such associations for purchasing agents, nurses, industrial engineers, and the like. These groups may begin largely for social reasons, then move on to aid members to advance themselves and the status of the occupation. Finally, some begin to consider bargaining directly with the employer for improved salaries and working conditions. For example, the American Nurses Association took on aspects of a bona fide union when it decided to engage in collective bargaining.

Bargaining

It is easy to believe that without unions, everyone would work together in harmony for common organizational objectives. Actually, bargaining is a way of life in nearly all organizations, even where there are no unions. As we shall see later, supervisors often exchange favors or make "deals" as a means of gaining cooperation from their subordinates. Large organizations include many different specialized groups even within management itself, and these groups negotiate with one another, "trading off" one advantage for another (see Chapter 16).

Outsiders

The typical management fears the union as an outside force with different goals from those of the firm. After all, the union is interested primarily in its own growth and survival. However, companies have grown used to dealing with many "outsiders." For example, government officials, recommend (or demand) special accounting or quality control procedures, outside contractors work inside firms, and countless examples could be cited of places where an organization's boundaries have become permeable.

Differing Perceptions

Management often argues that there are no real conflicts of interest between workers and the company. Both stand to gain if profits and productivity improve. This is often true, but the significant point is that employees *believe* that there is a conflict of interest, say, between profits and wages. Although their over-all interests may not always be in conflict, workers and management tend to see problems from a different vantage point. To the manager a new machine may represent a saving in labor cost, but to the employee it will appear as a threat to his job.

> It is now a well-established uniformity of organizational behavior that wherever groups of people occupy widely differing positions in a hierarchy (vertically arranged organization structure) and carry out different activities, they are bound to see their interests as being different.[1]

Conflict

At one time it was believed that a harmonious consensus within an organization was normal and that only unions introduced intergroup conflict. Yet given the inevitable differences among groups within an organization (between production and sales, for example), conflict and differing objectives permeate modern organizations. Of course, these internal conflicts do not result in the actual breaks in relationship that occur in strikes, but they are similarly obstructive to organizational effectiveness.

---

[1] William F. Whyte in an unpublished paper, "Models for Building and Changing Organizations" (mimeo, 1965).

Unions are not a new phenomenon in American life. There were scattered efforts to form trade unions early in the nineteenth century and, by the close of the century, the American Federation of Labor was well established in a number of skilled crafts. Yet until the 1930's union membership outside these crafts was highly unstable. Though unskilled workers sometimes joined unions in time of prosperity, they abandoned them when hard times returned. This pattern began to change drastically during the great depression of the 1930's, when a relatively large, permanent trade-union membership emerged not only in the traditional crafts where workers had found it easier to organize, but also in mass-production industry.

Certain changes in the American economic and political environment coincided with this growth:

1. The depression cost American business a great deal in terms of prestige and employee confidence. The unions, on the other hand, gained in prestige. Many observers regarded them as a healthy check on business power (a check that might help to moderate the business cycle). Gradually, unions began to escape the stigma of being somehow un-American.

2. Government at both the state and federal levels, which had traditionally handicapped union organization (for example, by unfavorable court decisions and the use of injunctions), became more favorably disposed to labor. In fact, new legislation like the Wagner Act (1935) actively encouraged union organization.[2]

3. A substantial segment of the working population began to accept as permanent the role of wage-earner, realizing that it was not just a temporary stop on the road to owning one's own business. As we observed in Chapter 1, the American dream of moving constantly along to better jobs had lost its luster for some and was replaced by a desire to protect the present situation. With this acceptance came an interest in improving one's lot as an employee through union membership.

4. The decline in immigration and the rise in educational standards tended to make our population more homogeneous. Relatively high standards of education raised the level of employee aspirations. No longer satisfied with just having a job, they demanded more and more from their jobs. And they regarded the union as a valuable ally in getting what they wanted.

---

[2] The basic federal statute protecting the right of workers to join unions and prohibiting employers from interfering with the organization of unions is the National Labor Relations Act of 1935 (the Wagner Act) as amended by the Labor-Management Relations Act of 1947 (the Taft-Hartley Act) and the Labor-Management Reporting and Disclosure Act of 1959 (the Landrum-Griffin Act).

Union membership in the United States since 1900.

5. The unions' growth provided some of its own impetus. Greater acceptance of unions by the community, and increased union prestige as a result of participation in civic and governmental affairs, increased the attractiveness of membership, as did identification of the steadily rising wage level since the beginning of World War II with increasing union strength.

WHY EMPLOYEES JOIN UNIONS

Almost every union member is also an employee and has joined his union because he hopes it will better his relationship with his employer. Why does he feel this move is necessary? Many managers have two oversimplified explanations of why workers join unions: The first is that the company has been foolish or selfish, or both. By providing unsatisfactory working conditions and wages, by permitting supervisors to play favorites, management has actually encouraged its employees to seek out a union. Such conditions undoubtedly stimulate the growth of unions. But what about the many well-managed organizations that have been unionized? What has motivated the workers of these companies to join unions?

Here is where the other explanation comes into play. Unionization, it says, must be the result of outside agitators, rabble-rousers, and radicals, who by lies and deceit stir up an otherwise satisfied work force. This reason also is an oversimplification. To be sure, professional organizers from the outside have a great deal to do with bringing workers into the union fold. And they often make use of a small number of strategically located insiders who are willing to take on the task of agitating for the new union. But this is only a small part of the total explanation. Below we have summarized the opinions of many careful observers of union organization.

Desire for Better Economic
and Working Conditions

Most people want to increase their income—even in top-paying companies. Seldom do we find a man who is convinced that the economic returns and physical satisfactions provided by his job are perfect and quite beyond improvement. In the United States, the greatest growth period of unions coincided with a rapidly rising income level for workers. Whether the unions have really obtained higher wages and better pension, insurance, and other benefits for their members, or whether these would have come anyway through normal economic and social processes, is not the point. The point is that an impressive number of employees *believe* that unions are responsible for improving their economic lot.

Desire for Control
over Benefits

In our society, many employees are unhappy when they are completely dependent on someone else for the satisfaction of their needs. Even when that "someone else" is very good, as many managements have been, and provides good wages, steady employment, and desirable working conditions, workers tend to be uneasy when they have no power to control the benefits received. In fact, management makes matters worse by emphasizing how much it has "given" its employees (that is, benefits provided at the discretion of the company, not offered because they *had* to be). In telling people that they should be thankful for what has been voluntarily given them, a company is also saying that what it has given can also be taken away.

Even in organizations where employees have always been treated with complete fairness and justice, stories circulate that John Jones over in Department 16 has been severely penalized for something he didn't do because a supervisor "had it in for him." In any situation where we lack the power to control what happens to us, we are more than ready to believe these "atrocity" stories and think, "Next time that could happen to us." The truth or falsity of the rumor may be unimportant.

Furthermore, in a large company where top management is many levels removed from the individual employee, the individual's sense of dependency and lack of control over what happens to him is magnified.

Desire for Self-Expression and
Communication with Higher Management

Many an employee feels that, as far as his company is concerned, he is nothing more than a time-clock number. Though many would not want the responsibility of management, they would like greater opportunity to express themselves. In part, this is just the desire to complain when hurt. But more importantly, as individuals we all have a need to express our point of view— not just to "get more" for ourselves, but to enjoy the feeling of being a whole person instead of a pair of hired hands.

Without a union, most employees feel they have no means of "safely" going over the head of their boss with a problem. After all, they must rely on this man to do many things for them. There are a hundred and one ways in which a supervisor can make their working life unpleasant and unrewarding. Discretion is frequently the better part of valor; when the supervisor says "No," most employees accept it as the final word.

This feeling of helplessness is particularly acute when the immediate supervisor is unsympathetic to their demands, either because he has no decision-making authority of his own (a point that will become clearer when we discuss organizational problems in Chapter 15), or because he has a natural unwillingness to reverse his own decisions. If only they can gain access to higher levels in the organization, employees reason, they may find someone with the authority to satisfy their requests.

The union promises a worker an opportunity to protest inequities, to believe that if something goes wrong he will have a chance to be heard. The union offers a direct road to participate, for its leaders have access to the top decision-making levels of the organization.

The Union Shop

Many employees, of course, do not have a choice about joining a union. Approximately nine-tenths of unionized blue-collar workers labor under a "union shop" agreement, that is, they are required to maintain their union membership in their present employment.

Precipitating Causes

We have been describing some of the underlying reasons for the growth of unions. But how can we explain why a union is organized in a particular company at a specific time? Here are some typical precipitating causes:

1. A change in the top management of the plant. Employees fear that the new management will be less friendly and will not preserve the favorable conditions they are used to.

2. Specific problems arising from incentive-payment systems, particularly new standards or new work assignments.

3. The cutting off of promotional ladders—for example, requiring that all new supervisors have college degrees.

4. Sudden cutbacks and layoffs.

In recent years union growth has slowed almost to a halt. Unions have been more successful in the older and more heavily populated industrial centers of the East and Midwest. They have been less successful in the South. Small towns in that region have been hostile to unions for a variety of historical and social reasons. On an industry basis, manufacturing, mining, transportation, and public utilities have been relatively well organized. Approximately 80 to 90 per cent of the eligible employees in manufacturing and public utility plants in the more heavily industrialized sections of the country are union members. On the other hand, office workers and those in the service industries and in wholesale and retail trade have not been receptive to union organization. Except in the largest cities, the proportion of employees unionized in these industries hovers around 10 per cent. Women and professional workers have also tended to shy away from union membership.

Yet the greatest growth in employment in recent years has taken place in service industries (schools, stores, banks, insurance companies, government work) where white-collar work predominates. Not only has relative employment declined in manufacturing, the stronghold of union organization, but many companies have had absolute decreases in employment as a result of technological improvements.

Since union membership is associated with blue-collar work, many white-collar employees fear that joining a union would lower their social status. Many of these employees work in close proximity to management and hope to move into management positions themselves. Further, the fact that they are broken down into small, uncohesive groups makes it difficult for them to develop the kind of consensus necessary for union organization.[3] Professional and technical employees tend to believe that they can get along "on their own" and that their individual chances for advancement should not be tied to the status of the whole group.

Nevertheless it should be noted that a heavy proportion of the relatively small recent union growth has been in the white-collar area. Unions of government employees (teachers, among others) have expanded their membership significantly. And professional and occupational associations which do not call themselves unions have been taking on union-like functions. Indeed, these "quasi-unions" seem to be growing much faster than have unions of the orthodox sort.

Organizations of functional staff groups, such as the National Association of Purchasing Agents, though not engaging in bargaining, have become increasingly active in advancing their members' occupational interests.

---

[3] Interestingly, engineers join unions when they work closely together in large undifferentiated groups, as in some of the huge aircraft and electronics plants.

The recent slowdown in union expansion may also be attributed to the exposure of corruption in a small number of unions. Corrupt leaders threaten strikes and boycotts if company officials refuse to hand over sums of money for their personal use. They can also organize unions and collect dues, yet do nothing to aid the membership; this small number of unscrupulous leaders may also tap accumulated dues and premiums paid to health and welfare funds by employees and employers. As a result of such disclosures, the union movement lost some of its reputation for crusading for improvements in the status of the common man.

At the same time, the legislation encouraging union growth has been modified, and in some ways organization has been inhibited. In addition, many employees have forgotten the preunion period of the 1930's when management personnel techniques were less well developed and unions had a larger number of obvious grievances to win and contract gains to acclaim.

Of course, employees have new worries: increasing company mobility and automation are threats to jobs. Further, there has been sharp management resistance to union demands for improved economic benefits and to increased union decision-making in matters affecting day-to-day production. Management opposition to union gains, emanating in part from increased competitiveness in product markets and decreased shortages in labor markets, has also served to detract from the union's momentum and prestige.

INTERNAL ORGANIZATION OF THE UNION

The Local Union

Now let us look at the rather complex structure of the unions themselves. Some employees are organized on the basis of the company or plant in which they work—for example, all the employees of the Carter Chemical Company's Atlanta plant are eligible to join a local industrial union whose membership is restricted to these employees. Frequently the white-collar clerical employees of such a company, or its most highly skilled maintenance employees, may belong to separate local unions. Industries that employ several clearly defined trades are usually not organized by unions on a plant or company basis. Rather, all employees in a given geographic area, usually a community, who have the qualifications to practice the trade, are eligible for membership in a local craft union—for example, all unionized bricklayers in Rochester, New York, belong to the same local, regardless of which employer they work for. Community-wide locals are also found where the employer unit is relatively small (for example, all the dry-cleaning plant employees in town might belong to a single local of the Teamsters), or where employees are likely to shift from one employer to another (for example, in the needle trades).

Why do we emphasize this difference between unions that are organized on the basis of an employer unit and unions that are organized on the basis of a geographic area? Because the governments of these two types of local union are quite different. Where the membership is derived from many different companies in a clearly defined geographical area, the union is likely to vest a great deal of authority in an elected business agent, who works full time on the negotiation of contracts, grievance problems, and the protection of the union's job jurisdiction.[4] Since these agents service many widely dispersed members who work for a variety of employers, they are very powerful, and management must be willing to deal regularly with them. Unfortunately, most of the corruption mentioned above has arisen in this type of union, and, because of the growth of so-called service industries in the United States, this type is expanding at the expense of unions organized by employer units.

By contrast, in unions organized on a company or plant basis, authority usually is dispersed among a number of leaders, many of whom continue to work at their regular jobs.

The Local Leadership

The local union has two types of officer: *Executive-board members* handle the union's internal business—finances, administration of election procedures, appointment of committee members, social functions, and so forth.[5] *Grievance officials* handle relationships with management—the union's collective-bargaining business. These latter officials have a variety of titles, depending on the union and their rank—business agents, committeemen, stewards, grievancemen, chief stewards, and so forth. Most of these officials continue to work for the company in their regular jobs while they are serving in their union capacity, and the company often pays for the time they spend handling employee grievances. Larger and wealthier locals, however, may engage full-time elected officials to handle their grievances and negotiations.

The Membership

The most active union members—the elected officers—are employees who have more energy and ambition than they can expend on their jobs. Essentially discontented and anxious to get ahead, they often turn to the union when their drives are frustrated elsewhere.[6] Many of these men may also be excellent workers, and management frequently finds that leadership in the union may provide a clue to supervisory ability.

This active group, together with members who do not hold office but who attend union meetings and participate in the local's political life, is likely to

---

[4] Unions organized on the basis of an employer unit are usually not active in getting jobs for members, nor are they concerned with making sure that no job in the community for which one of their members is qualified is filled by a nonmember.

[5] In some unions, the executive board is involved at some stage of the grievance procedure as well.

[6] Leonard Sayles and George Strauss, *The Local Union* (New York: Harcourt, Brace & World, 1967), pp. 56-70.

include no more than 5 per cent of the membership, and frequently a good bit less. Most of the members prefer to "let George do it" when it comes to taking an active role. They pay their dues as they would pay premiums on an insurance policy and they have little to do with the organization except when a grievance arises or when a strike takes place.

Few members seem to feel that union membership conflicts with their loyalty to the company that provides them with job and wages. For many, the union is a way of "making the company better." Of course, unions also attract members with deep-seated hostility toward management, workers who seek to embarrass their supervisors through union activity. Such persons are likely to be most active in the original organization of the union. Advocating a union where none exists typically requires stronger emotions than accepting it after the union has become established. However, many of the "firebrands" who helped bring in the industrial unions during the 1930's and 1940's are nearing or have reached retirement. Newer members may feel less commitment to an organization they did not help or observe get started.

The International Union [7]

Most local unions are affiliated with an international union that provides them with certain services. You are probably familiar with the names of many of these organizations: The Steelworkers, the Autoworkers, the Teamsters, the Carpenters [8] (all with close to a million members each!). Primarily, the internationals deal with union problems that are out of reach of the local, such as company-wide bargaining problems, government relations, and organizing the unorganized.

The international union usually hires "international representatives" to help the local union get established and to present local bargaining problems directly to management. These officials often participate in the later stages of the grievance procedure (which is described in the next section). Their most important job, however, is usually the handling of contract negotiations. The decision-making body for the international union is the convention, which is held once every year or two, or even more infrequently.

A large number of American international unions have joined together in the AFL-CIO, which serves as a general trade union organization.[9] It has almost no direct power over collective-bargaining matters, for most of its activities concern problems of the labor movement and relationships with government. There are other units in the union movement, such as city councils and state federations, which are organized to deal primarily with various levels

---

[7] Many a national organization is usually referred to as an "international" union in recognition of the fact that it may have members in Canada.

[8] These are not the formal names of these international unions, but the unions are commonly referred to in this fashion.

[9] However, several important international unions are not included in the AFL-CIO, such as the West Coast Longshoremen, the Teamsters, and the Mineworkers.

of local and state government. The international union, however, is by far the strongest unit.

The Union as a Political Body

If management is to deal with a union successfully, it must recognize that the union is a *political* body. Nearly all union officials—at both the local and international levels—are elected, and many union decisions, particularly at the local level, are made by direct vote of the membership. Thus, most decisions do not necessarily flow from top down as they do in management; officers cannot guarantee that the members will do as they are told, particularly in democratic unions, and members can always engage in wildcat strikes. Consequently, in order to win elections, officers must always win something in their negotiations with management. For this reason, they sometimes go through the motions of pressing grievances in which they do not believe.

Still, there is widespread apathy among union members—for example, the local union meeting, which is the major decision-making forum for the local, is usually very poorly attended. And yet, in spite of this apathy, management must recognize that what the union leaders do must at least appear to the members as satisfying their needs. Failure to recognize this fact may lead to a serious miscalculation of the behavior of union leaders. Whereas a top-management official in a negotiation may be able to make firm decisions on his own, a union negotiator may have to get membership approval before he can make a binding commitment. Unions are certainly not models of pure democracy, but in most unions an aroused membership can turn out its leadership in favor of another group. Discontent of this sort contributed to the defeat, in 1965, of David McDonald and James Carey, long-time presidents of the Steelworkers and the International Union of Electrical Workers, respectively.

Intergroup Conflicts

An important component of the political life of the union is struggle *between* groups within the rank and file: Each wants improved benefits for itself and each wants to protect itself from the encroachments of other groups. Members of each group feel the union is theirs. It is easy to be misled into thinking that the local union is a single, cohesive unit with a leadership that can speak for all members. But look at the kinds of issues on which there can be coercive comparisons leading to internal disagreement:

> Younger employees want their leaders to get higher wages while the older employees want negotiating efforts to go into improving pensions.
>
> Higher-paid workers want "percentage" wage increases and lower-paid workers want the same hourly increase to go to everyone "across the board." [10]
>
> Management adds a new finishing process. Workers in Department 35 claim

---

[10] For example, with a 5 per cent increase, employees earning $2.00 per hour would get 10¢ and those earning $3.00 per hour would get a 15¢ increase.

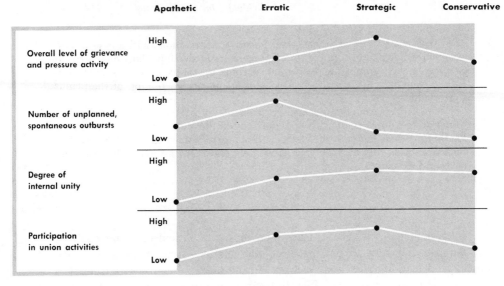

	Apathetic	Erratic	Strategic	Conservative
Overall level of grievance and pressure activity	Low		High	
Number of unplanned, spontaneous outbursts		High	Low	
Degree of internal unity	Low		High	
Participation in union activities	Low		High	

Summary of work-group differences.[11]

jurisdiction over this work while the employees in Final Assembly insist that the new work ought to become part of their department.

Such conflicts are not surprising when we reflect on the degree to which job satisfactions or dissatisfactions are felt in relative, not absolute terms (see Chapter 1). Thus, the leadership must balance off the claims of one group against those of another in the light of their relative political strength as well as the real equities. For example, some groups, if they don't get their way, will be able to defeat the officers at the next election or even to mount an illegal wildcat strike that will embarrass the officials in their dealings with management. Other groups put up no resistance if they lose their demands.

Varieties of Work-Group Pressure

Work groups seem to react to problems in different ways, depending on the kinds of jobs they do. At least four varieties of groups may be identified:

Apathetic Groups are least likely to pressure the union into fighting for them. They are often made up of men with low-status, relatively unskilled jobs who lack internal cohesion and leadership.

Erratic Groups at times exhibit very bellicose behavior, even walking off the job. Other times, with just as important problems facing them, they seem to be uninterested in any union actions on their behalf. These groups often include assembly line and crew workers, where there is a great deal of interdependence in work operations.

Strategic Groups are the most calculating and self-conscious groups within the rank and file and frequently exert pressure for more benefits for themselves.

[11] Leonard Sayles, *Behavior of Industrial Work Groups* (New York: Wiley, 1958), p. 39. The other material in this section is also drawn from this source.

They are never satisfied, always feel "relative deprivation" and know how to exert effective political pressure on the union leadership. The most typical workers in such groups are individual machine operators who work independently, not in crews. They also hold jobs near, but not at, the top of the plant's status ladder.

Conservative Groups are seemingly content with their high-status position. These groups only occasionally feel the need to pressure the union to do battle for them. When they are dissatisfied, they are restrained and very rational in their approach. Often, maintenance workers and other skilled craftsmen demonstrate this pattern.

THE UNION-MANAGEMENT RELATIONSHIP

Union-management relations are seen most dramatically during contract negotiations, when the parties meet together to determine the wages, fringe benefits, and working rules that will prevail until a new contract is negotiated one, two, or more years thereafter. But the negotiation of labor agreements takes much less time than the handling of grievances.

Even when a union exists, management continues to make most of the personnel decisions: who shall be hired, disciplined, promoted, given an increase in pay, have his working conditions or hours of work changed, and so on. Very few such decisions are ever made jointly, although the contract is designed to establish certain limits or checks on the decisions that management can make in these areas. After a manager takes action, however, the union can challenge the decision and file a grievance claiming that management is acting in violation of either the contract or of past practice (which becomes the equivalent of the contract).

John Jones Has a Grievance

Let us examine a hypothetical case to illustrate the ramifications of what may appear to be a simple grievance. Notice especially the number of people who are involved and their diverse points of view.[12]

The employee's problem: John Jones works as a laboratory assistant in the animal experimentation station of a large drug company. His work involves feeding, washing, and weighing animals, building cages, and occasionally cleaning them. Recently, Jones has noticed that he is required to spend much more time cleaning cages than are the other assistants. Since this is the least pleasant and lowest-status of all his tasks, he thinks it is unfair that he should have to do so much of it.

---

[12] This case does not describe the exact procedure by which every employee complaint would be handled. The number of steps and the union and management personnel who become involved at each step vary greatly from one labor contract to another. But this case is typical. Many "grievances," however, do not get written down and processed through a formal procedure; they are handled verbally in the regular, day-to-day contacts of union and management officials.

The supervisor's reaction: When Jones discusses his problem with the supervisor, Brown, he is told that job assignments are arranged in order to use the work force most efficiently. All assistants are hired with the understanding that they will be doing one or all of the tasks noted above. Brown feels that some of the other men are more skilled in handling the animals and doing minor construction work. So it seems a better use of manpower to have Jones spend more of his time cleaning cages.

Enter the union: Unsatisfied by Brown's answer, Jones considers calling in the union for help. He hesitates for a while, for fear that such a step may antagonize his supervisor and win him the reputation of troublemaker. Then he decides that, after all, help is what he pays dues for. So Jones contacts the union steward for the laboratory, who happens to work in an adjacent building. The steward discusses the problem with Brown and reports back to Jones the next day:

> "Brown refuses to do anything. He says it's his job to make decisions like this one, and he is not trying to discriminate against you. I'm not satisfied with his answer. I'll see the chief steward tonight at the union meeting and see what he says."

Note what has happened: The steward has tried unsuccessfully to represent the worker and now has turned the case over to a higher level in the union which can contact higher management.

The union's reaction.   The steward goes to the chief steward and describes the case. Here is the chief steward's reaction:

> "This is not a simple case; we have to be careful. In the first place we have to consider the reaction of the other men in the department. Jones is the newest employee; they may get pretty sore if more of this cleaning work is thrown at them. Secondly, the whole thing may backfire. Our present contract is weak on this point. There is actually nothing to prevent the company from changing a man's work, and if they start giving him a lot of the dirty jobs if they want to be mean about it, they might be able to justify paying him less money since his work may now be less skilled than before. Our only chance to win would be if we could show that the supervisor was doing this to Jones because he didn't like him. That would be covered by Clause 14. Discuss it with Jones and, if he has some evidence on this, get him to sign a grievance."

Note the implication behind this reaction: The union is not just the representative of the individual worker. It also has to think of its total membership. Actually, as you have already learned, many grievances and worker demands are directed against other employees, not against management. The union depends on the support of its total membership; dissatisfied members may succeed in ejecting officers or in overthrowing the union itself. Clearly, the union must consider the over-all implications of each grievance and demand.

Moreover, the union has to consider its strategic position vis-à-vis management. The union has certain institutional objectives. For example, it is seeking to strengthen its own position in the company somewhat independently of particular employee or group needs. Creating a fuss about Jones' complaint might lead management to insist on its contractual right to change jobs as it sees fit. Of course, the union might be aroused to seek a stronger contract at the next negotiations.

The middle steps of the grievance procedure: Jones agrees to sign the formal grievance papers charging Brown with discrimination. He notes on the printed form that his assignment to excessive cleaning duties followed an argument with Brown over new coveralls. "When I complained that my coveralls (supplied by the company) were too torn, Brown said I was always complaining and ought to have something to really complain about for a change." The grievance is also signed by the steward; the supervisor himself signs it, but only after adding this note: "Grievance refused—employee has not been discriminated against." Then the chief steward sends the grievance to the laboratory manager, asking for an appointment to talk the matter over.

Management's reaction: After the manager receives the grievance, he calls in the supervisor, Brown, to get his version of the case; he also checks with the personnel director to see whether similar cases have established precedents in this area that would affect the settlement.

The manager is at first concerned that this might be a case of discrimination. The company has a firm policy that no supervisor is to allow personal feelings to enter into personnel decisions. Having satisfied himself that Brown was right, the manager feels that he cannot grant the grievance. To do so would be to open the door to a stream of union challenges of work assignments. The manager tells the chief steward that, even though a man may feel he is getting more than his share of the unpleasant jobs, it is up to the supervisor to make such decisions in accordance with his own work requirements and the available manpower. So, while he will caution Brown to make sure such assignments are dictated by work needs and not by his personal feelings toward particular employees, the grievance will have to be refused. He writes: "No contract violation, supervisor was acting within normal management prerogatives."

Higher levels of the grievance procedure. The next move is clearly up to the union. The chief steward and the steward explain to Jones that he has a weak case. No one has heard the supervisor threaten Jones and, even if the supervisor admitted using threats, that would not prove he was discriminating. Well, yes, there are some other steps that might be taken. The union's business agent could take the case up with the division manager of the drug company. If the company still refused to agree to divide the work up more equitably, the case could then be taken to arbitration.[13]

---

[13] Most union-management agreements provide for the introduction of a third party, an impartial outsider, to decide grievance issues that have not been resolved through the normal grievance procedure. Arbitration is designed to preclude the use of strikes or lockouts in the grievance procedure, although these economic pressure weapons are retained for use during disputes over new contracts.

The chances of winning, however, are not good, Jones is told. The chief steward advises Jones to be alert for other evidence of discrimination that would enable the union to reopen the case. He promises that the union will also try to obtain a contract clause next year to prohibit, without specific union approval, changes in work assignments that are equivalent to job transfers.

Even though the chances of success were very slight, the chief steward might have decided to push the case anyway. Grievances provide interesting, challenging work and relieve the monotony of his highly routine job in the company. And yet most union leaders are not anxious to build up a reputation for pressing "poor cases" too vigorously. They want their opposite numbers in management to believe that they are sensible men who can tell the difference between just and unjust claims—but that they are also tough, of course.

IMPACT OF THE UNION ON MANAGEMENT

What over-all effect does the existence of a union have on the organization as a whole and on the management of personnel? The following discussion, which goes beyond the specific grievance problems we have described, will also suggest some of the reasons why many companies have resisted unionization.

Challenges to Management Decisions

The existence of a union means that all personnel decisions are subject to close scrutiny and, perhaps, active challenge. In a nonunion situation, employees may grow dissatisfied and harbor a sense of injustice or injury, but they are not necessarily willing to express their attitudes. The union gives them a means of taking action, not only by approaching the immediate supervisor, but also by reaching higher in the management structure with their demands. For the manager who relishes unchecked authority, this is an unpleasant experience. Almost any manager would prefer to have his orders and decisions go unchallenged.

Competition for Loyalty

Furthermore, the union is in a strategic position to compete with management for the loyalty of employees. For example, it may try to claim credit for any improvement in wages or vacations—even implying that these benefits had to be wrung from an unwilling management. Particularly in the organizational stage, when the union is trying to establish itself, it may caricature company executives and their "desire to sweat labor." Such charges of dishonesty and high-handed tyranny come as a rude shock to executives, particularly to those who think of themselves as benevolent, thoughtful employers. These managers are likely to fear that the union will deprive them of the opportunity to serve as protectors of their employees.

Review of Personnel Policies

The awareness that the union is ready to challenge its actions stimulates management to exercise more care in shaping personnel policies. Mistakes can be costly, not only in terms of the time and goodwill lost through grievance-processing, but also in terms of the new contractual demands that are likely to spring from employee dissatisfaction. For example, in one company the supervisors made a habit of asking workers just before quitting time to work overtime and pressured those who had other commitments either to stay or face the consequences. Here the union later demanded and won a clear-cut contractual prohibition against mandatory overtime work. At times this policy handicapped management.

Over-all, the growth of unions has been an impetus to the development of better personnel policies.

Threats to Efficiency

Management fears that the union may want to introduce barriers to efficient work methods, reduce work loads, and, in general, hold back productivity. For example, the union usually wants to introduce rigid rules preventing one man from doing another man's work. If a manager is prevented from assigning work in a way that will take advantage of the employees' aptitudes and experience, management reasons that labor costs are bound to go up.

Some observers argue that the increased costs that result from union pressures "shock" management into finding more efficient work methods.

Centralization
of Decision-Making

A manager who fails to understand the contract may inadvertently prompt an embarrassing grievance. It may set a precedent that will be very costly to the company for a long period of time in other departments and strengthen the union's argument that the company is "unfair." For example, in our hypothetical case above, the laboratory manager was anxious to avoid establishing the precedent that work assignments were not a management prerogative. Fearing such contingencies, many companies have withdrawn from lower-level supervisors the authority to make certain personnel decisions. This authority has been delegated to higher levels of management and, in many cases, to staff departments with specialists trained in labor relations.[14]

---

[14] The problems created by the changing organizational position of the supervisor and the growing importance of staff departments are analyzed in Chapter 16.

Introduction of "Outsiders"
into Labor Relations

As we have seen, an "international" union usually embraces members from a number of different firms.[15] Not only does the union have institutional goals distinct from those of the company (it wants to grow and prosper and its officers want to be re-elected), but it is also concerned with more than one employer. The union seeks wage increases in one company to set a precedent that will make it easier to negotiate a favorable contract elsewhere. Frequently, arbitration decisions set precedents affecting labor relations in many companies. As a result, many company officials feel that the problems to which union officers force them to devote time are not restricted to the interests of the particular organization and its employees.

Business agents and international representatives are not employees of the firms with which they negotiate. Although, in principle, many managers resent the fact that the union brings "outsiders" onto the scene, in practice, they often find that the outsiders are more dispassionate and better able to understand the company's side of a grievance than their own employees would be.[16]

EVOLUTION OF SOUND
UNION-MANAGEMENT RELATIONS

There is little question that the introduction of a union may prove a traumatic experience for management. At the outset, the union may try to dramatize every company mistake, and the early days may be spent in destructive warfare rather than in the constructive solution of problems. In many firms this period may drag on for years in a kind of "armed truce," with both sides trying to capitalize on the other's mistakes. While grudgingly accepting the existence of the union, managers may seek to sharply limit its influence in the company and compete actively with the union for the loyalty of the membership.[17] Yet many companies and their managements develop a more harmonious relationship and admit that the union can have a beneficial effect on the organization if dealt with properly.

---

[15] Many independent unions, however, which are not affiliated with international unions, have no organizational relationships beyond the company in which they are organized.

[16] Managers even find themselves facing this dilemma: Some unions which are not democratic, where the officers are not directly responsive to the demands of the membership, are easier to negotiate with than more democratic unions. Because the leadership in the latter group must face constant political criticism, they must be more careful of the agreements when the political pressure becomes great—e.g., when a wildcat strike seems to be gaining widespread membership support.

[17] In recent years this type of active opposition to increasing union power has come to be called "Boulwarism" after the former head of labor relations of the General Electric Company. Its tactics and point of view are best described in Herbert Northrop, *Boulwarism* (Ann Arbor, Michigan: Bureau of Industrial Relations, University of Michigan, 1964).

Opportunities for Improved
Human Relations

The most important factor contributing to sound labor relations is the recognition by management that its own actions and policies have a major impact on union behavior. Some observers even go as far as to generalize that "a management gets the kind of union it deserves."

To the management that is willing to explore new techniques, the introduction of a union into the organization need not be a catastrophe. The union can actually help management improve employee relationships.

Labor relations involve a problem that every company must face, whether or not its workers are unionized: this is the problem of adjusting the needs of the individual to the needs of the organization. Without a union, employees may find other means of protesting what they think is unfair: slowdowns, sabotage, or quitting. The union provides a peaceful means of resolving such disputes or differences in a way that will maintain productivity and preserve the work force intact.

Increasingly, managers are recognizing the merits of informal discussion of common problems. Even on subjects solely within the area of management prerogatives, they are learning that the union can serve as a channel of communication with the work force and can provide an aid in discovering and correcting weak spots in the plant.

Supervisors who are sensitive to human relations prefer to obtain group agreement before initiating changes in work procedure. Rather than deal with a large number of individuals with diverse points of view, they realize that it is far more efficient to sit down with a responsible union leader. He is the single spokesman who presumably represents the unified opinion of the entire work group and can subsequently sell his analysis to the group. In a sense, strong local unions are a guarantee that agreements will be honored.

Management learns that it can introduce changes in working conditions with much less friction if it consults with the union beforehand. Rather than sit back and wait for the union to raise problems, the company can make the first move and involve union officials in clearing up potential trouble areas.

> "We knew we were going to have a lot of squawks over new job assignments when we brought automation into the department. This could have meant a hundred grievances and months of wasteful talk. Instead we went to the union and told them what our plans were, how many of what kinds of jobs there would be after the change. We got them to work with us in deciding who was going to stay in the department and how transfers would be arranged. We also negotiated the rates on the new jobs."

Consulting with the union prior to the development of grievances often produces a valuable by-product. As we have seen, union officials are typically active men who want to keep busy. If they can be involved in handling constructive questions, they are less likely to seek out problems and grievances.

The Manager's Role

The chances of converting hostility-ridden, destructive labor relations into a constructive pattern depend largely on the manager's ability to adapt to the existence of the union. When a union is first established, the manager may have difficulty dealing with subordinates who are also active union organizers. At the outset, he needs to distinguish between the outspoken rabble-rouser and the genuine informal leader. The free-wheeling organizer may be motivated by deep-seated personality problems or personal grievances. Often he does not have the confidence of the group as a whole.

Instead of assuming that aggressive talk and behavior are in themselves evidence of valid leadership, the supervisor should give the members of the group an opportunity to decide whether the man who tries to usurp leadership is in fact the man they want as a leader. If they perceive that he is prompted by selfish motives and is overbearing and clumsy in his approach, they may reject him voluntarily. On the other hand, if the supervisor attempts to punish him, he may become a martyr and actually gain the group's support.

The supervisor should recognize that most employees experience no serious conflict between loyalty to the union (which they see as a sort of insurance program to protect them against future contingencies) and loyalty to management (to whom they owe appreciation for their jobs and economic well-being). So, if the manager rejects or becomes suspicious of everyone who expresses pro-union sentiments, he may alienate a number of very capable employees who, were they accorded responsibility and trust, might have identified themselves strongly with the company.

The manager also should be alert to the special problems affecting the union leader's behavior: He may be under conflicting pressures, one group wanting him to do one thing, another group insisting on something else. The manager should recognize the political position of the union leader and learn how to cope with him intelligently rather than bemoan the fact that unions are political institutions.

> Management representatives quickly learn to differentiate between the grievances on which the union leaders face strong political pressures and those which they are merely "going through motions" of pressing. . . . A shrewd management learns not to embarrass union officials before a close election. . . .
>
> We have observed many episodes such as the following telephone call by a union leader to a personnel director:
>
> "Look, Bill, we'll admit that Charlie Jones was drunk last week. Frankly we don't have a leg to stand on. If you'll take it easy on him—after all this is his first offense—we'll waive the formal hearing. And that'll save you a lot of time and money. . . ."
>
> These are not collusive dealings but rather part of the flexible process by which both sides adjust to new problem situations which could not have been foreseen when the contract was written.[18]

---

[18] Sayles and Strauss, *op. cit.*, pp. 9-10.

Thus, as time passes, the union abandons its role as a *competitor* for the loyalty of the worker. It takes on the role of a *policeman* who calls "halt" when a company representative makes a mistake, but who also keeps the member-employee within the bounds of legal decisions and practices. In some companies, this evolutionary process advances to the point where the union becomes a genuine *collaborator*, sharing with management the problems of improving efficiency and productivity.

CONCLUSION

The problems of labor relations are not distinct from other human-relations problems that arise in an organization. Although the union cannot eliminate management's responsibility for the conduct of personnel administration, it can become an integral part of the employment relationship. Even though its roots lie outside the organization, its existence reflects employee needs and dissatisfactions. Some human-relations problems, particularly in larger organizations, may be almost beyond the ability of management to solve, and the manager need not feel that the establishment of a union is evidence of his own failure. Thus, it is unrealistic to think of personnel administration as an *alternative* to unionization.

Union-management relations provide another challenge for management. In many companies, the necessity of working through these problems is just as much a part of the managerial job as developing budgets and work schedules, and issuing orders. While negotiation and consultation are time-consuming, frequently frustrating, and certainly threatening, they require some of the same supervisory skills and persistence that are necessary to carry out other management functions. These responsibilities cannot be avoided, nor would it be healthful for the organization if they could.

PROBLEM 1

UNION AND U.N.

Following is a description of the functioning of the United Nations. How comparable is the role of the union in the organization?

"There are, to be sure, other important functions which the U.N. performs. One of them is that it provides a public forum in which the weak nations can talk to the great powers and get back some kind of accounting. Although the debates in the General Assembly do not produce the purest candor or the highest wisdom, and are in fact often ignorant and foolish, it is better that the grievances and accusations be brought into the open than that they should be left to fester in the dark. But, while the public forum is useful and indeed necessary, the indispensable activity of the United Nations is what goes on privately and off the record. It goes on in the corridors and lounges of the U. N. . . .

"There is no other place where conversation is possible at any time of the day or night among the contending and quarreling peoples of the world. . . .

"This network provides an element which, while it has always been indispensable in the conduct of diplomacy, has become rare and difficult under the white lights of modern publicity and of democratic government. This indispensable element is the ability to try out proposals without being publicly committed to them, of letting them be accepted or amended or rejected without public debate, without any need to explain them or justify them if they do not work."[19]

PROBLEM 2

WILDCAT STRIKE

During the 20 years Harold Keller has worked for the James Company, he has risen to the top of his promotion ladder: a machinist first-class and one of the highest-paid nonsupervisory employees in the company. About five years ago, the workers in the company were organized by a union; Keller played no active part in the organizing campaign. About a year ago, Keller developed an illness that was difficult to diagnose; although he lost strength and energy, he was able to continue at work. Because of his good record and long service, the company found a number of special assignments for him and maintained his wages until he regained his health.

Just recently, the men in the machine shop in which Keller worked staged a wildcat one-day walk-out that did not have the formal authorization of the local union. Employees in other departments were not involved. The men in the machine shop claimed that their wages had declined relative to wages in many other departments because they had had no opportunity to work more than 40 hours a week. Men in many of the other departments were working 45 hours and 50 hours a week.

Much to the surprise and disappointment of the machine-shop supervisor, Keller not only participated in this protest demonstration, but actually appeared to be one of the leaders.

1. Does Keller's action seem reasonable in light of the consideration management accorded him during his illness?
2. What should the supervisor do with Keller now?
3. How typical do you think this case is?
4. What is your reaction to the complaint of the men in the machine shop?

PROBLEM 3

A CHANGE IN SCHEDULE

The company guards at the Rembrandt Company were among the last groups to join a union, but they had always expressed a great deal of dissatisfaction over their work schedules. For many years there had been charges of favoritism in the assignment of work hours. Guard work had to be carried on around the clock, and employees who were assigned to the less desirable shifts or to week-end duty complained that they should have better working hours.

The issue of "fair working schedules" was plugged hard by the new union in signing up new members, and it was one of the first questions raised by the union leaders when they met with management to negotiate their first labor contract. In fact, this issue took up the first two weeks of negotiation.

---

[19] Walter Lippmann, "The Indestructibility of the U.N.," *Newsweek* (October 25, 1965), p. 27.

When the issue was finally settled, management discovered that the agreement with the new guard union specified a work schedule that was almost identical with the one that had existed prior to unionization. Nevertheless, the union and the membership seemed satisfied with the agreement, and there was no longer the heavy stream of complaints about work assignments.

1. How do you explain this strange development? Were the employees dissatisfied before and, if so, why did they appear satisfied after the agreement was made?
2. What scheduling difficulties may the union leaders have become aware of during their two-week discussion with company representatives?

LEADERSHIP AND MOTIVATION

Up to this point we have been dealing with the "ingredients" of the business organization: people and their needs, technology and its impact, groups, and unions. In the following chapters we shall talk about the manager, the person whose job it is to blend all these ingredients in such a way as to enable the organization to satisfy its basic needs for production and profit.

What is a manager? A manager is one who is responsible for getting a job done that is too big to do by himself—a job that he can accomplish only through other people. True, he must have some technical ability. But it is the fact that *he must get his work done through others* that sets him apart as a manager and that creates the problems that we shall discuss in this section.

Clearly, management is not just a matter of giving orders or overseeing subordinates to make sure they follow rules. Management means building an effective work force and motivating each member of it to turn in his best performance. This is the job of every manager whether he is president of the company, a regional sales manager, or a foreman on the line.

To be sure, managers have other functions besides dealing with subordinates. Depending on their level in the hierarchy, they may have to make decisions relating to finance, marketing, production, research, advertising, scheduling, quality control, or public relations. Technical, analytical, and imaginative skills may be as essential as human-relations skills. The manager may have to deal with customers, suppliers, government agents, superiors, staff representatives, and other supervisors on his own level. Yet one of the most critically important skills of any manager is skill in *leadership*, and in this section we shall emphasize the manager as leader.

What is the difference between a good leader and a bad one? Styles of leadership vary greatly from one situation to another. The techniques used by "a maid to control her man" are very different from those used by a drill sergeant. The political demagogue, the parish priest, the president of the senior class, the father of a family—all are leaders. And so are the unofficial, informal leaders we met in an earlier chapter. Each uses a style of leadership appropriate to his own situation. As we shall see, in business, too, there is a wide range of leadership behavior.

Every manager, however, faces the problem of motivation. When a man works for himself, either at his job or at a hobby, he works with enthusiasm and energy. How can we get him to work in the same way in our complex mass-production society, where men work not for themselves, but for others, and where the satisfaction derived from the work itself is often meager? As we shall see in Chapter 6, there are various means of "Motivating People to Work," some appropriate to one situation, others to another. Nevertheless, the most generally positive form of motivation, in circumstances where it is applicable, is what is called internalized motivation.

The effective manager has three tasks: he must decide how much to delegate and in what manner; he must exercise his authority in such a fashion as to maximize acceptance of his orders; and he must act as leader of his work team.

1. The manager should delegate decision-making authority to subordinates to the maximum extent the subordinates' abilities and the needs of the organization permit. Instead of issuing detailed instructions, he will lay down rules, set goals, and seek to indoctrinate subordinates in organizational objectives. All this is involved in "Delegation" (Chapter 7).

2. In the "The Exercise of Authority" (Chapter 8), the manager must develop effective day-to-day relations with his subordinates. He must also take into account their conceptions of what they feel to be the legitimate use of authority.

3. The manager and his subordinates are members of the same work group. The effective manager is in effect a team leader. His job is to strengthen the group (provided the group's objectives are not opposed to those of management), to consult with group members, both formally and informally, and to work through the informal group structure (Chapter 9, "The Manager and the Group").

Before we go on to discuss these three aspects of leadership, we must point out that no one form of leadership is equally good in all situations. What form is best suited to a given situation depends on many factors: the type of work; the cohesiveness of the group; the group's attitude toward management; the individual needs and personality of the subordinate; and the personality, experience, and technical ability of the manager. The best manager is the one who is sensitive to the needs of each situation and adjusts his style of management accordingly.

Motivating People to Work

One of the basic problems in any society is how to motivate people to work. In a mass-production society this is not an easy task, since many people derive only slight personal satisfaction from their jobs, and enjoy little sense of accomplishment or creativity. In large organizations people must work together, following orders they may neither understand nor approve, and obey instructions from superiors whom they had no part in selecting and may never see. Few have the opportunity for self-expression or the freedom from control enjoyed by the farmer or the independent businessman or the professional man. How can one motivate people who have boring jobs, little freedom to make decisions on their own, and the normal human quota of laziness and stubbornness? How can we create a situation in which employees can satisfy their individual needs while at the same time working toward the goals of the organization?

In this chapter we shall consider five alternative methods for motivating people: (1) the "be strong" approach, (2) the "be good" approach, (3) implicit bargaining, (4) competition, and (5) internalized motivation. (We make no claim to have exhausted the list of possible forms of motivation, and in practice most managers use combinations of all five.) [1]

BE STRONG

The traditional form of motivation in industry (and the one that seems to come easiest to most supervisors) emphasizes authority. At its crudest, this method consists of forcing people to work by threatening to fire them if they don't. The assumption behind this approach, of course, is that the only reason people work is to earn money, and that they will work only if driven to it by fear of losing their jobs. It ignores the fact, mentioned in Chapter 1, that people also want around-the-job and through-the-job satisfactions. Off-the-job, economic satisfactions are not enough.

---

[1] Our thinking in this chapter has been greatly influenced by Douglas McGregor.

This approach further assumes that since no one likes work, people will try to get away with doing just as little as they can. To prevent them from doing so, there must be close supervision. Management must tell every worker exactly what he is to do every minute of the day; it must spell out every rule and give the worker the narrowest possible range for discretion. Often rules are promulgated just to "show who's boss." Individuals are kept busy "to keep them out of trouble."

This thinking is inherent in some of the less sophisticated versions of scientific management: Men are hired to work rather than think, and the smallest possible segment of human ability should be used on the job. It is also related to what has been called the "commodity" or "contractual" theory of labor, which holds that labor can be bought and sold just like material supplies—and can be treated in the same way.

This approach paid off fairly well in the early days of the industrial revolution when workers and their families were so close to starvation that the material, off-the-job needs for food, clothing, and shelter were paramount. In recent years, however, people have begun to expect more from their jobs than sheer punishment. As a consequence, the "be strong" policy has become less effective as a motivating device. There are three major reasons for the decline of the authoritarian approach.

1. In the first place, as we discovered in Chapter 1, as our standard of living has gone up and our physical needs have become better satisfied, people have begun to look for social and egoistic satisfactions higher up on the need hierarchy. This is particularly true in times of full employment. (Or, to put it another way, we have used part of our increased productivity to provide ourselves with more material goods, such as bigger houses, better cars, and fancier cuts of meat; part to provide us with more leisure off the job, shorter hours, and longer vacations; and part to provide ourselves with a more decent work environment, which means among other things a slower work pace and less tyrannical supervision.)

2. Fifty years ago children were taught, both at home and at school, to show strict obedience to their elders. And so the child-grown-man found little difficulty adjusting to stern discipline in the office or factory. Recent years have seen a revolution in the way children are brought up. Freedom and self-expression are encouraged in the home; schools emphasize spontaneous discussion and individual expression. As a consequence, the young worker of today finds it hard to accept autocratic leadership on the job.

3. Basic to the philosophy of "be strong" is the expectation that if a man doesn't do what the boss tells him to do, he will be fired. Unions, however, have made it more difficult to fire a man; in effect, they have lowered the minimum a worker can get by with.

Application
to White-Collar Workers

We all know how "be strong" techniques are used by the bullying foreman. But the same policy may also be applied to executives, supervisors, and white-collar workers. With no union to protect them and with a keen interest in advancement, the fear of punishment (either through discharge or denial of promotion) may be quite effective in motivating these individuals.

It is common practice for top management to set goals (increased sales, lowered costs, and so forth) for their executives, and then to exert constant pressure to insure that these goals are met. The penalty for not doing so is usually the withholding of promotions or salary increases, if not outright discharge. Some companies deliberately set their goals too high. Every time a goal comes close to being met, management raises it even higher, hoping as a consequence to stir employees to work harder and harder. As one supervisor remarked, "My philosophy is, always give a man more than he can finish. That way you can be sure you are getting the most out of him."

This is one reason we hear so much about "pressure" in many business offices. A top executive described his use of the "be strong" approach this way:

> As soon as we examine the budget results and see a fellow is slipping, we *immediately* call the factory manager and point out, "Look Joe, you're behind on the budget. What do you expect to do about it?" True, he may be batting his brains out already on the problem but our phone call adds a little more pressure.[2]

The consequent feeling of frustration is intensified because the white-collar employee typically does not have the channels of redress or the opportunities to express aggression that are available to his blue-collar brother.

Impact on People

The trouble with "be strong" as a form of motivation is this: It ignores the fact that people are not passive, inert machines and that they often react in ways not intended by management.

1. This policy normally provides no incentive to work harder than the minimum required to avoid punishment. The minimum may be fairly low in the case of unionized workers who are promoted on the basis of seniority and who have a union to protect them if they are fired. (On the other hand, the minimum may be relatively high if the work is closely programed and if it is easy to see whether a man is falling down on the job. And in the case of executives whose chances of promotion and winning substantial salary increases

---

[2] Chris Argyris, *The Impact of Budgets on People* (New York: Controllership Foundation, 1952), p. 5.

are quite great, the policy of "be strong" may seem quite effective. However, as mentioned above, executives often find it difficult to work creatively when subject to the pressures which "be strong" involves.)

2. The essence of "be strong" is the application of pressure. But when subjected to *too much* pressure, employees fight back. When they can, they fight through their union. Even if they have no union, they engage in slow-downs, sabotage, and spoilage.[3] As one worker commented, "In my shop there is an undeclared war of nerves. If management won't treat us like men, we aren't going to show much respect for them."

Part of this "war of nerves" consists of workers' efforts to get away with doing as little as possible; there is no incentive for doing more than the minimum, but there is a great deal of satisfaction in making management look silly. Naturally, management reacts by deciding, "We have to watch these men like hawks if we are to get anything done at all." Both sides spend a tremendous amount of energy trying to outsmart the other. Production is lower than it might otherwise be, and management, in frustration, often strikes back irrationally, perhaps by imposing needless restrictions or by firing alleged ringleaders. Thus, a vicious cycle is set in motion, a cycle of restraints and evasions, more restraints and more evasions.

As J. S. Mill said a century ago, "Nor are the greatest precautions more than very imperfectly efficacious, where, as is now almost invariably the case with hired laborers, the slightest relaxation of vigilance is an opportunity eagerly seized for eluding performance of their contract."[4]

3. To protect themselves from pressure, employees organize groups and cliques, as we saw in Chapter 4. And already-existing groups may be drawn closer together and take on a new purpose, that of protecting themselves against management pressure. As we have seen, work groups frequently establish "bogeys" or standards of output that no member is expected to exceed—in spite of what management wants. Group members may even conspire to "cover" each other's mistakes and to punish "squealers." As a result, higher management is kept ignorant of what is happening on subordinate levels and therefore cannot inflict the discipline that is necessary if "be strong" is to succeed.

This policy of self-protection is openly practiced by hourly-paid workers; even executives, however, often band together in an implicit alliance to protect themselves against their own superiors. Such an alliance may be highly effective even though it is never actually talked about.

4. Probably the most serious trouble with "be strong" is that it ignores a basic factor in human behavior: When people are put under too much pressure they become *frustrated*. (Note: we say *too much* pressure. Most of us respond

---

[3] See Stanley B. Mathewson, *Restriction of Output Among Unorganized Workers* (New York: Viking, 1931).

[4] J. S. Mill, *Principles of Political Economy*, People's Edition (London: Longmans, Green, 1891), p. 68.

well to some pressure, but all of us have a critical point—which differs from one person to another—beyond which frustration sets in.[5])

When people become frustrated they react in strange ways that tend to reduce the effectiveness of the organization in its main task of getting out production. Often their behavior seems quite irrational, in the sense that it cannot be understood in terms of the apparent stimulus.

> Superintendent Jones' secretary usually does a fine, conscientious job. Today she forgot to type an important letter. Jones bawled her out unmercifully.

Jones is normally a kind man. Why did he act this way today? Certainly his behavior was not designed to get the letter out more quickly, or even to prevent his secretary from making mistakes in the future. The fact is that he had been trying to meet an important deadline with an inadequate staff of men, and his boss had just called him up to spur him on.

One response to frustration is *aggressiveness*, which expresses itself in many ways. Instead of bawling out his secretary, Jones might have picked a fight with another supervisor, had a hassle with his wife, or whammed a small, defenseless white ball around the country-club park. If his frustration became too intense, it might have led to psychosomatic illnesses, such as high blood pressure or ulcers:

> Once we observed a group of working supervisors who had been strongly pressured to increase production under difficult circumstances with no backing from management. There were nine men regularly assigned to the day shift. One had a nervous breakdown, another had a fatal heart attack that was generally attributed to overwork and fatigue. Of the remaining seven, five had serious illnesses and in most cases no organic cause could be determined. All this happened during a period of twelve months. Meanwhile, the men on the night shift, where pressure was much less, had an almost perfect health record.

There are many other reactions to frustration. Some people *repress* their feelings for a long time and then suddenly blow up without notice. Others *regress* to less mature levels of behavior. Everyone is familiar with the three-year-old who reverts to thumb-sucking when a baby brother arrives on the scene. Similarly, adults who are frustrated by excessive pressure may find it difficult to make decisions or react intelligently and may engage in juvenile (and aggressive) activities such as horseplay. Though employees may be dragooned into submission by the "be strong" approach, the consequent frustration may lead to a serious reduction in the quality of their decision. Under extreme frustration, they may simply fall into *resignation* and give up trying altogether. Possibly the underprivileged, floating employees mentioned on page 61, who despaired of trying to improve themselves economically, had reached a state of resignation.

Frustration may also lead to *scapegoating*—that is, picking on those who are weak and defenseless. It is not accidental, for instance, that racial tensions

---

[5] Evidence suggests that, up to a certain point, anxiety facilitates the performance of all tasks, but that anxiety is more effective with simple than with complicated tasks.

in plants are higher when times are bad and layoffs are pending. Another response is *fixation*, in which the individual persists in some fruitless activity, such as Lady Macbeth's handwashing, even though it obviously accomplishes nothing. When assigned a difficult problem, some supervisors spend their time shuffling papers rather than trying to work out a realistic solution.

Finally there is *sublimation*, in which the individual seeks to satisfy his frustrated needs in some more effective fashion. Thus, the executive who has been denied promotion may become active in a social club, just as the girl who has been jilted may seek to express her love in nursery school work.

The collective reaction of a group of workers to frustration may have a devastating effect on the entire organization. It may disrupt group solidarity and cooperation, turning departments, groups, and individuals against one another. It may lead to rumor, mistrust, and suspicion. It may result in unexplained wildcat strikes or a general state of snarling irritability. In most cases, the basic objective of the organization—*production*—is bound to suffer.

To put this whole problem another way, when a rider whips his horse he must remember that the horse may dash off in any direction. A high degree of control is required to make sure it goes where the rider wants. If the only form of incentive operating is the employee's desire to escape punishment, there is no guarantee that he will perform his job in the way management desires unless *all* alternative courses of action are blocked.

The Value of "Be Strong"

Thus, the effectiveness of the "be strong" technique of motivation is subject to significant limitations: (1) It motivates employees to do only enough work to keep from being fired (except where there are significant opportunities for promotion); (2) it motivates them to "get away" with as much as possible (often making a game of it), thus leading to a vicious cycle of further management restrictions and employee evasions; (3) it motivates them to band together in self-protection; and (4) it leads to frustration and in turn to a whole series of deleterious side-reactions that jeopardize production.

And yet, as we shall see, there are times when "be strong" works fairly well. It works better in the short run than in the long run. It generally works better with white-collar workers than with blue-collar workers. It is most effective in nonunionized situations, during depressions when men are desperate for work, with members of minority groups who find it a difficulty to find work elsewhere, and in highly programed work where deviation from rules may be easily spotted.[6] Even in these situations, though, there are undesirable side-reactions.

There are times when a manager, because of his position, must use threats,

---

[6] For a case study of a situation where "be strong" worked with a group of marginally qualified employees who would have found it difficult to find work elsewhere, see William J. Goode and Irving Fowler, "Incentive Factors in a Low Morale Plant," *American Sociological Review*, Vol. 14, No. 6 (October 1949), pp. 619-624.

either implicitly or explicitly. But a manager who relies solely on threats as a means of motivation is likely to develop a group of subordinates who at best are cowed into fearful rigidity and at worst are openly rebellious.

BE GOOD

As a substitute for "be strong," many managements have adopted the philosophy of "be good." They have sought to raise employee morale by providing good working conditions, fringe benefits, employee services, high wages, and decent, fair supervision.

We may distinguish between two forms of "be good," which may be called *paternalism* and *hygienic management*. The argument for paternalism holds that if management is good to employees, they will work harder out of loyalty and gratitude. The argument for hygienic management ignores the question of gratitude; it holds that liberal benefits, good working conditions, and friendly supervision make for satisfied employees, and that satisfied employees work harder.

Paternalism

Paternalism is pretty much outdated, having had its heyday in the 1920's. In part, its wide adoption at that time was the result of genuine interest by employers in their employees, as well as the belief that "be good" was a more effective form of motivation than "be strong." In part, too, its popularity was a reaction to the rise of unionism during and immediately after World War I. In any case, under the banner of the "New Industrial Relations," management became interested in a wide variety of projects, varying from cafeterias and recreation programs for employees to cooking classes for their wives. Some of these programs were designed to change the employees' personal lives as well as their on-the-job performance. The Sociology Department of the Ford Motor Company of an earlier day went further than most programs. Headed by a Protestant minister, this department was manned by 30 investigators.

> In what amounted to a brief reign of benevolent paternalism, these gentlemen and their house-to-house canvassers imposed ... a set of rules which blended good sense with Ford whims and Puritan virtues.
>
> On the positive side, the men ... behaved like the home visitor of the modern public welfare agency. They doubtless helped to "Americanize" Ford's vast body of immigrant workmen. Their charges were encouraged to start savings accounts and to budget their incomes. They were given elementary lessons in hygiene and home management. ...
>
> At worst ... its agents became, to some extent, collectors of tales and suspicions. ... Hearsay as well as fact found its way into a card catalogue where a record was kept of every worker's deviations. ... Frittering away one's evenings "unwisely," taking in male boarders, sending funds to the "old country"—these things came to be regarded as earmarks of "unwholesome living." The use of

liquor was forbidden . . . as was marital discord that resulted in a separation or divorce action.[7]

Ford's program was shortlived, but similar patterns of paternalism were developed in other companies. There is little evidence that any of them were particularly successful in eliciting gratitude, in motivating workers to do a better job, or even in staving off the development of unions. In fact, some of the companies with the best-known histories of paternalism later became scenes of bitter labor-management strife.

There are good psychological reasons for believing that if management expects employees to work harder out of gratitude for benefits, then paternalism will fail to accomplish its purpose. What actually happens may be this:

1. Paternalism may engender resentment rather than gratitude. People don't like to feel dependent on someone else. They prefer to decide for themselves what they want. Letting others decide what is good for them makes them feel infantile and lowers their sense of importance. In spite of stories to the contrary, most people prefer earning things for themselves to having everything handed to them by others. Unearned rewards given out of the kindness of the employer's heart often are regarded as slights to the employee's sense of self-esteem. Instances of "biting the hand that feeds one" are quite common.

> A dramatic example of "ingratitude" was shown in a branch factory of a nation-wide company located in a small hill town in the South. As was typical of the area, most of the houses in town were owned by the company.
> Some years back, the company president's wife, Mrs. X, passed through and was shocked by the poverty of the town and the ugliness of the factory. A religious woman, she convinced her husband that something should be done—and she was given a free hand to do her best.
> Her first step was to attack the diet problem. A dietician was imported from the North. When no one showed up for her classes, Mrs. X complained to the factory manager. Next session an impressive number of women "voluntarily" signed up for the program.
> Heartened by this victory, she made similar efforts in other directions. A model home was set up, and attractive (by big-city standards) modern furniture was offered for sale at wholesale prices. Mrs. X had little success as an order-taker until the factory manager accompanied her on her visits through the town.
> The next step was to paint the factory equipment in bright cheerful colors. Then one day potted geraniums appeared at the factory windows. This was the last straw. The men went on strike, threw the geraniums out the windows, and joined the union.

2. As time passes, the novelty of being given free "hand-outs" wears off, and employees begin to take their benefits for granted. Once they come to regard benefits as part of their regular compensation, management is obliged

---

[7] Keith Seward, *The Legend of Henry Ford* (New York: Holt, Rinehart & Winston, 1948), p. 59.

to provide increasingly impressive gifts. Otherwise the workers will turn resentful, and management will get no credit at all.

3. Paternalism incorporates some of the basic assumptions of "be strong." People are expected to be docile in return for their gifts, and work is still regarded as a form of punishment that people undergo only in return for a reward. Moreover, many of the rewards must be enjoyed *off* the job. Little effort is spent on making the job itself more rewarding.

Although paternalism emphasizes the positive nature of the gift, it also carries with it a negative threat: "If you don't do your job as ordered, your gifts will be taken away." In most instances, since the rewards are distributed without discrimination to everyone on the payroll, there is little incentive for the individual worker to do more than the minimum required to keep from being fired.

Hygienic Management

Today paternalism is seldom resorted to, except by smaller companies. Hygienic management, which, in a sense, is a more subtle version of paternalism, is quite common, however. Management showers workers with high wages, fringe benefits, good working conditions, good supervision, and all the rest, in the hope that they will have higher morale and *therefore* work harder.[8] The only trouble with this assumption is the *therefore*. Since everyone shares equally in these benefits, there is no reward for good work and no incentive to increase output.

The term *morale* has been used in many different ways; but if morale means the employees' attitude toward the company as a whole, there is little evidence that high morale is necessarily associated with high productivity.[9] Just the reverse may be true. Morale may be very low in a concentration camp, yet production very high. Similarly, workers may be well satisfied to "goof off" in a department where the work pace is extremely slow. A confidential study of a nationwide manufacturing company showed that the plant with the highest production rate had the highest morale, while the plant with the next-highest production rate had the lowest morale. Most studies indicate a rather low correlation between morale and productivity. Apparently, efforts by management to raise morale do not necessarily raise productivity.

---

[8] In psychological terms this hypothesis suggests that morale is an intervening variable between management behavior and productivity.

[9] One careful scholar concludes that there is little convincing evidence that individuals, within any group who have more favorable attitudes toward the company do a better job. See Arthur H. Brayfield and Walter H. Crockett, "Employee Attitudes and Employee Performance," *Psychological Bulletin*, Vol. 52, No. 5 (September 1955), pp. 396-424. Another survey of research suggests there may be a slight positive correlation between morale and productivity: Frederick Herzberg, Bernard Mausner, Richard Patterson and Dora Capwell, *Job Attitudes: A Review of Research and Opinion* (Pittsburgh: Psychological Service of Pittsburgh, 1957). For a study which lists some of the conditions in which low morale and high productivity may go together, see Harold Wilensky, "Human Relations in the Workplace," in Conrad Arensberg, *et al.*, eds., *Research in Industrial Human Relations* (New York: Harper & Row, 1957), p. 25.

A significant, but controversial, study has given us a new insight into the effectiveness of the "be good" approach.[10] In this study, accountants and engineers were asked to "think of a time when you felt exceptionally good or exceptionally bad about your job" and then asked to describe what happened and why they felt as they did. Interestingly, the factors which made people satisfied with their jobs were not the same (or the opposite either) as those which made them dissatisfied. Apparently, the presence of so-called "satisfiers" would act to increase an individual's satisfaction, but their absence would not make him actively dissatisfied, only apathetic. Similarly, the presence of so-called dissatisfiers made people feel they had a "bad" job; but the absence of dissatisfiers did not make a "good" job.

What were these satisfiers and dissatisfiers? The satisfiers were: achievement, recognition, work itself, responsibility, and advancement. Note that all these forms of satisfaction arise *out* of work. The dissatisfiers were: interpersonal relations (both with one's superiors and peers), the technical ability of the supervisor, company policy and administration, physical working conditions, and the individual's personal life off the job. Note that all these factors relate to the *context* or the *environment* within which the job is performed, but not to the job itself. (Interestingly, salary ranked both as a satisfier and a dissatisfier. In general, when a man indicated that salary helped make his job a bad one, he was referring to the system by which salaries were set; when salary was mentioned as making a job a good one, salary was looked on as a sign of achievement and recognition.)

What is the relationship between these factors and productivity? The evidence is quite tentative, but Herzberg suggests that the presence of satisfiers leads to higher productivity (and for this reason satisfiers have also been called motivators). Dissatisfiers, on the other hand, do not lead to lower production nor does their elimination tend to raise it. Their elimination may reduce active resistance to the job, but promote only a passive acceptance of it. This attitude is illustrated by an interview we once held with a blue-collar worker on a routine job. This worker said:

> "I got a pretty good job."
> Q: "What makes it such a good job?"

---

[10] Frederick Herzberg, Bernard Mausner, and Barbara Snyderman, *The Motivation to Work* (New York: Wiley, 1960). There have been a number of attempts to replicate this study with various degrees of success. See M. Scott Myers, "Who Are Your Motivated Workers?" *Harvard Business Review*, Vol. 42, No. 1 (January 1964), pp. 73-88. The research techniques have been subject to quite serious (and we think justifiable) criticism. Victor Vroom suggests that (1) the findings are inconsistent with other evidence and (2) people are "more likely to attribute the causes of satisfaction to their own achievements and accomplishments on the job. On the other hand, they may be more likely to attribute their dissatisfaction, not to personal inadequacies or deficiencies, but to factors in the work environment." *Work and Motivation* (New York: Wiley, 1964), pp. 127-29. The authors of this present volume feel that despite the drawbacks of the research technique, the Herzberg study does point to a suggestive new way to examine the problem of motivation. For a review of recent studies of this controversial topic, see Lyman Porter, "Personnel Management," *Annual Review of Psychology*, Vol. 17 (1966).

A: "Don't get me wrong. I didn't say it is a *good* job. It's an OK job—about as good a job as a guy like me might expect. The foreman leaves me alone and it pays well. But I would never call it a *good* job."

The experimenters called the factors which lead to this rather sterile, non-involved attitude "hygienic factors" (since they are used to avoid trouble). We shall accordingly call management which emphasizes these factors "hygienic management." Such a "be good" policy may provide a pleasant environment in which to work and a considerable amount of around-the-job satisfaction, but little satisfaction through the job, and little sense of enthusiasm or creativity.

The Value of "Be Good"

We have applied the term "be good" to the philosophy which holds that high wages, good treatment, and so forth will automatically motivate employees to work harder. And we have suggested that this is an oversimplified theory of human behavior. Does this mean that it is a complete waste of money to try to make the company a better place in which to work? Of course not. Properly presented, fringe benefits and employee services are an important part of any personnel program. Such benefits bolster the company's reputation in the community and attract better workers. They also help to reduce turnover, for good workers are less likely to leave the company's employ. Further, a feeling of security serves to reduce tension among employees and thus, to some extent, contributes to higher productivity.

Without question, efforts to make the company a better place in which to work do pay off in terms of better workers and more harmonious relations on the job. But they provide little *direct* motivation for workers to contribute more than a minimum effort. Thus, they provide only a partial answer to the problem of how to motivate workers most effectively.[11]

IMPLICIT BARGAINING

One of the most common forms of motivation today (though some managers may hate to admit it) is bargaining. In this approach, management encourages workers to put out a "reasonable" volume of work by making an agreement to provide, in return, "reasonable" supervision (though the bargain is usually a matter of implicit "understanding" rather than any explicit agreement on terms).[12] In a sense, management agrees not to use all the pressures at its command if the employees will agree not to restrict output unduly. The

[11] In terms of organization theory, "be good" provides motivation "to participate" but not motivation "to produce." James G. March and Herbert A. Simon, *Organizations* (New York: Wiley, 1958), Chapters 3 and 4.

[12] At times, of course, management does engage in explicit bargaining with the union over the level of production.

chief difference between this approach and the two forms of motivation already discussed is that the terms of the bargain (namely, what constitutes *reasonable* supervision, and what constitutes *reasonable* output) are agreed upon more or less voluntarily by both parties.

Thus, in practice the level of output and the conditions under which men work are not determined unilaterally by the supervisor, but through unwritten agreement between supervisor and subordinate. There is an assumption that the parties are more or less equal in power, so that the terms of the "effort bargain" [13] are agreed upon voluntarily. Just how favorable the final agreement is to each of the parties is determined by their respective bargaining power. Let us look for a moment at the weapons in the possession of each party.

The workers' major weapon is this: Either they can display cheerful cooperation and maintain high production or else they can indulge in excessive clumsiness, misunderstanding, or overt slowdowns or strikes.

The manager's most obvious weapon is his power to discipline workers who fail to produce. In practice, in the typical unionized situation, formal discipline is difficult to impose unless the worker's production is completely out of line. Still, the supervisor has at his disposal a whole arsenal of minor weapons: small but highly prized "plums," minor concessions, and petty but very real punishments. He can assign easy jobs or hard ones. He can make concessions in terms of time off and accept obviously false excuses for absenteeism or tardiness—or he can nag employees for minor offenses. He can provide the help that makes a job easier—or he can make work almost impossible (this is a particularly telling weapon where piece-work is involved).

Sometimes the immediate supervisor permits minor violations of rules as part of the bargain. Superintendents in one gypsum mill allowed workers to punch the clock a little early so they could make more overtime, and to take limited amounts of material home with them for their own repair work.[14] In other situations, employees are permitted to take coffee breaks, make personal calls on the company phone, or take home company pencils. In return for this "indulgency pattern," [15] they implicitly agree to work harder. Although such agreements are never put into words, they are tacitly understood by everybody concerned. As one worker put it:

> "Our policy is to live and let live. We give the foreman reasonable production. He protects us from the time-study man who tries to jack up the output rate and looks the other way if we take a smoke. We look out for each other."

These privileges are extended only so long as the supervisor feels that the subordinates are doing a satisfactory job. Otherwise they are withdrawn.

---

[13] Maurice D. Kilbridge, "The Effort Bargain," *Journal of Business,* Vol. 33, No. 1 (January 1960), p. 12.

[14] Alvin Gouldner, *Wildcat Strike* (Yellow Springs, Ohio: The Antioch Press, 1954), pp. 19-20.

[15] *Ibid.*

A case in point was the "no-floating around rule" which specified that workers must stay at their workplace, except to go to the washroom or eat. When foremen felt that things were going smoothly in their group, that their men were "doing a day's work" and were friendly and "cooperative," they would allow their workers to "sneak off" for a smoke, and they would make no caustic remarks if they wandered over to talk to a friend. If, however, a man or a group was felt to be "goofing off," or was being "snotty," foremen were more likely to invoke the "no floating" rule.[16]

An analogy may be drawn between the indulgency pattern and bank deposits. Both subordinates and supervisors build up credits by doing favors for the other party, and both expect to draw on their account when they need a favor for themselves.

In many situations this policy of "live and let live" is the most realistic approach available to the supervisor. For all its disadvantages, it does make possible a reasonably satisfactory level of production and reasonably harmonious worker-supervisor and labor-management relations. Employees enjoy a sense of independence that they are denied under "be good" and "be strong." To be sure, they are motivated in part by the fear that if they fail to produce the supervisor will withdraw their petty benefits. Probably equally important is the feeling that since the supervisor is "fair" to them, it is only proper that they put out a "fair day's work."

The picture we get from this point of view is not that of the worker crushed by the organization, but of one who fights it, copes with it, and retains his autonomy—making deals with it which satisfy both the individual and the organization. Yet unless bargaining is coupled with more positive forms of motivation, it suffers from many of the disadvantages of "be good" and "be strong." Work is still considered a punishment that one endures only for the sake of receiving the benefits that may accrue from living up to the agreement. Each side does something unpleasant in return for something pleasant. From management's point of view, bargaining offers little opportunity to raise production. Indeed, production is often stabilized at a fairly low level. On the other hand, as we shall discuss later, in some cases this may be the most that management can realistically expect.

COMPETITION

Another form of motivation is competition for the pay increases and promotions that go to the men who do outstanding jobs. Competition furnishes several forms of need satisfaction. The prospect of winning a promotion or a pay increase provides a meaningful goal to work toward. And actually attaining the goal means that the employee enjoys an economic reward, as well as a

---

[16] Alvin Gouldner, *Patterns of Industrial Bureaucracy* (New York: The Free Press of Glencoe, 1954), p. 173.

sense of accomplishment and completion, a sense of progress, and added social prestige. Less supervision is required on jobs where competition provides a reasonably satisfactory source of motivation, since each man is on his own to do the best job he can. There is no need to push him.

Competition is not particularly successful as a motivating device among factory workers, however. In union plants the principle of seniority substantially decreases the possibility of winning a promotion on the basis of hard work alone. The trend to reserve foremen's jobs for college-trained men has further reduced the factory worker's chance of rising into management. In theory, the incentive (piece-work) system does provide an opportunity for workers to compete with one another. In practice, however, they usually cooperate to restrict output and prevent competition.

Among blue-collar workers (or white-collar workers in mass-production offices), competition is often more effective among *groups* than it is among *individuals*. We have observed numerous incidents where competition has arisen almost spontaneously between groups to see who will put out the most work, make the biggest reductions in scrap losses, and so forth. Workers seem to enjoy the increased sense of group belonging, the excitement of the game, and the thrill of winning.

Competition among individuals is much more widely accepted on the white-collar and managerial levels. Indeed, among salesmen, it is the traditional form of motivation. Yet even among nonfactory employees competition as a means of motivation suffers certain limitations and undesirable side-effects:

1. Not everybody is equally interested in advancement. Some people are highly ambitious, but others—who may be just as competent and hardworking —seek to avoid situations where they have to "cut the other man's throat" to get ahead. Indeed, if books such as William H. Whyte's *Organization Man* are correct, competition among members of management is no longer as socially acceptable as it once was. And many people, reasonably satisfied with their present job and earnings, do not want to expend the extra effort necessary to win a promotion.

Many engineers and scientists are more interested in professional advancement than in promotions, particularly if the higher-rated job takes them from their laboratory and saddles them with administrative chores. In a sense, these men are competing, but they are competing for professional recognition rather than for the goals management has set for them.

2. Excessive competition has been known to disrupt an entire organization. "A football team may compete successfully with other teams, but it does not follow that it will compete best if its members are in competition with one another." [17]

As we shall see in Chapter 16, the modern industrial organization is being

---

[17] Harold Leavitt, *Managerial Psychology* (Chicago: University of Chicago Press, 1958), pp. 258-259.

broken down more and more into specialized activities, such as credit, sales, advertising, engineering, product development, and so forth, none of which can be carried on without continuous cooperation from people who are performing other activities. There are fewer and fewer one-man operations, particularly at the higher levels of management. As a consequence, cooperation is vital to sustained productivity.

3. On many jobs it is difficult to measure who has been most successful, since it is impossible to identify the output of each employee. Even when objective measures are appropriate they are hard to formulate, and using them as the primary basis for distributing rewards may itself lead to a distortion of effort through an overemphasis on the factors being measured (see Chapter 15). Yet unless there is some purely objective way of determining who should receive promotions and rewards, competition may make subordinates overly dependent on their boss. They may be more anxious to look good than to actually do a good job.

Overdependence tends to transform the subordinate into a "yes man" and "apple polisher" who is so fearful of making mistakes that he never has a chance to learn from them. The supervisor who is constantly looking upward toward his boss rather than downward toward his subordinates is likely to do a poor job of supervision, and he is certain to inhibit upward communication. But more of this in Chapter 15.

4. Efforts to encourage competition are often regarded as pressure, and, as we have seen, excessive pressure is frustrating. Aggression and regression are common by-products of the contests conducted by sales organizations. *Time* magazine writes that:

> Many firms have . . . enlisted salesmen's families in ulcer-building campaigns to spur the breadwinner on. One company regularly sends cards to the home showing the salesman's standing in the current company contest, gives wives tags to hang on furniture around the house to remind their husbands of the furnishings they can earn. Some firms have even sent buzzers and shrill whistles to salesmen's children; when dad asks what the noise is all about, the kids are instructed to tell him it's only a reminder to straighten up and sell harder. . . . Such constant pressure from home and office is bound to take its toll on even the strongest salesman. . . . "You can carry this business of pounding away at a salesman too far," says Republic Steel's General Sales Manager L. S. Hamaker. "It can be too demoralizing." [18]

Excessive emphasis on competition is particularly frustrating to the loser. Since most promotional hierarchies are shaped like a pyramid, with fewer jobs at the top than at the bottom, there are always more losers than winners.

Many work groups actually band together to protect themselves from attempts to encourage competition, either by formulating group standards of "fair competition" or by banning competitive practices altogether. (For examples, see Chapter 4.) This response is most common among hourly-paid workers, but employees at all levels apply pressure on the "eager beaver."

---

[18] *Time*, Vol. 72, No. 2 (July 14, 1958), pp. 75-76.

In conclusion, excessive competition may do more harm than good. In its pure form, the philosophy of competition as a motivating device seems to assume that work is itself uninteresting. When used in moderation, however, and in conjunction with other forms of motivation, competition among individuals may be useful, particularly with certain groups (salesmen, for example), and in situations where teamwork is not essential.

INTERNALIZED MOTIVATION

A fifth approach to the problem of motivation is to provide opportunities for need satisfaction through doing the job itself, and thus internalize motivation so that people will enjoy doing good work. Here, the better job an employee does, the higher his level of job satisfaction will be. This approach requires management to discard the assumption that work must be objectionable. It also de-emphasizes economic motivation and off-the-job and around-the-job need satisfactions.

Note how this approach differs from "be good." In that method the employee is *given* need satisfaction; here he *obtains* satisfaction *through his own work*—work that he enjoys and work that helps management. In "be good" it is assumed that greater satisfaction leads to harder work. Here the relationship is reversed: It is assumed that the harder work is the element which leads to greater satisfaction.

We have seen that in informal groups people work together and accept the orders of their leaders in order to achieve group objectives. In the same way, it is management's task to create conditions under which people "will willingly and voluntarily work toward organizational objectives" [19]—because they enjoy their work and feel it important to do a good job. This desirable attitude has been called by various authors "spontaneous cooperation" [20] and "Theory Y." [21] As J. S. Mill put it, "Nor are the greatest outward precautions comparable in efficacy to the monitor within." [22]

The preceding chapters have already given some hints about how these opportunities can be provided. Later chapters will make other suggestions, but we shall list the major themes here.

1. We have already seen how intrinsic job satisfaction can be increased through redesigning the job—through job enlargement, job rotation, greater understanding of how the work is coming along, feeling of the whole, and so forth.

2. We have also considered the importance of social satisfactions on the

---

[19] Douglas McGregor, *The Supervisor's Job.* Mimeographed; undated.

[20] See Elton Mayo, *The Social Problems of an Industrial Civilization* (Boston: Graduate School of Business Administration, Harvard University, 1945).

[21] Douglas McGregor, *The Human Side of Enterprise* (New York: McGraw-Hill, 1960).

[22] Mill, *op. cit.*, p. 111.

job. Opportunities can be provided to develop friendships and to work to-gether as a team. When members of the group can participate in solving work problems, they may become more involved in the job itself so that their productivity rises.

3. Equally, if not more, important is the style of leadership shown by management. In the next chapter we shall suggest ways in which the supervisor may engage in "general supervision." Workers may be given an opportunity to enjoy a feeling of accomplishment in their work and, in so far as possible, to be their own boss. Under such circumstances supervisors conceive of their job as a way of helping their subordinates rather than as a means of pushing them.

Glance back for a moment at Chapter 1 and notice some of the needs we listed there:

skill	understanding	acceptance
autonomy (being one's own boss)	knowledge of where one stands	attention self-confidence
achievement	praise	

These are the needs that the policy of internalized motivation seeks to harness.

STRIKING A BALANCE

For all its merits, internalized motivation is not a panacea, though some observers are more optimistic about it than the authors are. To our minds, those who are most unreserved in its praise tend to overestimate the possible gains from its use and to underestimate the costs involved in making it work.

As we have just discussed, the policies of "be strong," "be good," and implicit bargaining provide little motivation to produce more than a certain minimum amount of work. Yet on many routine jobs this minimum may be enough, since management may have no need for outstanding performance. What is outstanding performance in the case of the assembly-line worker? That he work faster than the line? That he show creativity and imagination on the job? Management needs none of these. *Adequate* performance (as set by implicit bargaining, perhaps) is all that can be used on the assembly line and on many other jobs in our society. Here the conforming, dependent worker (who is not *dis*satisfied) may well be the best.

Further, as we have seen in Chapter 1, many individuals center their lives off the job and have little desire for the challenge internalized motivation provides. There are those who argue that such individuals are immature personalities, and that they have adjusted to techniques such as hygienic supervision or "be strong" by becoming apathetic and dependent: Were the organization environment healthy, were internalized motivation available, the argument goes on, these individuals would react differently. But in many cases, these people's limitations stem from childhood or are present in the general culture. Even if the argument is valid, such individuals may be "too far gone" to react well to internalized motivation, and their attitude is not likely to be changed short of intensive psychotherapy.

In addition, the reliance on internalized motivation can be quite costly to the organization. To increase intrinsic job satisfaction may require the use of job processes which are technologically inefficient. Increased teamwork may not be useful to the organization if employers unite to keep production low. To make general supervision work, many of the old-line autocratic supervisors must be retrained or replaced; this is an expensive process which may result in the demoralization and elimination of the organization's technically most competent individuals.

Since it is extremely difficult to develop internalized motivation on many routine jobs, once the traditional, external sanctions (implicit bargaining, fear of discharge, and so forth) are removed, *net* motivation may, on balance, fall. Furthermore, it is fairly meaningless to talk of permitting exercise of discretion to assembly-line workers or girls on punch-card operations; the very nature of technology requires that all essential decisions be centrally programed. There are those who suggest that such programed jobs should be redesigned to permit job enlargement, and thus greater challenge and discretion. Yet, as we have discussed, such technological changes can be made only at a substantial cost in terms of productivity.

Internalized motivation works best where the nature of the job permits the employee to enjoy autonomy (there may be little opportunity for it on the assembly line, but a good deal in professional work); where employees accept the organization's objectives (it might work better with managerial than blue-collar employees); and among those who make the job their central life focus (it might work poorly with women whose primary interest is finding a husband or bringing up their children).

In any case, the philosophy of internalized motivation is somewhat idealistic. It assumes that somehow the needs of the organization and needs of the individual can both be maximized at the same time, so that what is good for one will be good for the other. Clearly, this is rarely if ever, the case. Normally there must be some sort of trade-off, that is, if organizational needs are to come first, the individual will suffer to some extent, and vice versa. The most the manager can expect to provide is a reasonable satisfactory level of satisfaction for both parties. Conflicts of interest will continue to exist between management and employees and it is totally unrealistic to expect to eliminate them altogether. Employees will want more satisfaction, management will want more production, and where the balance is to be poised between the two "is a matter to be solved by bargaining, not by scientific evidence." [23]

---

[23] Herbert A. Simon, "Authority," in Conrad Arensberg, *et al.*, eds., *op. cit.*, p. 114.

One of the central problems of any organization is to motivate its members to work for the organization's over-all objectives. In the family, the primitive society, or the voluntary social club, this may be a relatively easy matter. But in the larger organization of our society, motivating employees is a difficult problem.

Traditionally, management has resorted to "be strong." With the growth of unions, a rising standard of living, and changing patterns of discipline in home and school, this approach has become less effective. It motivates people only to produce the minimum necessary not to get fired (though in some cases this minimum may be adequate). Moreover, it creates frustration and other undesirable side effects. In practice it is often tempered with a large dose of implicit bargaining.

"Be good" removes some of the harshness of the authoritarian approach. It may help recruit employees and make them more willing to accept their jobs. As a consequence they may not be dissatisfied. But "be good" alone provides little motivation to do more than the minimum amount of work to avoid being discharged.

Implicit bargaining seems a somewhat more realistic approach, particularly where there is a union situation. It provides an atmosphere of live-and-let-live, but it rarely furnishes any motivation to *increase* production.

Competition has only limited effectiveness as a motivating device on jobs where there is little opportunity for promotion or where seniority prevails. Excessive competition may actually disrupt teamwork and lead to frustration and a host of undesirable side effects.

From many points of view, internalized motivation is the "best" form of motivation, since it provides the greatest opportunity for individuals to satisfy their needs and to develop their personalities. Yet internalized motivation can rarely be applied alone, and it is considerably more appropriate with some sorts of people and jobs (for example, jobs which require individual discretion and commitment) than it is with others.

(Since all chapters in this supervisory section are closely related, we have grouped all the relevant problems together at the end of Chapter 9.)

Delegation

A manager makes decisions in some areas by himself; in other areas he delegates to his subordinates. In this chapter we are concerned with the means by which the manager delegates and with the conditions under which delegation is feasible. Our next chapter will deal with how the manager may exercise authority in the areas where he makes decisions on his own.

Delegation on the face-to-face, supervisor-subordinate level is often called *general supervision;* [1] on the organization-wide level it is called *decentralization.* General supervision involves giving increased autonomy to individuals; decentralization involves giving it to organizational subunits. The discussion in this chapter is primarily concerned with the face-to-face level, but much of what we have to say will apply to organization-wide decentralization as well.

THE MEANING OF DELEGATION

In applying delegation a manager makes relatively few decisions by himself and frames his orders in broad, general terms. Delegation is really a form of job enlargement, for it gives each subordinate a sense of being his own boss and exercising control over his own work environment. Thus, it seeks to provide internalized motivation, and tends to offset the monotony and lack of autonomy that technology has built into many jobs.

The manager who delegates is interested primarily in results, and he permits his subordinates to work out the details for themselves. He sets goals, tells his subordinates what he wants accomplished, fixes the limits within which they can work, and (in cases where the subordinates are adequately trained) lets them decide how to achieve these goals. Instead of rattling off a list of orders, he is likely to communicate helpful information or make suggestions. He

---

[1] Some scholars think of general supervision in terms of a pattern of interaction (or face-to-face contacts) and define delegation in terms of the location of formal decision-making powers. For our purposes here we will look upon delegation and general supervision as equivalents.

explains *why* he wants things done and points out how the subordinate's contribution fits into the over-all plan. In other words, he gives each subordinate the maximum freedom he can handle consistent with the aims of the organization. A successful plant manager exaggerated only a bit when he said:

> "I never make a decision by myself. Oh, I guess I have one or two since I have been here. If people know their job, I believe in letting them make their own decisions. Of course, if there is anything which affects the entire plant, the assistant managers, the staff chiefs, and sometimes the assistant staff chiefs come in here and we discuss it. But I don't believe in saying, 'This is the way it is going to be done.'"

Other managers seem to be unable to take this approach. They are inclined to give detailed instructions telling subordinates exactly how, and in what sequence, they want things done. They "were found to check up on their employees more frequently, to give them more frequent instructions, and in general to limit their freedom to do their work in their own way."[2]

Compare, for example, the difference in approach used by two office managers as they handed out the same assignment.

> *Office Manager A:* "Call Jones Office Equipment and the Wilson Supply Store. Get them to quote you prices on all the office dictation equipment they will. Ask them to give you a demonstration. Invite two managers to the demonstration, Ellis and Conrad, and let them try it out. Get them to put their reactions on paper. Then prepare me a report with the costs and specifications of all the equipment. Oh, yes, be sure to ask for information on repair costs...." (And so on.)

> *Office Manager B:* "I'd like to do something about our stenographic system. A lot of the executives who don't have secretaries of their own are complaining that it takes them too long to get a girl who can handle their dictation. Could you check up on some of the various kinds of dictating machines, find their prices, advantages and disadvantages, and give me a recommendation as to what we should do? I think we can spend $2,000. Possibly you could talk to some of the executives to get their ideas."

Office Manager A tried to think of all contingencies, and in doing so, gave his subordinate the feeling that she was little more than an errand girl. Moreover, he took so much trouble in trying to think of all the possibilities that he might as well have done the work himself.

Use of Pressure

One difference between what might be called close and general supervision lies in the use of pressure. Note how these managers "push" their men:

> "I handle the amount of work given each clerk, watch the dates and time the work so that everything gets out on schedule. If a letter comes in late, we

---

[2] Daniel Katz and Robert L. Kahn, "Human Organization and Worker Motivation," in L. Reed Tripp, ed., *Industrial Productivity* (Madison, Wisc.: Industrial Relations Research Association, 1951), p. 157.

have to speed up handling it—give it special attention. It has to be rushed along —handled in a different fashion than the usual run. I have to watch this to see that we make up time lost in other departments." [3]

"A factory is not a kindergarten. We've got schedules to meet and my job is to make sure that we meet them. . . . If you start babying the men, they will take advantage of you. They expect you to be tough."

Apparently, the supervisors quoted here have little trust in their subordinates' initiative or judgment, and feel that they have to check up on them constantly to make sure that they carry out instructions.

Note the difference in attitude reflected by this comment made by a supervisor who did exactly the same job as the first supervisor quoted above.

"If you keep your employees from feeling hounded, they are more likely to put out the necessary effort to get the work done on time. . . . I tell them, 'if you feel the job is getting you down, get away from it for a few minutes.' " [4]

Implicit in these different attitudes towards subordinates are distinct assumptions about human motivation. The close supervisor often seems to believe in the philosophy of "be strong," in effect, "Work is punishment. If I were to leave the shop, everyone would stop work." (And, no doubt, in his case, exactly this would happen.)

But the general supervisor seems to be saying, "As far as I am concerned, the average man wants to do a good job—at least until proven otherwise. If I walk away, production will continue as usual." (And in his case, this, too, will probably happen.) One study of supervisors with such attitudes comments as follows: "These foremen clearly believed in the willingness and capacity of their men to do a good job, and accordingly acted towards them with this assumption in mind. The men, therefore, tended to react in ways which justified the expectation held of them." [5]

It should be emphasized that the absence of pressure does not mean that subordinates are free to set their own standards. As we shall discuss shortly, delegation is rarely possible unless subordinates are given some sort of direction. High standards are essential if the organization is to be effective. They are also important from the standpoint of morale, since most people derive satisfaction from completing a difficult task. "In an organized production situation, workers expect to be asked to produce and be helped to reasonable levels of output. Furthermore, if the supervisory pressure is not excessive, workers'

---

[3] Daniel Katz, Nathan Maccoby, and Nancy C. Morse, *Productivity, Supervision, and Morale in an Office Situation* (Ann Arbor: University of Michigan, Institute for Social Research, 1950), p. 18.

[4] Rensis Likert and Daniel Katz, "Supervisory Practices and Organizational Structure as They Affect Employee Morale," in Schuyler Hoslett, ed., *Human Factors in Management*, 2d. ed. (New York: Harper & Row, 1951), p. 92.

[5] Charles R. Walker, Robert H. Guest, and Arthur N. Turner, *The Foreman on the Assembly Line* (Cambridge: Harvard University Press, 1956), p. 16.

morale goes up with increasing pressure!"[6] By setting exalted standards the leader indicates that he has confidence in his men. Throughout history, effective leaders have inspired their followers to strive for seemingly impossible goals.

In one sense, the general supervisor does apply pressure when he sets the goals he expects his subordinates to achieve. This is a very different kind of pressure, however, from the nagging, "breathing down a man's neck" type of pressure exerted by close supervisors. If subordinates accept the goals of the organization as valid, they tend to feel that the pressure to do a good job *originated* from the goals themselves, rather than from the supervisor. But we shall discuss this point later on.

The Advantages of Delegation

What are the advantages of delegation?

1. Few supervisors have the time to handle both their own job and the jobs of their subordinates. The close supervisor who tries to make every decision by himself frequently exhausts himself physically and mentally. Furthermore, his decision may not be as good as those of his subordinates, since the man who is closest to a problem usually understands it better than anyone else.[7]

2. A subordinate can take pride in results that are directly attributable to his own judgment. He feels little involvement in his work when someone else makes all the decisions.

3. Delegation helps to develop the talents and abilities of subordinates. It is hard to train people to take the risks of decision-making without putting them in a position of making decisions on their own. Over-close supervision makes it difficult for people to learn, even by making mistakes.

SUBSTITUTES FOR DECISION-MAKING BY THE BOSS

Effective delegation does not mean that subordinates are permitted to do exactly what they want. Quite the contrary. Delegation is feasible only when there are means available (other than the superior's making the decision himself) which can insure that subordinates will make decisions which are at least "adequate" from the viewpoint of the organization. To use a fashionable term, subordinates must be "programed" (or directed) to insure that they

---

[6] Robert Dubin, "Supervision and Productivity: Some Empirical Findings and Theoretical Considerations," in Robert Dubin and others, *Leadership and Productivity* (San Francisco: Chandler, 1965), p. 28.

[7] As we shall discuss in Chapter 15, the spread of computers has somewhat reduced this advantage of delegation. Provided information can be translated into computer language, electronic data-processing makes it possible to communicate the information quickly and accurately from subordinates to the data-processing center, and the computer itself never becomes exhausted from making too many decisions.

conform to patterns of behavior which are consistent with organizational needs.

The extent of programing necessary, whether it is tight or loose, may depend on a number of factors which we shall discuss later. First, however, we shall consider four types of programing (or four means of avoiding direct orders) which are available to management. The first three are *rules, goals,* and *indoctrination.* The fourth, on a somewhat different level, is the influence of *technology and work-flow.* Let us look at these in turn.

Rules

Rules are a means by which the decision-making activities of subordinates are programed so that it is unnecessary for every decision to be referred to the supervisor. Thus, rules save time for the executive. His subordinates do not have to consult him on routine matters, for the rules lay down principles in advance. Decisions can, therefore, be made more quickly and at lower levels.

Rules set up standard operating procedures. They may be written or unwritten; they may be established by supervisory edict, by training, by implicit bargaining, or through consultation. The significant points are that rules (1) restrict subordinate behavior, and (2) are enforced, in one way or another, by management (and, as we shall see in Chapter 9, sometimes by the subordinate's peers as well). Though many people disparage rules (particularly written rules) as "red tape," they are essential if an organization is to operate effectively.[8]

Rules serve to limit the freedom of subordinates. Naturally, the greater the area of freedom given the subordinate, the greater the feeling of autonomy he will have. Unfortunately, the subordinate cannot be given authority to do *everything* he wants: Well-understood limits or rules make it possible for him to exercise freedom within these limits. Sometimes, of course, these rules are implicit and need not be spelled out in detail.

> Suppose you are the office manager and the Big Boss tells you: "Go ahead, use your discretion in redecorating the office. Anything you say, goes!" Beware! He doesn't really mean that. There are certainly clearly understood rules within which you must work. You must abide by the city building codes and the union contract. You cannot exceed your budget. Further, you must go through the purchasing department, fill out the proper forms, and so forth.
>
> Also, if you are smart, you know that redecorating must play second fiddle to keeping production going. Unless you are on Madison Avenue, the office better wind up looking like an office, not a ladies' lounge or a Japanese garden.

Where there is room for doubt, the supervisor should state the rules clearly, sometimes even in writing. As we shall note later, it often seems that people are objecting to responsibility, when they are really objecting to uncertainty.

---

[8] For an excellent discussion of the relationship between rules and organizational efficiency, see Alvin Gouldner, *Patterns of Industrial Bureaucracy* (New York: The Free Press of Glencoe, 1954), pp. 167 ff.

Rules have both advantages and disadvantages, as the following sections discuss.

Establish consistency. Particularly in large organizations, rules serve to make the behavior of the parts consistent with the needs of the whole. They reduce the possibility that personal feelings rather than organizational objectives will predominate in decision-making. For instance, in an effort to achieve uniformity, management frequently promulgates standard lists of penalties for disciplinary infractions. Thus, excessive absenteeism will result in the same penalty in every department, even though managers may not agree about the seriousness of this offense. The alternative would be to have one man handle all discipline.

Reduce personal dependency. Rules are impersonal and, in effect, reduce the power of both the boss and the subordinate. This makes it easier for the subordinate to obey and for the boss to exercise authority. An office manager put it:

> It sure helped me when top management put in a rule that everyone must fly tourist class. This way when I turn down expense accounts with first class fare, the men know it isn't my fault (and almost no one puts it in any more).

Rules also protect the subordinate from arbitrary actions on the part of his boss. They are useful in defining employees' duties and responsibilities. They enable subordinates to predict the consequences of their actions—an ability that is essential to personal security. Well-thought-out rules establish limits within which employees are free to act on their own. Persons on higher levels step in only when one of these limits is violated, or when a question comes up which is not covered by existing policy. As a result, the position of employees is strengthened all down the line.

Permit routinization. Rules require the manager to initiate orders only once—when he lays a rule down. Most people prefer not to receive constant initiation, particularly when they cannot return it. But once rules are established for how a man should do his job (and once he is adequately trained in the meaning of these rules), then the job can be reduced to a routine. And "routinization protects the ego of those who would otherwise be continually ordered around." [9]

The value of rules in establishing routine was brought sharply to our attention in a training class for telephone supervisors. We asked a chief operator if she found it hard to delegate or give autonomy to operators since the nature of their job provided them little opportunity for discretion. "Oh, no," she said, "once a girl is trained, I let her completely alone. She knows her job and

---

[9] Henry Landsberger, "The Horizontal Dimension in Bureaucracy," *Administrative Science Quarterly*, Vol. 6, No. 3 (December 1961), p. 309.

knows what she is supposed to do. She has complete freedom as long as she does her job."

Many employees apparently do experience a feeling of autonomy under such circumstances. Usually it is a situation characterized by constant change that requires most direction:

> In their drive for change and progress, many executives overlook the stabilizing nature of work routines that can be built up and carried on by workers without constant attention from their supervisors. They fail to see that frequently imposed changes not only upset work habits of individuals, but also have a disturbing effect on the pattern of human relations that ties workers to each other and their supervisors.[10]

Excessively rigid rules. Rules may be too specific and detailed, however, and they may be applied too rigidly by subordinates who fail to use good judgment in handling specific cases. This is one symptom of what some people call "bureaucracy" (though sociologists apply this term to any hierarchical organization that makes use of uniform policies).

Unnecessary rules are difficult to enforce, and inadequately enforced rules may lead to a general breakdown of discipline. Even when they are enforced, if there are too many rules, men may live up only to the minimum requirements of the rules, feeling they have done all the company can reasonably require. Particularly when the reasonableness of the rules is neither self-evident nor well explained, they tend to make a man feel restricted, to breed resentment and aggressiveness, and at times to provoke a desire to break the rules just to prove one's independence.

Excessively rigid rules also discourage individual discretion and initiative, and make it difficult for an organization to adapt to changing conditions. They give the petty tyrant a shield behind which he can vent his vindictiveness. They provide the inept supervisor with a crutch to lean on and enable him to avoid the conflicts and uncertainties of making decisions on his own. They subject the able supervisor to endless frustration and make it impossible for him to operate with the flexibility required for peak efficiency. At the very least, they lead to red tape and wasted effort. Here is the way the personnel director of a small branch plant described the effect of excessively rigid rules:

> "The company employment procedures require us to check all references. This may be OK for some of the big plants with operations different from ours. But in this community with our type of work it is silly. We have written the top office a dozen times asking for an exception to be made for us. All they say is that it has to be uniform throughout the company. Why? Well, we go through the motions, but it really is a waste of time. *And in my job this kind of thing happens again and again.*"

Rules give the insecure supervisor a means of "passing the buck" for unpleasant decisions: "The office just issued a strict new policy—no more days

---

[10] William F. Whyte, *Human Relations in the Restaurant Industry* (New York: McGraw-Hill, 1948), p. 263.

off unless a man is sick; my hands are tied." The supervisor hopes, by blaming higher managers with whom the subordinate does not have any regular contact, to maintain his own good relationship with his subordinate. The result is a general weakening of the immediate supervisor's leadership position as well as damage to the employee's respect for the organization.

Rules have a tendency to become ends in themselves, particularly if those who carry them out forget the reasons for which they were promulgated in the first place. Consider this case:

> In order to prevent salary increases from getting out of hand, top management decides that one per year is the limit for any employee. An exceptional employee does an outstanding job. To prevent him from accepting a better offer from another company, his supervisor tries to offer him an extra salary raise. The personnel department automatically turns the supervisor's request down and the man quits.

We have no way of knowing, of course, whether this particular man should have been given an extra increase; we would need additional facts before deciding that. But it is clear that further investigation was called for before a decision was made.

Rebellious employees can cripple an organization by following every rule to the letter. In recent years, for example, "follow-the-rules" campaigns have been successfully used by employees of the British Post Office and the Long Island Railroad as alternatives to strike as means of putting pressure on management.

Correct use of rules.   Rules are designed to set a general direction, to insure some measure of uniformity and consistency. But the basic reason for rules is not to restrict the individual, but to further the general welfare of the organization and the attainment of its goals. When a particular rule prevents this organizational objective from being attained, then it must give way, an exception must be made.

The important point is that an exception must be clearly identified as such. Establishing a rule is like setting the course of a ship.[11] There may be times when the ship runs off course—in bad weather, for example—but the ship's officers need to know when and by how much they are departing from the prescribed course if the ship is to reach its destination.

In summary, intelligently devised rules grant the individual in a large organization considerable freedom to make decisions on his own. To insure that his decisions are not completely unfettered, however, his actions need to conform to the goals of the total organization. This insurance is provided through setting limits—that is, through establishing rules. These rules or policies can free higher-level managers from the necessity of handling many time-consuming aspects of the routine business of the organization. Subordinates do not have to check back with their boss each time an action or a decision is

---

11 Peter Drucker, *The Concept of the Corporation* (New York: John Day, 1956).

called for—they know the limits within which they can operate. The higher manager need step into a problem situation only when one of the pre-established limits has been violated by a subordinate or when a case comes up that is not covered by existing policies. The danger is that the existence of rules makes it possible for the inept or autocratic supervisor to avoid his responsibility for making difficult personnel decisions by interpreting rules in an excessively narrow fashion and "passing the buck."

Goal-Setting

By setting goals the manager can avoid the necessity for either making specific decisions or laying down detailed rules. This approach, which is in sharp contrast to detailed, minute-by-minute supervision, is often called "management by exception." It permits the subordinate to experiment, to adjust to novel situations.

Definite assignments.   The manager who practices close supervision gives his subordinates detailed orders but sets no over-all goals towards which to work. As soon as the subordinate finishes one task, the manager gives him another. The manager's only goal seems to be to "keep the men busy." Few practices can be so destructive to morale.

> The engineers studying a factory operation said the men could produce 500 units a day. The men said this was impossible. But one day, under the plant manager's urging, they really made an effort and reached their quota 30 minutes before the end of the shift. While they were congratulating themselves on their accomplishment, the plant manager saw them "loafing" and sent them back to work, saying that if they could complete 500 units in 7½ hours, they ought to be able to get up to 550 or 600 tomorrow. And that is what he was expecting! Next day, production went down to 350.

When employees have the experiences of this sort day after day, they develop attitudes that have disastrous effect on output. "Work hard and what rewards do I get? More work. I might as well just *look* busy." [12]

Delegation can be more effective when subordinates can be given definite assignments in terms of results expected. If an employee knows exactly how much he is expected to do, he has a goal to work for. He knows if he works hard now, he will have the reward of an easier time later on. He won't have to look busy just to keep out of trouble. (Once an employee told us, "I'm always in trouble because I work hard and finish up, so the boss sees me doing

---

[12] Although employees often resist time-study and other forms of work measurement as means of "speed-up," a report from IBM suggests that work measurement and the establishment of output standards may actually result in higher morale, where such standards are seen as providing "stability of work expectations" and a protection against managers who would otherwise constantly cry for "more, more." David Sirota, "A Study of Work Measurements," *Proceedings of the Sixteenth Annual Meeting* (Madison: Industrial Relations Research Association, 1963), p. 160.

nothing. The man next to me has no trouble with the boss; he's slow and it looks like he is always working.")

On jobs which provide little satisfaction, leisure may be a strong reward. Some organizations allow employees who have finished their days' work to go home and still collect eight hours' pay. In England this practice is known as "job and finish." In America, electric-meter readers, postmen, and garbage-men often work on this basis. In all these occupations close supervision is almost impossible. (Of course, if a man finishes much too soon, the supervisor has an indication that the work has been assigned inequitably. Still, management must be careful not to kill incentive by using a few free minutes as an excuse to give a man extra work.)

On managerial levels, goals are also used. Thus, in many companies each department is considered a "profit center" for accounting purposes, and the departmental manager is given the goal or making the "planned profit" or of not exceeding "planned costs." Sales quotas are, of course, frequently assigned to salesmen. In each of these cases management must be careful not to destroy incentive by raising the goals too quickly after they have been reached.

Naturally, many assignments cannot be as specific as "Process 150 forms a day" or "Sell $500 worth of toothpaste a month." Some must be more general, such as "Wait on all customers who come to your counter" or "Handle all union grievances which come to your level." The latter sort of assignment does not, in itself, constitute a definite goal to work toward (unless it is put this way: "Take care of all these customers or grievances and you will have a few minutes break till the next group comes.") Still, a general assignment (such as "take care of all customers") provides more autonomy than does a host of specific instructions. There is real satisfaction in knowing "This is my job. Here I am in charge. As long as I do it adequately, no one will interfere with me. I will be judged on how well I do."

A number of companies have experimented recently with goals which are jointly set by the boss and his subordinates or by the subordinates themselves. Many of these experiments have been on the management level. There is considerable evidence that goals set in this fashion are at least at high as those set by the boss alone—and that subordinates are more likely to feel such goals are fair and to be motivated to meet them.

Supervision by results. Typically, when supervision by goal-setting is practiced, management interferes very little, so long as the goals are met, except perhaps to give subordinates praise, promotion, or some financial reward. Only when serious trouble develops does higher management step in. The establishment of standards has advantages from the point of view of both management and the individual employee.

1. The very fact that employees know their efforts are being measured may stir them to work harder. Statistical measures are sometimes more effective in insuring high output than are specific rules. To require each supervisor to

make a monthly report on scrap loss may be more effective than a whole series of regulations or exhortations on avoiding waste. Such controls may also provide a swift means of altering the behavior of subordinates. Notice how this approach worked with interviewers in a public employment agency:

> Formerly, statistics were kept only on the *total* number of interviews carried on per month by each interviewer. This system motivated the interviewers to make a large number of *interviews,* but it gave them no incentive to find *jobs* for applicants. There was an immediate change in their behavior when statistics were also kept on the percentage of applicants who actually got jobs. In a two-month period the percentage of jobs filled jumped from 55 to 67. As one interviewer put it: "There is no tendency to get rid of an applicant as there was before. . . . Since they are measured by placements, everybody tried to get a job for every applicant." [13]

2. Supervision by results makes each man feel that he is his own boss. He understands what is expected of him and is encouraged to show initiative and develop his potentialities. He has a goal to work for and a feeling of completion when he reaches it. This approach encourages competition between individuals and groups—though excessive competition has certain disadvantages, particularly when individuals are expected to work together.

3. The existence of a clear-cut set of performance standards makes it easier for superiors to criticize the shortcomings of their subordinates. Employees are often resentful when their boss talks about their personal failings: It is quite another matter when the criticism is couched in terms of helping them improve their record. In fact, the mere existence of such records tends to reduce the need for the supervisor to prod employees; they know automatically when they have fallen down on the job.[14]

4. This approach to supervision makes it possible for higher management to discover when departments are having trouble and to take remedial measures quickly. As we shall discover in Chapter 15, this is a form of feedback, or upward communication.

5. Similarly, supervision by results makes it possible to evaluate the effectiveness of employees and supervisors and to decide who should get promotions or pay increases.

On the other hand, supervision by results can be attacked as over-emphasizing the individual at the expense of the group; as encouraging competition and passing the buck rather than fostering cooperation; as substituting for the single boss the more pervasive control of a number of "auditing departments" (such as accounting and quality control—see Chapter 16); and as placing excessive emphasis on immediate measurable results, as opposed to significant but immeasurable intangibles such as morale, good will, and employee development. Some of these problems, particularly as they relate to statistical controls, are discussed at greater length in Chapter 15.

---

[13] Peter M. Blau, *The Dynamics of Bureaucracy* (Chicago: University of Chicago Press, 1955), p. 37.

[14] For further discussion of this point, see *ibid.*, p. 40. Also, George Odiorne, *Management by Objectives* (New York: Pitman, 1966).

Indoctrination

When employees fully accept the goals and values of the organization for which they work, they are said to be indoctrinated. Such persons are willing to subordinate their personal views to the higher interests of the organization as a whole. Indoctrination, in a sense, is a means of establishing organizational loyalty and commitment.[15] Indoctrination makes it easier to delegate authority, since highly indoctrinated individuals all think in roughly the same terms and make their decisions on the basis of the same premises as their superiors. In other words, if a manager's subordinates are indoctrinated, he can feel sure that they will solve their problems in roughly the same way that he would himself. As a consequence, he has little need to be specific about rules or goals which his subordinates know as well as he does himself. They also know which goals are important and which can be broken when they conflict with others of higher priority. Ideally, then, with indoctrination, an organization can permit innovative flexibility as to *means,* knowing that there will be uniformity as to *ends.*

Many of the most effective organizations—such as the Marine Corps or the Catholic Church—rely on indoctrination to a high degree. A well-trained Marine can be relied on to "fight like a Marine" even in situations where he cannot be supervised by his superior officer. The Catholic Church operated for centuries on a decentralized world-wide basis, long before the advent of modern communications, largely because the strength of its priests' faith made it unnecessary for them to receive constant instructions from Rome. To a lesser degree many large corporations try to train their employees so that everyone in the organization can take a more or less consistent point of view towards their job. (Large corporations develop characteristic modes of operations and ways of thinking among their employees, and a General Electric man may well approach problems in a very different fashion from that of a man from Jersey Standard.)

As we pointed out in Chapter 3, professionals are also indoctrinated, but in terms of professional, not organizational, values. As long as the two are consistent (for example, as long as the company wants the scientist to engage in pure research or the company doctor to do his best to maintain employee health), decision-making power may be delegated to professionals with little need for external controls. But when professional and organizational objectives conflict (for example, when a scientist oriented towards pure research [16] is told to work on applied research), then some sort of closer control may be necessary. Skilled craftsmen are indoctrinated in much the same way. Their internalized sense of pride in craft motivates them to maintain high standards of workmanship as well as to put out a fair day's work.[17]

---

15 Philip Selznick, *Leadership and Administration* (New York: Harper & Row, 1957).

16 We do not subscribe to the myth that every scientist wants to do pure research. Many find considerable satisfaction working in the applied area.

17 See, for example, Robert Blauner, *Alienation and Freedom* (Chicago: University of Chicago Press, 1964), pp. 175-76.

Indoctrination usually requires a long period of hard training: The Catholic Church has its seminaries, the Marine Corps has boot camps, many companies have management training programs,[18] professionals, for the most part, learn their values in universities, and craftsmen in apprenticeship. Indoctrination is usually most effective, however, in organizations with high purposes and long traditions.

Indoctrination is far from being a universal cure-all for every management problem. Indoctrination can be really effective only when individuals internalize management's objectives and make them their own.[19] The Church, the Marine Corps, and other such noneconomically oriented organizations have ideological appeals which make it possible to demand almost complete loyalty from their members; but business firms will rarely, if ever, win such perfect dedication.[20] Religious zealots may be willing to sacrifice their personal ambitions to advance the True Faith. But the typical corporate manager seeks to advance only *himself;* faced with a choice, personal success is more important to him than are corporate profits. And the typical worker has less interest in advancing the company's interests, particularly when he sees them as conflicting with his own. Thus, indoctrination in business may have a meaning considerably different from what it has in nonprofit institutions.

Still, indoctrination may be useful for instilling in organization members a common approach to problems which may reduce the need for restrictive rules. It is more effective, however, on the management level than among rank-and-file white- or blue-collar workers.

Technology and Work Flow

The nature of the work to be done restricts subordinates in much the same way as do direct orders, rules, and other supervisory techniques.[21] The auto assembler's pace is set by the speed of the assembly line; the bank teller's

---

[18] The function of management schools in providing managers with a common point of view has been described by IBM President Thomas J. Watson, Jr., as follows: "These schools were not only to teach general management, but—most important—they were to give our managers a feeling for IBM's outlooks and beliefs. After a time we found that the schools tended to put too much emphasis on management, not enough on beliefs. This, we felt, was putting the cart before the horse. We felt it was vital that our managers be well grounded in our beliefs. Otherwise, we might get management views at odds with the company's outlook." *A Business and Its Beliefs* (New York: McGraw-Hill, 1963), p. 91.

[19] As a sociologist puts it, "Compliance in normative organizations in which there is a high personal commitment not based on force or possible economic gain rests principally on the internalization of directives accepted as legitimate." Amitai Etzioni, *A Comparative Analysis of Complex Organization* (New York: The Free Press of Glencoe, 1961), p. 40.

[20] In addition, the Church and the Marine Corps are able to isolate their members from conflicting pressures and values in a way which most businesses cannot. However, frequent transfers may reduce the strength of the business executives' loyalties to relatives, community, and social organizations.

[21] A recent study suggests that, particularly in process industries, technology imposes obvious directives which all can see, thus reducing the necessity for higher management to give orders. Joan Woodward, *Industrial Organization: Theory and Practice* (London: Oxford University Press, 1965).

by his customers; the tool crib attendant's by his fellow workers. In none of these cases does the superior have to tell his subordinates *how fast* to work; in each case controls are very simple: It becomes immediately obvious when a man falls down on the job.

Also, customers, fellow workers, and the demands of the work situation may tell the employee *what* to do; there is no need for the supervisor to initiate orders. This is true, for example, in a hospital operating room:

> Although innumerable orders have been precisely responded to, most of them have flowed from the dictates of the patient's presence and condition. In a very real sense, few of the directives during surgery are arbitrary decisions on the surgeon's part. Rather, in the last analysis, the patient's needs have been the controlling element in the entire situation. Thus the person who seems to be the least capable of exerting authority—the supine, unconscious object—has in fact assumed the star role and preponderant influence in the course of the drama.[22]

Electric utility substation operators, who often work completely by themselves, report feeling that they are completely their own bosses, when in fact they have to respond to "orders" issued by dials and meters. In the same way, factory maintenance men work only when equipment breaks down, and how they do their work is normally determined by the nature of the emergency, not by the boss's instructions. As long as the subordinates are adequately trained and the technology remains relatively constant (two determining constraints), the boss intervenes only when there is obvious trouble. The most important problems involve lateral rather than boss-subordinate relations (we shall discuss lateral relations in Chapter 16).

When a man knows his job well, the mere giving of information serves as a substitute for an order. Note the difference between these two statements: "Bill, bring some parts over to Machine 16," and "Bill, Machine 16 is down to six parts." The second provides Bill with the information he needs to make his own decisions—and it assumes that he will make the correct one. It enables him to serve Machine 3 first if it has fewer parts than Machine 16. In addition, providing a man with abundant information (all that he seeks and requests) has a positive effect on morale, even if he doesn't need all the information to do a good job.

Jobs can be rearranged so as to reduce the number of "human orders." We once observed a factory in which there was constant friction between operators and inspectors; the main trouble was the operators' resentment of what they felt was the inspectors' constant badgering to keep up quality. Only one inspector was able to keep up good relations. The secret of his success was that he rarely *told* a man he had made a mistake; instead, he showed him the offending part with the proper dimensions marked in chalk.

It should be emphasized that the various forms of programing just discussed are, in effect, substitutes for one another and for close supervision. As one

---

[22] Temple Burling, Edith Lentz, and Robert Wilson, *The Give and Take in Hospitals* (New York: Putnam, 1956), p. 262.

form is strengthened, another may be weakened. For example, in times of rapid change, close supervision may be required, since goals are no longer well defined, the requirements of technology are not clearly understood, and new rules have yet to be devised and accepted. If indoctrination breaks down, then new rules must be enforced. When work becomes routine, then there may be less need for elaborate measurement of results because bottlenecks become immediately obvious, and perhaps just as immediately straightened out by those involved without need for intervention by higher management.

GENERAL SUPERVISION IN PRACTICE

By our definition, general supervision involves a high degree of delegation of authority and, in most cases, requires some indirect means in insuring that employees' behavior conforms to management's needs. We have emphasized that the general supervisor does not give constant orders nor does he spend a large part of his time checking up on employees or putting pressure on them to keep working.

What does the general supervisor do with his time then? As we shall discuss in Chapter 18, spending less time giving orders to each individual subordinate may permit a general supervisor to manage larger numbers of subordinates (in terms which we will discuss later, he can expand his *span of control* and have a *flatter organization*). Even where this does not occur, the activities of the general supervisor may differ substantially from those of close supervisors. General supervisors are more likely (1) to do work different from that of subordinates, (2) to concentrate on long-range rather than short-range problems and, (3) to engage in training. Let us look at these activities in turn.

Different Work
from That Done by Subordinates

There is an old tradition that the good supervisor is the one who rolls up his sleeves and works alongside his subordinates, often setting an example by his efforts. The evidence suggests that this is a myth. Of course, in an emergency the good supervisor will always pitch in to help. And there are certain supervisory jobs that require close technical coordination, jobs such as that of orchestra conductor or engineering project manager. With these exceptions, however, research indicates that the high-productivity supervisor devotes much of his time to activities that pay off only in the long run, such as planning, improving human relations, and co-ordinating activities with other departments.[23] The low-productivity supervisor is more likely to do the same

[23] Much of the most interesting work in this area has been done by the Institute for Social Research, University of Michigan. For summaries of this work, see Robert L. Kahn and Daniel Katz, "Leadership Practices in Relationship to Productivity and Morale," in Dorwin Cartwright and Alvin Zander, eds., *Group Dynamics, Research and Theory* (New York: Harper & Row, 1953), pp. 612-627; and Rensis Likert, *New Patterns of Management*, (New York: McGraw-Hill, 1961).

sort of work as his men, and to concentrate on paper work and short-term activities such as checking up on his subordinates or arranging for materials.

How can we explain these differences? In the first place, the close supervisor may seek to avoid the personal contacts required for effective leadership. He may feel more secure working with his hands or mind than trying to cope with human-relations problems. This is particularly true of the man who has come up through the ranks and to whom the supervisory position has been given as a reward for hard work, technical competence, and seniority rather than as a recognition of leadership abilities. Faced with an entirely new and confusing set of problems that he is ill-equipped to handle, he retreats to a behavior pattern in which he feels secure. The following account describes what happened to head nurses in a hospital—but it applies equally well to business situations:

> In some hospitals women were raised to positions of authority over nursing floors because they had worked there the longest and had proved to be excellent craftsmen. Sometimes they had no experience whatsoever in organizing the work of others. Such a person, since her field of competence lay in the art of nursing rather than in supervision, tended to do what she was best at, which was to give direct bedside care. She put off the other parts of her job, resenting the time spent on paper-work, supervision and teaching. Sometimes a head nurse would have so much pride in her command of nursing skills that she found great difficulty in accepting the less perfect work of subordinates. She would follow each student or auxiliary around, picking up where they left off and finishing the job for them. . . .
>
> Another type of retreat was that taken by the head nurse who centered all her attention on paper work. Sometimes this was an older woman who looked upon her promotion to this post as a graduation from hard labor, a kind of semi-retirement from the strains of bedside nursing.[24]

The very fact that the supervisor works alongside his men means that he must engage in close supervision. His presence provides a form of "pace-setting," and his men may well feel that his directions and example are a reflection of his belief that they cannot be left to do the job on their own.

True, it is difficult for a manager to avoid close supervision of this sort. Every supervisor feels a strong temptation to fix up a subordinate's mistakes himself rather than explain what should have been done.[25] Doing something oneself is usually easier than teaching. As a supervisor in an engineering laboratory put it:

> "Frankly, I've had a lot more experience than anyone in my section. Most of the time when I hand out a problem I can get the solution very easily. It requires superhuman control to let those guys take three times as long as I would to get the answer. But how else can they learn?"

The close supervisor either keeps nagging his subordinates, feeling that constant pressure is the best way to get results—or does the work himself and

---

[24] Burling, Lentz, and Wilson, *op. cit.*, pp. 113-114.

[25] For a discussion of some of the personality problems involved in obtaining effective delegation, see Chapter 18.

thus tries to avoid personal contacts.[26] The general supervisor, however, tries to provide explanations and motivate his employees to improve their performance. Instead of rushing in and taking the job into his own hands, he is patient enough to help a subordinate who has failed.

Concentration
on Long-Range Problems

There is a significant difference between the way the general supervisor and the close supervisor spend their time on their job. The close supervisor is a man who runs from crisis to crisis putting out fires. He is concerned exclusively with the here and now (or perhaps checking on the past). He has no time for anything but short, specific instructions. Often he dispenses even with these, and pitches in to do the job himself. The general supervisor, on the other hand, looks to the future. He spends more time on planning, working to improve relations with other departments, setting goals, and training subordinates so they can meet emergencies without coming to him. In a sense he is making a capital investment of his time from which he will derive gains in time saved over the long run.

When employees are well trained and when work is delegated, the supervisor has time to concentrate on the over-all problems of his department and to develop new, more permanent solutions rather than just to cope with each crisis as it comes along. For instance, how does the supervisor react when a severe problem suddenly arises that calls for several men to work overtime? Does he go to each man in the department to ask him whether he is willing to stay late? Or does he develop a method of getting people to indicate in advance when they want extra work? The time the supervisor saves by adopting the second approach can be used for many useful purposes, including the improvement of relations with his boss, with staff sections, and with other departments with which his own department has to cooperate.

A study at General Electric reported this observation:

> The least effective foremen spent the greatest percentage of their time finding immediate solutions to short-range production problems, while the most effective foremen spent the greatest percentage of their time on activities which involved planning and organizing the longer-range aspects of the job. The less effective foremen spent more time checking on work progress or status, securing materials, supervising materials or production movement, and similar activities which successful managers apparently delegate. Probably because of their greater emphasis on training employees, their belief in their abilities to carry out their assigned tasks without checking, and greater success in organizing the work of their groups, better foremen did not find it necessary to continuously check the conditions in their area.[27]

---

[26] The term "close supervision" may seem inappropriate when applied to the man who avoids personal contacts and shuns supervising. Yet when this individual does supervise, he is likely to supervise in detail.

[27] General Electric Company, Public and Employee Relations Service, *The Effective Manufacturing Foreman* (processed, 1957), p. 47; see also Quentin D. Ponder, "The Effec-

Here is a summary of the findings on how the two groups of GE foremen spent their time.[28]

	FOREMEN	
Activity	*Effective*	*Ineffective*
Production	20%	40%
Personnel administration	23	12
Equipment and methods	14	8
Quality	6	6

There were similar differences in the pattern of communication between supervisors and their work groups: [29]

	FOREMEN	
Type of Communication	*Effective*	*Ineffective*
Giving *specific* work orders	3%	15%
Giving *general* work orders	5	1
Passing information to the group or engaging in two-way discussions with members of the work group	67	47
Receiving information from workers	25	37

The study comes to this conclusion:

> When the more effective foremen found it necessary to give direction to the work of their employees, they would do so in a general way, giving explanations and suggestions, but leaving details of method and sequence up to the worker. The less effective foreman, on the other hand, gave a far greater number of direct work orders, without explaining why a job should be done, or how the specific order related to the over-all work pattern.[30]

General supervisors seek to develop an atmosphere in which workers feel free to bring their problems to them. In this atmosphere subordinates ask for help and information when it is needed, thus reducing the supervisor's need to give instructions. As one foreman told us:

> "As far as getting action is concerned, it doesn't make much difference whether you *tell* a man what to do or he *asks* you. But it makes all the difference in the world in how he feels. So I try to be available for questions instead of telling people."

The GE study found that effective foremen were aware of this difference: "The lower-rated foremen spent more time seeking information from others, while

---

tive Manufacturing Foreman," in *Proceedings of the Tenth Annual Meeting* (Madison: Industrial Relations Research Association, 1957), pp. 41-54. Findings roughly similar to the General Electric study are reported in Paul R. Lawrence, *The Changing of Organizational Behavior Patterns* (Boston: Harvard University, Graduate School of Business Administration, 1958), and in Emanuel Kay and Herbert M. Meyer, "The Development of a Job Activity Questionnaire for Production Foremen," *Personnel Psychology*, Vol. 15, No. 1.

[28] Ponder, *op. cit.*, p. 47. The percentages do not add up to 100 because a number of miscellaneous activities are omitted.

[29] *Ibid.*, p. 52.

[30] *Ibid.*, p. 52.

the higher-rated foremen spent more time answering requests for information." [31]

The General Electric study revealed that there was little difference in the *total* amount of time spent by the two types of supervisor with their subordinates, but that the effective supervisors had fewer and therefore longer contacts than ineffective supervisors. The short contact is sufficient for an abrupt order or a question; more time is required if there is to be a meaningful explanation or a two-way discussion. The very fact that the general supervisor permits his subordinates greater freedom means that fewer contacts are required.[32]

In addition, this study found that more effective supervisors spent a greater proportion of their time improving their relations with their bosses, staff sections, and other departments. Here is a summary of how these supervisors spent their time.[33]

| | FOREMEN | |
People Dealt With	Effective	Ineffective
Staff and Service People	32%	20%
Own Subordinates	19%	17%

This distribution is consistent with other findings that one of the most important functions of the supervisor is to represent his work group to other groups in the organization.

What picture of the general supervisor emerges from all these observations? The picture of a man who is abreast of his job, who gives his subordinates a broad range of freedom, and who is regarded by them as being available for help rather than being a source of pressure. In the studies cited, the supervisors who exhibited these characteristics were also the ones who had the most effective, productive subordinates.

Training

We have already mentioned that the manager who engages in general supervision places considerable emphasis on training his subordinates. Well-trained men have no need for detailed instruction. It has been said that the test of a good manager is what happens when he is away from his department. If his men have been trained well, everything goes so smoothly that he is hardly missed. Even where there is a formal training department in the organization, the most valuable training still comes from one's immediate boss, for

---

[31] *Ibid.*, p. 51.

[32] The average length of a supervisor's contact depends in part on the technology of the work he is supervising. Supervisors on an assembly line, for example, may well have shorter average contacts than maintenance supervisors. See Walker, Guest, and Turner, *op. cit.* We would hypothesize, however, that if technology is held constant, high-production supervisors in most cases will have fewer and longer contacts.

[33] Ponder, *op. cit.*, p. 50.

he is the one who provides the on-the-spot cues to what should or should not be done.

The close supervisor and the general supervisor adopt very different approaches to training. The close supervisor tends to equate training with the never-ending issuance of specific instructions; to him training and detailed supervision are identical. He has no interest in helping his subordinates learn so they can do without close supervision.

The general supervisor explains the *why* of his instructions; he gives his subordinates the theory, the over-all framework within which this particular instruction fits. Provided with this framework, subordinates can cope with unusual problems without having to run to their boss for new instructions every time a problem arises. Patient explanation and demonstration by the manager is frequently an essential first step.

But in many areas it is more effective if the trainee is given an opportunity to think out his problems by himself—under guidance. For instance, when giving a new assignment the manager should try to avoid saying, "I want you to do it this way." Instead he might ask, "Do you have any ideas how this should be done?" and then encourage the subordinate to work out the problems involved. Possibly the manager can listen to the subordinate as he thinks through the problems out loud. If the subordinate cannot arrive at a satisfactory solution on his own, of course, the manager offers suggestions. But he is careful to give the subordinate maximum opportunity (consistent with his ability) to figure things out by himself.

This approach to training is substantiated by two psychological principles: (1) Active learning is more effective than passive learning in bringing about a change in attitude and behavior. People learn more easily when they work out solutions for themselves than when they are provided with ready-made answers. (2) Learning is more effective when they see the results of their actions and can correct their own mistakes. In other words, "feedback" is an important element in learning.

WHEN DOES GENERAL SUPERVISION WORK BEST?

We have spent our time so far contrasting close and general supervision, but, with the exception of the GE study, we have said very little about what sort of supervision is most effective, principally because this is still a highly uncertain area. There has been a good deal of research in the area, but much of it is inconclusive and the most we can say is that there is no simple answer.[34] It does seem that a broad range of people (but not everyone) finds delegation

---

[34] One reason for caution in this area is that the relationship between cause and effect is rarely clear. A study may find that close supervisors have less efficient departments, but this does not prove that close supervision *causes* low efficiency. It may be that in departments where efficiency is low, close supervision is the most intelligent way of getting it back to normal.

satisfying. But this does not mean that delegation necessarily results in higher productivity. About all we can say is that the extent to which delegation will be effective varies with the circumstances. What are the circumstances? Here, the research data is very scanty and the best we can do is to offer some hypotheses only partly supported by evidence.[35]

It would seem that general supervision works best (1) where the work provides intrinsic job satisfaction; (2) where the work group accepts management's objectives; (3) where worker and union-management reactions are harmonious; (4) where consistency and coordination are relatively unimportant; (5) where technology permits individual discretion; (6) where subordinates desire responsibility; (7) in the long run rather than in the short run; and (8) where the pattern of supervision is consistent throughout the organization.

Where the Work Provides Intrinsic Job Satisfaction

There is some evidence that general supervision is most effective where the job is challenging, where the work cycle is long, and where there is an opportunity for intrinsic job satisfaction. In contrast, where there is little opportunity for creativity and internalized motivation, employees are less likely to perform effectively when left by themselves.[36] One study suggests that, compared to unskilled workers, skilled workers feel more involved in their jobs and are more anxious for an opportunity to participate in making decisions relating to it.[37] Another indicates a less positive relationship between general supervision and productivity on jobs where the work is machine-paced than on jobs where the men pace themselves.[38] Thus, in some cases, job enlargement may be a precondition for effective delegation.

General attitudes toward work are relevant here. Journeymen printers, for example, are very proud of their craft. They have internalized management's objectives of putting out high-quality work, and have a long tradition of self-regulation. With such a group anything but general supervision would be resented. On the other hand, relatively less benefit might be derived from general supervision in the textile industry, where workers generally have low aspirations, place little value in self-expression, display an "indifferent attitude toward the meaningfulness of work," [39] and do not have work as a central life interest.

---

[35] For an excellent discussion, see Harold Wilensky, "Human Relations in the Workplace," in Conrad Arensberg, and others, eds. *Research in Industrial Human Relations* (New York: Harper & Row, 1957), pp. 25-50.

[36] Nancy Morse, *Satisfactions in White Collar Jobs* (Ann Arbor: Survey Research Center, University of Michigan, 1953), p. 46.

[37] Howard Vollmer, *Employee Rights and the Employment Relationship* (Berkeley: University of California Press, 1960), Chap. 4.

[38] Michael Argyl, Godfrey Gardner, and Frank Cioffi, "Supervisory Methods Related to Productivity and Labor Turnover," *Human Relations*, Vol. 9, No. 1 (1958), p. 38.

[39] Blauner, *op. cit.*, p. 176.

The fact that a given job may offer *some* people intrinsic job satisfaction is not enough to motivate *everyone* to work hard at it. If a man does not feel his job offers challenge to *him*—if he does not value the skills the job requires—then delegation is not likely to lead to higher productivity.[40] One would imagine, for example, that musician who is working temporarily as a salesman would react less well to general supervision that would one who considers himself a career salesman.

Where the Work Group Accepts Management's Objectives

The general attitude of the work group towards management's objectives is also significant in determining whether delegation is realistic. If the group is indoctrinated to support these objectives, then a high degree of delegation may be feasible. But, as we shall discuss in Chapter 9, if the group does not support these objectives, then more autocratic techniques must be used to get the work done. A higher degree of delegation is possible in a hospital or a social agency, where presumably the organizational objectives are highly valued by the participants, than might be possible in a jail or concentration camp.[41]

Where Work and Union-Management Relations Are Harmonious

Obviously, general supervision is difficult to practice in the face of a militantly antimanagement union or where subordinates are bitterly divided on ethnic or other grounds. Similarly, it is hard to elicit cooperation in communities where there is a long tradition of hostility to management and where everything a "boss" does is automatically looked upon with suspicion.

Where Consistency and Coordination Are Unimportant

In many instances the nature of a job requires that subordinates follow a uniform pattern of behavior, for example, where the job permits outsiders to compare behavior among employees. Thus, in a firm that deals with hostile unions, responsibility for labor relations is far more likely to be centralized than is training (which is a purely internal matter). Similarly, internal revenue agents are checked closely by top management in the Treasury Department to insure that there is a common, nationwide policy toward interpreting the law.

The nature of internal work-flow is another important factor. More delegation is feasible where there is "parallel" specialization than where specialization

---

[40] Victor Vroom, "Ego Involvement, Job Satisfaction, and Job Performance," *Personnel Psychology*, Vol. 15, No. 2 (Summer 1962), pp. 159-178.

[41] Etzioni, *op. cit.*

is "interdependent." [42] Parallel specialization occurs where work activities are assigned so as to minimize the amount of coordination required, that is, where there is relatively little work-flow among individuals and departments. Interdependent specialization exists where the day-to-day functioning of the job of one individual or department is closely related to that of other individuals or departments. For example, in the programing of computers there may be a number of programers who each do part of the job. Since their respective activities must fit perfectly into one another, the manager must specify in great detail how each is to proceed.

An automobile assembly line, with its closely coordinated work flow, is a prime example of interdependent specialization, whereas a university represents parallel specialization. Indeed, academic freedom is possible largely because each professor can proceed on his own in research or class with only a minimum of coordination with others in the university.

Where the Technology Permits
Individual Discretion

Technology often limits the amount of discretion which subordinates can be given. Some equipment can be operated only in one way; once it is put in place employees have no choice but to follow the prescribed routines. In some work, mistakes can be so expensive that higher management feels obligated to check subordinates constantly.[43]

The need for decisive decision-making on many jobs leaves little room for delegation. The conductor of a symphony orchestra must exercise strong leadership and there is little opportunity for delegation or participation (a jazz combo on the other hand may practice considerable participation). Decisive decision-making is also required of a surgeon in the operating room, an aircraft pilot, and a ship's captain. In each of these cases subordinates are likely to get their satisfactions from the excellence of their performance as a team rather than from the opportunity to exercise discretion. As we shall discuss in Chapter 8, in these cases human-relations ability may well be subordinate, in the eyes of subordinates, to technical ability.

Technology also determines how managers might best interact with subordinates. A study of parcel delivery service indicated that drivers, who see their boss only for a few minutes each day, are more likely to prefer bosses with strong authoritarian attitudes, whereas positioners, men who handle parcels on the dock and who work in close contact with their boss all day

---

[42] Interdependence is related to what some organizational theorists call complementarity. See, for example, Jacob Marshak, "Efficient and Viable Organization Forms," in Mason Haire, ed., *Modern Organization Theory* (New York, Wiley, 1959), p. 317.

[43] For a study which suggests that continuous-process technology requires closer supervision than batch or unit technology, see Robert Dubin, "Supervision and Productivity: Empirical Findings and Theoretical Considerations," in Robert Dubin and others, *Leadership and Productivity* (San Francisco: Chandler, 1965).

long, prefer those who are not authoritarian. Since drivers spend only a short time with their boss, apparently they prefer someone who is decisive.[44]

Where Subordinates Desire Responsibility

There are substantial differences in the amount of responsibility people are willing to accept on the job.[45] One person may flourish under supervision that another might find extremely restrictive. One of the authors learned this lesson the hard way when he was working in a government agency some years ago and was assigned an elderly secretary. Imbued with the principles of good human relations, he explained in detail the background of every letter he dictated, asked for her comments on style, and even suggested that, if she wished, she could draft some of the letters herself. At last she burst out. "I'm not paid to do that kind of work! That's your job."

Psychological research provides evidence that the nature of a person's personality affects his attitude toward supervision. There are some employees with a low need for achievement and high fear of failure who shy away from challenges and responsibilities.[46] Many seek self-expression off the job and ask only to be allowed to daydream on it. (For example, women who look upon their job as only a brief interlude before marriage may have relatively little desire for autonomy.) [47] One study, for example, suggests that people who have a high need for independence and weak authoritarian attitudes are likely to respond to consultation with their supervisors by being more satisfied with their work and turning out a better performance; those with low needs for independence and strong authoritarian values are much less likely to respond in this manner.[48] In addition, there are many who have become so accustomed to the authoritarian approach in their culture, family, and previous work experience that they regard general supervision as no supervision at all. They abuse the privileges it bestows on them and refuse to accept the responsibilities it demands.

Consider the case of two hospital floors supervised by two very different head nurses.[49] The first head nurse (Miss Smith), though extremely courteous, was strict and uncompromising with nurses who violated regulations. She

---

[44] Victor Vroom and Floyd C. Mann, "Leader Authoritarianism and Employee Attitudes," *Personnel Psychology*, Vol. 13, No. 2 (Summer 1960), pp. 125-140.

[45] People may also differ in the areas in which they wish responsibility. Some individuals may accept a great amount in their home life and in community organizations, yet not wish much on the job.

[46] For a study which suggests that there are substantially different needs for achievement among various classes, cultures, and ethnic groups, see D. C. McClelland, *The Achieving Society* (Princeton: Van Nostrand, 1961).

[47] Howard Vollmer, "Supervising Women is Different," *Personnel Journal*, Vol. 34, No. 7 (December 1955), pp. 261-263.

[48] Victor H. Vroom, *Some Personality Determinants of the Effects of Participation* (Englewood Cliffs, N.J.: Prentice-Hall, 1960).

[49] This case is based on the research of Dr. Edith Hamilton.

insisted that conversations be kept to a minimum and handed out detailed, unambiguous work assignments to her nurses.

The second head nurse (Miss Rogers) had a much more informal, almost kidding relationship with her subordinates and patients. She consulted with her nurses about problems and changes, and succeeded in developing a strong feeling of camaraderie on the floor.

Now you might suppose that all the nurses would have preferred Miss Rogers' floor to Miss Smith's—but they didn't. The hospital let nurses choose which floor they wanted to work on; both floors were quite popular, but with different groups of nurses. In general the older women liked the security of Miss Smith's floor, where everything went according to predetermined routine. As one older nurse put it:

> "I honestly feel I need a responsible person nearby to supervise me. I need guidance and therefore I prefer to work where there is fairly close supervision. . . . I like to do things in an orderly way. . . . (on Miss Rogers' floor) things are done too sloppily."

Most of the younger girls preferred the independence allowed them by Miss Rogers.

Why these differences? For one thing, nurses' training in recent years has become less strict than it once was, and the younger nurses have never experienced close supervision. More important, these differences may reflect an attitude toward authority that the younger girls developed in their formative years at home and at school, an attitude influenced by the wide range of freedom permitted to modern children. Indeed, subordinates' feelings toward their boss are often colored by the relations they had with their parents and the emotional maturity and security they developed as children.

Different groups develop different attitudes toward work. College graduates, for example, expect a great deal of responsibility and freedom. Certain ethnic groups, on the other hand, have trouble accepting the concept that people should make decisions for themselves, particularly decisions concerning work.[50] Some Indian tribes are brought up in a cultural tradition which teaches one not to take the initiative. "In their passivity, restraint and expectation of immediate results . . . there is scant evidence that the average adolescent, once he leaves [the reservation] will acquire the inner ambition that helps to produce a high standard of living."[51]

Americans have often run into trouble trying to apply general supervision abroad. Peasants from Latin countries who have worked for years under the control of *patrons* may find a sudden dose of independence extremely un-

---

[50] For examples from various countries see Heinz Hartmann, *Authority and Organization in German Management* (Princeton: Princeton University Press, 1959); James Abegglen, *The Japanese Factory* (New York: The Free Press of Glencoe, 1958); and Frederick Harbison and Eugene Burgess, "Modern Management in Western Europe," *American Journal of Sociology*, Vol. 60, No. 1 (July 1954), pp. 15-23.

[51] Frank C. Miller and D. Douglas Caulkins, "Chippewa Adolescents: A Changing Generation," *Human Organization*, Vol. 23, No. 2 (Summer 1964), p. 159.

settling. Since the employees are not prepared for this kind of treatment, they think something is wrong with a boss who doesn't act like a boss.

A recent study compared a group of "Town" workers in rural or small-town surroundings with a group of "City" workers (mostly with Italian and French-Canadian backgrounds).[52] The Town workers tended to react positively to work requiring greater skill and the acceptance of greater responsibility. The City workers, on the other hand, preferred simpler, less challenging tasks. This surprising contrast is hard to explain. It does seem that work and achievement (the so-called Protestant ethic) are more central to the life interests of those with a rural background than they are to those from certain ethnic groups in the city. Certainly those brought up on a farm are introduced to chores (now a rarity in city families) at an early age. For them work and discipline are easily taken in stride. The City workers, on the other hand, seem to value more highly social satisfaction on and off the job.[53]

In the Long Run
Rather Than the Short Run

Even under close supervision a work group may be highly productive, particularly in times of widespread unemployment when men are fearful of losing their jobs. In fact, management has often found that the best way to get an immediate increase in production is to increase pressure and to impose close supervision. In the long run, however, close supervision may well lead to a deterioration of morale and productivity and to what one author calls "a liquidation of human assets." [54]

> One experiment involved four divisions of a large company, each of which had about 100 clerical employees.[55] In two of these divisions managers and supervisors were trained in the principles of general supervision. In the other two divisions management cut the number of employees by 25 per cent without reducing the work load and systematically intensified the pressure and closeness of supervision. By the end of twelve months both groups had increased productivity. But the closely supervised group had increased theirs by 25 per cent compared with a 20 per cent increase for the group under general supervision. The employees under general supervision, however, showed significant improvements in measures showing loyalty, feeling of responsibility, and involvement in work. In the other group these same indices declined dramatically.

[52] Arthur N. Turner and Paul R. Lawrence, *Industrial Jobs and the Worker* (Boston: Harvard University, Graduate School of Business Administration, 1965).

[53] The evidence so far is slim, but see for example B. C. Rosen, "Race, Ethnicity, and the Achievement Syndrome," *American Sociological Review*, Vol. 24, No. 1 (Feb. 1959), pp. 47-61; Melville Dalton, "The Industrial Rate Buster: A Characterization," *Applied Anthropology*, Vol. 7, No. 1 (Winter 1948), pp. 5-18.

[54] Rensis Likert, "Measuring Organizational Performance," *Harvard Business Review*, Vol. 16, No. 2 (March-April 1958), pp. 41-50. See also Nancy Morse and Everett Reimer, "The Experimental Change of a Major Organizational Variable," *Journal of Abnormal and Social Psychology*, Vol. 52, No. 1 (January 1956), pp. 120-129.

[55] *Ibid.*

Of course, lowered morale need not lead to a decline in production. But increased pressure may well result in resistance on the part of individuals, informal work groups, and the union; in restriction of output; and in all the familiar symptoms of aggression that we discussed earlier. Under these circumstances management is often tempted to enter into the vicious cycle of closer and closer supervision, to which the employees reply by sabotage, wildcat strikes and ever-tightening output restrictions.

On the other hand, the sudden introduction of general supervision is unlikely to lead to an immediate increase in production where the individuals involved have become accustomed to close supervision. If, because of their previous experience, workers expect to be pushed into work, chances are that they will abuse any relaxation of pressure unless the process is handled with great skill. They may look upon the manager who tries to apply general supervision as weak and flabby.[56] At times the manager who is being trained to use general supervision is regarded by his subordinates as threatening because his behavior is unpredictable. Employees sometimes find it easier to work for a hard-bitten so-and-so whose behavior is more predictable than one who seems to be changing his behavior every day.

Where the Pattern of Supervision
Is Consistent Throughout the Organization

The *over-all pattern* of supervision is more important than any one aspect of it. There is a danger that managers may adopt certain features of general supervision and disregard others. A manager who delegates authority but neglects to train his subordinates to exercise it intelligently may well have worse results than the manager who retains all authority for himself.

More important than any particular manager's style of leadership is the general pattern of human relations that prevails in the organization. It is very difficult for a supervisor to practice general supervision if his boss and his fellow managers all practice and expect close supervision, particularly if the boss fails to back him up and show tolerance for his mistakes.

CONCLUSION

General supervision is an approach to management which is based on delegation to subordinates of wide authority to make decisions. It assumes that people will work harder if they are given freedom to make their decisions, and it relies on internalized motivation, the satisfactions people get from being free to do a good job more or less in their own way.

---

[56] For an excellent discussion of some of the problems involved in introducing general supervision into an organization, see Lawrence, *op. cit.* The point made above is discussed on pp. 196-197.

Delegation is rarely absolute. Delegation is possible only under conditions when management can be reasonably sure that subordinates will behave in a relatively satisfactory fashion and, if they make mistakes, that these will not be too dangerous to the organization. To insure that subordinates do behave adequately, management must provide some sort of guidance. Rules, goals, indoctrination, and even the requirements of technology tend to provide such guidance.

There is a good deal of research which suggests that general supervision results in higher productivity. As we have indicated, this is not always true. The feasibility of delegation depends on a number of factors: the nature of the work, individual personality and background, over-all management practices, employee acceptance of management goals, union-management relationships, and the organization's needs for coordination and consistency. Unless these factors are favorable to delegation, delegation may not increase motivation substantially. Even if it does, the cost to the organization in terms of impaired coordination, and so forth, may be greater than the gains in terms of motivation.

Clearly, there is no one best method of supervision applicable to all situations.[57] There are a number of means of delegations, some of which are applicable to routine work, for example, and others of which work best where a high degree of initiative is required. Only in rare instances is delegation enough in itself. Even the general supervisor must exercise authority. The problems this involves will be discussed in the next chapter.

[57] See, for example, Warren G. Bennis, "Leadership Authority and Administrative Behavior," *Administrative Science Quarterly*, Vol. 4, No. 3 (December 1959), pp. 259-301. Also, Robert Tannenbaum and Warren Schmidt, "How to Choose a Leadership Pattern," *Harvard Business Review*, Vol. 36, No. 2 (March 1958).

The Exercise of Authority

The manager must make many decisions on his own. He must do so when he sets the rules and goals previously discussed. And if the rules are violated or the goals unmet, it is the manager who must somehow restrain or reprimand the subordinates responsible for falling short. In some cases, subordinates may not be competent to make decisions because of lack of information, training, or understanding of over-all organizational needs. In other cases, as we have seen, subordinates may not be motivated to make the proper sorts of decisions or to exercise freedom in a manner consistent with organizational objectives. Often the manager must arbitrate disputes among subordinates.

In all the above situations the manager must exercise authority. But being given the right to do so doesn't mean that he will be effective. To get subordinates to respond to his authority requires that the manager both skillfully handle his relations with subordinates *and* establish himself as a legitimate source of authority. These are two separate considerations. The manager must have effective day-to-day relations, but more than this is required. Based on previous experiences, subordinates have developed perceptions of what leadership should be like. They expect that anyone to whom they give their allegiance will have characteristics and behave in a fashion consistent with this image.

Thus, this chapter will approach the exercise of authority from two points of view. First, we shall look at the day-to-day relations or interaction patterns between bosses and subordinates. Second, considering the problem from a longer-run point of view, we shall examine the conditions under which subordinates will view the manager's exercise of authority as legitimate.

DEVELOPING EFFECTIVE RELATIONS

Subordinates can hardly be expected to forget that their boss (or someone at a higher level of management) has the power to discharge them or withhold benefits and promotions. Regardless of how effectively the relationship between subordinates and superior is cloaked in democratic procedure, no one forgets for a moment that there are very real differences in power between them. In every work situation, problems of reward and discipline inevitably arise, and these problems often lead to frustration and bad feeling. One of the manager's goals should be to minimize this frustration and to try to create conditions in which people will accept authority with the maximum of enthusiasm and the minimum of resentment.

Ambivalence toward Authority

The manager's job is always complicated by the fact that people feel a certain ambivalence toward authority. In Chapter 1 we talked about egoistic and social needs, or independent and dependent needs. Among the many independent ones we listed was the need for a sense of accomplishment, autonomy, and skill. To illustrate dependent needs we mentioned the need for praise, fair treatment, and approval.

As Eric Fromm has suggested, most of us have complicated, mixed feelings toward independence and dependence. We value freedom but sometimes feel lost and anchorless when we have too much. We like protection but we don't like interference.

If management fails to provide enough independence on the job, employees will exercise independence on their own by resorting to absenteeism, union activity, slowdowns, and the like. On the other hand, employees find it difficult to adjust to too much independence, for no one can stand completely by himself. Most of us like to be assured that we are doing the right thing and that we will receive help when we are in trouble. On occasion we even like to have people make tough decisions for us.

To put it another way: People are generally willing to tolerate, and may even be anxious for, a few areas of their life which are unpredictable and exciting, but they insist that most events occur as expected. A research scientist, for example, may relish the novelty and uncertainty of laboratory work, but he insists that his secretary be always on call, that his technician give predictable responses, and that his car start with complete regularity.

The policy of "be strong," under which employees know that they are expected to do exactly what they are told, minimizes the sense of independence. The policy of "be good" fosters dependence, for it regards the ideal employee as the "loyal worker" who follows instructions to the letter without a thought of his own. Delegation, on the other hand, helps satisfy the need for independence that is present to some extent in everyone. Even so, some accommodation must be made to the people who require the security and assurance of knowing that someone is interested in them, and to others who must be restrained lest they abuse their freedom.[1]

Working in a large-scale organization requires that every subordinate be

---

[1] For a strong statement of this view, see Robert N. McMurry, "The Case for Benevolent Autocracy," *Harvard Business Review,* Vol. 36, No. 1 (January 1958), pp. 82-90.

to some degree dependent on the organization generally and on his supervisor in particular; individual independence must be sharply restricted.

We shall now consider some of the ways in which the manager can exercise authority effectively, but without being unduly restrictive. The kind of personal relations he develops, the way he gives orders, his fairness in handling problems, and his manner in handling mistakes—all have a significant impact on subordinates' attitudes toward authority.

PERSONAL RELATIONSHIPS

The personal, man-to-man relationships between a boss and his subordinates have a lot to do with the way subordinates view their jobs. Since employees are dependent on their boss, it is all-important for them to feel that he approves of both their work and themselves as individuals. A feeling of approval is an adult version of the child's feeling that his parents love him. It is the assurance that "though the supervisor may chastise me for my mistakes, he values me as an individual. He is not out to get me. He is out to help me."

Creating a Feeling of Approval

The supervisor can foster a feeling of his approval of subordinates in many different ways: taking an active interest in subordinates, listening to their problems, giving praise when justified, showing tolerance when mistakes are made, and so forth. Notice that we say *feeling* of approval. We are talking about the over-all supervisory pattern rather than about any one specific act. In fact, the existence of such a feeling helps determine how individual acts are interpreted. *If* such a feeling exists, employees may tend to excuse their boss's mistakes; if it does *not* exist, they may exaggerate his mistakes out of all proportion. For instance, in the absence of a feeling of approval, a boss's attempt to show interest in his employees may be seen as meddling.

> When the supervisor is interested in the welfare of his subordinates and is accepted by them as a member of their "team," then his close attention to what his subordinates are doing is welcomed by them. When the supervisor is around and showing interest in what they are doing, subordinates may be eager to please him and win his approval. On the other hand, when the supervisor is held by subordinates as indifferent to their welfare, or even as a hostile outsider, then his close supervision will probably meet with apathy and resentment.[2]

Thus, the over-all pattern of the supervisor's behavior is infinitely more important than any specific gesture. Take kindness and courtesy as an example. Obviously, saying "please" and "do you mind" is important, but employees soon see through superficial gestures if they conflict with the rest of the supervisor's behavior. In some situations cusswords are better evidence than

---

[2] Martin Patchen, "Supervisory Methods and Group Performance Norms," *Administrative Science Quarterly*, Vol. 7, No. 3 (December 1962), p. 290.

icy courtesy that the boss likes you. Although most human beings like approbation, they are suspicious of indiscriminate praise.[3] Further, praise for good work is not enough. People have bad days as well as good; a real feeling of approval assures the individual that his boss will show tolerance for an occasional mistake.

In short, the existence of a feeling of approval means that the supervisor has demonstrated a personal loyalty to his subordinates. Until he has done so, he cannot expect loyalty to flow the other way.

Note, though, that approval means different things to different people.

> We once interviewed two lacquer-mixers who worked pretty much by themselves at opposite ends of a long factory floor. They did the same job and were under the same foreman (who said both did a good job). The first mixer said: "I've got a good boss. He knows I know the job so he leaves me alone, he never bothers me." The second mixer said: "My foreman doesn't care whether I'm dead or alive. He's a bum foreman who doesn't show any interest in his men or how they are doing."

Obviously, these two men looked upon supervision very differently. The first saw supervision as restrictive, to be avoided if possible. The second expected help and reassurance from his boss. Both men were anxious to win approval and acceptance, but what came through clearly as acceptance to one man seemed outright rejection to the other. The manager must be alert to these subtle differences in the manner in which his behavior—however well intentioned—is interpreted; he should try to adjust his behavior pattern to his subordinates' individual personality needs.

Developing Personal Relations

A feeling of approval is more likely to result if the boss shows personal interest in his subordinates. Consequently, an effective manager "makes" time to get to know his subordinates and to help them with their problems both on and (to a limited extent) off the job.

Need for personal relations. People like being treated as individuals. Yet, as far as the typical company is concerned, the average employee is nothing more than a time-card number or a job specification. The company is impersonal; only the immediate boss can make management personal. Particularly to a new employee, the immediate supervisor *is* the company, and what he does helps mold the individual's conception of the company as a whole. An insensitive manager can easily counterbalance all the company's efforts to create a good impression through public relations and fringe benefits.

Home problems affect efficiency on the job. So a good manager listens to his employees' problems, and in some areas actually offers assistance. Ordinarily,

---

[3] Praise given in public may give rise to charges of favoritism—and those who are not praised may feel that the supervisor is resorting to an undercover form of criticism against which they cannot defend themselves.

all he can do is listen, but even this interest provides some relief to an individual in distress. In any case, the more the manager learns about the people who work for him, the better he can understand their behavior and how to deal with it. (Of course, the manager should not seem to pry or meddle, as we shall discuss in Chapter 11.)

Even more important, good informal relations on matters that are not directly related to the job set the stage for better communication between manager and subordinate on problems related to work. Any social barrier will create a communications barrier. An employee rarely feels completely free and easy when talking with the boss about the work in hand, for he is quite aware that the boss is the one who hands out rewards and punishments. But when they talk about the employee's fishing trip, the employee is an *expert* for the time being, even if there is no true feeling of equality between them. Some of the air of permissiveness and informality created in discussing baseball or the weather may carry over to on-the-job affairs. Once the manager and the subordinate know each other as individuals, both will feel freer to bring up mutual problems.

To put it another way: As we said earlier, the good manager tries to reduce the number of orders he gives by encouraging people to ask him questions rather than by telling them what to do. For this approach to succeed, however, the subordinates must feel confident and secure enough to go to their boss when difficulties arise.

Setting the tone. Obviously, it is the superior who sets the tone of the relationship, not the subordinate. First, the manager must make himself available to all comers. The boss who barricades himself behind a wall of formality or is always "busy, busy, busy" is not likely to develop satisfactory informal relationships. Nor is it enough to be a good fellow a few times a year. In most companies the permissive atmosphere of the annual Christmas party stands out in sharp contrast to the distant relationship that is normal for the rest of the year.

The manager must take the initiative by maintaining regular and frequent contacts with subordinates. Some managers make periodic "howdy rounds," talking to each employee in turn. Even if these encounters consist only of idle chatter, still they provide an opportunity for employees to bring up problems that are bothering them. In other words, the manager opens up the contact and lets the subordinate decide what topics should be covered.

Certain very real dangers are likely to arise when the manager develops excessively close personal relations with his subordinates, particularly in circumstances where he must rely on close rather than general supervision. There are situations where a manager is forced to rely largely on formal authority to maintain discipline. Then he can hardly afford to be a "good guy." As we shall discuss later in this chapter, one reason for the carefully maintained social barrier in the armed forces is that officers do not want their men to question decisions or initiate action.

In any case, there is more to being a good boss than being a nice fellow. Although many employees respond favorably to the "glad-hand" approach, most are suspicious of insincerity. After all, the manager must develop a *long-term* relationship, and over a period of time it is easy for subordinates to detect whether his apparent interest is sincere. It is better for an introvert to be naturally reserved than artificially friendly. In today's cynical world, people are highly suspicious of overfriendliness: They are constantly afraid of being manipulated. They easily see through what has been variously called "false personalism" or a "skin-deep relationship." Unless the manager combines good informal personal relations with good job-oriented relations, he will be judged a hypocrite: "He'll try to butter you up. But watch out, he'll stab you in the back."

JOB-ORIENTED RELATIONS

Some early studies of managerial behavior contrasted "job-centered" with "employee-centered" supervision. The job-centered manager is interested almost exclusively in getting his job done; the employee-centered mangager is interested chiefly in satisfying the needs of his subordinates. In the terms used in some studies, the job-centered manager is high in what was called "initiating structure" (running the job), whereas the employee-centered manager is more concerned with "consideration." Regardless of what terms were used, it was believed that these two qualities are on opposite ends of a continuum. Later research suggests that these characteristics are not mutually inconsistent.[4] An effective manager is interested both in his employees as individuals and in the work they do. An interest in one does not preclude an interest in the other. A good manager, then, has effective job-oriented relations with his subordinates.

In one sense, this entire volume is concerned with job-oriented relations. At this point we wish to stress that, where feasible in directing the job, an effective manager will keep open the lines of communications with his subordinates, both upward and downward. He will provide them with information, consult with them, and listen to their suggestions. Let us consider each of these points in turn, although we have already seen something of the over-all pattern in our discussion of the General Electric study in the previous chapter.

Providing Information

Few of us are content to be at the mercy of forces we do not understand. We all tend to feel insecure in poorly defined situations. Research indicates that high-production supervisors tend to give their subordinates as much information as possible about what is expected on the job and what is likely to happen to them in the future. This information helps the subordinate do

---

[4] For a good discussion of this point, see Robert L. Kahn, "Productivity and Job Satisfaction," *Personnel Psychology*, Vol. 13, No. 3 (Fall 1960), pp. 275-287.

better work by enabling him to make wiser decisions; moreover, it heightens his sense of security.

Understandably, employees are keenly interested in knowing what they are required to do on the job. For some, this need is satisfied only when they receive explicit direction in every aspect of their work. You will remember the nurse who said, "I need guidance and therefore I prefer to work with a fairly strict supervisor."

> The older girls on Miss Rogers' floor complained because they did not receive enough detailed instructions; the younger girls on Miss Smith's floor felt insecure because Miss Smith failed to provide enough information for them to make decisions on their own, and had a habit of issuing unexpected and seemingly arbitrary orders.

Even those who value the freedom to make decisions themselves feel more self-confident in a well-structured situation. When they are given an order, they want some explanation of what is to be done, why it is to be done, and what limits will be set on their freedom—as well as any background information necessary to help them do a better job or to satisfy their natural curiosity. They prefer that the boss be easily available to answer questions or to provide assistance when asked.

The subordinate is especially curious to know *where he stands with his boss.* For white-collar workers in particular, "getting ahead" is of paramount importance. The subordinate constantly asks himself, "How am I doing?" and tries to divine from the boss's tone of voice or facial expression whether his performance is finding favor. The subordinate is directly dependent on his boss, he wants to please him, and he wants some sort of feedback or evaluation to indicate how his efforts are being received.

Finally, employees are keenly interested in knowing about anything that will have an effect on their future prospects or their work. "What's the production level likely to be next week?" "Has the supply room received the forms I need?" "Are the rumors true that this department will be automated?" "How will this affect me?" "How bad are the squawks down the line about the bum job I did yesterday?" To the employee who is deprived of this sort of information, the future seems uncertain and sinister.

Consulting with Subordinates

The way a manager issues an order influences the way it is received. With routine orders there is usually little trouble. But before a manager issues an order that will have a major impact on his subordinates, or an order that they are likely to resist, it is better for him to discuss it with them than to impose it unilaterally with no opportunity for questions or objections. Even if the manager may wish to make the final decision himself, he may wish to increase the subordinate's sense of involvement through permitting him to influence the final decision.

The wise supervisor explains such "critical" orders orally at first, though later he may put them in writing for permanent reference. To be sure, it may take more time to issue instructions orally than in writing. Yet, as we will see in Chapter 10, voice communication is often more effective than the written word. It permits the supervisor, if necessary, to present a detailed explanation of what he wants and why he wants it—and in a way that is tailor-made to the needs of the individual subordinate.

The effective supervisor also permits the subordinate to comment and to ask questions (at least within the limits set by other demands on the supervisor's time). This gives him a chance to judge how the subordinate is reacting to the proposed order and enables him to answer objections, explain points that are not clearly understood, or make arrangements for exceptional circumstances that may require special procedures. Moreover, the subordinate may come up with suggestions that will make the proposed order more workable—or he may object so strenuously that the supervisor will decide to withdraw the order altogether.

Doesn't the supervisor lose respect when he modifies or withdraws an order in face of his subordinate's objections? Yes—if his original instructions were stated in terms of "this is what I order you to do." No—if he has said, "I have been thinking about this and would like your reaction." There is a gain even if the supervisor eventually decides that he must impose an order over his subordinate's objections, for at least the subordinate has had a chance to be heard and to let off steam.

Finally, a subordinate is more likely to carry out an order if he has specifically agreed to do so, for he is then committed to take some action. If the supervisor closes the discussion with the question, "Are you willing to give it a try?" he is likely to get assent. Even though this assent may be enforced, there has been an explicit agreement to go along. Suppose the subordinate refuses to assent? In most instances it is better to bring the resistance out in the open at the outset than to assume that the order will be carried out when in fact it will be sabotaged.

Listening to Suggestions

Although there are many areas in which the manager cannot give his subordinates freedom to make decisions by themselves, he can encourage them to make suggestions. This practice provides the manager with many useful ideas and a more accurate feeling for what his subordinates are thinking. It provides subordinates with an opportunity to express themselves and to feel that they have made a valuable contribution to the operation of their organization.

The manager should not only listen to the suggestions that are brought to him; he should actively seek them out. There are many areas in which the manager doesn't have all the facts that he needs to make important decisions. Or perhaps he feels perfectly confident that he can make a good decision, but has some doubts about whether his subordinates will accept it. Under such circumstances it may pay for him to ask for suggestions. This approach will certainly result in better acceptance of the decision, and it may improve its quality as well. There is no obligation for the manager to accept all the ideas presented, so long as he considers them seriously. If he rejects all suggestions out of hand, however, his subordinates will soon see through his pretense.

Many of the suggestions made by subordinates are remarkably valuable. Understandably, the man who works close to a job day after day often knows more about it than his boss.

People derive great satisfaction from knowing that their suggestions are being considered and even more if they are actually put into use. Everyone is enthusiastic about implementing his own ideas.

But what happens when management is obliged to reject a suggestion? Even here the suggestion has served a purpose. First, the subordinate did have a chance to express himself and to be heard. Second, by explaining why the suggestion was rejected, the supervisor can improve the subordinate's understanding of the problem and perhaps stimulate him to produce better suggestions in the future.

FAIR TREATMENT

Since subordinates are directly dependent on their bosses, they are understandably anxious to receive fair treatment from them. "The highest praise a worker can give his foreman is to say 'he's fair.'"[5] The boss can demonstrate his sense of fair play by letting each employee know exactly what is required of him, and by exercising consistent discipline. He can base his decisions on grounds that are accepted as legitimate by his subordinates, he can provide an appeals procedure (see Chapter 15), and, above all, he can make an all-out effort to treat them equally, so that the rewards he dispenses seem proportional to their contributions.[6]

"Treating people equally" is not as simple as it sounds. The conscientious manager is torn between two conflicting, though universally accepted, platitudes: "Avoid favoritism" and "Treat people as individuals, in accordance with their special needs." He can never forget that each individual has special needs, but at the same time he must realize that what appears to be inconsistent treatment will create endless bad feeling within the group.

With all the good will in the world, the manager may begin to play favorites unconsciously and to follow the normal tendency of either favoring the passive, dependent, "good" employee or paying the most attention to the aggressive individual who fights for his demands, to "oil the wheel that squeaks the loudest." The manager must avoid both extremes.

---

[5] George Homans, "Effort, Supervision and Productivity" in Robert Dubin, *et al., Leadership and Productivity* (San Francisco: Chandler, 1965), p. 65.

[6] George Homans calls this meeting the requirements of "distributive justice." See his *Social Behavior: Its Elementary Forms* (New York: Harcourt, Brace & World, 1962).

The manager should be careful to bestow favors only when the employee needs them. If, for instance, the boss decides to lend a hand at a time when the subordinate feels he is doing his job adequately, the subordinate may either look upon his help as meddling or accept it as the normal thing and complain when he doesn't get it.

Making exceptions. What about making exceptions in special situations? Obviously, treating people fairly does not mean treating everyone in exactly the same way. It does mean that when an exception is made, it must be accepted as legitimate by all members of the group. There is a general rule, for example, that vacations must be taken during the summer months. Bill Lawrence's wife is sick, so the boss lets him have February off to take her to Florida. Is this favoritism? Only if Bill Lawrence's fellow employees think so. An exception of this sort will be accepted as fair if the group (1) knows why it was made, (2) accepts it as justified, and (3) is confident that another employee in the same situation would receive the same treatment.

Granting special favors when the circumstances permit not only lessens a subordinate's feeling that the organization is arbitrary and "heartless"; but it may also lead to an "exchange of good turns." As a worker in an assembly plant described it: [7]

> "My foreman knows the traits of human nature and acts accordingly.... He came in one morning and it was bitterly cold. He went out to the cafeteria and bought two big cans of hot coffee and gave it to the men. While we can't be bought the thought was there and we appreciated it. As a result the men picked up lots of jobs that ordinarily they would have let go through to be picked up by the repair man."

The assumption behind this approach is that if the manager does more for his men than is absolutely required, they will respond in kind. It means, for instance, that if Jack comes to work with a sprained ankle, the foreman will find him some work that he can do sitting down; if a waitress is suddenly deluged with customers, the hostess will relieve some of the pressure by setting up tables and pouring water. The hope is that when an emergency arises the subordinates will reciprocate by doing more than is normally required, by working overtime or by producing more than the usual "bogey." Thus, an atmosphere is created in which both supervisor and subordinate exhibit a flexible attitude toward their mutual obligations.

HANDLING MISTAKES

In the previous chapter we suggested that managers should set realistic goals for their subordinates, train them to do the best job they are capable of

---

[7] Arthur N. Turner, "Foreman—Key to Worker Morale," *Harvard Business Review*, Vol. 35, No. 5 (September 1956), p. 77.

doing, and then give them a wide margin of freedom. But this does not mean that management should sit idly by when employees violate rules, turn out sloppy work, or fail to do their job. Quite the contrary. Not only is such laxity bad for production (after all, the company exists to make a profit); it is also unfair to the conscientious worker who carries out his assignments effectively, and it even serves to encourage the "culprit" in his bad work habits.

The manager cannot ignore mistakes. But the manner in which he handles them may determine whether his subordinates will resent his use of authority or will come to look upon him as a source of help.

Blame or Help?

Research studies reveal that the difference between high-production and low-production managers lies not in their interest in eliminating mistakes, but in their *manner* of handling mistakes. Note the difference between these two comments: [8]

> "My boss thinks that whenever anything goes wrong it's always my fault. . . . He never says what he can do to help you, but he always picks your job apart. He tries hard, but he is too ready to condemn rather than help."

> "My boss is the best man I have ever worked for. He finds out what's troubling you before he tells you what to do, and he'll ask why. . . . Other supervisors come down here and start yelling at you before they find out what's wrong. But not him."

When something goes wrong, the low-production manager is interested above all in fixing blame and bawling out the person responsible. ("Well, what sort of excuse do you have?") He has a tendency to look to the past, to "cry over spilt milk," and to assume that all negligence is deliberate. What is the effect of such an approach? The subordinate denies responsibility, tries to pass the buck to someone else, or at least to find some sort of excuse to show that he really wasn't at fault. This approach encourages the "stool pigeon" and tends to make the development of harmonious groups almost impossible. If the group *does* succeed in working together in such an atmosphere, it directs its efforts *against* the manager.

The policy of blame-placing often defeats its own purpose: It makes employees so tense and insecure that they make even more mistakes. And it motivates them to cover up errors and spend their time trying to avoid *looking* wrong. As a result, upward communications is impaired and higher management can never get a clear picture of what is really happening below. A kind of game develops: In an effort to uncover the deceptions of subordinates, higher management sets up inspection systems and elaborate control reports, while the subordinates become increasingly adept at hiding mistakes.

In contrast, high-production managers tend to look forward, rather than

---

[8] Charles R. Walker, Robert H. Guest, and Arthur N. Turner, *The Foreman on the Assembly Line* (Cambridge: Harvard University Press, 1956), p. 45.

backward. They are interested in discovering what happened, why it happened, and what can be learned rather than in fixing responsibility. They look upon mistakes as an opportunity to provide training.[9]

Mistakes as a means of learning.   If the manager insists that subordinates must never make a mistake, he is also insuring that they will never assume any real responsibility. Not that the subordinate should be encouraged to make mistakes. Far from it. But if he feels that one mistake is disastrous, he will be completely inhibited from taking any responsibility or initiative. The boss who feels that every mistake is a calamity must abandon all hope of improving the performance of his subordinates.

Actually, doing something wrong is often the most effective way of learning to do it right. Getting "burned" a few times may be the only way for us to learn that some of our pet ideas really won't work. In effect, a subordinate should have freedom to fail. A superior should weigh very carefully the cost of a mistake against the value of having the subordinate learn both (1) that he has the freedom to act on his own, even to make mistakes, and (2) that the particular way he has chosen was wrong. Overprotection by the superior means underdevelopment by the subordinate.

In effect, when mistakes are overpunished by severe criticism, people learn not just to avoid *specific* behavior, but to avoid *any* situation where a mistake is possible. When a subordinate has taken the initiative and his action has turned out badly, the supervisor can buttress his sense of independence by saying, "You made some mistakes in handling this, but I am glad you were willing to experiment and to take responsibility on your own." Of course, if the subordinate continues to make mistakes or exceed his authority, then it may be necessary to take disciplinary action.

Some managers react to a subordinate's mistake by taking the job over themselves because they find this course easier than training the subordinate so he won't make the mistake again. Obviously, with an approach like this the subordinate will never learn, and he will become increasingly reluctant to take on responsibility on his own.

Calling Mistakes to Subordinate's Attention

When to call a mistake to a subordinate's attention depends both on the situation and on the subordinate's personality.

"Many times workers recognize their own mistakes and take steps to remedy them before the supervisor steps in. If, then, the manager pushes his criticism

---

[9] For two studies which show that supervisors who engage in nonpunitive handling of mistakes have higher production, see Michael Argyl, Godfrey Gardner, and Frank Cioffi, "Supervisory Methods Related to Productivity, Absenteeism and Turnover," *Human Relations,* Vol. XI, No. 1 (1958), p. 38; and Robert L. Kahn and Daniel Katz, "Leadership Practices in Relation to Productivity and Morale," *Group Dynamics,* Dorwin Cartwright and Alvin Zander, eds. (Evanston, Ill.: Harper & Row, 1953), p. 621.

anyway, the worker becomes resentful. It is only when workers are unaware of their mistakes or seem not to be profiting from them that the supervisor should step in." [10]

On the other hand, it is clearly foolish to let a subordinate continue to make mistakes when he is obviously making no progress in solving them or when they are causing great harm to the organization. Leaving a subordinate in the dark when he is doing a poor job is unfair both to him and to the organization as a whole.

Some managers find it temperamentally difficult to correct their subordinates. They are unsure of the soundness of their own judgment; or they resist accepting the responsibility of "playing God" and judging other men; or they are reluctant to risk injuring the personal relations they have established with their men. As a consequence, one often hears managers defending their failure to offer constructive criticism: "You shouldn't correct anyone until you are 100 per cent sure you are right. You have got to get all the facts." But this is an exaggeration of the problem. There is no need to prove the other man *wrong*. The question of guilt is irrelevant. What *is* relevant is to discuss the trouble in terms of "What happened? What can be done about it?"

Investigating mistakes. Some observers say that a manager should never try to correct a subordinate unless he can offer a better alternative. The cautiousness implied in this approach is commendable, and yet little harm is done when the manager says, "There seems to be something wrong here. Frankly, I don't know the answer, but perhaps we can work it out together." Certainly this is better than letting anger and suspicion mount until one has "all the facts." Lack of frankness between superior and subordinate cannot help but generate tension and misunderstanding.

> When a mistake is made, ask the worker how it happened. *Let him tell you.* If his explanation is weak, he'll recognize it in telling the story, and so will you. You won't have to rub it in, in most cases, because he knows what is expected of him and is willing to recognize his own failings—when he isn't pushed and prodded with them.
>
> Then ask him to *tell you* how the mistake can be avoided in the future. You don't have to accept his solution but, with this approach you are more likely to get him to accept responsibility for his actions and to try to do something constructive.[11]

Letting the subordinate explain what went wrong and then work out his own solution has a definite educational value. As one manager put it, "When you go to them that way and let them explain, they feel a lot better. Sometimes they will come to you and tell you when they make a mistake, and you can really talk it over. That's very important." [12]

---

[10] William F. Whyte, *Human Relations in the Restaurant Industry* (New York: McGraw-Hill, 1948), p. 270.

[11] *Ibid*, p. 269.

[12] *Ibid.*, p. 268.

Often the problem involves the entire group and can best be handled by group discussion. But there, too, the manager can refrain from trying to pin the blame on one or two individuals and concentrate instead on working out a solution for future activities that is satisfactory to everyone.

Criticism

Most mistakes are due to ignorance or lack of skill, and can be handled through training without resort to overt criticism. Some mistakes, however, are clearly due to negligence; here the manager has no choice but to let the subordinate know that he is dissatisfied with the subordinate's level of performance. But unless the manager is tactful in making his criticism, he will jeopardize his relationship not only with the subordinate but with the whole work group as well. Whyte suggests some useful rules:

> 1. The criticism should be voiced in a matter-of-fact manner. Emotional heat on the part of the critic seems to beget a defensive reaction on the part of the subordinate. Only when the subordinate refuses to act on the criticism does it seem advisable to apply the heat.
> 2. The criticism should be focused on the job operation and should, as much as possible, avoid placing of personal blame.
> 3. After it has been stated, the criticism should be dropped—unless the mistake has not been corrected. Men speak of the emotional tensions they have been under when working for a [supervisor] who would not only criticize you but would then seem to be "down" on you for a long time thereafter. One man described the more effective approach in this way:
>
>> "Ed will tell you right to your face how he wants it done. Oh, sometimes we might have a little argument about it, but when the argument is over, it is really over and forgotten. He never gets down on you. You like to work for a fellow like that."
>
> 4. Criticism should be balanced by giving credit for good work. No matter how skillfully a man makes his criticism, if he has only critical remarks to make, he destroys cooperation.[13]

It should be added that criticism of this sort is best offered in private.

Some mistakes, of course, are due to improper training, failure to understand instructions, or severe problems at home. In situations of this sort, the manager may be able to get at the root of the trouble only through skillful interviewing. And he may have to resort to formal discipline if the subordinate fails to respond to criticism and training. The problems of interviewing and discipline will be discussed in Chapters 11 and 14.

In our discussion to this point we have dealt with day-to-day manager-subordinate relationships. But in doing so, we gave a somewhat oversimplified picture. Having read this far, you might well conclude that there is one sort of boss-subordinate relationship which is best for all conditions. Obviously this

---

[13] William F. Whyte, *Leadership in the Work Team* (mimeographed, 1956), pp. 12-13.

isn't so. Let us look at the exercise of authority from a broader perspective and examine why subordinates follow their superiors in the first place. In so doing, we will gain some insight into how the means by which authority is effectively exercised may well differ from one situation to another.

From a purely formal point of view, the manager receives his authority from above, from his superiors, who define his powers and responsibilities and who sometimes put a statement of these in an organization handbook. Another view is that the manager receives much of his *real* authority from below, from his subordinates, and that the statement of authority which he receives from above is merely a hunting license; for in spite of his statement of formal powers, if his subordinates are not willing to obey him, then he has no real authority.[14]

How can the manager induce subordinates to obey him? Of course, he can use bluster, force, and the policy of "be strong." If enough pressure is applied, then his subordinates will comply. But as we saw in Chapter 5, their compliance may well be grudging and resentful.

Alternatively, subordinates may wish to comply because the organization is doing what they want to do themselves. Individuals lost in the wilderness gladly take directions from a leader who seems to be taking them back to civilization. Orchestra members exercise little autonomy, but they follow their conductor willingly because they want to create good music. Similarly, a junior research scientist will obey his boss with enthusiasm if he sees his boss's directions as helping him solve his own research problem. Note that in all these cases the subordinates would have followed their boss's instructions even if he didn't have the formal title. They obey because their ends are identical with those of their leader.

Relatively few cases involve either sheer coercion or the boss telling subordinates to do what they really wanted to do in the first place. Most situations occupy a middle ground: Subordinates obey their boss because they respect the legitimacy of his order, that is, because according to their norms and values it is expected and proper for the boss to give his particular order and for them to obey it.

Thus, the leader must establish a series of relationships with subordinates which support his legitimacy. But he must also recognize that the process of legitimization occurs in a group and cultural setting, for what any one individual perceives as legitimate depends largely on the views of his associates. The group makes it easier for the boss, though, for it often informally disciplines those who violate group expectations by not obeying legitimate orders.

14 For a recent summary of the literature on authority, see Amitai Etzioni, *Modern Organizations* (Englewood Cliffs, N.J.: Prentice-Hall, 1964). For a somewhat different approach, see T. T. Patterson, *Glasgow, Ltd.* (Cambridge: Cambridge University Press, 1960).

As we mentioned in Chapter 4, every group has customs, proprieties, and expectations that its members believe are proper. A manager who violates these standards acts in an "illegitimate" fashion, and does so at his peril: Subordinates can retaliate in numerous ways, ranging from refusal to do more than their normal share in time of emergency, to wildcat strikes and sabotage. In contrast, the manager who respects the group's standards often wins its cooperation and, at times, finds that the group will modify its standards in management's favor. To take an example of the impact of such standards:

> Train crews in a marshaling yard were handling 150 trains a day. Through short cuts (often violating safety rules) they were able to finish their work in six hours. The rest of the time they could sleep or read.

We can identify several standards in this situation: (1) 150 trains a day represent a proper work load; (2) the remaining time can be spent as the men wish; and (3) certain rules will not be enforced.

> Then management decided that since the men had so much free time they could handle 200 trains. Immediately the men began to follow all the rules. They would never move a train even a few feet without having someone to go to the rear and wave a red flag. As a result, the men put in a full day's work, but productivity fell to 50 trains a day. Soon management gave up its demands for 200.

Here management violated group standards and acted in what the group felt was an illegitimate fashion, and the men retaliated in a way that left management helpless.

In the remainder of this chapter we shall consider what the group views as the legitimate use of authority. In the next chapter we shall consider how the manager can best deal with the group. First, however, a word of warning: though we shall use the word "group" rather freely here, you should remember that social groups tend to overlap and that any given employee may belong to several groups with varying expectations (see Chapter 4).

How can a manager exercise power legitimately? The answer seems to depend on at least three factors: (1) his job legitimacy, that is, on his right to hold his power in the first place; (2) the way be behaves on the job; and (3) the demands he makes on subordinates. These three factors are obviously interrelated; for example, the manager can ask more from subordinates if his right to hold his job is legitimate, and if he makes his demands in a legitimate fashion.

Job Legitimacy

To some extent people obey leaders just because they are invested with the symbols or titles of authority. Soldiers are trained to obey those who wear officers' insignia, regardless of the individual merits of the wearer. Royal coronations and presidential inaugurations are ceremonials which symbolize the transfer of a certain "magic" to kings and presidents.

Nevertheless, every group has definite expectations about what qualifications their leader should possess. If the leader fails to live up to these expectations, then his subordinates feel that he is not "fit for his job"—and this holds true whether he is a foreman or President of the United States. The important thing is that the leader be respected.[15]

Background. Certainly there are expectations about the leader's background. He may be expected to belong to a certain ethnic group, to be a graduate of a certain college, or to have a certain degree (thus a Dean without a Ph.D. or a hospital director without an M.D. can find it harder to win support from subordinates). Recall our discussion of status inconsistency in Chapter 4. It is hard for a person who has low status in terms of sex, age, seniority, ethnic background, and so on to win respect as a supervisor.

The nature of the qualifications subordinates expect in their leaders will, of course, vary substantially from job to job. Thus, in many American companies the fair-haired boy who is promoted solely on the basis of family connections will find it hard to win cooperation. On the other hand, family connections are almost essential if one is to be considered a legitimate king (and, in some European firms, a legitimate company president). In some organizations a man is expected to work his way up through the ranks, and an outsider who is brought in over the head of someone subordinates feel deserves the job will have to face strong resentment (though "proper" behavior may ultimately win him respect). In other cases, it is traditional for leaders to be brought in through special channels; thus, for a long time in the Army, officers won greater respect if they started their careers in West Point, rather than as privates. But traditions can change: In recent years the Army has made it easier for enlisted men to become officers; on the other hand, many large companies have increasingly reserved management ranks for college graduates.

Technical ability. It is important for the supervisor to be technically skilled in his work, even if he rarely practices this skill on the job.[16] Indeed, subordinates often subject a new supervisor to a period of testing and initiation to determine whether he measures up to their standards. If subordinates feel their supervisor is master of skills they themselves regard as important, then in a way he has beaten them in a fair race—he has earned his job and is respected for doing so.

The feeling that the boss should show technical skill is particularly strong among men who take pride in their work and closely identify with their occupation (building tradesmen, for example, or college professors). Supervisors who do not possess the relevant skills have a hard time, indeed.

Technical skill is very important in certain types of work where close co-

---

[15] Respect need not mean liking. As Machiavelli advised his Prince, it is often better to be feared than to be loved.

[16] The leader's technical skill need not duplicate that of his followers. A pilot can't overhaul an engine; perhaps a conductor can't play all the instruments in an orchestra; yet both derive status from their technical ability.

ordination is required between members of the work team—as in flying a plane, conducting an orchestra, or operating on a patient. In such cases, "unpleasant personal characteristics are often overlooked if competence is high enough. The irascible surgeon who is, nevertheless, highly respected for his skills is almost a legend. Colleagues and nurses judge doctors according to the mastery they exhibit." [17]

To summarize, we are discussing here what Herbert Simon calls the "authority of confidence." [18] Or, to put it another way, the manager will find his authority more easily accepted if he is an authority *on*, as well as an authority *over*.

Managerial Behavior

Subordinates normally have well-defined expectations about how a "good" manager should behave, both on and off the job, though these may vary greatly from one situation to another.

In the giving of orders, for example, authority may be emphasized or underplayed. As we discussed earlier, North Americans tend to resent the outward display of authority, and often feel it proper that their bosses go through the forms of consulting with them. Engineers, scientists, and professors seem to hold this expectation particularly strongly. Australians seem to resent authority even more than do North Americans. But there are many other cultures in which a boss is expected to be firm and to know his own mind.

Of course, all supervisors are expected to be fair and to treat people in a "nice way." But the nice way in the university would be very out of place in the Army. An officer, for example, is expected to have a "military bearing," and a professor to display a "scholarly attitude." Some groups expect their supervisor to "act like a boss," and the men take advantage of him if he doesn't rule with an iron hand; in other groups it is a great compliment to say that the supervisor "doesn't act like a boss." In some situations a good boss is expected to "let his men alone"; in others he should be available every minute of the day—that is, he should be "in there pitching and providing leadership."

This much is clear: A manager should become familiar with his subordinates' expectations as soon as possible. The manager may eventually wish to change these expectations, but he must recognize the likelihood of resistance (see Chapter 13).

Social distance. Perhaps the most subtle of these expectations about managerial behavior concern the social distance (or status differentiation) which the boss should keep from his subordinates: Military officers should be aloof from their men; deans should invite all new faculty to dinner; plant

---

[17] Temple Burling, Edith Lentz, and Robert Wilson, *The Give and Take in Hospitals* (New York: Putnam, 1956), p. 266.

[18] Herbert Simon, "Authority," in Conrad Arensberg, *et al.*, eds., *Research in Industrial Human Relations* (New York: Harper & Row, 1957), p. 106.

managers are expected to make "howdy rounds" in the plant and to be good fellows at the company picnic (but perhaps only there); supervisors should show interest in their subordinates' home life (and in some plants go out drinking with their men on pay day). In most situations a boss is expected to "be friendly" (and this is particularly true where the American tradition of equality prevails), but the meaning of friendliness varies greatly from one situation to another. To violate these expectations may well lead to trouble.

A wide variety of factors is relevant here. Life insurance agents feel under great pressure from their job and their boss, and as a consequence, according to one study, fear that if he gets too close to them he will criticize them.[19] At sea there has been a traditional social gap between officers and men. This distance is maintained by means of separate uniforms and separate eating and sleeping arrangements. Yet, on smaller ships this traditional formality tends to break down. Moreover, there is more formality in the navy, where men are subject to danger, than there is in the merchant marine. And there is a decidedly different attitude in the American merchant marine, where most men rise from the ranks, than on European ships, where officers and the men they supervise usually come from different social classes.

The question of expected social relationship is closely tied in with technological considerations. In a scientific laboratory a premium is placed on widespread communication of information and widespread participation. Here status differences are expected to be played down, and social relations are close. But in military organizations where the "technology" requires instant obedience, social relations are kept distant. Indeed, it is feared that if enlisted men become socially close to their officers and learn of their personal inadequacies, they may begin to question the officers' orders.[20]

When businessmen and government officials go to foreign countries they run into all sorts of unanticipated problems of social distance. An anthropologist describes how: [21]

> "British respect for rank and maintenance of formal distance seems to have fit well with chieftainships and aristocracies in some parts of traditional Africa and the caste system in India. American equalitarian biases, on the other hand, have seemed to fit poorly in some parts of Oceania, where rank and social distance seem important. . . . With secularized Hindus, nationalist change-oriented Africans and others sensitive about the possible social connotations of superiority in the maintenance of social distance, American informality—even "backslapping"—have been seen as desirable traits in the relationship. Some Latin

---

[19] L. G. Wispe and K. E. Lloyd, "Some Situational and Psychological Determinants of the Desire for Structured Interpersonal Relations," *Journal of Abnormal and Social Psychology,* Vol. 55 (1955), pp. 57-60.

[20] Technological change, however, has largely outmoded the brave infantrymen of Tennyson's day, whose job was "not to reason why," and put in his place a technician who is expected to make decisions on his own. Along with this the social aloofness of the officers has tended to decline. See Morris Janowitz, *The Professional Soldier* (New York: The Free Press of Glencoe, 1960).

[21] Robert N. Rapoport, "Some Notes on Para-Technical Factors in Cross-Cultural Consultation," *Human Organization,* Vol. 23, No. 1 (Spring 1964), pp. 8-9.

Americans have even felt Americans to be cool and remote by their standards —more like the image we would have of the stiffly correct Britisher."

The manager must be concerned with his off-the-job contacts as well as those on the job. In a small community, for example, there are bound to be many unplanned after-hours encounters, and a manager's failure to meet the normal community standards of friendliness and politeness will not be excused. In a large city, however, off-the-job meetings must be arranged in advance by the manager. If he goes out of his way to be "one of the boys," he may set up a pattern of expectations that cannot be maintained on the job.

Social distance is intimately connected with the manager's style of leadership. If he maintains informal, permissive relationships off the job, it will be hard for him to exercise autocratic supervision on the job; on the other hand, if he avoids all social contacts not directly connected with work, he will find it difficult to develop a free-and-easy relationship in discussing job-related problems. Certainly, snubbing people, particularly those with whom one has frequent work contacts, violates our democratic standards.

Work customs. A manager should also be sensitive to the indirect effect of his actions on work customs. Take status, for example. Assigning younger workers to the newest equipment may enable them to earn higher bonuses than their seniors, thereby splitting the work force into two hostile groups. Innocent decisions about parking lots or the arrangement of tables in the cafeteria may upset delicate social relations, and may lead to turmoil and antagonism.

Time-honored work customs sometimes conflict sharply with management's formal rules. In a gypsum board plant, for example, it was a well-established practice for workers to take "extra" boards home with them for personal use. When a new manager decided to enforce the rules against "stealing," he helped precipitate a wildcat strike.[22]

Work Demands

On most jobs there is felt to be an implicit contract between boss and subordinates which governs what the boss may legitimately demand in the way of work.[23] If he restricts his demands to those that are believed legitimate, then obedience is almost automatic. On the other hand, if he makes demands that are felt to be excessive, he must be prepared for resistance. Implicit bargaining plays a very important role here.[24]

Most employees realize that they assume certain obligations when they

---

[22] Alvin Gouldner, *Wildcat Strike* (Yellow Springs, Ohio: The Antioch Press, 1954).

[23] Some readers may recognize that this is related to what Chester Barnard calls the "zone of indifference" (*The Functions of the Executive*, Cambridge: Harvard University Press, 1950), and Herbert Simon calls the "zone of acceptance" (*Administrative Behavior*, New York: Macmillan, 1947, Chap. 7).

[24] Simon, *op. cit.*, also suggests that the existence of the "zone of acceptance" is made possible, in part, by subordinates' inertia—their reluctance to make decisions on their own.

accept a job, and acknowledge that the boss has a right to insist on a "fair day's work." In effect, they feel, "Since I work here I must obey orders and try to do a job. I realize that it is the boss' job to get work out and the company's job to make money. So I'll do my *fair* share."

But employees have definite expectations of what constitutes their "fair share," a notion often embodied in a "bogey." They resent what they regard as "being taken advantage of." As we saw in the train marshaling case, they resist doing more than their bogey, and those who do so are subject to punishment by their peers.

Employees generally question working outside the limits of their customary job description (whether written or not), particularly if the boss's demands seem to threaten their status. Regardless of the union contract, for example, a group may consider it unacceptable for a maintenance man to be asked to do production work—or vice versa.

As we have seen in Chapters 2 and 3, craftsmen and professionals tend to have well-developed internalized standards of how they should do their jobs. Craft and professional pride lead them to turn out work which is of generally high quality and in at least fair quantity. On the other hand, they vigorously resist efforts by managers without the requisite craft or professional skills to interfere in what they feel is their area of craft or professional autonomy.

A manager's instructions are more likely to be accepted if they seem to be concerned with getting the job done, rather than with the arbitrary exercise of authority for authority's sake. Employees object to being given busy work after their "fair day's work" is done. In general, subordinates reject orders as unfair if they are not reasonably related to the purpose for which they were hired.

Indoctrination leads men to resist inappropriate assignments. The more strongly an individual is indoctrinated in the organization's objectives, the more willing he is to accept work assignments which he feels are helping to achieve those objectives, and the more strongly he resists assignments which he feels are irrelevant to them.

On the other hand, technical instructions concerned with the job are considered legitimate—unless the individual making them is felt to be incompetent. Similarly, subordinates accept orders which are obviously required by the situation. They resent rules that are imposed for no apparent reason. Thus, no-smoking rules are hard to enforce unless employees are convinced there is a real fire hazard. The manager must be able to justify rules as essential to getting the job done, maintaining plant safety, and so forth.

Conversely, subordinates often feel that their boss is remiss when he fails to enforce legitimate regulations. Mine workers in one situation placed the blame for accidents on a foreman, since it was his job to see the rules are followed.[25]

---

[25] Alvin Gouldner, *Patterns of Bureaucracy* (New York: The Free Press of Glencoe, 1954), p. 195.

[Employees] know that, as a group, they are incapable of making quick decisions; if the organization is to function effectively, there must be leadership in making decisions and putting them into effect . . . They have no respect for the supervisor who gives orders timidly and with uncertainty. And, strange as it may seem, they like discipline—when they see that it is important in getting the job done.[26]

Employees often expect the boss to show *leniency,* to ignore minor or technical violations of rules as long as the job is getting done. As we have seen they also expect that under unusual conditions (say, when they have bad days) the boss will give them a break and not insist even on the fair day's work. As we have seen, this expectation involves a form of implicit bargaining, for in exchange for this "good turn" the employee may feel some obligation to work extra hard in genuine emergencies.

A System in Equilibrium

To conclude, we have seen that legitimacy is largely determined by subordinate expectations, and that these expectations in turn are established and enforced *in part* by the various forms of implicit bargaining discussed in Chapter 6. At first, the bargain established in this fashion may be little more than an armed truce, but over time, expectations arise that the bargain *should* be observed by both parties. Gradually, expectations "harden" and acquire what anthropologists have called the "crust of custom."

Thus, the manager-subordinate relationship can be conceived of as a system in equilibrium: There are strong forces operating against all parties to restore them to equilibrium should they ever stray away. The manager is confined and restricted by his subordinates' expectations. As long as he is content to accept them, his job is rather easy. The manager who ignores or flouts these expectations does so at his risk, though sometimes—if the organization is to deal successfully with external challenges—the risk must be taken. Before doing so, however, the manager should pause and consider what he intends to do, or perhaps devise an approach that will achieve his objectives without a frontal attack on what subordinates feel to be right and proper.

It should be emphasized that expectations arise through other means besides implicit bargaining. Some expectations are established by the culture generally and efforts to change them solely through the group are doomed to failure. The manager's task is made even more difficult because his subordinates may belong to a number of different groups, each with its own set of expectations. Indeed there are times when expectations are quite difficult to determine. Certainly a manager is misconstruing his function if he is trying to win a popularity contest.

---

[26] William F. Whyte, *Human Relations in the Restaurant Industry* (New York: McGraw-Hill, 1948), p. 259.

Although delegation may reduce a manager's need to exercise authority, he cannot abandon it altogether. The boss remains a boss. In fact, there are some people who, because of personality or background, expect their boss to provide firm, detailed leadership, and there are situations where delegation is not enough to get the job done. Knowing *when* (and when not) to use firmness is one of the critical criteria for effective leadership.

It is also important to know *how* to use authority: The manner in which it is used may spell the difference between resentment and acceptance. The effective supervisor maintains good communications with his subordinates. He develops personal relations which indicate that he accepts and values them as individuals. Although he may make decisions which his subordinates don't like, he endeavors to consult with them, to listen to their suggestions, to provide them with wanted information, and to treat them fairly. Even the handling of mistakes may provide an opportunity to strengthen supervisor-subordinate communications. Such methods may not generate positive enthusiasm for management's objectives, but will reduce resistance to authority. At the minimum they provide the hygienic supervision discussed in Chapter 6.

Subordinate acceptance of authority (though not necessarily enthusiasm) is facilitated when the manager's right to a job, his behavior on the job, and the demands he makes on subordinates—all are accepted as legitimate. His claim to legitimacy is judged in a group and cultural setting, however, and expectations may vary substantially from one situation to another.

Though subordinate expectations (or concepts of legitimacy) do place limits on a manager's discretion (limits which he may at times wish to expand), within the "zone of indifference" he often has a considerable degree of freedom. Certainly a manager should not show exaggerated concern for what his subordinates think. Effective leadership requires an understanding of social pressures, but a true leader does not become a prisoner within them; instead he makes use of them to work toward organizational objectives. In the next chapter we shall consider the relationship between the manager and the subordinate work group within which many of these social pressures are generated.

The Manager and the Group

Our discussion so far has been concerned primarily with the relationship between the manager and individual subordinates. But as our analysis of legitimacy demonstrated, boss-subordinate relations do not occur in a vacuum. Men belong to groups, and these greatly influence their expectations and behavior. Thus, this chapter will consider some of the problems involved in developing the work group into a team which works effectively for management objectives. We will consider the desirability of building cohesive groups and the methods by which this can be done, the development of group participation (and the controversial question of group decision-making), and how the manager can work through the informal organization.

BUILDING A WORK TEAM

Not long ago a nationally known concern distributed to its supervisors a pamphlet entitled "Deal with Individuals, not Groups." Its message was simple: Individuals, if properly handled, will work for management's objectives; groups will inevitably oppose management. Cater to the worker's competitive spirit, reward his individual efforts, and break up his attachment to the group, the argument ran, and you will be surprised how much work he puts out.

The fostering of competition is not the only means that management can use to break up group cohesion. As we saw in Chapter 4, groups can be made so large and heterogeneous that "team spirit" becomes difficult to develop. Similar effects can be obtained by modifying technology and work arrangements. In restaurants even the height of the counter separating waitresses from countermen affects their ability to work together.[1]

But is it wise for management to try to splinter the informal organization? There is no absolutely clear answer to this question. To be sure, cohesive groups show greater teamwork. Its members gain greater social satisfaction

---

[1] William F. Whyte, *Human Relations in the Restaurant Industry* (New York: McGraw-Hill, 1948), Chapter 6.

from working together. Morale is higher. Turnover and absenteeism are frequently lower.[2] Further, it may be easier to supervise a closely knit group, since the supervisor need not repeat information and orders to every member; the informal leader will act as an effective channel of communication to and from the supervisor. A quarreling, disorganized group finds it hard to work together and may direct its aggressiveness against management in the form of poor workmanship, sabotage, grievances, and wild-cat strikes.[3]

On the other hand, certain dangers arise when the work group becomes too tightly knit. Such a group may be reluctant to accept new employees as members and, though there may be more cooperation within the group, cooperation with outsiders may suffer. Thus, competition and ill feeling may develop among rival groups.

But does cohesion increase productivity? Several studies suggest that cohesive groups produce either substantially more than the average or somewhat less.[4] Particularly where the job requires close cooperation among the members of a work team, the mere existence of cohesion makes work more efficient. In general, however, cohesion results in higher productivity only if the group accepts management's demands for higher production as legitimate. If the group is unified for the purpose of protecting itself against management, then greater cohesion will mean less production. All cohesion means is that the members will adhere more closely to the group standards, whatever they are.

Where management finds that there is no possibility of developing groups with goals that are compatible with the objectives of the organization, it may become necessary to resort to measures that will weaken or eliminate informal groups. Continuous movements of personnel, particularly those showing leadership potential, and supervisory patterns that stress dealing with the individual are two possible ways of keeping strong groups from developing.[5] In most instances, however, given a sound over-all program of human relations, it is in management's interest to promote teamwork.

What can the supervisor do to develop teamwork? Most important, he can develop a sensitivity to the facts of group life discussed in Chapter 4. He can familiarize himself with the social geography of the group he supervises and

---

[2] Elton Mayo and George F. F. Lombard, *Teamwork and Labor Turnover in the Aircraft Industry of Southern California* (Boston: Graduate School of Business Administration, Harvard University, 1944).

[3] Cohesive groups may do the same thing, but their efforts are better coordinated, more carefully thought through, and less erratic than those of the disorganized group. Leonard R. Sayles, *Behavior of Industrial Work Groups* (New York: Wiley, 1958), pp. 7-40.

[4] Stanley Seashore, *Group Cohesiveness in Industrial Work Groups* (Ann Arbor: Survey Research Center, University of Michigan, 1954); Daniel Katz and Robert Kahn, "Human Organization and Worker Motivation," *Industrial Productivity*, L. Reed Tripp, ed. (Champaign, Ill.: Industrial Relations Research Association, 1951), pp. 161-162; Morton Deutsch, "The Effects of Cooperation and Competition on Group Process," *Group Dynamics*, Dorwin Cartwright and Alvin Zander, eds. (Evanston, Ill.: Harper & Row, 1953), pp. 319-353.

[5] These were among the techniques used by the communists during the Korean War to break down the morale and cohesion of American prisoners.

learn to identify the patterns of status, leadership, friendship, and cliques that exist within it. Understanding relations can help in a host of ways:

1. He can avoid putting enemies together by carefully assigning men to work positions—thus reducing the possibility of personal friction.

2. He can put friends together. True, this arrangement may lead to more talking on the job, but the evidence suggests that more work will be done too, particularly where the work requires cooperation. One study showed that carpenters and bricklayers who were allowed to choose among themselves whom they would work with outproduced those who were not permitted this choice.[6] Similar results were obtained when laundry workers were assigned on the basis of sociometric preference,[7] and where air-force pilot-training groups were selected in this fashion.[8] (On the other hand, sociometric selection of work teams may be inconsistent with an organizational policy of racial integration.)

3. He can provide special help and attention to isolates—the lonely workers who make no friends. Careful recognition of the position of such employees and the use of clique leaders to help them win acceptance may do much to improve their performance and to prevent them from quitting.

4. He can assign men in such a way as to avoid the growth of competing subgroups.

> A study of social organization in the merchant marine suggests that watches (work teams) were most effective when (a) the entire group came from the same social background, or (b) every member of the group came from a different background. When two sharply different cliques formed, efficiency was impaired.[9]

5. He can cut down on excessive transfers *between* departments, within the limits of union seniority rules.

6. He can rotate jobs within the group in order to strengthen each employee's identification with the team as a whole rather than with his individual job.

7. He can try to set up situations in which the employee can make his job easier by cooperating with others.

> In restaurants we studied, management trained the waitresses to work together and help each other. They were taught to consider two, three, or more stations as a unit and to divide the work among themselves in the most efficient manner.

---

[6] R. H. Van Zelst, "Sociometrically Selected Work Teams," *Personnel Psychology*, Vol. 5, No. 3 (Autumn 1952), pp. 175-185.

[7] John H. Jacobs, "The Application of Sociometry to Industry," *Sociometry*, Vol. 8, No. 2 (May 1945), pp. 181-198.

[8] L. D. Zeleny, "Selection of Compatible Flying Partners," *The American Journal of Sociology*, Vol. 52, No. 5 (March 1947), pp. 424-431.

[9] Stephen Richardson, *The Social Organization of British and United States Merchant Ships* (mimeographed; New York State School of Industrial and Labor Relations, 1954), p. 54.

... The waitresses are told to help only those girls who will return the favor. ... The girl who helps nobody can get nobody to help her, and she drops behind and has trouble with her service. The girl who gives help gets help in return.[10]

8. He can provide financial incentives: Group incentives may do more to encourage cooperation than individual bonus plans.

9. He can make sure that new workers are carefully introduced to the group. Many companies have a "big brother" system in which every new employee is assigned an older employee to help him become familiar not only with the formal requirements of the job but also with the informal mores of the group. In his social contacts with the group, the supervisor should be careful not to exclude the new employee.

10. He can provide employees such as maintenance men or internal auditors, who are constantly moved from department to department, some opportunity to work together as a common group and to feel they have a home.

DEVELOPING GROUP PARTICIPATION

Many high-production supervisors have discovered that they can obtain better results by giving a group an opportunity to participate in decision-making, either through consulting with the group or by allowing it to make and implement decisions by itself.

Industrial engineers in a metal-plating department had been trying for a long time to figure out an equitable way of dividing up the girls' work. The operation was unusually complex and erratic, and every time the engineers made a suggestion the girls were quick to prove that it was unfair to someone. The engineers were about to give up in disgust when the girls asked, "Why not let us decide?" In a short while they had worked out job allocations that even the engineers agreed were superior to theirs.

Naturally everybody gains from this sort of participation. The girls win the satisfaction of exercising greater control over their work environment, as well as the feeling of success from having accomplished something by themselves. Management gains in that better decisions are often made by people close to the job. There is less need for the supervisor to exercise authority or to follow the philosophy of "be strong"; individual employees are more likely to obey rules they themselves have established.

Employees who are given the freedom to regulate themselves are far more capable of making sound decisions when emergencies arise. Since they make the decisions by themselves, there is less need for them to refer every problem to the manager. As a consequence, he can concentrate on long-term planning and handling relations with other departments.

When subordinates are given the necessary freedom, they often do an

---

[10] Whyte, *op. cit.*, p. 214.

impressive job of working out their own methods of scheduling, quality control, and so forth. They may even set production goals for themselves and discipline those who fail to live up to expectations. Sometimes these goals are surprisingly high.

> Groups that participate in setting goals for themselves often make higher demands for themselves than supervisors and methods engineers consider practical. A furnace cleaning job was cut from four to two days; tardiness was set at less than 3 per cent when formerly it was 10 per cent; service calls were reduced from one in 14 to one in 21 ... repairs per man per day rose from 8.5 to 12.5 when the crew planned the service; and over a period of three years men worked more days when they decided whether or not the weather was inclement than when the supervisor made the decision.[11]

The mere fact that the group is given the power to enforce and implement rules increases the likelihood that they will accept the rules, even rules to which they might otherwise object. In other words, whether or not a group accepts management's objectives depends not only on *what* is demanded but also on *how* it is demanded.

> The superintendent of a machine operation was convinced by his Safety Department that long-sleeved shirts were a safety hazard even when rolled up. So he posted a notice that beginning the next Monday morning wearing long-sleeved shirts on the job would be prohibited.
>
> Monday morning four men showed up with long sleeves. Given the choice of working without shirts or cutting off their sleeves, they refused to do either and were sent home. The union filed a sharp grievance, asking for back pay for time lost.
>
> Then the Personnel Department stepped in. The rule was suspended for a week and a special meeting was called with the union grievance committee. The safety director explained that if a worker got his sleeve caught in a machine his whole arm might be ripped off. The union agreed to the rule provided that it was extended to include management (who originally had been exempt on the grounds that they didn't get close enough to the machines).
>
> Next Monday the rule went back into effect. A few men, forgetfully, arrived in long sleeves. The other men handed them a pair of scissors and insisted that the offending sleeves be cut off on the spot. Later in the afternoon a union vice-president and a company time-study man were treated in the same way.

Summarizing, these examples suggest that permitting the group to participate in decisions—through actually making the decisions, enforcing them, or being consulted about them—may result in genuine advantages for management. Employees take more responsibility for minor problems without constantly running to the supervisor with questions, they set production goals (at times at higher levels than would be set by management), they enforce their own rules, and they even modify their group standards in a way they might not otherwise do. In addition, of course, members of the work group gain many satisfactions from participation: a chance to be creative, to feel a sense of accomplishment, to show leadership, to let off steam, and so forth. Further-

---

[11] Norman R. F. Maier, *Principles of Human Relations* (New York: Wiley, 1952), p. 172.

more, there are situations where the group expects management to consult with it; if management fails to do so, subordinates may feel that management is behaving illegitimately.

How can the manager stimulate participation of this sort? To some extent he can permit it to develop naturally, merely by refraining from close supervision. However, if he goes too far, and simply says "Take over," fumbling and confusion are bound to result. In the following two sections we shall see that managers can encourage the group to develop effective participation through (1) holding meetings with subordinates to consider mutual problems, and (2) working through the informal organization of the group.

HOLDING MEETINGS

Many an effective manager calls his subordinates together whenever he has a problem of common interest. Of course, individual problems can be discussed and worked out in private conversations, but *group* problems require *group* discussion. Such meetings need not be formal. Indeed, meetings range all the way from a regular session of the board of directors to an informal discussion between a foreman and a couple of mechanics around a machine that has been causing trouble.

Meetings of this sort may be used for three different purposes:

For information-giving.   This meeting is simply a substitute for posting a notice or speaking to subordinates one by one. Obviously, taking the whole work force away from their job is an expensive procedure, but it insures that everyone will be notified of new directives or information which are important to the whole group. Furthermore, such meetings give subordinates a chance to ask questions, raise objections, and discuss the implications of the announcement.

For consultation.   Just as a manager can ask individuals for suggestions on how to solve a problem (see p. 181), so he can call a meeting for the same purpose. Though the manager will make the final decision on whether or not the suggestions are accepted, people derive great satisfaction from knowing that their ideas are being considered and even more if they are used. A group of individuals exchanging opinions and experiences often comes up with better suggestions than any one person working alone. A suggestion that has evolved from the contributions of many members of the group is more likely to be implemented with enthusiasm by the entire group than is a suggestion that is the brain child of one person, whether he is the manager or an individual subordinate.

For group decision.   Just as a supervisor can delegate authority to individual subordinates to handle problems that involve them alone, so he may call a meeting and delegate authority to a group to handle problems that involve the group as a whole. Of course, there is little difference between a meeting called to solicit suggestions and a meeting called to enable the group to make decisions on its own. But, by waiving its veto power, management thrusts upon the group the responsibility for choosing between alternatives.

Group Decision-Making:
Subject for Controversy

Most business meetings are called for the first two purposes mentioned above—for information-giving or for consultation. Yet, the greatest amount of interest and conflict about group meetings centers on the third purpose, group decision-making.[12] Some observers seem to feel that group decision-making is almost a cure-all for every business ill. There are books on human relations and supervision devoted almost entirely to this one process. The controversy revolves around three basic questions: (1) whether group decision-making will lead to decisions which from management's point of view are proper, (2) whether group decision-making is a form of unfair manipulation, and (3) whether group decision-making is more effective than individual decision-making.

Can meetings be trusted?   Critics make this objection: "Very well, group decision-making has some value, but can you be sure the group can be trusted to make what is from management's point of view the right decision? Won't subordinates avoid responsibility and try to get out of work? If given the power to make decisions, won't they wander over into areas that are none of their business?"

Actually, there are many areas in which management does not care what decision is made, so long as there is no excessive dissension. For example, management is unconcerned with how men divide up the dirty work so long as the work is done—or how rest periods or vacations are scheduled, so long as the time allotted is not exceeded. Since no vacation schedule can satisfy everybody, hard feelings are bound to result. The manager who can pass the responsibility on to the group saves himself a major headache.[13]

In other areas the manager's objectives coincide with those of the group—

---

[12] For example, see Alfred J. Marrow, *Making Management Human* (New York: McGraw-Hill, 1957); Maier, *op. cit.;* W. H. Whyte, Jr., *The Organization Man* (New York: Simon and Schuster, 1956); Chris Argyris, *Personality and Organization* (New York: Harper & Row, 1957); Herbert Thelen, *The Dynamics of Groups at Work* (Chicago: University of Chicago Press, 1954). Rensis Likert, *New Patterns of Management* (New York: McGraw-Hill, 1961); George Strauss, "Some Notes on Power Equalization," in Harold Leavitt, ed., *The Social Science of Organization* (Englewood Cliffs, N.J.: Prentice-Hall, 1963), pp. 41-84; Robert Dubin, "Business Behavior *Behaviorally* Viewed," in Chris Argyris and others, *Social Science Approach to Business Behavior* (Homewood, Ill.: Irwin-Dorsey, 1962).

[13] Note, however, that the manager still must preside over the process by which the men make the decision. If the manager merely says, "You decide," without helping to establish a procedure by which the decision can be made, there will be endless bickering and confusion. It is the manager's responsibility to help the group resolve its internal disputes.

in matters of accident-prevention or avoiding jam-ups in the parking lot, for example. Possibly management should reserve a veto power over decisions in such matters, although it is unlikely that the group will make decisions that are, from management's point of view, far wrong.

The manager, of course, is interested not only in getting a sound decision but also in getting one that is accepted by the group. An *adequate* solution that is enthusiastically implemented by the group may well be better than a *perfect* solution that meets with stubborn antagonism. Thus, the group-decision process is of particular value when management is more concerned with getting *acceptance* of a decision than with its *quality.*

How can a manager keep a meeting from encroaching on areas of decision-making that are not its proper concern? One way is to set clear *limits* to the group's area of freedom. (These limits are similar to the authority-delegating limits we discussed in Chapter 7.) Suppose management is interested in re-furnishing the ladies' lounge. The experienced manager might say, "We have $500 allowed us. How should we spend it?" rather than "What should be done?" or, even worse, "How much should we spend?" Similarly, instead of asking "How much vacation time should you get?" the manager might ask, "How many people can we spare at any one time during vacation and still maintain production? Who should go when?"

If there is no agreement on basic objectives, however, even the setting of limits provides no absolute safeguard against what management might regard as irresponsible decisions. Children balk at being asked, "Which do you want, milk of magnesia or castor oil?" and their parents also object to being asked to make that sort of choice. Normally a group will refuse to make a decision on "We've got to lay off 20 men. Who should they be?" unless there is some previous agreement among the parties that *someone* will be laid off. There must be a mutual acceptance of objectives before a group decision is possible.

Ideally, management provides broad areas of freedom in which subordinates can regulate their own behavior (this is simply teamwork). However, there are bound to be areas of basic conflict between superiors and subordinates, between the organization and its members. In approaching these areas, the most a manager can do is explain why he has made a particular decision and perhaps ask for questions. At one time or another, every supervisor must face the inevitability of making and announcing distasteful decisions.

Manipulation? Some observers feel that group decision-making is nothing but manipulation or even brainwashing—a device by which management imposes its will upon the group without the group's realizing what is happening. Certainly, many managers look upon participative techniques as a means of getting subordinates to accept decisions which are not in the subordinates' interest, or as a way of making them feel that there is no real conflict between their interests and those of management.[14]

14 Raymond E. Miles, "Human Relations or Human Resources?" *Harvard Business Review,* Vol. 34, No. 4 (July 1965), pp. 148-163.

Much of the argument is exaggerated. Group decision-making works best in those areas where management is really willing to accept the group's free decision. True, management may pretend that the group has more freedom than it really has. And it may try to manipulate the discussion process so that employees seem to agree when they really do not. But experience suggests that subordinates quickly see through "mock democracy" of this sort. Such attempts at brainwashing may be successful at first, but in the long run in a free society they are likely to backfire, giving rise to mistrust and resentment.

It must be remembered that group decision-making is a form of delegation and is subject to the limitations we discussed in Chapter 7. It works best on jobs which are of intrinsic interest to those who do them, and it works much less well with those whose central life interest is away from the job. Similarly, it works best where participation is encouraged consistently throughout the organization and less well where the objects sought by participation are inconsistent with the subordinates' basic values.

For example, since academicians, professionals, and members of higher management are likely to have roughly the same objectives as do their bosses, participation with these groups may well be effective over a wide range of subjects.[15] On the other hand, among workers who lack intrinsic interest in their work, participation may be effective only over a narrow range. Thus, group discussion among secretaries about when to hold a coffee break may lead to acceptance of the agreed-upon time and perhaps to fewer breaks at other times. It is more problematical, however, whether such a discussion will lead to their working harder.

Genuine group decision-making on the low levels of an organization may well be confined normally to what may seem to be rather trivial matters, which are, nevertheless, often of considerable importance to those directly involved. Group *consultation* may have a wider role at this level, provided the manager makes it clear at the outset that the final decision will be his.

Group vs. individual decision-making. Even apart from possible differences in objectives, is group decision-making more effective than individual decision-making? The answer seems to depend on the nature of the group, the problem being considered, and what is meant by "effective." Groups sometimes turn out higher-quality solutions than do individuals, although this isn't always the case. In solving problems where there is one definite solution, a group is more likely to be accurate than an individual. Furthermore, group problem-solving has the advantage of enlisting a variety of backgrounds and experiences; thus, the range of solutions is usually greater, and the group solution is more likely to represent a balanced point of view. Meetings are particularly useful when the participants represent various departments whose coordination is required to implement the final decision, for the discussion tends to force the

---

[15] Participation may be particularly effective for academicians and professionals, since these groups value highly the concept of "colleagueship."

departmental representatives to look at the problem from an organizational rather than a departmental point of view.[16]

Individual decision-making, on the other hand, is more likely to be firm than to represent a compromise. Individuals are more capable than groups of handling subtle relations—whether in threading a needle or in developing a complex theoretical formula.[17] Great works of art are almost without exception the products of single individuals. "Could *Hamlet* have been written by a committee," it has been asked, "or Mona Lisa been painted by a club?" [18]

In addition, meetings are awfully time-consuming. Decisions reached in them take longer than do those of individuals, particularly if time is computed in terms of total man-hours expended. Sometimes, of course, the higher quality and easier acceptance of decisions reached through meetings makes them worth the extra time involved. On the other hand, managers on occasion pass the buck to meetings when they are psychologically unprepared to make decisions themselves. Meetings under these circumstances rarely accomplish much.

There is the risk, too, that presenting a problem to a group to discuss may lead to greater conflict than existed before—and skillful leadership is required to prevent this [19] (as we shall see in Chapter 12). The danger of conflict is particularly great where vested interests are involved (for example, when a group is deciding whether "soft jobs" should be rotated or assigned on the basis of seniority). The less cohesive the group, the greater the difficulty in reaching agreement, though experience in making decisions of this sort may help cohesion develop.

The advantages and disadvantages of group decision-making through committees are effectively summarized in contrasting remarks by well-known executives from two companies with vastly different attitudes toward the use of committees:

> "If you can name for me one great discovery or decision that was made by a committee, I will find you the one man in that committee who had the lonely insight—while he was shaving or on his way to work, or maybe while the rest

---

[16] But, one experienced executive warns, the over-all manager who chairs the meeting should still make the final decision, for by his very position he is best suited to look at the problem in terms of the needs of the organization as a whole. Wilfred Brown, *Explorations in Management* (London: Tavistock Press, 1960).

[17] Thus, groups may be more efficient than individuals in solving crossword puzzles, but individuals are better at devising them.

[18] Donald W. Taylor, Paul Berry, and Clifford H. Block, "Group Participation, Brainstorming, and Creative Thinking," *Administrative Science Quarterly*, Vol. 3, No. 1 (June, 1958), p. 27.

[19] In addition, there is the problem that if the boss consults with his subordinates regarding one area of management, they may establish expectations of being consulted in regard to other areas, too. Since it may not be possible to consult everybody in a large organization, perhaps it might be better not to start a process which is difficult to control. See Robert Dubin, "Psyche, Sensitivity, and Social Structure," in Robert Tannenbaum, Irving R. Weschler, and Fredrik Massarik, *Leadership and Organization* (New York: McGraw-Hill, 1961).

of the committee was chattering away—the lonely insight that solved the problem and was the basis for the decision." [20]

"It stands to reason that if you get five men together and one man is wrong,
the mistake will be picked up. Or if one man has a good idea, the others will
contribute to it and develop it. And if they have good ideas, what comes out
may be better than the separate ideas added together." [21]

Group Consultation
on a Day-to-Day Basis

The preceding discussion may have given the impression that the use of
meetings involves a drastic change from traditional management practice.
Quite the contrary. In some companies most major decisions have long been
made by committees, particularly at the higher levels of management. (Sometimes this practice is called "multiple management.") And at lower levels it is
now accepted practice for supervisors to hold regular meetings at which
subordinates can raise questions, discuss common problems, and consider new
developments. Increasingly, such meetings are being held even on the hourly-
paid level, though they are still probably more common in service organizations such as restaurants,[22] hospitals, stores, schools, and libraries than in manufacturing plants.

Some organizations require that regular meetings be held as a standard
practice at all levels. Unfortunately, supervisors may call these compulsory
meetings merely because they are told to do so: They go through the motions
but never become involved in the spirit of consultation. An office girl once
described her experience to us:

> "We have meetings once a month. The office manager asks us if we have any
> questions or suggestions. Sure we have lots of complaints, but no one has the
> courage to bring them up. Once in a while one of the girls who is looking to
> make a good impression asks some silly question, although she already knows
> the answer.
>
> "Most of the meeting is spent by the office manager telling us we ought to
> cooperate more, we ought to be neater in our work, and so forth. Frankly, I
> always resent these meetings—they take you away from your work. And I hate
> the way the office manager talks about our smooth-working loyal group when
> I despise her and so do the other girls."

Actually, the mere act of holding formal meetings is less important than
the manager's willingness to consult with subordinates informally when
problems arise. Status differences create less of a barrier to communication
when consultation takes place around the drawing board, over the machine
that has broken down, or in the cafeteria—than at a formally called meeting.

---

[20] Ralph J. Cordiner, former Chairman of General Electric, as cited in Justin G. Longen-
ecker, *Principles of Management and Organizational Behavior* (Columbus, Ohio: Merrill,
1964), p. 206.

[21] Frank Abrams, former Chairman of Standard Oil of New Jersey, as cited in *ibid*.

[22] For a good description of such a meeting in a restaurant, see Whyte, *op. cit.*, pp.
236-240.

It would be impractical for a manager to call a meeting every time he has a problem to solve. Often he can work out a solution by himself, taking into account the standards and expectations of the group. But at other times the successful manager will make use of the informal organization of the group.

Informal Leaders

As we mentioned in Chapter 4, groups evolve their own leadership. Informal leaders play key roles in every organization, and without their cooperation management must face an uphill battle against sabotage and apathy.

W. F. Whyte tells the story of two settlement-house recreational directors who handled the same problem in different ways.[23] The problem was this:

> The younger boys were to use the play center till 9 o'clock, then they were to leave and make room for the older boys. But, instead of going home, the younger boys would hang around the door, bang on the windows, and generally create a nuisance.
>
> Again and again the first recreational director asked the boys as a group to go away—but with no results. Faced with the same situation, the second director turned to one member of the group and merely said: "Listen, Joe, the time's up. Be a good fellow and take your gang out of here." Joe, who was the informal leader, complied immediately and the group left.

Why was the second director so successful? He recognized the informal leader's special status, and gave him an opportunity to gain still more status through proving his power to the director. Under the first director's approach, the informal leader could exhibit his power only by opposing the director's will; had the group obeyed the director, the informal leader would have lost status.

The situation is very much the same in business and industry. A supervisor can either fight the informal organization and its leaders or work with them. If the informal leaders fail to win recognition by working *with* management, they will get it by working *against* management.

Management is often heard to complain, "All our trouble is caused by a few ringleaders. If we could only get rid of them, our trouble would disappear, morale would rise, and our employees would be loyal once again." Unfortunately, these "ringleaders" are often informal leaders; the trouble they cause reflects the desires of the group. It is particularly important to work with informal leaders of *strategic* groups (see p. 113). In dealing with them, a

---

[23] William F. Whyte and Burleigh B. Gardner, "The Man in the Middle: Position and Problems of the Foreman," *Applied Anthropology*, Vol. 4, No. 2 (Spring 1945).

certain amount of bargaining is often required. Eliminate the informal leaders, though, and the group may become still more antagonistic to management, morale may fall even lower, and new ringleaders will step to the fore. In a nonunionized situation it may be possible to eliminate ringleaders one by one till finally nothing is left but a cowed, disorganized mass of individuals who docilely obey orders. However, such individuals never show a gleam of initiative or teamwork.

What is the alternative to firing ringleaders? Working with them. There are numerous ways in which a manager can build up good relations with the informal leaders working under him. Among other things he can pass information along to them first, ask their advice on technical or human-relations problems, and assign them to train others.

There are, however, several dangers that the manager must guard against:

1. The informal leader is often hard to identify. The outstanding man who does the best work and cooperates most readily with management may *seem* to be the informal leader, whereas these characteristics may actually make him a social isolate. On the other hand, the "loud-mouth" may serve as the group's *spokesman* rather than its actual *leader*. The group may even have different leaders for different purposes. Sometimes the members of the group will follow one individual when they act in cooperation with management and another when they are antagonistic. Finally, there may be no identifiable informal leader at all.

2. The very fact that the informal leader works closely with management may result in his losing status with the group: He will be known as a "company man." This danger is particularly acute when there is antagonism between the manager and the work group generally and the informal leader is asked to do things that the group does not accept as legitimate.

3. Carried too far, cooperation becomes favoritism. It is one thing for the manager to give the informal leader information and to ask for his advice. It is quite another to give him easier work or special favors. Nothing could be more effectively calculated to drive him from his leadership position.

The Working Supervisor

The working supervisor is a group member to whom a manager may show special attention without giving rise to charges of favoritism. There are two kinds of working supervisor. The most obvious is "the straw boss," sometimes called the working foreman, leadman, keyman, or group chief. He is the leader of a group of men who do roughly the *same* sort of work. He shares their work and performs certain quasi-supervisory duties as well.

The other sort of working supervisor exercises his authority by virtue of his technical position on the work team, because his work is *different* from that of the others and requires more skill. Working supervisors are common in process industries and also in some of the older, more traditional industries in which craft skills still prevail. For an example from a traditional industry:

> In glass-blowing shops where high-quality crystalware is manufactured for the luxury market, each work team is headed by a gaffer. The gaffer, the top man in a six-step hierarchy, is a craftsman of considerable skill and long seniority in his trade who does more intricate work than either members of his team. He is accountable to management for the quality and quantity of the ware produced by his team and has almost complete authority over their work performance.

The supervisory power of these top-status crew members rarely receives such formal recognition from management. Instead, it exists because of tradition and because supervisors have found these men to be effective assistants in running the department.

Since the working supervisor often gains status because of his seniority and technical proficiency, subordinates will be more willing to accept orders from him than from the foreman himself. This is particularly true where the foreman has not come up from the ranks himself, where coordination of the work force requires a high degree of technical skill that can be acquired only through years on the job, or where constant attention and order-giving are required, as with a fast-paced steel-mill crew.

We have observed situations in which management has impaired output and demoralized the work group by deliberately or inadvertently taking away some of the working supervisor's power and prestige.[24] This often happens when a college-trained foreman pays too much attention to the formal organization chart and not enough to traditional relationships between workers and management.

Actually the relationship between foreman and working supervisor is a highly personal one and cannot be established simply by top-management edict. In many cases, the supervisor can substantially increase his effectiveness by consulting with the working supervisor and channeling orders through him.[25]

The Union Steward

The union steward is ordinarily an informal leader who commands respect outside union matters. Provided the over-all union-management relationship is friendly, the manager may wish to pass on information to the steward first, use him as a sounding board for proposed changes, and even ask his advice. Again if relations are good, this consultation can be handled outside the context of formal collective bargaining and in a way that will not lead to the loss

---

[24] See George Strauss, "The Set-Up Man: A Case Study of Organizational Change," *Human Organization*, Vol. 13, No. 2 (Summer 1954), pp. 17-25.

[25] Charles R. Walker, Robert H. Guest, and Arthur N. Turner, *The Foreman on the Assembly Line* (Cambridge: Harvard University Press, 1956), p. 45.

of the manager's power or the establishment of precedents that management may later regret. Such consultation has the great advantage of permitting the steward to participate in solving technical and human-relations problems in a constructive, positive fashion; otherwise, in order to display his status, the steward has to resort to the essentially negative activity of processing grievances. In a strongly unionized situation, the supervisor will never be able to develop cooperative relations with his subordinates if he bypasses or ignores the union.

CONCLUSION

The manager rarely interacts with his subordinates in isolation. Usually this occurs in a group setting. In handling group problems the effective manager will consult with subordinates before taking action and in some areas will encourage them to make their own decisions. He may meet with the group as a whole or channel his activities through the group's informal structure. He may work with informal leaders, working supervisors, and union stewards.

A strong case can be made for participative management, in which the manager makes a practice of encouraging his subordinates as a group to discuss a wide variety of significant work-related problems. Ideally, participation of this sort will lead both to greater cohesion and to greater acceptance of management's objectives. To the extent that such a cooperative relationship can be established, the gains are substantial for both employees and for management. An atmosphere of cooperation provides essential need satisfactions for subordinates: the social satisfaction of working together, a feeling of identification with the group and the over-all organization, and a pride in accomplishment. Belonging to a group reduces the feeling of anonymity and provides a sense of identity.

For the manager, such cooperation, if achieved, makes life a lot easier. There is less need for him to check on his men, for they make their own rules, take care of emergencies by themselves, and may even discipline their own team members. Participation is particularly useful during periods of change.

There is a danger of being Pollyanna-ish, however. We have tried to suggest the limits of participative management. There are many areas in which there are conflicts of interest between subordinates and management. Subordinate acceptance of the legitimacy of management's demands and behavior does not necessarily mean that these subordinates will "internalize" and work enthusiastically for management's objectives. It may only mean that they will put in a "fair day's work." What is such a fair day's work is largely determined through implicit bargaining and may be fairly low. To the extent that subordinates expect to be consulted, participative techniques may provide merely hygienic management (see Chapter 6) rather than positive motivation to work.

In a sense, strengthening group cohesion through participation may make management's task harder, for the group will now develop expectations that its acquiescence is required for what management does. Meetings take up a lot of time. If they are given genuine freedom to make important decisions, there is no guarantee that the decisions will be those which management wants (and the very process of discussion may lead to internal friction among group members). If the meeting is manipulated so as to come to the "right" conclusions, the members will eventually see through such mock democracy. In fact, many of the benefits of participation can be obtained without formal meetings, merely through working with subordinates on an informal basis.

LEADERSHIP: A LAST WORD

In our discussion of leadership we have tried to emphasize that there is no one pattern of management that is universally appropriate. Instead, the pattern of management that is most appropriate to a given situation depends on a number of factors:

1. The personality and background of the manager. *Example:* A manager who is brought in from outside the organization will almost of necessity maintain a greater social distance from his new subordinates than will one who has risen from the ranks.

2. The personality and background of the subordinates. *Example:* Professional engineers expect and require a higher degree of delegation than do older nurses with a rural background.

3. The type of work. *Example:* Assembly-line workers, who have relatively little opportunity to obtain need satisfaction from their work, may require closer supervision than do maintenance men.

4. Urgency of getting results. *Example:* If quick results are required, there may be no time to develop a cooperative, cohesive work group.

The sensible manager will take all these factors—and many more—into account before he decides how to behave in a particular situation. Even in a given situation, however, there is a broad range of leadership approaches that will be successful if properly implemented. For instance, in Example 1, a manager brought in from outside might very quickly develop close social relations with his subordinates and thus increase rather than decrease production. Or, in Example 3, a maintenance supervisor might get excellent production in complete violation of the principles of general supervision.

It is important to remember that many successful businessmen have violated all the principles discussed here. They have been successful in spite of their human relations—or perhaps because they have so inspired their subordinates to identify with the company and its success that employees have given their all in spite of supervisory actions that would be resented in almost any other context. (We are talking here about what some sociologists call the difference between "instrumental" and "expressive" leadership.)

In fact, the ability to supervise is only one of the many characteristics of a good manager. The company president, for example, must be effective in dealing with his subordinates. But this is only one part of his duties: He also makes plans, evaluates the recommendations of others, represents the company to outsiders, and so forth. He must have technical and administrative as well as human-relations abilities. In fact, as we shall discuss in later chapters, getting along with still higher management may be more important for him than getting along with subordinates. It has been suggested that the primary function of any top executive is to adjust the goals of his organization to the needs of his times.[26] The ability to sense the main current was the central genius of Washington, Lincoln, Franklin Roosevelt, Queen Elizabeth I, and Churchill. It is also the genius of the business executive who decides at the opportune moment to switch his company's operations from wholesaling to direct sales— or the man who steals a march on the market by making plans for the mass production of a new chemical though the laboratory tests are far from complete.

Certainly we would admit that the executive's ability to make critical decisions of this order is more crucial to the survival of the organization than his particular skill in dealing with people.[27] An organization permeated with inappropriate [28] human-relations practices, however, is unlikely to remain profitable for long, regardless of the personal brilliance of the man at the top. An organization can be successful even if some of the individuals in it, even those at the very top, lack important skills, *provided* there are others in the organization who can fill in for them. The president may be inadequate in dealing with people, but the organization will be little harmed provided he channels his contacts through someone high in the management hierarchy who is skilled in this area. Available evidence suggests that the quality of supervision in itself is often relatively unimportant in determining levels of productivity—particularly where production rates are determined by technology or by group standards.[29]

Similarly, on lower levels it would be unrealistic to expect management to promote men entirely on the basis of their leadership abilities. What is important is not that every manager be a good leader, but that the structure of the organization and management policies be such as to encourage sound human-relations practices.

At this point you may complain, "A few chapters ago you seemed to state a strong preference for delegation. Now, many hedges later, haven't you

---

[26] Philip Selznick, *Leadership in Administration* (Evanston, Ill.: Harper & Row, 1957).

[27] Though we would argue that major critical decisions must be made in the field of personnel administration just as frequently as in such fields as marketing, production, or finance.

[28] Note we use the term *inappropriate*. The appropriate practice for the given situation may be the unrestrained use of authority.

[29] Robert Dubin, "Supervision and Productivity: Empirical Findings and Theoretical Considerations," and George Homans, "Effort, Supervision, and Productivity," in Robert Dubin and others, *Leadership and Productivity* (San Francisco: Chandler, 1965).

worked yourself into a position where it doesn't seem to make much difference what kind of supervision is used?" By no means. We think that the healthiest, soundest, most profitable organization will be the one in which delegation can be used effectively. But to make it possible to use delegation effectively, it may be necessary to revamp the whole organization through changes in organization structure, delegation, improved communications, and even, as we suggested in Chapter 2, substantial changes in the technological processes of production. Changes of this sort may well create cumulative changes in the over-all organization that will make general supervision possible.

As a consequence, the face-to-face relationship between supervisor and subordinate cannot be considered in isolation from the other factors that we will consider in later chapters. First, however, we should define more closely some of the skills required by the supervisor.

PROBLEM 1

THE PRESIDENT'S LETTER

The following letter was sent to the *Harvard Business Review* by the president of a medium-sized insurance company. The president is explaining why his company has so few immediate personnel problems in its Home Office (which, we may assume, houses about 500 employees, most engaged in routine, clerical operations.) [30]

> The reason lies not in the attitudes of workers but in the attitude of management. It is true that lavish offers of fringe benefits give no assurance of mollified workers. This company has gone far in the fringe area, but I have never felt that what we did accounted for the remarkable *esprit de corps* our people show. I feel it is how we do it.
>
> By that I mean that for eleven years since I came to head this company my first objective in dealings with our people has been to dignify them as individuals and to express a feeling of pride in them which quickly won their recognition. This is the pattern followed by my staff. Supervisory attitudes—management's real intent—are quickly observed and evaluated by employees. My company takes this seriously.
>
> Alex Osborn of B.B.D.&O. is an old friend of mine. You may have seen his two recent books, one captioned "Your Creative Power," and the other more recent one entitled "Applied Imagination." These books have been widely circulated among our officers and supervisory people, and many things have come out of them. For example, we took a longer look at our suggestion plan and approached it on the basis that whatever the quantity or quality of suggestions, the Suggestion Committee must deal, not only with an open mind, but liberally, with suggestions in the first year. While we get many suggestions that cannot be given dollar awards, we make sure that occasionally a good suggestion gets a walloping return. We now invest a rather substantial sum in suggestion awards, and I submit we get a great deal of genuine interest and benefit. Our plan works well and it costs us about the same as one qualified clerical person.
>
> I am interested in the local orchestra, and a few years ago it was brought to my attention that there were several unsold boxes. I hit upon a plan evolved from Osborn's thinking that pays off three ways, and it has been most successful. Our people are encouraged to bring flowers from their garden to decorate the lobby

---

[30] Vol. 32, No. 6 (November 1954), reproduced by permission of the author and publisher.

of our building. They are given a credit line for so doing and feel good about it; secondly, our hobby is as attractive as any you will find; and thirdly, those who add to its beauty are rewarded by pairs of tickets to the concerts. The orchestra benefits as do our people. The plan appealed to every bank and insurance company in this town, save two, and there are no unsold boxes. Parenthetically, I maintain a box adjacent to that purchased for the employees. I am usually there and find an opportunity to visit either before the concert or during intermission with my people and their husbands and wives and friends.

Perhaps the most significant thing we have done is one which has given dignity to every person in the building and it happens to be in the field of philanthropy. In 1947, I was General Chairman for the Community Chest Campaign, and the slogan adopted by the company's employees committee that year was "PAR FOR E.A.R." [E.A.R. is the president], and in that year there was 100% giving. The company became pleasantly notorious throughout the city for this 100% accomplishment; and believe it or not, with a constantly changing personnel, the record of 100% giving—every officer, every employee, every cafeteria and building maintenance worker—has been maintained through the years since. Every year the drive is completed on the first day and a telegram sent to the general chairman. In the public meetings which follow, our people are photographed and feted. Every individual feels personally responsible for the result.

Our pay scales are measured by objective job analysis and careful performance rating. Our hours are the best, our working conditions as good as any, and there is a constant effort to be humane in all matters.

We have had interesting conversations with the group acting as the Board of Governors of the "Employees' Club" over the years, and we have met every reasonable request they have made. Biweekly pay was one of the requests which we adopted costing us about 8% more in salary, smoking in work areas which we permitted, music in work areas which we maintain. We are always willing to listen to our people. If they want something that will help them in their work and in their happiness here we will go far to supply it.

Ours is not a perfect shop, and I may be lulled into thinking it is happier than I suggest, but of one thing I am sure, while most of our officers have had collegiate experiences, there isn't one who came into the world with a gold spoon in his mouth, and that may account for their interest in people and their problems.

I have a great feeling of intimacy with our employees. I write dozens of longhand letters to those who do me and this company favors, and I write a specially dictated letter to each person on his reaching a fifth, tenth, etc., anniversary.

We make a good deal of a Christmas Party that is really a family affair. There is no drinking in connection with it, though we are not opposed to drinking as such. We bring in the families and children of all people who wish to come. It is a very successful affair.

Similarly we take an interest in our retired people and annually give them the finest dinner and entertainment in the best place available. We encourage them to visit the office and to attend the functions held by active employees.

If our people should become upset about anything I am prepared to say it would be my fault, because there is nothing reasonable they could urge that we could afford to do, that we aren't doing, or be willing to do. If we could not do it my experience with them has been that we could spell out the reasons convincingly and acceptably.

We take good care of our older people and pay an extra service allowance for length of service which is quite considerable in the case of the older and in some cases, less productive people. We have meetings in which the dignity of the individual is advanced with deliberate care.

Morale cannot be won in a day or purchased at any price. It takes a long time to develop good morale and it takes constant planning to preserve it. On the other hand, I could lose it all in one day's misbehavior. All I would need to do would be to walk through a work area and complain about the posture of a couple of people and ask whether it was necessary to burn as many lights. It would help to turn on lights but it would never do to turn one off.

The important thing is that the work be congenial; and if that is not so, liberal rules and wage scales become of less importance. Care must be taken in the employment of people and more care in the treatment of them later. We try to take that care and that I think is why we apparently do so well in our company.

1. Evaluate the effectiveness of this company's program.
2. How are the various forms of motivation, which were discussed in Chapter 6, utilized in this company?

PROBLEM 2

THE TOOL CRIB ATTENDANT WHO READS

Bill Smith works as a tool-crib attendant at the Acme Company. A tool-crib attendant has a fairly responsible job: He has to keep tabs on who gets what tools, keep the tools in order, make minor repairs, and order new tools when the stock runs low. At the beginning and end of each shift there is a lot of work to do, but most of the time the men have relatively little to do, especially on the night shift. Nevertheless it is one of the highest-paid nonskilled jobs in the plant. (To work up to a skilled job, a man has to start as an apprentice in his twenties.)

Until last year Bill held an important union office and used his free time and the strategic location of the tool crib for political purposes. Last year he was defeated; those who opposed him felt his aggressive attitude toward the company was merely provoking trouble.

Shortly thereafter Bill was caught by his foreman reading a newspaper on the job. The following exchange took place:

Foreman: You're supposed to be working now. We're not paying you for reading.

Bill: I'm doing my job. I've got nothing to do now. How does it hurt you if I read?

Foreman: If I let you read, then the men on production will want the same privilege. If I stop them, they will say I'm discriminating against them. You pushed a grievance case just like that yourself. In fact, since I'm dealing with a legal eagle like you, I'll give you a written warning just to cover myself 100 per cent.

Bill: Why do I get the warning? I'm not the only one who's been reading papers. You're picking on me just because I made you eat a lot of dirt when I was a union official.

Foreman: No, I'm warning you because you're the first man I caught. I'll warn everyone else I catch too.

Bill: You can't give me a warning. There's nothing in the plant regulation about reading newspapers. We've never received any notice and you're punishing me for a rule you've just set up. That's poor personnel policy.

Foreman: OK, I'll post a written order too—and this warning is just to make double sure you know about it.

Bill: OK, I'm filing a grievance. By posting the notice you're admitting this is a new order. I don't want any warning in my file that you can hang over my neck from now till doomsday.

Bill filed his grievance, but his steward, who was a political opponent, never "found time" to push it. Shortly afterward, Bill's wife got a job as a night telephone operator on the 11:30 P.M.-7:30 A.M. shift. Bill's own shift ran from 8:00 A.M. to 4:00 P.M. Bill's plan was to pick his wife up after she finished work, then drive down to the Acme Company, where he would turn the car over to her and go to work himself.

Acme and the phone company were on opposite sides of town and Bill began to come in late for work. After this occurred several times, his foreman gave him a written warning that if he came late again, he would be fired. From then on, whenever he saw he couldn't get to the plant by the starting whistle, he went home, reported sick, and took the rest of the day off. Technically, management could have required a doctor's certificate from him, but this was never requested unless a man had been out of work for several days.

Finally, the situation got to be too much for Bill and he requested a transfer to the midnight shift in accordance with the seniority provisions of the union contract. The foreman turned him down on the grounds he did not possess sufficient "fitness and ability" to work the night shift since there was provision for only one tool attendant on the night shift and Bill's poor tardiness, absentee, and newspaper-reading record would mean that the company would often be caught short.

Bill did not explain the real reason for his absenteeism, fearing that it might bring him punishment. Instead, he caught the plant manager at the plant gate and said to him:

Bill: Mr. Struthers, I just asked my foreman to give me a transfer to the "mid" shift and he turned me down. I got the seniority, but he said I couldn't make the move because I've been absent too much. That's true: My wife's been sick once in a while and I've had to stay home to take care of the kids. If I can work the night shift, my sister can take over when my wife's not feeling good.

Mr. Struthers: OK, Bill, I'll see what I can do.

Next day Struthers had the following phone conversation with the foreman:

Mr. Struthers: Is it true you turned down Bill's transfer application because of his absentee record?
Foreman: Yes I did. I don't think he can be trusted on the job.
Mr. Struthers: Well, I'm willing to take the chance.

The following day Struthers told Bill his transfer would go through shortly.

Meanwhile the day-shift foreman told the night-shift foreman, "You're going to get a guy named Smith who will give you a pack of trouble. Watch him like a hawk."

Six o'clock the first morning of Bill's new shift, the foreman dropped in on him, sure that Bill would be asleep. Instead Bill had spent the whole evening washing down the walls and building a new cabinet for his equipment. Since that time the foreman has checked on him only at infrequent intervals. Bill is fairly satisfied with the new work:

"Of course, it is just as boring as can be. I had out about ten tools a night. I've repainted and completely straightened out the crib, but you can't do that forever. I can't read my paper in the spare time, so lots of times I go to sleep, often for six hours. I have an arrangement with the fellows in the shop that if anybody from management comes they'll make some noise and wake me up."

1. Was management wise in instituting the no-newspaper-reading rule? List the arguments that could be presented *for* and *against* this course of action. (Assume management may not increase Bill's job duties.)
2. What was wrong with the way the order was issued? What would you have done?

3. Suppose you were night-shift foreman and word came to you through the "grapevine" that Bill was sleeping on the job. Would you have done anything? What? Why?
4. Go through the rest of the case and point out other mistakes made at different levels of management.

PROBLEM 3

FILLING A VACANCY FOR FOREMAN

Management has been having a great deal of trouble in the cone-making department in the Ashford Plant. Cone-making used to be done entirely by hand and required considerable skill. Today much of the skilled work is handled by machinery, but the cone-makers still put in a good deal of physical effort in feeding the machines, and the work process involves heat and fumes. The department is isolated from the rest of the plant in an older, rather dilapidated building.

For years management has pretty much let the cone-makers have their own way, though, on occasion, the men have gone on slow-downs or wildcat strikes over petty grievances. Their foreman, Mike Malone, has looked upon his job chiefly as that of protecting his men from management pressure. In recent years, productivity has tended to fall and costs in this department are considerably higher than in comparable departments in other plants. In part because of anticipated employee resistance, management has been reluctant to install new production methods and it is giving some thought to shutting down the department eventually. Malone is ready to retire and management must find a successor. Among the possibilities are:

a. *John Callahan,* age 50, who has been with the department for 33 years. He knows cone-making backwards and forwards, is well liked by the men, and has been union steward for years.

b. *Gus Nowak,* college graduate, age 32, who has done an outstanding job in cutting costs as foreman of the assembly department, a department of low-skilled workers which includes many women and has always had considerable turnover.

1. Is this a cohesive group?
2. Why might it resist change?
3. What are the relative strong and weak points of each candidate for foreman? Which one would you select?
4. Assuming Nowak is selected, what advice would you give him?
5. Assuming Callahan is selected, how should the plant manager try to handle him?

PROBLEM 4

THE SAFETY GUARD

While walking through your department, you notice that one of the operators a couple of aisles over seems to be working with the safety guard up. However, as he catches your eye, he fumbles with a piece of stock and knocks the safety guard into place—at least that is how it looks to you. This is a serious offense. When an employee commits this violation (often in order to speed up his operation and make it a little easier), the usual penalty is a three-day layoff. Several people have been seriously injured by failure to use the safety guard.

1. How would you approach the employee?
2. What would you say?
3. What would your objectives be in your discussion with him?

THE POOR WORK OF JANE SMITH

Jane Smith has been a slightly better-than-average employee, though not an outstanding worker. Recently, the quality of her work has been declining, for no apparent reason. You have just checked some of the parts she has been working on and decide that nearly half of them are unsatisfactory. This is about the worst performance you have ever spotted.

1. How would you approach Jane?
2. What would you say first?
3. Should you first compliment her on her work?

INFLAMMABLE MATERIAL

Through the years your company has had a no-smoking rule that has been largely ignored. Recently some of your departments have begun working with rather inflammable material, though there is still almost no fire danger in most of the departments. You are plant manager.

1. Describe the steps you would take to handle the danger of fire and yet maintain sound human relations.
2. Why would you take these steps rather than others?

HOSPITAL ORDERLIES

Hospital orderlies are often homeless older men who accept hospital work in spite of its low pay because it offers them free room and board. Their duties normally include various sorts of dirty work, such as moving beds and carrying stretchers—work that is too hard for women.

A. In some hospitals each orderly is assigned to a ward or group of wards where he works under the direction of the head nurse and does any work that the nurses, student nurses, practical nurses, and nurses' aides on the floor request. When he is through with one assignment, he waits around for another.

B. In other hospitals all orderlies work out of a central orderly room. When a head nurse wants an orderly for a specific job, she calls the head orderly, who dispatches men as needed. When an orderly finishes his assigned task, he reports back to the orderly room.

1. What special human-relations problems would you find in situation A which you wouldn't find in situation B and vice versa?
2. Compare the two situations in terms of the special skills required by the head nurses to deal with orderlies.

TIME TO SLEEP

The Merrimac Corporation sells, rents, and services electronic data-processing equipment and employs a large staff of servicemen to keep its customers' equipment in order. The 30 servicemen who work out of the St. Louis district office (which covers most of the Midwest) all live in the St. Louis area and are often required to travel to customers in distant locations; usually they travel by air. A given trouble call may take several hours or even days of work.

A problem has arisen from the fact that, when an assignment is completed, the men fly back to St. Louis and often arrive home late in the evening or even after midnight. Under these circumstances management has always allowed the servicemen to take a few hours extra sleep and not report to the office the first thing in the morning. Recently there have been signs that the men have begun to abuse this privilege. A few men have developed the habit of taking the entire morning off after every out-of-town trip, even if they arrive back at their home by 5:00 the previous evening. And other employees are beginning to wonder whether they might do the same.

Management has considered imposing a hard-and-fast rule that all service-men must report for work at 9:00 A.M. regardless of what time they got in the night before. But in some cases this would impose an obvious hardship, and it might encourage the servicemen to spread their work out so that instead of finishing their job in the afternoon and returning home late they would slow down and work through the next morning, returning home in the afternoon.

Above all, management is anxious not to disturb the employees' high morale and interest in their work. These servicemen are paid a salary, receive liberal fringe benefits, being treated almost like members of the management.

Advise management on how to handle this problem.

MANAGERIAL SKILLS

In this section we shall look more closely at some of the skills that the effective manager must possess. Obviously, before a manager can supervise his subordinates he must be able to communicate with them. Yet communication is not a simple matter. The words uttered by the sender of a message may have a different meaning for him than for the man who receives them. Particularly when subordinates are insecure, hostile, or suspicious of their superiors, they may ascribe unintended meanings to messages from above. To prevent misunderstanding, the senders of messages, at all levels of the management hierarchy, must be careful to fashion them so that their meaning is clear to the receiver. This is the problem we shall discuss in Chapter 10, "Communications."

Effective communication is a two-way process. The good manager must also be a good listener. Interviewing, which is merely deliberate listening, is an essential skill if the manager is to get to know his subordinates. In addition, merely by listening the manager may help subordinates solve their own problems or at least induce them to become more receptive to what he has to say (Chapter 11, "Interviewing: The Fine Art of Listening").

Because the manager must deal with groups as well as individuals, committee meetings and informal conferences are becoming increasingly important as a means of communication in industry. As we shall see, the skills of conference leadership are closely akin to the skills of interviewing (Chapter 12, "Conference Leadership").

Chapter 13, "Introducing Change," considers a problem that is directly influenced by the quality of communications within the organization. As we shall see, it is the meaning that is communicated by a proposed change that most often leads to resistance. Effective use of communications, interviewing, and conference leadership—as well as of some of the managerial skills discussed earlier—helps insure that change will be readily accepted.

What happens when change is rejected? When subordinates refuse to obey new rules—or, for that matter, old rules too? Then discipline is required (Chapter 14, "Discipline"). In a way, discipline is also a form of communication: The message management is trying to transmit is that it really intends to enforce certain rules. To make discipline accepted and meaningful, the rule and its penalty must be carefully communicated, and the offender must be made to understand that the reason for his being disciplined is the fact he broke the rule, not personal animus on the part of the manager.

Considered together, these are some of the skills that an effective manager uses in implementing the philosophy which we discussed in the preceding section of this book.

Communications

"But I didn't think you meant I was to inspect *every* unit."
"How did I know he was serious about quitting?"
"Our employees are always misinterpreting what we say. . . ."
"You can't trust management to tell the truth."

There is hardly an aspect of management's job that does not involve communications. Serious mistakes are made because orders are misunderstood. Casual kidding leads to anger. An off-hand remark by the big boss leads the plant manager to adopt a get-tough attitude with the union. All spring from a breakdown in communications.

In this chapter we shall be concerned largely with face-to-face communications between individuals. In Chapter 15 we shall look at communications in terms of the over-all organization.

On the surface, face-to-face communications would seem to be simple. Have you ever listened to two old friends talking together? Rarely do they use complete sentences; often a single word, a grunt or a groan, or a raised eyebrow communicates as much meaning as lengthy speeches would convey between casual acquaintances. A few syllables go a long way.

But successful communication does not necessarily take place automatically whenever two people get together. Let's examine a situation more typical of business life. The shop-clerk tells his boss with pride, "This is the heaviest day we've ever had." But the boss thinks the clerk is lazy and looking for an excuse not to unload new stock. So he answers angrily and the subordinate concludes that the boss is an overbearing, ungrateful so-and-so.

The basic problem in communications is that the meaning which is actually received by one person may not be what the other intended to send. The speaker and the listener are two separate individuals living in different worlds; any number of things can happen to distort the messages that pass between them.

The human sensory apparatus does not transmit an exact duplicate of reality from the outside world into the mind of the observer. Our needs and experiences tend to color what we see and hear. Messages we don't want to accept are repressed. Others are magnified. Still others are created out of thin air (for example, the "faults" in a person we dislike) or are hideously distorted from their original reality.[1]

What are the causes of breakdowns in communications? What can be done to overcome them? We shall consider each of these questions in turn.

WHY COMMUNICATIONS BREAK DOWN

Hearing What We Expect to Hear

What we hear or understand when someone speaks to us is largely shaped by our own experience and background. Instead of hearing what people tell us, we hear what our minds tell us they have said. These may be the same things—or very different. We all tend to have preconceived ideas of what people mean; when we hear something new we tend to identify it with something similar that we have experienced in the past.

> The manager tells an employee that the company has lost some important orders. Now this employee has had other jobs, and whenever a company has lost business he has been thrown out of work. So he "hears" the manager's statement as, "You can expect to be laid off in the near future." When the man announces that he has quit to work elsewhere, the supervisor may be surprised to learn that the man thought his job was in danger.

Psychologists have said that individuals are motivated to obtain information which is consistent with their conception of themselves.

An extreme form of letting expectations determine communication content is *stereotyping*. For example, we may expect athletically inclined, big-muscled people to be rather dull, and when they say something we say to ourselves, "Well there is another typical remark made by someone who is all brawn and no brain." We grow up believing that Rarutanians (or some other group) are shiftless and lazy. Bill Jones is a Rarutanian. When Jones comes up with an intelligent short cut on his job which took a great deal of time and energy to develop, we take it as proof that "he's always looking for a chance to loaf, just like all the rest of them." Though ridiculous, such stereotypes are stubbornly preserved even in the face of conflicting evidence.

Although this is short-cut thinking, "one of the most time-consuming pastimes of the human mind is to rationalize sentiments and to disguise them as logic." [2]

---

[1] Our discussion is greatly influenced by Alfred Korzybski, *Science and Sanity* (Lancaster, Pa.: Science Press, 1933).

[2] Fritz Roethlisberger and William Dickson, *Management and the Worker* (Cambridge, Mass.: Harvard University Press, 1939), p. 88.

Ignoring Information That Conflicts with What We Already "Know"

Most of us resist change. We tend to reject new ideas, particularly if they conflict with what we already believe. In some ways our communications-receiving apparatus (sense organs and brain) works like an efficient filter. When we read a paper or listen to a political speech, we tend to note only those things that confirm our present beliefs. We may even comment that it is "good to get that additional information." On the other hand, we tend to ignore anything that conflicts with our beliefs; sometimes our filters work so efficiently we don't hear it at all. And even if we do hear it, we either reject it as a fallacious notion or find some way of twisting and shaping its meaning to fit our preconceptions. Because we hear and see what we *expect* to hear and see, we are rarely disappointed.

Communications sometimes fail to have the desired effect because they run counter to other information that the receiver possesses. Management may insist that the company must reduce costs if it is to survive. Everyone is urged to work harder and cut expenses to the bone. But some of the employees shrug off the announcement, for they know that salesmen still receive lavish allowances for "entertainment expenses." These expenses may be justified as a means of obtaining orders, but this is something the employees are in no position to appreciate. The same reaction would set in if they saw wasteful methods of manufacture countenanced week after week without being corrected.

Similarly, statements that hard work leads to promotion are likely to be ignored in a company where promotions in fact often are made on the basis of seniority or favoritism. A guarantee that "the company never cuts an incentive rate because employees are earning too much" is disregarded if rates have in fact been cut as a result of minor engineering changes. Even if the company is perfectly justified in retiming a job after the method or product has been changed, the employee may be convinced that this is simply an excuse for cutting the rate.

> The story has been told that, while the U.S. was able to break the Japanese top-secret code before Pearl Harbor and thus had information concerning the projected attack, this data was ignored because it did not fit into the working hypotheses of some key government officials. The record of World War I is filled with similar examples of information being ignored that was inconsistent with plans and policies that had been drawn up by the French and German General Staffs.[3]

Evaluating the Source

"The first time I met Bill Smith he tried to impress me that he was a big shot. Ever since, I have discounted everything he says because I know what kind of blowhard he is."

---

[3] Barbara Tuchman, *The Guns of August* (New York: Macmillan, 1962).

Not only does the receiver evaluate what he hears in terms of his own background and experience, he also takes the sender into account. How reliable is he as a source of information? Does he have an axe to grind?

Often the receiver ascribes nonexistent motives to the sender. This is particularly true in labor-management relations. Many union members, convinced that management is trying to weaken the union, interpret every company statement as an attempt to deceive them. Similarly, management often regards every union grievance as a political maneuver designed only to win votes. Both sides are sometimes right, of course. But this mental set makes mutual understanding and agreement more difficult.

One experimenter clipped a cartoon from a union publication illustrating "The Four Goals of Labor" and pasted it up with a caption indicating that it had come from a publication of the National Association of Manufacturers. When the clipping was shown to union members, they were overwhelmingly critical of it as an unfair, biased representation of labor's goals. Having accepted the source as antilabor, they automatically drew the "obvious" conclusions.[4]

This sort of bias is one of the reasons why company newspapers (so-called "house organs") find it difficult to gain worker acceptance. Once employees become convinced that the paper is just a management mouthpiece, many will believe nothing it prints, no matter how objective or verifiable. So, too, with pamphlets and other give-aways. If these are tagged as propaganda, all the information they contain becomes suspect, even useful information about health and household safety.

Similarly it is hard for a manager to shed a reputation for being hardboiled or unfair. Suppose he goes through a training program and emerges with every intention of turning over a new leaf. Subordinates may well be extremely suspicious of his motives and assume that his new approach is just a trick. If so they will distort and misconstrue every move he makes. He is now unpredictable.

A manager who receives a suggestion from a colleague or subordinate may assume one of two things: (1) Here is an alert, intelligent employee who is anxious to make a contribution to the efficiency of the organization, or (2) here is somebody who is trying to show me up by suggesting something he figures I was too foolish to think of myself. And which of the two motivations he attributes to the subordinate will have a substantial effect on what he actually "sees" in the suggestion.

In short, it is extremely difficult for us to separate what we hear from our feelings about the person who says it.

Halo Effect

One aspect of stereotyping and evaluating the source is the tendency to ignore the "greys" and to react in "black or white" terms. Thus, when someone

---

[4] William H. Whyte, Jr., *Is Anybody Listening?* (New York: Simon and Schuster, 1952), p. 223.

is speaking who has gained our trust or who begins a speech by saying something with which we agree, we will hear nearly everything he says as good and correct. On the other hand, someone we distrust will be ignored or heard to say nothing worth attending to. The failure to make appropriate discriminations between the "good" and "bad" that may be intermixed within a single person and his comments is often called the "halo effect."

Different Perceptions

People interpret the same stimulus in different ways, depending on their previous experience. Take the case of a supervisor who is watching a group of employees laughing.

> 1. To the manager who believes that work must be painful in order to be productive, the laughter communicates to him that time is being wasted, and perhaps assignments are too easy.
> 2. To the manager who believes that contented employees work harder, the laughter communicates that he is succeeding as a manager.
> 3. To the manager who is personally insecure, the laughter communicates that the men are ridiculing him.

Clearly, the group with which we identify ourselves—the "reference group," as psychologists call it—tends to build in a bias. As advertisers discovered long ago, an individual rarely changes his mind by himself. His attitudes toward politics, music, recreation, work pace, and all his other activities and interests are largely colored by the group with which he identifies. As we mentioned in Chapter 9, the supervisor is wasting his time trying to convince an individual employee to work harder when there is a strong group standard to the contrary. The employee would be risking ostracism if he went along with the supervisor's request. Management often uses slogans and posters to indoctrinate workers with the ideas of promoting safety, cutting scrap losses, making suggestions, or engaging in good housekeeping. They even send personal letters to employees' homes. The trouble with these efforts is that they are directed to the *individual,* whereas the basic attitudes and convictions are determined by the *group.* Thus, if an employee's fellow workers see the supervisor as harsh and unfair, chances are he will feel the same way.

Even the categories of thought used by different groups may be widely divergent. It may well be that trying to convince an hourly employee to improve his *industriousness* will be less effective than trying to convince him to improve his *skill.* Employees can distinguish differences in skill but can't always distinguish differences in industriousness.[5]

In a large organization, the difficulties of perception are compounded. An announcement may go to dozens of groups with different occupational and status interests. What each group "hears" depends on its own interests. An announcement that the company has purchased the plans for new products that

---

5 Harry Triandis, "Categories of Thought of Managers, Clerks and Workers about Jobs and People in Industry," *Journal of Applied Psychology,* Vol. 43, No. 5 (1959), pp. 338-344.

will be manufactured in a new plant on the West Coast may be heard in these different ways:

> *Design engineer:* "This may be an indication that the company prefers to go outside the organization for new ideas, and that is bound to hurt our status."
> *Production engineer:* "This new product will mean more work for us. Some of us may have a chance to move out West."
> *Worker:* "The new products aren't going to be manufactured in the home plant. That means if business should get slack, we're likely to get laid off. A bad trend."

Or take this example.

> The head of marketing has recently spent a great deal of time convincing the company president that they are losing business because competitors' prices are lower. Thus, when the president requests new cost-saving efforts, the marketing manager hears the news as a significant policy statement. On the other hand, the production manager, who does not contact customers, "hears" this as another platitude.[6]

This is one of the most serious sources of friction in industry. With all the sincerity in the world, we try to frame a message that will break the communications barrier and carry an appropriate meaning to those to whom it is directed. But in many instances we know too little about their point of view, and our efforts miscarry.

The trouble may be simply that a subordinate doesn't understand what sort of information his boss wants him to supply. Consequently, the subordinate has no way of knowing what he should tell his boss, or when or where he should speak. Inevitably, the boss complains that vital facts have been kept from him or that he is being deluged with useless information.

The reverse situation is just as troublesome. In training a subordinate, a superior often tries to communicate information before the subordinate is ready to understand it.

In conclusion, it is very difficult to understand information that is outside our experience, no matter how simply and clearly the information is presented by the sender.

Words Mean Different Things to Different People

This is the so-called "semantic" problem. Essentially, language is a method of using symbols to represent facts and feelings. Strictly speaking we can't convey *meaning;* all we can do is convey *words.* And yet the same words may suggest quite different meanings for different people. The meanings are in the people, not in words.

When management says that profits are essential if the business is to sur-

---

[6] For more cases of how organizational location and prior experience determines perception see Margaret Chandler, *Management Rights and Union Interests* (New York: McGraw-Hill, 1964), p. 298.

vive, it is thinking of profits as a means by which the company can buy new equipment, expand, and provide more jobs. To management, profits mean a successfully operated, growing enterprise. But to employees, the word profit sometimes suggests a picture of excess funds piled up through paying inadequate wages. No matter how often management explains the need for profits, employees may persist in attaching the meaning of "excess," "unearned," or "unfair" to the term. Any attempt to communicate about profits must surmount the barrier of established meanings attached to the word.

We find this problem arising in the "economic education" programs conducted by many companies. These programs try to give workers an understanding of how profits and productivity are related to job security and high wages, and an awareness of the advantages of our economic system over others. It has been estimated that companies are investing $100,000,000 each year in such attempts.[7]

Here again the difficulty is that the management which sponsors these programs and the employees for whom they are produced live in different worlds. Abstractions like "profits," "capital," and "productivity" have real meaning in the world of management, but they may have little meaning to the employee (or very negative associations).

In addition, the "psychological distance" that separates the rank-and-file worker from top management impedes understanding. They have little experience in dealing directly with one another. When they do interact, the contact tends to be highly restrained, formal, and artificial—unsuited to real communication.

This problem is especially acute with abstract terms. But even simple concrete words and phrases often lead to trouble; again because the sender and receiver live in separate worlds. For instance:

> The foreman spots oil on the floor and tells a machinist, "Get that oil wiped up as soon as you can; it's a real safety hazard." The machinist nods that he will. Ten minutes later an inspector slips on the very same spot.
> The supervisor is enraged by this needless accident. When he prepares to penalize the machinist for failing to follow instructions, he is told, "But I was going to do it *as soon as I could,* as you told me. I thought you could see that I was working on a delicate cut, and I had to finish that first."

To the supervisor "as soon as you can" meant immediately; to the operator it meant as soon as it could be done without endangering his work. It is foolish to try to decide who was right. Here we see the fallacy of the simple "tell them what you want them to do" approach. Simply telling people isn't enough when the sender and the receiver give the words different meanings. Confusion arises even when words are selected with great care.

Symbols. For some people, a particular word or phrase may have a symbolic meaning that others overlook. When we use words of this sort, we may find ourselves communicating things we had no intention of saying.

---

[7] Whyte, *op. cit.,* p. 7.

> When the manager tells a new supervisor that the parking lot is too crowded for him to have a parking sticker, something more is being communicated than simple information on parking conditions. What the new supervisor hears may be this, "You are not accepted as a member of management, and everyone will soon know it."

The manager's reference to parking stickers carried far more meaning than he had intended.

Observers of collective bargaining have noted that violent antagonism develops in discussions about "management prerogatives" or the "union shop." Again, these are terms that have great symbolic significance. While the manager is talking about prerogatives to the union, he is really trying to say that the very basis of the managerial function and perhaps of the free-enterprise system is involved. Similarly, the union leader arguing for the union shop feels that acceptance or rejection symbolizes the real place of the union in the plant —is it a permanent, accepted institution or merely a temporary nuisance that is being tolerated? Compromise on such issues is difficult, for both parties feel that their vital interests are at stake.

Argot

Occupational groups and sometimes social groups tend to develop their own special language, called "argot." Sometimes group members forget this when they are talking to an outsider who doesn't share these "insider" meanings.

> The new supervisor was dismayed when a subordinate told him that a customer's shipping request had been "pickled in oil." The men used this term to mean giving an order extra-special treatment.

Although argot simplifies in-group communication and provides a sense of belonging and sometimes status to those who use it, there may be other motivations involved in its use. Individuals may seek to impress people with their complex technical knowledge—for example, by talking about "I/O" (input-output) equipment instead of computer printers. In a sense, they use words that will communicate something about themselves by not communicating about the subject under discussion!

Similar to argot is the use of special techniques of speaking and acting that only insiders understand. For example, Americans often tease each other, feigning extreme criticism when it is not meant seriously. Someone not used to this joking style might take seriously, with disastrous results, a comment like this maintenance supervisor's (to one of his mechanics): "That certainly is the crummiest piece of work that ever took a man so many wasted hours to get done!" Overseas, such joking is often not appreciated.

Of course, teasing and joking perform another function in communication that is often forgotten. Many people learn to impart in this fashion delicate or sensitive information that would be unacceptable (or cause an antagonistic reaction) if it were said straightforwardly.

Nonverbal Communication

In trying to understand what another person is trying to say to us (and thus to predict their future behavior) we use many *cues* beside language. Looking at the eyes, the shape of the mouth, the muscles of the face, even bodily posture may tell us more about what the other person really thinks than the words he uses. The reverse is that we ourselves often communicate things unintentionally. Arriving at the office angry because of a traffic jam, a disgruntled manager may be "telling" his subordinates by his general appearance that he is dissatisfied with their work, although that was never intended.

Styles of dress, tone of voice, even our manner of speaking often communicate a good deal about us. The noncollege-trained employee may have a difficult time adjusting to a company in which most employees have degrees because he always seems "different." He must learn a number of subtle bits of behavior that are assimilated during college and that communicate to others that one is sophisticated, or well educated, or reasonably high in status. It is not easy to learn all these hidden cues, which communicate even more than what we think we are saying.

Effects of Emotions

When we are insecure, worried, or fearful, what we hear and see seems more threatening than when we are secure and at peace with the world. Rumors of all sorts spring up when management makes a change of any kind without adequate explanation, even a change as simple as moving desks around the office. This is particularly true during an economic recession. Then statements and actions that under less trying circumstances would have passed unnoticed become grounds for fear. "Yes, Joe might be right, they are going to double the work load." "I saw the foreman looking at the seniority list; I guess the rumors are right, a lot of men will be laid off because of the new equipment."

By the same token, when we are angry or depressed, we tend to reject out of hand what might otherwise seem like reasonable requests or good ideas. Our gloom and despair color everything we do and see. Similarly, when elated, we may not "hear" problems or criticisms.

Noise

Living in a world of words and being deluged by sounds all the time, individuals learn to "tune out" many things. While a mother usually hears her child crying, the father often sleeps through, although he would hear his wife call. Many things a manager says are ignored, actually never heard, because they sound so much like what he always says: "Work efficiently," "This order is very important," "Save materials," "The company is depending on us." Thus, before individuals can hear a message, they must learn to discriminate between background noise (that is, what is always being said) and what is significant and relevant new information and worthy of attention.

Summary

Barriers to communications among members of an organization cause breakdowns, distortions, and inaccurate rumors. They plague the daily life of the manager who must depend on accurate transmission of orders and information for efficient operation. The implication is clear: Don't assume that every message that you send will be received in the form you intended it to be.

OVERCOMING BARRIERS TO COMMUNICATION

Up to this point we have purposely presented a discouraging, one-sided picture: pervasive problems and no solutions. But the picture need not be this bleak. We now know many techniques for improving communications, even though—it should be emphasized—none is a cure-all. Perfect understanding between people is impossible.

Among other things, good communications requires solving simultaneously two quite different problems. The manager must learn to improve his *transmission*—what words, ideas and feelings he actually sends to the other person. At the same time he must cope with his own *reception*—what he perceives the other person's reactions and statements to be. We shall devote the rest of this chapter to a discussion of several methods by which a manager can maximize his success in communicating. At first glance, these techniques may appear mechanical substitutes for mutual trust and understanding. However, a wide variety of research confirms the efficacy of considering communications as a type of engineering problem—the problem of transmitting information from one point to another.

Utilizing Feedback

Perhaps the single most important method of improving communications is *feedback*. This term, adopted from engineering,[8] refers to the ability of certain complex machines (technically, systems) to check on their own performance and to correct it if necessary.

We all use this principle of feedback in our human communications—perhaps without realizing it. Even in casual conversations we are constantly on the alert for cues to whether we are being understood (such as attentive nods

---

[8] For sophisticated analyses of how principles of electronic communications may be applied to human communications, see Norbert Wiener, *Cybernetics* (Cambridge, Mass.: Technology Press, 1954); Colin Cherry, *On Human Communication* (New York: Wiley, 1957); Claude E. Shannon and Warren Weaver, *The Mathematical Theory of Communications* (Urbana: University of Illinois Press, 1949).

from the other person). Similarly, a good teacher is always interested in audience reaction among his students. If they seem confused or drowsy, he knows his lecture isn't getting across. The good supervisor is equally conscious of the need to determine his subordinates' reactions to what he is trying to communicate.

An interesting study illustrates the importance of feedback. Two students were placed in different rooms and one was asked to communicate to the other the position of an interconnected series of dominoes placed on a grid. Both had identical grids in front of them. The sender was permitted to explain to the receiver, in any way he saw fit, the relative positions of the dominoes. Yet it was impossible to complete the task successfully when the receiver was forbidden to respond—that is, when communications were entirely one-way. No matter how painstakingly the sender explained the pattern, the receiver never understood all of it. Apparently some opportunity to ask for further information, at least to answer "yes" or "no" to the questions of the sender (e.g., Did you understand what I said?), is essential if complex information is to be communicated. Without feedback, false perceptions creep in, and even a small error that goes uncorrected may become magnified into a major distortion.

This experiment also revealed that communications gain in speed and efficiency as more and more feedback is permitted. Limiting the receiver to "yes" or "no" responses is less effective than allowing him to expand his comments to whatever he deems appropriate.

Using Many
Communication Channels

How do we know if the person to whom we are communicating understands, agrees, or sympathizes with us, or is indifferent, hostile, or confused? There are several techniques for maximizing feedback.

Observation. In a face-to-face situation, we can observe the other person and judge his responses by his total behavioral set. We can watch for nonverbal cues—the expressions of puzzlement, anger, or comprehension that flicker across the face of the listener, or the subtle body motions that reveal impatience, animosity, or agreement. These cues give eloquent expression to attitudes that the receiver may be reluctant or unable to express in words.

Indeed, by their posture and facial expression, the set of their lips, the movement of an eyebrow, people often tell us more than they do in hours of talk or scores of written memoranda. A subordinate is seldom eager to challenge the orders of his superior. But in the course of informal, face-to-face discussion, an alert supervisor can detect the subordinate's lack of enthusiasm by his tone of voice and his general physical behavior.

Few of us appreciate just how much valuable information these nonverbal cues transmit. As one social scientist has observed, "When communication is at peak efficiency, in the most intimately shared situations, words are often superfluous. Good examples of this are the hospital operating room, the jazz band, and some small interdependent work teams in industry." [9] The close coordination necessary for these groups to achieve their goal is attained exclusively through occasional nods and glances.

Listening with a "third ear."   We must listen carefully if we are to discover what a person is trying to say. Though few of us can qualify as psychiatrists, we can learn to listen with a "third ear" by asking ourselves such questions as: "What did Joe really mean when he told me he was 'fed up'? Was it his assignment? His family? His chances for promotion? Me, as his boss? Why did he remain silent when I asked him for details?"

There is a hidden content in many communications that can only be inferred by the listener. (This underlying element is frequently referred to as the *latent* content as distinct from the *manifest* content.) Although the listener should keep his imagination in check, he should try to go beyond the logical verbal meaning where there is some evidence that emotional feeling is involved. Most communications are in fact a combination of fact and feeling.

A good example of this hidden content is provided by the word "communications" itself. An office manager complains to the personnel director that all his human-relations problems stem from "poor communications." If the personnel director wants to be of assistance, he will try to get behind the manager's use of the word "communications." The manager might mean that there are divisive cliques that tend to distort his orders or that he, the boss, never hears the "real truth" about what is going on in the office. He might be using the word communications to mean that cooperative teamwork is lacking, or to mean many other things. The point is that the words used by a speaker may not be very informative until we have an opportunity to question him on what he really means in terms of actual observable behavior. The listener must try to get back to the *referents* of the speaker and to avoid the easy assumption that both people are attaching the same meaning to abstract words.

Adjusting rate of speaking.   To facilitate communications it is important to become aware of differences in speaking patterns. Some people, for example, speak with long-drawn-out pauses between thoughts or sentences. If such speakers are interrupted by someone who becomes impatient sitting passively so long, they will often fail to reveal all of their original ideas. Also, interruptions can cause anger, which impedes communication, as already noted.

In conversation, a listener's attention is often lost by a speaker who insists on talking too long a time without allowing the other person to respond. Many individuals have such verbal energies that the words come out like a torrential downpour, and, in the process, they lose their audience. On the other hand, the natural style of speaking for some people is in short bursts. These people are only comfortable and able to say all that they want to if the other individual replies each time they stop.

---

[9] From a lecture by Dr. Robert N. Wilson, University of North Carolina.

Failure to adjust, to synchronize, to the speaking patterns of the other person causes breakdowns in communications because of lost ideas as well as the discomfort and emotional reactions associated with interruptions or long silent periods.[10]

Using Face-to-Face Communications

Face-to-face communications are superior, under most circumstances, to written orders, printed announcements, or business letters. Only when the sender is able to experience direct feedback from the receiver can he really know what the receiver is hearing and what he is failing to hear. How else can the sender become aware of the hidden meaning—the symbolic significance the receiver is ascribing to his words? How else can he bring out into the open contradictory information already in the receiver's mind that may cause him to reject or ignore the communication?

Another reason for the greater effectiveness of voice communications is that most of us communicate more easily, completely, and frequently by voice.

Probably the greatest advantage of voice communications is that they provide immediate feedback. Merely by looking at the audience, the skillful speaker can judge how it is reacting to what he is saying. If necessary he can modify his approach or vary the intensity of his voice. (The human voice can provide a wider variety of emphasis and pace than any printed page, regardless of the number of type fonts used.)

Even better feedback is possible if the recipients of the message are allowed to comment or ask questions. This gives the supervisor an opportunity to explain his meaning or to consider unexpected problems. (Printed material can provide explanations, but few writers can anticipate all the questions that might be asked.)

For example, it is almost impossible to criticize someone's performance in writing without their taking serious offense. The cold type or words always sound more harsh and condemnatory than they may have been intended, and such written criticisms often provoke strong emotional counterreactions. The result is that the recipient tends to reject the entire message as having come from a hostile source. The same criticism discussed in a face-to-face exchange can be made much more acceptable and thus will be heard.

Furthermore, we usually ascribe more credibility to what we hear someone say than to words attributed to him in print. Employees conditioned to the "slick" releases of public relations offices tend to discount many of the printed announcements they read. Actually hearing the boss say that the company is in serious trouble, however, may carry a great deal more weight than would

---

[10] A more precise explanation and description of how people differ in the physical pattern of their interaction is provided by the researcher who has done most of the studies in this field. *Cf.* Eliot Chapple and Leonard Sayles, *The Measure of Management* (New York: Macmillan, 1961) pp. 114-141.

a statement in the house organ, particularly if employees have an opportunity to ask the boss direct questions.

A Secretary of State explained why he frequently left Washington:

> "Well, I fly because I go to meet heads of government, foreign ministers of other countries, and in a few minutes or at most a few hours of personal consultation you can achieve a much better understanding than you can possibly achieve by working through notes and writing to each other." [11]

Does all this mean that written messages have no place in the organization? Not at all. In fact, they are often indispensable. Lengthy, detailed instructions must be put in writing so that the person to whom they are addressed can have a chance to study them at leisure. The spoken word exists only for an instant, and then vanishes. The written message provides a permanent record to which the receiver can refer to make sure he understands what has been said, and to which the sender can refer as evidence that he has in fact said it. Frequently, too, the relative formality of written communications gives the message greater weight than it would have if it were delivered orally.

For very important messages, both the spoken and written word may be used in combination. For instance, if a new procedure is to be introduced, the supervisor might call a meeting of his subordinates to give them a rough outline of the change. At this point he could (1) explain why the change is necessary, (2) answer their questions, and (3) perhaps make adjustments to meet objections. Once general agreement has been reached, the new procedure can be reduced to writing for future reference.

Sensitivity to the World of the Receiver

It is extremely difficult to get through to a listener when what you are trying to communicate contradicts his expectations and predilections. If your typist has been in the habit of preparing only a single carbon, you must *stress* a request for two carbons. If being sent to the front office is regarded by employees as a sign of impending discipline, you must take pains to communicate that this is not the reason, if in fact it is not.

In short, you must be sensitive to the private world of the receiver, try to predict the impact of what you say and do on his feelings and attitudes, and tailor your messages to fit your receiver's vocabulary, interests, and values. Managers who work with a variety of groups in the organization must learn techniques of "simultaneous translation" to avoid misunderstandings. The greater the gap between your background and experience and that of the receiver, the greater the effort you must make to find some common ground of understanding. If the supervisor really wants to communicate with the

---

[11] Dana Adams Schmidt, "Instant Diplomacy and the New Diplomats," *Columbia University Forum* (Fall 1958), p. 36.

sweeper, for example, he must find a way of (a) fitting his remarks to the sweeper's attitudes and beliefs, (b) making some appeal to the needs of the sweeper, and (c) constantly testing (via feedback) whether his message is being received.

The Detroit Edison Company has adopted an interesting approach. Its house organ features a "rumor clinic" in which top management deals candidly with questions raised by employees on such subjects as: alleged pay and vacation inequities, why some employees receive company-bought clothing and others do not, the quality and price of cafeteria food, and the reasons for layoffs or overtime. In answering questions submitted by workers, management has an opportunity to communicate information about the company's economic conditions, engineering and sales problems, and so on—and in terms of direct interest to employees.

Sensitivity training.   Recognizing the crucial role of communications and the widespread incidence of misunderstanding, many organizations have sought to improve the ability of managers to *empathize*. Empathy is defined as the ability to put yourself in someone else's place and thus to understand better what they feel and are trying to say. One of the best ways of doing this is to learn the impact that your own way of speaking and behaving has on other people. Although associates, and certainly subordinates, are understandably timid about candidly revealing how they react to a manager's style of interaction, special training groups assess openly one another's interpersonal shortcomings. This procedure has been given a name, *sensitivity training.*[12] The objective is not only to minimize distracting and disturbing behavioral characteristics but to help managers see how individual differences affect communication. As the poet Robert Burns once said: "The giftee . . . to see ourselves as others see us."

Awareness of Symbolic Meaning

As we have seen, symbols play a vital role in the "private world" of the listener. Here is a case in which effective communication was blocked until symbolic meanings were taken into account:

> To help in the preparation of market analyses the District Sales Manager asked the salesmen to compute correlation coefficients from their records. These coefficients could be calculated quite simply and painlessly by use of a simple formula. But the salesmen refused to do what they were asked. One excuse followed another: The computations were too complicated, it was clerk's work and not part of their job description, the coefficients were really useless, and so on. There seemed to be no way to convince the men to perform this simple task, and their persistent refusal seemed out of all proportion to the issue at hand.

---

[12] For an extensive treatment of this subject see Leland Bradford, Jack Gibb, Kenneth Beane (eds.), *T-Group Theory and Laboratory Method* (New York: Wiley, 1964).

Why was this modest request greeted with such stubborn resistance? The very degree of the salesmen's reaction was the key to the problem. Investigation revealed that coefficient correlations had been tried three years earlier, when the department was headed by an inept supervisor who had earned the universal dislike of his subordinates. Among other things, he had tried to revamp all the departmental procedures and in the process had introduced this statistical technique. Ever since, the salesmen had associated the term "coefficient correlation" with autocratic supervision. To them it had become a symbol of oppressive management. Once the company had plumbed this seemingly irrational attitude, it was a simple matter to develop a different terminology for the operation, to conduct training in how the computations should be carried out, and to gain ready acceptance for the whole activity.

The moral of this story is clear: If there is extraordinary, unexpected resistance to a proposal, try to find out whether some symbolic meaning is associated with it.

Timing Messages Carefully

We have already noted that our current beliefs often distort the meaning we ascribe to what we hear or see. There is an analogy here to the concept of "noise" as used by the communications engineer. The supervisor must recognize that when he is trying to tell his subordinate something, other things are being heard simultaneously that may distort his message.

One way of limiting the amount of noise or distortion is to communicate your message before those other beliefs or attitudes come into play. Then the communication will meet less resistance and your chances of getting it accepted will be greatly increased.

> Management announced that Foreman Green would retire in a few months and would be replaced by a man named Williams from another department. One of the men felt that Williams had done him an injustice years ago, and spread the word among his fellow employees that Williams was a tyrant who played favorites.
>
> Long before Williams set foot in the new department, a petition was sent to top management requesting that a different foreman be assigned. And once Williams showed up, everything he said and did was fitted into the picture the employees had already established. Every job assignment he made was scrutinized for favoritism. Even harmless statements were often interpreted as threats.

A situation like this is an ideal breeding-ground for misunderstanding and unrest. Yet management could have minimized the problem by taking positive action before the picture of the new supervisor got established, perhaps by having the employees meet him as soon as the announcement was made.

In other words, a message is more likely to be understood when it is not competing with other, potentially conflicting messages. Of course, this was the basis for "brainwashing" during the Korean War. Some of our captured soldiers were isolated from their buddies and exposed to repeated anti-American stories. A more moderate application of the concept of minimizing *noise* would involve the isolation of a group of executives at a mountain-top conference center. Without the interference of normal communications they would be more likely to "hear" a major departure in corporate policy that was being announced.

It is worth remembering that people listen when they are motivated to hear. As many staff experts have discovered, fellow managers actually tend to hear the good ideas that the expert has only when the manager has a problem for which the idea might provide a solution. Training sessions similarly are most effective, for example, *after* an employee has been faced with the kind of problems which would cause him to recognize the need for additional training. Earlier "messages" may be ignored or not heard because they are competing with so many other stimuli reaching the individual.

Reinforcing Words with Action

Words by themselves are suspect. Employees are more likely to accept new propositions when they observe an actual change in behavior or participate themselves in the process of change. For example, supervisors in one company were told that they would have the final say in granting individual pay increases. This was a radical departure from past practice. Most of the supervisors were skeptical about whether management really meant what it said. But this feeling disappeared when they began filling out recommendation forms themselves and sending them to the Personnel Department (a minor clerical job that in the past had been done in the superintendent's office). The consistent reinforcement of verbal announcements by action increases the likelihood that the communication will be accepted.

Employees learn that their supervisor, not the Personnel Department, controls pay increases when they see him taking this action and hear directly from him that they are to receive the increase. Where Personnel does the notifying, they perceive otherwise.

Management must be careful not to allow supersalesmanship techniques to dominate its thinking in communicating to employees. Because employees are able to judge for themselves the quality of the relationship they enjoy with a company, sustained repetition of slick slogans will not be effective. One cannot advertise one type of personnel program and deliver another. In the same vein, low-pressure statements are probably more effective than high-pressure pronouncements. Instead of telling workers how generous their pension benefits are, it may be more effective to give them the facts (comparative data on pension plans for the industry or community) and let them draw their own conclusion. It is difficult if not impossible to communicate "values"; facts can be transmitted with some success, but even facts are subject to distortion.

Once management has acquired a reputation for accuracy and reliability in its communications, it can do a more effecive job of communicating information on new problems. The British learned this lesson during the war.

> Early in World War II, when the radio stations of most countries were widely suspected of distorting the war news, the British Broadcasting System adopted a policy of frankly reporting Allied setbacks. This gave the British an advantage in morale and tactics over their enemies when the tide turned in favor of the Allies, for Europeans of all nationalities were ready to believe the news of the German rout—simply because it came from a source that had proved itself trustworthy.

Using Direct, Simple Language

Written communications should be as intelligible and readable as possible. Rudolf Flesch, one of the foremost proponents of simple, clear, direct writing and speaking, urges that multisyllable and erudite words be avoided, that lengthy sentences be broken down into more manageable units, and that metaphors, irony, and other indirect devices be shunned.[13] He has developed various scales by which the readability of material may be related to the education and comprehension level of different groups of readers.[14] Flesch and others who have specialized in research of this sort also advocate the use of words and phrases that personalize the material and make it more concrete and immediately intelligible.

Every manager must insure that his announcements, public statements, and directives are couched in simple, direct language. Government agencies have been the favorite butt of jokes about "gobbledegook," but many private organizations also are guilty of torturing simple statements into complicated puzzles, and of using specialized and complex jargon. Low readability is undoubtedly a factor in the breakdown of communications. (And since most people talk more simply than they write, it is another reason for using face-to-face communications whenever possible.) High readability, however, is not an answer in itself to the fundamental barriers to communication that we have discussed.

Introducing a Proper Amount of Redundancy

Communications engineers have developed techniques for measuring the amount of "redundancy" in a message—roughly the amount of repetition it contains. The supervisor who wants to give a direct order or transmit technical

---

[13] Rudolf Flesch, *The Art of Plain Talk* (New York: Harper & Row, 1946), and *The Art of Readable Writing* (New York: Harper & Row, 1949).

[14] For instance, the Flesch index for this section is 5.45 or difficult. According to Flesch, it should have a potential audience of 24 per cent of all readers, *op. cit.*, p. 205.

information should make sure that his message includes substantial redundancy. Then, if any word or phrase is misunderstood, there are other elements in the communication that will carry his point. To give a very simple example:

> A firm manufacturing several thousand varieties of chemical compounds used a numerical coding system to refer to each of the products. Increasingly, management found that mistakes were creeping into the ordering system. When a supervisor requested a shipment of compound #28394, a clerical error would occasionally result in a wasted shipment of #23894. Each digit was crucial, and the slightest mistake was costly. Eventually the firm adopted individual names for each compound and these words had a great deal of built-in redundancy, as do nearly all words. If a clerk ordered "calitin" instead of "calithin," the shipping department knew what he meant.

If each word is crucially important, it pays to say the same thing in several ways. In giving complicated directions, for example, it is wise to repeat them several times, perhaps in different ways, to guarantee successful transmission.

At times, however, a manager may want to avoid redundancy, and concentrate instead on introducing novelty or originality into his communications.[15] We tend to ignore many of the messages we receive simply because they sound so familiar. Most of us are guilty of repeating our favorite clichés to the point where people no longer listen to what we say because it is all so predictable. ("I know what the boss is going to say the minute he starts on that line about us all being one big happy team.")

There is some need for surprise, in modest doses to be sure, if we are to gain the attention of those with whom we wish to communicate. This is particularly true when our message contains something that contradicts expectations. For instance, to repeat our previous example, if your typist has been in the habit of preparing only one carbon, you must stress your request for two carbons.

Thus, the supervisor needs to balance carefully the redundancy and surprise elements of his communication.

CONCLUSION

Nearly every aspect of human relations and of supervisor-subordinate relations involves communications. When a selection policy is geared to admit people with similar backgrounds and interests, some of the problems we have discussed in this chapter are minimized. Similarly, carefully planned training and orientation programs help establish a common point of view and reduce misunderstandings that arise from differing frames of reference. Even the structure of the organization—affecting as it does status relations and the number of levels between top management and the worker at the bottom—has a

---

[15] Cherry, *op. cit.*, p. 14.

most significant effect on the ability of people to communicate easily and quickly.

The swiftest, most effective communication takes place among people with common points of view. The supervisor who enjoys a good relationship with his subordinates has much less difficulty in explaining why air-conditioning equipment cannot be installed for another year than does the supervisor who is not trusted by his men. When people feel secure, they can talk to one another easily. Where discontent is rife, so is misunderstanding, misinterpretation, rumor, and distortion. In this sense, communication is a dependent variable. Where there is mutual trust and human relations are good, it is easy; where there is distrust, it is almost impossible. Therefore, the communications area is *not* the place to start improving supervisor-subordinate relationships.

Nevertheless, the problem of communicating accurately and effectively in each contact makes a supervisor's job more difficult. He must guard against the natural inclination in our highly verbal society to assume that simply *telling somebody* is enough to insure successful communication. Fortunately, as we have seen, the supervisor can resort to a number of techniques to facilitate the transmission of understanding between people in their day-to-day activities.

One must be careful and not draw the conclusion that "the more communication the better" is always true. There are limits to how much an individual can absorb and be responsive to. Employees need to be protected from needless

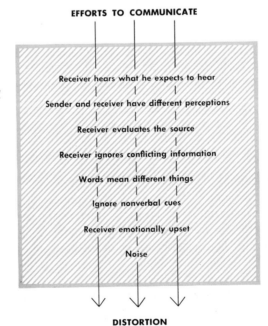

Barriers to successful communication.

EFFORTS TO COMMUNICATE

Receiver hears what he expects to hear

Sender and receiver have different perceptions

Receiver evaluates the source

Receiver ignores conflicting information

Words mean different things

Ignore nonverbal cues

Receiver emotionally upset

Noise

DISTORTION

Feedback

Many channels

Face-to-face communication

Sensitivity to receiver

**EFFORTS
TO
COMMUNICATE**

Awareness of symbolic meanings

**CLEAR
MESSAGE**

Careful timing

Reinforcing words with action

Simple language

Redundancy

Techniques for improved communication.

information so that they concentrate on important data. Also, there may be private fears, hopes, and hostilities within an organization that ought not to be communicated because they would only engender adverse reactions.

Communications is a matter of both transmitting and receiving. This chapter has emphasized transmitting. In Chapter 11 we will consider one of the most useful techniques for receiving information: interviewing.

PROBLEM 1

"WELCOME ABOARD"

This was Joe Phelan's first day on the job, and he was anxious to learn as much as possible about what was expected of him and what kind of company he was going to be working for. He had been hired as a technical writer primarily to prepare manuals to help customers operate the complex industrial equipment the company manufactures.

He was somewhat apprehensive since this was the first time he had ever worked for a large corporation, and this company had a reputation for being impersonal and bureaucratic.

No one greeted him when he came in a few minutes before nine this Monday morning, but remembering the man's name he was replacing, he found the office that he assumed was to be his. The desk still contained a few candy bars and a rather worn blotter. There was also a note to call his supervisor, Cal Thompson.

He followed instructions, and in a few minutes Thompson appeared:

"We certainly are glad to have you aboard, Phelan. Hope you like your new office. By the way, here are half a dozen manuals we issued during the past few months; I think if you read them you'll learn a lot about the work we do. Later this morning my secretary will bring over a lot of background material on the new Series 18 machine which you'll be working on, and tomorrow you'll meet the engineer in charge of the project. Oh, yes, don't forget to go down to the Medical Office sometime today; they want to complete your records. If you have any questions don't hesitate to call me, but I've got to go to a meeting now myself.

Joe thanked him and said he looked forward to getting into the project. "Also, I wonder if I could meet some of the sales people who work with the kind of customers I will be writing for?"

Although Thompson thought that Phelan seemed a little over eager to make a good impression, he only replied, "In due time," and left the room. Thompson's tone of voice convinced Phelan he had spoken out of turn.

Just then Thompson's secretary called to tell him that the normal lunch hour for the department was from 12:30 to 1:30 and that if he had any typing to do he should send it to her and she would transmit it to the typing pool. Phelan, without thinking, replied, "I thought lunch was at noon and I've already agreed to meet an old friend then. And, by the way, could I see the Series 18 file?"

> *Secretary:* "I assure you, Mr. Phelan, I am correct when I say 12:30, but whether or not you wish to observe that, of course, is up to you. I am not your secretary, by the way."
>
> *Phelan:* "Yes, I know that, but Mr. Thompson said you would have those materials."
>
> *Secretary:* "If he said that, he must have forgotten to give them to me. When he does, I assure you that you will get them immediately."

1. Note all the communications breakdowns that occurred and in each consider what misconceptions each party received.
2. How much of this could have been avoided if Joe Phelan had been less apprehensive?

PROBLEM 2

THE CASE OF THE DISAPPEARING FURNITURE

Carlin Mailaway specializes in reproductions of New England antiques and sells them by means of a nationally distributed catalog. The company, located in Great Barrington, Massachusetts, has won a dominant position in the market it serves.

Recently, Carlin instituted a more formal inventory system. The results were appalling to the General Manager, James Coffin. According to the second quarterly inventory, at least $2,000 worth of merchandise had disappeared "mysteriously" during the preceding three months. Almost simultaneously the warehouse supervisor found several pieces of merchandise wrapped as trash in a refuse barrel—as though they had been placed there by someone who intended to retrieve them later.

As soon as the figures were confirmed by a sample rechecking, Coffin dictated a letter to the Warehouse Supervisor, and sent copies out to every one of the 28 employees working in the warehouse. The letter read as follows:

> Our auditing procedures have just disclosed a shocking loss of goods in our warehouse. In the future, no unauthorized personnel are to be allowed into the warehouse section of our building and all employees working in the area will be expected to refrain from carrying packages in or out of the department and permit close scrutiny of their persons as they leave work.
>
> In no sense should any of our loyal, faithful employees interpret this as a slur against their characters. We know that they would want these stern provisions to be introduced to eliminate any possibility that they might be implicated.
>
> We will appreciate your cooperation and thank you for your help in the past.

1. As a long-service employee in this department, how would you "interpret" this letter? Would others interpret it differently, do you think? Which ones and why?
2. What would you think the General Manager's motives were in writing this letter?
3. What alternative procedures might have been considered? What would their shortcomings and advantages be?
4. Might the Manager's letter have been better conceived and written?

PROBLEM 3

FAIR EMPLOYMENT POLICY

For many years the Brace Machine Works had employed Negroes only in menial jobs. After deliberation, and in part as a result of the passage of new state legislation, top management decided to adopt an unambiguous policy of offering equal employment opportunities for members of all nationality, racial, and religious groups.

The president of the company called in the personnel director for his counsel on how to announce this new policy in a way that would not only assure Negroes of equal employment opportunities but would also guarantee that they would not be discriminated against in opportunities for promotion to better-paying, more skilled positions.

1. If you were the personnel director, what advice would you give the president?
2. In helping him frame his approach, what questions would you ask, what information would you need, and what knowledge about the company would be useful to you?

Interviewing: The Fine Art of Listening

"My boss doesn't give a hoot about me. As far as he is concerned I am another piece of machinery."

"I'll say this about my boss: No matter what your problem is, he'll hear you through."

"Though I'm supposed to be in charge of this department, it's my people who do the work. I try to remember that to himself each person is absolutely different from anyone else. He wants special recognition. So I try to pay attention to him, listen to his problems."

Effective communication requires effort both by the sender of the message and the receiver. The last chapter was devoted largely to the sending of messages. In this chapter we shall be concerned with an important aspect of receiving them—with listening.

Listening is one of the most important of all management tools. Yet even though people learn to listen before they learn to talk, relatively few listen well—few have learned the art of *interviewing*.

What do we mean by "interviewing"? Most people think of interviewing in the sense of the formal interviews connected with getting a job. By interviewing we intend much more than this: we mean deliberate, active listening whose purpose is to draw the other person out, to discover what he really wants to say, and to give him a chance to express himself fully.

HISTORICAL BACKGROUND

Management first became aware of the value of interviewing in industrial relations during the 1920's as a consequence of studies conducted at the Hawthorne plant of the Western Electric Company.[1] These studies were

---

[1] For the most thorough review of these studies, see F. J. Roethlisberger and W. J. Dickson, *Management and the Worker* (Cambridge: Harvard University Press, 1939). For a critical analysis of these studies in the light of later research, see Henry Landsberger, *Hawthorne Revisited* (Ithaca: New York State School of Industrial and Labor Relations, 1958).

primarily concerned with the determinants of morale and productivity. However, in their attempts to uncover basic feelings regarding these factors, the researcher found that direct questions designed to find out how the subjects felt about specific aspects of their jobs resulted in superficial, "lifeless" answers. Even worse—or so it seemed at the time—instead of giving "straightforward" responses, some of the people interviewed tended to talk about what interested them most at the moment.

Following this clue, the interviewers tried a radically new experiment: They sat back and decided to let the interviewees direct the interviews. Now they discovered that people began to express their *feelings* as well as give factual answers. Employees launched into long tirades (to which the interviewers patiently listened) revealing attitudes that might otherwise have been kept carefully guarded. In fact, some employees expressed attitudes that they had not been consciously aware of themselves. As a consequence, the interviewers got a much better picture of the psychological geography of the plant. They discovered surprising relationships about which they would never have learned by asking direct questions.

More important: The employees benefited greatly as well. Just by talking freely in the presence of a sympathetic listener, they got their problems off their chest and felt better. They experienced what psychologists call *catharsis* (from the Greek: to make pure). In addition, merely by talking things over, the employees began to gain insight into the nature of their own problems. Once they had relieved their feelings by speaking openly in a receptive environment, they were able to look at their problems more objectively. And their clearer understandings, supplemented by further discussion, often enabled them to work out solutions (at least to those problems that they were in a position to solve themselves).

Impressed by the value of the Hawthorne experience, Western Electric instituted a program of formal counseling. Specially chosen counselors were trained in the use of *nondirective* interviews. (By nondirective interviews we mean—as we shall explain later—a type of interview in which the interviewer encourages the interviewee to express his own thoughts with considerable freedom—as contrasted to directive interviewing, in which the interviewer asks direct questions and tries to keep the discussion within predetermined limits.)

These "free-floating" counselors were given no regular supervisory duties; they were completely separate from the normal management hierarchy. Their function was merely to listen to employees' problems without giving advice or taking action. Other companies rapidly followed Western Electric's example. Particularly during World War II counseling was very popular. Many employers assigned "free-floating" counselors throughout the company, especially to help women workers.

The counselors faced a tough ethical problem of what to do with the information they received. If they repeated to management what they had been told, the workers would no longer trust them. On the other hand, if they could use their information in a discreet manner, they might be able to eliminate the causes of trouble. Often the counselors compromised by giving management general reports without revealing details that might identify individuals.

In recent years the use of such counselors as a personnel tool has declined. It was discovered that this technique has many drawbacks, including the following:

1. Although counseling might help an individual make a better adjustment to a poor environment (say to an inept supervisor), it didn't improve the environment itself. Employees often began to feel that they were wasting their time talking to a counselor who could do nothing for them, and ended up almost as frustrated as before.

2. Counseling is directed almost entirely toward changing *individual* attitudes and behavior, in spite of other evidence from the Hawthorne study itself that group attitudes are often more important than individual attitudes.

3. The counseling system gave subordinates a chance to bypass and tattle on their supervisors. Naturally, the supervisors objected.

4. In some cases employees began to compare the "good" counselor with the "bad" supervisor. Supervisors felt they were entitled to the undivided loyalty of subordinates.

5. The counselors discovered that they were spending most of their time with a few disturbed individuals who really needed deep psychotherapy rather than counseling.

The basic trouble with "free-floating" counseling was its separation from line management. Line management emphasized downward communication. Counseling provided upward communication. But the two forms of communication went along different channels.

Management began to learn that effective communications must go both ways. Upward communication and downward communication, listening and order-giving, are both more effective if done by the *same* person. Furthermore, if they are merged into the same process, something new and better emerges. Thus, there has come the realization that counseling or interviewing or listening (which are really all the same thing) is not a special technique for use by personnel experts only, but a vital aspect of good management generally.

LISTENING AS A MANAGEMENT TOOL

To list the circumstances where interviewing is useful would be almost like listing the functions of management itself. Indeed, all through our discussion of general supervision and methods of correcting mistakes we constantly emphasize the importance of listening. The following example indicates what might happen when this approach works at its best.

Suppose you are a division manager and you want to introduce a new system of quality control. Although you have not as yet consulted with the production supervisor, you have heard through the grapevine that he has strong objections to the new system. Yet his cooperation is essential if the system is to succeed.

You feel pretty certain that your plan is good and that the production supervisor's objections are not well grounded. You are the boss, of course, and you could give him a direct order to put the plan into effect. (Question: How would the supervisor react to this order? How loyally would he carry it out?)

Instead, you decide to listen to his point of view. In spite of the grapevine you can't really be sure you know what his objections are until he has spoken to you personally. If you are at all sincere, you must admit to yourself that his objections may have some merit. (Question: What would happen if you had already made up your mind, and just went through the formalities of listening?)

So you explain the proposed change to him, being careful to emphasize that you still have an open mind, and ask him to comment. You listen attentively and encourage him to express himself fully. As he speaks, he relaxes and explains his point of view with more balance and restraint than he would if he felt he were on the defensive. Instead of trying to answer his arguments, you encourage him to tell you everything he thinks and feels about the change. When he finishes, you briefly summarize what he has said to make sure you understand—and also to indicate *to him* that you have understood.

After speaking his piece, the production supervisor feels free to listen to your point of view—which may have changed since you heard his objections. You fill in some of the areas where you feel he was mistaken, indicate the points on which you have changed your own thinking, and explore with him any adjustments that seem necessary. Even if he is still not fully convinced of the wisdom of your plan, he is more willing to try it out and probably feels pleased that you consulted him and listened to his objections.

The above example suggests the flexibility of the interview technique (though we must emphasize that the results are frequently not as good as we have pictured). It is obviously well suited to formal interviews, such as those used for hiring, exit, and requests for transfer. But it is also appropriate in less formal situations, such as the following:

Low morale: finding out the cause of employee dissatisfaction, turnover, or absenteeism.

Discipline: discovering why employees are performing unsatisfactorily and helping them to evolve means of correcting themselves.

Order-giving: getting reaction to and acceptance of orders, to see that the person who receives the order really understands it.

Resistance to change: gaining acceptance of new techniques, tools, procedures.

Merit rating and evaluation: helping an employee correct his weaknesses.

Training: finding out how much an employee knows and what difficulties he experiences in learning.

Grievance-handling: finding out the real causes of a union grievance and getting the union officers to agree to a constructive solution.

Settling disputes: finding out the causes of the disputes between employees and getting them to agree to settlement.

The interview approach is not something to be applied only when dealing with specific problems. It is a general attitude which the manager can apply day in and day out in his dealings with fellow supervisors, subordinates, and his boss. In a nutshell, it is a matter of always being ready to listen to the other fellow's point of view and trying to take it into account before taking action oneself. If this attitude is absent, then communications may become blocked, as they did in one company:

> The most frequent complaint was that although orders and instructions about work traveled easily enough, it was difficult to take up ordinary feelings, especially if they were critical about the job or about life in the factory. The main stumbling block in getting such feelings resolved was the reticence about communicating them upwards. The reticence was said to be due to the fact that if a person tried to express to his superior his feelings about the job, or about the superior himself, it was all too likely that the superior would argue with him and try to show him that his feelings were unreasonable and that they did not tally with the facts. Having the existence of one's feelings denied in this way only made things worse. The person was not only left with the original feeling but in addition had a resentment against his superior for not understanding him and not helping him get at what was disturbing him.[2]

Establishing Confidence

The supervisor must take the initiative in encouraging subordinates to come to him with their problems (see our discussion in Chapter 8). He must show that he is willing to hear them out. Otherwise minor irritations may grow to tremendous proportions, even before the manager has become aware of the danger. For example, the manager does something the subordinate doesn't like. The subordinate doesn't feel free to talk about it. Gradually his irritation grows and he begins to see his superior in a new light. Everything the supervisor does may now seem threatening and unfair. The subordinate's antagonism grows stronger and stronger, until at last there is a serious breakdown in his relationship with the supervisor.

If the initial interview is a pleasant experience for the subordinate, he will come back more freely and more regularly when new problems arise. If it has been an unpleasant experience and if he feels he has been "put on the spot," he will be reluctant to reveal what is on his mind in the future.

The manager should be aware that some of the men who report to him will be easier to get to know than others. Some will talk to him quite freely and easily. Others will hold back because of fear or natural timidity. The manager must be careful not to spend all his time with those to whom it it easy to talk.

To avoid the charge of favoritism, and to insure that he is able to deal with the problems of all his employees, the supervisor must go out of his way to make contact with employees who are reluctant to come to him. The manager must recognize that there is an invisible barrier which separates him from his subordinates. For some, this status difference is of little importance, but for many it makes effective upward communication much harder.

---

[2] Elliot Jaques, *The Changing Culture of a Factory* (London: Tavistock, 1951), p. 133.

Off-the-Job Problems

Managers sometimes use interviewing to help employees solve personal off-the-job problems. Normally stable individuals may have unexpected trouble and seek to use their supervisor as a wailing wall. However, the manager should be careful not to give advice or get himself saddled with the responsibility for running his subordinates' personal lives.

The manager should be particularly cautious when sensitive areas are reached in the course of an interview. In situations like this, what most people want is a sympathetic, understanding listener rather than an adviser. They may ask for advice, but actually they want only a chance to talk. Even when advice-giving is successful, there is the danger that the employee may become over-dependent on his manager and run to him whenever he has a minor problem.

The manager should be still more careful when deepseated personality problems are involved. In such a case it is wise to refer the person to a professionally trained specialist rather than to play amateur psychologist. The average manager is not equipped to do counseling, nor is this part of his job. The patient-psychiatrist or client-counselor relationship is just not consistent with that of subordinate and boss. And the subordinate may resent being conned by the nondirective technique into blurting out confidences which he later regrets having revealed.

THE USE OF THE NONDIRECTIVE APPROACH

The type of interviewing we shall discuss here has been called "nondirective" because it emphasizes permitting the interviewee (rather than the interviewer) to direct the interview, at least in the early stages. What can this approach accomplish? The nondirective interview has three functions:

1. From the point of view of the interviewer, it helps provide clues to what the interviewee is really thinking and what lies at the root of the problem. Thus, for a manager, the interview is a means of getting information on which he can base decisions.

The first answer an employee gives to an involved question may not be the whole truth. He may not be exactly lying, but he finds it difficult to express just how he feels. True, if the manager starts to fire direct questions, he will usually get direct answers, and they may *sound* reasonable. But they may represent only a small, inaccurate sample of the interviewee's total feelings.

Most of us have trouble expressing our real feelings to others. In part this is so because we are fearful or ashamed of what the other person will think. We want to make a good impression. This reluctance to reveal our true attitudes is also a product of our inability to understand our own complex, often conflicting, and even unconscious feelings. Consequently we often say things we don't really mean.

Patient, prolonged, skillful listening is required to help another person express his feelings. Good interviewing, then, is essentially a technique to encourage expression which is uninfluenced either by the preconceived notions of the interviewer or by the need of the interviewee to make a good impression.

2. It helps the interviewee achieve catharsis, a feeling of relief. There are many sources of frustration in modern industry, and unless frustration is relieved it may lead to aggression, regression, and other undesirable responses. The interview provides a channel through which frustration may be partly drained away, even though the causes of the frustration remain.

3. Nondirective interviewing helps a man develop greater insight into his own problems. Turning his questions back and encouraging him to talk enables him to answer them himself. We often think better when we think out loud—when we have to organize and weigh our thoughts—than when we are thinking to ourselves.

In arranging his thoughts before presenting them to a sympathetic listener, the interviewee may bring his problem into sharper focus and, without additional help, actually change his own attitudes. At this stage one hears comments such as, "You know, the more I talk about this, the more I think I have been on the wrong track." Solutions reached in this fashion are much more likely to be implemented with enthusiasm than are those suggested by the supervisor.

Stages in an Interview

In understanding how the nondirective approach should be used, it is helpful to think of the interview as running through three stages: feelings, facts, solutions.

1. Feelings. The interviewee is encouraged to release his feelings; the interviewer is concerned with helping the interviewee express himself. This stage is the most purely nondirective, for the interviewer still has little idea where the discussion will go.

2. Facts. Having blown off steam, the interviewee is now ready to look at the facts rationally. In this stage the interviewer can be more directive and may even use "probes" (to be discussed later) to bring out information that the interviewee has not already volunteered. In fact, the interviewer may contribute additional information on his own.

3. Solutions. Once the facts have been assembled, the interviewee is in a position to weigh alternate solutions and pick the best one. As we have mentioned frequently, it is preferable to help the interviewee work out his own solution; however, the supervisor may have to be rather strongly directive to make sure that the solution is consistent with the needs of the organization.

These, then, are the three major stages of the interview, although it may switch back and forth from one stage to another as different problems are considered. Still on a given problem the interviewer should stick to the order indicated: feelings, facts, solutions. Certainly he should avoid the common human tendency to jump to a solution before getting all the facts.

Equally important, he should not waste his time trying to isolate the facts before the interviewee has had a chance to express his feelings, to blow off steam. Why? Because feelings color facts, and as long as a man is emotionally excited he is unlikely to approach problems rationally. Furthermore—and the point is subtle—the feelings of the people concerned in the situation are themselves facts that must be considered. For instance, the office manager has been having trouble getting Mary to do a full day's work. The most important fact in this solution may be the manager's intense dislike of Mary as a person. Until the manager's feeling is recognized as a complicating element, "facts" he presents will be distorted by his antagonism toward Mary.

Does this mean that the interviewer should never express himself—that he should never try to correct the other person if he is wrong, or try to change his opinion? Of course not. It may be enough for the psychiatrist or the professional counselor merely to listen. The supervisor must also take action. But in most cases, before he takes action he should wait until he has heard the interviewee's whole story.

Suppose a subordinate comes to you and says, "Boss, you've got to transfer me from this job. I can't stand it any more." If he insists on his request, you will have to give him some kind of answer. Only antagonism will result if he gets the impression that you are trying to put him off. But there is no need for you to commit yourself before you have heard him through.

The nondirective approach is not a magic solution to all human-relations problems, of course. There are times when a supervisor may have to be quite firm and directive in the solution stage of the interview to make sure that the solution is consistent with the needs of the organization. For instance, the supervisor may listen patiently to the subordinate's objections to a new system; the subordinate may persist in his resistance; and the supervisor may still have to overrule him, explaining why, and insist that the system be used. However, the subordinate will have had the satisfaction of being consulted, of knowing that he had his day in court to present his side of the story.

INTERVIEWING TECHNIQUES [3]

Skillful interviewing is an art, and like all arts it requires training and experience. It can be learned better by practice than by reading a book, especially when the practice is supervised by an experienced instructor. Fortunately, one can gain unsupervised practice every day of the year.

Each interviewer must develop a system that is comfortable for him and that fits his personality, but he should avoid using the same technique with

[3] Three excellent and very different treatments of interviewing are: Carl Rogers and others, *Client-Centered Therapy: Its Current Practice, Implications and Theory* (Boston: Houghton Mifflin, 1951); Robert L. Kahn and Charles E. Cannell, *The Dynamics of Interviewing* (New York: Wiley, 1957); Stephen Richardson, Barbara Dohrenwend, and David Klein, *Interviewing: Its Forms and Functions* (New York: Basic Books, 1965).

all people and for all purposes. An interview held for disciplinary reasons will naturally be different from an interview held for the purpose of order-giving.

Regardless of the form of the interview, here are a few hints that may prove useful.

Encouraging the Interviewee to Talk

Your primary objective is to get the interviewee to talk freely, *not to talk yourself.* The best way to find out what the other person wants to say is to listen, and the best interview is usually the one in which the interviewer talks least.

But listening is not easy, for our natural impulse is to talk. This is particularly true when we feel threatened by what is being said to us—for instance, when we are being criticized. Under these circumstances our normal impulse is to defend ourselves rather than to listen.

Listening is more than just not talking, however. It requires an active effort to convey that you understand and are interested in what the other person is saying—almost that you are helping him say it. A friendly facial expression and an attentive but relaxed attitude are important. A good interviewer also makes use of phrases such as "Uh-huh," "I understand," "That explains it," or "Could you tell me more?"

Even silence can be used to keep a man talking. When he pauses in his discourse, he is either being polite and giving you a chance to talk, or else he wants you to comment, to evaluate what he is saying. Merely by not taking up his challenge, by waiting through his pause, you indicate that you have nothing to say at the moment, that you want him to continue talking.

Even if you plan to use the nondirective approach, it is vital to set the stage properly, to indicate to the interviewee what you want the interview to cover. For example, if you wish to talk to a worker about sloppy work, you might start with, "Bill, you seem to be having a little trouble with the blue-edge gadgets."

Reflective Summary

One of the most effective devices to encourage the other person to talk is the *reflective summary,* in which you try to sum up the feelings a man has expressed, disregarding the factual details and incidentals. For example: "The reason I want to quit is that so-and-so foreman keeps pestering me. He won't give me a chance!" Then he stops, wondering whether he has got himself into trouble by saying too much. Your response, "He won't give you a chance?" encourages him to tell the rest of his story, but it does not commit you in any sense. Such a summary serves a number of purposes:

1. It shows the worker that you are giving his ideas careful consideration and that you understand him—in other words, that you are being fair.

2. It gives him a chance to restate and elaborate his attitudes if he feels that you haven't quite grasped his point.

3. It serves to highlight what he has really been saying. Often people are surprised to learn what their words have meant to someone else, and are rewarded with deeper insight into their own attitudes.

The reflective summary is particularly effective if you reflect not only what the man has actually said, but can somehow put into words what he has tried, unsuccessfully, to express. Be careful, however, not to hear more in his words than he intends to put into them. For if he finds you reading things into his words that he did not mean to be there, he will be doubly careful to watch what he says.

Your summary should indicate neither approval nor disapproval of what the interviewee is saying. It should simply indicate that you are listening attentively. For instance, he says, "It's got to the point where I may lose my temper and take a poke at the foreman." If you were to say, "Well, that's quite understandable," you would almost be inviting him to carry out his threat! A far more satisfactory response would be, "You are really sore at him because. . . ."

Probes

The "free-floating" counselor is interested primarily in getting at the interviewee's underlying feelings. And as a supervisor you too are interested in the feelings of your subordinates. But if you know that you must act on the basis of what you learn in the interview, you will also want to get all the facts, the whole story.[4] This means that after the feeling stage has passed, you should to some extent direct the interview. Tactfully and calmly, you should steer the conversation, but without forcing the interviewee into an area he does not want to enter, and with no hint that you have already made up your mind.

One way to direct the interview is to build on what the interviewee has already said. By repeating certain words selected from what he has said, you can indicate that you would like him to talk more about this particular area. This device is called a "probe." For example, in explaining how a fight started between himself and another employee, the man being interviewed says, "Joe was always riding me. When he picked up my lunch bucket, that was the last straw." Now if the supervisor wants to find out more about what Joe has done to arouse this man, he has a good chance to insert a probe: "You say Joe was always riding you?" Then he stops and waits for the man to go on. Notice that the interviewer does not say: "What did Joe do to make you so sore?" Rather, he simply repeats the employee's own words. Chances are this approach will encourage the man to tell more about the "riding" than he would if he had been asked a direct question.

---

[4] In other words, your interviewing is "organization centered" not "client centered." See Rogers and others, *op. cit.*

Less subtle probes are: "Could you tell me more about ... ?" or "I am interested in what you said about. ..."

Weighing Alternatives

Sometimes it is enough if the interview helps you find out how the employee feels about the situation and what the essential facts are as *he* sees them. In other instances, however, you may wish to help him devise a solution. How can you do this without seeming to impose your own ideas on him? The following approach may be useful both in individual interviews and in group meetings:

Let us assume one of your managers wishes to discipline severely one of his employees who has been a troublemaker. The manager's first suggestion, for example, may be that he should go right out to the shop and fire the troublemaker. If you keep asking for additional suggestions, he may suggest lesser penalties. Finally, he may even come around to suggesting certain changes in his own behavior.

Now, after the manager has offered all these suggestions, you would attempt to get him to examine each one:

> What would its probable effect be?
> How would the men react?
> How would it help him solve his problem?

By helping the interviewee think through his problem, you may succeed in having him come to a conclusion that is *his,* not yours. And if it is his, he will be much more likely to act on it with enthusiasm.

Direct Questions

One of the most frequent errors made by inexperienced interviewers is transforming the interview into a game of "twenty questions." A man has fallen into the habit of coming to work late and his supervisor is anxious to straighten him out before discipline becomes necessary. Having had some training in human relations, the manager suspects that a home problem is involved. His end of the conversation may run something like this:

> "Do you have trouble starting your car?"
> "Is there any trouble at home?"
> "Does your alarm clock go off on time?"
> "Did you have a drink too many last night?"

To each question Bill replies, "No, it isn't that." And to himself he says, "That's none of his business." And then another question is shot at him.

Here the manager, not Bill, is directing the interview. Note that every one of these questions is phrased in such a manner as to put Bill immediately on the defensive and make him over-cautious in what he says. Some of the questions, such as, "Did you have a drink too many last night?" he may feel are insulting.

The interviewer rarely knows the right questions to ask; if he did, he would probably know the answers as well. The interviewee's problem is usually more complex than it seems at first glance, and direct questions tend to narrow it down too quickly.

To complicate matters, most subordinates try to say what they think will please their supervisor. Direct questions often imply the kind of answer the supervisor wants, or at least give the subordinate an "out." For instance, the question "Did you have trouble starting your car?" provides a ready excuse for a tardy worker.

If the supervisor wants to find out what the subordinate really has on his mind, he should leave the situation as free as possible to permit the subordinate to emphasize the things that are important to *him*.

If possible, the interviewer should avoid questions that can be answered with a simple yes or no. "Well, do you like your job?" "Do you think the tools are in bad shape?" Questions of this sort shut off discussion because they can be answered by a relatively meaningless "Oh, I guess so," "I suppose you might say that."

THINGS TO AVOID

Too Much Warm-up

Many people feel that before getting down to the subject of an interview, particularly if it is an unpleasant one, they should try to place the interviewee at ease by discussing some irrelevant topic—baseball, fishing, the traffic problem, or what have you. Thus, a foreman calling a man in to lay him off may chat about the Dodgers for a few minutes before settling down to the nasty task.

This approach may relieve the foreman's anxiety, but it intensifies that of the worker, particularly if he has some idea of why he has been called in. While he is on the "hot seat," he may be thinking, "Why doesn't this character get down to business? Why does he have to play cat-and-mouse? What's this building up to?"

Such "warming-up" is useful at times; however, the interviewer should be careful to use it only when it actually reduces anxiety. Often when the supervisor initiates the interview, "beating around the bush" merely increases the suspense. Similarly, if the employee comes to the supervisor with a problem, he probably wants to get down to business without delay.

Premature Judgment

The interviewer should avoid giving any indication that what the subordinate says either pleases or displeases him. In other words, he must refrain from passing judgment before all the facts are in. This restraint is extremely important because subordinates look for verbal or facial cues that will tip them off to what the superior wants or does not want to hear. (Of course, unconsciously we are always forming impressions, even on the most meager facts. However, the supervisor should be aware of his predispositions and try to keep them from warping his judgment or his communication.)

Criticizing or moralizing puts the interviewee on the defensive. Even if he does not argue back, he will begin to edit what he says in order to win the interviewer's approval. He will concentrate on proving that he is right rather than on giving an honest explanation. Certainly putting a man on the defensive makes is harder to find out what he really thinks.

Even praise or sympathy should be avoided until the end of the interview, for it makes the interviewee think his present approach is correct and encourages him to avoid the hard work of thinking the problem through.

Arguing

Little is gained from argument, at least in the early stage of the interview. Yet everyone has a strong human tendency to correct the other person when he says something that is obviously wrong. Moreover, if the interviewer himself is attacked personally, he must exercise tremendous restraint not to answer back.

For example, an employee says he is having trouble doing the work because the stock has been changed. "The company must be buying cheaper material these days." Now if you know that there has been no change whatsoever in the materials, you will be strongly tempted to "set the employee straight" on this point, although his complaint may be a symptom of something much more basic. If you give way to this temptation, you may simply transform the interview into a fruitless argument. If you just continue to listen, however, the employee may move on to more basic problems and difficulties that he finds more troublesome to discuss.

Excessive Psychologizing

Sometimes managers abuse the nondirective technique by shifting the discussion from the technical aspects of the question at hand to the subordinate's motives in dealing with it.[5] Such abuse occurs most commonly when the manager has a psychology or social work background. For example, a subordinate may have a sound practical objection to something his boss may want to do. Instead of listening to the objections themselves, the excessively psychologically-oriented boss may look upon the subordinate's attitude as an example of hostility and may seek its emotional basis. Obviously such an approach often adds to the hostility it is designed to alleviate.

---

[5] For a good discussion, see Peter Blau and W. Richard Scott, *Formal Organization* (San Francisco: Chandler, 1962), pp. 188-89.

Advice-Giving

When you finally get the complete picture as the employee sees it, you may be able to provide advice or information that has not previously been available. But again it is often better to help him work through his own problems. In any event, you should hold off giving advice until *after* the interviewee has told his entire story—until you have all the facts.

Masterminding

Many people go through the motions of the nondirective interview but violate its spirit. They hope by asking shrewd questions to manipulate the interviewee into believing that he is thinking through his problem by himself, though the way questions are worded inevitably forces the interviewee to arrive at the interviewer's own predetermined conclusion.

Masterminding is used with various degrees of sophistication. One of the less subtle forms makes constant use of the leading question, the "don't you feel?" approach: "Don't you feel it would be better for the company and your own future if you came to work on time?"

Questions like this usually permit only one answer. They are thinly veiled forms of advice, judgement, or just plain bawling out. They are even more directive than an overt, straightforward statement. The interviewee is often free to reject outright advice, and even if it is clear that he must accept it (in other words, when the advice is really an order) he may be unhappy about it, but willing to be a good soldier. Masterminding, however, not only requires the interviewee to do what the interviewer wants, but also to say that he likes it. The interviewee is treated like a child and the alleged interview degenerates into a form of brainwashing.

There are subtler forms of brainwashing in which the interviewee may actually feel convinced of something at the time of the interview, only to realize that he has been duped after he has had a chance to think things over. Conversion at a forced rate seldom lasts. As the poet Robert Burns once said:

> He who is convinced against his will,
> Is of the same opinion still.

People change their attitudes slowly, and only when they are ready to do so.

CONCLUSION

Interviewing is a form of communications, and like other forms of communications it is most effective when it is two-way. A good interview is more than a one-way process in which the interviewee tells his story to the interviewer; the interviewer must in turn be constantly communicating his interest in the interviewee as a person and in what he has to say.

It is not enough for the manager to understand his employees; he must also give them the feeling that he is sincerely trying to help them. The manager must not only listen, but must also communicate the feeling to his employees that they are being listened to.

The basic purpose of nondirective interviewing is to enable the interviewer to find out how the individual sees the problem or situation at issue, and then to help him think and, above all, *feel* his way through to a solution. The goal of this whole philosophy is for the supervisor to be perceived as a source of help—as a man who can assist the subordinate to develop and do a better job.

It has been argued that the interview approach would be fine if a manager had nothing else to do all day except serve as a wailing wall, but that in practice he just doesn't have time to do much listening. Realistically, pressure and other demands may make him abrupt and unsympathetic in his dealings with subordinates. And yet the manager who "makes time" to listen may find not only that his human relations are better, but that in the long run he will save enough time by having fewer personnel crises to deal with.

The nondirective interview is not a cure-all for every situation. Effective interviewing requires considerable skill, and even a good interviewer discovers that many people find it difficult to discuss their problems. Moreover, many problems involve several people and require group discussion. Finally, certain problems cannot be decided at the manager-subordinate level. Still, in spite of these reservations the interviewing technique is a general-purpose tool for every manager.

PROBLEM 1

INTERVIEWING DRILL

In each of the following cases, which of the responses suggested would be more likely to lead to a constructive solution of the problem? Remember that these represent the opening of the interview.

1. You have come home from a hard day and your wife greets you with:
   "What a day I've had. The baby was crying all morning. The washing machine broke down and I had to do the things by hand. Then I went downtown to buy a hat and had to wait twenty minutes for a bus. I couldn't find a thing I liked and everybody was so pushy and the store was so crowded. When I got back the baby-sitter had let the stew burn— and I'd worked on it so hard. I'm so mad I could cry. And I've got to go downtown tomorrow again to look for a hat."

   a. "You must have had an awfully hard day."
   b. "Your old hat looks pretty good to me."
   c. "I'm tired too. You should hear what happened to me. First. . . ."
   d. "Don't say another word. Put on your glad rags and I'll take you out for dinner and don't mention it."
   e. "You know, maybe we ought to get another baby-sitter."

2. A worker has been late three times in the last two weeks. You ask him why and he replies:

"I just can't seem to get up in the morning. Frankly, I've lost my enthusiasm for the job. It doesn't interest me any more. So when I do get up I've got to rush like mad to get here."

  a. "Don't you think you are letting the company down?"
  b. "Do you have an alarm clock?"
  c. "You've got to lick this problem or I've got to lay you off and give you some time to think it over."
  d. "The job doesn't interest you any more?"
  e. "Are you having any trouble at home?"
  f. "Have you thought of going to bed earlier?"

3. A worker who has been making little progress tells his boss:

"I just can't seem to get the hang of things. I try to find out what I'm supposed to do, but no one tells me. The other guys don't pay any attention to me and I can't figure it out by watching. Maybe I ought to quit."

  a. "Why don't you give the job a chance? Most people take a while to learn it."
  b. "Why don't you try harder? You can't get ahead without hard work."
  c. "If I were you I would ask the other fellows to help you."
  d. "Do you have any ideas why the other fellows don't help you?"
  e. "I'll assign one of them to instruct you."
  f. "You feel that the other fellows don't pay any attention to you?"
  g. "Let me show you how to do it."

4. A toolmaker tells his foreman:

"I've had ten years' experience and no one ever told me I did a bum job. Sure I make a few mistakes, but why do I get all the blame?"

  a. "All I want you to do is be a little more careful in your work."
  b. "You feel the standards are too high?"
  c. "I'm not saying it is your fault. I am just asking you to please do the piece over."
  d. "You feel you are unfairly blamed?

PROBLEM 2[6]

THE EXTRA HALF PLUM

Scene I

Mary, a salad girl, is seated at a table backstage by herself, thumbing through a magazine. She is off duty. Miss Jones walks on stage from the right and stops at Mary's table.

Miss Jones: Mary, may I speak to you for a moment?

Mary: All right.

Miss Jones: It's about your work. I feel that you're a hard worker but there are times when you seem to grow a bit careless. I've noticed lately that sometimes your salads are a trifle sloppy in appearance, and you don't always check your recipes carefully enough. For example, the fruit salad calls for two halves of plums. I saw you putting three on some of the

---

[6] We wish to express our thanks to Professor William F. Whyte for permission to use this case, which was prepared by him.

salads today. If you just check up on things like this, you'll do the job I think you're capable of.

(Mary does not answer. She shuts the magazine, gets up, and walks away. Miss Jones looks startled, then walks toward the office of Mr. Black, the manager, downstage left, and knocks on the door.)

Scene II

Black: Come in. (Miss Jones walks in and sits down.) Hello. What is it, Miss Jones?

Jones: I'm worried about Mary Stevens. I thought maybe you'd want to talk to her.

Black: What seems to be the trouble?

Jones: Well, she's a hard worker, but sometimes she just doesn't seem to have her mind on her work. Now that wouldn't be so bad if she'd let us correct her, but the girl won't take criticism. I just asked her to be a little neater in putting up her salads and I checked her on putting an extra half plum on the fruit salad. I put it just as tactfully as I know how, but she wouldn't even answer me. She just sat still until I was finished and then walked right out on me. It was a deliberate insult.

Black: Yes, that's bad. . . . Do you think she is quitting?

Jones: Well, I don't know. But I don't see how I can use her when she behaves that way.

Black: Do you want to get rid of her?

Jones: Well, you know how short we are at that station. I can't really spare her and she can do a very good job when she wants to. Maybe it's some trouble at home. I don't know. But I thought you might be able to help her.

Black: I'd be glad to talk to her for you. She'll be coming in for her paycheck tomorrow. I'll see her then.

Jones: Thanks. That'll be a big help to me.

Scene III

(Black's office. Black at desk; Mary comes in.)

Black: I was hoping you'd come in to see me. Won't you sit down, Mary?

Mary: (hesitates, then sits down) Well, I suppose you know all about it.

Black: Miss Jones told me something about it, but I want to get your side of the story. After all, we want to be fair with you. I've always done my best to see the employee's point of view. We want you to feel satisfied with your work here, and if there is some problem I can help out on, I want you to feel free to talk things over with me.

Mary: Well, I don't suppose I should have walked out, but I just couldn't take it.

Black: You mean, you can't take criticism?

Mary: Well, not exactly. But this is such a nerve-wracking job. And Miss Jones is always picking on you. She doesn't seem to appreciate the work you do.

Black: Mary, don't you think you're being a little unfair to Miss Jones? Now, I happen to know that she thinks very well of you. She wants to help you.

Mary: She doesn't act that way. I mean—well I know she has to see that the work gets done right, but it seems she's always looking over your shoulder to catch you or something. And such little things, too, she—

Black: Mary, you have to remember that the little things add up together to make something pretty big. If we neglected the little things, we wouldn't be in business very long. Now that extra half plum—it may seem like nothing at all to you, but we have to work out the prices and portions to make a small profit on that salad. If we put in an extra half plum, we're really giving it away. If we sell 100 of those salads a day, that mounts up. We're doing all the work for nothing. Now, I'm not criticizing you, but I just want you to understand the importance of these things. Do you see what I mean?

Mary: Well, if I did put on an extra half plum, it was only on 2 or 3, not 100. I don't remember every one, but I know it was only 2 or 3.

Black: Sure, that's what I'm getting at. You were just a little careless. That's all. Miss Jones was trying to correct you. Now, you don't blame her for trying to see that the work is done right do you?

Mary: Sure, she wants it done right, but she doesn't realize what we're up against. It's one thing to know just how to make a salad. It's another thing to have to make hundreds of them in a rush, like I have to. If Miss Jones had ever worked behind the counter like the rest of us, she'd know what it's like.

Black: But Miss Jones did work behind the counter when she was getting her training.

Mary: That's different. You weren't so rushed then like we are now.

Black: Yes, that's true. But I'm not trying to defend Miss Jones to you. I'm just trying to help you to get this thing straightened out. Now, you didn't like the way Miss Jones criticized you. But let's look at both sides of it. Do you think you were fair to her?

Mary: I know what you think. You think I wasn't polite to her. All right, I wasn't. I lost my temper. If I had said anything, I would have told her what I thought of her. So I thought it would be better not to say anything. Well, what of it? It's done, and I'm through now. Give me my paycheck and let me out of here.

Black: Your check is here for you, Mary, but let's not be hasty about this. Remember your aunt has worked here a long time. She hoped you'd fit in too. If you just walk out this way, it'll be quite a blow to her.

Mary: I don't care about her or Miss Jones or you either. I've got my own life to live. I'm tired of having people always pick on me and tell me what to do. I know what I want to do now. I want to get out of here. Give me my check!

Black: Well, if that's the way you feel about it—(hands her the check).

1. Comment on how Mr. Black handled his conversation with Mary.
2. How should he have handled it?
3. What mistakes did he make?

Conference Leadership

Among the most valuable skills of the modern executive is the ability to function as an effective conference leader or committee chairman. In fact, meetings have become so common in modern business that many observers are worried lest "group think" replace individual initiative. In some companies all important decisions are based on group consensus. A standing joke is, "All we do is meet all day and never get time for work."

Why this emphasis on meetings? As we have seen (in Chapter 9), one reason is the growing realization that people are more enthusiastic about carrying out plans that they have helped draw up than they are about implementing plans that are simply announced from above. Moreover, as business activities grow increasingly specialized it becomes more urgent to coordinate departments and encourage subordinates to volunteer advice.

Conference skills are useful, of course, even when the participants are not sitting around a table at a formal meeting. The manager needs these skills in his day-to-day activities whenever he is talking to a group of subordinates or equals and trying to reach some sort of agreement. Suppose three workers are quarreling over their vacation schedules and come to the foreman for a solution. He could listen and play judge. But it would be better if he could somehow get them to work out a schedule themselves that they could all accept.

In Chapter 9 we distinguished three types of meetings: those called for the purpose of giving information, those called to elicit suggestions, and those called to arrive at decisions. Although we shall be primarily concerned with decision-making meetings in this chapter, the skills we discuss are useful in the other types of meeting as well.[1]

Let us start with an example:

> The Plant Manager has called a special meeting of his top staff to consider whether a new cafeteria should be built. The present cafeteria is 40 years old and too small for current needs.

---

[1] For an excellent discussion of conference leadership generally, see Norman R. F. Maier, *Problem Solving Discussions and Conferences* (New York: McGraw-Hill, 1963).

It is 2:45 P.M. and the meeting is getting nowhere fast. It has been in session since lunchtime and the participants have been alternately bored and annoyed with each other. There has been a lot of hot air but little real progress. Everyone has his pet point of view and so far there has been no semblance of agreement.

Of course the Plant Manager could put a stop to all this talk by proclaiming his own opinion, but at least on this issue he doesn't want to act without the close support of his staff. To this moment he has failed as a conference leader. Yet unless he can induce the group to accept a common solution there will be no new cafeteria.

Why all this trouble? What are the pitfalls that make running a meeting such a difficult art to learn? For one thing, there are invisible currents (sometimes called the "hidden agenda") in every discussion that must be recognized and mastered if agreement is to be reached. It is the ability to identify these currents and to direct them into proper channels that constitues the strength of a good conference leader.

The success of any meeting, particularly one called for the purpose of decision-making, depends largely on three interrelated factors: (1) the development of unity and teamwork within the group, (2) the chairman's ability to handle the meeting, particularly his skill in maintaining the proper degree of looseness or tightness of control, and (3) the participants' observance of an agenda designed for the orderly consideration of the problem at hand.

Many of the concepts we shall discuss in the following pages were developed by R. Freed Bales of the Harvard Laboratory of Social Relations,[2] by the Research Center for Group Dynamics, and by the National Training Laboratory for Group Development [3] (sometimes called the "Bethel group," after Bethel, Maine, where the Laboratory conducts an intensive summer training program).

INTERNAL UNITY AND TEAMWORK

In addition to carrying out their formal tasks, the members of every meeting carry on an informal social life among themselves; if this informal life is unsatisfactory, the formal tasks will not be performed successfully. In other words, before we can have a smoothly working committee we must have a smoothly working social group.

As we discussed in Chapter 4, a new group is a collection of strangers, each of whom is anxious to establish a position that meets his personal needs.

---

[2] Over the years Professor Bales, using a room with one-way glass to permit observation of meetings in session, has developed ingenious devices to measure interaction among committee members. See R. F. Bales, *Interaction Process Analysis* (Cambridge: Addison-Wesley, 1950), and R. F. Bales, "In Conference," *Harvard Business Review*, Vol. 32, No. 2 (March 1954), pp. 44-50.

[3] See Leland Bradford and John R. F. French, eds., "The Dynamics of the Discussion Group," *Journal of Social Issues*, Vol. 4, No. 2 (April 1948).

When people are confronted with each other, they must first find the place where they fit in. This involves being in or out of the group, establishing oneself as a specific individual, and seeing if one is going to be paid attention to and not be left behind or ignored. This anxiety gives rise to individual-centered behavior such as overtalking, extreme withdrawal, exhibitionism, recitation of biographies and previous experience.[4]

Much of the early history of a group consists of attempts to establish pecking orders or status hierarchies. Only when these relationships have coalesced and a well-defined informal organization has been established can the group settle down to work. Gradually the members of the group develop friendships and teamwork, and the aggregation of self-conscious individuals grows into a real group.

The success of the conference depends a great deal on the needs and interests of the people who take part in it. "The problems on the conference table are really not as difficult to deal with as the people around the table." [5] Let us look at some of these needs and interests, using as an example the cafeteria meeting we mentioned earlier.

Outside commitments of the members.   It is just human nature for committee members to think first about how a new proposal will affect them and the people with whom they work. Mr. A, the assistant controller, is worried lest he give the impression that he has committed his boss (who is not present) to spend money on the cafeteria.[6] Mr. B, from the main office, wants the cafeteria located near where he works. Even though the arguments for building it elsewhere are very persuasive, he is worried about how those who work for him will react to having to take a long walk to lunch.

Differing perceptions of the issue.   Mr. C has been sold on the desirability of a new cafeteria for a long time and feels that the only question left is how to design it. Mr. D, on the other hand, feels pressured by any discussion of design, since he hasn't been convinced that a new cafeteria is needed in the first place. Mr. C and Mr. D have obviously started out with different assumptions as to the purpose of the meeting. These differences will undoubtedly lead to friction.

Equally troublesome are the differing perceptions of the assistant controller and the personnel director. One thinks purely in terms of cost, the other in terms of improving morale. Moreover, different commitments are likely to cause differing perceptions, so that people see the same "facts" differently.

---

[4] William C. Schultz, "The Interpersonal Underworld," *Harvard Business Review,* Vol. 36, No. 4 (July 1958), p. 132.

[5] William M. Sattler and N. Edd Miller, *Discussion and Conference* (Englewood Cliffs, N.J.: Prentice-Hall, 1954), p. 149.

[6] In a situation like this it is sometimes a good idea to adjourn the meeting for a few days before trying to reach final agreement—or else make it clear that "representatives" do not bind "principals."

Obviously, what is needed at the outset is an agreement on the basic nature of the problem (or, in most cases, problems) and the setting up of an agenda so that each problem will be considered in turn. Certainly the chairman should refrain from stating baldly, "Gentlemen, *this* is the problem," for his perceptions may differ from everyone else's. Instead, he should find out from the participants what *they* think the fundamental issues are and then try to establish a common basis for discussion.

Personal needs.   People do not stop acting like people just because they are at a meeting. They abandon neither their personal idiosyncrasies nor their status position in the organization. Mr. E has just had a fight with his wife. Mr. F is an assistant division manager and *expects* to receive respect. Mr. G wants to show up well in the discussion so that he will be promoted. Mr. H enjoys an argument of any kind. Mr. I is just shy.

Reactions to individuals rather than to ideas.   Mr. J talks too much; consequently the group habitually rejects his ideas. Mr. K is disgusted by all this chatter and keeps his mouth shut. Mr. L, who is on the opposite side of the political fence from Mr. M, is almost automatically against whatever Mr. M is for and would love the chance to make M look silly. L and M are leaders of opposing cliques. When cliques develop in a group, the members tend to evaluate a new idea on the basis of how it will affect their prestige rather than on the basis of its real merits.

Thus, members bring to the meeting what sociologists call their respective roles—their points of view and patterns of behavior. It is the chairman's job to handle these various roles in such a way that individual viewpoints are dovetailed for the good of the group—in other words, so that teamwork develops.

So long as a committee has an unsatisfactory internal life, the members will go out of their way to look for matters of substance on which they can disagree, to make mountains out of molehills. On the other hand, a closely knit group will not be disrupted even by differences of policy. Each member feels assured of the acceptance and respect of colleagues. Social activity and good-natured kidding help build solidarity. Furthermore, once a matter has been fully aired, the minority is willing to go along with the majority, for there is group pressure to conform. At the same time, the majority respects views that are strongly held by the minority and is reluctant to override them. Mr. J's need for security no longer forces him to talk all the time. Mr. I's shyness no longer prevents him from offering suggestions. All the members show willingness to listen to each other's points of view, and to accept each other's foibles.

Once the members begin to experience the subtle transformation that marks the emergence of an effective team, they begin to take on new roles related to the functioning of the meeting itself. Some of these roles have to do with the *content* or subject matter of the meeting. Others have to do with the *process* by which the discussion is carried out. Here is a suggestive, though by no means complete, list of these roles (note that not all of them are constructive): [7]

CONTENT ROLES

Initiator—makes suggestions
Information-seeker—asks questions
Blocker—objects to other people's suggestions for action
Expert—knows the facts
Destructive critic—tears other people's ideas apart

PROCESS ROLES

Summarizer—summarizes where the group stands
Task-setter—tries to get the group to move on, emphasizes what
    still has to be done
Decision-announcer—announces decisions after the group has
    reached agreement
Traffic cop—decides who talks when
Encourager—encourages others to contribute
Mediator—tries to narrow differences
Playboy—kids around (and sometimes reduces excess tension)

(In addition to the roles we have mentioned, there are also inactive roles, such as follower, listener, and daydreamer.)

Does this mean that every member of the group plays only one role at a time? Not at all. Members frequently switch from one role to another and may play several roles simultaneously. Similarly, any one role may be played by several people at once.

If certain key roles are neglected—that of initiator or summarizer, for example—the whole meeting will suffer. But overemphasis on any single role should be avoided. Clearly, everyone cannot serve as an initiator or a harmonizer. In fact, a meeting in which everyone is careful not to step on anyone else's toes never accomplishes anything. Similarly, "rigidity of role-taking" [8] is undesirable, for team spirit is shattered when one person insists on always acting as destructive critic or demands parliamentary procedure regardless of the situation.

One of the responsibilities of the chairman is to help people fit their roles together for the good of the group. He wants to insure that the meeting will enjoy the full benefit of Bill's skill as a summarizer, Joe's expert knowledge, or Dick's special skills by calling on each at the *proper* time.

In summary, a successful meeting requires that members subordinate roles based on personality needs, outside commitments, and so forth, and accept

---

[7] See "Training in Member Roles," *Adult Leadership*, Vol. 1, No. 8 (January 1953), pp. 17-23; and Kenneth D. Beane and Paul Sheats, "Functional Roles of Group Members," *Journal of Social Issues*, Vol. 4, No. 2 (Spring 1948), pp. 41-50. Although we use the same types of role as Beane and Sheats, we categorize them differently.

[8] Beane and Sheats, *op. cit.*, p. 47.

roles, both content and process, which will help the meeting move toward its objectives. In other words, from an aggregation of individuals a work group arises which both satisfies the social needs of its members and works in reasonable harmony in solving problems.

The chairman himself plays a variety of roles: traffic cop, mediator, decision-announcer, and so forth. Indeed the success of the meeting depends to a large extent on the skill with which he plays these roles.

The so-called "autocratic" chairman plays both content and process roles: that is, he acts as an advocate of one point of view and also tries to get the meeting to reach agreement. His "democratic" counterpart is concerned primarily with process and tries to remain neutral when it comes to a question of content. But even the democratic chairman will be flexible in how he uses process roles, depending on the kind of problem being considered, the nature of the group, and the amount of time available. At times he must keep tight control over the meeting (that is, keep many of the process roles for himself); at other times he may exercise only loose control and try to spread responsibility throughout the group.

With this brief introduction, let us look more closely at various approaches to the chairman's responsibilities.

Should the Chairman Assume Content Roles?

It has been argued that the chairman's job is to help others express their point of view while keeping his own to himself. His function has been defined as "interviewing the group," helping it work through its own problems and reach its own decisions. Like the interviewer, the chairman needs to be permissive and unbiased. He is a catalyst who serves to bring out ideas already present in the group.

Certainly it is true that if he takes sides or expresses his own opinions other members may hesitate to take issue with him (particularly if the chairman happens to be the boss). In fact, any value judgment offered by the chairman may inhibit or distort communication.

> We have observed this problem at union meetings where the local president serves as presiding officer. The president seems to have a split personality. During most of the month he must act on his own initiative, like the commander of an army. Here his success depends on personal forcefulness, ingenuity, and ability. But in the meeting he is expected to be completely impartial even when his policies are under attack. Such switches in role are extremely difficult to make. The members are confused too. Bob Jones starts to criticize the president's activities as chief executive at the wrong point in the agenda—and is then called out of order. Bob can hardly avoid suspecting that the president is being less than impartial.

It is frequently unrealistic, however, for the chairman to remain completely neutral. Naturally, it would be foolish for the chairman of a three-man committee to keep his opinions completely to himself (although at times this is what a mediator does in labor relations). And if the chairman is an expert on the subject under discussion, it would be senseless for him to withhold his factual knowledge and his informed opinions—though if the subject is touchy he should be careful to distinguish his role as expert from his role as chairman.

What about the meeting in which the chairman is also the boss and has already made up his mind about what he wants to do? Should he pretend to remain impartial throughout the meeting, even though he knows very well that he may ignore the group's recommendations as soon as the session is over? Or should he try to mastermind the group into thinking that his ideas are really their own? Experience suggests that it rarely pays for the chairman to play cat-and-mouse with the group, for people resent being manipulated. Nor is it wise for him to exaggerate the amount of freedom that is actually being bestowed on the group. In such a situation, it is probably best for the chairman to open with something of this sort: "I'm thinking of doing so-and-so. What are the loopholes in this plan? Will it or won't it work?" The chairman should then try to answer questions and objections and must be willing to accept constructive suggestions.

In meetings where the members in fact enjoy a wide range of freedom, the chairman should normally try to stay neutral. However, it is often hard for a chairman to restrain himself, particularly where he is also boss. Feeling that he is expected to act as a vigorous initiator and decision-maker, the boss may fear that if he were to sit back and listen his behavior would be interpreted as a sign of weakness and indecision. And so, if the chairman is really anxious to let his subordinates make their own decision, he must learn to control his desire to take a dominant role.

With the important exceptions noted, then, the chairman is usually wise to avoid assuming content roles. What about process roles?

Should the Chairman Assume Process Roles?

It has been argued that the chairman should not assume process roles. When the field of group dynamics was first explored, there was a great deal of interest in what are known as "leaderless groups." It was felt that in a really mature group there would be no need for a formal chairman. Instead, every member would share the responsibility for steering the meeting and would automatically exercise the self-discipline needed to make the meeting a success. Strong leadership, it was argued, is undemocratic and tends to prevent the group from reaching its maximum potential.

Leaderless groups have proved useful in psychotherapy, as a technique for selecting leaders, and in what is known as sensitivity training. And almost every day we all participate in groups that get things done with only informal leadership or with no apparent leadership at all. Nevertheless there is strong evidence that if a group must meet over a period of time,

> there is need for a stable structure of group organization if the group is to move ahead on the tasks before it. . . . When the leadership is in doubt, the members will become preoccupied with the leadership problem and with their relations with each other in general, and they will not be able to move ahead towards their goal until progress can also be made in the development of a regular pattern of interaction.[9]

In other words, the chairman performs an essential function in developing a pattern of teamwork that will lead to the efficient handling of problems. Sometimes an informal leader, acceptable to all the members of the group, will emerge naturally—though there is always the danger there will be a long, nasty struggle for power. But usually, time will be saved if a chairman is formally elected or appointed.

One study has suggested that groups without formal leaders are less effective in solving mathematical problems than groups with leaders.[10] Apparently the significant difference between such groups is that the formal leaders give minority opinions a chance to be expressed, and often it is the minority opinions that lead to a correct solution. In leaderless groups, however, minorities have less opportunity to speak up. Another study showed that as leaders become better trained, the quality of group discussion improves.[11]

Thus, it seems that the chairman makes an important contribution to making discussion effective. Now let us look more closely at what he does.

The Chairman's Dilemmas

The chairman is beset by dilemmas. The goals of a meeting are (1) to devise what seems the best solution to the problem under consideration, (2) with the greatest amount of unanimity, (3) in the shortest period of time. Obviously these three goals sometimes conflict.

1. The quality of the final decision depends both on the amount of time devoted to hammering it out and on the degree of freedom the members enjoy to make comments and suggestions. Too much haste or too zealous an attempt to work out a compromise acceptable to everyone may result in an unsatisfactory solution.

2. It is wise to give everyone a chance to participate in decision-making, particularly when the committee members are expected to implement their

---

[9] William F. Whyte, *Leadership and Group Participation*, Bulletin 24, New York State School of Industrial and Labor Relations, pp. 19-20, 25.

[10] Norman R. F. Maier and A. R. Solem, "The Contribution of the Discussion Leader to the Quality of Group Thinking: The Effective Use of Minority Opinions," *Human Relations*, Vol. 5, No. 3 (August 1952), pp. 277-288.

[11] Norman R. F. Maier, "The Quality of Group Decisions as Influenced by the Discussion Leader," *Human Relations*, Vol. 3, No. 2 (June 1950), pp. 155-174.

own decisions. "A few words [on each member's part] will serve to express and solidify his involvement, and to avoid his subsequent dissatisfaction." [12] The chairman should try to persuade the minority to go along with the majority, or, at times, try to induce the majority to accommodate objections that the minority feel to be extremely important. But this takes time and may result in a less satisfactory solution.

3. Most business meetings run under a time limit—either implicit or explicit. Even where there is no limit, the members become bored or frustrated if the meeting lasts too long. However, time can be saved only at the cost of less participation and a less carefully considered solution.

These conflicts among the basic goals of the meeting present the chairman with some perplexing problems. He must somehow manage to obtain general participation, but he must *also* keep the discussion relevant and directed toward the agenda, and he must *also* insure that the meeting will move steadily along toward its ultimate purpose—the making of a decision. How can the chairman keep all these balls in the air at the same time?

Obtaining General Participation

Probably the chairman's hardest job is to encourage nonparticipants to speak up and to persuade those who talk too much to give others a chance to be heard. The man who sits cloaked in silence all through the meeting is often either apathetic or secretly opposed to the solution being discussed. Bring his objections out into the open and they may either be answered or the program may be modified to gain his support. Only through active participation can he get the feeling that *we* made the decision.[13]

This does not mean that the conference leader should strive for absolutely equal participation by all members. Naturally, on any given subject some people are likely to be better informed or to have stronger feelings than others. Even though each member of the meeting has a single vote, the members are rarely equal in fact. "In bureaucracy, ideas do not stand on merit alone. It is not only an opinion or an idea which wins but also a man." [14] Furthermore, evidence suggests that the man who talks most in a conference tends to have the best ideas and tends to approach problems in the most constructive manner.[15]

How can the conference leader stimulate participation? His general attitude is important. He should accept everyone's contribution without judgment and should seem to want everyone to participate. He should try to ask questions

---

[12] Bales, "In Conference," p. 46.

[13] E. Paul Torrance, "Function of Expressed Disagreement in Small Group Processes," *Social Forces*, Vol. 35, No. 4 (1957).

[14] Victor Thompson, "Hierarchy, Specialization and Organizational Conflict," *Administrative Science Quartery*, Vol. 5, No. 4 (May 1961), p. 503.

[15] R. F. Bales, "How People Interact in Conferences," *Scientific American*, Vol. 192 (March 1955), p. 18.

that are specific enough to stimulate a spirited response, even controversy. Once discussion is underway, he can use the reflective response to keep it going: "Jack thinks we can afford new equipment only if we can count on a large increase in sales. What do the rest of you think?" As in interviewing, here the reflective response serves to acknowledge Jack's contribution and to spur the others to join in.

A more elaborate technique for involving everyone in the discussion is the so-called "buzz session," in which the conference is broken down into small committees, each meeting in a separate part of the room. Each committee is instructed to discuss an assigned question and report back to the meeting as a whole after a specified period of time. Among the advantages of the buzz session are: forcing people to think for themselves, getting people to talk who would remain silent in a larger group (in fact, it is the only way in which all the members of a very large group can participate), and, often, saving time because a lot of discussion gets boiled down into a brief report. Buzz sessions are particularly useful in a larger conference.

Another technique of eliciting discussion is for the chairman to start at one side of the room and ask each conferee in turn to give his thoughts about the problem at hand. This device is particularly useful at the beginning of the meeting.

Sticking to the Agenda

The chairman must also keep the meeting from wandering off into a discussion of irrelevancies. Otherwise progress will be slow and morale will fall.

One of the most effective techniques for keeping the discussion moving along in the right direction is to record on a blackboard or flip chart both the original agenda and the essential steps that are taken as the meeting progresses. Keeping a visual record of the unfolding discussion serves three functions: (1) It acknowledges contributions and encourages people to speak up, (2) it prevents repetition of what has already been said, and (3) it encourages participants to ask themselves whether their contribution will be relevant before they start talking.

Other, more specific techniques (besides the blunt "You are out of order") may be used by the chairman to keep the session marching along at a brisk pace:

> ... Comment, "That's a good point. Do you mind if we take it up later?" (And perhaps point to the appropriate spot on the posted agenda.)
> ... Repeat or write down only the relevant part of each contribution.
> ... Ask, "How does this fit in with what we are discussing?" (Perhaps you yourself are at fault for not recognizing its relevancy.)
> ... Summarize what the group has accomplished and what still must be done, so that the participants can decide for themselves what is relevant at the moment.
> ... Ask a member to do the summarizing, thus spreading responsibility for keeping the discussion on the track.

The chairman should not be too dictatorial in ruling people out of order. After all, what seems irrelevant to the chairman may seem perfectly relevant to the majority of the members. And even an apparent irrelevancy may spark a completely new approach to the problem. In fact, to the man who made it, the contribution must have seemed relevant or at least associated in some manner with the problem under discussion. If the chairman cracks down on a member now, he may inhibit this member's contribution in the future. Moreover, some irrelevancies, such as wisecracks or funny stories, actually help relieve tension and create a relaxed atmosphere.

Keeping the Conference Moving toward Its Goal

As we have pointed out, the chairman faces a dilemma in keeping the conference moving toward its proper goal. If he moves too fast, some of the participants may feel pressured and resentful, and may not feel involved in the group's decision. On the other hand, if he moves too slowly, some members may grow restless and apathetic. The fact that most conferences operate under the pressure of a time limit helps the chairman keep the discussion moving, but it also obliges him to be less permissive than he would otherwise be.

As we shall see, a carefully prepared agenda helps the group progress, particularly when it is supplemented by periodic summaries to remind the group of what is still to be accomplished. A blackboard listing of matters still to be covered can gently coerce participants to move faster.

Through experience, the chairman learns to sense the opportune time to move on to the next point. Certainly it is time when the members start repeating gossipy irrelevancies. Having decided that the discussion has stalled, the chairman may resort to various techniques to motivate the group to move on. Note the difference in urgency between "Does anybody want to add anything" and "Unless someone has something else to say, I'd like to take up. . . ." A short summary also helps close off one topic and lead the way to another.

The Chairman's Tightness of Control

How tight should be the chairman's control over process? To refer back to our discussion of process roles, certainly the chairman must perform the function of traffic cop. In addition, he may decide to assume all the other process roles: mediator, encourager, task-setter, and so forth. But if he does, he must realize that he will be exercising extremely tight control over the meeting, and he will run the risk of appearing dictatorial. Even if he does this in a highly benevolent fashion—by drawing others out, acknowledging contributions, and so on—the members may become resentful under his paternalistic rule.

Perhaps the best solution is for the chairman to try to induce the members to accept a share of the procedural responsibilities. The more fully the members share in the work of making the decision, the more likely they will be to carry it out with determination.

The comparison shown in the illustration on the opposite page suggests some of the differences between groups in which the leader exercises tight control and groups in which the leader exercises loose control.

THE AGENDA

The chairman is responsible for steering the group step by step toward the final decision.[16] Before the meeting gets under way he should give careful thought to his over-all strategy—to his agenda. But he must not insist that his plan be followed rigidly, for he cannot predict exactly how the members will react to the questions that come up. Consequently he must be flexible enough to adjust his strategy to the ever-changing demands of the group. He must remember that what may seem to him the most efficient way to analyze a problem may not meet the psychological needs of the group.

The chairman who exercises tight control normally decides on his over-all plan in advance, even though he may apply it with flexibility. He may even circulate copies of the agenda before the meeting as a means of helping the members prepare for the discussion. The chairman who exercises loose control may let the group itself decide on the agenda. Or he may listen to a preliminary discussion of the problem and then propose an agenda that seems to cover the main issues raised.

The productive meeting seems to pass through successive stages of development. If these stages are ignored or taken in the wrong order (for instance, if there is an attempt at decision-making before the facts are evaluated), the meeting will take longer and be less productive.

There are certain standard procedures for analyzing problems, such as (1) assembling facts, (2) evaluating them, and (3) making a decision. But such neat formulas are often too simple to be of any real value. Instead, the course the discussion takes should be determined by the chairman's (or the group's) evaluation of what the crucial issues are. Here, for example, are three alternative agendas for a discussion of the problem of tardiness.

Agenda I

1. Should we have a firm rule against tardiness?
    a. What advantages?
    b. What objections?
2. How could such a rule be enforced?

---

[16] One experiment showed that groups which follow "developmental" plans for discussion (that is, agendas) came up with higher-quality decisions than groups which permitted "free discussion." Norman R. F. Maier and P. A. Maier, "An Experimental Test on the Effects of 'Developmental' v. 'Free' Discussion on the Quality of Group Decisions," *Journal of Applied Psychology*, Vol. 41, No. 5 (October 1957), pp. 320-323.

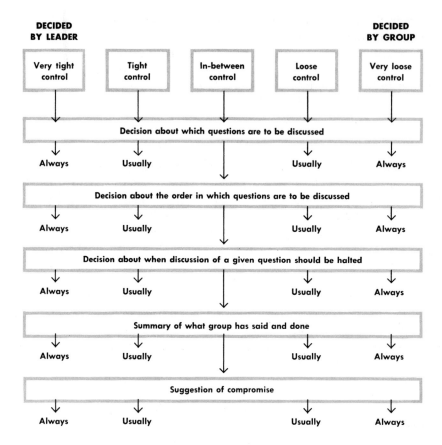

DECIDED BY LEADER				DECIDED BY GROUP
Very tight control	Tight control	In-between control	Loose control	Very loose control

Decision about which questions are to be discussed

| Always | Usually | | Usually | Always |

Decision about the order in which questions are to be discussed

| Always | Usually | | Usually | Always |

Decision about when discussion of a given question should be halted

| Always | Usually | | Usually | Always |

Summary of what group has said and done

| Always | Usually | | Usually | Always |

Suggestion of compromise

| Always | Usually | | Usually | Always |

The chairman can exercise tight or loose control in a number of different ways.

Agenda II

    1. Why are people late?
    2. What can be done to handle each reason for lateness?
    3. How can these suggestions be put into effect?

Agenda III

    1. How much of a tardiness problem do we actually have?
    2. What can be done about it?
    3. What are the advantages and disadvantages of each suggestion?
    4. Which one should we adopt?

Note the differences among these three agendas. Agenda I concentrates on one solution of the problem: a definite rule. Agenda II tries to find the basic causes of the problem and makes it possible to explore alternative solutions. Agenda III goes even deeper by exploring whether a serious problem really exists. Each of these agendas will lead to a different kind of discussion. Which agenda is best, of course, depends on the immediate situation.

With this warning against the dangers of too standardized an approach, let us sketch roughly the steps through which a typical problem-solving meeting might progress. (Note that we do not say *must*.)

Preparation.   There is no need to repeat the standard injunction that the chairman should make sure of his arrangements beforehand—a suitable room, a blackboard, and so forth. But it is just as important for him to remember that advance briefing of the members on the main topics that are likely to be covered may stimulate them to do some thinking before the meeting. A preliminary caucus of those who are most concerned with the problem may be useful, provided it does not suggest to the others that the meeting has been rigged.

Social warm-up.   Remember that a committee cannot become an effectively functioning work group until it has first become a comfortable social group. An opportunity must be given for new members to be introduced and for old members to go through the standard social ceremonies of banter and kidding (though when the participants see each other regularly, this period may last only a few seconds). To regard such social activities as disruptive or extraneous is to misunderstand completely what happens within a normal group. If the opportunity for socializing is not given before the meeting, chances are that it will occur during it.

Statement of the problem.   The chairman's initial statement of the problem sets the stage for what is to follow. If there have been earlier meetings, he may simply summarize what has transpired so far. If it is the first meeting on a particular problem, the chairman's opening statement may cover: the general nature of the problem, its importance, its background and history (if necessary), the range of freedom the group will have in making a decision, and, possibly, a tentative agenda.

Free discussion.   There is real value in having a free, unrestricted discussion before settling down to the systematic analysis necessary for decision-making. By free discussion we mean a chance for the participants to talk about those aspects of the problem that seem most important to them, regardless of whether the comments have any logical relevance to each other. In our tardiness conference, for example, A may brag that there is no lateness in his department; B may insist that he can't stop tardiness in his department until the other supervisors do something to put their deparments in order.

Many a member comes to the meeting burning with a pet idea that he *must* get off his chest before he starts listening to anybody else. He is bound to bring it up at the first opportunity, even when it is obviously not relevant to the topic of the moment. (Thus, even if the chairman tries to start the discussion by asking, "Why are people tardy?" Mr. C would insist on talking about the side issue of how to enforce rules.)

Unrestricted discussion of this sort makes it easy for people to warm up to the problem and to start participating. It gives the chairman a chance to survey the psychological atmosphere, so that he can plan his strategy and anticipate the crucial issues. Finally, the free-discussion period provides an opportunity for participants to get to know each other's position; it is in every sense a warm-up before people start "keeping score."

Adopting the agenda. When the free discussion has served its purpose, it is time for the chairman to propose an agenda or ask the group to suggest one. In either case it is important that the agenda be made explicit.

Getting the facts. Too often meetings flounder because members are arguing from conflicting factual premises. Facts may be hard to obtain but at least they are subject to objective inquiry, and it is usually easier to get agreement on facts than it is to get agreement on opinions. Actually, one may lead to the other.

> A rich background of common facts lays the groundwork for the development of common inferences and sentiments, and out of these common decisions can grow. No decision rests on "facts" alone, but there is no better starting point.[17]

Listing alternative solutions. Logically, the next step is for the group to suggest alternative solutions to the problem at hand. The chairman will normally want to elicit as many suggestions as possible, to insure that no good idea is overlooked and that no participant feels neglected.

In recent years a technique known as "creative thinking" has come into use as a means of stimulating suggestions. Although it has had its most enthusiastic following in advertising and public relations, its principles are sometimes useful in other fields. The advocates of this approach insist that all alternatives should be listed before any attempt is made to evaluate them, since premature judgments may interfere with getting the maximum range of ideas.[18]

The heart of creative thinking is "brainstorming," a process in which the members throw out ideas as they occur to them. No attempt is made to evaluate the suggestions at this point. Instead, the chairman writes them down as fast as they are made. The emphasis is on unorthodox, "free-wheeling" ideas, or on "hitchhiking"—that is, using another person's ideas as a springboard for a completely different one of your own. On a question such as "What can be done to stimulate sales of government savings bonds?" a good group can think of as many as a hundred ideas in five minutes. "Brainstorming" has been compared with free association in psychoanalysis, where the patient is expected to give expression to everything that comes into mind. Brainstorming has been

---

[17] Bales, "In Conference," p. 47.

[18] The creative-thinking movement is largely the brain-child of Alex Osborn, co-founder of the advertising firm of Batten, Barton, Durstine and Osborn. See his *Applied Imagination* (New York: Scribner's, 1953).

criticized, though, as leading to fewer suggestions than would be produced by the same number of people working alone.[19]

Evaluating alternative solutions. Having listed the alternative solutions, the next step is to evaluate them. Although the method of evaluation will naturally depend on the nature of the problem, evaluation normally proceeds by stages. One approach is to discuss the advantages and disadvantages of each proposal in turn (along with suggestions on how to overcome difficulties), and then to compare one proposal against another.[20]

Notice how this approach differs from typical parliamentary procedure, in which each suggestion is considered separately and accepted or rejected in turn with no explicit consideration being given to possible alternatives.

During this evaluation period the chairman should try to help the group guard against the normal human tendency to think only of objections without trying to figure out how they can be overcome, or to take a black-and-white position for or against each idea, without trying to weigh alternatives realistically.

Narrowing the alternatives.[21] The group's function is to narrow down the many conceivable alternatives to the one or more on which general agreement can be reached. Normally, the more adequate the evaluation has been, the easier it will be to reach agreement. Yet the process is not automatic.

The first step is to determine which alternatives can be eliminated by unanimous consent. The remaining alternatives, which presumably have some supporters in the group, can then be narrowed down (1) by their proponents becoming persuaded that they are wrong, (2) by mutual concession—that is, by a negative compromise in which everyone gives up something, or (3) by synthesis—that is, by a constructive or positive compromise that incorporates what every member regards as significant and that leaves out nothing that anyone feels is important. Probably the third alternative is the best, and the second the worst.

In the process of working out a solution, the chairman may take entirely upon himself the function of conciliator or "middleman." But there will be greater acceptance of the final decision if there are other "middlemen" in the group who assist in finding a constructive synthesis or compromise.

One of the chairman's most difficult problems is to help the minority surrender its position without loss of face. Agreement is easier to achieve if the chairman is able to convince each of the factions that the final decision incorporates some of their ideas and that each has won a partial victory.

---

[19] For an excellent review of the research in this area, see Marvin Dunnette, "Are Meetings Any Good in Solving Problems?" *Personnel Administration*, Vol. 27, No. 2 (March 1964), p. 12.

[20] This is an elaboration of the "risk technique," which is discussed in Norman R. F. Maier, *Principles of Human Relations* (New York, Wiley, 1952), pp. 62-73.

[21] Note that the techniques suggested here are the same as those listed by successful labor-management mediators.

At times agreement is not reached because the members misunderstand each other's position, or because they disagree over the facts themselves. To forestall unnecessary stalemates, the chairman may ask "Is this what you mean?" There are enough clear-cut problems to be settled without letting semantics cloud the issues.

> People often think they disagree when actually they simply are not talking about the same experiences. In such cases they do not draw each other out enough to realize that, although they are using the same words, they are talking about different experiences.[22]

The chairman can also invite the protagonists to restate their position in a constructive, positive form (avoiding criticisms of their opponents), by asking clarifying questions, or perhaps by summarizing the various positions in a way that will emphasize the areas of agreement. If none of these work, it may pay to refer the problem to the committee, or to recess while the members think things over.

One observer has proposed a "procedure for coercing agreement" to be used when the chairman feels the conference is bogging down in emotional argument. Here the chairman takes a firm stand and entertains only questions and answers designed to ascertain facts, to clear up details, and to distinguish one proposal from another.[23]

Taking a vote.   Should the chairman insist on working through to a unanimous agreement no matter how long it takes, or should he terminate the discussion by taking a vote? Traditionally, voting has been regarded as the democratic way to make decisions, and the practice has taken on almost ceremonial overtones. In fact, a vote is often taken even where there is no opposition, just to show the group's solidarity.

And yet it can be argued that voting sometimes makes agreement more difficult to attain, since it plays up the differences among members and makes side-taking unavoidable. The trouble is that once a man has publicly committed himself to a position it becomes awkward for him to change his mind. Moreover, the man who is flatly overruled by a vote may be less likely to carry out the group's decision with enthusiasm. The public recording of each member's position tends to split the group into opposing factions, and encourages the members to pay more attention to the arguments of those who are on "their side" than to the arguments of the opposition.

It can even be argued that in a sense majority rule is actually undemocratic, since it shows no respect for the minority. The Quakers, for example, insist on unanimity, and any member can block a decision until he is convinced of its validity. Consequently, whenever action is finally taken it enjoys unanimous support.

---

[22] Bales, "In Conference," p. 49.

[23] See Irving J. Lee, "Procedure for 'Coercing' Agreement," *Harvard Business Review*, Vol. 32, No. 1 (January 1954), p. 39. For criticism of this approach as being autocratic and mechanical, see Harold P. Zelko, *Successful Conference and Discussion Techniques* (New York: McGraw-Hill, 1957), pp. 152-153.

If [the group] can reach unanimous consent . . . the effort is well worth while, for there will be no disgruntled minority which refuses to support or reluctantly supports group action. The search for unanimity places a premium on trying to understand a person rather than arguing him down.[24]

Insistence on absolute unanimity, however, has certain disadvantages: (1) It makes for unduly long meetings and delays essential action, (2) in a sense it lets the dissenter make the decision (since he decides whether there will be a decision or none at all), and (3) the common-denominator compromise that suits everybody is rarely bold, imaginative, or capable of arousing enthusiasm. The unanimity rule may work well enough in a religious community (particularly one in which the members have a strong sense of social values),[25] but in industry quick decisions are often of the greatest importance.

The chairman should seek unanimity whenever possible, of course, and on most issues this is not too hard to obtain. The chairman can usually sense when agreement has been reached, and then he needs only to state the "decision" and ask if everyone agrees. Unanimity should not become a fetish, however. If the cost in time and frustration promises to be too great, the leader should call for a vote. A minority that loses after having had ample opportunity to sway the majority frequently accepts the results without too much ill feeling. To do otherwise in our society is considered poor sportsmanship.

Releasing tension. Arguments, decision-making, and undertaking commitments naturally result in the building up of tension within the group. The Bales study has suggested that after a decision has been reached it is important to give people a chance to release this tension by relaxing and engaging in informal social activity. The chairman who ignores this need by rushing the members back to work will find that until they let off steam they just won't settle down to business.

SELF-EVALUATION

Successful group cooperation does not occur spontaneously. Group members must learn to work together. This process can be speeded up if the group sets aside some time to examine the effectiveness of its own activities—in other words, to learn from itself. Self-evaluation enables the group to improve its performance constantly.

Evaluation of this sort is usually more successful if there is some sort of feedback.[26] For example, one member of the group may be designated as a "process observer." He takes no active part in the meeting; instead, he makes a series of running notes on what is happening and then reports his observa-

---

[24] Frank S. Haimon, "Group Think or Group Thinking," *Adult Leadership*, Vol. 1, No. 10 (March 1953), p. 12.

[25] Even Quakers, however, sometimes feel frustrated because of a hold-out objector. See Whyte, *Leadership and Group Participation*, p. 35.

[26] See David H. Jenkins, "Feedback and Group Self-evaluation," *Journal of Social Issues*, Vol. 4, No. 2 (Spring 1948), pp. 50-60.

tions during the evaluation period. "The observer can act as the eyes for the group leader, who because of his own responsibility for discussion, is unable to attend as closely to the difficulties in the group process and to be as objective about his own feelings." [27] A typical observer's report might start this way:

> "Discussion was slow at first. No one was sure what the problem was. Then Bob presented his ideas and almost everyone started contributing. Jack sidetracked us a bit by talking about . . . and the rest seemed bored until Jim (the chairman) very tactfully suggested that Jack defer his comments until later. I notice that Gus and Mike have been very quiet."

Even this small segment of the report would provide plenty of meat for self-evaluation:

1. How could the problem have been stated better at the beginning?
2. How did Jack feel about being called out of order? (When discussed in the evaluation session, this would permit Jack to let off steam, might persuade him to show more self-discipline next time, and would help the chairman evaluate his handling of Jack's irrelevancies.)
3. Why were Gus and Mike so quiet?

Indeed, the chairman can interrupt the meeting for a special report from the process observer whenever he thinks discussion has bogged down. The role of the observer should be rotated in order to give everybody a chance to observe the group from outside.

Another aid to self-evaluation is a "post-meeting evaluation form," which is filled out by each of the members. A simple form might include questions such as these:

1. On the whole, how did you regard the meeting?
   Excellent—— Very Good—— Good—— Fair—— Poor——
2. What was good about the meeting?
3. What was bad about the meeting?
4. Was the chairman too strict? Too easy?
5. Do you feel you had sufficient opportunity to talk?

PARLIAMENTARY LAW [28]

Parliamentary law is a formalized procedure designed for large deliberative bodies. Consequently it rarely has much value in small committee meetings, and even in large meetings it should be applied with flexibility. If a group tries to follow the letter of the law, it will fall into interminable, meaningless wrangles, resulting in the frustration of everyone concerned.

Strict observation of parliamentary law demands that the group vote for or

---

[27] *Ibid.*, p. 57.

[28] For a sharply contrasting view on the value of parliamentary law, see Malcolm Knowles, "Move Over Mr. Robert," *Adult Leadership*, Vol. 1, No. 2 (June 1952); Robert W. English, "General Robert Replies," *Adult Leadership*, Vol. 2, No. 2 (June 1953), p. 29; and Zelko, *op. cit.*, pp. 151-152.

against each proposal, with no provision for making a systematic comparison of alternatives. Parliamentary procedure is supposed to save time and to produce a more orderly meeting, but its rigid rules often do just the opposite, particularly since few people understand their intricacies.

Nevertheless, parliamentary procedure does have one major advantage for large meetings: It keeps control over process firmly in the hands of the members themselves. Only the group as a whole can decide when to stop debate, to make a decision, or to move on to the next question. The chairman's power is restricted to recognizing speakers and calling members out of order (and even this is subject to appeal).

CONCLUSION

The ability to act as an effective chairman or a productive committee member is becoming increasingly important in management. The same basic rules of conference leadership apply when the company president sits with the board of directors in mahogany and velvet surroundings as when the foreman calls his men together in the locker room to discuss a production technique.

Good meetings don't "just happen." They require skillful leadership on the part of the chairman and sincere cooperation on the part of the members. When the members are unable to integrate their individual needs and roles, meetings tend to degenerate into futile wrangles. A feeling of solidarity and common purpose is required before members will evaluate ideas on their merits rather than in terms of self-interest.

The chairman plays a variety of roles, depending on the purpose of the meeting. The more effective chairman minimizes content roles. If he is a strict chairman, he will assume strong process roles; if he is a loose chairman, he will not.

The chairman faces a constant dilemma in deciding how tight a rein to keep on the discussion. Too tight control may frustrate the natural development of ideas, force people to conclusions before they are ready, and generate resentment. Too loose control may result in a feeling of aimlessness and confusion.

The chairman must constantly keep in mind that the goals of meetings (high-quality decisions, general acceptance, and economy in time) often conflict with one another. He must encourage participation and yet at the same time keep the discussion both relevant and moving toward a conclusion.

The successful meeting proceeds smoothly from stage to stage. The chairman senses the invisible currents at work within the group and decides on the proper moment to move on.

If a meeting is to achieve its objective there must be a carefully devised agenda to insure an orderly, efficient procedure for discussion and decision-making. An effective agenda takes advantage of the natural stages through which a meeting passes, and is flexible enough (1) to meet the needs of the particular problem, group, and time limit, and (2) to be modified during the course of the meeting as the need arises. An agenda that has been accepted by the members serves many purposes: It insures that every point of view has been considered; it allows for maximum participation, and (hopefully) it enables the meeting to make its decision within the time allowed.

In a broad sense, the first three chapers of this part have been concerned with communication problems: those involving transmission of messages (Chapter 10), the reception of messages (Chapter 11), and improving the flow of messages among members of a meeting (Chapter 12). In each of these areas, as the following table illustrates, certain principles have emerged which dovetail neatly with similar principles from other areas.

Communicator	*Interviewer*	*Conference Leader*
1. Directs message to the world of his audience.	Tries to understand how interviewee sees problem.	Helps each member understand how others see problem.
2. Pitches remarks in terms audience can understand; takes into account what words mean to the audience.	Tries to understand what the words of the interviewee mean to him.	Helps members understand what each other's words mean.
3. Tries to discover the audience's emotional state and takes this into account in framing message.	Helps interviewee release feelings before getting down to consider facts.	Allows group to express feelings before getting down to decision-making.
4. Tries to indicate to audience that he understands their problem.	Tries to indicate that he understands interviewee's problem.	Tries to indicate that he understands a conference members' problems.

PROBLEM

STAFF MEETING

Role play a meeting of the Dooley Division Staff (Chapter 16, p. 396) discussing a proposal by the new purchasing agent to introduce a formal requisition or inventory-control system. Various members of the group may take on the roles of Dooley, Wallace, the chief engineer, the controller, the general foreman, and the purchasing agent. Assume that Dooley has no strong preference, either for or against the new system, but that he is anxious to get a fairly unanimous agreement within his staff.

Introducing Change

We live in a world of change. We Americans in particular have learned to expect change as part of our everyday life. We pride ourselves on being modern and up-to-date in our habits and behavior. Still we may be more traditional than we think. To be sure, we accept and even welcome changes in terms of material things, such as household gadgets or cars. But we tend to resist changes in our interpersonal and job relations, because these changes threaten the security of the orderly and familiar ways we have known in the past, and often our status as well.

If a company is to survive today, it must be able to react to changing conditions by changing itself. In fact, it *must* anticipate environmental changes by altering its own policies and structure in time to meet these new conditions as they arise. The ability to introduce change with a minimum of resistance is a key managerial skill. In this chapter we shall discuss (1) why there is resistance to change and (2) what can be done to deal with it.

TYPES OF RESISTANCE TO CHANGE

Of all the types of resistance to change, perhaps the one most commonly recognized is the resistance of many employees to technological change—to automation, for example. Such resistance is readily understandable. In some instances, technological change means that employees must agree to work on faster machines with increased workloads. In others, it requires the acquisition of new skills and even a new approach to work; for example, the worker must learn to watch and adjust equipment rather than to operate it manually.[1] In still others, as in the case of locomotive firemen and flight engineers, it may mean the loss of work altogether.

But there are many other forms of change which are also resisted: changes

---

[1] See Charles R. Walker, *Towards an Automatic Factory* (New York: Harper & Row, 1957).

in organizational structure, methods of compensation, and so forth. Take the case of a clothing store, once famous for its high-quality merchandise, which is located in an area from which high-income customers have moved. A new owner resolves to introduce a lower-priced line and to induce his salesmen to engage in high-pressure salesmanship. The salesmen are likely to react violently to changing well-established patterns.

Resistance to change is sometimes as deep-rooted at the managerial level as it is at lower levels. In many companies one hears constant complaints about "old fogies" who are hampering progress. As we explore elsewhere,[2] there are problems involved in re-educating managers to improve their supervisory practices, to give higher priority to accident prevention, and so forth. Indeed, managers tend to resist the introduction of almost any new personnel practice. They may regard a new system of job evaluation as a threat to existing status relationships, or the introduction of tests in hiring as a threat to their traditional prerogative to hire whomever they wish.

Resistance to change may show itself in unexpected ways, for instance in aggression, regression, and in all the negative reactions discussed in Chapter 6. It may appear as absenteeism, resignations, requests for transfer, and as "the expression of a lot of pseudo-logical reasons why the change will not work." [3] One clear sign of resistance is a series of apparently "emotional" or "irrational" objections to minor changes; these often indicate that more deep-seated problems are involved.

It should be emphasized that not all change is resisted. Some forms of change are welcomed (such as pay increases). Aerospace companies, for example, engage in constant technological and organizational change with relatively little resistance. It is not change itself which causes the resistance, but the meaning of the change for the people involved. Thus, one should expect greater resistance to change in a company which is contracting or stationary in size than one would in a company which is expanding, even though the expanding company has a larger number of changes—the reason being that in the expanding company the changes are less likely to threaten employees' social or economic status.[4]

WHAT CAUSES RESISTANCE TO CHANGE?

Economic Factors

The most obvious reason is economic. Workers resist automation when they fear they will lose their jobs; they are unimpressed by arguments that

---

[2] George Strauss and Leonard R. Sayles, *Personnel* (Englewood Cliffs, N.J.: Prentice-Hall, 1960), Chapter 24.

[3] Paul Lawrence, "How to Deal With Resistance to Change," *Harvard Business Review*, Vol. 32, No. 3 (May 1954), p. 49.

[4] Michael Stewart, "Resistance to Technological Change in Industry," *Human Organization*, Vol. 16, No. 3 (Fall 1957), pp. 36-39.

in the "long run" there will be more jobs in other parts of the country. What concerns them most is the economic welfare of themselves and their families.[5]

Similarly, a craftsman may fear that new developments will reduce the economic value of his skill. In the same way, managers themselves oppose a change that helps the company as a whole but hurts their individual promotional opportunities.

Sometimes the economic factors underlying resistance to change are obscure and not immediately apparent. In one plant the employees began to damage parts they were sending to a new plant overseas; formerly the parts had been shipped to a domestic plant. Was this blind resistance to change? Not at all. Investigation revealed that the employees were afraid the company was shifting more and more of its operations to the overseas plant and feared that eventually they would lose their jobs.

We must, however, guard against the common misconception that workers generally—and particularly their unions—blindly resist all forms of technological progress. The Hat Workers and Clothing Workers unions, for instance, have developed special programs designed to encourage management to introduce such changes. They recognize that only through rising productivity can their wages be raised. Similarly, John L. Lewis and the United Mine Workers cooperated with coal-mine owners in an extensive mechanization program which has resulted in substantially fewer jobs in the coal fields, but higher earnings for those who remained. Foreign visitors to this country express surprise at the extent to which American workers have learned that technological change redounds to their benefit and is the source of rising wages. There is, however, a significant gap between the intellectual recognition of this relationship and the acceptance of change in a particular case.

Inconvenience

Equally understandable is the resistance to change that threatens to make life more difficult. A worker fights the assignment of extra duties; he has learned his old job so well that it requires no attention any more, while the new job requires surface attention. Similarly, executives dislike the inconvenience of being reassigned from one location to another. Even if the company pays their expenses, there is the bother of buying and selling houses, packing, and readjusting to new work and a new environment.

All of us develop a vested interest in our usual way of doing things. Our everyday habits provide us with a certain security in our life. Some of these are quite trivial: We drive to work by a fixed route every day, even though other routes are equally good; when our usual route is temporarily blocked, we are annoyed by the inconvenience of having to change our pattern.

Learning new ways requires the expenditure of energy, and human beings

---

[5] For similar reasons, workers may object to bigger workloads, even when there is no demand for greater physical effort. They reason that they may work either themselves or their friends out of a job or that management is getting "something for nothing."

are generally lazy. Even for the simplest job there are "tricks to the trade" that take time to learn. When a man is thrown into a new situation his tricks no longer apply and he loses the security of the familiar.

Uncertainty

The new way is always strange, threatening, and laden with uncertainties—even if it is an improvement over the old. We have a chance for a new job at higher pay. Should we take it? Maybe not. How hard will it be? How long will it take to learn? Will we be able to meet the challenge? Who will our friends be? The opportunity may be very good indeed, yet there is a strong tendency to let well enough alone.

One reason for this fear is the lack of factual information. We know our present circumstances; we don't know what the new ones will be. Some people are gamblers by nature, but the average person hesitates to venture into uncharted waters. The uncertain is always threatening.

New equipment is introduced into the plant. What will it mean to our job, our status, our security? A new boss is assigned to the department. What will his policies be? How will they affect us? Often the rumor mill exaggerates the potential threat of a change. Until management clarifies the impact of the change, such rumors can panic a group of employees.

Uncertainty caused by lack of information may be corrected simply by providing answers to questions—assuming that management is aware of what questions are being asked. But there is another kind of uncertainty that cannot be dissipated by providing information: the anxiety that springs from the individual's fears about how *he himself* will react to the new situation. Every draftee is assailed with doubts the night before his induction. What will army life be for me? Every veteran is delighted to provide information, but no one can predict how *I* will react. For this sort of uncertainty there can be no quick remedy.

Symbols

Symbols raise special problems. Remember that a symbol is something which stands for something else. The flag symbolizes one's country; the Bastille, pre-revolutionary oppression in France; the supervisors' parking lot, their special status; the restaurant's white table cloth, its general excellence. A symbol cannot be eliminated without threatening in people's minds the things for which it stands. Note, for example, the widespread emotional reaction to the change in the Canadian flag, or the following case from industry:

> The new manager of the Integrity Insurance Company had little difficulty with his "modernization" program until he decided it was a waste of money to print policies on high-quality parchment paper. His proposal to substitute a cheaper but still durable paper led to a storm of protest from the company's insurance agents: The new paper wouldn't look or wear well, it didn't look

right, the customers would think it cheap. Investigation revealed that to the agents the parchment paper was a symbol of Integrity's reputation as a leader in the industry. They began to fear that these changes would mean that Integrity would be just like any other insurance company.

Small changes may symbolize big ones, particularly when employees are uncertain about how extensive a program of change will be. When a situation begins to shift, subordinates search for indications of what lies ahead. For Integrity's agents, the cheaper paper was a convincing sign that management intended to degrade the company's prestige. A symbol represents a whole framework of treasured relationships and values; subordinates unite to protect it against attack just as if everything it represented were actually in danger.

Threats to Interpersonal Relationships

As we mentioned in Chapter 4, anything that disrupts the customary social relationships and standards of the group will meet with strong resistance. In particular, employees oppose changes which threaten their status or their painfully acquired, socially valued skills.

> For example, vests and coats in one clothing center are made by separate groups of tailors, though to an outsider their skills seem readily interchangeable. Over the years the demand for vests has fallen off while an acute shortage of skilled coatmakers has developed. Yet in spite of the combined urging of union and management, the vestmakers refuse to transfer to coatmaking. As a result the vestmakers lose over $30 a week. Why do they persist in this apparently illogical attitude?
>
> The vestmakers are a small, tightly knit clique of friends who are proud of their skill. They have a long-established union local of their own. They fear that if they were transferred to coatmaking their clique would be broken up, they would become the *least*-skilled coatmakers rather than highly skilled vestmakers, and they would lose the protection of their local. Thus, the change is a threat to their prestige, their ability to meet their social needs, and their union protection.

Even when no change in physical location is involved, most changes tend to upset interpersonal relations. Take the situation in a small firm that had just hired a new purchasing agent.

> Previously each department head had ordered his own supplies. Now the department head merely filled out a purchase order and the purchasing agent decided on the supplier and negotiated the price. Though this policy saved the department heads from being pestered by salesmen and saved the company money, the department heads were highly antagonistic. They missed the feeling of importance that came from dealing directly with salesmen; the purchasing agent was far less obsequious to them than the salesman had been, and he threatened their authority by suggesting at times that they might use cheaper, lower-quality material. This fact may help explain why they began complaining about red tape and about how the purchasing agent made their jobs harder, not easier.

Every supervisor develops patterns of informal relations with his sub-ordinates. And every new supervisor requires a long period of initiation before he is accepted by his subordinates as their legitimate leader (see Chapter 8), in part because they fear that he may not follow his predecessor's patterns of informal relations. In fact, *any* new member of a group has a hard time until he develops satisfactory relations with his colleagues—and one of the reasons why people resist being transferred to new jobs is that they dislike the disrup-tion of old relations and the work of establishing new ones.

Other changes may threaten a man's opportunity to provide leadership. For instance, before automation a crew chief on a press directed the men who worked with him; after automation there was less need for teamwork and less opportunity for him to issue orders. Or the change may mean that the man who used to call the signals waits passively for someone else to take the initiative. Under the old scheme the maintenance man scheduled his own work; under the new scheme he must wait until someone calls him, thus reducing his discretion and status and substantially changing his social relationships with others.

Individuals adjust their pattern of social relations to fit their own special personality needs, just as they adjust other elements of their life in the forma-tion of habits. Over a period of time, assuming an employee is not anxious to quit his present job, he has probably developed a good fit between his person-ality needs and the requirements of the job. The man who wants to boss others around, even if he is not officially a supervisor, has probably found a position in the work group that permits him to initiate activity; the worker who wants to avoid social pressures has probably found a job where no one can push him, not even the man who works next to him. Changing work procedures and systems, and introducing new equipment, upsets these convenient, pleasant job patterns. The sequence of work may be so drastically changed that the man who was formerly isolated must now work with a high-pressure colleague, and the leader is left with no one to lead.

Resentment toward New Orders and Increased Control

Whenever management institutes change, it must substantially increase the number of orders it gives to subordinates. This results in a change in interpersonal relations, and this second change, in turn, may well lead to resistance.

Some people resent taking any orders at all. Others have become accustomed to a certain level of control from higher management but resist any attempt to strengthen this control. On routine jobs or on jobs where employees are used to being their own boss, direct orders from management are relatively rare. When change occurs, they become subject to all sorts of unusual pressures from supervisors, engineers, and the big boss. Suddenly they find that some-one is checking up on them and barraging them with far more orders than usual. This sharp increase in control reduces their feeling of autonomy and self-reliance. It emphasizes their dependence on management.

Similarly, members of management often resist change when it is initiated by staff people who normally have little control over (or even contact with) the line people who must carry out the change. Staff people have a strong incentive to promote change because it increases their prestige and influence; for almost these very reasons, however, line people have a tendency to resist change.

Resistance of this sort occurs even in the relations between staff groups. Engineers, for example, often resist suggestions by purchasing agents to utilize new materials which have come to the purchasing agents' attention through salesmen. Engineers feel that they should have exclusive authority to specify the material used, and that they should tell the purchasing agent what sorts of material should be used—not vice versa. So when purchasing agents try to influence the engineers, they are reversing the usual channel of communication. (We shall discuss this problem at greater length in Chapter 17.)

When told that they *must* change their behavior, people sometimes become stubborn. They seek to defend themselves and become more committed than ever to their old attitudes. As we shall see, change is easier when the people who are to be changed are consulted beforehand or have a chance to participate in making the decision—and thus do not feel pushed.

It has been argued that one of the main problems in introducing change is to keep it from being introduced in an intermittent fashion. The organizations that have greatest difficulty are often those that make changes only once in a while. The trick, it is claimed, is to make change almost continuously, to make change for the sake of change, even if there is no compelling reason for change at the moment. Perhaps this suggestion is too extreme. Still it does emphasize the point that living under change is very different from leading the same placid existence day after day.

Union Attitudes

Unions are also likely to resist change unless management consults with them, either formally or informally. It is not enough to inform individuals or consult with them. Every union has certain institutional needs that must be met if it is to retain its members' loyalty. If management makes a point of working with the union, the union may cooperate in introducing the change. If management ignores the union, the only way the union can preserve its status is by opposing management.

What happens when management decides to introduce new equipment that will require men to learn new jobs and assume new responsibilities? The typical approach in some companies is for the industrial engineer to make all the necessary plans, perhaps in consultation with the foreman. When the equipment arrives, the foreman assigns men to the new jobs and the personnel department computes the new pay rates. Almost inevitably, the union will find something wrong with the change and will file a grievance—and perhaps even sponsor a slow-down or wildcat strike. Why? If the union were to accept management's action passively, it would in effect be abandoning what it regards as its proper role. The only way to save face is to fight the proposed changes.

In other companies, management customarily informs the union of proposed changes long before they are made, asks for suggestions on how the seniority clause should operate when men are transferred, and bargains over wage rates for the new job. The union's status is preserved, and it assumes responsibility for resolving what might be a bitter dispute over who will be assigned to the new jobs. Of course, in bargaining over wages the company may have to make concessions, but the over-all cost may be less than the expense of trying to force the change over the union's objection, for workers are in an ideal position to insure that unwelcome change will prove unsuccessful or costly.

Change and the Over-all Organization

So far we have dealt with change as if it occurred in a vacuum. Obviously, this is not so. "Since every group is a social system, any change in one of its component parts is likely to require or result in alteration or rearrangement of other parts." [6] Apparently simple changes may involve a host of people who at first may not seem concerned. For example, a change may appear to affect only Mr. A, but it affects his relationship with Mr. B, who becomes upset, thus hurting his relationship with Mr. C. Mr. C in turn deals with Mr. A in a less friendly fashion than usual, which further upsets Mr. A. Eventually, a comparatively minor change touches off a major crisis.

Change must be seen in organizational terms. Rarely are a manager and his immediate subordinates the only ones involved. Very often the need for change develops first: Profits decline, competition adopts new products or production processes, equipment begins to wear out and get out of date, and so forth. Management may cling to its traditional ways at first, even though to an outsider the need for adjustment may be obvious. Eventually, one group within management (usually a staff department) may become aware of the problem and propose a solution. Now it must sell its solution to other groups within management. Line personnel may resist because they have the difficult task of implementing the change. Other staff men may resist also: the controller, for instance, because the change is too expensive, or the personnel director because it would disrupt a tricky union relationship.

While the plan is under consideration, rumors fly, restlessness increases, and sometimes exaggerated fears arise. When the plan is finally tentatively adopted at higher levels, management must now try to win the acceptance and co-operation of those at lower levels, and sometimes from the union. Often the

---

[6] Paul C. Agnew and Francis L. K. Hsu, "Introducing Change in a Mental Hospital," *Human Organization*, Vol. 19, No. 4 (Winter 1961), p. 199.

change may have widespread and unexpected ramification and may disrupt precariously balanced relationships.

The process should not be considered entirely a one-way street which runs, for example, from staff to line to subordinate employees. Line management will seek additional information from staff, it will raise objections, and it will suggest modifications in the proposed plans. Staff people may now be the ones who are resisting the changes proposed by line. Subordinates will react in the same way, openly if they are permitted to speak out, otherwise on an undercover basis. (For example, they may "modify" management's plans through outright sabotage.) Often subordinates propose change which higher management will "resist" in turn.

In organizations where human relations are sound, however, change is usually taken in stride. But in organizations where tensions and dissatisfactions are high, changes will be more difficult to accomplish. For example:

> The high degree of [social] integration, the relative lack of conflict, and the level of job security in the chemical industry provide an atmosphere in which technological change is more accepted by workers and management than in the automobile industry, where, because of its history of labor-management strife and its irregular employment patterns, workers are naturally suspicious of the motives and effects of technological innovation.[7]

In some situations, stresses which are not obvious in ordinary circumstances become evident when change is introduced, almost as if the change is the straw which breaks the camel's back. Consider the following ingenious study conducted at General Electric: [8]

> The experiment was concerned with two sets of groups of workers, all doing repetitive, no-attention work. First these employees went through a "manipulative period" of several weeks. One set of employees, the "Favored Groups," received praise and friendly help from their bosses and were protected from disruption. The other set, the "Disfavored Groups," were nagged and pestered by management in a number of annoying ways. As might be expected, the Favored Groups developed positive attitudes toward their treatment while the Disfavored Groups expressed feelings of considerable aggravation. Nevertheless, neither treatment seemed to have a significant effect on the various groups' output rates.
>
> At the end of the manipulation period, all special treatment stopped, except that shortly thereafter slight changes were made in each group's production methods. In both sets of groups both quantity and quality of output went down but the effect was very significantly greater in the formerly Disfavored Groups than it was in the Favored Groups.

---

[7] Robert Blauner, *Alienation and Freedom* (Chicago: University of Chicago Press, 1964), p. 153.

[8] Stanley Schacter and others, "Emotional Disruption and Industrial Productivity," *Journal of Applied Psychology,* Vol. 45, No. 4 (August 1961), pp. 201-213. The above description of the experiment is somewhat oversimplified, but gives the essential picture of what was done.

The lesson for management here is that, although morale may have little impact on productivity under normal conditions, it may well have the effect of making change more difficult.[9] The impact of change upon an existing organization is always difficult to predict.

Violation of Expectations

One concept may help summarize much of what we have said about resistance to change. In previous chapters we suggested that in most well-established groups there are generally accepted (legitimate) norms about the rights and responsibilities of both managers and subordinates—and that the nature of both these rights and responsibilities are established by implicit bargaining. Change, however, violates the implicit bargain. Unless the manager is careful in how he introduces change, his action is likely to be regarded as illegitimate, and subordinates, through resisting the change, will seek to restore the previous equilibrium.

REDUCING RESISTANCE TO CHANGE

Let us examine the problem of introducing change in still another framework. Take a situation in which workers are producing at 70 per cent of the efficiency that might be expected on the basis of purely technical considerations. Obviously, certain forces are operating to hold the rate down. For instance:

1. Dislike of work.
2. Fear of working oneself out of a job.
3. An informally set "bogey."
4. Dislike of the supervisor.

Yet another set of forces must be operating to keep the rate *as high as* 70 per cent. These may be:

1. Fear of losing one's job—or at least fear of losing special privileges.
2. Pressure exerted by the supervisor.
3. Financial incentives (if there is piece work).
4. Fear of being caught idle.

Presumably, at the 70 per cent rate of production, the two sets of forces have reached a balance which has been called a "quasi-stable equilibrium."[10] That is, a system has been established in which one set of needs is balanced off against the other. (See A in the diagram.)

---

[9] For another study which leads to the same conclusion, see Chris Argyris, "Organizational Effectiveness Under Stress," *Harvard Business Review*, Vol. 38, No. 3 (May 1960), pp. 137-146.

[10] This concept of quasi-stable equilibrium was developed by Kurt Lewin. See his "Frontiers in Group Dynamics," *Human Relations*, Vol. 1, No. 1 (1947), pp. 5-42.

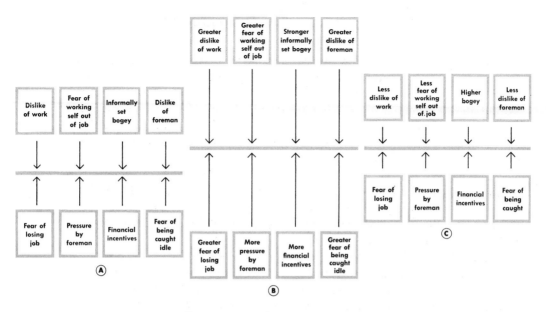

A *shows quasi-stable equilibrium; B shows higher equi- librium with strengthened upward forces; C shows higher equilibrium with weakened downward forces.*

Now, if management wants to increase production, the typical approach is to strengthen the upward forces (B in diagram), perhaps by having the fore- man apply even more pressure or by installing piece work. This method of introducing change we shall call *overcoming resistance*. Of course, the higher production climbs, the more workers' resistance is raised, until finally a new equilibrium is reached where the two sets of pressures are once more in balance. However, and this is a crucial point, at the new equilibrium, stronger forces are operating on each side, and tension is at a higher level. Frustration is greater, and employees are more likely to devise techniques to insulate them- selves from the pressures acting on them. From management's point of view this is an inefficient way of doing things. It is like trying to stop a car by using the brakes without taking one's foot off the gas.

Fortunately, there are more efficient ways of accomplishing the same ob- jective. Instead of strengthening the upward forces, management can weaken the downward forces (C in diagram), perhaps by making the work less dis- agreeable, or by inducing workers to change their bogey, or by reducing their dislike of the foreman. This method we shall call *reducing resistance*. Here, too, a new equilibrium will be reached at a higher level of production, but at a lower level of tension. It is like stopping a car by taking one's foot off the gas, but by not using the brake.

Though method 2 (reducing resistance) frequently cannot be used without some of method 1 (overcoming resistance), the former places the least strain on human relations.

In overcoming resistance, management seeks to apply enough pressure on a man to induce him to do what is expected. For instance, the most obvious way to overcome resistance to change is simply to threaten to fire a man if he doesn't adjust, or promise to pay him more if he does.

But this threatening approach leads to all the problems we discussed in Chapter 6 under "be strong." A man may respond to threats either by quitting altogether, by sabotaging the change once it has been introduced, or by implementing it in a half-hearted manner.

What about trying to deal with resistance by promising a man an economic reward if he will accept the change? If the reason for resistance in this case is largely economic—and in many cases it is—obviously an economic reward is a good answer, for it helps reduce the cause of resistance and thus helps get the change accepted with less tension.

On the other hand, economic rewards are less successful if the reason for resistance is noneconomic. For instance, an executive may be offered a salary increase to move to a new location. Let us assume that the executive's immediate reaction to this offer is that the new location is very unpleasant and that he has misgivings about the type of work he will be doing and the type of men he will be associating with.

Confronted with such a choice, the executive will probably experience painful indecision. Indecision is always frustrating even between attractive alternatives. He may even try to get the salary increase without leaving town, perhaps by going to work for another company. And regardless of what he decides, for years to come he may resent having been forced into the decision. If he stays, he may deplore his economic sacrifice every time he pays a bill. If he goes, his attitude may make it difficult for him to adjust to the new situation.

> A large chemical company used quite a different approach in manning a new laboratory in a remote section of the country. Their approach emphasized reducing causes of resistance. First, the company publicized the importance and challenge of the new laboratory's work and hinted broadly that assignment there would offer great opportunities for promotion. Then it invited a small core of experienced engineers to accept positions in the new lab and told them that they could invite less-experienced men to join them. However, management made it clear that those who were invited were free to reject the invitation. The potential candidates and their families were brought together from all over the country at the site of the new lab and were given a chance to get to know one another and to investigate housing possibilities. As a consequence, the firm had little trouble recruiting able men to work in the new location.

In the discussion that follows, we shall seek to emphasize methods of reducing, rather than overcoming, resistance.

Through Economic Incentives

As we mentioned earlier, much of the resistance to change has an economic motivation. Either men hear that the change will result in an immediate loss of job or earnings, or else they fear that it will affect their long-run job security or chances for promotion. The easiest solution in such a case is simple but expensive: Guarantee that these fears are groundless. For instance, if a man refuses to work on a new machine merely because he fears a loss of piece-work earnings, management might guarantee him that his earnings will be no lower on the new machine. It is quite common in union contracts today for management to guarantee that no one will be displaced by technological change. Certainly, too, if new equipment is to be introduced that will displace men, the change should be made in a period of expanding employment when the displaced employee can be offered another job that offers equally good security and pay.

Such guarantees are extremely useful in smoothing over change. The difficulty is their expense. The very reason for change may be the desire to cut costs because of economic necessity. Even in such a case management may reduce resistance if it can truthfully show that the change will be an improvement in the individual's own (not just the company's or the other workers') economic prospects in the long run.

Though the bulk of this chapter is concerned with noneconomic means of handling resistance, you should not draw the wrong impression from our allocation of space. *Economic motivation is very important in our society.* And when the cause of resistance is economic, all the noneconomic techniques that we are about to discuss will be meaningless. True, an employer may successfully manipulate an employee into acquiescing to a change that is not in the employee's best interest. But in the long run, in a free society such attempts at brainwashing tend to backfire against their instigators. We emphasize this point because there are employers who feel that if proper "human relations" are applied, employees will be willing to do without a fair wage. Such misuse of human relations is, in our opinion, highly immoral; fortunately, it is rarely successful.

Through Two-Way Communication

Resistance to change that springs from fear of the unknown can be reduced simply by providing appropriate information. This information should explain not only *what* is to happen but also *why*. And it should be sent to the whole organization, to those both directly and indirectly involved.

This question of communications raises all the problems that we discussed in Chapter 10, particularly: (1) Is the information really understood? And (2) does it answer the questions actually being asked? Here, as in most areas of human relations, only *two-way* communication will serve the purpose. When major change is contemplated, supervisors and subordinates should sit down and discuss the proposed plan in a way that will bring doubts and questions out into the open where they can examine and answer them. After all, even though management's ideas may work in theory, employees may have the know-how to make them work in practice. Indeed, what management diagnoses as *employee* resistance to change is sometimes really management resistance to listening to employee suggestions.

Through Group Decision-Making

We have seen that most people have a strong desire to participate in decisions that affect them directly. Group decision-making involves subordinates actively in the process of introducing change and enhances their sense of control over the environment.[11]

> One group-decision experiment was made with girls who were learning machine-paced work and who were failing to keep up with the required pace.[12] In discussions with their foremen, the girls requested that they be allowed to determine the pace themselves. A dial was installed that allowed them to set their own speed. It was discovered that the girls set up a work pattern which varied with the time of day, but that the *average* speed was considerably higher than the *constant* speed previously set by engineers. Yet the girls reported that their work was easier, and their total output was between 30 and 50 per cent higher than expected.

Unfreezing attitudes. People often resist change because they hold certain fixed attitudes or stereotypes to which they adhere in spite of all evidence to the contrary. Group decision-making helps them *unfreeeze* these attitudes so that they can be re-examined.

> An example occurred in a pajama plant.[13] During World War II the company's staff psychologist tried to persuade management, in view of the general manpower shortage, to abandon its policy of not hiring workers over 30. The top-management group immediately opposed this suggestion, insisting that older women took too long to train, had a higher absenteeism rate, and never worked at top speed. When the staff psychologist mentioned the good performance of older women currently employed, management dismissed them as exceptional cases.
>
> Shifting to another approach, the psychologist tried to involve management in a minor research project to find out how much money the company was losing through employing older women. Management itself determined the criteria to be used (production rates, turnover, absenteeism, and learning speed) and also decided how the data were to be gathered. In short, management became actively involved in the project. To management's surprise, the data showed that older women were better on all counts. Highly excited by these findings, management changed its policy and even spread the word of its shift to other companies.

---

[11] See, for example, Lester Coch and John R. P. French, "Overcoming Resistance to Change," *Human Relations*, Vol. I, No. 4 (1948), pp. 512-532; Kurt Lewin, "Studies in Group Decision," Dorwin Cartwright and Alvin Zander, eds., *Group Dynamics* (Evanston, Ill.: Harper & Row, 1953), pp. 287-301; and various articles in *Journal of Social Issues*, Vol. 1, No. 3 (1945). It should be noted that not all the "group-decision experiments" have been able to be duplicated. For an example of failure, see John R. P. French, Joachim Israel, and Dagfin Äs, "An Experiment in Participation in a Norwegian Factory," *Human Relations*, Vol. 13, No. 1 (February 1960), pp. 3-20.

[12] William F. Whyte and others, *Money and Motivation* (New York: Harper & Row, 1955), Chapter 10.

[13] A. J. Marrow and John R. P. French, "Overcoming a Stereotype," *Journal of Social Issues*, Vol. 1, No. 3 (1945), pp. 33-37.

Notice that the psychologist failed when he tried to attack management's stereotypes head-on. But he succeeded when he induced management to unfreeze its old attitudes by engaging in the research study. By doing this, management opened its mind to objective evidence. In a sense the approach used was like double-clutching. Instead of shifting directly from one attitude to another, the group went first into "neutral" before taking up its final position.

Establishing new group standards. In Chapter 4 we mentioned that groups develop certain standards of proper conduct and that individuals who fail to live up to these standards are subjected to pressure to conform. When an individual member of a group decides to accept a change imposed from above, he fears that his fellow workers will criticize him for playing along. But when the entire group is involved in the decision leading to the change, just the opposite occurs: The man who *refuses* to accept the change is pressured into accepting the group decision. In effect, group decision-making may lead to the establishment of new group standards that are rigidly enforced.

Commitment. Group decision-making commits each member of the group to carry out the decision that is agreed on. Even if a member has reservations or second thoughts, he is under strong pressure to implement the decision. Providing employees with information and arguments may influence them one way or another, but they themselves must decide whether to accept or resist a proposed change if they are to experience any commitment to the ultimate decision.

Though group decision-making may serve as a useful tool in reducing resistance to change, it is by no means a cure-all for management's problems. It works effectively in areas where management is relatively indifferent to what the group decides; for instance, management may not care how the work is divided up so long as the job is done. Group decision-making may also prove effective when management and employees have overlapping but not conflicting interests. But when no community of interest exists, or when participation is foreign to a group's experiences, group decision-making is of little use in reducing resistance to change (see Chapter 9).

Through Bargaining

How does bargaining differ from group decision-making? In group decision-making, management gives the group freedom to make its own decisions (though within limits). Bargaining implies a willingness to talk things over and to make compromises in an effort to get the group's approval of proposed changes. However, management does not agree in advance to accept any decision made by the group. Normally, it accepts only some of the group's proposals and only as a *quid pro quo* in exchange for the group's accepting the rest of what management wants.

Sometimes bargaining is implicit (as we mentioned in Chapter 6)—that is, unspoken understandings are reached on how much management will demand in the way of change, and subordinates in effect agree to accept a limited amount of change as long as management is "reasonable" in its demands.

Often, explicit and open bargaining is more useful, particularly in a unionized situation. As we have seen, unions insist on being consulted on every matter that affects the welfare of their members. Some changes, such as pay cuts, may clearly require union approval. In other instances, management may have the power to make a change on its own, but may be caught up in a swarm of grievances if the union does not approve of what was done. When workers are transferred from one job to another, for example, the union may charge that the seniority clause of the contract has been violated. When workloads are increased, the union may charge that there is a violation of the health and safety clause of the contract or of established past practices.

Many managements insist on their "prerogative" to make all decisions by themselves. When the union attacks their actions, they try to limit the discussion to the strictly legal question of whether the contract was in fact violated. They feel that once the union is given a say, it will be difficult or impossible to operate efficiently or to make any decisions at all.

There are times when management probably should stand on principle, particularly to show that unrelieved obstinacy on the part of the union can provoke equal obstinacy on the part of management. But management should set an example of reasonableness—at least to the extent of listening to the union's point of view.

Management loses little of its essential power when it informs the union well in advance of proposed changes and shows a willingness to listen to objections. But these gestures may not be enough in themselves. The union is seldom satisfied just to be informed or to be given an opportunity to air its objections, if these objections always prove fruitless. If management wants to win the union's support in introducing change, it must give careful open-minded attention to grievances brought up by the union. And it may even let the union participate in the decision-making process itself.

Regardless of whether management lets the union participate in decision-making, management must be prepared to make concessions and to accept union suggestions that it may not feel fully desirable, on the theory that a reasonably adequate solution enthusiastically supported by the union is better than a perfect solution strongly opposed by the union.[14]

Many of these same principles apply to dealing with nonunion groups. The

---

[14] This is not the place to enter into a full discussion of the techniques of collective bargaining. We might observe, though, that in dealing with a union it is rarely wise to adopt a take-it-or-leave-it attitude. In fact, if the union is to survive politically it must win some sort of "concession." Management may sometimes adopt an extreme position at first, just to give the union a chance to win an apparent victory. Also, management should not insist that the union give immediate answers to its proposals; rather, it should give the union leadership a chance to consult with its rank-and-file membership.

interests of management and subordinates often conflict. Regardless of how assiduously management uses the techniques of consultation and group decision-making, there will be occasions when subordinates are unwilling to accept everything management wants. Under these circumstances it is only common sense for management to make some concessions to the subordinates' strongest objections, if only as a means of winning more complete acceptance of other aspects of the proposed change.

Collective bargaining is difficult with nonunion groups, for there is no established mechanism to rely on. With small nonunion groups, however, it is at least possible to discuss problems with the group as a whole, and with larger nonunion groups management can deal with informal leaders or specially selected committees. It should be emphasized, though, that such meetings are useless unless all participants feel free to express their objections openly.

Management is under no obligation to bargain over every change it wants to initiate. On occasion it must push proposals through without regard to the objections of subordinates. But whenever management acts this way, it should be fully aware that it may be preparing the way for costly resistance later on.

Handling Symbols

How can management minimize resistance when it becomes necessary to change or eliminate some feature that has acquired symbolic meaning? First, management should indicate clearly that changing the symbol is not the same as attacking the values for which the symbol stands. Thus, in switching from parchment paper for insurance policies (see case on p. 288), the sales manager might emphasize that the change will help create the modern, up-to-date atmosphere that customers of the Integrity Company expect.

Sometimes it is possible to replace one symbol with another: When a new state is added to the Union, the old flag is discarded, but a new one takes its place. Similarly, if it becomes necessary to move foremen's cars from the front to the rear parking lot, special areas might be reserved for them, marked with special signs.

> We have been told of an interesting example of this technique used by the administrative staff of a hospital.[15] Members of the resident medical staff often had guests in the hospital cafeteria for Sunday dinner. Due to crowded conditions they often found it impossible to find a whole table for themselves. They had the cafeteria director place a sign on a group of tables: "Reserved for Medical Staff." Immediately several other high-status groups asked for similar consideration. To avoid the inflexibility and embarrassment that would arise if a majority of tables were specially reserved, the director changed the notices to read: "Medical Staff Are Requested to Use These Tables." This request could be justified on the grounds that it would make doctors easier to reach in case of emergency calls—and it also minimized the feeling that this was an additional symbol of the doctors' higher status.

---

[15] We are indebted to Dr. Robert Wilson for this case.

Making Changes Tentative

When the individuals concerned are permitted to participate in making the final decision on whether or not to accept a change, it is sometimes useful to ask the group to go along with the change on a tentative, trial basis at first. This approach has two advantages:

1. It enables employees to test their own reactions to the new situation, and provides them with more facts on which to base their decision.

2. It helps to "unfreeze" their attitudes and encourages them to think objectively about the proposed change. A change introduced on a trial basis is less threatening and generates less resistance than a permanent change.

However, where the individuals concerned do not participate in making the final decision, tentative changes may be unwise. They prolong the period of uncertainty and tension and the length of time in which the group is supervised closely. And there is always the chance that employees will in effect "participate" in the final decision—by resisting it or sabotaging it.

Slow Change or Quick?

Should change be introduced slowly or quickly? The answer is not clear. Many people believe in "making haste slowly," on the grounds that slow changes are less disruptive than fast changes and provide greater opportunity for adjustment. Given time, the new will blend with the old—as, for example, in the British constitution.

Fast changes, if forced on people, may lead to violent resistance, and the resulting shock may disrupt the entire organization. There may be some resistance to slow change, but it will be less intense at any given time. Indeed, if the change is introduced slowly enough, it may not even be perceived—or else the organization may become accustomed to constant, gradual change as a natural process, as the fashion industry has.

Slow change entails certain dangers of its own, however. Every change has widespread ramifications, and it is bound to be less effective if it is just patched onto the existing set of practices. In introducing change it is far better for management to consciously re-examine the entire process to determine what adjustments should be made. Unfortunately, however, when management introduces slow change, total re-evaluation is rare (often because management wants to avoid "trouble"), and practices are continued that become increasingly inappropriate to the changed situation.

The story is told of how during World War II the British army ordered a time study of their standard procedure for firing artillery.[16] Most of the opera-

---

[16] Elting Morison, "A Case Study of Innovations," George Shultz and John R. Coleman, eds., *Labor Problems: Cases and Readings*, 2nd ed. (New York: McGraw-Hill, 1959), p. 264.

tion seemed efficient enough, except that just before the gun went off two men came to attention. When the time-study man asked why, he was told, "We've always done that." Only after considerable research did he discover that the original purpose was to keep the horses from jumping (though horses had not been used for years).

When change is so gradual that people do not recognize that it has occurred, they may well continue to behave in a way that was appropriate only to the old situation.

> We observed this tendency in a factory where management sought to strengthen the power of the foreman. Formerly the set-up men were the ones who gave orders to the operators; the foreman had little direct contact with his men, concerning himself chiefly with over-all administration. It was decided to make this change gradually, "so they won't realize what is happening," and the foreman began giving all the orders on his own and to refuse to support the set-up men's decisions.
>
> As time passed, both the set-up men and the operators became increasingly confused. The set-up men tried desperately to maintain their traditional prestige and resisted the foreman every inch of the way. They met each new slight to their authority with growing indignation. Production gradually slumped until the foreman himself gave in and began once more to channel his orders through the set-up men.

If change is to be made slowly, management would be wise to give everyone concerned an over-all picture of what is eventually intended. Otherwise employees will begin to wonder, "Something is happening, but we don't know what," and exaggerated fears will arise about where the change is leading.

Actually, if employees fully understand and accept the change, there is little reason not to make the change rapidly. Adjustment is required only once, and there is small likelihood of anachronistic holdovers from a former period. Fast change eliminates the need for the constant series of adjustments which are required by slow change and which leave the organization in an endless state of turmoil.

Other Techniques

One of the most common and most difficult problems in introducing change is that of bringing in a new manager to head up an existing department in an established company. Ordinarily, if the old manager has been well liked, the new one will have two strikes against him, for none of the employees will believe that he can be as good as his predecessor. At the outset, everyone wonders what changes the new man will make. His most inconsequential acts are carefully examined for clues to his future policy, and may be exaggerated into foreboding of future disasters. His subordinates may resent him as an outsider and prepare themselves to reject everything he does.

Let us examine this problem and how it was handled in a specific situation;

our example will illustrate several techniques that may be helpful in introducing change in a wide variety of situations. W. F. Whyte describes how a new supervisor was introduced into a large restaurant: [17]

> Since the old supervisor had developed warm relations with her subordinates, the restaurant manager was afraid that her departure might have a bad effect on the morale of the whole organization. Consequently he prepared the way for her successor with great care. First, he discussed the problem of a replacement with both the old supervisor and the chef, her chief assistant. The chef proposed a candidate for the job; though this candidate had to be rejected, the reasons for the rejection were fully explained to the chef.
>
> When the new supervisor was finally selected, she was introduced to her subordinates at a general meeting. The manager announced that the old supervisor was leaving and went on to say how much she meant to the restaurant. The old supervisor spoke with great emotion about how sorry she would be to leave her associates. Then she introduced the new supervisor, extolled her virtues, and asked her employees to show the new woman the same cooperation they had given to herself. Finally, the new supervisor promised to do her best to follow in her predecessor's footsteps.
>
> For the next few days the new supervisor followed the old one around, getting to know people and trying to learn the supervisor's routine and methods of dealing with people. On the old supervisor's last day, the whole kitchen staff gave her a farewell party.
>
> Although the new supervisor decided that she would eventually make certain changes in the operation, she spent her first few weeks trying to follow the human-relations pattern established by her predecessor. Only after she was fully accepted by the group did she begin making changes.

What techniques were used here to win acceptance for the new supervisor? How might these techniques be used in other situations?

Consultation.   The manager respected the key position of the chef in the informal organization and requested his opinion on the change. When he felt the chef's opinions had to be rejected, he was careful to explain why.

Other organizations may use similar techniques to involve key subordinates in the selection process and thus substantially increase their acceptance of the final decision. Universities, for instance, typically appoint faculty members to the committees that choose presidents or deans.

Induction.   The old supervisor was careful to introduce the new supervisor to all key personnel and to explain the customs of the organization. Doubtless this did much to save the new supervisor from making social *faux pas*, to help integrate her into the social pattern of the organization, and to minimize the amount of disruption caused by the change in command.

---

[17] Adapted from *Human Relations in the Restaurant Industry* (New York: McGraw-Hill, 1948), pp. 319-331. For another example of a successful handling of what sociologists call a "succession crisis," see Robert Guest, *Organizational Change: The Effect of Successful Leadership* (Homewood, Ill.: Dorsey-Irwin, 1962).

Ceremony. The meeting at which the new supervisor was introduced, and the farewell party for the old supervisor, both served a ceremonial or symbolic function. They formalized the fact of change and helped the old supervisor pass on some of her prestige to the new.

There is a tendency in our cynical society to play down the importance of ceremony. Yet it is no coincidence that throughout history every strong, stable institution—be it church, state, university, or company—has been noted for the ceremonies by which it helped focus individual loyalty on the organization as a whole.

Ceremonies are particularly important in time of change. Take, for example, the traditional ceremonies observed at the crucial moments of our life: birth, graduation, marriage, and death. The presence of relatives and friends and the giving of gifts and flowers help symbolize friendship and the unity of families. By involving ourselves in the formalized rites of the ceremony, we somehow protect ourselves from some of the fears and pains of moving from one stage of life to another. The heightened emotional atmosphere helps prepare individuals for major changes in their relationships with others. Indeed, we have learned to expect really important changes to occur in this way.

Probably more important, the use of ceremony is a public proclamation that in spite of apparent change the basic values remain the same; the new pays obeisance to the old. The English cry, "The King is dead; Long live the King." The French say, "Plus ça change, plus c'est la même chose." In primitive countries, oil companies may hire medicine men to sprinkle holy incense on new oil wells—thus showing their willingness to come to terms with the other culture.

Avoiding change until acceptance is assured. The new supervisor avoided making changes until she had developed informal, social relations with her subordinates. This is in conflict with the old adage that a new broom should sweep clean—or that a new manager should make all his changes at once. True, as we suggested earlier, it is sometimes (but certainly not always) desirable to complete change quickly rather than to let it drag on. Even so, it is usually wise for a new manager to wait before taking action until he knows more about the organization and the people with whom he is dealing.

In earlier chapters we distinguished between the supervisor's formal and informal authority, pointing out that the first arises from his official position, the second from the respect accorded his technical and leadership skills. The man who has both informal and formal authority can win acceptance of his ideas more easily. But the new manager has only formal authority and in effect must force his ideas on his subordinates. After a few months he begins to accumulate informal authority; as he becomes trusted as an individual, his ideas meet with less resistance.

Building on the past. In the restaurant case cited above, the new supervisor made it clear that she had no intention of throwing out past practices wholesale. As anthropologists and missionaries long ago discovered, it pays to learn the customs of the people with whom one works, particularly their ceremonies, symbols, and expected ways of doing things. Changes can be introduced more easily if an adjustment is made to the past. There are times, of course, when one may wish to cast out all the old patterns of behavior and start completely from scratch. However, in doing so one also casts out the good with the bad, the baby with the bath.

CONCLUSION

Change is among the most common of management problems. Yet management suffers from selective perception: Too often it is so concerned with the technical aspects of change that it fails to consider the human-relations problems which many changes generate. It fails to recognize that even a seemingly small change may have profound ramifications and that people sometimes resist change even when it is in their economic interest. They have vested interests in the old ways; they fear the uncertainties of the new. They give strange meanings to change, and dislike having their traditional customs, symbols, and patterns of dealing with people violated. People seldom resist change just to be stubborn; they resist it because it hurts them economically, psychologically, or socially.

Management often regards resistance as something essentially irrational, forgetting that apparently irrational attitudes or behavior may be symptoms of deep-seated problems. Or management may seek to overcome signs of resistance without knowing why the resistance exists. Too often management assumes that winning acceptance of change merely requires good salesmanship or one-way communications. Just as management plans the technical aspects of change, so must it consider in advance the impact on human relations. It must seek to find out how change will affect the people involved, and particularly how it affects their interrelationships.

The first step in dealing with resistance is to bring the real problems out in the open, to establish genuine two-way communication. After all, management has the responsibility not only of generating new ideas, but also of getting them accepted. Those who are seeking to initiate change would be wise to listen carefully to questions, objections, and suggestions for modification. Questions should be answered. Some objections and proposed modifications may be useful and their acceptance will improve the over-all quality of the proposed change. Other objections and modifications may not be of high quality themselves, but their acceptance in the spirit of bargaining may make it easier to win acceptance for the over-all change. Symbolic meanings must be considered and an intelligent judgment made on whether change should be introduced quickly or slowly.

SMALL FASHIONABLE STORE

A small, fashionable clothing store with about 25 long-service employees has always catered to the wealthy classes. Traditionally it has closed at 5:00 P.M., but a new manager is considering whether it might be more profitable to stay open two nights a week until 9:00.

He is concerned about how he would distribute evening work, particularly since each salesclerk has her own clientele. Also, he is far from sure whether any of his present customers would prefer to come in during the evening. The salesgirls work on commission.

Advise him on what he should do about the employee-relations aspect of his projected change. In particular, discuss why the employees might resist this change and what might be done to reduce **each form of resistance.**

NEW MARKETING MANAGER

You have recently been hired by the Winspear Corporation as Marketing Research Director with instructions to rejuvenate the entire research program. When your predecessor started the program 30 years ago, he had advanced ideas, but in the years prior to his retirement he seemed to slow down both physically and mentally. He handled a few projects himself, but the rest of the staff (12 employees) gradually began to look for guidance to Heath Bailey, Assistant Marketing Research Director. Bailey ran the department in a competent but unimaginative manner.

Your talk with your new subordinates indicate that they are quite capable, and in general get along together well. However, two of the youngest men in the department, Bob Hertel and Jim Delevan, seem restless and anxious to try out new ideas.

At present Bailey handles all administrative matters himself. Following the practice developed under your predecessor, the staff reports to him, he hands out assignments, makes decisions, and then at long intervals tells you what he has done.

By now you have a number of research projects that you would like your research staff to begin. Some are quite different from anything the staff has done before, and several require a good deal of travel—which is also new.

1. Are the human relations in this department sound?
2. Should you try to change Bailey's key position in the organization? Why? How would you go about making the change?
3. What sort of relationship would you like to develop between yourself, Bailey, and the rest of the staff?
4. How should you handle Hertel and Delevan?
5. How do you intend to introduce the new research programs?

Discipline

We have purposely left discipline to the end of this part so that we could discuss other problems first. Discipline is required only when all other measures have failed. Suppose you have clearly instructed an employee on his duties, have listened to his problems, have tried to help him to do better, and have tactfully criticized his performance (as discussed in Chapter 8)—yet he still fails to meet standards. Then what? Then, reluctantly, you are forced to resort to discipline.

But can discipline be made consistent with what we have said about general supervision? We think it can.

In the first place the best discipline is self-discipline, the normal human tendency to do one's share and to live up to the rules of the game. Once people understand what is required of them, they can *usually* be counted on to do their job effectively and with good cheer. Yet some people (perhaps most of us) find that the possibility of discipline lurking in the background helps our "better selves" win out over our "lazier selves." As one man put it:

> "If you can get away with small things you keep trying to get away with bigger and bigger things until, finally, you are caught and you are in trouble. Just for example, if you can sneak nuts and bolts out of the plant in your lunch box, you start trying to take spare parts and accessories out next. . . . It's much better if you know that they are going to check your lunch box every night and you can't even take out the smallest thing. Then . . . you don't get into bad habits." [1]

Ordinarily, if employees feel that the rules by which they are governed are reasonable, they will observe them without question. That is to say, they will respect the rules not because they fear punishment, but because they believe in doing things the *right* way. Coming to work on time; following the supervisor's instructions; avoiding fighting, drinking, and stealing at work; punching the time clock—all these are accepted by a majority of workers as reasonable rules, as necessary conditions of work.

---

[1] Daniel M. Colyer, "The Good Foreman—As His Men See Him," *Personnel,* Vol. 28 (September 1951), p. 142.

Standards accepted by the group are frequently enforced by the group. (See, for example, our story on page 201 of how machinists enforced the rule against long-sleeved shirts.) Still, it is useful for management to back up the group when it is seeking the same objectives as management. The following quotation from a worker on an automobile assembly line illustrates a common feeling:

> "If a man is late all the time, the guys just try to avoid him. They have no use for a guy like this. He just makes it hard for us all because the utility man [the substitute for all jobs on the lines] cannot do the work as well as the regular man, and so we have to work harder just to keep the work up. Of course, if a guy is just trying to give a smart aleck foreman a hard time, we are all for him. . . . But if the fellow is just a slacker, the foreman should straighten the man out for the sake of everybody." [2]

Most employees are tolerant when a man has an occasional off day, provided he does his part the rest of the time. But they resent seeing someone else "get away with murder" while they are doing a full day's work. As one man said:

> "[Management] should be able to trust men, not have to watch them all the time. But you don't like to do your best and work hard while the other guy goofs off, loafs, and is always busy while you swing the job. It burns you." [3]

In fact, unless the culprit is disciplined the rest of the group may adjust to his low level of performance.

Thus, consistent proof that all rules are being enforced serves to strengthen the informal group's efforts at correction. Clearly, good supervisory practices will vastly reduce the need for discipline. But if employees realize that infractions of rules will be disciplined, good supervision will become even better.

When new rules are introduced, management must make every effort to convince employees of their reasonableness and legitimacy.[4] For instance, as we mentioned in Chapter 9, management should avoid introducing too many rules or rules that seem unrelated to doing the job at hand. No organization would survive if its only means of winning acceptance of correct procedures was to discipline all violators. Our disastrous experience with Prohibition shows the futility of trying to enforce a law that the majority feels to be unreasonable. In other words, management should try to establish what has been called "positive discipline," an atmosphere in which subordinates willingly abide by rules which they consider fair. In such an atmosphere the group may well exert social pressure on wrong-doers and reduce the need for the "negative" punitive discipline discussed in this chapter.

---

[2] *Ibid.*, p. 143.

[3] *Ibid.*

[4] One of the problems of introducing new industries into underdeveloped areas is that the new industrial employee, fresh from the farm, has no conception of factory "etiquette." In India, for example, employers find it difficult to teach employees that they have to report to work regularly.

How severe should the penalty for wrong-doing be? In recent years many companies have provided what is called "progressive" or "corrective" discipline, which calls for increasingly severe penalties each time a man is disciplined. Except for very serious wrong-doings, an employee is rarely discharged for a first offense. This is particularly true if the firm is unionized, since arbitrators insist that a man be given a second chance unless the offense is particularly bad. Ordinarily, the sequence of penalties under "progressive" discipline is as follows:

1. Oral warning.
2. Written warning.
3. Disciplinary layoff.
4. Discharge.

Oral warnings, as a form of correction, were discussed in Chapter 8. When a man fails to maintain standards, or has broken a rule, a clear oral warning that repetition may eventually call for discipline is in order. The supervisor should, of course, concentrate on helping the subordinate figure out ways to prevent his troubles from recurring.

Written warnings are the first formal stage of progressive discipline. Psychologically, perhaps, they are not different from oral warnings, but they are made part of the employee's record—and they can be presented as evidence if more serious penalties follow or if the case is taken to arbitration. Written warnings, sometimes called "pink slips," are often prepared in four copies—one each for the foreman, steward, personnel department, and the disciplined individual.

Disciplinary layoffs (to be distinguished from layoffs caused by lack of work) are next in severity. Usually they are for several days or weeks; layoffs in excess of a month are uncommon. Some companies skip this stage of discipline altogether, particularly when it is hard to find a trained replacement, on the grounds that it is too cumbersome to replace a man for just a few weeks. Moreover, the disciplined employee may return from his layoff in an even nastier mood than when he left.[5] On the other hand, there are some employees who pay little attention to oral warnings, but to whom actual punishment, such as loss of income, is convincing proof that the company means business. For them a layoff may be the shock that serves to bring them back to their sense of responsibility.

Discharge remains the ultimate penalty, and one that is being used less and less commonly. The expense of training a new employee makes the loss of an experienced man very costly to the company, and the hardships that face a

---

[5] For the argument in favor of eliminating layoffs as a step between warnings and dismissal, see John Huberman, "Discipline Without Punishment," *Harvard Business Review,* Vol. 42, No. 4 (July 1964), pp. 62-68.

man who has been discharged make arbitrators and unions increasingly un-willing to permit its use. Many arbitrators, indeed, refer to discharge as "in-dustrial capital punishment"—and for good reason.

> Consider the impact of a discharge on a man of say 55, with 30 years' senior-ity. In the first place, he may lose pension rights worth $15,000 or more, plus substantial vacation benefits. Few high-paying employers would be willing to hire a man of his age, especially after they check his references and discover his discharge. Certainly he can expect less pay than he was getting from the job to which his 30 years' service had carried him. Further, as a low-seniority man, he is now fully susceptible to all the winds of economic misfortune. Assum-ing he loses $1.50 an hour for the rest of his life, his financial loss may be as high as $50,000.

No wonder one arbitrator told us: "I am very reluctant to let a man be fired unless I feel the company's grounds are justified, both morally and legally. I think the employee should have every chance to mend his ways." Faced with this attitude among arbitrators, companies are being forced to place greater emphasis on their selection and training programs. Workers who are discharged today are often individuals who simply don't care for their jobs, younger em-ployees with no family responsibilities, or persons with severe behavior problems, such as alcoholics or psychotics.

Because of the serious implications of discharge in the modern economy, some companies authorize their foremen only to "suspend" employees for a five-day period, and reserve to higher management the final decision on whether they are to be discharged.

Demotion is seldom used as a disciplinary measure; it is ordinarily reserved for situations in which an employee has been mistakenly promoted or is no longer able to perform his job. As a disciplinary measure, demotion has a number of disadvantages. Losing pay over a period of time is a long, slow form of constant humiliation, as compared with the sharp slap of a layoff. Also, if a company is going to retain a trained man in any capacity, it makes more sense to use his highest skill.

Managers whose performance is below standard are rarely given layoffs or formal demotions. Instead, they are often quietly transferred without cut in pay from responsible jobs with substantial promotional opportunities to dead-end jobs with little or no opportunity for salary increase or promotion.

Most firms find that it is best not to treat either managerial or hourly paid employees so harshly that they give up hope or lose motivation.

THE "HOT-STOVE RULE"

Inflicting discipline puts the supervisor in a **dilemma. How can he expect** his subordinates to continue to regard him at a source of help, when discipline is by nature painful? Can he impose discipline without generating resentment? We think so—through what Douglas McGregor called the "hot-stove rule." This rule draws an analogy between touching a hot stove and undergoing discipline. When you touch a hot stove your discipline is *immediate*, with *warning, consistent*, and *impersonal*.

Let's look at these four characteristics as applied to discipline. When you burn your hand you are angry with yourself. Sometimes you are angry with the stove too, but not for long. You learn your lesson quickly, because:

1. The burn is immediate. There is no question of cause and effect.
2. You had warning. Particularly if the stove was red hot, you knew what would happen if you touched it.
3. The discipline is consistent. Everyone who touches the stove is burned.
4. The discipline is impersonal. A person is burned not because of who he is, but because he touched the stove.

In short, the act and the discipline seem almost one. You are disciplined not because you are bad, but because you have committed a particular act. The discipline is directed against the act, not against the person. There will still be resentment against the source of the discipline, but the more automatic the discipline becomes, the more this resentment is reduced. As one worker put it: "I really had it coming to me. I was looking for trouble. I can't blame the foreman. His job was to enforce the rules. That's what he is paid for."

Put another way, "the purpose of discipline should be to obtain compliance with established rules of conduct—that is, to correct improper conduct. It should not be punitive in nature, that is, to discipline solely for the purpose of getting even with the employee." [6]

Let us see how the "hot-stove rule" works out in actual practice.

Immediate Discipline

The supervisor should begin the disciplinary process as soon as possible after he notices a violation of the rules. (Of course, if he has lost his temper he should wait until he has cooled down.) Note what happens if he delays action:

> Joe Jones has a bad tardiness record. He comes in a half-hour late, but thinks the supervisor hasn't noticed it. By noon, Joe decides he has nothing to worry about.
> The supervisor *has* noticed it, but he is busy on another problem and he figures it might be a good idea to let Joe "stew awhile." Late in the afternoon, just before closing time, he calls Joe into the office to give him a two-day layoff.

Naturally, Joe feels he has been treated unfairly and resents both the discipline and the supervisor. He assumes the supervisor has been saving his grudge instead of "having it out like a man." In the future, he will never feel secure with the supervisor and will always wonder, "What's he going to pull on me next? Why does he have to play this cat-and-mouse game with me?"

---

[6] H. D. Garrett, *Building a Responsible Work Force* (Ann Arbor, Mich.: Bureau of Industrial Relations, University of Michigan, 1955, multilith).

Further, the more quickly the discipline follows the offense, the more likely it is that the offending person will associate the discipline with the offense rather than with the person imposing the discipline—that is, the more automatic the discipline will seem.

Of course, immediate discipline does not mean that a man should be judged without full investigation. But it does mean that the supervisor should take notice of the offense as soon as possible and push the investigation with all due speed.

> For instance, a man comes in to work after two days' absence. According to your records, he never called in to report sick, and, therefore, he is subject to discipline. "Immediate discipline" requires that you call him into your office for an explanation as soon as he gets to work. However, if he claims he was unconscious under a doctor's care during this period, you obviously are not going to discipline him until you have a chance to investigate. Even here you should push your investigation as rapidly as possible.

When the facts of a case are not clear, and yet immediate action is necessary, many companies provide for suspension. The employee is told that he is "suspended" and that he will be informed later about what discipline will be imposed. This technique may be used where tempers are so high that calm appraisal is impossible, or where the guilt is obvious but the amount of penalty can be determined only after further investigation. Suspension also makes possible a consultation among various levels of management before the final penalty is determined. Since suspension is a form of layoff, however, it should not be used unless the offense calls for at least a layoff. If the suspension is longer than is justified by the offense, arbitrators will usually order back-pay.

Advance Warning

If discipline is to be accepted without resentment, both the man who is being disciplined and his fellow workers must regard it as fair. And *unexpected* discipline is almost universally considered unfair. This means that (1) there must be clear warning that a given offense will lead to discipline, and (2) there must be clear warning of the amount of discipline that will be imposed for a given offense.

Assume that a rule has been posted for several months but that the supervisor has never disciplined anyone who violated it. Clearly, no one expects that the rule will be enforced in the future either. Now the supervisor grabs one man and makes an example of him. The victim might well cry, "Why me?" Discipline without warning violates the workers' expectations of fair supervision.[7] Further, if the case were taken to arbitration the company might lose.

Does this mean that once an order is laxly enforced the company can never again enforce it? Perhaps, in a unionized situation, for an arbitrator may rule that a *precedent* of no enforcement has been established. If, however, there

---

[7] See Alvin Gouldner, *Patterns of Bureaucracy* (New York: The Free Press of Glencoe, 1954), p. 170.

has been at last some enforcement of the rule (that is, if the company has not given clear evidence of its acquiescence to nonenforcement), the company can begin strict enforcement once it has issued clear warning of the change in policy.

> Suppose, for instance, the company has been very lax in requiring men to be at work on time. Before starting to penalize tardy workers, the company should give clear warning that it is tightening up on enforcement. The foreman might call the men together and, after appropriate discussion and explanation, say "From now on I'll expect you to come to work on time. Anyone who is more than five minutes late without adequate excuse will receive a written warning. If you receive more than two written warnings in any 30-day period, you will get a day's layoff."

We have already discussed the need for effective communications within the organization. Once more, let us emphasize management's responsibility to make sure that all employees really know what the rules are and how they are to be enforced. A failure to communicate such information deprives employees of clear warning. A communications program might include, among other things, the following:

1. Upon induction, the immediate supervisor can explain the rules to all new employees, perhaps with the help of the personnel department.
2. Notices can be posted on the bulletin board, and handbooks distributed to employees.
3. In some cases, lists of penalties can be included in the union contract.
4. When rules are changed, the immediate supervisor can call a group meeting or notify individuals informally.
5. When a rule is about to be violated, or actually is violated (provided it is a minor, first offense), the supervisor can issue an informal warning.

Many arbitrators, interpreting the legal meaning of the contract, might say that posting a notice on a bulletin board constitutes clear warning. But from the point of view of human relations, this is not enough. Written communications should be supplemented by oral communications. The better job management does of explaining a new rule and why it is necessary, the easier it will be to enforce it—simply because workers will be more likely to accept it as reasonable. Regardless of the legal requirements of arbitration, management is clearly to blame if the men unwittingly violate rules because they don't know what is expected of them. Good communications pay off by significantly reducing the amount of discipline that must be imposed.

Consistency

If two men commit the same offense and one man is more severely disciplined than the other, naturally there will be cries of favoritism. One of the quickest ways for a supervisor to lose the respect of his subordinates and to lower the morale of the work group is to impose discipline in a whimsical, inconsistent way. Consistent discipline is considered fairer and is far more likely to be accepted by the workers involved. Indeed, consistency is basic to good human relations.

Management must always keep in mind the educational function of discipline (and also of nondiscipline). Consistent discipline helps to set limits (that is, to inform employees what they can and cannot do); inconsistent discipline inevitably leads to confusion and uncertainty. Consistent discipline is essential if the work environment is to be kept stable. When some rules are permitted to go unenforced, employees may either (1) decide to ignore all rules, or (2) become confused about what is really required of them.

> Whenever we are speeding on the highway, we must feel this same sort of anxiety. After all, we are breaking the written rule; on the other hand, it isn't often enforced. Maybe this is a place, or a set of policemen who don't take the rule seriously, and we can speed a little. But still there is a lurking insecurity, because the police may, at any time, decide to enforce this particular rule.[8]

For instance, one day the boss lets Mary, his secretary, get by with handing in a report that is full of erasures. The next day he bawls her out for a sloppy report that is actually less sloppy than the previous day's. Under the circumstances, it is hard for Mary to know what standards are expected of her. She may well decide that the discipline has nothing to do with her act and "learn" only that the boss has a personal grudge against her. Not only won't she learn the rules, but she will be resentful as well.

Every individual wants to know the limits of permissible behavior, and one way to establish these limits clearly and dramatically is to punish those who exceed them. We all tend to be unhappy and insecure in a situation where we are not sure what is expected of us. Child psychologists, for instance, have learned that children are not necessarily happier when they are given absolute freedom. One reason they get into so much mischief is that they are trying to find out how much they can get away with, at what point Daddy will spank. Grown-ups are the same way. They want to know "How far can I go? What can I do? What can't I do?"

Consistency is hard to maintain. Some people we like—others we don't. Sometimes we see a rule violation as a personal insult, a direct challenge to our authority. Other times, prompted by our natural instinct to be understanding and kindhearted, we are tempted to tell the rule-breaker, "Well, I'm going to let it go this time, but don't do it again."

Dissatisfaction may arise over excessive leniency as well as over excessive harshness.

> The office had a rather strictly enforced rule that employees could not leave without permission until the end of the work day. Braden was caught by his supervisor in the hall heading for the exit about ten minutes before quitting time. Upon review the normal penalty of a two-day layoff was suspended be-

---

[8] Mason Haire, *Psychology in Management* (New York: McGraw-Hill, 1956), p. 60.

cause the following week was Christmas. However, a petition was signed by the other employees protesting this decision as showing favoritism and thus being discriminatory! They felt that since he was obviously guilty, he should receive the same penalty others had received.

One source of inconsistency is management's tendency to be stricter in slack times and to ignore rule violations when manpower is short.

> Crawford had a terrible absenteeism record. He missed work for two days without a legitimate excuse. Normally, given his record, his offense would justify an immediate two-week layoff. However, Crawford's services were badly needed on a rush job. No one else could take his place. So the supervisor added the incident to Crawford's personnel record and warned him that a further violation would lead to discharge.

Keeping Crawford on solved the immediate problem of maintaining production. But the long-term effects might have been more serious. What did Crawford and the other workers learn from this incident? One of several things: (1) The absentee rule was not to be enforced strictly, (2) the supervisor was playing favorites, or (3) strict discipline in time of slack work was merely a dodge to get around the seniority provisions of the contract. In any case, the employees' respect and trust for their supervisor probably took a nose dive.

Often a supervisor finds it easier to transfer a problem employee to another department than to face the hard task of disciplining him. In one case a man who had consistently failed to live up to company rules had been transferred 11 times without any record of disciplinary action appearing in his personnel folder. This employee could hardly be blamed for not knowing what standards of behavior were expected of him. No one had taken the trouble either to help salvage him or to rid the company of a constant expense.

Consistency in enforcing discipline may be expensive in terms of lost production, but inconsistency may be even more so. Although the evidence is incomplete, it would appear that automobile plants which are most hesitant about enforcing rules against wildcat strikes (work stoppages not officially authorized by the union) have had the worst record of such strikes. Yet if a whole department goes on strike, it may be very costly to discipline everyone. Not only will the company lose the production of that department, but the men in other departments may walk out in sympathy.

Wildcat strikes are set off by a variety of causes (frustration with the work or slow handling of grievances, for instance). Obviously it is better to eliminate the causes than to punish the symptoms.[9] Still, if no discipline is imposed, the men "learn" that they can engage in such strikes with impunity. Companies that have been willing to sustain the short-run costs have found that wildcat strikes have decreased. Further, when management takes a firm stand, the

---

[9] Indeed, if workers are prevented from wildcatting they may release their aggressions in other ways—through slowdowns and absenteeism, for example.

union finds it easier to discourage its members from taking matters into their own hands. Many union leaders have told us candidly that they find it hard to observe the "no-strike" provisions of their contracts when management doesn't take the initiative in disciplining violators. "We can't be more against strikes than management."

Consider another problem involving consistency of discipline. We have heard foremen say, "I can only catch a small proportion of the rule violators, but those I catch I punish severely." Is this fair? Many men consider it a form of "Russian roulette." Adventurous souls may make a game of this procedure and try to see how much they can get away with. Furthermore, scattered instances of discipline hardly constitute clear warning.

If a rule is on the books, the supervisor should make an effort to enforce it (and enforce it uniformly). If he finds it impossible to do so, the rule may have to be revised or dropped altogether. Sloppy enforcement of one rule encourages employees to disregard other rules.

In some situations, of course, 100 per cent consistency is impossible. For instance, unless everyone is searched as he leaves the plant, stealing may be impossible to stamp out. However, such searches are expensive and deeply resented by employees. The company may have to rely on stern punishment of anyone who is accidentally caught stealing. Since workers generally accept antistealing rules as reasonable, there will be little resentment of this policy, inconsistent though it seems.

Does consistency require that the penalty should be determined entirely by the offense, regardless of the personal history and background of the person who committed it? Of course not. We have already said that it is common industrial practice to be more lenient on first offenses. Arbitrators are reluctant to let "industrial capital punishment" be imposed on a man unless a reasonable effort has been made to rehabilitate him. Certainly each case should be considered on its own merits. As a top industrial-relations executive put it:

> "There is no precise mechanical formula. . . . Each instance of misconduct must be viewed . . . individually. . . . This, of course, is a matter of judgment, but . . . four principal factors should be taken into consideration . . . first, the seriousness and circumstances of the particular offense; second, the past conduct record of the employee and his length of service; third, the lapse of time since his last misconduct for which disciplinary action was taken; and fourth, the plant practice in similar cases." [10]

For example, three employees are caught gambling. One has been disciplined for the same offense before, the other two have not. The first man is discharged, the other two are given written warnings. This, we would argue, is being consistent as it may first appear. Although each case should be considered on its own merits, the over-all disciplinary program must be kept consistent. Certainly if two individuals with the same personal histories commit the same offense, they should be treated equally.

---

[10] Garrett, *op. cit.*, p. 5.

How long should a rule violation be held against an employee? Current management practice tends toward disregarding offenses committed more than a year or two ago. Thus, an employee with a poor absenteeism record would start afresh if he maintained a good attendance record for a year.

The rules of fair warning and consistency require that discipline be neither greater nor less than expected. If the degree of discipline comes as a surprise, the company may have failed to give adequate warning; if it is less than expected, the company will have difficulty in gaining acceptance of a more serious penalty in the future. When there is uncertainty and misunderstanding about whether the offense is to be punished and how much the punishment is to be, then the policy is inconsistent. If the rule-breaker sees the supervisor as wielding arbitrary discretion, then he may blame the supervisor for his discipline rather than himself.

There has been considerable discussion in industrial-relations circles about whether or not good personnel policy requires the posting of all rules and the setting of standard penalties for violations. For example: "Rough-house: First offense, warning. Second offense, one-day layoff. Third offense, one-week layoff. Fourth offense, discharge."

Those who favor such lists argue that they provide effective warning and greater consistency. Those who oppose them feel that they make it harder for management to distinguish between various degrees of guilt. Mandatory discharge for stealing would mean that the employee who is seen taking a box of safety clips would receive the same penalty as one who was caught robbing the safe. One company with a rigid series of penalties was obliged to impose only a one-week layoff on an employee who had altered his output records—this was the standard penalty for inaccurately reporting production figures. Actually, the employee had been doctoring his records for years and had received hundreds of dollars in unearned incentive payments as a result. Had the company not set up a specific penalty in the rule book, it could have imposed a far more severe penalty.

Some companies insist that unless they maintain a uniform list of penalties they are unable to justify discipline to the union. Others say that such lists enable the union to force the company into excessively legalistic decisions on discipline. For instance, if the company had no specific rule against loafing, legally it couldn't discipline a man no matter how lazy he was.

Impersonality

We have said that a good supervisor encourages his subordinates to express themselves freely and tries to play down differences in status. He tries to build up the feeling that he and the worker are on the same team. Doesn't the imposition of discipline seriously endanger this relationship? It may. In fact, the disciplined employee might easily murmur, "That so-and-so. I thought he was my friend. I'd rather have a foreman who wasn't such a hypocrite and then you'd know where you stand."

It is not easy to impose discipline without causing the person disciplined to feel resentful and aggressive. But the supervisor can minimize the danger to the relationship by imposing dicipline in as impersonal a way as possible.

> Discipline is most effective and has least negative effect on individuals, if the individual feels that his behavior at the particular moment is the only thing being criticized and not his total personality.[11]

In its opening stages, the disciplinary interview is not much different from most other forms of interview. First, state the problem as you see it; then encourage the subordinate to state his point of view. Let him tell you his story. Ask *how* it happend, not *why*. Give him every chance to explain himself. Try to avoid this sort of exchange:

> *Foreman:* Late again, I see. Didn't I tell you yesterday, if you were late once more this month, I'd give you a layoff. . . .
> *Employee:* But . . .
> *Foreman:* (ignoring him) Well, you've had your last chance. You better go home.
> *Employee:* But I did get here on time—only the superintendent called me in to his office to discuss the Savings Bond drive.

Instead, do your best to draw the man out and try to discover the real story. Use the interview technique. Don't ask him for his excuse, but concentrate on the *basic* reasons for his rule violation. Is he having trouble at home? Has he been poorly instructed on the job? Has he lost his motivations? Why? (Of course, you should have asked yourself some of these questions long before the employee's misconduct led to discipline.)

Sometimes your interview will give you all the facts you need. In other cases you may need to investigate further, perhaps by checking with other members of management. Avoid making a decision until you have the whole story, but reach your decision as soon as possible.

Once you have decided what discipline is appropriate, impose it quietly and impersonally. For example, suppose in a lateness case that the employee shows general irresponsibility, and that his only excuse for his latest tardiness was that he forgot to set his alarm clock.

> *Supervisor:* Well, I can see how it happened. But from the company's point of view, not setting your alarm clock is not an adequate excuse, particularly since this has happened three times this month.
> (Pause—in which to listen to objections.)
> You have already received two written warnings this month and the rules now require that you receive a day's layoff.
> (Pause—again for objections.)
> Jim, you've got to figure out a way to get here on time. You do a fine job when you are here, but the rule (and I think it is a fair one) is that if this occurs again within 30 days you will receive a week's layoff and if it occurs

---

[11] Chris Argyris, *Executive Leadership* (New York: Harper & Row, 1953), p. xiii.

again you will lose your job. I don't want this to happen. Now what can be done about it?

(Then discuss positive means of avoiding trouble in the future. Try to get him to suggest a workable plan—or suggest one yourself. Even if this doesn't work, end with:)

Jim, will you try harder to get here on time in the future?

(The answer is bound to be "yes" and you have, for what it is worth, a positive end to the interview and a positive commitment to do something.)

Note that the discipline here has been imposed impersonally and the employee has been given every chance to express his objections. After imposing discipline the supervisor reverts to his role of *helping*. The interview ends on a positive note.

After disciplining a subordinate, you may understandably tend to avoid him or to alter your attitude toward him in subtle, hardly noticeable ways. But these shifts in attitude are particularly dangerous, for they generate corresponding alterations in the subordinate's attitude. He concludes, "You hurt me and you know it." Eventually, the whole relationship may be destroyed. By contrast, if you treat the man as you always have, you indicate that by-gones are by-gones, that it was the act that was punished, not the man.

Simple as this advice may seem, it is hard to carry out in practice. Both parties are upset by what has happened. It is easy to understand why the person who has been disciplined is resentful, but the act of imposing discipline is also emotionally distasteful to the person who imposes it. Most of us hate to hurt other people, and when we do so we feel guilty—even when such a feeling is not justified. To protect ourselves from guilt feelings, we have to build up a feeling of anger. But, since we fear the anger of the person we have disciplined, we become unapproachable and cold after we have imposed the penalty. As a result, we seem to be disciplining the other person *as a person*, rather than as the violator of a specific rule. Naturally his response is, "He doesn't like me."

Two mistakes are common in imposing discipline: the supervisor either apologizes or bawls the offender out.

APOLOGETIC DISCIPLINE

Supervisor: Jim, I'm sorry I have to do this, but the rule says I must. How would the other fellows feel if I didn't do something?

Subordinate: (to himself): Even the boss doesn't think it's a good rule. Boy, I sure have tough luck. *Or:* He doesn't have guts enough to back up his own rules. *Or:* Why does he worry about the other fellows? I know they won't care if I get off. *Or:* Who's he kidding?

PERSONAL BAWLING OUT

Supervisor: I've given you every chance, gone out on the limb for you, and you haven't helped at all. You told me last time that you would really make sure you'd leave home early, and you broke your promise. Well, I've done all I can for you. You are letting the company down. You aren't being fair to them or to the other men. You've got to wise up or you'll really be in trouble, and I won't bail you out.

In the second case, the superintendent is being overpersonal, possibly because he feels a little guilty. There is no need to remind the employee over and over again of what he has done, to rub his nose in the dirt. Instead, it is much better for the supervisor to make it clear that he wants to let by-gones be by-gones and that he assumes the man will mend his ways.

It requires a great deal of maturity to approach discipline without a sense of guilt or hostility, particularly if you feel that a man's disregard of the rules is a reflection on your own supervisory abilities.

THE ROLE OF THE UNION

As yet we have said little about the role of the union in matters of discipline. We have observed in our research that unions rarely object strongly to discipline provided it is applied consistently and provided the rules are clearly publicized and generally considered reasonable. Of course, union officers may go through the motions of filing a grievance at the request of a disciplined member, much as a lawyer defends a client even though he is wrong. But in doing this, they often feel as this union officer did:

> "I've got to go to this grievance meeting and fight for that so-and-so. He had it coming to him and got what he deserved. How can he think he is so much better than anyone else he doesn't have to follow the rules?"

Management should not expect the union to discipline members who violate the contract.[12] When the union does impose discipline, it is abandoning its traditional role as the worker's defender, and management is failing to assume its responsibilities. A management spokesman makes this point:

> "The union cannot maintain its proper function of representing the employee and protecting his interests if it assumes any part of management's function of setting disciplinary penalties. If the union agrees with management as to what a proper penalty should be in a particular case, it forecloses its right to protest the penalty. Union representatives should be in a position to protest any disciplinary action taken by management against an employee on the grounds that the discipline is unfair, unjust, discriminatory, lacks cause, or is too severe. Any procedure which forecloses the right of the employee to have his case aired in the grievance procedure is basically unsound." [13]

Management must also be realistic about the union leader's political position. Often union leaders feel obliged to defend members whom they themselves think are guilty; to do otherwise would be to risk defeat at the next election. Once management recognizes that union leaders must often perform what is for them an unpleasant job, life becomes a good bit easier for both management and the union.

---

[12] There are a few exceptions in the building and clothing trades, where powerful unions may discipline members who violate the contract.

[13] Garrett, *op. cit.*, p. 1.

Management may be able to reduce the number of grievances prompted by disciplinary action by bringing the union into the earlier stages of the disciplinary procedure.

> Bill Jones has been absent frequently. According to accepted plant practice, after five no-excuse absences, he can be laid off for a month. Jones' foreman informs the department steward that he intends to enforce the rule against absenteeism and that the steward might try to "straighten Jones out" before he gets into real trouble. Where the foreman-steward relationship is a good one, the steward will often warn the man informally that continued violations may lead to a penalty that the union will find difficult to get reduced.

In this way the union is given an opportunity to play a constructive role without being burdened with the responsibility for applying discipline.

Quasi-Legal Procedures

The presence of a union need not impair management's efforts to maintain a satisfactory disciplinary policy. But it may force management to adopt what might be called a "quasi-legal" procedure.

Most union contracts require (1) that the company may discipline employees only for "just cause," and (2) that any employee who feels he has been unjustly disciplined may appeal to higher management through the grievance procedure, and, if management's answer is unsatisfactory, to arbitration. The arbitrator makes the final decision on whether the discipline was for just cause. He may be able to sustain the company's action completely, or reduce the penalty, or decide the penalty was entirely unwarranted and eliminate it altogether.

The grievance procedure provides a valuable protection to the individual worker, awkward though it may be for management. Since Magna Carta, an established principle of Anglo-Saxon law has been that an individual shall not be judged by his accusers. Management has the right—one might even say the *duty*—to establish the rules under which the organization shall operate. But a channel of appeal must be kept open from management decisions on whether or not these rules have been violated. Thus, the grievance procedure operates as a means of enforcing consistency.

In our Anglo-Saxon tradition, a man is assumed innocent until proved guilty, and in establishing guilt the burden of proof is almost entirely on management. For instance, to prove that a man has been loafing on the job, more than the supervisor's unsubstantiated word is required. Management must be able to produce objective, factual data which show that other employees on comparable jobs consistently produce more than the alleged offender. And it must show that the worker's low production was not due to poor material or faulty equipment. Similarly, the union may challenge any rule that has not been clearly communicated to the employees or consistently enforced.

As a consequence, disciplinary matters must sometimes be handled in a legalistic, courtroom manner, particularly when they reach the arbitration stage. Unfortunately, both union and management may find themselves devoting more energy to legal intricacies than to dealing with the human problems involved. Each side tries to build up an air-tight case and to poke loopholes in the case of the opposition. The billowing clouds of legal technicalities often serve as a smoke screen that obscures the underlying human problems. Fortunately, the company that maintains a generally fair disciplinary policy as part of its standard procedure is less likely to become involved in the legalisms of arbitration.

The existence of the grievance procedure means that the supervisor's disciplinary penalty may be reduced or eliminated, either by higher management or by an arbitrator. It is even possible that a man, who the supervisor is sure has flagrantly violated the rules, may be totally exonerated. Under these circumstances the supervisor naturally may feel frustrated when his decision is not "backed up." However, such possible miscarriages of justice are the price that must be paid for development of a judicial system which permits every accused employee to have his "day in court." A basic tenet of our society is that it is better for a guilty man to go free than for an innocent man to be convicted.

The reason why "guilty" employees are acquitted at higher stages of the grievance procedure is usually that the supervisor has failed to gather evidence, to be consistent in his application of discipline, or to communicate the requirement of the job to employees. Hence it is important for higher management to train and advise supervisors on the requirements of a sound disciplinary policy.[14]

CONCLUSION

Basically, discipline is a form of training. When disciplinary problems arise, it may be as much management's fault as the workers'. Many disciplinary problems grow out of management's failure to inform employees what is expected of them.

On the other hand, effective discipline depends on more than one-way communication in which the supervisor tells employees what to do and punishes them if they don't. Employees may be aware of a rule, yet refuse to accept it. For instance, if there are large numbers of employees taking extra-long lunch hours or using sick leave as a vacation, the problem is not to punish the guilty but to get group acceptance of a new standard. We must initiate discipline by winning acceptance of the standard (a process discussed in Chap-

---

[14] For a good analysis of the problems of effective disciplinary policies in unionized companies see Orme Phelps, *Discipline and Discharge in the Unionized Firm* (Berkeley and Los Angeles: University of California Press, 1959). Also see Lawrence Stessin, *Employee Discipline* (Washington, D.C.: Bureau of National Affairs, 1960).

ter 9). Once this has been accomplished, discipline will be provoked only by the small minority of recalcitrants.

For discipline to be accepted, the rules must be effectively communicated and the penalties inflicted must be consistent. Discipline helps employees learn the requirements of their job; and if discipline is applied impersonally, without personal animus, the respect shown the supervisor by his subordinates may actually be increased.

PROBLEM 1

DISCUSSING MISTAKES

Suppose an employee has been making a series of small mistakes. Is it better for the supervisor to (1) discuss each mistake with him as it occurs, or (2) discuss his *over-all* record with him from time to time?

PROBLEM 2

THE DRUNKARD

Dave Thatcher comes to work drunk. The foreman sends him home with another man, intending to speak to him when he is sober. As soon as Dave comes in the door the next morning, he drunkenly picks up a high-pressure hose and squirts the foreman in the face. The company discharges him for insubordination, assault with a deadly weapon, intoxication, and violation of company rules. There are no posted rules or penalties.

The union doesn't deny that Dave was pretty high. However, it alleges that (1) he has been having trouble with his wife, (2) his record has otherwise been excellent, (3) he was sent home but not otherwise given a warning on the first day, and (4) in other cases of drunkenness that occurred this year the men were referred to Alcoholics Anonymous.

The company answers: (1) The wife trouble is irrelevant, (2) Dave's work has not been good, even though he has not received previous formal discipline, (3) he was in no condition to appreciate a warning on the first day, and (4) the men referred to Alcoholics Anonymous were quiet drinkers who hadn't committed major violations of company safety rules. It adds that Alcoholics Anonymous is for alcoholics and, aside from the two-day spree, there is no evidence that Dave is an alcoholic.

1. Was the company's position correct?
2. What sort of penalty should be imposed?

PROBLEM 3

THE AUTO THIEF

The company's employment application says "Falsification of this form will be grounds for immediate discharge." Among the questions on the form is this one: "Have you ever been convicted of a crime?" Howie Bowman was employed three years ago and has a perfect record. Suddenly the company finds out that 15 years ago, when he was 17, Howie was convicted of stealing an automobile and given a suspended sentence. He had not mentioned this fact on his application.

1. Should Howie be disciplined?
2. How long should the company hold this rule violation against him?

FIGHT

The foreman catches two men fighting. Smith had been kidding Jones about his hillbilly background. Jones took a poke at Smith. Smith hit back. Both have had a good record in the past.

While some companies try to determine who really started a fight, others feel they will get nowhere trying to settle personal feuds between workers, but should exercise discipline only when one party resorts to his fists to settle differences. What do you think? Should both men receive equal punishment? Should Jones be punished more severely for starting the fight—or Smith for provoking it?

NO GAMBLING

A foreman says, "We have rules posted against gambling. Of course, we don't enforce them against small bets and there is some card-playing for money in the washroom at lunch break. However, we have the rules posted as a standby measure if things get out of hand."

Do you agree with this foreman's approach?

THE BOOKIES

A company has a posted rule against gambling. Six months ago two men were given written warnings about shooting dice. One day the local police arrest two other men on plant property for bookmaking. There is evidence that they have been collecting bets on horses in the plant. The men plead guilty before the judge, who gives them a suspended sentence. When they return to the plant they are discharged. To date, both men's records have been perfect.

If this case were carried to you as an arbitrator, what would you decide?

ORGANIZATION

Up to this point we have been talking about some of the components of the organization: individual workers and their jobs, supervision, informal groups, and unions. Each of these is an integral part of the organization, but there is a missing element still to be considered: the organizational system itself, within which all these components interact. In this section, therefore, we consider the impact of the organization on human behavior.

As long as people work in small groups where they see each other almost continuously, little thought need be given to defining in advance how they are to relate to one another. They develop patterns of relationship almost spontaneously: Few formal plans need be made except to insure a high quality of supervision.

As more and more people are added to the organization, however, the management of personnel becomes more complex. In order for work to be done efficiently, an orderly pattern (or system) of human relationships must be evolved. This pattern is commonly referred to as *organizational structure*. A company such as General Motors, for example, must coordinate the activities of hundreds of thousands of people doing thousands of different tasks in dozens of locations. In large organizations, merely giving consideration to the needs of *individual* workers and the requisites of face-to-face supervision is not enough.

Our primary questions, then, are these: What patterns of human relationships enable an organization to function most efficiently? What problems arise in the attempt to establish these patterns? What type of organizational structure is most likely to motivate people to work toward management's objectives? How can structure be evaluated in human-relations terms?

In a very real sense, an organization is a set of human relations. Every organization has a hierarchy of authority. The men at the top give orders to the men beneath them and so on down the line. The purpose of the hierarchy is to make it possible for a large number of people to work under the over-all control of a relatively small number of managers.

Organizations also spread out horizontally. Rather than having one person do the total job—for example, designing a new machine—many people are brought together and their activities are coordinated so that, although each does only a small part of the total job, finished engineering drawings are produced. This is the familiar principle of division of labor. By assigning only a limited number of tasks to each specialist, the organization hopes to attain greater productivity than when each person does the whole job by himself.

These two principles—(1) control exercised from the top down through successive levels of hierarchy, and (2) specialization of function—are the source of a host of challenging human-relations problems that management must somehow solve. Indeed, failure to develop an adequate organizational structure may nullify the benefits of effective supervision. Careful planning in this area must precede any other management program.

Within the broad field of organization, we shall concentrate our attention on several types of problem. Perhaps the most obvious one, but certainly not the simplest, concerns the ability of a many-leveled organization to control itself—the ability of upper levels of management to direct the efforts of employees whom they never contact directly and probably do not even know. Chapter 15 ("Hierarchy") discusses these "vertical" relationships, the passing down of orders and information through a series of levels, and the efforts of management to develop systems by which information from below will flow upward to these same levels.

Many organizations that resort to the use of specialists in their attempts to achieve maximum productivity find that the alleged benefits of specialization are simply not forthcoming. Coordinating all the specialized parts so that they fit together neatly into a productive organization gives rise to many human-relations problems. These problems of coordination are described in Chapter 16, "Specialization."

Within management itself and for work involving the collaboration of many specialized, trained professionals, it is often impossible to construct small autonomous work groups within the organization. Successful completion of their respective missions requires a large number and wide variety of "lateral relationships" that cross department and functional lines. By looking at two extended cases, one involving the role of purchasing agents in manufacturing organizations, the other, the difficulties encountered by a development engineer in getting other groups to cooperate with him, we hope to portray realistically the difficulties inherent in lateral relationships. (Chapter 17, "Case Studies of Lateral Relationships.")

A number of answers have been proposed to the human-relations questions associated with large organizations. These proposals are analyzed in Chapter 18 ("Minimizing the Human Problems of Larger Organizations"). We shall devote particular attention to efforts to provide greater decentralization, whereby lower levels of the organization are assigned self-contained tasks that limit their need for contact with other levels of the organization.

Hierarchy

Heretofore our discussion has concentrated on a two-level organization: an employee and his supervisor in direct face-to-face contact with one another. However, it should be apparent that as the size of an organization increases, there will have to be more than two levels. No longer can a single manager supervise everyone. With the addition of a number of managers comes the need for supervising and coordinating the work of the managers themselves: managing the managers. Thus, another level is introduced into the organization, and with it relationships which do not involve face-to-face contact. More and more levels will be introduced as the organization grows in size.

In this chapter we shall be looking at the human problems associated with multi-level organizational structures. First we shall want to consider what these organization structures look like in the real world. Then we shall examine in turn the distinctive problems of leadership and communication in this type of organizational setting.

CHARACTERISTICS OF HIERARCHIES

The term hierarchy refers to this multi-leveled, vertical structure. A hierarchy tells us who outranks whom within the organization, who must defer to whom; in other words, the formally prescribed status differences. The result can be summarized in the familiar organization pyramid.

For coordinating the activities of large numbers of people, some form of pyramidal organization is inevitable, simply because there will always be fewer people with very high status than with moderate or low status. Only in this way can order be maintained:

> In all organizations of any size at all, the flows of materials, people, and messages quickly fall into patterns, or "channels." One has only to make a circle of a hundred points and to connect each point with all the others by a straight line to realize how quickly an unpatterned flow of communications and transportation would break down; even in a small organization, this has

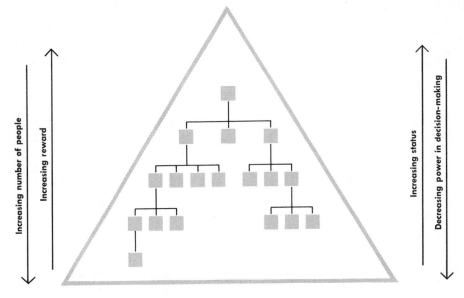

The organizational pyramid.

the makings of a colossal traffic jam. The simplest way to order these flows is to establish a chain, so that each individual only communicates with two others, but this is both slow and highly vulnerable to breakdown that paralyzes the entire organization. It is safer, faster, and more economical to divide the members of the organization into groups having individual spokesmen through whom all flows into and out of the group nominally pass, and to gather the spokesmen into groups with spokesmen of their own, thus establishing the familiar pyramidal hierarchical form. This arrangement permits comparatively fast contacts from top to bottom without overburdening anyone, for it reduces the number of contact points considerably, yet it permits most of the organization to continue operations even when part is cut off. The pyramidal distribution pattern of most large organizations develops, in short, because it has significant advantages over the alternatives to it.[1]

Thus, it is easy to understand the emergence of a pyramidal structure when the efforts of more than a small number of people must be coordinated. However, there is disagreement about what its actual shape or form should be.

Those students of management whose views have been labeled "scientific management" or "bureaucratic theory"[2] conceive of a very regularly shaped pyramid. The table of organization or organization chart that is so familiar (see the figure above) represents this pyramid. The actual relationships among members of organizations are presumed to be consistent with this structure with the results that:

---

[1] Herbert Kaufman, "Why Organizations Behave as They Do: An Outline of a Theory," Papers Presented at an Interdisciplinary Seminar on Administrative Theory, University of Texas (Austin, Texas, 1961), p. 47.

[2] For a brief description of the bureaucratic, or rational, model of organization, see Victor Thompson, *Modern Organization* (New York: Knopf, 1961), pp. 73-77.

1. Nearly all contacts take the form of orders going *down* and reports of results going *up* the pyramid.
2. Each subordinate must receive instructions and orders from only one boss.
3. Important decisions are only made at the top of the pyramid.
4. Each superior has only a limited "span of control," that is, he supervises only a limited number of individuals.
5. An individual at any level (but the top and bottom) has contact only with his boss above him and his subordinates below him.

Under the impact of recent research, this traditional view of the organization pyramid is undergoing modification. Let us look at each characteristic of the pyramid theory and compare it with recent research findings.

Up and Down Contacts

Traditional view. The only significant contacts in an organization are those between superiors and subordinates: giving orders (downward) or reporting back on results (upward) or requesting information (up or down).

Recent research. Researchers are becoming increasingly aware of the importance of horizontal or lateral contacts in activating organizational goals (see Chapter 16). For some time, organization theorists referred to these horizontal contacts as the "informal organization," implying that they were not really required or anticipated by management when it designed the "formal organization" (or the pyramid). To be sure many "informal" relationships are primarily social contacts that take place largely within informal groups (Chapter 4), yet other contacts are work-oriented, such as: [3]

1. Work-flow contacts among people who must collaborate to get a job done.
2. So-called "staff-line" relationships (see Chapter 16), which can be envisioned as diagonal contacts.
3. Appeals to higher management by those on lower levels for modification of decisions made by their direct bosses.

One Source of Orders

Traditional view. The manager or boss is viewed as the one source of *legitimate* power to which subordinates should respond. Other sources (such as informal groups) are viewed as illegitimate.

Recent research. Since staff groups are in a position to reward friends and to make life less pleasant for enemies, they too exert power. Though staff's requests may be called "advice," line learns that this is advice which it is

---

[3] One of the earliest analyses of these nonpyramidal contacts is provided by Conrad Arensberg. See his "Behavior and Organization: Industrial Studies," in John Rohrer and Muzafer Sherif, eds., *Social Psychology at the Crossroads* (New York: Harper & Row, 1951), pp. 324-352.

perilous to ignore. In addition, fellow employees with roughly the same status in the organization exert pressure and even give orders. For example, when an engineering group requests some drawings from drafting, engineering is giving what amounts to an order, even though the two departments may be of equal formal status.

Decisions Made on the Top

Traditional view. All important decisions are made by top managers since these are the best informed and most competent people in the organization and so can set broad policies for the organization as a whole. The policies they make are passed down through successive levels of the organization and, as they are passed down, are spelled out in increasing detail and transformed into operating instructions.

Recent research. The traditional view may have been realistic when companies comprised a small number of trained (and educated) managers and a large number of relatively unskilled, untrained workers. Today, organizations hire many managerial, professional, and technical personnel. Since they are often better informed on technical subjects than their superiors, the latter must abdicate certain key decisions to them. This view has been expressed as follows: [4]

> ...the business enterprise of today is no longer an organization in which there are a handful of "bosses" at the top who make all the decisions while the "workers" carry out orders. It is primarily an organization of professionals with highly specialized knowledge exercising autonomous, responsible judgment. And every one of them—whether manager or individual expert contributor—constantly makes truly entrepreneurial decisions which affect the economic characteristics and risks of the entire enterprise. He makes them not only by "delegation from above" but inevitably in the performance of his own job and work.

As companies move toward process automation, the relative number of managerial personnel increases dramatically. There may be three to four times the number of managers for a given number of nonsupervisory employees in companies employing this type of technology, compared to those with older methods of production! [5] The existence of relatively large numbers of staff personnel and department heads can produce pyramids that are quite "middle heavy" (or that bulge in the middle) as distinct from the rather tall, thin structures envisioned by traditional theory.

Further, the modern organization is not a unified, homogeneous entity directed toward one set of objectives. As we shall see in Chapter 16, individual departments and groups compete with each other for status and recognition.

---

[4] Peter F. Drucker, "Long-range Planning, Challenge to Management Science," *Management Science*, Vol. 5, No. 3 (April 1959), p. 242.

[5] Joan Woodward, *Industrial Organization: Theory and Practice* (London: Oxford University Press, 1965), pp. 56-57.

Each group develops its own special objectives which may sometimes conflict with the goals of the larger organization.

Limited Span of Control

Traditional view. An effective organization requires tight control. The supervisor is responsible for coordinating the work of his subordinates. To do this he must have a very limited span of control. The fewer subordinates, the better the management. This point of view results in quite steep pyramids. In large companies it is not unusual to find ten levels separating the hourly employees from top management.

Recent research. As we have already seen, under many circumstances subordinates perform more effectively with limited supervisory order-giving and controlling. Also, coordination can often be enhanced if employees contact one another directly (that is, through lateral not hierarchical relationships). "Flatter" organizations, involving broad spans of control, thus are often desirable.

Whereas traditional management theorists assumed that there were fixed maximum numbers of subordinates who could be supervised effectively, new research suggests that the desirable number varies, depending on the basic technology of the enterprise. A study of 90 English companies showed the following differences: [6]

KIND OF TECHNOLOGY	MEDIAN SPAN OF CONTROL OF FIRST-LINE SUPERVISORS
Unit or small-batch production (fabricating "one of a kind" products such as custom-designed suits or electronic equipment)	23 subordinates for each supervisor
Mass-production and assembly-line work	49 subordinates for each supervisor
Process production (continuous processing of chemicals and other fully automated "flow type" manufacturing)	13 subordinates for each supervisor

These striking differences in span of control are maintained at higher levels of the organization. For example, the most successful *process-production* companies in the above study all had ten or more subordinates reporting to the chief executive. However, in *mass-production* plants only half this number reported to their respective chief executives.[7]

Another way of predicting the "span of control" of supervisors is to observe the frequency with which the manager has to check how operations are proceeding, issue new instructions, and answer questions, or in any way get in-

---

[6] *Ibid.*, p. 69.
[7] *Ibid.*, p. 71.

volved in the work process. The more routinized are operations or the more responsibility that can be delegated to subordinates, the greater the number of subordinates that can be supervised.[8]

No Bypassing

Traditional view. Contacts in the organization are supposed to follow the table of organization. An individual restricts his relationships to his immediate boss and his immediate subordinates. As a result every manager has full information about the activities and people he is responsible for.

Recent research. For reasons that will become clear in the latter parts of this chapter, timely communication often requires bypassing certain steps in the hierarchical chain. Also, every organization needs an *appeal channel,* a mechanism by which subordinates can go over their boss's "head" when they feel a serious injustice has been done to them.

SPECIAL PROBLEMS OF EXTENDED HIERARCHIES

Although we have been critical of the simple, traditional view of organizational hierarchies, it would be a serious error to ignore the importance of rank differences. There clearly are successively higher levels in the modern organization, with fewer occupants of the levels as one moves upward. And clearly, too, status differences make leadership and integration possible, and promise rewards that encourage employees to seek advancement by effective performance.

These differences also pose some rather special problems, however, particularly for extended hierarchies (that is, structures with many levels). We shall first want to look at the impact of the hierarchy on the position and problems of the immediate supervisor and on his relationship with subordinates. Secondly, we shall assess the impact on the efficiency of operations and communications.

**The Manager
as a Man in the Middle**

Our emphasis in earlier chapters—and the emphasis in current research, training, and management thinking—has been on the relationship between supervisors and their immediate subordinates. In actual day-to-day activities, however, many supervisors spend less time with their subordinates than they do with superiors, staff, and others at their own level. And as we saw in

---

[8] See Robert Dubin, "Leadership and Productivity: Empirical Findings and Theoretical Considerations," in R. Dubin, G. Homans, F. Mann, and D. Miller, *Leadership and Productivity* (San Francisco: Chandler, 1965), pp. 14-17.

Chapter 7, there is empirical evidence that the effective supervisor spends a greater proportion of his time on upward and horizontal contacts than the ineffective supervisor does.

Every manager, except for the company president, belongs to two groups: the work group of which he is the leader, and the higher-management group of which he is the immediate representative. The manager is thus a man in the middle, endlessly beset by conflicting loyalties and demands. The ineffective manager allows himself to be squeezed by these conflicting pressures; the effective supervisor resists them and serves as a communications link between those above and those below him.

Transmittal of supervisory styles.[9] Supervisory styles are "handed down" from level to level; good supervision at the top is reflected by good supervision at the bottom. The evidence suggests that those who receive general supervision are more likely to practice general supervision themselves, and that those who are supervised closely will supervise their subordinates closely.[10]

It is perfectly natural for a manager to reflect the supervisory style of his boss, for the boss is the one who hands out rewards. His actions are looked upon as clues to the behavior he expects from his subordinates.

If a supervisor is subjected to pressure by his own boss, he has a strong tendency to pass it on to those below. Transmitting pressure—and perhaps increasing it a bit in the process—is a time-honored way of relieving frustration and soothing a wounded ego. Moreover, when the boss applies pressure on the man directly below him, he is saying in effect that he wants immediate results regardless of the long-run effects on subordinates farther down the line. As a consequence, many supervisors decide:

> "I can't afford to have any mistakes made in my department or my boss will get me in trouble. He's likely to quiz me on everything that happens. So I better check up on everything and have all the facts and explanations at my finger tips. This means I have to keep close tabs on my men."

Furthermore, no supervisor can permit his subordinates to exercise freedom in areas in which he does not have freedom himself. Some top managements, for instance, issue strict rules which describe in detail what they want subordinates at all levels to do in almost every conceivable situation. Under such

---

[9] See Rensis Likert and Daniel Katz, "Supervisory Practices and Organizational Structure as They Affect Employee Productivity and Morale," Personnel Series 120 (New York: American Management Association, 1948); Daniel Katz, Nathan Maccoby, and Nancy Morse, *Productivity, Supervision, and Morale in an Office Situation*, Part I (Ann Arbor: Institute for Social Research, University of Michigan, 1950); Robert Kahn and Daniel Katz, "Leadership Practices in Relation to Productivity and Morale," in Dorwin Cartwright and Alvin Zander, eds., *Group Dynamics* (New York: Harper & Row, 1953).

[10] See Edwin Fleishman, "The Description of Supervisory Behavior," *Journal of Applied Psychology*, Vol. 37, No. 1 (February 1953), pp. 1-6; Edwin Fleishman, "Leadership Climate, Human Relations Training, and Supervisory Behavior," *Personnel Psychology*, Vol. 6, No. 1 (Summer 1953), pp. 205-222; Charles R. Walker, Robert Guest, and Arthur N. Turner, *Foreman on the Assembly Line* (Cambridge: Harvard University Press, 1956), p. 25.

circumstances the supervisor has little discretion himself and cannot delegate any at all.

On the other hand, the supervisor who receives general supervision from above feels free to let his subordinates make decisions by themselves. Knowing that he will be judged by over-all results, he encourages his subordinates to experiment and does not penalize them for making unintentional mistakes. He is confident that his own boss will back him up when his judgment is questioned, whether by subordinates, by other supervisors, or even by top management. He recognizes that as long as he produces results his boss will back him up and refrain from meddling with petty details. Imbued with a sense of confidence and freedom, he operates in what we have called an "atmosphere of approval." Here we have an extension of the principle of delegation of authority. In effect the boss is saying, "I really mean it when I tell my subordinate that I am giving him authority. I won't interfere with his decisions so long as the final results are good."

One reason for an ineffective manager's poor performance is his personal insecurity. Uncertain about where he stands in the eyes of his boss and his company, fearful that the axe will fall any minute, and anxious to avoid the boss's displeasure, it is little wonder that he is reluctant to experiment or to encourage his subordinates to develop their own ways of doing things.

Representing subordinates.   Employees are quick to recognize that their immediate supervisor has limited powers. The levels above make many crucial decisions that will affect their welfare.

Therefore, the effective supervisor must act as a spokesman and protector for his subordinates, and must represent their interests to higher management. (You will remember that, in our discussion of informal leadership in Chapter 4, we mentioned that the informal leader functioned as "an outside contact man" for the group. The effective supervisor fills a similar role.)

In a sense, the effective supervisor serves as a shock-absorber, shielding his men from outside influences that jeopardize their welfare and productivity. As one foreman put it:

> "If I treat a man right and he figures a way of doing a job which gives him a little rest, then so much the better for him. My boss doesn't understand that, so that you might say I am a concrete wall between the general foreman and the men. I have to take it one way, but not give it out the same way." [11]

He accepts responsibility when things go wrong. When someone on a higher level asks for explanations, he does not say, "That's Joe's fault; I'll speak to him." Instead, he takes the "rap" himself rather than involve Joe with higher-ups. (Whether Joe knows about this specific favor is irrelevant; the group will know the results of the policy, and that is what is important.) He tries to ameliorate the rigid requirements imposed by higher management, in an attempt to make life easier for his subordinates.

---

[11] Walker, Guest, and Turner, *op. cit.*, p. 26.

Moreover, he speaks out for the interests of his men when he thinks that management has made a wrong decision. He acts as spokesman for subordinates who have little opportunity to contact higher levels of authority. Note what one worker said:

> "My present foreman is the nicest guy I ever worked for. The other foremen respect him also. I saw him stick his neck out with the general foreman over work loads. . . . He'll argue a point with the general foreman if he thinks he is right." [12]

In other cases, acting as spokesman for the group may mean fighting for promotions, cutting red tape to get an employee immediate benefits under an insurance plan, or pointing out to the time-study engineers that their controls are too "tight."

However, the manager cannot fight for his men or take a critical attitude toward management decisions if his boss forces him to be a "yes man." In battling for the interests of his group, the manager may have to tread on a lot of toes; he may even have to disagree with the boss himself. But he can behave in this way only if his boss permits him to do so, if the boss in turn listens to his suggestions and backs him up when he gets into trouble with other departments.

Much depends on the supervisor himself, of course. Being a spokesman for the group is not enough. The supervisor must be successful in getting results.[13] This means he must have the skill to make effective presentations to his boss and to other departments: he must be a good listener and a good communicator. And, since it takes time to develop good relations, he must be able to plan his work and train his men well enough so that he doesn't have to be constantly present in his own department.

Thus, the effective supervisor has what has been called "influence" [14]—that is, other levels of management respond to his requests. When the supervisor is successful, the confidence of his men is reinforced. When he is perpetually turned down, his men become disillusioned with his effectiveness in exerting influence.

In fact, general supervision *without* influence may lead to poorer results than close supervision *with* influence (or at least to more dissatisfaction).[15]

Conflicting loyalties.   Do effective supervisors feel greater loyalty to their subordinates or to their boss? Often members of management complain, "We've got to make our supervisors feel they are company men. They're always taking the employees' point of view." This may not be too regrettable a situation.

---

[12] *Ibid.*, p. 27.

[13] At an insurance company, supervisors of the less productive departments were more likely to recommend promotions; but supervisors of the more productive departments won the promotions. From Katz, Maccoby, and Morse, *op. cit.*, p. 27.

[14] Donald Pelz, "Leadership within a Hierarchical Organization," *Journal of Social Issues,* Vol. 7, No. 5 (1951), pp. 48-55.

[15] Nancy Morse, *Satisfactions in White Collar Jobs* (Ann Arbor: Survey Research Center, University of Michigan, 1953), p. 164.

There is evidence that at least on the first level the good supervisor identifies as closely with his subordinates as he does with management.[16]

In a study of the Prudential Insurance Company, supervisors were asked questions designed to determine whether they identified more closely with the company or with employees. As the following table indicates, employee-identified supervisors had the more productive sections: [17]

| | IDENTIFIED WITH | |
	EMPLOYEES	COMPANY
High-production supervisors	9	2
Low-production supervisors	4	8

This same company had separate dining rooms set aside for supervisors. The high-productivity supervisors, reflecting the attitude of their employees, objected to this form of segregation. The low-productivity supervisors went along with it.[18]

Still, the employee-oriented supervisor's loyalty is not undivided. He is also loyal to upper management—or, to be more precise, he is motivated to carry out the assignments that have been delegated to him. As a result, he may sometimes find himself in conflict with the men he supervises and have no choice but to act restrictively. And yet he must somehow manage to keep his dual role intact, for he will sacrifice his effectiveness if he becomes too interested either in meeting management's production demands or in safeguarding the interests of his men.

> If management fails to recognize this duality and attempts to enlist a supervisor's undivided loyalty, he may lose his ability to act as a representative of his employees and eventually his effectiveness in helping management gain its objectives.[19]

Although personality and experience differences affect loyalty too, there is some tendency for lower-level managers to be more downwardly oriented than their higher-level counterparts.[20] This divergence can be explained by the likelihood that the farther down you go in the hierarchy, the more cohesive the

---

[16] Katz, Maccoby, and Morse, *op. cit.*

[17] *Ibid.*, p. 23.

[18] *Ibid.*, p. 25. High-producing foremen in a tractor factory were more critical of company policies and their bosses than were low-producing foremen. Kahn and Katz, *op. cit.*, p. 222. Higher-rated Forest Service supervisors were more likely to be critical of their superiors than were lower-rated supervisors. A. L. Comrey, J. F. Pfiffner, and H. P. Beem, "Factors Influencing Organizational Effectiveness: The U. S. Forest Service," *Personnel Psychology*, Vol. 5, No. 4 (Winter 1952), pp. 307-328.

[19] F. C. Mann and J. K. Dent, "The Supervisor: Member of Two Organizational Families," *Harvard Business Review*, Vol. 32, No. 6 (November 1954), p. 112.

[20] For an empirical exploration of some facets of this problem, see Peter Blau and W. Richard Scott, *Formal Organizations* (San Francisco: Chandler, 1962), pp. 159-163.

work groups are. As we have seen in Chapter 4, the greater the cohesiveness, the more effective is the group in being able to pressure their superior.

The special problem of the first-line supervisor. First-line supervisors probably suffer more from being men-in-the-middle than do the members of any other supervisory group. Their subordinates, whether they are production workers, office girls, or engineers, do the actual work of the organization. These subordinates have no one to supervise and often little chance for promotion. As a consequence, even if they are paid salary or commission, they are less likely to identify with management. In fact, since they normally do not compete with one another, they have a tendency to join together in defense against higher management.

The first-line supervisor can ignore this potentiality for revolt only at his own peril. His subordinates, as a group, are in a strategic position to embarrass him. By following his instructions too literally and by failing to use common sense, they can spoil work, damage equipment, and waste materials. By slowing down in unison they can prevent him from meeting schedules; through a hundred different subterfuges they can increase his costs and make him look bad in the eyes of his superiors. Thus, though the first-line supervisor is subject to many pressures from above, he cannot pass these pressures down to lower levels; if he tries to do so, he will only make matters worse.[21]

The inevitable result is that the first-line supervisor must somehow come to terms with his subordinates. He must be particularly careful to insure strong, continuing motivation, primarily through bargaining and on-the-job need satisfaction. Often, too, he must make deals with the union steward involving special concessions to the men in return for their implicit agreement to keep production high.

As might be expected, expedient arrangements such as these are rarely acceptable to higher management. Consequently supervisors sometimes become "two-faced," turning one face to management and another to their subordinates. Caught inescapably in the middle, they must cope with all the problems of higher levels of management and at the same time resolve all the problems that are peculiar to their own position in the hierarchy.

Personal Contact between
Higher and Lower Levels

Even with effective representation, there is evidence that employees like to have some personal contact with higher managment. Some such contact facilitates identification with the total organization.

We are all familiar with generals, kings, and presidents who on occasion

---

[21] For a description of the reaction of foremen in a situation where high management imposes pressures which they cannot pass on, see Chris Argyris, *Executive Leadership* (New York: Harper & Row, 1953), Part II.

mingle with the "people." An actual view of the leader, perhaps hearing his words directly, even touching his hand or coat, is meant to impart confidence in his human or organizational qualities. Particularly if the head of the organization has a strong personality, he can impart a sense of identification with himself; he in turn personifies the total organization. In an effort to recreate the personal intimacy between hierarchical levels that characterizes small organizations, many managers try to cultivate the feeling of "one big happy family." They resort to such devices as:

> Personal appearances by top management before employee groups.
> Special, personal letters from the company president to employees on anniversaries with the company, or after special accomplishments (*e.g.*, a new patent).
> Christmas parties, bowling teams, golf tournaments, and other events at which various levels of the organization meet informally.

All these efforts are designed to counteract the impression that the company is impersonal, to give the feeling that top management consists of flesh-and-blood individuals who are wise decision-makers and genuinely interested in the welfare of the people who work for them. But two factors seriously limit the effectiveness of this approach as a means of communication.

As we noted in our discussion of communications, lower levels of the organization may suspect or distort management's motives. And this type of communication is directed primarily downward. Nevertheless during crises (for example, when labor relations are strained) these direct "lines" to the top may be utilized extensively.

As with other aspects of supervisory behavior, such personal contacts by higher management cannot be evaluated in isolation; they take on meaning only in the over-all context of human relations. If the president's "personal" birthday card fits into the employee's previous perception of his relation to the president, fine. If not, the birthday greeting may seem hypocritical. Similarly, it is waste of effort for the boss to be a mass of smiles at the annual picnic if he is completely unapproachable at other times of the year. Under such circumstances, gestures that are intended to be warm and personal may well be perceived as merely mechanical or hypocritical.

Multilevel organizations have certain advantages over smaller organizations in reducing tension over the exercise of authority. Depending upon an individual's needs, upper levels—far removed from his immediate experience—can be seen as composed of either saints or sinners. If immediate supervision is unsatisfactory, subordinates can say: "If only the old man (the president of the company) really knew what was going on he would straighten things out." On the other hand, many blame unpopular decisions on top management rather than the immediate boss. (However, supervisor who maintains good relationships with subordinates by always blaming his superiors is not doing his job effectively.)

If we turn from the impact of hierarchy on leadership to day-to-day operations and communications we shall discover still other human-relations problems.

At the beginning of the chapter we concluded that a hierarchical form of structure is necessary to move directions and information efficiently through a large body of people. It would be incorrect to assume, however, that this dissemination is the same process as communication within the small group. The multiple levels introduce problems, for orders are not simply passed downward through one subordinate manager and then another until they reach the lowest level in the structure.

Unfortunately, when we draw boxes and connect them with lines, we have a tendency to believe that the system we design will function like a physical model—that is, we think of an organization as though it were a system of interrelated pipes and reservoirs. Water starting at the top always reaches the bottom in exactly the same quantity and quality as when it started out—if everything is connected correctly, that is. Thus, the model suggests that someone at the top issues an order or makes a policy decision, and the next person in the hierarchy passes the instructions along to the men who report to him, and so on down the line.

Similarly, significant information from "down the line" is reported upward through the same system of "pipes" so that those at the top will have at their finger tips all the information they need to administer the affairs of the organization. This constant circulation of information up and down the chain of command provides the lifeblood of the organization and keeps it in a healthy state of alertness and efficiency. Each employee at the bottom is supposed to respond in some predictable way to plans originated at the top, regardless of the number of linkages through which orders must flow before reaching him, and regardless of how many layers his ideas and experiences must pass through before reaching the top again.

But an organization is not made up of mechanical parts or pipes. It consists of *people,* whose attitudes and behavior are affected by the system of human relations in which they function. These people upset the simple mechanistic working of the hierarchical model. They introduce distortions in both the downward and upward transmission of information. Here we shall concentrate our attention on these distortions and on the human-relations problems they create.

Distortion in Downward Communications

In a sense, we are now dealing with the problem of exercising good supervision where there are more than two levels of authority. As we shall see, the supervisory practices we recommended previously appear simple in contrast to the complexities of motivating and directing people in a multi-level structure.

Let us start with an example. Top management decides that racial discrimination in employment shall be eliminated. What happens as this policy is passed down the line through successive stages of the hierarchy? By the time the policy reaches the individuals who do the actual hiring, it may have been transformed almost beyond recognition, for example: "Hire *some* Negroes at each location, so that the company appears to be nondiscriminatory."

In part, this sort of distortion is caused by the communications problems we discussed in Chapter 10. People may "hear" the new policy in ways unintended by top management. The result is wide differences in interpretation, which grow increasingly wider the more broadly the policy is communicated.

But the organization itself complicates matters further. The order-giver is a long way from the final recipient. You may have played the game in which a story is passed from person to person in a group. Each person alters the facts slightly to fit his own needs and preconceptions, often without intending to do so. When the story finally re-emerges, it has been distorted beyond recognition. Information passing through many status levels can be more confused.

Complex statements of policy, whose accuracy depends on subtle shades of meaning, are particularly vulnerable to distortion as they move "down the line." A fairly simple company decision to grant every employee with more than six months' service a two-week vacation with pay could probably be communicated down through several levels without major alteration. But an announcement of policy on union matters, or on promotions, is often badly mangled or downright misleading by the time it filters down through the levels of the organization.

Two sorts of distortion are particularly common. The first is *exaggeration*. Every subordinate is highly dependent on his boss's goodwill, for the superior has countless ways of making his job either easier or harder. Consequently,

Prescribed channels of communication.

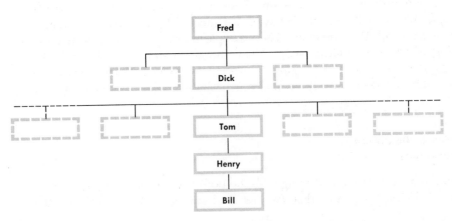

most subordinates are highly sensitive to the boss's every whim and seek to anticipate his desires, sometimes before they are expressed. This constant search for clues to what the boss wants often leads to strange results.

> Nearly every company is familiar with what happens when one of the members of top management makes a visit to an outlying installation. If local management hears through company gossip that the visiting dignitary is likely to be impressed by the physical appearance of the organization, a sudden redirection of effort takes place. Employees are taken away from their regular jobs to do housekeeping chores which are normally neglected. Equipment and buildings take on an unusual "shine."

Many a subordinate asks the boss's secretary, "What is he gunning for today? Is it safe for me to mention ... ?" The authors once observed a personnel department hectically preparing to run a morale survey (though the department doubted that it was a good idea) purely because a top official had read a short article in a popular management magazine and had remarked to the personnel director, "This looks like a good idea for us."

The second common type of distortion is just the opposite: the *playing down* of directives. Lower management drags its feet in carrying out an order, or follows the letter but not the spirit. For example, we once observed the reaction of middle and lower management to a top-management directive to install a supervisory performance-evaluation program. This program required each superior to rate his subordinates every six months, and then to discuss his ratings with them. With few exceptions, the managers were reluctant to adopt this new program, which they felt would breed more antagonism than good will. So they procrastinated, in the hope that the program would gradually be forgotten by all concerned.

Distortion of this sort occurs when the subordinates as a group feel strongly opposed to a new policy and feel that top management is not really serious about implementing it. Many subordinates show sheer genius in endlessly evading directives without becoming overtly insubordinate, making sure that nothing can be "pinned on" them (that is, feigning acceptance).

In short, employees frequently receive mystifying directives that have been passed down from higher levels of the organization. For example, managers are told costs must be cut. But how should a priority be placed on this order compared to other instructions that have been issued? Should other objectives that have been established—for example, smooth labor relations or safe working practices—be ignored? Or modified? Or given a lower priority? When directives appear to conflict, as they often do, or priorities are unclear, as they often are, employees spend a great deal of time and energy "researching" the problem: What is top management really thinking now and what group has the most influence on the president's thinking?

Obviously, in small organizations, where orders come from immediate supervisors with whom the subordinate has almost continuous contact such problems are minimized. Over time the manager's scale of values and personal priorities become clear and his changing preferences are easy to interpret.

To summarize, the larger the organization, the more difficult communications are, and top management finds it harder and harder to maintain firm control over the lower levels of the hierarchy simply by issuing orders. Top executives are never really sure of what is happening below, and those at lower levels become uncertain about what is expected of them. As a result, management's decisions often become vitiated or distorted as they move down the line.

Short-Circuiting
the Lines of Communications

Going through channels: the red-tape problem.   The typical large company has not one but a number of separate hierarchies with parallel lines of upward and downward communication. Each hierarchy represents a specialty. Since, in theory, these specialties are completely independent of one another, except for coordination at or near the top, one might think that there would be very little need for contact between them. Nothing could be further from the truth.

Take a typical problem: A group of plumbers are working on the air-conditioning equipment in the accounting office. The men stop work a half-hour before quitting time and engage in extensive "clean-up" operations. After this has been going on for several days, the clerks begin to grumble that they should have the same privileges.

How can the accounting supervisor handle this problem? In theory, he must report the matter to his supervisor and so on up the line until it reaches the common boss over both accounting and maintenance. Then the matter descends down the maintenance chain of command till it hits the plumbers.

In this case it might take six supervisory contacts before the problem could officially come to the attention of the supervisor who is directly responsible. If there were a need for frequent adjustments between the accounting section head and the plumbing foreman, the number of contacts would soar astronomically.

In one sense, this cumbersome procedure is desirable. If the accounting supervisor were to start giving orders directly to the plumbers, the plumbers would be subject to all the evils of "too many bosses." A clearly defined sequence of supervisory contacts, by contrast, helps to bring order into interpersonal relations.

But in emergencies the need to go through channels can be costly in terms of managerial time and may only complicate the problem. Days and weeks may pass before a serious problem can be attended to. Think what would happen in a hospital: ". . . Suppose a piece of oxygen equipment goes out of order. If the nurse were to report it to the head nurse, she to the chief engineer, and he to the repairman, the patient would probably be dead before the equipment was fixed." [22]

As you can see, it becomes more difficult to move swiftly and effectively on challenging problems within the specialized organization. Particularly in large companies, the burden of going through channels, in terms of the sheer number of interactions that must take place for every problem, tends to slow the organization and creates endless frustrations and conflicts. It is under these circumstances that one hears that "red tape" or bureaucracy is defeating the purpose of the company.

As a result, there is a widespread temptation to short-circuit the chain of command. In the case above, the accounting supervisor might go directly to the plumbing foreman. But those who are left out—those who get "short-circuited"—are understandably resentful of such violations of the chain of command and feel their leadership position threatened.[23]

Bypassing. A manager may become so frustrated by the time-consuming process of going through channels and the apparent inability of subordinates to carry out instructions precisely as they were intended, that he bypasses intermediate levels and goes straight to the men involved. For instance, the superintendent goes directly to an employee to find out why a new machine is

---

[22] Temple Burling, Edith Lentz, and Robert N. Wilson, *The Give and Take in Hospitals* (New York: Putnam, 1956), p. 323.

[23] *Cf.* George Homans, *The Human Group* (New York: Harcourt, Brace, and World, 1950), p. 430.

Accounting and maintenance hierarchies.

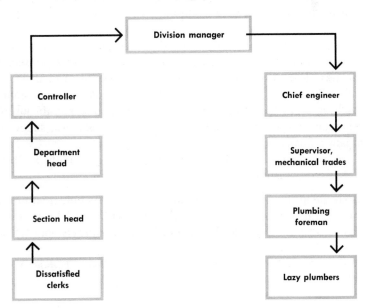

producing so much scrap, or the division manager calls in a salesman to tell him to give special attention to a customer who is threatening to take his business elsewhere. Often top-management expediters are sent as temporary replacements for lower managers who are in trouble. Here is a description of a top executive (former President of Curtiss-Wright) who is particularly well known for taking direct action and cutting through red tape:

> Hurley is chief expediter at C-W and chief executioner of good ideas with bad cost records. He seldom "moves through channels." He figures that the division manager doesn't have any more idea than he has of what is wrong or the figures would not have been negative in the first place. So instead of waiting for a briefing, Hurley moves directly to the spot, right down to the machine on the floor if that is the heart of the problem. Many a division manager has discovered hours later that the boss has been in his department and long since moved on. And many department heads have discovered that an important job has been given to an employee they hardly know, and without consulting them. Hurley spots a man who seems bright and says, "You do it." That the job may be completely unrelated to the employee's work is of no concern to Hurley.[24]

Attractive and dramatic though bypassing may seem, we must remember that sticking to the formal channels has one great advantage: It insures that everyone who is supposed to be informed actually is informed.

Mass communications.   In many companies the word *communications* refers not to the transmission of orders and information through normal hierarchical channels, but to what we would call mass communications: the company newspaper ("house organ"), bulletin-board announcements, direct mailings to employees, fillers in pay envelopes, movies, a loudspeaker system, and so forth. Almost every large company has a special staff assigned to preparing material of this sort.

Mass communications are seldom used by themselves to convey messages that are really important. When management wants to raise production or cut costs, it sends clear, unmistakable orders down the line, and makes sure that every subordinate understands them. Mass-communications techniques are used chiefly in areas that are peripheral to management's main job of getting the production out—areas such as safety, personnel policies, suggestions, and the company's financial position.

Why are mass-communications techniques used so widely in these areas? There are several reasons:

1. Often the information to be transmitted is of a technical nature. If details of a new insurance scheme, for example, are transmitted by word of mouth from top management through the various levels of supervision, they are bound

---

[24] William B. Harris, "Curtiss-Wright Throws Away the Book," *Fortune*, Vol. 57, No. 1 (January 1958), p. 115.

to be badly distorted by the time they reach the rank and file. Further, management may feel that the supervisors are not qualified to explain such involved matters as why depreciation must be deducted from profits to give an accurate picture of the company's financial position, therefore top management must communicate directly with employees.

2. Since messages of this sort do not have A-1 priority, management wants to insure that they will not be distorted or forgotten by lower supervision. Lower supervision is chiefly interested in getting out production, and messages relating to "fringe" areas may be laid aside or given perfunctory attention. The supervisor tells his men at the end of a meeting, "And, of course, as you know, I'm supposed to tell you once a week to be sure to wear your safety hats."

Many of the messages sent through mass-communications channels are sponsored by staff departments, such as finance or personnel. And these departments have learned through sad experience that if they have to trust line management to carry their messages, the information will never reach lower-level employees.

3. Finally, in contrast to what we said earlier, some messages are so vitally important that it is essential that details not be distorted by transmission through channels.

> A large, geographically dispersed corporation, recently made a number of vital changes in salary policy affecting every one of its 75,000 employees. To insure uniform and simultaneous reception, loudspeakers were installed in every location and work stopped for 15 minutes to permit the company president to address the entire workforce.

As is probably already clear, it is unwise for management to rely excessively on mass communications. With the exception of movies and loudspeaker announcements, mass communications involve the printed rather than the spoken word; they are always one-way rather than two-way. You will remember from our discussion in Chapter 10 that printed one-way communications lack flexibility and the opportunity for the feedback of the face-to-face spoken word. A man can't ask questions of a bulletin board, nor does a letter repeat itself if the reader is drowsy or inattentive.

If the message is of any importance at all, the use of mass communications tends to reduce the status of the immediate supervisor. In effect, top management is saying, "We don't trust you to explain complicated problems." Often, too, if the message is of importance, the subordinate has questions to ask about it. If his boss can't answer them, then the subordinate's respect for him will drop even more.

On the other hand, the fact that messages are sent through mass communications channels rather than through the line may indicate to the employees that the message is really not important. If the boss says "work faster" and the bulletin board says "work safer," the subordinate will be more likely to pay attention to the boss than to the bulletin board.

Improved mass-communication methods.   In order to overcome these difficulties, many companies are using mass communications with greater finesse. For example, top management may (1) give higher supervisors advance notice before relaying messages to lower levels, (2) urge the immediate supervisor to add a few words to supplement the formal message, and (3) encourage subordinates to address questions concerning these materials to their immediate boss. Such efforts preserve the advantages of specificity and uniformity, enable the immediate supervisor to retain his status, and encourage feedback from subordinates.

The grapevine.   Though not consciously designed by management, the grapevine is frequently an extremely effective means of communication. "Being flexible and personal, it spreads information faster than most management communications systems operate. With the rapidity of a burning powder train, it filters out of the woodwork, past the manager's office, through the locker room, and along the corridors." [25] Often subordinates learn of top management's decisions through the grapevine long before anything is put into writing. And when formal messages are transmitted, rumor "helps" explain and interpret them. Since the grapevine is personal, spoken, and permits feedback, it often has a far stronger impact on the recipient than do other forms of communication.

Many times the grapevine is surprisingly accurate; in fact, exaggeration is less common than simplification and abbreviation.[26] Of course, individuals in a position to initiate the process—for example, a key executive secretary—gain status and influence in the informal organization.

Many managers feel that rumors should be stamped out, on the grounds that they are often false, exaggerated, malicious, and even give away management secrets. Yet the grapevine performs a very useful function: It tends to correct some of the shortcomings of formal communication. Bill and Joe are in totally different divisions of the organization, but their work is closely tied together. A change is made in Bill's department that will vitally affect Joe. It may take weeks for the message to go up through the formal channels of communication and then reach Joe—possibly much distorted. But if Bill passes the word along to Joe on the job, the message is transmitted efficiently and accurately.

Actually it is unrealistic to expect that rumors can be stamped out. The grapevine fills a vital human need. Gossip gives people a social outlet and a chance to exercise their imagination. It gives an opportunity to relieve fears of the unknown by expressing anxiety in the form of stories. Above all, it allays curiosity.

---

[25] Keith Davis, *Human Relations in Business* (New York: McGraw-Hill, 1957), p. 244.
[26] *Cf.* Theodore Caplow, "Rumors in War," in *Some Theories of Organization*, Albert Rubenstein and Chadwick Haberstroh (eds.) (Homewood, Ill.: Dorsey, 1960), pp. 280-287.

The grapevine is bound to exist in any organization. If facts are available, it will transmit them effectively, though often with some distortion. If facts are not available, the grapevine may invent them. From a few clues, vastly perverted images may be constructed. Rumors rarely cause trouble where facts are readily available.

The best way to minimize undesirable rumors is to improve other forms of communication. Untruthful rumors rarely get started if the boss announces his intentions in advance, and if his subordinates feel free to ask him questions.

We have been talking about three somewhat different techniques used to short-circuit formal downward channels of communication: bypassing, mass communications, and the grapevine. More generally, we have been discussing the whole process of downward communication as a means of coordinating people in the organization, the reasons why this communication sometimes fails, and what can be done to improve it.

Communication and Supervision

It is useful, for a moment, to look at the relationship between hierarchical communication and patterns of supervision. The aggressively authoritarian manager may have difficulty even in communicating *downward*. Sometimes subordinates seek to impress the boss by doing more than he has requested and thus exaggerate his orders. Alternatively, they may object to the boss's order, yet fear to express their objections openly. Instead, they "play down" the order and systematically sabotage it or give it only token compliance. Subordinates may be afraid to ask their boss questions even when they fail to understand what he has said. In the last two instances, it should be noted that the boss's failure to encourage upward communication makes downward communication more difficult.

Often, this type of manager has little confidence in his subordinates, so he discourages downward communication, particularly through the regular channels. He doesn't trust subordinates to convey information or orders and, not trusting them with information, he doesn't see why they need more than the minimum amount required to do their job. His idea of good communication frequently is in terms of what we have called mass communications.

PATTERNS OF UPWARD COMMUNICATION

A healthy organization needs effective upward communications as much as it needs effective downward communications—and for two primary reasons:

1. *Obtaining information.* Top management depends on a steady stream of information from subordinates in order to make intelligent decisions. How well are we doing on Line 7? Is that new quality-control man working out

OK? Are we going to have to hire some more junior engineers? Without some sort of reporting system, top management can never find out what orders are needed or how effectively its orders are being carried out. Effective upward communication furnishes management with quick and accurate reports on what is happening at lower levels.

Successful upward communication requires that management's questions be truthfully answered. More than this, it requires that vital information be transmitted upward even if management has never requested it; it requires that *management be willing to listen to unsolicited messages.* The men on the top do not always know the right questions to ask or the right instructions to give. Subordinates frequently have useful suggestions to make, questions to ask, or problems of which their supervisors are ignorant. Unless subordinates feel free to communicate these matters upward, management will lack some ot the data essential to sound decision-making.

2. *Maintaining morale.* It is psychologically unsound for the initiation of contacts to run in only one direction—always from superiors to subordinates. No one is happy when he is always on the receiving end. We all want some opportunity to express ourselves, particularly to those who control our activities and welfare. When we are disturbed or under pressure from others—for example, when an earlier deadline has been unexpectedly imposed, or another department is demanding speedier service from us—the need to express ourselves becomes even more urgent.

Difficulties
in Upward Communication

Effective upward communication is difficult to obtain, particularly in larger organizations. In a small firm, the informality that usually prevails between the employees and the top boss produces a feeling of intimacy and personal satisfaction. Indeed there is a certain amount of censorship at each level in a large organization. Let us examine this difference in detail.

Covering up. Subordinates have a natural tendency to withhold unfavorable information from their superiors, or to filter the information as it is passed up the line. Often middle- and lower-level managers conspire with subordinates to hide from higher levels serious mistakes, deviations from standard procedures, or unsolved problems. Sometimes these deceptions are deliberate falsehoods to avoid blame; sometimes they just take the form of failure to report self-incriminating information. (For example, because an operator was not properly instructed, an entire batch of chemicals had to be thrown out, but the waste was disguised as garbage.)

The subordinate's fear of sending unfavorable information upward also reflects his lack of certainty concerning what top management wants. Recognizing the imperfection of downward communication, and not sure of what is expected, he tries to avoid reporting anything that might give an impression of failure. (Thus, poor downward communications often make upward communications harder.) [27]

Status problems.   In an effort to maintain his superior position, and to ration his scarce time, the manager may isolate himself from his subordinates by setting up barriers. An advance appointment, appropriate dress, passing the scrutiny of an officious secretary—all may be necessary before a man can ask the boss a modest question.

A department head calls in one of his subordinates to give him special instruction on handling an important project. The instructions are confusing, but the subordinate makes no attempt to ask clarifying questions. Why? Simply because he is afraid that the supervisor will interpret his questions as evidence of slowness or stupidity. He is not sure that the questions he will ask will be "good ones"—that is, the kind of question an intelligent, competent man is supposed to ask. So rather than risk hurting his reputation, he remains silent.

Strangely enough, this common cause of breakdown in upward communication is also one of the easiest to remedy. The solution is simply for the supervisor to encourage questions, indicating that they are expected and appropriate —in fact, giving the subordinate the feeling that asking questions indicates a high degree of alertness.

Pressures
for Upward Communication

In a small organization the manager can see for himself how his decisions are being carried out. In the large organization, managers can "see" only through the eyes of others. Top management normally relies on "auditors" and the reports of managers at the next level in the hierarchy, who in turn must rely on those reporting to them, and so on down the line of command. But top management finds it very difficult to discover what is really happening on the levels below. One often hears executives asking, "We wonder what is really going on at the work level."

Quite revealing are the apocryphal stories about the efforts of navy captains to learn what is happening below decks. In the typical tale the captain disguises himself as a seaman and wanders through the ship, or invites a seaman to his cabin for drinks and talk.[28]

On the other hand, employees are often anxious to bring their problems to the attention of higher management. Joe feels that his manager is discriminating against him and wants a fair hearing from someone higher up on why

---

[27] One would expect upward communication to be much more effective in a company that practices general supervision. Here subordinates are more likely to feel free to discuss problems with their bosses without fear of being bawled out for mistakes. The close supervisor, on the other hand, tends to build a wall of suspicion between himself and his subordinates.

[28] James F. Downes, "Environment, Communications and Status Change Aboard an American Aircraft Carrier," *Human Organization*, Vol. 17, No. 3 (Fall 1958), p. 14.

he has been denied a promotion. Jack has thought up a new fixture that he is sure will cut machining time by one-third, but his foreman brushes him off with a curt rejection. Bill feels at ease with his immediate supervisor, but realizes that it is pointless to complain to him about his salary when someone higher up makes the decisions. In effect, all these men are saying, "If only someone in top management would listen to us!"

Appeal Channels and Bypassing Techniques

Appeal channels. Most organizations have some form of appeal channel by which a member can challenge his immediate superior's decision.[29] Some procedures are quite formalized, as with the establishment of a union in a company or with the use of the Inspector General in the armed forces. Since a superior has so much power over his subordinates, it is not surprising that these channels have been carved out. They give subordinates a greater sense of security and provide higher management with useful information.

However, organizations have also been successful in using less formalized procedures. Many companies have experimented with the "open-door" policy whereby every employee is guaranteed the privilege of walking into the office of any manager at any level in the organization to voice his complaints. In some companies this policy has succeeded in opening up a worthwhile channel of appeal. More often, however, subordinates take advantage of the privilege only rarely. Why? One reason, of course, is the deterrent of social distance—the fear that keeps the buck private from complaining to his colonel that he has been assigned to KP too often, even though the colonel makes himself available. More than this, the subordinate realizes that once he exercises the privilege of appeal, he will have jeopardized his whole future with his immediate superior.

A subordinate knows intuitively how his supervisor feels about the open door. He calculates that if he walks through this portal he has only a slim chance of winning anything and a good chance of losing a great deal. After all, the immediate superior controls many things that the complainant holds important—job, salary level, work assignments, and so forth. The risk is too great, so the open door is rarely entered.

In at least one very large and successful American corporation the formal open-door policy works. There is a well-publicized series of appeal steps, almost like a grievance procedure, that ends in the president's office, which is many hierarchical levels above the average employee. Each year a significant number of employees get to see the president with their personal "grievances." He has so frequently supported them and reversed decisions of lower levels of

---

[29] A very interesting analysis of appeal systems in business, the military, the U.S. Government, the UAW, and the Catholic Church is contained in William G. Scott, *The Management of Conflict* (Homewood, Illinois: Richard Irwin and Dorsey Press, 1965).

supervision that, not surprisingly, there has been a morale problem among supervisors! Nevertheless, it should be stressed that this is not the typical case, but it does indicate what a management can do in creating a viable appeal channel.

Understandably, a supervisor is upset when a subordinate decides to go over his head with an appeal to a higher level in the organization—this behavior spotlights his own deficiencies. The supervisor also begins to worry lest the subordinate reveal practices or mistakes that he has carefully tried to cover up. And he recognizes that if the top boss does decide to grant the complainant's demand, a steady stream of complaining subordinates may carry appeals over his head, and thus seriously endanger his leadership position.

In spite of what we have just said, a boss can always, if he wishes, encourage employees to bring problems directly to him, bypassing their direct supervisors. Many times a higher-level manager will be contacted informally—perhaps while he is walking through the office—by an employee who has a special request or protest. The frequency with which this occurs depends more on the attitudes of higher management than on any announced open-door policy.

What is a boss to do when the subordinate of one of his supervisors comes to him with a problem? If such bypassing is encouraged, the effect on the supervisors' morale may be disastrous. Yet if it is completely banned, the effect on the workers' morale may be equally harmful. Probably the best approach is to listen to at least a summary of the problem and then to suggest tactfully that the subordinate see his immediate superivsor.

But suppose the man has already seen his supervisor? One solution would be for the boss to call the supervisor and subordinate together and hear them out. Such a meeting, however, might aggravate the tension between them, and inhibit both of them from talking freely. The supervisor might have had confidential reasons for taking the disputed action. Above all, the fact that the subordinate is implicitly making charges against his supervisor tends to make the supervisor feel that he is on trial, that he must defend his every action. To make a meeting of this sort successful would required unusual human-relations skills on the part of the boss.[30]

Probably a better approach is for the boss to listen carefully to the subordinate's problem, without committing himself one way or the other, and then promise to discuss it with the supervisor. In his meeting with the supervisor, the boss should try to minimize his interference with the supervisor's freedom to make decisions within the limits of his delegated discretion. If the problem is serious enough, the boss may use the nondirective technique to help the supervisor talk through his difficulties. If possible, however, he should leave the final decision to the supervisor. In the event that he feels compelled to reverse the supervisor's decisions, he should be careful to give the reasons

---

[30] For an example of a boss who was able to make such meetings successful, see William F. Whyte, *Human Relations in the Restaurant Industry* (New York: McGraw-Hill, 1948), pp. 298-300.

why. Further, in order to preserve the supervisor's prestige, he, not the boss, should be the one to explain the final decision to the subordinate.

Attitude surveys. Many companies use morale or attitude surveys as a means of finding out how their employees feel about their job, their supervisors, specific policies, or the company as a whole.

Today the making and interpretation of such surveys is a growing but specialized field. Psychologists in colleges, in management consulting firms, and in individual companies have become highly skilled in preparing, administering, and evaluating questionnaires.

Some experts argue that standardized surveys (which can be purchased from firms specializing in psychological services) are the best, for they make it possible to compare firms and departments and to point out significant deviations from "norms" that have been developed on the basis of experience elsewhere. Other experts argue that special questionnaires should be devised to meet the needs of each particular company.

Most surveys consist of written questionnaires that may be filled out on the job or at home. (As might be expected, a high percentage of the "take-home" questionnaires are never returned.) In either case, care is taken to preserve the anonymity of the respondent.

Many questionnaires require the employee to indicate the degree of his feeling in regard to each point. For example:

I feel fairly well satisfied with my present job:

_____ strongly agree   _____disagree
_____ agree   _____ strongly disagree
_____ undecided

Other questions may invite the employee to choose among various alternatives:

The following items describe different conditions that may be bothering you in your work. Check the ones that need to be improved: [31]

Ventilation	( )	Unpleasant noise	( )
Lighting	( )	Faulty unsafe equipment	( )
Too cold	( )	Dirty work station	( )
Too hot	( )	Lack of sanitation	( )
Drafts	( )	Too far from rest room	( )
Sun glare	( )	Unpleasant dust	( )
Dampness	( )	No union	( )
Unpleasant odors	( )	Other _____	( )

Some surveys try to elicit more detailed (and perhaps deeper) answers through so-called "open-ended" questions, such as, "What would you say are

---

[31] Roger M. Bellows, *Psychology of Personnel in Business and Industry*, 2nd ed. (Englewood Cliffs, N.J.: Prentice-Hall, 1954), p. 155.

your most serious dissatisfactions with your present job?" A modification of this technique is the sentence-completion procedure, in which the respondent is requested to complete sentences like "The most serious complaint I have about my present job is _____."

Because employees are sometimes reluctant to reveal their deeper feelings and may not even be able to express them, attempts have been made to adapt psychiatric techniques to industrial use. For example, rather than using verbal questions, the respondent may be shown cartoons of people in the organization talking, but with the traditional little "balloons" over their heads left empty. The respondent is asked to fill in the balloons with what he thinks the people are saying to each other. These more sophisticated forms of survey are far more expensive to score than the check-your-answer forms, and are less frequently used.

Once the forms have been filled out, the results must be tabulated and analyzed. Simple, so-called "straight runs" (e.g., 70 per cent of the men like their jobs) are usually less useful than cross tabulations, such as:

	AMONG MEN WHO LIKE THEIR JOBS	AMONG MEN WHO DISLIKE THEIR JOBS	TOTAL
Foremen speak to them often	85%	15%	100%
Foremen speak to them rarely	45	55	100

The survey results are then presented to top management, which sometimes disseminates them to lower levels. Indeed, some companies use survey results as a springboard for supervisory training.[32] On occasion, the results are specific enough to dictate immediate action, as in the case of a survey which revealed that many employees misunderstand the details of a new pension plan. More often the results are ambiguous. They raise a host of questions but the answers, if any, must be found through careful re-examination of policies and behavior in the affected areas.

Thus, surveys point up broad problems, but rarely suggest solutions. They are a rather artificial form of upward communication and their findings are subject to serious forms of distortion. Employees may purposely or unconsciously misinterpret questions and give misleading answers. By their very design, these surveys make no provision for communicating the specific problem of specific employees. Often they are expensive and time-consuming. For all these reasons, attitude surveys are a valuable adjunct to, but not a substitute for, more unambiguous, direct means of upward communication.

---

[32] For an interesting example of the use of feedback from morale surveys to change supervisory attitudes (as they learn what their subordinates believe and perceive), see Floyd Mann, "Studying and Creating Change: A Means to Understanding Social Organization," in Industrial Relations Research Association, *Research in Industrial Human Relations* (New York: Harper & Row, 1957), pp. 146-167. A more complete analysis of the theory behind the use of survey data as a means of upward communication is contained in Rensis Likert, *New Patterns of Management* (New York: McGraw-Hill, 1961).

Committees. Management sometimes sets up special conference groups or committees to find out what is on the minds of employees. These committees give lower-ranking personnel a chance to express their attitudes directly to top management, thus bypassing intermediate levels. For example, the first-line supervisory group may elect representatives to meet weekly or monthly with the general manager to discuss current problems. The representatives are encouraged to ask about the rumors floating about on their level, ask questions, ventilate gripes, and give management some ideas of the unsolved problems in their departments.

Some companies have used similar devices for hourly-paid personnel.[33] Here caution needs to be exercised to insure that these committees do not conflict with existing unions or violate the provisions of the National Labor Relations Act, which prohibts employers from assisting in the formation of employee organizations with union-like functions.

Other techniques. Suggestion systems are used by many companies as a means of collecting specific ideas for improving company efficiency. Ordinarily, suggestions are presented in such a way as to bypass the intermediate levels of management.

> The experience of one company highlights the manner in which suggestion plans bypass normal communication channels. An employee suggested that the installation of a coin-operated coffee machine would reduce the half-hour coffee break to a few minutes. The employee wrote out his proposal and dropped it in the "Suggestion Box." It was the first indication top management had ever had that half-hour coffee breaks were being permitted at lower levels.

In a sense, a union itself provides a very important channel of upward communication by bringing the average worker's problems directly to the attention of top management. Many cost-sharing union-management cooperation plans bring committees of workers face to face with top management in discussions of production problems.

Staff specialists provide another upward channel because of the ease with which they can contact higher management. They may hear of good ideas that have been smothered by unsympathetic superiors or good men who have not received adequate recognition. (Of course, their "mobility" can be a source of conflict between these specialists and the line manager.)

This last is worth expanding on briefly. The weight of the hierarchy, of tradition, and the impact of controls that we shall be discussing next may be all on the side of preserving the status quo. Individuals with a great deal of initiative and new ideas may be discouraged from doing or saying things that

---

[33] For a description of how one company makes use of overlapping committees that blanket the entire organization, see Elliot Jacques, *The Changing Culture of a Factory* (New York: Holt, Rinehart and Winston, 1952).

would "rock the boat"—would in the short run create new problems for their supervisor. As organizations come to depend more and more on new technical knowledge, on research findings and ideas, they must protect themselves against the possibility that originality will be summarily rejected. Often the supervisor cannot judge the intrinsic quality or usefulness of a man or his idea, and both need to be exposed to higher levels of the hierarchy.

STATISTICAL CONTROLS

Now let us explore what is probably management's most effective means of upward communication—statistical controls. Normally, management introduces statistical controls in order to further coordination, pinpoint responsibility, and find out what is actually happening at the operating level. Since figures are harder to distort than subjective reports, higher management insists on receiving a constant flow of data on production, sales, costs, quality, grievances, salary increases, turnover, and so forth.

Functions of Statistical Controls

Through cost accounting, for example, "standard costs" are developed for every item produced or service rendered. If the standard cost of an item is 35 cents and the foreman can make it for 33 cents, he is making a "profit" (part of which may accrue to him, personally, as a bonus). If he spends 37 cents to make it, he is incurring a "loss." These departmental profit and loss accounts, called *variance accounts*, provide standards by which higher management can measure departmental efficiency. Other standards may be set in terms of quantities produced, man-hours expended per unit, sales, scrap loss, turnover, and so on.

To insure that these data reach headquarters rapidly and without distortion, they are ordinarily collected by staff departments, such as accounting, quality control, and personnel. Because these departments operate at least semi-independently of the line, the data can be reported directly to the top without being filtered through intermediate steps of management that may have reputations to protect. Computers enormously increase the amount of data that can be assembled and the speed with which they can be transmitted to top management.

In addition to providing top management with the information it needs for decision-making, statistical controls serve many other functions described briefly below.

Supervision by results. Statistical controls eliminate the necessity for close, detailed supervision, and provide the evidence needed for supervision by results. Through reports on profits, sales, and so forth, top management can evaluate the effectiveness of subordinate departments without checking on every detail of their work. Without satisfactory statistical controls, decentralization is difficult.

Standards. Statistical controls also make it possible for management to set standards for achievement and to emphasize areas that require special attention. For instance, if top management is anxious to focus attention on a scrap-reduction program, it will begin asking all subordinate departments to report each month how much they have reduced scrap losses over the preceding month. Thus, statistical *controls* are a means of downward communication and exerting pressure.

Personnel evaluation. In turn, they help develop goals and provide motivation and measures of success for those whose work is measured by controls. Statistical controls that measure individual performance provide a means for selecting, appraising, and compensating employees.

Difficulties in Measurement

Yet statistical controls should not be considered as a magic cure for all organizational ills. Improperly handled, they may create as many problems as they cure. Elements like department costs, efficiency, and productivity are difficult to measure fairly, while the very act of measurement may distort effort.

Naturally if employees are to be evaluated largely in terms of their success or failure in meeting these goals, it is important that the goals be fair and reasonable. Establishment of such goals is a highly technical and often inaccurate procedure. It is all too easy to set standards that are too "tight" or too "loose." (It should be obvious, too, that the greater the reliance on statistical measures of efficiency, the greater becomes the power of the staff departments which prepare them.)

Many types of work are so general and intangible that it is almost impossible to devise an adequate technique for measuring them. How is one to measure the effectiveness of the personnel department? [34] Surely not in terms of cost, because low cost may simply mean that nothing is being accomplished. Not in terms of turnover, number of strikes and grievances, productivity, and so forth, for all these things are related to over-all plant policy or the organization as a

---

[34] Or how does one measure the efficiency of a university professor? By the number of students who take his courses? But this may depend on whether the professor makes it a "snap course" or on the nature of the subject matter (witness the rise of physics). By student rating? Perhaps, but teaching ability is more than being a good showman. By relative scores on an identical exam which is jointly graded and given to all students in the same course? Possibly—but note the motivation this gives the professor to cover only those points likely to be on the exam. In many colleges promotion is largely based on the number of scholarly articles published, with an obvious effect on the relative time spent on research as against teaching. How does one compare the relative efforts of a classics professor with one in chemistry? Obviously, direct measurement has its limitations in the university as well as in industry.

whole. Roughly the same sort of objections can be raised against any direct rating of staff departments. And there are other departments, such as research, where meaningful results become apparent only in the long run.

> In talking to engineering supervisors in a large research organization, we heard this common complaint: Supervisors had a hard time evaluating their subordinates, and subordinates didn't know what was required to get a pay raise or promotion. One supervisor put it this way: "An engineer is constantly making decisions in which he is balancing time against efficiency against cost. It is practically impossible to know whether his judgment is good. Also, if a man doesn't get results, how are you to know whether he has been 'goofing off' or been up against a streak of bad luck?"

Even more severe problems arise in attempts to make a comparative rating of various departments. How does one rate costs in division A, which makes the same product year after year, against division B, where the product is always undergoing change? Some department stores try to measure departmental efficiency in terms of sales and profit, but the level of sales in any department may depend on its location in the store, the weather, and the business cycle more than on the individual efficiency of the department manager.

Unfortunately, the measures selected to evaluate performance may be a reflection of what is easy to measure, rather than the real criteria of effective performance.[35] Because of the problems of dealing with short-run and long-run factors, situational exceptions, the combination of personnel, production, financial and marketing effectiveness, one often sees organizations using overly simplified controls, devices which are not much different from worker incentive plans that just measure raw output.

Distorting Behavior

If excessive emphasis is placed on statistical controls, compared to other forms of upward communication, the very act of measurement may lead subordinates to distort their efforts and work less efficiently.

Overemphasis on the items measured. Departments will normally concentrate on the items that are being measured rather than on the job as a whole. Successful banks realize that good customer relations are vital and that a very poor impression is created when a teller refuses to serve a customer until he has finished adding up his figures. Yet "the teller has found all his rewards in the past for careful balancing of the books. . . . He has never been rewarded or punished for his treatment of customers." [36]

Top management rarely realizes how alert subordinates are to adapting

---

[35] *Cf.* Kenneth Arrow, "Control in Large Organizations," *Management Science*, Vol. 10, No. 3 (April 1964), p. 400.

[36] Mason Haire, *Psychology in Management* (New York: McGraw-Hill, 1956), p. 17.

their behavior to the reward and punishments implied in the controls being used. Very slight changes in what is measured are magnified into very substantial changes in behavior.

> In the past the development engineers in the ABC Chemical Company had devoted themselves to helping line managers solve day-to-day production problems. A new head of Engineering for the company was very interested in the new mathematical techniques of operations research and "model-building" techniques. As the "word got around" that he appreciated very sophisticated analytical reports, most of the engineers gave up their efforts to aid line managers and began working on quite advanced "theoretical" research projects. This changed drastically the relationships the engineers had with production, and they were no longer perceived as a source of assistance.

Supervisors are supposed to maintain both high morale and high productivity. Morale is intangible and difficult to measure, but productivity and costs can presumably be measured to a tenth of a decimal place. As a consequence, productivity comes first; good employee relations are a luxury to be enjoyed only when there is nothing wrong with output.

Token compliance. Supervisors may greet statistical control with token compliance—that is, by striving to *look* as if they were meeting their standards. Unfortunately, the effect of keeping up appearances may well be to lower overall performance.

As part of a drive to cut excess inventory, the divisional superintendents in one company were required to give a monthly report of supplies on hand. What happened? There was a scramble to use up all the stock before the end of the month and to insure that no new supplies were delivered until after the beginning of the next. But the average inventory over the month remained just about the same.

Inefficient scheduling of work. Sometimes the existence of standards results in a long-run deterioration of real performance, *even on the items being measured.*

> Because management in one company paid so much attention to end-of-month efficiency ratings, department supervisors left no stone unturned to get as many units into finished stores as possible. They even resorted to such expensive and disruptive processes as "bleeding the line"—that is, stopping operations in order to complete more units by the deadline. This process is summarized by what another foreman said:
> "For the last two weeks of the month we're driving hell out of the men. We have to get pieces out and we are always jammed up at the end of the month. . . ." [37]

---

[37] Frank Jasinski, "Use and Misuse of Efficiency Controls," *Harvard Business Review*, Vol. 34, No. 4 (July 1956), p. 107. This problem is even more serious in Russia where "storming" (as it is called there) during the last week of every month is done at high pressure. David Granick, *The Red Executive* (Garden City, N.Y.: Doubleday, 1960), pp. 267-270.

Even where employees are not subjected to such hectic pressures, the mere existence of standards may induce them to schedule work less efficiently. A claims adjuster once told us, "Of course, some claims are harder to handle than others, but as far as the quota is concerned they all count the same. So I always try to keep a few easy cases aside to handle at the end of the month if it looks like I won't be able to meet the quota without them. I try not to turn in too many cases in any month or they'll always expect me to work that hard." Piece-workers also build up "banks," to equalize their earnings over the week.

Emphasis on short run rather than long run.   The use of statistical controls often produces short-term results at the expense of the organization's long-term good. Managers often complain that supervisors are "department-centered" and show no loyalty to the organization as a whole. For instance, department managers in retail stores are rewarded for high sales and profits in their *own* departments. By pushing shoddy merchandise they can sometimes get high sales for themselves at the expense of the goodwill of the entire store. Yet under these circumstances, what other sort of motivation could be expected? Similarly, salesmen, conscious of the importance of an impressive sales record, may ignore the store's public relations—showing themselves unwilling to spend time with indecisive or dissatisfied customers—in favor of the easy, free-spending customer.

Covering-up.   Faced with the necessity of having to look good on paper, the natural impulse of employees is to try to "adjust " the reported statistics. At times plain lying is sufficient, but sometimes it is necessary to hide the evidence. In one department the men put defective parts in refuse cans and covered them over—with the foreman's full knowledge. In another, the fore-man himself came back to the department at night to pick up damaged equip-ment and drop it in the local quarry.

Thus, controls may injure upward communications, or what is called "the intelligence function." Ironically, the more reliance is placed on control meas-ures, the less top management may find out about what is really happening.

> In the midst of a safety campaign, one employee suffered a slight injury at the end of his shift which might have kept him home for several days. The foreman begged him:
> "If you can possibly come to work tomorrow I will guarantee you will not have to do a lick of work until you really feel up to it. I'll pick you up at home and drive you back. But for the love of Mike, let's not have a lost-time accident on our record."

Passing the buck.   Another unfortunate by-product of excessive emphasis on standards is an added inducement to pass the buck. If parts turn out de-fective, there is always an argument about which department should be charged with the cost or repair. Similarly, there may be endless haggling over whether time spent in training new employees, or in the handling of grievances, should be charged against the particular department or against the personnel department.

In a well-known national company, accident-prevention is so strongly emphasized that regular tribunals have been established to determine whether an accident will be "charged" against the foreman of the department in which it occurred. In one case, all sorts of internal political pressures were used to influence the panel members in their decision. These tribunals seem more concerned with fixing responsibility than in determining and eliminating the causes of accidents.

Impaired teamwork. Statistical controls and supervision by results rest on the assumption that each individual supervisor should be held responsible for the efficiency of his own department. Within limits it is healthy to encourage individual responsibility. Yet overemphasis on individual performance may lead to excessive individualism and selfishness, particularly in departments that are highly interdependent.

> In one large company, maintenance and repair charges assessed against production departments were "adjusted" by management. Departments that were "friendly" to maintenance received low charges, while unfriendly departments received not only their own charges, but those left over after the special reductions.[38]

Reduction in discretion. Insofar as statistical data are used as the basis for evaluating the success or failure of managers and departments, they serve to reduce the discretion of the immediate supervisor. As one researcher has noted:

> The evaluation of subordinates is a major responsibility of supervisors. If this evaluation were based entirely on statistical indices, this responsibility would be reduced to a clerical task, the application of a mathematical formula to a set of data. This would not only make the job of supervisor less interesting for him but also undermine his authority over subordinates.[39]

Another expert points out the need for preserving supervisory discretion:

> The practical effect of this high-handed behavior [excessive reliance on statistical controls], oddly enough, is not to make top management the boss, rather, the accountant with his rows of figures becomes the dominant voice in the company. He becomes a manager by default, as it were, because knowledge is power, and the knowledge on which action is based is what the accountant puts into his reports.
>
> The fact is that the day accountants can devise a balance sheet or graph which encompasses total reality, we can do away with executives—but not until then.[40]

---

[38] Melville Dalton, *Men Who Manage* (New York: Wiley, 1959), p. 37 ff.

[39] Peter Blau, *The Dynamics of Bureaucracy* (Chicago: Univ. of Chicago Press, 1955), p. 41.

[40] Jasinski, *op. cit.*, p. 111.

Effect on centralization. The introduction of electronic data-processing apparatus has a similar effect on the position of the supervisor. Such equipment makes available to top managers vastly more data than they have ever had before, and permits them to make detailed decisions affecting the smallest department in the company—thus completely bypassing middle management.

Some observers, however, believe that improved processing of statistical control data can strengthen the decision-making ability of lower levels of the organization. Used properly, computers can also process information that communicates directly to first- and second-level supervisors rather than to higher management. One manager of data-processing operations described the situation in his company:

> [In the old days] many decisions were of necessity made at the plant manager's level because the superintendent didn't have the local facts.
>
> Now the superintendent makes the decisions and they're better decisions because information is more complete, more accurate and available when the manager needs it.
>
> Take the foreman. Decisions he used to make about stock each day were based on not much more than experienced intuition. Now that he knows the answers these decisions are easy—almost automatic. He can concentrate on areas like personnel relations, performance, on schedule and operating efficiency.[41]

Standards as a form of pressure. Without question, management uses standards as a means to apply pressure. The techniques, of course, vary with the supervisor, as these contrasting quotations indicate:

> "I go to the office and check the budget every day. . . . If it's OK, I don't say anything. But if it is no good, then I come back here and give the boys a little—well, you know, I needle them a bit."

> "You know, it is a funny thing. If I want my people to read the budget, I just lay it on my desk and leave it alone. They'll pick it up without doubt." [42]

Notice that both approaches use standards as a form of pressure. Basic to both is the assumption that failure to meet a quota is prima-facie proof of falling down on the job. In effect, the standards are transformed into an extremely arbitrary boss. Many a supervisor says, "I don't want excuses, just get the job done." It does little good for the subordinate to reply, "But I did get the job done—only the profit figures don't give the complete picture." When standards are boss, all explanations are regarded as excuses.

> Perhaps one of the [supervisor's] greatest criticisms of budgets was the fact that they never included the reasons *why* they were not achieved. . . . Supervisors disliked intensely the fact that their departments would look "sick" in

---

[41] *For Line and Staff Supervisors* (New York: National Foremen's Institute, July 1959).
[42] Chris Argyris, *The Impact of Budgets on People* (New York: Financial Executives Foundation, 1952), p. 24.

the budget while the reasons for the "sickness" were never published along with the results.[43]

Controls are not omnipotent.   In most organizations there are other pressures at work "balancing off" the pressures exerted by the use of standards. As we have observed, the work group, unions, and colleagues have standards or norms of their own which may conflict with the requirements being imposed by top management. Then the supervisor, charged with the responsibility of making a good showing in the eyes of his boss, finds himself caught "in the middle."

This phenomenon even occurs in totalitarian states, where consumers, community groups, and employees can exercise some influence because of their ability to withhold or give enthusiastic cooperation. For example, a notable study shows that in Russia the factory manager tends to resist standards imposed from *above* because of informal pressures being exerted from *below:*

> These informal pressures constitute standards of which the manager must take cognizance, pressures to which he must adjust, in order to maintain such relations with his "working community" as will permit him to meet standards directly set and enforceable by superiors. . . .
>
> [The manager reacts to pressures from above by] providing for a safety factor; simulation, or feigning the meeting of standards, and *blat,* or the use of personal influence to obtain favors.[44]

Improved Use of Controls

The use of control measures is an essential part of management's job in any large organization. No top manager can know everything he needs to know without quantitative data that summarize what is happening and that compare actual results with expected or planned results. When carefully presented, these data enable him to detect trouble-spots almost instantly, without reviewing every facet of day-to-day operations. All he need do is look for the variances, the departures from the quantitative limits that he has set for his subordinates—the number of units to be processed, the amount of permissible overtime, the number of merit increases, and so forth.

The challenge for the manager is also to develop methods of using control channels of communication that do not have the serious drawbacks described above. If he is successful, the rewards can be substantial—greater autonomy, job satisfaction, and better performance for subordinates at each level.

Since the controls themselves often originate with staff specialists who are not the direct superiors of the managers being appraised, conscious attention must be directed to their relationship. One study urges that accountants and line managers establish a human-relations pattern of give and take:

---

[43] *Ibid.*, p. 11.

[44] Andrew G. Frank, "Goal Ambiguity and Conflicting Standards: An Approach to the Study of Organization," *Human Organization,* Vol. 17, No. 4 (Winter 1958-59), p. 9.

On the other hand, if a definite program is set up, involving regular assignments for accounting personnel requiring them to contact operating supervisors for information, the accountant may begin to arouse the interest of the operating executives in possible uses of accounting data. They may also obtain a better understanding of these executives' needs for data. When this occurs, the operating heads will generally encourage or seek out more frequent contacts with the accountants. Each begins to gain a more thorough understanding of the vocabulary, problems and methods of the other. This cycle continues until a fairly high degree of communication and use of accounting data is attained.

This provides the controller's department with an opportunity to show that it really intends to provide data in useful and usable form, in terms of operating departments' need, so that when it is asked for help, it meets such requests promptly.[45]

One test of good usage is the organization's response when a man fails to meet standards. Is his failure regarded as evidence of incompetence, perhaps meriting discipline? Or is it just a cue for management to find out how badly he has fallen down, to help him find out why, to stand ready to give him whatever assistance he needs? Management must decide whether to use controls as a means of "catching" people, or as a means of identifying problems and allocating the resources of the organization to provide assistance. Management's choice is dictated in part by its approach to setting standards in the first place. Standards are probably most effective when they are set by the supervisor and subordinate working together. They are least effective when they are imposed by staff officials or top managers who have relatively little understanding of the specific department. Standards are particularly troublesome when they are used as a basis for setting compensation (as in a bonus system) without appropriate appeal channels.

In summary, statistical data do not necessarily give a complete picture of "results." Failure to achieve "results" should always raise the question "*Why?*" "What has happened to cause this departure from what we anticipated?"

> In the words of the old saw, "Figures don't lie." Maybe they don't lie, but that doesn't mean that they are capable of dictating action without the aid of managerial judgment bolstered by information gleaned from multiple sources.[46]

Such comments become even more important in an age of computers.

CONCLUSION

Organizational structure is more than a series of interconnected boxes and lines on a chart. It is a pattern of human relationships—planned and unplanned —that has evolved over a period of time in response to the human and technical problems of the firm.

---

[45] Herbert Simon, *et al., Centralization vs. Decentralization in Organizing the Controller's Department* (New York: Financial Executives Foundation, 1954), pp. 49-50.
[46] Jasinski, *op. cit.*, p. 106.

As organizations grow in size they also grow in "height," in the number of managerial levels they contain. On paper these hierarchies look quite simple and logical, but they do not function as simply as many theorists have stated. Recent research suggests that:

1. There are many important human relations that contribute to the operation of the organization that are not "hierarchical." (These will be discussed in greater detail in the next chapter.)

2. In the modern organization, individuals receive instructions and pressures from other people besides their boss.

3. With complex technology has come the greater likelihood that important decisions will be made at relatively low levels of the structure.

4. There is no simple formula for determining the right "span of control" for a manager and it is *not* true that the smaller the number of subordinates, the better.

5. Bypassing, meaning skipping levels in communications in both upward- and downward-direction contacts, is a relatively common occurrence.

The manager of any large organization faces a most difficult task of getting all employees (frequently including many levels of supervision as well) to coordinate their efforts and to follow his leadership and direction. To accomplish this objective he must make use of both downward and upward channels of communication—he must both give orders and assess their effectiveness. Yet the systems of human relations that he depends on for transmission are far from foolproof. Organizations often do not function as planned. Serious distortions are introduced by the necessity of communicating through many levels; interpersonal contacts inevitably are limited and restrained between employees at different levels.

The individual supervisor also has his problems in dealing with the hierarchy. The leadership techniques he can use are limited by the methods of management used by his manager and his manager's manager. He must learn to balance the conflicting demands of those over him with those underneath. If he succumbs completely to either (for example, by failing to represent vigorously the interests of his subordinates to higher levels), his leadership position is weakened, if not destroyed.

In an effort to duplicate some of the communication advantages of the smaller organization, modifications are introduced in the hierarchical structure. These include, among others, techniques for bypassing and short-circuiting, such as mass communications, attitude surveys, and special committees. Multi-leveled organizations have special needs for protected appeal channels by which those at lower levels who feel an injustice or believe they have been unfairly treated can get a hearing at key decision-making levels without depending on their immediate supervisor to represent them. Unions and open-door techniques help to fill this need. However, there is a danger that these modifications can be as injurious to the organization as the problems they are supposed to remedy. Usually they threaten the leadership position of the immediate supervisor.

Large organizations cannot depend upon the ability of management to oversee everything directly. Therefore, a variety of control measures are developed which serve to both measure and motivate performance. While they are supposed to communicate to upper management accurately and impartially what lower levels have accomplished they are susceptible to a variety of distortions. Perhaps more than any other factor, the problems surrounding the utilization of controls typifies the complexities for human relations associated with multi-leveled hierarchies.

Two distinctive features of large, many-leveled organizations are the use of rules (or policies) and quantitative controls. Poorly administered rules and controls can throttle initiative, destroy job satisfaction, and create debilitating inflexibility. However, they can be used to advantage by the administrator who is sensitive to their impact. Rules and controls developed with care insure that employees will know what is expected of them, what criteria they will be judged on, and what discretion they have to make decisions. All the way up the line, supervisors are relieved of the time-consuming and morale-damaging necessity of interfering in the work of subordinates in order to make sure it is going as planned. (Rules and policies were discussed in Chapter 7.)

PROBLEM 1

BAD FIXTURE

Telephone Conversation—(Plant Manager phones, somewhat excitedly, to one of his superintendents)

PM: "Say, this morning when I was walking through one of your departments, one of the setup men, Joe Smith in Department X, stopped me and said the fixture he was using on his machine was no good. It had to have a couple extra clamps on it which slowed production down on his machine by 10%. What are you doing about this?"

Supt.: "I don't think I know anything about the situation you're talking about. I'll have to check into it."

PM: "But the setup man said that this has been going on for two days now. Haven't you heard anything about it?"

Supt.: "No, I guess I wouldn't hear anything about it unless it involved a problem that the foreman out there thought he couldn't handle."

PM: "Well, get on it as soon as you can, and let me know what you find out as soon as you do."

In Superintendent's Office

Supt.: (to Foreman) "I've called you in to ask whether we are having any serious trouble with the fixtures over in Joe Smith's area."

Foreman: "Well, I've been with Engineering on this. They're designing an entirely new-type fixture, so we're getting along with this the best we can in the meantime. I know it's costing us something to limp along this way, but I figured it was cheaper than ordering a replacement for the old fixture at a thousand dollars and have it become obsolete in the couple weeks it would take them to develop the new one. I feel this new design is going to really save us some money. Why, is there anything wrong?"

Supt.: "Yeah, the boss wants to know what we are doing to take care of it. Maybe this is something I should have known about since the boss was so interested."

Foreman: "Oh yeah, I remember yesterday when the boss came through; Smith and he started talking. I guess I should have gone over to see what was up. And the next time, on something like this, I'll check with you immediately."

Supt.: "Did the setup man know what was being done with Engineering about the fixture?"

Foreman: "Sure. I told him yesterday. He knows the whole story. I wonder what he's trying to pull—griping to the boss."

Supt.: "Well, I'll call the boss and you take care of Joe."

Foreman: "O.K."

1. Why was the PM disappointed that the Superintendent did not know about the malfunctioning fixture? Should he have been upset?
2. What effect did the PM's call have on the methods of supervision that would be used in the future? Describe the probable changes in the relationship between the PM and Superintendent, between Superintendent and Foreman, and between Foreman and setup man.
3. Did the Foreman handle Smith correctly? Is there anything the Superintendent can do to review this problem with the Foreman that will not discourage the Supervisor in taking responsibility and initiative?
4. Assume that the whole incident could be repeated. What should the PM do after learning about the operating troubles in Department X? Be specific in describing what should take place in the contacts between:

> PM and set up man
> General Superintendent and Superintendent
> Superintendent and Foreman
> Foreman and setup man

5. What might Smith's motives have been in this case?

PROBLEM 2

THE ASSISTANT'S DILEMMA

Bill Adams was hired to fill a new job as assistant to Alfred Grozia, the laboratory head and research director. Adams' assignment was to handle all the administrative details for a very busy executive-scientist.

After about six months on the job, Adams was on good terms with nearly everyone in the lab. In the course of a conversation, Adams learned that one of the ablest metallurgists, Isaac Carroll, was seriously considering quitting. Carroll's boss, Felt, a project director who reported directly to the research director, had been giving Carroll a great deal of extra routine work to do. Not only was Carroll finding it difficult to complete his regular research activities and earn recognition for the quality of his performance, but he also found the additional work tedious and unsatisfying. Carroll had asked for a technician to serve as an assistant, but this request had been turned down.

Adams was unsure of what to do. He was convinced that Felt was unaware of Carroll's extreme dissatisfaction. Felt had a reputation for "pushing" people, although he was technically competent. But Adams was reluctant to broach the question to Felt; the two had never hit it off, and Felt had made it clear that he wanted no interference from the boss' assistant. Moreover, Adams was reluctant to speak directly to Grozia, for fear that he might be regarded as a "spy," and cause Carroll serious embarrassment. If word got out, Felt would feel that Carroll had gone over his head. At the same time, Carroll's resignation would be a serious and needless loss to the organization.

How would you handle this situation if you were Adams?

PROBLEM 3

QUITTING TIME

Eggert is the general manager of a large Eastern department store, with responsibility for directing most of the operating departments. For years, two of these departments—packaging and merchandise-marking (ticketing)—have been afflicted by a high turnover rate, failure to meet deadlines, and employee grievances.

Recently the situation in marking has improved significantly, although it is still far from satisfactory. Apparently the present supervisor in the marking department, Elsohn, is doing a good job—at least the selling departments are no longer complaining about incorrect ticketing or failure to have merchandise ready for floor display on time.

Recently Colson, the head of the packaging department, complained to Eggert that all sorts of disciplinary problems were being created by the way Elsohn was running his department. The two departments were physically adjacent, and Colson's employees noticed that the people in marking consistently stopped work 15 to 25 minutes before the end of the day to freshen up, gossip, and relax. There was a clear store rule that all personnel were to work until the closing bell had rung; ample time was provided during the day for employees to take breaks.

Colson said he could hardly enforce this rule in his own department so long as it was being flagrantly violated next door. Eggert promised to "look into the situation."

1. What would you do if you were Eggert? What information would you need? What criteria would you use in evaluating new data?
2. What are the dangers here?

PROBLEM 4

A LETTER TO THE PRESIDENT

The company president has received a long letter from an employee in the shipping department, complaining that he did not get a promotion to which he felt himself entitled. The reason, claims the employee, is that his supervisor has a grudge against him. Moreover, he claims, the supervisor's judgment cannot be relied on. In his letter, he discloses a number of violations of company policy that the supervisor has countenanced, and a number of private deals that have been worked out in the department.

What should the company president do with this information?

THE FRIENDLY DIVISION MANAGER

"I'm the manufacturing superintendent of the Snyder Division of the Amherst Corporation. I've been on the job in this plant for six months and I have a big problem—my boss, Clarence Akron, who has been Division Manager for about fifteen years. Clarence loves his job and he loves people. He knows all 700 employees in the Division by name and he spends a great deal of time wandering about, listening to people's problems and helping supervisors out of trouble. He's even pitched in on the assembly line when we've had a tight schedule.

"All this is fine—except for two things. He spends so much time talking to individual employees and to first-line supervisors that he never has time to spare for his office work and the long-range problems. And his whole approach makes my job—keeping the manufacturing end of the Division going—much harder. I never know what he has told the men—so in a way he's more on top of *my* job than I am. I'm just a figurehead. Frankly, I'm ambitious. I'd like to do a good job here, but his attitude makes it hard—though he's always been friendly and personally helpful to me. The other men on my level, the chief engineer, the sales manager, and the office manager, all have the same troubles I have, though they've been here longer and have got used to it.

"What should I do? Should I talk to Clarence alone? What should I say to him? Should I try to get the rest of management to see him as a delegation? Should I talk to the Vice President (I know him rather well) next time he pays us a visit from Corporation headquarters? Or is there some other approach?"

Specialization

Seldom is an organization composed of people who all do the same type of work. The typical pattern is for individuals and groups to *specialize* in one function or activity, leaving other functions to their colleagues in other departments or divisions. In fact, specialization has become so common in contemporary life that we tend to take it for granted. In this chapter, however, we shall see that the use of specialization as a means of increasing output and efficiency has many repercussions on the patterns of human relations in the organization.

Specialization creates two kinds of problems:

The first you should be familiar with, based on the discussion in Chapter 2—the effect on job satisfaction.

The second effect, to which most of this chapter will be devoted, is the problem of coordination.

SPECIALIZATION AND JOB SATISFACTION

Actually, we can think of two kinds of specialization: specialization by task and specialization of people.[1] Task specialization, the most familiar, involves breaking jobs down into their finest components (as suggested by Taylor and his disciples). Task specialization requires *less* training. The concept behind task specialization is simple enough: It is more efficient to have each employee perform a single function than to have everybody do a little of everything. For example, as soon as a service station has enough volume of business, one man concentrates on selling gasoline, another on lubrication, and others on repairs.

More specifically, task specialization has these clearly recognizable advantages:

---

[1] Victor Thompson, *Modern Organization* (New York: Knopf, 1961), pp. 25-27.

1. It reduces training costs, for a worker learns more quickly when he concentrates on a single function.

2. It avoids the waste of time involved in shifting a man from one kind of job to another, and enables each man fully to develop his skills for a particular job.

3. It makes unnecessary the duplication of equipment that would otherwise be used on only a part-time basis.

4. It enables the company to purchase more specialized equipment.

5. It simplifies the problem of developing job controls.

6. It reduces wage costs by making it possible to hire less-skilled workers.

People specialization, on the other hand, involves hiring employees with high levels of training: product designers, reliability engineers, market researchers, and the like.

Task specialization, as we saw in Chapter 2, can create serious morale and motivational problems. In the typical white- or blue-collar factory, many employees have little sense of accomplishment, autonomy, or identification with work; their fragmented jobs yield both monotony and drudgery. Further, these workers realize they can be easily replaced.

Individual specialists, on the other hand, often work on depth-attention jobs, identify strongly with their work, and may even enjoy professional status. And they enjoy substantial job security, as we saw in Chapter 3.

Each has a specialized task to do which is not the result of breaking down some larger, more complex task. Indeed, some of these jobs did not exist before new activities and responsibilities in business required their addition.

THE NEED FOR COORDINATION

Managers sometimes believe they can get something for nothing. They can get the advantages of increased specialization by dividing up more complex jobs into simpler jobs or by hiring additional trained specialists. But they ignore the possibility that the problems of coordination so created may more than outweigh the advantages gained. Dividing up work is easier than putting the parts back together again. The purpose of any organization is to complete work: the production of goods or services. Individual task performance is only useful insofar as it serves to facilitate the attainment of the over-all objective of the enterprise. No matter how hard an employee works, his efforts are wasted unless they integrate with those of his fellow workers.

Acme Distributors used telephone operators to take phoned-in customer orders. The operators formerly typed up the forms for use by central billing and the warehouse. The company recently added a group of special typists to transcribe the operators' pencilled notes. Now there is conflict because some operators use abbreviations and have poor handwriting. Also, some operators fail to look up in the catalogs the serial numbers of special items, thus requiring the transcribers to do extra work. None of these problems existed, of course, when one girl did a total job.

How specialization creates unproductive work has been described in a popular spoof on the internal workings of large organizations, *Parkinson's Law*.

Parkinson's Law.   Parkinson argues with adroit satire that the number of people employed in a given department within an organization has no relationship to the amount of work that needs to be done. In order to improve their own position vis-à-vis others in the organization, managers are motivated to expand their staffs needlessly: "An official wants to multiply subordinates, not rivals." However, this grand strategy for self-aggrandizement rarely reveals itself because the new personnel make work for one another—with the organization's strong propensities for division of labor. Parkinson describes how seven officials can keep busy doing work that was formerly handled by a single employee of an English ministry, Mr. A.

> For these seven make so much work for each other that all are fully occupied and A is actually working harder than ever. An incoming document may well come before each of them in turn. Official E decides that it falls within the province of F, who places a draft reply before C, who amends it drastically before consulting D, who asks G to deal with it. But G goes on leave at this point, handing the file over to H, who drafts a minute that is signed by D and returned to C, who revises his draft accordingly and lays the new version before A.
> What does A do? He would have every excuse for signing the thing unread, for he has many other matters on his mind. Knowing now that he is to succeed W next year, he has to decide whether C or D should succeed to his own office. He had to agree to G's going on leave even if not yet strictly entitled to it. He is worried whether H should not have gone instead, for reasons of health. He has looked pale recently—partly but not solely because of his domestic troubles. Then there is the business of F's special increment of salary for the period of the conference and E's application for transfer to the Ministry of Pensions. A has heard that D is in love with a married typist and that G and F are no longer on speaking terms—no one seems to know why. So A might be tempted to sign C's draft and have done with it. But A is a conscientious man. Beset as he is with problems created by his colleagues for themselves and for him— created by the mere fact of these officials' existence—he is not the man to shirk his duty. He reads through the draft with care, deletes the fussy paragraphs added by C and H, and restores the thing back to the form preferred in the first instance by the able (if quarrelsome) F. He corrects the English—none of these young men can write grammatically—and finally produces the same reply he would have written if officials C to H had never been born. Far more people have taken far longer to produce the same result. No one has been idle. All have done their best. And it is late in the evening before A finally quits his office and begins the return journey to Ealing.[2]

---

[2] C. Northcote Parkinson, *Parkinson's Law* (Boston: Houghton Mifflin, 1957), pp. 5-6.

Technology and Human Relations

Buried here is an important principle of organizational behavior: **The division of labor is responsible for a predictable pattern of human relations.** Anything that changes the specialization is going to change human relations. For example, if we give A some additional assignment it is likely to change *whom* he sees, *when* he sees them, *how often,* and *what* he must do in relation to other people he contacts.

Managers are often insensitive to how profoundly rather small changes in technology, by altering jobs, can change human relations. Take, for example, the division of labor in a restaurant.[3] Generally, a single bartender prepares drinks in response to the verbal orders of waitresses who have just come from their customers. The result is usually a group clustered around the hapless bartender asking when their order will be ready. To complicate matters, there may be misunderstandings concerning what combination of drinks was ordered by a specific waitress. Is it the fault of the inadequately enunciated requests of the waitress or the poor memory of the bartender?

---

[3] William F. Whyte, *Men at Work* (Homewood, Illinois: Dorsey Press), pp. 128-129. The analysis here has also benefited from Elias Porter, *Manpower Development* (New York: Harper & Row, 1964).

Change in technology provides change in human relations.

Before

Bartender or counterman

After

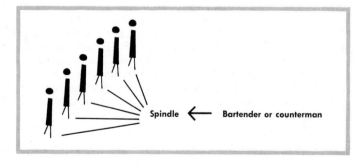

Spindle ← Bartender or counterman

Now look at the changes in the pattern of relationships if the restaurant changes technology by insisting that all waitresses write their orders and place them on a spindle to await the bartender:

1. Contacts between waitresses and bartenders are reduced by the buffer action of the spindle and written orders.

2. The bartender can now exercise more initiative by rearranging and combining waitresses' orders in such a way as to make his own job easier or more pleasant (for instance, mixing all the Manhattans at the same time). (In the words of modern computer theory, serial-order events have been transposed by providing a display device with possibilities of random access, the spindle.)

3. Waitresses no longer have to wait in line to place their orders; the spindle becomes a "queuing device" for holding their orders in place.

4. Disagreement over who ordered what can be resolved by written evidence rather than more fallible individual memories. Furthermore, differences in voice characteristics and in ability to demand service are cancelled and greater equality among waitresses is maintained.

Coordination among Specialists

Management anticipated that, if well-trained, highly motivated specialists could be hired or trained and if each did his job correctly, coordination would take care of itself. But if we watch these staff and technical specialists at work, we see the same human-relations problems in coordination that we glimpsed both with the operators and transcribers and the bartenders and waitresses.

Clearly, the problems of coordination have increased as more specialists have been created, more tasks subdivided, and thus more human relations created. Coordination is a human-relations problem: How to get A to do his job so that it fits into the way B and C are doing their work. The modern organization is characterized by ever greater interdependence, at all levels of the hierarchy. There are more human-relations problems to be resolved if work is to be accomplished and over-all organizational goals attained.

To express it another way: Specialization has increased the relative importance of lateral relationships, as distinct from hierarchical (superior-subordinate) relationships. Both managers and nonmanagers alike spend a great deal of their time in contact with other people in the organization (and some outside the organization, as well, such as with government, unions, suppliers, customers) who are neither their boss nor their subordinate. Many of these relationships involve people at roughly the same status level. In one organization, for example, managers had to maintain close working relationships with as many as 70 or 80 people who were not superiors or subordinates.[4]

---

[4] Leonard Sayles, *Managerial Behavior* (New York: McGraw-Hill, 1964), p. 43.

But we can go further than noting simply the lateral-relations explosion that characterizes the modern organization. By watching the interaction of managers, professionals, technicians, and blue-collar people in large, complex organizations, we can identify certain recurring patterns of relationship. These patterns encompass the ways in which specialists in the organization come together, the recurring problems they face, and the feelings these problems generate.

Research suggests that there are at least five distinctive patterns: [5] Work flows, service flows, advisory flows, audit flows, and stabilization flows. Each poses problems that are distinct from the supervisory problems already dealt with. These relationships will be described in turn.

Work-Flow

Nearly every employee is in an intermediate position in the flow of work: He depends on those who precede him to prepare supplies, papers, or semi-finished parts for him to work on; those who follow him similarly depend on him. For example, a factory clerk may collect and summarize production data; he then sends it on to an accountant who processes the data further. Or, the waitress gives her order to pantry personnel; they in turn are served by runners from the kitchen; the cooks and their assistants in turn prepare the food for the runners. Each of these is an example of a work-flow sequence. Note that employees who must time their actions to coincide with the needs of others may not work near one another; they may not even have a common supervisor. Naturally these relationships generate problems.

Who is at fault? Friction is normal on any job, for work rarely goes as planned. And when things go wrong in a specialized organization, people are tempted to avoid accepting responsibility and to pass the buck to others involved in the work sequence. For example:

> A shortage of material develops on the night shift. When asked why, the night-shift workers protest that the day shift failed to keep the material bins full. They insist the day shift never does its share; they just used up the stocks provided by the night truckers.

> The accounting department is criticized for failure to meet its schedule for making reports. It blames the production department for failing to provide needed data on time.

---

[5] The discussion here draws on the work of George Strauss in "Tactics of Lateral Relationship: The Purchasing Agent," in *Administrative Science Quarterly*, Vol. 7, No. 2 (September 1962), pp. 161-186, and "Work Flow, Interfunctional Rivalry and Professionalism," *Human Organization*, Vol. 23, No. 2 (Summer 1964), pp. 137-149, and of Leonard Sayles, *op. cit.*, pp. 93-103.

This natural tendency of each person to defend his own interests hurts the organization as a whole. Employees sometimes devote more energy to proving that another is at fault for some problem than in trying to solve the problem. This difficulty is accentuated when higher management pressures subordinates for results at any cost, and imposes heavy penalties. Thus, the system of rewards built into the organization frequently motivates its members to think only of their own personal interests. In so doing, they make it more difficult for others to do their job.

Status complications.   Normally, higher-status employees give orders to lower-status employees, and not vice versa. This is true throughout life. We expect to have to respond to persons of higher prestige than ourselves; in fact, we are often very reluctant to try to approach them first. We wait to be approached, and similarly we expect to initiate action to people we feel occupy positions of less prestige than ourselves.

Sometimes the work-flow patterns *reverse* this normal relationship. We have all seen situations such as this:

> A clerk or office boy is sent by the department head to ask a skilled crafts-man in another group if it would not be possible to speed up his work on a particular job. The employee bristles when approached in this manner by a mere "clerk" and may, if anything, slow down his operation.

This is a critical source of human-relations difficulties in the restaurant industry. Whenever female waitresses give orders to male bartenders, or when young pantry personnel give orders to veteran chefs, periodic blow-ups hurt productivity as well as job satisfaction.[6]

---

[6] William F. Whyte, *Human Relations in the Restaurant Industry* (New York: McGraw-Hill, 1948), pp. 105-108.

Work-flow contacts.

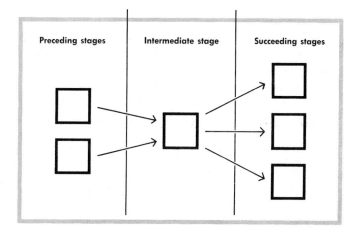

| Preceding stages | Intermediate stage | Succeeding stages |

Uneven patterns. Most people want to achieve some equilibrium in their dealings with others: They don't want two people asking them to do something one day and 25 the next. Employees are willing to tolerate a certain amount of variation in this contact pattern from day to day as the work load varies; however, this range of tolerance can be exceeded only at the expense of much tension and discontent. Unfortunately, work rarely flows evenly through an organization. There are usually periods of crisis when everyone feels under tension, tempers are short or nonexistent, and normally suppressed conflicts break out into open hostility.

Some of the crises are periodic. At the end of the month clerks in the billing department work under high pressure; store clerks rush to spruce up their display before the monthly visit of the district manager. Many organizations go through annual cycles. In a toy company, for instance, design changes must be made in the spring; production works hardest from July to October, while shipping is under greatest pressure till the first of December. Other crises are unplanned. A vital piece of equipment breaks down, a rush order comes in from an important customer, the "brass" from the main office arrives on a surprise inspection trip.

In each of these situations the normal level of contacts is left far behind as members of the organization scurry around to get other individuals and groups on whom they depend to get their work out faster, cheaper, or more impressively. When work routines are interrupted, management becomes worried, and frequently many levels of the hierarchy descend simultaneously on some small group of employees, thus making matters even worse.

Design and development decisions. Sometimes problems between specialized departments arise not from the actual flow of work but from the need to coordinate decisions. Here we are faced with many of the problems we have already discussed, plus some others that we have not as yet considered.

Increasingly in modern industry, the work of each department is so closely coordinated with that of the other departments in the organization that each department's decision affects all the rest; and yet no department can make a decision without knowing what the others are doing. Problems of this sort resemble simultaneous equations, where no one part of the problem can be solved without solving all the rest. In industry, such problems often arise in large engineering laboratories that design new products, or in "job shops" that are constantly planning the production of items to the customer's special order. Each department or group controls a part of the "answer"—but these parts must be assembled before the organization's problem is solved.

To see these problems in action, let us look at the process of designing a new-model TV set, as we observed it in one company. The Engineering Department is, of course, the one most directly concerned, and it consists of five sections. *Electrical* determines in theoretical terms how the set will be made (technically: what the over-all "system" will be). *Mechanical* tries to fit the components together; it often finds that Electrical's theoretical plans are impractical or even that one Electrical engineer's theoretical suggestions are incompatible with those of another. *Chassis* designs the cabinet; close coordination is required if the components are to fit into the cabinet. This is not as easy as it sounds, since Electrical and Mechanical are constantly designing improvements which give better reception, but which conflict with the company's over-all goal of producing an ever-thinner, lighter set.

Automation designs the machinery which makes the printed circuits and attaches the tubes to it; in contrast to Electrical, which wants an ever-more "sophisticated" set, Automation wants one that is simple enough to be reduced to printed circuitry and put together mechanically. *Industrial Engineering* determines the techniques by which the set will be manufactured (other than the operations that are 100 per cent automated). Like Automation, it seeks to eliminate what it feels to be unnecessary frills.

Further complicating over-all coordination are the pressures brought by outside departments: Sales wants an attractive product that will sell easily, and Manufacturing wants a set that is easy to put together. And management as a whole is interested in keeping costs low, profits high.

Note that in this case no one section can make modifications without affecting all the others. A change in cabinet, for instance, may require adjustments by every other section, yet each adjustment may in turn require further compensating adjustments elsewhere. Each section has its own vested interest. Electrical, with its goal of technical perfection, conflicts, for example, with Industrial Engineering's goal of manufacturing ease.

Since a new model must be designed each year, intergroup conflicts tend to reach a crescendo as the time for a final decision approaches. During the early part of the year there is little pressure to resolve agreements, and each section is free to work on its own pet projects. As the deadline draws near, an increasing number of compromises and adjustments must be made, tempers grow raw, and human-relations problems begin to complicate the technical ones. Each engineer likes to feel that he has *completed* his end of the job and hates to reconsider his position just to please another section. No engineer likes to sacrifice his own brainchild.

Complicating all these problems are the changing status relationships between departments. When TV was new, the major problem was to design a workable set, and Electrical was the highest-status section. Today the emphasis is on sales appeal and manufacturing ease. Electrical still thinks its function is the most important one, but management seems to favor other sections when it makes critical decisions and hands out promotions.

We have gone into the problem of this TV engineering department at some length because we think its problems are typical of many in management. When an organization is small, and specialization at a minimum, the problem of coordination can be solved by one man who keeps all the details in his head and can predict by himself all the possible ramifications of each possible change. Once the organization passes a certain size, however, no one person can keep track of all the variables. At this point, good communication among the specialists becomes all-important—both to enable each person to get all the information he needs to make a decision, and also to help preserve organizational morale.

Service Relationships

Often an organization centralizes auxiliary functions such as maintenance, purchasing, laboratory analysis, and computer processing. These "service relationships" between the suppliers of services and their in-company "customers" involve distinctive human problems.

Bottleneck operations. Intergroup competition may manifest itself in a struggle to corral as much as possible of a "scarce resource." The incident below involving interdepartment competition for scarce maintenance facilities, as described by a departmental supervisor in a large industrial plant, will help illustrate what we mean:

> "Whenever we need equipment repaired, we put a tag on it saying what we think is wrong and send it to the Repair Department. We have a series of different-color tags which we can use. We use a white tag for a routine job. Yellow tags mean important but not top priority. A red tag means the repair is highly urgent and production will be held up until the piece is returned. Well, we suddenly burned out one vital unit and I sent it down with a red tag because we needed it back desperately. When I didn't hear from them for several days, I really got mad and decided to check on what was holding us up. Well, you can imagine how burned up I was when I entered the Repair Department to see that every piece they had down there was red-tagged."

This approach, of course, simply makes scarce resources become scarcer. When one supervisor decides that he may not have all the supplies or repair facilities available that he might need in the future, he takes steps to build up an ample reserve. When other supervisors follow suit, a potential shortage becomes an actual scarcity and the whole priority system breaks down.

This kind of situation strains relations among the individuals and groups that are competing for the scarce resource, and each accuses the other of selfishly trying to grab more than its share. Needless to say, the common supervisor to whom these groups report constantly will have to mediate among them and resolve intergroup disputes.

Unbalanced pressure. In organizational terms, pressure springs from the efforts of *others* to originate action for you when you are unable to originate for others. Pressure is great when one person repeatedly and consistently attempts to do so (the supervisor who comes back constantly to ask why a certain job has not been completed), or when a relatively large number of people come to you with conflicting demands (as was the case in the repair department described above, and in most service departments).

In either instance, the endless pressure is bound to keep you in a state of unrelieved discomfort. Look back to the "Case of the Red Tags" from the point of view of the repair department. Imagine the pressure the repairmen are under who control the scarce resource! Here is an example of a job subjected to constant pressure, as described by the supervisor in charge:

"We are part of a special purchasing division that services the engineering department. It is our job to order parts and materials for the various research projects the engineers undertake. Well, it has gotten so that nothing is routine anymore. The engineers are always engaging in rush projects—you know, someone gets a brainstorm and they want to get it under way immediately. So they come down with the orders they want filled. First they try to get you to tell them it will be done within an hour. By the next morning they're calling the boss to complain you are not working on it fast enough, and by the next afternoon they are in the office themselves trying to get you to put their order ahead of someone else's. They can't seem to understand that it all takes time and we've got lots of other rush jobs. It seems as though we are always under pressure; someone is always asking for greater speed than we can give them. Let me tell you, I have never experienced such tension; I don't know how much longer we can take it."

Reaction to pressures. The tensions created by these pressures take their toll in departmental efficiency. The rate of personnel turnover is often high, while those who stay usually resort to one or the other of the following patterns of defense or adaptation:

1. Some workers affect an air of resignation, though they may be seething inside; they work off their tensions on their families, friends, or themselves (in terms of psychosomatic illness).

2. Others fight back. They give vent to their frustration by dealing with their tormentors in an aggressive fashion. One observer has related a classic

Pressure resulting from conflicting demands.

case of how a group defends itself against excessive pressure from other groups:

> The Ship's Store department on a large ship found that certain groups were always demanding rapid service on complicated requisitions. The Ship's Store workers, moving with speed and efficiency, merely announced that these offending groups would have to fill out in perfect detail the multicopy, excessively complicated formal requisition sheets that were required by an official, but rarely observed, rule. These same pressuring groups also were denied their share of the personal items that were distributed, in part, at the discretion of the Stores department: stationery, film, etc.

Unfortunately, this response may further reduce organizational efficiency and lead to additional pressure.

3. Still others develop a cordial personal relationship toward the offending groups in the hope of cutting down the pressure. The expert at this approach uses a mixture of kidding, sympathetic listening, and sincere concern. This is the approach followed by the men's store that hires a delectable blonde to handle complaints.

4. Finally, some workers establish their own system of priorities and firmly resist all efforts to violate it. This is what the rushed butcher does when he asks his customers to take a number and wait until it is called.

Employees who work side by side day after day often work out their own systems for accommodating the demands they make on one another. These systems may be reinforced by group norms that forbid fellow members to push or pressure one another. Large, specialized departments, however, even when they are located close together, seldom develop such informal patterns of accommodation.

The supervisor's responsibility.   The alert supervisor is sensitive to the impact of the organization on his subordinates. What can he do when this is the source of trouble? Here is one easy solution:

> Joe Santini was in charge of the central offices of a diversified manufacturing company. As one of their miscellaneous duties, some of his men were assigned the job of moving office equipment when departments were relocated. Santini discovered that one of his most loyal subordinates, in charge of this operation, was about to quit, claiming that he couldn't take the "strain of his job any more." After investigation the supervisor discovered that the man who was ready to quit had been subject to a series of conflicting pressures. The company had been undergoing rapid change and expansion. In the process everyone wanted their facilities moved at the same time, each claiming that their job had priority and that the "President is vitally interested in our getting into our new quarters as soon as possible." This man had no way to resist their demands—he was many levels below all the managers who came into his office to get service. Santini's solution was a direct one. He got top-management approval for a new policy: All requests for moves were to come directly to his office and he would assign a priority to them based on date of submission and company needs. Because of Santini's relatively high position in the organiza-

tion, he could not be intimidated as his subordinate had been, and in turn, the subordinate found that there was no longer so much pressure in his job.

This solution represents just one small example of reorganizing the pattern of interpersonal contacts required by the division of labor as a means of solving certain morale problems.

Advisory Relationships

Modern organizations employ many technical experts to provide advice. An internal advisor can help solve questions such as the following. To the plant engineer: "We seem to be getting more machine breakdowns on line 24 than on any of the others; what's wrong?" To the company lawyer: "Our largest customer is threatening to shift to a competitor; is it legal for us to give him a special price advantage?" To the packaging department: "We're getting a lot of breakage in shipments; what's wrong with our packing methods?" Note that most of these questions concern recurring problems that the normal organizational procedures have not been able to cope with successfully.

The personnel department has a typical advisory relationship (although it may have other nonadvisory functions, as well). Using this department as a case study, let us examine some of the human problems inherent in the advisor's role.

What is "advice"? Many theorists draw a sharp line between line and staff. The staff man is expected to provide technical information or advice and counsel (because he is an expert in the field), but he does not make decisions. In practice, however, these theoretical distinctions are blurred, and the technical expert performs all three tasks.

When providing information, the personnel manager simply furnishes the facts that will help the manager make sound, well-informed decisions. For instance:

1. The disciplinary clause of the union agreement means thus and so.
2. The "going rate" for engineers like Jones in our present labor market is $850 per month.
3. Other companies in the metropolitan area require their carpenters to move small machinery when necessary in the course of their work.

Or he may play a more active role and furnish advice:

1. You are likely to provoke a wildcat strike if you give Bill Williams a disciplinary layoff.
2. On the basis of the record, Jones looks like a better bet for the promotion, since the man on the job will have to assume a good deal of initiative without close supervision.
3. If you hire Smith at that salary, you are going to have some dissatisfied older employees in your departments.

Finally, he can make decisions:

1. Don't discharge Brown; give him a warning slip.
2. Hire Green to replace the man who left.
3. Pay White $100 per week for that new job.

Sometimes there is a very narrow line between providing facts and providing advice. Thus, by selecting his facts carefully, the personnel manager can actually sway the line manager's decision one way or the other. Also, what is given as "advice" may be interpreted by the recipient as a decision.

The temptation to exceed the advisory role.   Historically, management has tended to turn over more and more functions to well-trained experts who have specialized knowledge in a relatively narrow field. When experts were first used to supplement the skills of line supervisors, the distinctions between information, advice, and decision-making were rarely made. Further, management showed a readiness to accept expert advice uncritically. Often, since management was very anxious to avoid trouble with the unions, for example, the industrial relations department actually *told* supervisors whom to hire, what to pay them, and how to answer their grievances. The result was often disastrous to the prestige and status of supervisors.

In practice, it takes a strong-willed personnel manager to resist the temptation to become a decision-maker. Once he has grown accustomed to providing advice and counsel, he may find it irresistible to take the next step and actually make decisions. Even when the personnel manager is careful not to usurp the line supervisor's responsibility, his actions may still be misinterpreted. The following case illustrates this problem:

> A grievance was filed against Gus Homes, a departmental supervisor, for failing to divide overtime equally. Homes argued that employees who failed to meet production standards on regular work should not be given overtime. The union contract said nothing about overtime, although general plant practice sanctioned equal division. The personnel director of the company, anxious to avoid any union bargaining on the overtime issue, urged Homes to change his mind. Homes refused. Some weeks later, Homes was transferred to a less desirable job. The plant grapevine reported that the manager had "given him the axe" on the recommendation of the personnel director. The truth of the matter was that the manager had believed for some time that Homes should be removed from his department. The overtime situation was just one among many reasons that seemed to justify the move.
>
> From this point on, other supervisors thought twice about refusing the personnel director's "advice." His recommendations had become cloaked with line authority; he had become another boss.

When the manager wants more than advice.   Line managers, themselves, may encourage staff experts to broaden their range of activities. The willingness of the personnel man to help out on a difficult problem, for example, may provide the supervisor with welcome relief from burdensome responsibilities. In effect, he says to the personnel man, "Good, you handle the personnel and I'll take care of all the technical problems." Then, if a decision backfires, the line supervisor can simply point out that he was following personnel's advice. What a pleasant relief this excuse provides!

And so it is easy to understand the line supervisor's reluctance to question the expertise of the specialists whom top management has hired. The subordinate manager who challenges their ability runs the risk of making a bad decision for which he will have to bear all the responsibility. He may even prefer to interpret "advice" as a decision in order to avoid assuming responsibility and in order to pass the buck to the expert.

Paradoxically, a manager may resent an advisory group's power and at the same time grumble that it is failing to take responsibility for decisions. As one supervisor expressed it:

> "We stay away from the industrial relations department as much as possible —they're always trying to sell you on some new program that makes more work for you. But then when you go to them with a problem you can't get a straight answer from them; they won't tell you how to handle it. They give you a lot of pros and cons and stuff that leaves you more confused than when you went in."

Broader contacts.   Staff advisors are in position to short-circuit the usual chain of command and to communicate with people at all organizational levels. Frequently they have *top* management's ear, and this fact increases lower management's reluctance to disregard staff's advice. Staff men may also develop close relations with men at the *lower* levels of the organizational ladder. For example, personnel people often provide a more sympathetic ear for the disturbed employee than does his own supervisor, and he may prefer to take his troubles to them. If this happens too often, the line manager will lose contact with his employees and their respect as well. For instance, a manufacturing superintendent once told us, "My foremen have learned that they can get action a lot faster if they go to staff than if they see me. Except when there is trouble I am pretty much a figurehead—and then I am the one who has to bear the blame."

Caught in this dilemma some managers take the easy way out—they pass the buck to higher management and to staff. In effect, they say, "Don't blame me. Blame the other guy."

Conflicting advice.   We have simplified, of course, by implying that at one time only one advisor (the personnel man) is involved. In fact, in the modern organization, expertise is distributed among many specialized groups and a given problem can call for knowledge of engineering, standards, methods, personnel, and finance. The boundary lines are never clear and each group feels that theirs is the real "answer" to the difficulty. Thus, a manager may be deluged with helpers, many of whom are inclined to remind him of their associations with higher management in order to encourage his adoption of a particular solution to the problem.

Audit Relationships

In traditional theory a manager watches everything his subordinates are doing to be sure that they are not violating the rules or standards of the organization and that they are achieving their work goals. In large organizations, however, it is often difficult for the manager to make these observations directly. For one thing, where the work is highly technical, the manager may not be trained to evaluate its adequacy.

For example, even an engineering manager who is not a specialist in circuits may be unable to answer the questions: "How good is the new design for that circuit?" Lack of adequate technical knowledge may also prevent the manager from assessing the adequacy of subordinates' financial and personnel skills.

Similarly, the rules, procedures, and standards of an organization may be so complicated and extensive that no single manager can administer all of them. Just imagine how many personnel, engineering, and financial procedures alone there may be in the typical large manufacturing company. Such procedures have been developed over the years to facilitate coordination among departments and jobs on the assumption that carefully circumscribing the jobs of specialists will make it less likely that they will do things that handicap the work of others.

Finally, the manager has difficulty overseeing the observance of standards because of the tendency of subordinates to hide or distort unfavorable information (see Chapter 15). Not being able to evaluate everything himself and not fully trusting all that he sees and is told, the manager in the large organization must use specialists who help him appraise and evaluate the work of subordinates. Yet their work, in turn, creates a host of human-relations problems.

Standards are ambiguous.

The engineers inspecting a finished piece of electronic equipment claimed that it would not operate in a room kept at 100 degrees temperature. The department that built the equipment argued that the humidity was too high in the room and that if the air had been dryer it would have held up, as the standards require, and operate at 100 degrees.

Standards conflict.

The inventory control department told the production supervisor to ask people to work overtime because his output is below scheduled requirements. However, the accounting office has issued an ultimatum that all overtime work must cease since the budgeted overtime allowance has already been exceeded for this particular accounting period. The supervisor spends a good deal of time going back and forth between these two "audit" groups, trying to get one or the other to concede.

Auditing generates suspicions and distrust.

> Quality-control inspectors often say that bad work is hidden so that it won't be discovered and reported, thus making the job of checking quality that much more difficult. In trying to do a thorough job and overcome the hurdles that are put in their way, the inspectors appear to be overly eager to find trouble. Many operators and their managers assert, "Inspectors have to find a certain number of errors to justify their existence and their fancy budgets."

Additional problems are created because these relationships are often so sporadic that there isn't an opportunity to develop regularized patterns of inter-action.[7]

Stabilization Relationships

Somewhat similar to the audit pattern is the stabilization relationship, except that the contacts are more frequent and regular. These relationships grow out of the need to coordinate the separate parts of an organization, each of which pursues its own objectives. As with auditing, this function would have been performed by the manager himself before the age of specialists. Let us look at some typical examples:

> A manager would like to reduce his output tomorrow because two machines will be down for repairs. He can't make this decision himself, however, because it will obviously affect other departments in the flow of work, departments that rely on those parts for their assembly requirements.

> A manager wants to give an employee a large raise to keep another employer from bidding him away. The raise is an unmixed blessing for the particular manager, but it could hurt other managers who have to explain why their best employees are not getting comparable increases.

In the first case, the manager will have to have his production schedule checked with production-control department. In the second case, a salary administrator will have to give approval. Thus, stabilizing relationships involve getting approval for certain critical decisions from experts who are supposed to keep the total organization's needs in view. As in auditing relationships, the needs are often not absolute and fixed; there is much room for differences of opinion. What will actually happen may be the product of the respective negotiating skills of the individuals involved. Possibly, as some have argued,

---

[7] A good analysis of these problems with some solutions is presented by Herbert Simon and others, *Centralization vs. Decentralization in Organizing the Controller's Department* (New York: Financial Executives' Institute, 1954).

in the future computers will determine the true optimal course of action, thus eliminating any need for haggling.[8]

A persistent problem is that both auditing and stabilization relationships force managers to contend with multiple sources of influences all pulling in various, often inconsistent directions. For example, the personnel department may urge managers to utilize lower-skilled employees because they are easier to hire in a tight labor market while at the same time the engineering department may be demanding more exacting work. The astute manager learns to sense which requirements are the most dangerous to ignore and adjust his behavior accordingly. At times, personnel considerations predominate, then engineering, and perhaps later on financial.

ORGANIZATIONAL IMPLICATIONS OF INCREASING SPECIALIZATION

As noted before, many people think of the organization as a pyramid with all decisions being made at the top and all orders passing down from the top, to be obeyed by the subordinates below. But reality is more complicated. As specialization has increased, so has the need for obtaining effective cooperation and coordination between specialized work groups, if work is to move smoothly through the various stages of production, if service groups are to be spared overloading, and if advisors, auditors, and stabilizers are to be used properly.

With hierarchical relationships it is clear who is boss and who is subordinate; but lateral relationships are less clear since no one is clearly superior to another. Hence, lateral relationships lead to much intergroup friction and competition for status and influence. Unless managers are effective in mitigating these conflicts, great inefficiency results.

Specialists often identify more with their respective groups than with the organization as a whole. One reason, of course, is that the members of each group interact with one another more frequently than they do with persons outside the group. This identification with an informal group provides an important need satisfaction for employees who might otherwise feel lost in the larger organization (see Chapter 4). It enables them to relieve themselves of pent-up hostility and bolsters their self-confidence. These satisfactions can contribute to over-all efficiency, but, as we know, a price must be paid for these advantages.

What happens when groups of specialists concentrate on their own narrow interests rather than on the interests of the organization as a whole? Each group is intent on growing as influential as it can. Each seeks to impress its own point of view on the total organization. Each wishes to enhance its relative status or prestige. Though the competitive struggle may help keep each group

---

[8] Harold Leavitt and Thomas Whisler, "Management in the 1980's," *Harvard Business Review*, Vol. 36, No. 6 (November 1958), p. 47.

on its toes, it may also get out of hand, leading to destructive friction between groups, and doing serious injury to the organization as a whole.

Department In-Breeding

As time goes by, each specialized group—the accountants, the production men, the engineers—comes to adopt a distinctive point of view or "organizational character." [9] Each develops a certain dominant value or goal that shapes its entire way of doing things.

The "in-breeding" that develops within these specialized units makes it difficult to hammer out common agreement on interdepartment problems. Since representatives of each specialty have been conditioned to think in a characteristic way, they find it hard to work together with others as a team. (As we discovered in Chapter 12, these outside commitments present the committee chairman with one of his most difficult problems.) Here is a good description of what happens:

> We've refused to recognize or admit that the various components of our industrial machine are driven by different people with different motives. Sales, for example, is always looking for something to add to the product in order to gain competitive advantage . . . sales presses for changes to get an edge over competitors. Engineering wants changes too, but for an entirely different reason. They're always fighting for easier, cheaper production. Where Sales wants to add to the product, Engineering wants to simplify it. Production has a totally different idea. They know that their salvation lies in keeping the men at the machines doing the same thing over and over again. Any production man will tell you how and why repetitive work is the secret of mass production. And he'll fight changes at the drop of a suggestion.
>
> Thus we have three major divisions of one business looking at the same product from three conflicting points of view. Each of them tries to impress on top management that its contribution is the most important and in the process it pushes under the rug anything that might lower its own status, and slyly points up the faults of its "competitors."
>
> Is it any wonder that we have friction? And, mind you, this friction exists when people are working together with the best intentions. [10]

A sociologist looking at the same problem draws a similar conclusion, but in somewhat different terms:

> The over-all managerial problem has become more complex because each group of management specialists will tend to view the "interests of the enterprise" in terms which are compatible with the survival and the increase of its special function. That is, each group will have a trained capacity for its own function and a "trained incapacity" to see its relation to the whole. [11]

---

[9] For an excellent discussion of this point, see Philip Selznick, *Leadership in Administration* (New York, Harper & Row, 1957), pp. 38 ff.

[10] Bernard Davis, "The Pill's Grim Progress," *Esquire*, British edition, Vol. I, No. 3 (August 1954), p. 55; cited by Lt. Col. Lyndall F. Urwick, "The Span of Control—Some Facts about the Fables," *Advanced Management* (November 1956), p. 11.

[11] Reinhard Bendix, "Bureaucratization in Industry," in A. Kornhauser, R. Dubin, and A. Ross, *Industrial Conflict* (New York: McGraw-Hill, 1954), p. 170.

Earlier we noted some possible sources of conflict between advisory groups such as personnel departments and line management. This was but one example of a more general problem affecting the status particularly of first-level supervisors or foremen. Let us look at the impact of specialization on the foreman. Although we shall be discussing foremen in the following pages, most of the observations are just as relevant to office supervision at the first level.

Fifty years ago. A half-century ago, the foreman had almost absolute power. He did all the hiring (there were no personnel departments in those days) and he expected his men to show gratitude for being selected. If he picked friends or relatives, no one was in a position to object. The workers were completely dependent on him and naturally catered to his every whim. Often they even felt obliged to give him Christmas presents. As one old-timer put it:

> "In the old days the foreman used to be King—he really *was* a big shot—he'd walk down the plant floor like he really owned the place and you better do what he wanted fast—or you'd be looking for another job."

He had the sole power to discharge employees, for unions were rare and personnel standards nonexistent. If the stories of old-timers are to be believed, it was not uncommon for a foreman to fire a man "just to show who was boss and to keep people on their toes." Single-handed, he took care of all the activities that are now called scheduling, methods, safety, wage administration, and quality control (though many foremen of those days would not have known what the terms meant).

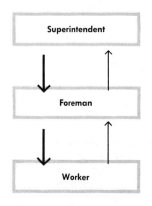

Foreman fifty years ago.

Scientific management. The first blow to the foreman's prestige was the scientific-management movement. The doctrine of specialization preached by its apostle, Frederick Taylor, meant that the foreman's job would be broken up into functional specialties. By 1930 many of the foreman's functions had been taken over by staff departments. *How* men worked was decided by the methods department; the *sequence* in which they handled products was decided by production control. Quality-control inspectors came into the foreman's shop to check on quality. A special organization arose to handle safety, and another was set up to take care of maintenance. In many cases even the hiring of workers—the foreman's traditional prerogative—was taken over by the personnel department, thus usurping one of the foreman's main sources of prestige and loyalty.

The union. During the 1930's the union made its first appearance in many plants. No longer was the worker obliged to humor the foreman in order to protect himself from being fired. Union membership sapped the loyalty of employees to their immediate supervisor, making it harder for him to make his orders stick. A radically new style of supervision was required, to which it would take the foreman years to adjust.

Worse, another official was added to those who could give the foreman "orders"—this official was the union steward, who was technically the foreman's subordinate.

Further, largely as a means of protecting itself against the union, management began to centralize the functions of discipline, promotion, and salary administration in the personnel department. Management's reasoning went this way: The union filed grievances whenever the foreman violated the contract or showed favoritism; and whenever a foreman in one plant made an unfortunate decision, the union regarded it as a precedent that could be used against the company in its other plants. Very well, said the company, we will centralize all these functions in the hands of experts, to insure a uniform, consistent policy.[12] What little power the foreman had left was now restricted by specific rules.

As a consequence, the foreman was exposed to conflicting orders and pressures from all sides. His fall from power was almost complete.

Loss of opportunity for promotion. The next blow fell when the foreman was deprived of his opportunity for promotion into higher management. More and more companies now began to recruit their future executives from among college graduates. In some companies the foreman was faced with a dead-end job.

The war. Next came the war period, with its frantic pressures to perform miracles with untrained help. And then the final blow: The advent of wage controls meant that in many cases the foreman's wages fell below the wages of some of the men he supervised, particularly the men on piece work. By the end of World War II, foreman morale was at an all-time low.

The foremen join a union. To protect themselves against this steady erosion of their prestige and power, a number of foremen decided to establish a union of their own. The Foreman's Association of America spread like wildfire.[13] The foreman reasoned that if other workers could bolster their position by joining a union, he would be foolish not to do the same thing himself. He

---

[12] Even nonunion companies adopted this policy, in an effort to eliminate possible causes of unionism.

[13] This was the period during which the National Labor Relations Board gave it the same status as other unions, a condition that was reversed by the Taft-Hartley Act. Foremen joined unions also to obtain the advantages of the wartime wage and salary stabilization programs.

felt himself excluded from management, relegated to the status of a mere messenger boy.

Management rediscovers the foreman.   The rapid spread of the Foreman's Association came as a traumatic shock to management. It was bad enough to lose workers to the union; if the first-line foremen were to defect as well, how could management hope to control its men?

Management's first reaction was an all-out attack on the Foreman's Association. The biggest battle was at Ford, where after a lengthy strike the Association was completely crushed. (Some companies are still suspicious of foremen's clubs of any kind, even those run by the YMCA.[14])

On a more constructive level, measures were taken to induce foremen to feel once again as though they were members of management. One measure was largely social: Management clubs, management dinners, and other activities were arranged at which foremen could mingle on a supposedly equal level with their superiors. Management also made an effort to improve downward communications by means of newsletters and meetings designed to help the foreman feel that he was "in the know" on company developments—hopefully, before the union learned of them.

But management's major efforts to rehabilitate the first-line foreman were in the area of training. At the least sophisticated level, the newly instituted

---

[14] At times with reason: we were present at one foreman club's "annual gripe session," to which management was invited. The interchange sounded remarkably like collective bargaining.

The growth of staff.

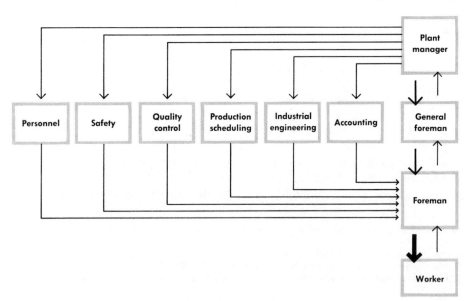

training programs consisted of trite exhortations to feel and act like management (though, as one foreman put it, "it is more important to be treated as management than to be told that you are management"). The better-conceived programs helped to equip foremen with the attitudes and skills necessary to lead men rather than drive them.

More substantial than any of these measures was the decision taken by some companies to cut down on the power of staff and restore it to the foreman. In many instances foremen were given the final say over hiring, discipline, and promotion. Some of the safety and quality-control departments, along with much of personnel, became advisory, with the foreman exercising actual control in these areas.

A few large companies have experimented with creating a kind of super-foreman. The number of employees reporting to the foreman have been doubled or tripled but he has been given a number of assistants and an advisory staff who report directly to him. Thus, for example, he has his own industrial engineer and personnel assistants. They assist him in setting work standards, dealing with grievances, scheduling, and so on. With his own staff the foreman no longer has to negotiate with outside staff departments.

All these efforts reflect a recognition that the foreman leadership role cannot be fractioned. If the foreman is to have the confidence, loyalty, and respect of his subordinates, he must have some significant control over those areas of decision-making that most affect his people. Surely work standards, grievance handling, and wage increments and similar subjects are examples of such crucial subjects. As we have seen elsewhere in this chapter, the challenge is to provide the advantages of specialization (and expert knowledge) without destroying the human relations necessary for a well-functioning organization.

CONCLUSION

Organizational human-relations problems often are mistakenly thought of solely as a by-product of autocratic supervision or uninteresting jobs. But normal frictions between specialist groups also contribute to human-relations problems. With increased emphasis on specialization in the modern organization and on "lateral relations" have come increasingly difficult problems of coordination.

We do not question the contribution of specialization to productivity. However, this chapter has emphasized that a manager's problems do not end when he has broken a single job into parts that can be handled by specialists. Managerial success depends on being able to put these parts together again and on developing coordinated cooperation among various individuals and subgroups so that the total organizational goals can be achieved.

The division of labor and the technology prescribe a pattern of human relations; change one and you change the other. Management typically underestimates the human relations consequence of even slight changes in specialization or layout or equipment. Yet these have an immediate impact on who must do what with whom, when, and where, and thus ultimately on the total job.

We examined in some detail the relationship conflicts inherent in five different patterns of on-the-job relationship prescribed by the division of labor. These were the work-flow, service, advisory, auditing, and stabilization patterns. We noted that any given manager must spend as much, if not more, of his time and energy engaged in these lateral types of relationship as he does dealing directly with subordinates and superiors. Over the years, the position and status of the first-line supervisor has been endangered by these new specialists, and new organizational arrangements have become necessary to avoid further deterioration.

Employees learn to identify with their own specialty and frequently lose sight of the over-all organization. Specialists tend to develop close ties with members of their own specialty and to develop distinctive points of view that clash with the points of view of other specialties. Employees who are supposed to integrate their work activities so that ideas, materials, or papers pass smoothly from department to department often engage in struggles for their "fair share" of rewards and prestige. Very often these clashes are not resolved by fixed rules or by top management decision but by bargaining. The weapons used in these intergroup struggles are techniques that enable men to avoid responsibility, to "pass the buck." Extreme specialization increases the likelihood of bottlenecks in the work flow, and those who are caught in the bottlenecks are subject to heavy pressures from fellow employees, such as mutually conflicting demands from other departments for quick service.

On the positive side, the increased emphasis on negotiations, the multiplicity of relationships that have to be maintained (compared to just dealing with superiors and subordinates) also gives much greater challenge to managerial jobs in the modern organization.[15]

We have suggested certain "short-term" remedies that may help to ameliorate some of the pressures arising from specialization. In Chapter 17 we shall consider the possibility of making basic changes in the organizational structure designed to eliminate some of the underlying causes of discontent.

PROBLEM 1

THE DOOLEY CASE

You were just promoted from a buyer at headquarters to the job of Purchasing Agent of the newly acquired Dooley Division of the General Products Company. In most companies the job of P.A. is to negotiate for the purchase of needed equipment and supplies on the basis of requisitions submitted by user departments. Most P.A.'s feel that at the plant level they should report to the plant manager.

As you left your old boss in central purchasing, he cautioned you,

---

[15] *Cf.* Leonard Sayles, ed., *Individualism and Big Business* (New York: McGraw-Hill, 1963).

"Be careful now. Remember, that division was pretty much a one-man firm till we bought them out. Bill Dooley would never have sold out if he didn't need capital for expansion. His outfit is a big money-maker and as Division Manager he is still the boss there. As long as he brings in the profits, no one from headquarters is going to interfere with his decisions. He's never had a P.A., and you are the only man sent from headquarters except the controller. The Big Boss [company president] persuaded him that having a P.A. was the fashionable thing to do, but I'm not sure if Dooley knows what purchasing is all about."

You arrived at the new plant—miles away from the main office. Dooley turned out to be a likable bundle of nerves of about 45. He showed you around, or tried to, because it seemed that he couldn't take a step without someone running to him for a decision—mostly on technical questions. The administrative problems he seemed to push off on Bob Wallace, the manufacturing superintendent.

As you went around, you noticed a sanding belt that was not of the latest design. So you commented that one supplier had developed a new product that was both cheaper and better. Dooley seemed delighted: "Well, get us the new product. That's what we have you here for." Wallace seemed a little unhappy but said nothing.

You were shown your new office, next to Wallace's and personnel's in the factory building; Dooley, the accounting office, and engineering were in the new building.

When Dooley left, Wallace sat down with you and began to speak haltingly. "To tell you the truth, I'm not sure how we will be able to use you. We never had a P.A. before. Dooley brought you in because headquarters said you might help out here. We are really a very small outfit with only 200 people, and we just don't believe in paper work. We have always worked so well together that we really don't need it. Now as I see your job, it is to keep the salesmen off Bill's and my shoulders—except for the few with whom we have developed very good relations—and to buy our supplies at the lowest possible cost."

Before you could comment, he was off on an errand, having instructed a general foreman to show you around. You asked what you felt were shrewd questions about costs and output, some of which the general foreman seemed reluctant to answer. You noticed several parts that it would seem better for the company to buy rather than make. When you suggested this, the general foreman answered, "This is a small firm, mister, and a lot of people depend on this work."

You tried to talk to the chief engineer. He showed a lot of interest in your background, your family, your housing arrangements, but he seemed to freeze up when you mentioned his work.

"It's highly technical . . . making big advances which are hard for a layman to understand. . . . Yes, we make up the blueprints and tell the shop what to make. They're a good lot. All local boys, been with us a long time, take care of the troubles before they come up. . . . Specifications? Well, insofar as we have them, we draw them up with Dooley; he tells Wallace what to buy . . . I guess you'll be helping Wallace on that. He handles all the paper work. He needs help. Things have been getting pretty busy recently."

The controller gave you a different picture.

"I'm going crazy here. Been trying to get some sort of cost analysis, but don't make any progress because there are no records kept of anything. If I want specific information, I can usually get it from Dooley or Wallace—they keep it in their heads—but I can't develop anything systematic. If I try to pin Dooley down on a new system of some type, he seems to listen, but he's off on a new problem before I get an answer. I just can't get cooperation from anyone."

Next day Wallace started giving you instructions. "Get in touch with some of the coal firms in town and see what price you can get. Maybe we can buy cheaper. Call up Louhurst Bros. and ask them to send over 10 gallons of Sherman-Williams white paint."

You asked if a purchase order was needed. He answered, "No. When the bill comes in, Mary in the office will call Jack in receiving, and if it came in OK, she'll send out a check. . . Oh, Bill or I sign it."

Just then the phone rang. It was Wallace again. "I'm sending over a salesman from the MM Company, who is going to make some widgets for us and it's a big order, so make up some kind of contract with him—he'll tell you what we agreed on—and send it to me to check over and sign."

1. How much could you realistically expect to accomplish during the next three months?
2. What problems would you face in getting acceptance of a real purchasing program?
3. How is your problem complicated by the personalities and vested interests of these people?
4. How do the various parties—Dooley, Wallace, the general foreman, the chief engineer, and the controller—view you?
5. What plans could you make for handling each of them?
6. What mistakes did you make at the outset?
7. How has the absence of specialization, rules, procedures, and so forth helped or hindered the Dooley Division?

PROBLEM 2

MAKING QUOTA

Just before their pre-Christmas business reached its maximum, the Cantor Toy Company installed a new conveyor line which provided a more mechanized means of spraying and drying their toy soldiers. Simultaneously they placed the operation on a three-shift, round-the-clock basis to meet the heavy influx of customer orders.

A group of six sprayers worked on individual fixtures and placed the sprayed soldiers on a conveyor belt which went into a drying chamber. The drying cycle took about two hours, so that the same sprayers were able to take off dried units and box them. The job description and the incentive plan under which the sprayers worked took into account the fact that each sprayer was both a sprayer and a packer. There were continuous shifts so that the next shift would package soldiers that had been sprayed during the last couple of hours by the previous shift and so on.

Management observed that during the first hour or so of each shift the sprayers always seemed to be in trouble and behind their quota (if they were to actually make a bonus for the day). On closer examination it became apparent that each shift was normally careful to place sprayed soldiers on the conveyor belt in such a way that they could easily be removed for packaging without interrupting the spraying operation. However, toward the end of the day, when the sprayed units would no longer be packed by themselves (because the drying cycle ran over into the next shift), they grew careless in their haste to make their own quota. The next shift would then find them bunched and unevenly spaced, would fall behind, and, in turn, would take a careless attitude toward the spacing of the pieces they rushed through to make their quota during the last couple of hours.

1. To what extent is this production problem due to poor attitudes toward work and to what extent is it the result of the technology—the organization of work?
2. Have you any suggestions for eliminating this problem?

PROBLEM 3 [16]

TECHNICIAN POOL

The Bellows Chemical Laboratories were engaged in the development and production of a number of organic chemicals used in the printing and textile industries. As a result of the growing acceptance of the company's product line, the research laboratory experienced a major expansion.

In this company the job classification of "laboratory technician" referred to persons who performed routine tests at the direction of professionally trained employees. A variety of tests was involved, and many of the tests required considerable skill to execute. All the technicians had completed high school and several had attended college for one or two years. Several technicians had also worked in the factory and had been transferred to the laboratory at their own request. The professionals in the laboratory were all graduate chemists or engineers.

The work of the laboratory was organized under the "project" system. The work was authorized by management, as required, and assigned by the head of the laboratory to one or, at the most, two professionals for execution. When the work was completed, the chemists or engineers involved were given new assignments.

Until recently, the size of the laboratory (both professional and technician groups), was small enough so that frequent interaction among the entire staff was possible. Desks of all personnel were located within a single "conversational" area, and everyone had fairly accurate knowledge of the goals and work requirements of the various active projects. When a chemist or engineer had a series of tests to be run, he would ask the technician who seemed least burdened with work at the time to undertake the assignment. On the whole, this arrangement worked smoothly. Delays in the work and manifestations of discontent among the personnel were infrequent.

Recently the demands on the laboratory have increased markedly. The number of active projects has increased by a substantial margin, and the number of professionals employed has approximately doubled. Also, several additional technicians have been assigned to the laboratory.

When it became apparent that the informal arrangement for scheduling technician time would not function adequately with the larger group, a "technician pool" was created and put in the charge of a senior technician. Professionals who desired tests run were to route their requests through the head technician, who in turn would assign technicians from the "pool."

The new arrangement has had two unexpected results. First, the number of technicians per professional employee has had to be increased to get the required work completed on schedule. Second, a considerable degree of discontent has developed among the technician group and to a lesser extent among

---

[16] We are indebted to one of our former students, Mr. E. W. Coleman, for the outline of this case.

the professionals. Not infrequently, conflict arises over priority in the use of equipment. Availability conflicts between the head technician and the chemists over technicians are becoming more numerous. One of the technicians has requested that he be transferred out of the laboratory. Whereas the old informal scheduling of technician time had become cumbersome and inefficient, the new technician "pool" has resulted in still further loss of efficiency and in open conflict.

1. To what extent were the new problems involving the allocation and assignment of technicians an inevitable product of expansion in the laboratory?
2. Why didn't some of these conflicts over priorities emerge when the laboratory was smaller? It is unlikely that there was a surplus of technicians, even then, and there must have been times when a chemist or engineer could not obtain personnel when they were needed.
3. "Pools" are used to conserve many scarce resources in the organization. They are supposed to insure that everyone has an equal opportunity to use facilities and that the facilities are not wasted. Why doesn't this reasonable explanation enable everyone in an organization, like the laboratory, to accept temporary shortages and inconveniences, since the total group is probably benefiting by the arrangement?

PROBLEM 4

A DROP IN QUALITY

The Wilton Company manufactures a small replacement part sold by automobile accessory dealers. The company is in a highly competitive industry, and recently has been losing ground to other manufacturers whose product sells for slightly less than that manufactured by Wilton. The Executive Committee of the company has decided to try to decrease their unit labor costs. The plant manager has indicated to the two division heads who report directly to him (the superintendent for fabrication and the superintendent for assembly) that they will be held responsible for tightly adhering to new output standards, which require about 5 per cent more work for approximately the same wage cost.

During the first week after the application of the tighter standards and the closer checking of department cost figures, a major disagreement arose between the two division heads. Since the matter of quality standards was also involved, the plant manager invited the head of the inspection department to attend the meeting. The chief inspector also reports to the plant manager, and serves in a staff capacity to the production departments.

The following exchange took place during the meeting:

Plant Manager: "I have called this meeting to find out what we can do about this awful production situation. As you know, it was just a week ago that we decided to try to up our output by about 5 per cent. I am certainly shocked at the results of our program. As you probably know by now, the figures for the week indicate that instead of some increase in output we actually suffered a 9 per cent decline over our average for the past two months. Apparently, a large share of this poor performance is due to low-quality work and scrap. How do you explain this?"

Superintendent for Fabrication: "I know what's holding us up! It's simple. Jack, here [superintendent for assembly] is sending back nearly one out of five parts that we send to him, claiming that they are not perfect, and he can't use them in his assembly operations. This is ridiculous; we are utilizing the same tolerances we've always utilized. There is no such thing as perfection, as he knows, but all our parts are within limits."

Superintendent for Assembly: "All I know is that we can't continue to meet our old output standards, no less meet these new ones, if we're going to have to use parts that are finished like these have been. If my foremen are going to be able to insist that each employee work along at 100 per cent efficiency, those employees have got to have parts that don't jam when they try to fit them together. Sure, if we had all the time in the world, we could fuss around with them to make them fit—they wouldn't have to be remachined—but we don't have all the time in the world and we've got to have good parts if we're going to have any decent level of output."

At this point the plant manager asked for an opinion from the chief inspector. His response was brief, and somewhat unexpected.

Chief Inspector: "All I want to say is that in the past week my inspectors have been under more pressure from both of your foremen than they have ever endured. Both in fabrication and assembly the inspectors have been pressured to pass work that was really borderline, if not below standard. I can assure you that we haven't succumbed to any of these pressures, but our job has just been made that much more difficult. I don't see why your production foremen can't stick to the standards and leave it up to our inspectors to find out whether or not the parts fit."

1. How do you explain the sudden drop in quality at the fabrication stage?
2. What is likely to be the effect on interdepartmental relations of this attempt to increase output?
3. What do you see as the basic problem in the manufacturing organization of the Wilton Machine Company? Do you have any suggestions for improving the organizational structure?

Minimizing the Human Problems
of Large Organizations

We have been looking at some of the problems that stem from extended lines of authority and the division of labor in the contemporary organization. By this time you may have decided that the "game is not worth the candle"—that too heavy a price must be paid in terms of human relationships to win the advantages of large-scale organization. There are those who look back nostalgically to the "good old days" when companies were small, when the boss knew all his employees intimately, when everyone worked together and did a whole job, when problems of coordination and communication were at a minimum. Neither horizontal nor vertical cleavages were particularly significant, and the work group and the company were synonymous. Many studies have shown that employee morale is higher in small groups than in large ones.[1] Supervision and job satisfaction are all easier to achieve in the more intimate setting.

The technological and economic advantages that come with size, however, mean that large organizations are here to stay. Size makes possible many of the economies of specialization (*e.g.*, mass production) and the introduction of expensive equipment (*e.g.*, electronic data-processing machines). As the organization grows, it usually gains what economists call "economies of scale"— that is, money can be borrowed at lower interest rates, supplies purchased in larger quantities, and so on.

Even from a human-relations point of view, large organizations possess advantages. Larger companies have pioneered in introducing personnel programs designed to eliminate many of the sources of unrest common to smaller companies. They have sought to regularize employment, to develop training and promotion programs stressing merit rather than nepotism, to introduce equitable wage and salary administration programs that adjust income to job

---

[1] See R. W. Revans, "Industrial Morale and Size of Unit," in Walter Galenson and Seymour Lipset, eds., *Labor and Trade Unionism* (New York: Wiley, 1960), pp. 295-300. See also Mason Haire, *Psychology in Management*, 2nd ed., (New York: McGraw-Hill, 1964), p. 28. Professor Haire also has included a stimulating section on the interrelationships of organization size, shape (structure), and functions (pp. 223-228).

responsibility, and to provide retirement and insurance programs to reduce the fear of illness and old age.

The basic problem is this: How can organizations gain the advantages that come with size and specialization without paying a heavy price in terms of reduced employee and managerial effectiveness? In the small organization where face-to-face relationships predominate, a manager of goodwill who likes and respects people may prove highly successful. In the large organization, good intentions are not enough; human relations needs to be *planned* to insure an environment conducive to productivity.

How can organizational structure be designed to minimize human friction? In answering this question, we shall try to show that the manager who plans his organizational structure intelligently and realistically can:

1. Reduce the number of levels in the organizational hierarchy, even though he does not reduce the total number of employees.
2. Improve the efficiency with which the immediate work group solves the difficult work-flow problems of coordination and cooperation.
3. Improve cooperation between groups within the organization.
4. Relate personality variables to job design.

FEWER LEVELS OF SUPERVISION

In Chapter 15, we mentioned that the existence of many levels within an organization complicates the problems of management. The individual employee feels lost because he is many steps removed from the key decision-makers who control his welfare, and both top management and the worker feel isolated from one another. Orders and information have to pass up and down through so many levels that there are countless possibilities for breakdowns and distortions in communication.

It is not uncommon for large corporations to have ten to twelve levels intervening between the hourly-paid employee and top management. And yet the number of levels required by the organization is *not* automatically determined by the number of employees. For instance, Sears Roebuck reported in 1950 that with 110,000 employees in their retail division, there are only four levels of supervision *between* the president of the company and the sales-people in the stores.[2] This "flat" structure is not accidental; it is a reflection of deliberate management policy to maximize the number of subordinates (the span of control) reporting to a given supervisor. The result is that the levels of supervision in the organization are kept to a minimum.[3]

---

[2] James C. Worthy, "Factors Influencing Employee Morale," *Harvard Business Review*, Vol. 28, No. 1 (January 1950), p. 69.

[3] There are other organizational techniques for reducing the number of supervisory levels, which we shall not detail here. The interested reader will find a description of them in an excellent case study of reorganization at the International Business Machines plant in Endicott, N. Y.: F. L. W. Richardson, Jr., and Charles R. Walker, *Human Relations in an Expanding Company* (New Haven, Conn.: Labor and Management Center, Yale University, 1948), pp. 32-48.

Flat vs. Tall Organizations

Fortunately, the Sears Roebuck Company has analyzed the effect of its organizational setup on human relations within the company. Sears operates many stores that have an almost identical number of employees doing highly similar jobs. In some of these stores, 32 department managers report directly to the store manager; in others, the department managers report to 5 or 6 division managers, who in turn report to the store manager.[4] Obviously, the first is a relatively *flat* type of structure; the second, a *tall* type. What has Sears observed in the operations of these two quite different organization patterns?

The tall organization tended to encourage close supervision. With a relatively small number of subordinates, each supervisor, whether he was the store manager or the division manager, was able to give very detailed instructions to and exercise strong control over every one of the people in his unit. But in the flat organization the relatively large number of subordinates made this type of supervision physically impossible. Each supervisor was obliged to rely on general supervision and good training; he just didn't have the time to keep a close watch on everyone. The delegation of responsibility in these stores encouraged subordinates to work on their own initiative and learn from their own mistakes. Since the supervisor could not make a decision on every problem that arose, subordinates achieved a high degree of self-reliance. The results showed themselves in the higher profits, better morale, and greater number of promotable executives produced by the flat organization.

Another obvious advantage to the fewer-leveled organization is the saving of managerial time: Problems are handled more quickly. Equally important are the better human relations associated with fewer levels. Communication is expedited; the individual employee finds it easier to identify with the work of his part of the organization.

Not every organization, of course, can arbitrarily increase the number of subordinates reporting to each of its supervisors. The ability of Sears to make use of a relatively "wide" span of control is a function of the following factors:

1. It was possible to develop efficiency measures (controls) for the various departments so that a manager could be left to make nearly all his own decisions and only have to account for the final results: in other words, supervision "by results."

2. Department store personnel receive a good part of their compensation in the form of commissions and bonuses based on sales performance. These incentives provide them with a high degree of motivation and decrease the need for close supervision.

---

[4] A good summary of the Sears experience may be found in William F. Whyte, *Men at Work* (Homewood, Illinois: Dorsey Press, 1961), pp. 88-93.

3. No great amount of coordination between department managers was required in these stores. In effect, each department could be operated relatively independently of the others, thus reducing the amount of supervision required by the store manager.

One other interesting facet of the Sears study is worth mentioning since it relates to what we shall say later about personality. The Sears organization found that certain managers *preferred* the "tall" organization and its attendant close supervision. Given their personalities, that was the way they wanted to manage. Others, if they were shifted into that kind of store, immediately set about to increase the number of people reporting to each supervisor. Their personality was such that they trusted people and didn't want to exercise close supervision.

BUILDING INTEGRATED WORK TEAMS: A SYSTEMS VIEW

Which jobs should be put together under a common supervisor? This is often called the departmentation decision. Naive managers assume that the answer is obvious:

> The drill presses and the punch presses have *always* been in separate departments.

> The sales engineers report to the manager of engineering; after all they're engineers, aren't they?

But, of course, such decisions are not obvious. Whereas many organizations rely on functional boundary lines (grouping together employees with similar job titles or "functions"), others are showing an increasing interest in a *systems view* of organization. In this approach, the manager looks at what people actually have to do in their relationships with one another if work is to flow smoothly. Those people who must coordinate their task are then placed together under a common supervisor.[5]

The significance of this approach was underlined by the problems associated with producing highly complicated military equipment like the Polaris submarine. A large number of separate tasks had to be integrated perfectly. If task No. 32 wasn't done, No. 33 couldn't begin—and there were thousands of these distinguishable design, manufacture, and assembly tasks. Further, the

---

[5] For a more complete and precise definition of these criteria, see Eliot Chapple and Leonard Sayles, *The Measure of Management* (New York: Macmillan, 1960), pp. 18-45.

sophistication of the technology required that each task be done in such a way as to intermesh perfectly with the others in terms of dimensions and operating characteristics.

Given these kinds of problems, new organizational procedures had to be invented. New *control* techniques like PERT (Program Evaluation and Review Technique) were given to managers to enable them to watch the progress of the work through its various stages and to identify where bottlenecks threatened. More importantly, managers were given responsibility for the development of a total weapons system rather than being divided up according to functions (such as design, development, manufacture, testing, and so on). This was the same "task force" procedure that had been utilized in the Manhattan Project, which developed the atomic bomb.[6]

In civilian work, this systems approach reflects itself in increasing emphasis on organization by *product* manufactured or service rendered rather than by *process* or function. But this distinction will be clearer if we look at an example.

The Ajax Company:
Customer-Order Processing Department

To illustrate how this reorganization can be accomplished, we shall describe a case in which changes in organization substantially altered the human relations of the situation. Notice particularly that the original emphasis on functional specialization, a characteristic of modern organizations, as emphasized in Chapter 16, was the chief source of the difficulty. The division of labor employed *before* the change looked logical and reasonable on paper; but when real people filled the jobs that had been created, continuous personnel conflict and inefficiency arose. Management's mistake was in assuming that people behave like the rectangles and lines of an organization chart.

Before

The Ajax Company manufactured small home appliances which it sold to retail outlets. Every order sent in by salesmen in the field had to be processed by four different groups of employees in the home office.

a. *Customer contact clerks* communicated with the customer if the salesman's order was unclear, if the merchandise ordered was unavailable, or if price changes had taken place.

b. *Billing clerks* checked the arithmetic on the order and entered correct charges and credits on the customer's account.

c. *Inventory checkers* checked to make sure that goods ordered were available for shipment.

---

[6] *Cf.* Richard Johnson, Fremont Kast, and James Rosenzweig, *Theory and Management of Systems* (New York: McGraw-Hill, 1963).

d. *Credit approval clerks* examined the customer's credit status in order to authorize shipping.

The Ajax Company placed each "functional" group of employees under separate supervisors, as in the diagram below.

Thus, each customer order passed through four distinct departments (and two divisions). Each specialist belonged to the organizational unit to which his function was *logically* related.

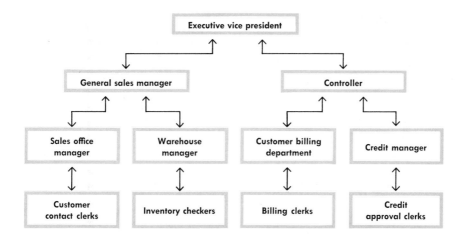

You can probably predict what happened. The design of the organization made no provision for the cooperation and communication required to complete the *total job* of customer-order processing. There was constant conflict among employees. Inventory checkers complained that they had to track down merchandise that might later be dropped from the order as a result of the discovery of a salesman's clerical error or inadequate customer credit. Customer contact clerks were in a constant dither because their letters were rendered obsolete by the work of the credit clerks or the inventory checkers. Responsibility for delays in processing orders were "passed" from one group to another. The billing clerks complained that the inventory checkers were always late with their information, and the inventory checkers retorted that their delays were the result of faulty information from customer contact clerks.

Higher management was always being called in to settle disputes. When conflict arose between an inventory checker and a customer contact clerk, for example, each would contact his superior, who in turn would take the battle up to the General Sales Manager. When the billing clerk complained that he couldn't get up-to-the-minute information from the customer contact clerks (and thus made embarrassing errors in customers' accounts), the problem might have to go to the Executive Vice President, who was their common supervisor. Even the Sales Manager and the Controller were constantly blaming one another for difficulties in each other's departments.

After

In a reorganization of these functions, all employees processing customer orders were placed under a single general office supervisor, who in turn had first-line supervisors for the various geographic areas served by the company. The new organization looked like this:

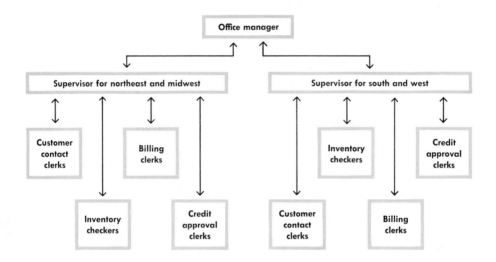

Under each of these supervisors, the same specialists continued to do much the same job they had done before. Now, however, any dispute could be settled face-to-face within the immediate work group, or, in exceptional instances, by the first-line supervisor. No longer was it necessary to channel complaints up the line through two or three levels of management. The new scheme saved a great deal of executive time, and made it possible to settle most problems by horizontal work-flow contacts between the employees themselves. The arrangement increased output enormously by eliminating many petty frictions.

The sales, warehouse, and credit managers now have a lateral, not a supervisory, relation to the office supervisor. Each was made responsible for establishing standards of performance for the clerical employees who did work involving their respective special interests, and for auditing to be sure that these standards of performance, that is, controls, were being observed.

Reduction in Number of Levels

Under the new systems arrangement, nearly every decision, and all information that has to be communicated, is handled either at the work level, among the employees themselves, or between them and their immediate supervisor: one of the two geographic office supervisors. The organization of this part of the business now consists of two relatively autonomous divisions, each of which can function almost entirely on its own.

In short, what happened at Ajax was this: (1) Management reduced the number of levels of supervision that had to participate in the solution of normal, daily work problems. And (2) it created more inclusive work teams that could handle problems on a face-to-face basis with a minimum of friction.

Improved Communications
and Coordination

Recall the recurring struggle and frictions among the customer contact, billing, and credit approval clerks and inventory checkers. There was little of the mutual help, loyalty, and protection that we described as characteristic of the informal work group in Chapter 4. Why? The employees who had to interact with one another in order to complete the assigned work of processing customer orders did *not* belong to the same group. The billing clerks, for example, may have had a fine relationship with one another, but unfortunately the people they had to work with were not other billing clerks. They were working with employees in other departments: inventory checkers, customer contact clerks, and so on.

The manner in which work activities are organized influences the quality of communications within the work group: People who work near one another and identify with the same group find it far easier to share the information they need to coordinate their jobs than do people who have infrequent contact with one another. In fact, much of our earlier discussion of flow-of-work problems could just as logically have appeared in a discussion of "communications problems." When two work groups have so much trouble understanding each other that communications are misinterpreted or go astray, or when top management complains that lower levels fail to understand the needs of the business—these are usually indications that the groups that make up the organization are too far apart. Because they report to different supervisors, they develop unique interests. Their separate worlds, their special skills, their special desires and activities, create barriers to effective communication.

Vast quantities of information are required to perform many of the jobs within the large organization, and the superior-subordinate relationship cannot possibly carry the burden of communicating all of it. If every employee had to rely exclusively on his immediate superior for information about the company and his particular function within it, the supervisor would have to spend full time "communicating" information.

Students of organization are often surprised by the amount of work-oriented information that is communicated during what appear to be social contacts. During a coffee break it is not unusual to hear a conversation of this sort:

> "Say, Joe, just out of curiosity, tell me what your guys are doing to mangle those parts we're supposed to put together in a minute and a half in our assembly operation."
> "Bill, you've got the wrong villain. Orders came down from the plant manager's office to loosen up on our tolerances. They figure we were rejecting too

many out-of-limits parts and wasting money. In fact, they claim that you guys have been having it too soft with our perfect parts; now you'll have to just work a little harder to put 'em together."

These semi-social contacts, which are normally a product of membership in the same group, are an indispensable supplement to the more formal channels of communication.

Research Studies
of Organization Change

Mining.[7]   Let us examine what happened when a natural work team in a coal mine was broken up. At one time all the operations at the mine face were performed by a small team which worked together on a single shift. Since they were in close contact with one another, it was easy to devise solutions for problems as they arose. Each member of the group felt responsible for the entire operation.

In the mistaken belief that it would increase efficiency, management combined these small groups into much larger ones working over larger areas. For example, one crew did nothing but prepare the new "face" for blasting. Others handled the recovery of the coal that came down after the dynamite had been set off; another crew worked on timbering and moving rail lines. This new division of labor was carried out on a three-shift, 24-hour cycle: Each shift performed a different function. Each worker became a specialist. As a result, no single group of workers felt responsible for the total operation; as problems arose, each shift developed the habit of shrugging them off and passing the buck to the next shift. Communications, which at best are very troublesome in a mine, were further complicated by the workers' being separated from each other in time and space. Previously, the small groups were almost self-supervising (motivated as they were by a group incentive plan); now, coordinating the various individual workers, none of whom had much motivation, became a complex management task. Even new equipment did not compensate for production losses due to work-flow problems.

Similar problems arise even when employees are not separated into different time shifts, as the next case suggests.

Textile mill.[8]   An Indian textile mill, which had undergone intensive "job re-engineering," did not attain satisfactory output levels. Each occupational group in the mill was assigned a work load based on a careful study of all the job components. For example, in one room containing 240 looms, the following assignments were made to the 12 types of specialist:

[7] E. L. Trist, G. W. Higgin, H. Murray, A. B. Pollock, *Organizational Choice* (London: Tavistock Publications, 1963).

[8] A. K. Rice, "Productivity and Social Organization in an Indian Weaving Shed," *Human Relations*, Vol. 6, No. 4 (1953).

1. Each weaver tended approximately 30 looms.
2. Each "battery filler" served about 50 looms.
3. Each "smash hand" was assigned some 80 looms.
4. Each of nine different categories of maintenance men was responsible for from 120 to 240 looms.

All these occupational tasks were highly interdependent, and the utmost coordination was required to maintain productivity. But the assignment of work loads militated against coordination. In effect, each weaver came into contact with five-eighths of a "battery filler," three-eighths of a "smash hand," and even smaller fractions of the other nine workers on whom he was at least partially dependent to keep his looms operating.

When the work was reorganized so that all interdependent workers were made part of the same work group, production soared. Work groups were reconstructed so that a single group of workers was responsible for the operation of a given bank of looms. The new interaction pattern produced regular relationships and communications among workers and led directly to the increase in output.

An automated power plant. With good fortune a team of social researchers were able to study the introduction of automation into a large steam power plant. Automation, with its integrated controls, served to break down the organizational boundaries between the independent boiler, turbine, and electrical departments. These groups of men had been responsible separately for steam generation, turbine operation, and the distribution of the resulting electricity. Automated processing permitted management to put a single foreman over the entire operating force and eliminate intergroup problems. In the research, the employees also reported:

> ... being significantly more satisfied with the amount of information they got about both the plant and the company [than a comparable work force in a nonautomated plant]. Reducing the number of people between the top staff and the employees appears to have eliminated one of the communication barriers between these ... groups ...[9]

Summary of cases. The conclusion to be drawn from these studies is that in designing the organization the administrator should provide each work group with a relatively autonomous task. Only under such circumstances can competent *internal* leadership and group responsibility develop.

Ideally, the individual worker should be permitted to coordinate his activities by himself (that is, through job enlargement). If the same girl does both the typing and the filing, problems in integrating the two processes are unlikely to arise. The next best thing is to have the coordination take place within the immediate work group, where each individual feels loyalty and

---

[9] Floyd Mann and L Richard Hoffman, *Automation and the Worker* (New York: Holt, Rinehart and Winston, 1960), p. 56.

responsibility to his fellow workers and is willing to adjust his pacing, the quality of his work, and his over-all efforts to the needs of the others.

Developing Identification
with the Total Job

The type of organization rearrangements we are considering have another valuable by-product. The new groups that are created are more likely to have high morale than are large, highly specialized work groups.

The structure of a work group has profound effects on the job satisfactions derived by its members. An employee who is just one of many, all doing the same operation, which operation in turn is only a small part of some larger activity, feels little sense of accomplishment or identification with the larger unit. However, in the semi-autonomous groups we have been describing, in which people who do complementary tasks are brought together:

> Employees have a much better opportunity to know each other, so that cooperation between individuals and departments can develop on a more personal, informal basis and not be so largely dependent on impersonal systems and administrative controls. Employees can see much more readily where they themselves "fit" into the organization and the significance of their jobs in the whole scheme of things.[10]

You will recall that this is one of the major sources of satisfaction under process automation as contrasted to mass-production technology (see Chapter 3). Employees see themselves as responsible for a total process, something with an observable output, and their jobs are designed to mutually facilitate the total effort rather than a fractional part.

When large numbers of people doing similar work are brought together in a single department, particularly if their work is unchallenging, personnel difficulties are likely to multiply. Typing pools, departments filled with hundreds of draftsmen or engineers doing identical tasks, all are sources of serious morale problems. To be sure, such a scheme may mean that the work can be scheduled more efficiently and that complex and labor-saving equipment can be used to handle the work of the entire organization. Yet the concentration of a large number of people, all doing the same job, tends to isolate them from the total organization. These groups become conscious of areas where their needs conflict with the rest of the organization. We have seen an occupational group that was satisfied with its pay and working conditions become a sore spot in the organization when the entire group was concentrated in the same department.

> In one large automobile manufacturing company, the draftsmen became a source of friction after they were all moved into one department instead of being scattered around among the departments that used their services. The new department became known as "Siberia."

---

[10] Worthy, *op. cit.*, p. 68.

It would be unrealistic, however, to assume that completely autonomous work groups can be developed. In the modern organization, work groups and departments have to cooperate with one another if the objectives of the enterprise are to be attained. Consequently, management has a responsibility to innovate organization changes that further intergroup cooperation.

Layout

Excessive physical distance among groups almost invariably reduces their opportunities to cooperate.

> "As accountants, our job is to help department heads improve their procedures and records to make their jobs easier and the results more effective. Oftentimes, however, we are not called in early enough when a new project gets started or some change is contemplated. The fault lies in our location—the laboratory accounting office is located in a small rented building several miles from the nearest research or development group. Being far away they never get around to calling us until their plans are already fixed; it takes so much longer to undo things than to get in on the ground floor. When we used to be located in the same building, these problems never occurred."

One way to improve opportunities for contact between groups that need to coordinate is to revise office and work-floor layouts. At the same time, the manager may also want to separate groups that do not need such intimate contact. Too easy access between such groups may encourage them to make unnecessarily frequent demands on each other.

Where for one reason or another such physical shifts are impossible for the manager to arrange, he may be able to devise special procedures to bring groups together that have to coordinate their activities but that are part of separate organizational families. We observed one company in which such procedures were hit on by chance. Two groups of engineers who reported to separate departments but who were working on interrelated drawings found that they needed to see each other more frequently than the normal flow of work allowed. Since there was no company cafeteria, the members of the two groups developed a car-pooling arrangement for traveling to and from lunch so that they could discuss their problems on the way.

Committees and Coordinators

Special committees are useful in facilitating exchange of information between groups that normally have little contact with one another:

> The members of one department were upset by another group's habit of sending in requests for "rush orders" that put tremendous pressure on everyone to do the impossible. They couldn't understand why these last-minute needs could not be predicted earlier in the day. It was only when cross-depart-

411

ment staff meetings were held that they learned about certain inherent technical problems in processing that made additional supplies necessary at the last minute.

Under the direction of a skilled chairman, committee meetings provide an opportunity for systematic, face-to-face discussion of problems and dissemination of information.

Increasingly, large companies make use of coordination or liaison specialists. For example, *product planners* have the responsibility for getting development engineering, manufacturing, and sales to work together. They work between each of these groups, persuading them to modify their efforts for the common good, that is, the design, production and distribution of a new product.

Training

As we have seen, many of the problems of coordination in specialized organizations arise out of the fact that each group has its own "vested interest," its own typical point of view or approach to problems. The engineer is interested in quality, for instance; his training and the nature of his work give him little interest in cost reduction. The accountant has just the opposite point of view. Such differences are inevitable (in fact, properly utilized by management they contribute to organizational strength).

An effective training program can help the engineer put himself into the accountant's shoes. It can show each group how its own actions sometimes cause unwitting but unnecessary affronts to other groups. It can show each group how it can communicate with others in understandable terms.

Clearly, then, provision must sometimes be made for communicating across department lines even though the departments normally have little in common, and even though they report to separate parts of the organization. Realistically, of course, this type of communication can never be as effective as face-to-face communication between members of the same work group.

Supervision

The good manager evaluates the status of intergroup relationships as part of his regular supervisory pattern. He seeks to identify potential and actual points of friction in the organization and to determine whether they are the result of poor organization design, personality problems, bad placement, or temporary operating problems.

THE MEANING OF DECENTRALIZATION

Some of the types of reorganization we have been describing might approximately be called shifts toward greater *decentralization*. Large, amorphous organizations in which nearly every decision must go up through many levels are highly *centralized*. They are the ones cursed with the problems of many-leveled hierarchies and specialization described in earlier chapters (like the Ajax Company before it was reorganized).

And yet centralization is not just a product of a particular managerial or supervisory philosophy, such as: "Close supervision is useful because people can't be trusted." Centralization also results from the design of the organization itself. When operations are highly specialized and departments finely sub-divided, decisions *must* be made by higher levels in the organization, and rigid rules *must* be employed. The reason, of course, is that no supervisor, any more than a single employee, is in a position to be "on his own." Because only a small part of the total job is done by any one employee or department, upper levels of management must step in to insure cooperation and coordination.

> Where the work of the organization is broken up into so many functional divisions again, cooperation can no longer be achieved spontaneously. After all, each functional unit was set up as a distinct entity in order that it might achieve a more efficient system. Each unit, therefore, tends to operate primarily in terms of its own system rather than in terms of the needs of the organization as a whole. Each unit becomes jealous of its own prerogatives and finds ways to protect itself against the pressures and encroachments of others. Conflict develops on the employee level as well as the supervisory level, thus forcing an extra administrative load on higher levels of management because of the need for constantly reconciling differences.[11]

Under decentralization, by contrast, management often considers a very different set of variables in deciding on organization structure. Rather than grouping employees together because they do similar work, management assesses the number and type of contacts required to complete a total operation. It designs work groups to facilitate coordination and cooperation between people who must interact frequently. When interrelated jobs are carefully grouped together, the supervisor can be left pretty much to his own devices. He can serve as an effective leader, since he has autonomy himself and can in turn delegate some autonomy to his subordinates.

There is some evidence that American industry is moving in the direction of greater decentralization. The Vice President of Manufacturing in a large oil company has described the organization of one of the company's new refineries in systems terms much like the automated power plant on p. 455:

> In this refinery all the men except the accountants and laboratory technicians are part of a single operating team. There is only one department—the Operating Department. The men have been trained somewhat as the crew of a submarine, in that every man can fill almost any breach. They are not concerned whether someone is doing their work, or whether they are doing someone else's work. Their interest lies, as a team, in keeping the operation going. All of the operating work is their work.

---

[11] Worthy, *op. cit.*, p. 71. Harold Leavitt titles an interesting description of this dilemma "The Jigsaw Puzzle of Responsibility," in his text *Managerial Psychology* (Chicago: University of Chicago Press, 1958), pp. 266-269.

There are ten on each shift. They run the entire refinery, including crude distillation, catalytic cracking and reforming, product testing, blending and shipping of products, and the utilities.[12]

Under this philosophy of management some of the large concentrations of staff groups that create problems of coordination for the line manager are being dispersed. Middle managers and sometimes even first-level managers may be assigned their own staff specialists (to assist in methods work, personnel, finance, tooling, and so on). That they can directly control the activities of the specialists makes coordination much simpler and helps train the supervisor to do his own control and planning work. In turn, as a manager gains skill and experience in these tasks which had been taken away from him (see Chapter 16, p. 413), his self-confidence and status are built up. This helps him deal more effectively with his immediate subordinates and superiors.

Decentralization means shifting "downward" the point at which all the employees necessary to do a complete job come together and report to a common supervisor. Again, this shift means that more responsibility can be delegated to the supervisor. Building the organization structure around the flow of work permits the large company to enjoy the human-relations advantages of the small company. All the operations that need to be integrated come under a common supervisor at the lowest possible level. This supervisor is able to communicate directly with everyone who has any impact on his ability to meet the goals assigned him. Workers and managers who must coordinate their activities are made members of the same team. Each employee is able to contact directly his real boss—the man who makes the important decisions.

In other words, an organization should consider its needs for *horizontal* communications before constructing its *vertical* or *hierarchical* lines of communication.

Limitations of Decentralization

This technique of decentralization is not a cure-all for human-relations problems, however. While companies like General Motors, Sears, duPont, General Electric, and others are enthusiastic about its virtues, others, like Chrysler, have tried it and moved away.

One of the reasons for this difference in experience may be that decentralization requires unusually able personnel—managers and employees who can accept delegation and general supervision and the responsibilities these entail. This means that management must devise good selection procedures by which it can accurately identify supervisory talent and must also provide for effective on-the-job training. Decentralization demands that all managers in the com-

---

[12] Clarence H. Thayer, Vice President in Charge of Manufacturing, Sun Oil Company, Philadelphia, Penn., "Automation and the Problems of Management" (address to the Wilmington, Delaware, Chapter of the Society for the Advancement of Management, delivered on October 14, 1958).

pany share a common understanding of the methods and objectives of the organization; otherwise autonomy may lead to anarchy.

There are other limitations that make decentralization something less than a cure-all for organization ills. Decentralized organizations may not be as effective in making quick decisions or in adjusting to rapid environmental changes. For example, it may be hard to get separate units to agree to manpower cutbacks unless the change is imposed from above. Many organizations are composed of parts that are too interdependent to allow for a great deal of autonomy—the opposite of the Sears Roebuck case described earlier. Interdivisional cooperation may prove deficient when each division concentrates primarily on its own objectives rather than on those of the organization. One division may be unwilling to share scarce technicians with another, although the needs of the latter are more pressing. A research laboratory that is completely autonomous may fail to coordinate its activities with the needs of the manufacturing divisions. In turn, the manufacturing divisions may fail to appreciate how they can make use of research. Finally, decentralization has many added hidden costs arising from duplication of specialized staff work and the costs of operating the necessary controls to keep top management informed.[13]

PERSONALITY AND ORGANIZATION STRUCTURE

Another key influence on job performance is personality. Particularly on jobs with a high human-relations content, where most of the working day is spent interacting with other people, personality is a major determinant of what will be done and how it will be done. This statement holds for store clerks and superintendents and industrial engineers as well as many other white-collar jobs. The role of personality is hardly surprising, however, since an important component of personality is an individual's capacity for dealing with other people.

Let us first look more specifically at how personality shapes job performance and then consider what can be done about the personality factor in order to improve organizational performance.

How Personality
Shapes the Organization

Traditionally, personality was ignored in organizational decision-making because jobs were dealt with in isolation. It was assumed that a job could be defined in terms of abstract "responsibilities" without giving much thought to

---

[13] For an excellent criticism of decentralization from the point of view of the accounting and finance functions, see John Dearden, "Mirage of Profit Decentralization," *Harvard Business Review*, Vol. 40, No. 6 (November 1962), pp. 140-148. Dearden details the extra costs associated with decentralization, particularly the increasing number of financial specialists that must be maintained and their costly battles with line officials over the "true" profit figures for each decentralized unit.

the relationships between jobs, what behavior was expected of the individual in relation to other people in the organization. Thus, it should make no difference whether the position "Product Engineer for Special Fabrics" is occupied by Mr. Ross or by Mr. Jones. Each should do it in exactly the same way, because that is the way the organization is designed to function.

But practice differs enormously from theory. The organization will undoubtedly not function the same way when Ross has the job as it did with Jones. Each man's personality will reveal itself in the way he works with his colleagues, his boss, his subordinates, and other departments. As a result, when the incumbent on a job changes, everyone has to adjust to a whole series of changes in the way work is accomplished.

In spite of organizational theory, it is naive to assume that employees fit themselves into the straitjacket of the job specification. As they try the job on for size they begin squirming a bit, pulling in here and pushing out there, until the job begins to fit their personality needs. The result is that the organization functions differently from the way the designers of the structure envisioned.

> Brown as purchasing agent is supposed to spend about half his time analyzing sources of supply and negotiating terms of purchase, and the other half managing the employees in the purchasing office. Brown enjoys negotiating, but is unhappy handling what he calls these "darn petty personnel problems." So he spends less and less time supervising and more time buying. Gradually the job of running the office is assumed by his chief assistant, since the employees need someone to turn to with their problems.
> In contrast, Smith is supposed to spend nearly all his time drawing up engineering specifications. However, he has a flair for dealing with people, and he soon finds that other engineers are coming to him with their personnel problems. He begins to represent them directly in contacts with the division head. As his reputation as a "fixer" grows, upper management uses him as a trouble-shooter. He does less and less engineering and more and more human-relations work. At the same time, his own boss, the section head who prefers puzzling over blueprints to worrying about employee relations, is by-passed and gradually loses authority.

What an organization *really is* reflects the personalities of those who hold key jobs. The personality of the chief executive officer permeates the entire company, and as we noted earlier, personal preferences of store managers at Sears determined whether "tall" or "flat" organizations evolved.

Similarly, supervisory styles, how subordinates are dealt with, is often a reflection of personality make-up. Here is one example: [14]

> Berg believed that a good supervisor should delegate as much responsibility as possible to subordinates. He couldn't understand why he was always being criticized for failures to delegate. If one watched him supervise the answer was

---

[14] This and the cases following are adapted from Eliot Chapple and Leonard Sayles, "The Man, the Job, and the Organization," *Personnel* (March-April, 1958), pp. 72-79.

clear enough. Yes, he would give orders that would allow the individual to assume a great deal of responsibility. But he was very impatient and never took the time to train a subordinate thoroughly before giving a new assignment. Often the employee didn't know the background of the problem he was expected to handle and how it related to other activities for which he was responsible. Lacking complete information and adequate training, he either went very slowly or made serious mistakes. When Berg observed this behavior he hastily moved in and handled the job himself, always saying "It's easier to do it myself; no one wants to take real responsibility any more." Thus, his method of handling order-giving (arising from his fast-paced personality), frustrated his own intellectual belief in delegation.

Using Knowledge of Personality to Solve Human-Relations Problems

When personality problems arise, a manager has three principal choices. He can endeavor to get people to modify their behavior to make their job performance more consistent with the needs of the job, or he can change the job, or he can replace the person. The last, of course, is the most drastic and frequently the most painful decision.

Modifying behavior. If the manager knows the proper behavior in a given situation, he may be able to persuade or train employees to adopt this pattern. Unfortunately, though, many managers are content just to tell their people, "delegate more," for example, rather than actually to observe how subordinates are dealt with.

In the Berg case cited above, Berg's manager was able to get him to recognize that he, in fact, did not delegate. Working with his personnel director, Berg became aware of his own propensity to "move in" too rapidly. He learned the importance of spending adequate time in giving assignments, to spend at least a half hour consecutively with a subordinate when a new project came in, and to wait several days before going back to the subordinate after making an assignment.

Many times conflicts occur between specialists who are supposed to collaborate. Because of personality problems, the jobs don't intermesh as they should as each comes to distrust or dislike the other. Here is an example of a conflict in industrial engineering:

> Two section heads in the industrial engineering department of a medium-sized company had been feuding almost since the day—two years before—when they both promoted to their present positions. One was the installations engineer. The other was a methods engineer whose primary responsibility was to develop new operations, to test them out in the experimental shop maintained in the department, and to turn the processes over to the installation section for testing. Whenever trouble broke out between him and the installation engineer, the methods man was convinced that the latter had changed the process or hadn't followed the method as he had spelled it out, while the in-

stallation engineer was equally convinced that the basic idea was wrong or that the methods engineer hadn't taken into consideration the practical requirements of the shop.

The methods engineer found making contacts with others difficult. He was slow to take initiative, easily upset by criticism, and tended to withdraw into his shell and become increasingly petulant. The installation engineer was a man with a great deal of energy and initiative. He liked to get things done quickly and usually had little difficulty dominating others.

Since both men were good engineers and did their job well, the chief engineer was unwilling to transfer either one out of the department. On the other hand, he became increasingly aware that the backbiting wasn't helping his relations with production since each man was enlisting others outside the department in the feud.

With the aid of the training director, the chief engineer took a hand in this situation. First, the two of them discussed with the installation head how he disturbed his opponent by being too quick to take the initiative and by dominating every time he tried to raise an objection. The installation engineer came to understand that it was his natural way of behaving, effective though this made him in the shop, which brought out these instinctive reactions in the other man. It would help matters, he was advised, if he genuinely tried not to jump in when the methods engineer was attempting to formulate an idea and if he could refrain from taking over the discussion until the methods engineer had finished making his point.

To the methods engineer, on the other hand, it was suggested that he should refrain from seeing the installation engineer on a day when he had too many other contacts or had been upset by other problems. The chief engineer also worked out a schedule whereby each man could plan his contacts instead of leaving it up to the installation engineer to take the initiative every time he thought he might have a problem.

In recent years management has been experimenting with a variety of other techniques such as "sensitivity training" [15] to get key personnel to modify their behavior when it is upsetting to other people and jobs.

Redesigning jobs. Many times it is easier to change the job than to change the person. Many behavioral attributes are too deeply ingrained to modify easily. Thus, parts of a job that are difficult for the individual to perform or on which he conflicts badly with other people may have to be removed. Jobs can, in fact, be viewed as flexible packages of component parts, at least some of which are shiftable in order to tailor the job to the needs and competencies of the individual personality who will be manning it.

A large aircraft firm employed a training director who had long years of experience and many skills in designing both programs and materials. However, he lacked the ability to develop effective working relationships with the managers of other divisions. Within his own department he was competent, but he was unable to make himself initiate contacts with the divisional managers often enough to build up effective relations with them. Nor was he able

---

[15] *Cf.* discussion of sensitivity training in Chapters 10 and 24.

to put over his program in the face of any opposition. Though management believed that training should be carried out at the divisional level, the training director found every excuse to stay in the central offices. Top management then evolved a plan to shift the "selling" parts of his job to an assistant and give the training director additional responsibilities for company publications.

Selection and rejection.   Many times the types of problems we have been describing are avoided by considering the behavioral requirements of the job in advance and selecting an appropriate personality to fill the job. Of course, when the selection turns out to be a poor one, when the individual is unable to develop satisfactory relations with subordinates or colleagues, he may be shifted to another job or leave the company. This course of action can be embarrassing and costly to all concerned and thus is used as a last resort. Thus, changing people (personalities) changes the operating characteristics of organization just as does any structural change.

CONCLUSION

Unfortunately, some managers believe that the prime requisite for a smooth-running organization is a clear-cut, symmetrical organization plan which shows each man who his boss is and what his responsibilities are. Or they assume that the most logical scheme is to bring together under a common supervisor all employees who do similar work—that is, to organize personnel according to a "functional" pattern.

The results of such approaches to organization may have a disastrous effect on efficiency and human relations. They consume a great deal of managerial time simply because many levels of supervision are regularly involved in the day-to-day problems of getting work done. They encourage intergroup struggles and make it difficult or impossible for supervisors to use the techniques of general supervision. Supervisors are compelled by the difficulties inherent in the organization structure to resort to close supervision and rigid rules; they cannot afford to delegate much responsibility. But the mere piling up of pressures, rules, and controls does not guarantee that all the parts of the organization will do "as they are told" and coordinate their activities effectively.

We have endeavored to show how some of the problems stemming from large, impersonal hierarchical structures based on the principle of division of labor can be ameliorated or solved. Care needs to be taken to insure that both work groups and department jurisdictions encompass as many as possible of those jobs that are closely interrelated. Cooperation that arises spontaneously out of the structure of the organization is far easier to maintain than that which is imposed by rigid rules, control, and close supervision. Furthermore, such decentralization leads to an enormous saving in managerial time and energy. It means that more of the day-to-day work problems can be solved by the immediate supervisor, rather than having to be carried up through one or even several levels to a common supervisor.

In short, organizations should be constructed from the *bottom up,* rather than from the *top down.* In establishing work-group boundaries and supervisory units, management should start with the actual work that must be performed, an awareness of who must coordinate his job with whom, when, and where. Making work groups as inclusive as possible discourages close supervision and fosters downward delegation. Rather than an amorphous institution in which people cannot understand the relationship of their jobs to the objectives of the business, the organization then takes on some of the desirable characteristics of the informal group, an organic human system.

In a somewhat analogous fashion the manager endeavors to build effective personality-job combinations. Jobs are analyzed in terms of what patterns of human relations will be required of the persons filling the job. An effort is made to find personalities compatible with the behavioral requirements of the job and to modify ineffective relationships. This can sometimes be done by transforming elements of the job (for instance, the training director helping the individual to observe where his activities are inadequate—such as the manager, Berg.)

We have traveled a rather long road to prove our point. At the outset, you will recall, we emphasized that to a substantial degree the human relationships in an organization are a product of its structure, as well as of the type of people, jobs, and supervision that make it up. In outline form, this is the pattern we have tried to develop:

Structure of the organization

> Personality
> Number of levels
> Type of specialization and controls
> Degree of centralization

↓

Shapes the pattern of human relations or interaction

> Social (informal group) contacts
> Up- and down-the-line contacts
> Flow-of-work (horizontal) contacts

↓

Whose product is

> Quality of teamwork
> Degree of cooperation
> Type of leadership
> Personal motivation

Traditionally in the field of human relations, these variables have been divided into those that compose the "formal" organization and those that make up the "informal" organization. The term "formal" connotes that these elements are specified or contrived by top management, whereas "informal" organization refers to those patterns of human relations that evolve out of day-to-day experiences. The diagram below may make this distinction clearer:

Formal Organization | **Informal Organization**

Division of labor (job definitions and specifications)

Personalities (filling the various jobs)

THE ACTUAL ORGANIZATION

Hierarchical structure (reporting relationships, rules, controls)

Informal groups (leadership, status relations, and norms)

The formal and informal elements interact to produce the actual pattern of human relations that can be observed: how work is actually performed in terms of who does what with whom, when and where, as well as who defers to whom, who initiates to whom, and what implicit rules of behavior govern these contacts. This structure of human contacts and communications provides the framework within which problems of personnel policy and decision-making can be realistically understood and dealt with by administrators.

PROBLEM 1 [16]

ALTERNATIVE ORGANIZATION STRUCTURES

You head a division of your company that will perform three primary functions or operations; "A work," "B work," and "C work." Since no major equipment is involved (*i.e.*, there are no economies of scale), each of these types of work is divisible into any size; however, the finished service or product requires one unit each of "A," "B," and "C." (One example might be machining, assembling, and inspection.) The total volume of output required of the department is such that there is need for three units of "A work," three of "B work," and three of "C work."

---

[16] This case is taken from material presented by James Worthy in his paper, "Some Aspects of Organization Structure in Relation to Pressures on Company Decision-Making," *Proceedings of Fifth Annual Meeting, Industrial Relations Research Association*, L. Reed Tripp, ed. (Madison, Wis.: Industrial Relations Research Association, 1953), pp. 72-76.

The organization could be structured in one of two different ways:

1. All of each type of work could be placed under a common supervisor, one unit having all the "A work," one all the "B work," and one all the "C work." Each of these supervisors would report to a common second-level supervisor, a superintendent.

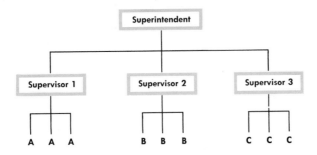

2. Alternatively, these nine units could be placed under three supervisors, each of whom managed one unit of "A work," and one unit of "B work," and one unit of "C work." Again, these supervisors would report to the superintendent.

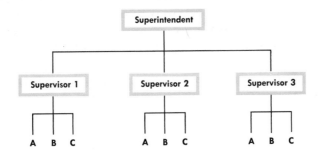

Compare the relative advantages of these two systems of organization. Consider the impact of each on the problems of supervision, coordination, the ability of the superintendent to delegate to his subordinates, the quality of personnel required for the various supervisory jobs, the amount of management development that would be accomplished.

PROBLEM 2

FRESH PRODUCE

The Freshway Supermarkets prided themselves on their policy of decentralization. Each store manager's bonus depended on the profit performance of his store. In general, each manager controlled his own purchasing, advertising, display, and clerical activities. The corporate offices of the chain provided certain essential services through pooled purchasing and staff assistance in technical areas: equipment selection, employee testing, techniques for reducing food spoilage, suggestions for improving advertising copy, and so forth.

Harry Alpert, the manager of the South Dayton store, earned the highest bonus of any of the midwestern managers. To a large extent this was the result of Alpert's technical ingenuity. By means of several inventions he was able to reduce the cost of his refrigeration equipment and to keep his fruits and vegetables looking fresher longer (thereby avoiding the waste of markdowns). He also developed a stock-handling system that was a significant improvement over the method recommended by the central-staff industrial engineering department. In fact, Alpert violated several of the routine procedures that had been established by central staff groups. However, he was careful not to disclose his techniques or deviations to others for obvious reasons.

1. From the point of view of the organization as a whole, how was Freshway's policy of decentralization working out?
2. Is there any way of rewarding individual managers for their initiative and ability that will not deprive the whole organization of innovations developed in any single unit of the system?
3. Is a central staff consistent with decentralization?

PROBLEM 3

A NEW FILE CABINET

Jane Hall, Director of Market Research for the Summertime Fabrics Company, looked out of her office to see why her secretary had not responded to the telephone-flashing signal. She was surprised to see three executives hovering around the secretary, obviously discussing some matter of great importance. After three-quarters of an hour had elapsed, the men left and Miss Hall was able to call her secretary. When asked what all the commotion was about, this is the story the secretary told:

"Since we have expanded the use of our sales office customer questionnaires, I am beginning to accumulate them in droves. They no longer fit in the file cabinets we have in the office, so I asked Mr. Frank, the office manager, if I could have another file. He said he would call Purchasing, and request that a new one be ordered. Apparently they told him they could not authorize the purchase without the approval of the Systems and Procedures Department. Mr. Frank then called them and they sent Mr. Otto over with a slide rule and lots of tables that tell you what shapes and sizes are most efficient for storing things. As Mr. Otto and Mr. Frank were interviewing me on just what items I wanted to keep in the files, their size, and how often I would be using them, Mr. Helpton came down from Purchasing. He said that frequently the most scientific file either wasn't readily available or was much higher in cost, and he usually found it moved matters along if he could get the Systems people to compromise on a unit they regularly order from a reliable supplier. Mr. Frank stayed in the conversation because he said that while he didn't want his budget to be charged with any fancy, unnecessary equipment, he wanted me to have the right file cabinet now, when I needed it. It took the three of them the good part of an hour to come to an agreement on what kind of file I should have."

1. What organization problems do you see here?
2. What is their source?
3. What organization changes could be introduced that would eliminate or minimize this type of situation?

The Role of Personnel Administration

The personnel function in management is especially concerned with the development of a highly motivated, smoothly functioning work force. True, this job is actually the responsibility of every manager, as is suggested by the oft-repeated phrase, "Management is people." Yet the *personnel department* has a special part to play in this field. And the fact that personnel is the responsibility both of the entire organization and of one special department makes the lateral relations between the personnel department and other departments particularly difficult.

In this chapter, however, we shall be concerned with the unique contribution of the personnel specialist and the personnel department. First, we shall endeavor to provide some historical perspective. Next will come a brief description of the scope and organization of the functions of personnel administration. Finally, we shall examine the organizational implications of these functions, concentrating on those that pose the most difficulties.

HISTORICAL BACKGROUND OF PERSONNEL WORK [1]

The Period 1900–1930

Response to problems of industrialization and urbanization. One of the first manifestations of organized concern with the personnel function in management was the pre-World War I industrial welfare movement. Certain benevolent employers sought to improve the lot of the working man. The Industrial Revolution having brought with it many deprivations, life was often brutish for workers, particularly in congested cities. Incomes were too low to meet basic human needs. Supervisors were harsh, and many employees were recent immigrants who knew neither their rights nor the ways of this strange land. To alleviate these conditions, some employers developed a wide range

---

[1] For a summary of the historical literature including a comprehensive annotated bibliography, see Frank Miller and Mary Coghill, *The Historical Sources of Personnel Work.* (Ithaca, New York: N.Y. State School of Industrial and Labor Relations, 1961.)

of paternalistic benefit programs, extending from loans in times of adversity to lectures on thrift and homemaking (see Chapter 6). Such employers often hoped that their employees would be grateful for their benefits and, being happier, would work harder.

Some more foresighted employers hired social workers to help with these problems of adjustment and to provide sympathetic guidance for those who found themselves suffering from extreme pressure or discouragement. Others sought means by which workers' interests could be systematically represented within the organization. Since workers were afraid they would be punished if they complained to their bosses, the personnel department was a place to go for a fair hearing. In fact, personnel people served as an upward channel of communication between employees and production managers and represented the interests of employees in the councils of management.

Many personnel departments, however, made their first appearances as record-keeping departments. They maintained employment records (such as date hired, background information, successive jobs held in the company, and disciplinary penalties imposed), and also time- and production-records for the purpose of preparing payrolls. These were relatively routine clerical tasks that other members of the organization were probably glad to have taken from their shoulders. These functions are still important, of course, in view of the growing emphasis on pension and insurance programs, seniority benefits, and in-company promotion and management-development programs. But many argue that this development has been a curse to the personnel field because record-keeping lacks prestige in management circles.

Response to new knowledge. The early decades of the twentieth century are associated with the scientific management movement. F. W. Taylor and his followers, dealing largely with production workers, showed that productivity could be improved through time study, the careful design of jobs and tools, and the use of incentives (see Chapter 26). Meanwhile, new psychological research made it possible for companies to improve employee-selection procedures (see Chapter 20) by looking systematically at human differences. Similarly psychological principles of learning could be useful in training.

Both scientific management and psychology taught management to realize that human problems required analysis and systematic attention. To minimize *ad hoc* or expedient decision-making, specific *policies* were drawn up, particularly in regard to personnel (policies toward wages, employment, and the rest).

Governmental innovations and legislation. Government led the way in some personnel developments. The Civil Service pioneered in certain aspects of job evaluation (see Chapter 25), and private industry followed. In World War I, the U.S. Army experimented with a variety of selection and placement techniques that were later taken up by industry.

Government also contributed to the personnel field by legislation. Since the 1910's, there has been a growing stream of protective labor laws, both state and federal, that regulate wages, hours, and safety and hygienic conditions as well as provide social security (see Chapter 30) and compensation for on-the-job injuries (see Chapter 29).

Response to unionization. Employer opposition to trade unions helped increase the status of personnel departments, for many early benefit programs were looked upon as means of keeping unions out. The peak of the antiunion drive among large corporations occurred in the 1920's, when the so-called "American Plan" became popular. Under this scheme, employee-representation plans (ERP's) were established to provide a type of grievance procedure and to give employees a voice in decisions affecting the work force. Although many ERP's were but cynical efforts to provide the shell of representation without the substance, some employers sought to use these plans in good faith as a means of improving communications with rank-and-file workers. (Ironically, some of the leaders who arose in ERP later were active in starting unions.)

In addition, in the hope that employees would recognize their common interest with employers if they learned first-hand about the role of profits and shared in their growth, profit-sharing plans were established by some firms. It was hoped that workers would seek to increase profits by contributing their suggestions for production improvements and to go beyond the status of the worker who only follows orders in a rote fashion.

The 1930's

The personnel decision-making stage. During the 1930's there was another shift of emphasis: in many companies the personnel department (with its title often expanded to read "industrial relations department") was now expected to take direct charge of all employee and union relations. Often it was given full responsibility for hiring, firing, wage determination, handling union grievances, and determining who should be transferred or promoted.

Why did the personnel department suddenly gain so much power? Partly because of a widespread recognition by management of the importance of human elements, but probably the threat of unionism was the chief factor. Unions were on the offensive all through the late 1930's. They charged management with setting substandard wages, with discharging long-term employees unjustly, with harboring foremen who acted as petty tyrants, with basing transfers and promotions purely on favoritism, and with paying little attention to the human dignity of the individual worker. Faced with such charges, many companies felt that the best way to keep unions out was to eliminate the grievances that made workers turn to them. Management believed that inept supervisors were largely responsible for what observers conceded were haphazard personnel policies. So in many companies management gave the personnel department broad powers to establish uniform personnel policies and to police and administer them.

Unions came into many large companies in spite of the personnel department's efforts. But this invasion only served to increase its status. Now it had the responsibility for negotiating the labor contract and handling grievances. And since unions constantly seek out chinks in management's armor and try to establish precedents in one department that can be used elsewhere, the personnel department was given still further centralized control over personnel activities throughout the organization.

Yet as the supervisor's standing as a leader declined, the question of the staff's proper role in the organization was asked more and more persistently. To the supervisor the enhanced power of the staff meant a usurpation of his authority, a weakening of his relationship to his own subordinates, and a forced dependence on a department that did not share his responsibility for meeting cost and production objectives. The demoralized supervisor complained that he was being asked to run his department without any effective power to select, discipline, or reward his subordinates. Furthermore, the industrial-relations department overruled his decisions so frequently that he often gave up all attempts to exercise supervisory judgment.

In many organizations, personnel departments made critical decisions concerning such matters as selection, wage and salary administration, and discipline. Other organizations became concerned with the impact of this fragmentation of the supervisor's job on his ability to exercise effective leadership. These companies believed that staff groups like personnel should restrict their activities to advising and counseling supervisors who request their assistance.

The Present

In recent years the influence and prestige of the personnel function has expanded, for many reasons. Management no longer conceives of personnel work solely as a series of techniques to keep hourly workers satisfied or to meet governmental obligations. Management itself is a work force (involving selection, remuneration, and promotion problems, to name but a few). There is also an increasingly large professional-specialist group within organizations, and these people have high expectations that must be responded to. Long-range manpower projections have become a crucial tool for management at every level of the organization, and training takes places at almost every level.

In addition, particularly in very large organizations, audit and stabilization functions that serve as a control on personnel-related decisions have increased in scope. Many of these are administered, as we shall see in this chapter, by the personnel department.

Wider use of social science.   Management has also become more sophisticated about human relations. Starting with the Western Electric researches, the results of which began to appear in the late 1930's, management has learned that productivity is not simply a matter of getting the right man on a well-designed job and paying him an equitable wage (with perhaps an incentive rate attached). Employees restrict output, informal groups oppose change, and status systems and personality problems complicate and distort communications.

In other words, the simple tenets of scientific management have come under question and the emphasis has shifted from individuals to groups, social systems, and communication networks. Increasingly, to solve productivity problems management is turning to supervisory-development programs, personnel research, and organization analysis (often bringing in concepts from sociology, applied anthropology, and political science).

Most recently, the onrush of automation, the rising costs of unemployment insurance and supplementary benefits, and demands from the community for more attention to the problem of the unemployed have caused management to rethink its manpower policies. New approaches have been made to the retraining of older or unskilled workers. Revised transfer policies, early retirement, and various techniques to stabilize employment levels have been tried.

Finally, there has been a growing appreciation of the effect of community attitudes toward the firm both on attracting suitable manpower and shaping employee behavior in the organization. In this connection, companies have explored methods of measuring community attitudes and public-relations programs to contribute to their formation.

THE SCOPE OF PERSONNEL ADMINISTRATION

Let us now take a look at the scope of personnel administration in the modern organization. Our first effort will be to paint with broad strokes the subject matter that might be dealt with in a very large company's personnel program. Below is such a listing, but it is by no means comprehensive or necessarily representative of the work of the personnel staff of any given company.

Recruitment, Selection, and Placement

　Contact with and evaluation of advertising media, employment agencies, and state employment services
　College and school recruiting
　Screening and testing techniques including physical examinations
　Assistance on in-company transfer, career development
　Assistance in layoffs and plant closings through job searches for redundant personnel
　Labor market surveys and projections of potential shortages
　Manpower planning—projecting future company needs

Job Analysis, Job Description, and Job Evaluation

　Development of methods that will facilitate personnel placement and assignment of dollar values to skill and experience
　Development of promotional ladders by means of job analysis
　Position guides for organization planning and information for new placements

Compensation and Appraisal Plans

Design and implementation of personnel appraisal plans

Wage and salary administration

Control of merit increases

Design and installation of incentive and bonus plans

Administration of deferred-compensation plans such as profit-sharing, bonus plans

Employment Records

Maintenance of job histories, skill inventories, and aptitude and education information

Maintenance of wage and hour records, output records, overtime, vacation payments, incentive earnings

Employee Benefit Programs

Administration of life insurance, pension, and health and welfare benefits programs

Approval of vacation, disability, and compensation payments

Suggestion and saving plans; credit union administration

Recreation and athletic programs

Cafeterias, employee clubs

Company medical services: first aid, preventive medicine, community referrals (psychiatric, alcoholic)

Counseling service

Special Services

Safety inspection; safety plans and controls

Company guards and protection services including fire fighting

Staffing of reception areas

Communication services: photography, printing, house organs, policy manuals, news releases, instructional manuals

Training and Education Programs

Liaison with public schools, training institutes, and colleges, with apprentice programs

Planning and administration of induction, on-the-job, after-hours, and development-training courses

Administration of education-rebate programs

Supervisory training and management-development activities

Assistance in the identification of training needs and personnel who might benefit from training

Validation of training usefulness

Grants to schools, scholarship programs

Labor Relations

Assistance in preparation for and participation in contract negotiations

Participation in grievance procedure

Internal organization of a large company's personnel department.

Analysis of grievances, contract terms

Continuing monitoring of legislation and court decisions in the labor area

Training of supervisors in contract interpretation

Assistance in preparing arbitration cases; maintaining labor relations services and consultant relationships

Maintenance of seniority lists

Shared trusteeship of union-management benefit program

Advice on contracting-out decisions

Public Relations

Company donation and gift policies

Liaison with community officials, various community groups, and social welfare agencies (e.g. Scouts)

Preparation of news releases on company events

Development of tour and information programs for visitors

Speech writing, lecture services

Assistance in the writing of articles by technical personnel for professional journals

Representation of company on special boards, inquiries and other community and governmental committees

Personnel Planning and Evaluation

Validation of the usefulness of various personnel techniques

Assessment of the strengths and weaknesses of company personnel policies and practices

Conduct of morale surveys, personnel audits

Assistance in organization planning, preparation of organization charts

Personnel research on persisting company problems

Retention of consultants

The way many of these activities are structured in a typical personnel department is shown in the accompanying diagram.

THE LATERAL RELATIONS
OF THE PERSONNEL FUNCTION

Traditionally, personnel work has been conceived of as a *staff* function, that is, as secondary or subsidiary to the major *line* functions of business (such as manufacturing or sales). The staff category also meant a lack of authority and, of course, low prestige (and often low compensation as well).

But, as we have already seen, this dichotomy is an oversimplification, both because staff groups do have power and because there are various patterns of relationships associated with those functions of the business that go by the title of "staff."

Let us apply our knowledge about these patterns of lateral relationship in the modern organization in order to learn more about how personnel work is actually performed. In the process, we shall also observe some of the conflicts and dilemmas inherent in the personnel function.

The Advisory Role:
Influence without Authority

Perhaps the most common behavior pattern of all, or at least the one most often associated with the professional personnel manager, is serving as an *advisor*. In such matters as the impact of labor legislation, appropriate techniques for dealing with the union, the availability of tests, and labor market sources for new recruits, the personnel man *on request* supplies technical information, counsel, and recommendations to *assist* another manager in making a decision or solving a problem. The scope for such advice is bounded by the recognized competency of the personnel man and the range of problems faced by line management.

As we observed in pages 384-385, one of the central problems of the advisory role is the temptation (and often the demand) to become an authoritative decision-maker.

A case example. But how can a personnel department exert influence without resorting to the use of authority? To put it another way, how can the staff man gain acceptance for his ideas without forcing them on the line manager under threat of punishment or promise of reward? Let us look at a typical case and then explore possible solutions:

> The personnel department has noticed that turnover is very high in Chet Anthony's department. Chet's boss, the vice president in charge of sales, urges the personnel director, Phillips, to do something to halt the loss of valuable personnel. What should the personnel director do? How should he approach Anthony?

What happens if he calls on Anthony to say that both he and the vice president are worried about his high turnover rate? Chances are that Anthony will react this way:

> "Here is someone representing the vice president. Phillips carries the boss' authority. All right, what do they want me to do? If they're willing to put up the money for higher salaries or take the responsibility for putting in some new-fangled ideas, that's up to them; it's no skin off my teeth."

Clearly, the battle is lost before it has begun, for Anthony has no intention of telling Phillips what his problems really are. From this point on, Anthony may "cover up" as much as possible and try to shift the blame for any future problems onto personnel.

And if Phillips makes suggestions, Anthony may term them "too theoretical" or "impractical," or else accept them superficially (perhaps just to settle the issue), only to destroy them in practice through subtle sabotage. For example, he may agree to introduce some technique of general supervision and even hold meetings with his subordinates and ask for their advice, but continue to hold the threat of punishment over the head of anyone who does not immediately accept his point of view.

How then can the personnel director influence the department head without "pulling rank"? Primarily by persuading Anthony to regard him as a *source of help.* Anthony has certain objectives that he is trying to achieve. He may be anxious to establish a record that will earn him a promotion, or to win prestige in the eyes of his fellow managers, or to minimize the amount of administrative red tape. Phillips can exert influence by convincing Anthony that his skills and knowledge will help him reach his goals.[2]

---

[2] We are indebted here to the excellent analysis of the role of the staff expert first presented by Douglas McGregor in his article, "The Staff Function in Human Relations," *Journal of Social Issues*, Vol. IV, No. 3 (Summer 1948), pp. 6-23.

The staff expert must keep in mind that Anthony's way of handling his department has evolved over a long period of time in response to his own particular needs. For any real change to take place, Anthony must discover for himself that his behavior is inadequate to the situation, and must be genuinely ready to accept help.

Phillips might start the discussion by commenting that he has noticed a rise in the turnover figure and is curious about what it signifies. Is Anthony having any trouble training replacements? Is there anything the personnel department can do to help? Using this as an opening, Phillips might encourage Anthony to explore the problem. While Anthony talks, Phillips should avoid seeming to judge him, or to be imposing a solution on him. Instead, Phillips should make it clear that he is merely trying to find out how the problem looks to Anthony and perhaps help Anthony view his problems and himself more realistically. Phillips should concentrate on creating an atmosphere that will permit a free and easy discussion of all the facts in the case and the possible alternative solutions.

In the process of working together on a variety of problems, Phillips can learn Anthony's attitudes toward his job and its problems. He also can present a picture of personnel's role and position in the organization. He can make it clear that the goals of the personnel department are to help other groups and individuals help themselves to deal with their human-relations problems, and to provide specific skills and techniques when they are called for by the line managers.

Next Phillips might encourage Anthony to consider the alternative solutions to the problem, and the probable success of each. This is the most crucial point of all, for Anthony must work through for himself the ramifications of suggested changes. He must regard as his own any programs that are developed, and must assume responsibility for implementing them. For example, Anthony may have to make a presentation before his boss to get a new appropriation to assist in solving this problem. "Role-playing" (see Chapter 24) then can be used to "try out" various approaches to the boss. Such training, counseling, and try-outs should be designed not only to increase the line official's skill but also to bolster his confidence in himself.

In effect, Phillips should try to use all his knowledge of individual needs and informal group behavior, of supervisory skills (such as interviewing and discipline), and of labor relations to *help* the line supervisor make *his own* decision.

In this case, Anthony may decide that his own supervisors need a training program to improve their managerial skills. But he would prefer to have the whole program handled by the personnel department—after all, this is "out of his field" and personnel are the experts. Phillips should be wary of such efforts to shift the responsibility to his department. Lacking responsibility for the program, Anthony would never be sure that it was exactly what he wanted; the supervisors participating in the program would not associate it with the "boss'" attitudes and desires.

Of course, Phillips must not be merely a passive listener. He must provide information and evaluations, when asked—though only as a means to help Anthony make a realistic decision. For example, he might reveal some of the dimensions of the problem by probing more deeply into the turnover statistics: Who is leaving—what age groups, from what occupational groups? How does turnover here compare with turnover in other departments? What are the possible causes: wages, supervision (including Anthony's), other factors in the work environment? Personnel, like any other specialist department, has analytical tools at its command—in this case, perhaps, a community salary survey or a review of department employment records.

Thus, a simple "yes" or "no" answer—a "do this" or "do that" response—by the personnel man to line problems wastes an important opportunity. Research in learning suggests that training is more effective and individuals more highly motivated to learn when they have immediate problems that they want to solve. The best time to help train a supervisor to make better decisions in the future is when he has an immediate problem.

Eventually, with the passage of time, subsequent discussions with the personnel department should enable Anthony to handle his personnel problems by himself, and to ask for help only when especially difficult problems crop up. The end result should be a better-informed supervisor with considerable skill in applying to his day-to-day problems the knowledge developed by personnel experts.

Characteristics of the advisory role.   Let us summarize the elements that seem to characterize a healthy advisory relationship:

1. The supervisor turns to the personnel man for help with his problems largely on his own initiative, with a feeling that he can discuss them freely with a sympathetic listener who is not in the line of authority.

2. The supervisor comes to understand the role and to utilize the skills embodied in the personnel group, and, in turn, the personnel staff grows familiar with the special interests and needs of the supervisory group it services.

3. The supervisor is helped by personnel to understand the dimensions and alternative solutions of his problems, and is helped to develop skill in evaluating alternatives.

4. The supervisor increases his own ability to cope with the human problems of his group. He regards problems as means of developing new abilities and insights.

5. The personnel staff develops greater acceptance for its ideas and points of view, not through putting pressure on the line supervisor to change "or else," but through developing confidence in the staff's "helping" role and through proving in practice that it can contribute to the supervisor's effectiveness.

6. The line organization receives credit for any improvements that result.

You will have realized, of course, that we have been describing an ideal staff-line relationship, one that is difficult to achieve in practice. Staff groups like personnel actively struggle within the organization to gain recognition and acceptance for their points of view and skills. While their efforts to contribute ideas and programs often fall on deaf ears, top management may still hold them responsible for evident failures in the company's personnel efforts. As a result, staff officials are caught in a dilemma: How can we exert influence and help ward off personnel problems in the organization when we don't have authority to get our recommendations adopted by the supervisors whose actions determine the company's personnel relationships? Efforts to escape this dilemma take many forms: attempts to "educate" supervisors or their bosses, guarded threats to report ineffective supervisory actions to higher levels in the organization, and a host of subtle or overt lobbying activities.

Audit and Stabilization Relationships

In terms of influence and power, audit and stabilization roles are at the other end of the spectrum from advisory relationships. An example of stabilization relationships for a personnel department is the requirement that it approve all requests for merit increases or interdepartmental transfers. Thus, managers must get the permission of Personnel *before* they can go ahead with their plans (presumably in order to assure that no line manager hurts larger organizational objectives by his actions).

Top management also asks Personnel to appraise, or audit, how well line managers are doing their job, *after the fact*. Relative wage costs, as between various departments or between the company and its competitors, or the effectiveness of department heads in "bringing along" (i.e., developing) junior subordinates, in maintaining employee morale, or in minimizing grievances—all can be audited by Personnel and reported up the line.

Behind these activities is the assumption that the organization has *standards* or *criteria* on which to base the evaluation of supervisory or departmental performance. For example, checking to see that the salaries paid for engineers in Department Z are "appropriate" requires that there be such policies. The same holds for appraisals of productivity, safety, and the results of labor negotiation.

Staff departments are often asked to develop indices that will keep upper levels of management informed. Personnel specialists, for example, develop measures of turnover that will enable individual departments to compare their records with those of other departments in the same company as well as in other companies. The same holds for accident records, absenteeism statistics, number of grievances, and similar personnel data.

Although personnel groups have technical expertise in activities of this sort, it is our view that they should *not* be permitted to establish the organization's criteria for supervisory success. All the policies, objectives, and standards of the company are so integrally related to one another that line management— and line management alone—must retain responsibility for determining them. The staff can provide information on which line can base its decisions, of course. For example, in establishing a salary policy for a branch unit in a new community, personnel department surveys of labor supply and salaries paid for comparable jobs will be an indispensable component of the final policy decision. But line management should decide what salary policy the company will adopt.

Problems When Personnel Wields Power

Conflicts with the advisory role. Perhaps the most serious problem that occurs where Personnel wields these types of powers is the likelihood that they will interfere with the advisory relationship. The latter requires complete openness, the willingness on the part of the manager to reveal his fears and shortcomings—if aid is to be forthcoming. Is it reasonable to assume that a manager will be open with a group that is also auditing aspects of his performance or whose permission he must obtain before he takes certain actions? Isn't he likely either to hide data or to exaggerate his needs?

Impairment of line responsibility. Another source of trouble is that line managers resent these restrictions on their freedom when they emanate from groups such as personnel staff who appear to have excessive authority with no concomitant responsibilities.

> Those guys tell me I can't give one of my key engineers a raise. They won't be blamed if I miss my schedule because the guy quits; *I* will!

Resentment may also arise if it is felt that Personnel is a lower-status group initiating action for a higher-status group.

And as another cause of trouble, see what happens when the supervisor is required to get the permission of the industrial-relations department before discharging an employee (part of a stabilization role). The supervisor now may be inclined to shrug off responsibility for the future performance of the man. "After all, I really wanted to get rid of him, but they made me keep him," reasons the supervisor. The supervisor has many difficult and risky decisions to make. This one may cause a work stoppage and that one may lose a valuable man. If management wants the supervisor to take responsibility for making difficult, unpleasant decisions, Personnel cannot take a strong hand in influencing these decisions.

Who is the boss? Another serious ramification of staff decision-making is the potential erosion of the supervisor's leadership position. As employees begin to detect that the personnel department is determining how hard they should work and at what rate of pay, who is hired and who is fired, they find little reason for dealing with their direct supervisor as the "boss." He, in turn, will find it increasingly difficult to motivate or control the behavior of his subordinates, since he no longer controls the rewards and penalties or determines the basic decisions in his department.

Often the personnel department becomes the "good boss" when employees discover that they can obtain relief from their supervisor's decisions by taking them "to personnel." In other cases the supervisor "passes the buck" to the personnel department; he tells a subordinate, "I'd be glad to give you that raise, but they (the personnel people) won't let me."

In either case the supervisor's relationship to his men is damaged. His subordinates decide that the personnel department, not the supervisor, has the power to influence their standing in the organization, and bend their efforts to finding ways of influencing the personnel department.

Seeing only part of the picture.   Further, most supervisory problems do not lend themselves to decisions by stabilization groups, largely because a single staff expert, by virtue of his job and his training, sees only part of the picture. Often a seemingly trivial decision concerning something like the change of one man's work schedule may involve questions of cost, production balancing, safety, quality, work-group stability, and a host of special circumstances that can only be known to the immediate supervisor in the department where the question has arisen. The supervisor can call on one or more experts like the personnel man for advice on parts of the problem, but rarely can the expert solve the whole problem.

"Passing the buck."   Of course, we should not forget, as noted in Chapter 16, that many line supervisors *want* Personnel to make decisions in these difficult human problems of administration. The readiness with which line officials surrender responsibility for unpleasant personnel matters has been described by Mason Haire:

> If we are assembling widgets we usually know just what to do. . . . However, at the next step up the hierarchy the job is very different. Now, although the superior is responsible for the number of widgets turned out, he can't assemble them himself. He must accomplish the production through a very uncertain medium that intervenes between him and the widgets themselves—the people on the production line. It is a medium that is changeable, unpredictable, and intractable. It is a little like trying to pick a cherry from the bottom of a tall glass with two wobbly straws. It is easy to see what you are trying to do, but the instrument with which you are working is very hard to control. In many cases it seems likely that it is because of the difficulty of the medium through which production must be accomplished that managers turn away from the medium itself, in an unconscious effort to escape the problem, and say, My job is production—I'll hire an expert staff man to worry about the people.[3]

The need for good working relations.   Line management may look upon Personnel's control activities (i.e., audit and stabilization) as just another form

---

[3] Mason Haire, *Psychology in Management* (New York: McGraw-Hill, 1956), pp. 49-50.

of pressure designed to make its life more difficult. At the operating level, the supervisor has to cope with informal groups, he has to adjust to the demands of his subordinates if he is to get them to accept his demands—and this means that he must often depart from the plans, procedures, and policies that top management has established. Understandably, he regards Personnel's control activities as a threat to his established ways of doing things. Line managers are motivated to hide their methods of operation, to juggle figures or seek excuses or shift responsibility in order to cover up deviations from standards (see Chapter 15). In the process, they develop an antipathy for the "checkers" who do not "understand the problems we face on the firing line."

Personnel is responsible for directing management's attention to human-relations trouble spots and for helping to develop remedial actions. But it can do neither job unless it enjoys a good working relationship with the line officials who must institute changes. Unless this relationship exists, the staff can prepare any number of lengthy reports and analyses, but most will automatically be filed away and never referred to again. Successful industrial-relations personnel have learned that they are more effective in improving line performance if they discuss the results of their evaluations with the supervisor involved *before* they send them on to higher management. This gives the supervisor a chance to improve his performance before the boss learns that he is doing a poor job. Rather than a pressure mechanism, the staff report then becomes a device to help the supervisor remedy defects in his operations and meet the standards established by top management. When most of the problems uncovered by staff investigations are remedied without recourse to higher levels of the organization, one usually finds that staff and line groups work together harmoniously.

Line managers also will be more willing to accept a staff control report if they can see how its contents will help them achieve their objectives and if it is timely. As a personnel director described his technique for dealing with the salary increase problem:

> If we wait until the manager gives out his increases, we are in trouble because then all we can do is "blow the whistle" on those that have exceeded the percentage top management has established. Also we get into a dog fight over whether or not special circumstances justify more increases in a particular case. So we concentrate most of our efforts on working with managers and showing them how to get the most mileage out of their budgeted salary increases and how to handle those whom they've got to disappoint in such a way that they don't become problem cases.

Service Relationships

In practice, it is impossible to draw a neat dividing line between Personnel's responsibilities for carrying out audit duties and responsibilities for carrying out *service* functions. The identification of a recurrent line problem often leads directly to the development of a new service program.

In performing a service activity, the staff department does something *for* the line department. Usually the relationship is quite amicable, for line departments have little interest or ability in these specialized areas and are glad to have staff relieve them of what they feel are "nasty headaches." For instance, the division manager is glad to have Personnel handle the writing of job descriptions. Many other examples of service relationship could be cited, notably recruiting, testing, and training programs. One of the earliest staff roles was to serve as the representative or stand-in of the manager who could not be personally present, and personnel department executives now often fill just such jobs: They represent the department head at a community dinner, the president on a fund-raising campaign, the company at a union contract-negotiation session. Because of their training and experience in interpersonal relationships, it is believed that they can handle speech-making, meetings with strangers, and negotiations more effectively than the typical line manager. As government and community relations become more important, the demand for this type of service work is likely to increase.

There are times, however, when the service relationship leads to friction.

1. The line department may ask the staff department to perform services that the staff feels are excessive or unnecessary.

2. Several line departments may compete with one another for a larger share of the staff department's services.

3. In contrast, the line department may resent the staff department's performing a particular service, either because line feels it can handle the service more effectively itself, or because it feels that the so-called "service" actually makes its job harder.

Line asks for too many services.   At times line management requests services that staff believes are unnecessary, ill-advised or that should be handled by the line. For example, a line department may ask the personnel department to run a training program for first-line supervisors, even though the personnel department is convinced that such a program will be useless until higher management itself participates in it. A supervisor may pass the buck to the personnel department in the handling of a ticklish disciplinary problem. Or line management may ask the personnel department to make the final decisions on union grievances, or even to handle the negotiations for a new contract.

Some of the services requested may appear wasteful. A training program is not always the answer to employee-relations problems. A bigger and fancier house organ may actually intensify the problems of poor employee-employer relations.

Personnel staff should try to persuade line departments not to request unnecessary services. In the last analysis, however, staff may have to provide such services if the line authority insists—at least, if line is willing to pay for them out of its budget. The skillful personnel official, without seeming to shirk his responsibilities, is able to demonstrate to the line official why a special new program will not answer his problems.

Conflicts over scarce services.   When line's demand for services becomes too great, the staff must somehow ration its limited time and energies among rival claimants. Department A wants Personnel to devote more of its efforts to recruiting engineers; Department B thinks Personnel should concentrate on finding better accountants. The staff department must show great tact in setting priorities, for every time it turns down one department's request for services it hurts its advisory relationship with that department. Preferably line-management establishes standards for these priorities.

Resistance to staff performance of services.   Some line departments, imbued with the "do-it-yourself" philosophy, object to having staff perform certain services. They feel that they could much more effective service if they could do their own recruiting, instead of having to channel their manpower requisitions through the personnel department. Certainly when the line department has direct control over a service, it does not have to compete with other departments for "scarce resources." Furthermore, line may feel that staff does not understand its special needs. Thus, the engineering department may feel that it should recruit its own engineers, since "the average personnel man doesn't know what makes a good engineer tick." Often, too, line supervisors are suspicious that Personnel wants to take over a service in order to increase its own importance and the size of its budget and its staff. Line's resistance is intensified if management charges the cost of the new service against the line department's budget, or if it requires line managers to spend time and energy on the new activity.[4]

> We once watched the difficulties encountered by the personnel department in one company that attempted to introduce a new management-development program. Line officials tried to sabotage the program, even though it was designed to help them develop more promotable subordinates. However, in another company an almost identical program was welcomed by line managers. Why the difference?
>
> In the second company, the firm's president had indicated that one of the new *controls* he would begin watching was the number of promotable executives produced by each department and the vigor with which each department set up training programs. Aware that this new factor would enter into their own appraisal, the line managers asked the personnel department to *help them* create management-development programs. In the first company, the initiative had come exclusively from personnel.

In short, line managers welcome staff activities that promise to help them achieve their own goals and resist those that do not seem intimately related to their needs.

Personnel initiates programs. Personnel departments sometimes find themselves engaged in service activities that they feel should really be handled

---

[4] It is common accounting practice to prorate the cost of service programs to all line departments according to some criterion like number of employees or gross sales.

by line simply because line refuses to accept responsibility for them. At other times, staff throws its energies into service activities seemingly as a compensation for its failure to develop satisfactory advisory relationships with line. One personnel director told us:

> "I handle grievances myself. I know you professors think this is wrong—it detracts from my supervisors' prestige and so forth. But I can't trust them to handle grievances properly—every time I let them try it I get into trouble. I've tried training programs, but I can't get them to change their ways. Some day our present supervisors will retire and I'll let the new men handle the responsibility. But for the moment I can't risk ruining my union relations just to back up a theory."

Staff often retreats into service activities because they do not require such close working relations with line management as do most advisory relationships. For example, a safety director may have tried in vain to get supervisors to attend a safety course, or to induce them to discipline employees who engage in unsafe practices. In despair he resorts to a safety poster campaign—not because he thinks posters can compete with a supervisor's order in changing employee behavior—but because he knows that no one will object to posters and at least he will have a sense of achievement and something to show management in the way of "activity."

> [One company] reports that it has developed an automated suggestion box which senses an employee who is approaching the box. When this occurs a music box attachment is "set off," playing a stimulating march tune and then a taped "pep talk" on the value of suggestion, and finally a shoe-shine device is activated which gives the employee at the suggestion box a free shoe shine.

Company resources are wasted frequently in these efforts.

Appropriate Division of Labor for Service Work

The table on page 442 represents what we feel is an appropriate division of labor and responsibility between staff services and line in the area of employment. As you check the distribution of responsibility between staff and line, try to analyze the reasoning behind it.

Centralized Company Services

Personnel departments also carry out service activities that are far removed from the day-to-day problems of other parts of the organization. Examples of this include the processing of claims and records relating to company welfare programs, the operation of company medical facilities, fire fighting, and plant-protection units, manning reception desks, administering suggestion plans, and running cafeterias. Sometimes Personnel becomes almost a catchall for activities that don't fit elsewhere.

Division of Labor for the Employment Function [9]

DEPARTMENT SUPERVISION (LINE)	PERSONNEL-EMPLOYMENT SPECIALIST (STAFF)
1. Prepare requisition outlining specific qualifications of employees needed to fill specific positions. Help create reputation that will attract applicants. [First step.]	1. Develop sources of qualified applicants from local labor market. This requires carefully planned community relations, speeches, advertisements, and active high-school, college, and technical-school recruiting. [Second step.]
2. Interview and select from candidates screened by Personnel. Make specific job assignments that will utilize new employees' highest skills to promote maximum production. [Fifth step.]	2. Conduct skilled interviews, give scientific tests, and make thorough reference checks, etc., using requisition and job description as guides. Screening must meet company standards and conform with employment laws. [Third step.]
3. Indoctrinate employees with specific details regarding the sections and jobs where they are to be assigned—safety rules, pay, hours, "our customs." [Seventh step.]	3. Refer best candidates to supervisor, after physical examinations and qualifications for the positions available have been carefully evaluated. [Fourth step.]
4. Instruct and train on the job according to planned training program already worked out with Personnel. [Eighth step.]	4. Give new employees preliminary indoctrination about the company, benefit plans, general safety, first aid, shift hours, etc. [Sixth step.]
5. Follow up, develop, and rate employee job performance; decide on promotion, transfer, layoff, or discharge. [Ninth step.]	5. Keep complete record of current performance and future potential of each employee. [Tenth step.]
6. Hold separation interview when employees leave—determine causes. Make internal department adjustments to minimize turnover. [Eleventh step.]	6. Diagnose information given in separation interviews, determine causes, and take positive steps to correct. [Twelfth step.]

9 Robert Saltonstall, "Who's Who in Personnel Administration," *Harvard Business Review,* Volume 33, No. 4 (July 1955), pp. 75-83.

The numbers of people supervised can be very substantial and the administrative requirements demanding. Many times professional personnel skills are diverted from more profound corporate problems. A typical frustrating example is company food services, always a fruitful source of complaint and frustration. There is some trend toward the contracting-out of such functions, which are so unlike the normal "business" of the organization, on the grounds that a specialized outsider can do it more efficiently and with less drain on in-company administrative talent.[5]

Personnel can also carry out specialized activities that are germane and central to its more traditional functions of working with other parts of the

5 Cf. Margaret Chandler and Leonard Sayles, *Contracting-Out,* Columbia University, Graduate School of Business, 1959.

organization. Many of the research activities of larger personnel departments fall into this category. Typical research problems include sources of employee motivation, effective supervisory styles, differential illness and accident propensities in the work force and relative usefulness of alternative safety devices and clothing.

Special Problems
in Decentralized Organizations

Staff departments in decentralized organizations face special difficulties: Their immediate supervisor is usually the line manager who heads the branch operation, but they also have a "functional relationship" to the central-office staff group. Thus, a personnel man in the Akron office of the Superior Insurance Company takes his orders from the District Manager in that office, but his chances for promotion also depend on whether or not he pleases the Vice President for Personnel in New York City. Conflict often arises when the central staff tries to get some new program adopted throughout the organization —for example, an employee-appraisal system. The local personnel man is urged by New York to lobby for the new program, but the management in Akron is far from enthusiastic about having New York interfere in local employee relations. The local staff man is caught up in a "role conflict," since he must try to satisfy the incompatible norms or standards of two distinct groups.

THE STATUS OF PERSONNEL WORK

Personnel work has had and continues to have its status problems within the organization. Its historical association with social work and record-keeping, its frequent responsibilities for a miscellaneous collection of peripheral activities, and the fact that shortsighted top managements often transfer less-than-successful executives to a "safe" Personnel position—all contribute to diminished status. On the other hand, few companies fail to recognize that the effective management of human resources is one of the most crucial factors associated with growth. Insofar as personnel managers prove themselves effective in contributing to this objective, their status and influence is assured.

In fact, in some companies there is extreme jealousy because of the mobility of personnel executives. In effect, theirs is a shorter hierarchy and they can more easily gain the attention of top management. Balancing this advantage, though, is the usual requirement that experience in line management is essential for promotion into top management. There has often been jealousy between the more academically trained industrial-relations man and the "experienced-trained" line executive. But this is disappearing as formal university training becomes a more common part of the background of all managers.

The future is never easy to foretell. An increasingly large number of companies have Vice Presidents for Personnel or Industrial Relations. At the same time, practitioners of new specializations—in systems, organization planning, and organization development—are competing with personnel professionals for the recognition and attention of top management.

The nature of the personnel function is often confusing and ambiguous. Personnel men engage in high- and low-status activities at the same time. Their roles as advisors may often seem inconsistent with their roles as auditors and stabilizers. Although personnel work is a separate speciality, it is also at the heart of every manager's job. Thus, a delicate balance must be kept between those aspects of personnel which should be handled by the line manager and those which should be handled by the staff specialist.

Close coordination must exist between Personnel and other functions of the organization. The successful personnel executive must gain the confidence and respect of his colleagues in other departments. He must persuade them that he is seeking to help them with *their* problems and to meet their objectives, that he is using techniques that are useful and valid, and that he is not seeking to embarrass or show them up. He is certain to run into trouble if he seeks credit for constant "victories" or is too concerned with status.

Further, the personnel man deals with complex and recalcitrant materials. Figures and materials are relatively manipulable; they "stay put" and there are reliable, highly workable theories by which they can be put to appropriate use. Despite much social research, the behavior of human beings is less predictable.

Thus, personnel men require unusual personalities. They must identify organization trouble spots and work with line management without creating antagonisms and without using threats. Their job is sometimes made particularly difficult by differences in their own background and training and that of line officials.

Many managers who wish that Personnel would step in and take over their human-relations troubles still resent Personnel's interference when it stops them from transferring an employee or giving a raise.

From one point of view, Personnel's chief job is to help line management learn to detect and solve its own problems. Line's motivation to learn is heightened when it is aware that it has a problem. As auditors, personnel men should be conscious of the difficulties which each manager faces in meeting the standards set for his unit by top management. By helping the manager think through his difficulties, and by providing him with new skills and techniques in coping with them, personnel can discharge its training responsibility. Sometimes the solution may be a totally new staff program or service. For example, recurring shortages of qualified applicants might be dealt with by having Personnel handle all recruitment.

Ideally, management should take advantage of staff's technical expertise, but it should keep the basic responsibility for managing the organization firmly and unambiguously in the hands of department supervision. Both line and personnel people must work together, and their activities must intermesh; but their roles in the organization should not be permitted to shift over time. Line must retain the basic responsibility for setting standards and executing plans.

PROBLEM 1

APPRAISING AND THE ENGINEERS

Growing out of a top management decision, the Development Division of Crowder Engineering has been required to implement an "obsolescence program." The policy that will be administered by the personnel department requires each unit head to rank all of his employees, thereby identifying each group's lowest 10%. The policy states that this low ranked group will be considered for discharge, transfer, or early retirement depending on further individual evaluations.

The corporate personnel man is very enthusiastic about this program and helped sell it to top management. The head of personnel for the Division has been less than enthusiastic about it on the grounds that the Development Division has a select group of employees; he also believes an across-the-board dropping of 10% is a serious mistake. Further, in his efforts to explain the program to unit heads within the Division, he has encountered great resistance.

Under the corporate timetable each unit head was to submit his rankings by July 1 to his Division manager. As of June 30 only 6 out of the 27 unit heads had submitted their forms. On that day the Division manager received a call from the executive vice president at corporate headquarters reminding him that these would be due the next day. The following dialogue took place after the manager excitedly called his personnel man to his office:

Division Manager: Harold, how come you let me down? Here we are just about overdue on those rankings, and you never alerted me that we were going to be in trouble on this. Your job is to keep me out of trouble with the head office on personnel matters. You are in contact with those unit heads, and if you spot that they are not doing something that they are supposed to be doing—come to me with it and come quick. Now what the blazes can we do this late?

Personnel Manager: This is one of the most unpopular policies that has ever come out of headquarters. I've been trying to convince our people to go along with it, but frankly I find it hard to be convincing! And, Joe, if I run to you and "squeal" on your people who may be violating some policy or other, they'll never have any confidence in me. They won't tell me things about their real personnel difficulties and I won't be able to provide that kind of assistance which you want me to provide to them and that will keep this operation functioning smoothly.

Division Manager: But you put me out on a limb when you don't keep me informed. I want you to "squeal" if you find someone who isn't doing his job in the personnel area; that's as much a part of your job as helping those guys. You're my eyes out there in the labs.

1. How can the personnel man reconcile the demands of his advisory and his audit responsibilities to the division manager?

2. The personnel man also has a "functional" relationship to the corporate personnel department. Evaluate that relationship.
3. What should the personnel man do when he has an unpopular policy to enforce which he himself has doubts about?

INFLUENTIAL PERSONNEL

The finishing department in a large paper-manufacturing plant has been the source of many grievances. The personnel director of the plant has evidence that the superintendent of the department is in part at fault. The superintendent, a member of the "old school," assigns heavy disciplinary penalties for the slightest violation of shop rules. The most recent grievance, which almost resulted in a strike, concerned a two-week layoff he had given to a man for "loafing on the job." Caught smoking in the washroom, the man had insisted it was common practice for workers to leave their machines for brief intervals when setup men were changing rolls. The union won its grievance and the employee received two weeks' back pay for the "unjustified" layoff.

This was just one of a series of such instances. To date, the finishing department has had two wildcat strikes and several slowdowns.

It is common knowledge in the company that the personnel director has had several discussions with this superintendent about his handling of disciplinary problems and his dealings with the unions.

The plant manager is primarily concerned about maintaining output levels. Competition is severe and stoppages impair the company's ability to fill orders. For this reason the plant manager has decided to transfer the superintendent of the finishing department to a considerably less important job. In doing this, he points out to the superintendent that the transfer is a direct result of his failure to follow good personnel practices, and that he has had ample opportunity to "mend his ways" with the help of the personnel director.

Word quickly spreads through the organization that the "word of the personnel director is law" and that supervisors violate his "suggestions" at the risk of transfer or discharge.

1. How can the personnel director, under these circumstances, retain his staff status and avoid "undermining" the authority of line supervisors?

A CASE FOR ROLE-PLAYING:
DEALING WITH A SUPERVISOR ACCUSED OF DISCRIMINATION

Role for Personnel Director.   You are convinced that the supervisor of the receiving and marking room is discriminating among his employees. There is now a union grievance on your desk charging that he has failed to equalize overtime in the department as required by the union contract. Two girls were passed over for Friday night work that involved an extra four hours (or pay for six hours), which amounts to about $10 lost wages for each girl, Miss Smith and Miss Jenkins.

The supervisor claims that he asked the girls on Friday whether or not they would like to work and they said they wanted to get an early start for a weekend trip. The union claims that the supervisor purposely waited until late Friday before announcing the opportunity in order to discriminate against these particular girls. In the past, the supervisor has indicated that he was dissatisfied with their work and attitudes.

In "playing" the role of personnel director, have clearly in mind the objectives you want to accomplish through your discussion with the supervisor.

Role for the Supervisor. You have been pressed to cut costs. Your department is a sort of "graveyard" to which women who have failed elsewhere are transferred. You don't like to admit this, however, because it lowers your prestige. In fact, you yourself may have been put in this department for the same reason! Where possible, you try to give the girls who do accomplish something a little extra break, feeling that it is the only way to encourage them, since all jobs pay the same. The work is unpleasant, though relatively easy and not fatiguing. The two worst shirkers are Miss Smith and Miss Jenkins. They are always baiting you and you are pretty sure they are telling other people in the department false things about you behind your back.

You did wait until late in the day hoping that they would refuse. You don't see how you can face them if they win the grievance and get back pay. You feel that would destroy any chance of improving the morale and efficiency of your department.

1. Role play the personnel director's interview with the supervisor.
2. Assuming that the personnel director is unsuccessful in his interview with the supervisor, what should be his next move?

MANPOWER AND EMPLOYEE DEVELOPMENT

We are now ready to consider the more traditional areas of personnel management. Since each supervisor faces almost identical problems in developing and maintaining effective employee relationships, and since the actions of one supervisor have an impact on all others within the same organization, progressive companies try to establish and publicize systematic policies for the treatment of personnel questions. These, in turn, regulate personnel decisions.

Few organizations can take for granted that there will always be enough workers available to fill all the jobs that must be manned. Consequently, one of the most pressing responsibilities of management is to attract to the firm and develop within the organization enough people to handle present positions and to move into vacancies created by changes in the company's business, retirement rate, and other factors.

A stream of qualified personnel must be kept flowing into the organization and through the various promotional, training, and transfer channels designed to allocate scarce human resources. This is a continuing responsibility, for no organization is static: Employees are always leaving; and shortages are always developing at certain points, surpluses at others. In this section we shall examine alternative methods for developing this "stream of manpower" and various criteria for judging the effectiveness of these methods.

The sequence of chapters in this section reflects the movement of employees throughout the total organization: Chapter 19, "Recruitment and Selection," discusses ways of bringing new personnel into the organization; Chapter 20, "Promotions, Transfers, and Seniority," takes the newly hired employees along the pathways by which they are assigned to appropriate jobs and rewarded for performance and service. "Technical Training," Chapter 21, concentrates on the psychology of learning as applied to the development of specific job skills, again at the non-managerial level. The next three chapters are concerned with the assignment and development of managerial talents: "Management Development," Chapter 22; "Performance Evaluation," Chapter 23; and "Management Training," Chapter 24.

In no one of these areas are there any pat formulas or fixed principles. However, there are methods of analysis that enable the manager to develop solutions consistent with his needs at a particular time, in a particular place. Thus in the chapters to follow in this section and in the next as well, we shall be emphasizing the questions that management must ask itself when seeking to develop policies and procedures. Personnel problems are never solved easily or permanently. Company-wide methods may minimize the human-relations problems of each supervisor, but each method has its limitations and requires constant adjustment.

Our objective is to ask the "right questions"—to identify the potential sources of difficulty in each situation, to know what data are necessary, and what method of analysis, to provide a workable (but, to be realistic, not a permanent) solution. Knowledge about the components of an organization—its people, jobs, unions, and structure—as well as an understanding of the skills of supervision, are necessary ingredients in gaining acceptance of these manpower policies.

In addition, these policies provide a fertile ground for employee misunderstanding. Tenure and promotion arrangements are matters of vital concern to all, for they have a direct effect on each employee's sense of security and progress. Unless management uses effective means of communication, bolstered by clearly defined, widely available, written statements of policy, rumors and half-truths will circulate freely throughout the organization. And in the murky atmosphere of rumor, both productivity and morale languish.

Recruitment and Selection

Logically, the first step in the development of a firm's personnel activity is to acquire the people to operate the organization. Not only is this first in theory, it is one of the most critical steps in the establishment and growth of a business. The supply of qualified people limits the success of a business just as sharply as does the supply of money, materials, or markets.

On close examination, personnel-acquisition policy emerges as an inter-related, ordered series of decisions: estimating manpower requirements, evaluating the potential of both external and internal (to the firm) labor markets, determining recruitment methods, and developing techniques for selecting among available applicants.

MANPOWER: SUPPLY AND DEMAND

Farsighted companies make careful analyses of their manpower needs. They take a long-term point of view towards manpower development. (See Chapter 22 for a discussion of executive manpower planning.) Rather than wait until there is an urgent need to fill a vacancy, they consider their existing work force, their promotional ladders, and the future vacancies that will be created by predicted turnover (through resignation, discharge, death, and retirement) and growth. The results of this analysis should provide time tables of personnel needs, specifying:

1. the jobs for which new employees are likely to be needed;
2. the skills which these jobs will require; and
3. the extent to which new employees should have the potential for promotion to jobs at higher levels.

Decisions must also be made on whether to hire all new employees at the bottom and then train them for promotion—or whether to fill vacancies at the level they occur by hiring from outside. If too few well-qualified people are hired at the bottom, management may be stampeded into promoting unqualified people in times of labor shortage. If too many people with high potential are hired at the bottom, low morale and high turnover may result because promotions are slow. (For further discussion of this dilemma, see Chapter 20.)

Two problems must be given particular consideration: turnover and present composition of the work force.

Turnover.   Recruitment problems differ greatly from one organization to another. A department store with a relatively large percentage of young, unmarried girls on its payroll may find that it has to hire two or even three times the total number of its employees each year. Not that everyone who is employed at the beginning of the year will have left before the end. Rather, some newly hired personnel will leave almost immediately, thus obliging management to hire several people to fill a single job for the year. On the other hand, in a large utility with a high percentage of male employees with at least 15 years of seniority, the recruitment problem is minimal.

Present work force composition.   Historical factors also enter into management's approach to recruitment.

> For example, during a period of labor scarcity, one company hired a great many people with very limited potential for advancement. As a result, the bottom rungs of the company's promotional ladders are now filled with incumbents who are unlikely to advance. Consequently, the company must now recruit a large number of people for the higher levels of pay and responsibility.

The Nature of the Labor Market

In recruiting new employees, management must consider the nature of the labor market. What sorts of potential employees are available and how do they look for work? Only when answers to questions such as these are known can management recruit intelligently. Economists have studied the labor market for years. What have they learned that is relevant to recruitment? [1]

Labor market boundaries.   A labor market consists of *geographic* areas in which the forces of supply (people looking for work) and demand (employers looking for people to hire) interact and thus affect the price of labor (wages and salaries). The actual boundaries of the market depend on the type and number of job candidates being sought. The labor market for certain unusual skills may be half or all of the United States. Top-quality hotel chefs may move from resorts in Maine to Florida when appropriate openings occur. At the other

---

[1] Students interested in further exploration of labor-market problems as they affect recruitment may consult the following: Lloyd G. Reynolds, *The Structure of Labor Markets* (New York: Harper & Row, 1951); Charles Myers and George Shultz, *The Dynamics of a Labor Market* (Englewood Cliffs, N.J., Prentice-Hall, 1951); Richard A. Lester, *Hiring Practices and Labor Competition* (Princeton, N.J.: Princeton University, Industrial Relations Section, 1954); Gladys Palmer, *Labor Mobility in Six Cities* (New York: Social Science Research Council, 1954), and Herbert S. Parnes, *Research on Labor Mobility: An Appraisal of Research Findings in the United States,* Bulletin 65 (New York: Social Science Research Council, 1954).

extreme, married women seeking clerical positions may be unwilling to take jobs that are not within a few miles of their home.

Knowing the boundaries of the labor market helps management estimate the available supply of qualified personnel which it might recruit. Many times the personnel director will draw a line around the work location and attempt to estimate the number of potential applicants who live within that area. The line will rarely describe a perfect circle, since few employees commute to work "as the crow flies." In fact, it may be more appropriate to define the area on the basis of transportation lines and commuting time. Over the years the time spent in commuting has tended to remain constant—that is, as transportation speeds have increased, people tend to live farther away from their work.[2] Rarely do more than 10 or 20 per cent of the employees commute more than 30 miles.[3] However, a company opening a new operation that will employ a relatively large number of people may find that people will be willing to commute very long distances and eventually shift their residences to take advantage of opportunities vastly superior to any nearer home.

Estimating potential applicants. Once the labor market has been identified, the next step is to assemble estimates on the number of potential applicants in the area. Most of those presently unemployed but seeking work are likely to be registered with state unemployment insurance offices. Chambers of Commerce, railroads and utilities, city and state departments of commerce and development, and larger firms in the area all accumulate statistics on both the numbers and types of workers within the geographic areas they serve. Most useful will be state and federal manpower agencies.

Specific Labor Market Factors

Most companies are not primarily interested in the gross number of workers available in the labor force. They want to know instead: (1) What skills are available? (2) How many workers with these skills are likely to apply at the rate we offer? (3) What are the attitudes toward the company of potential job-seekers in the community?

Available skills. Few companies hire "labor"; rather, they hire specific kinds of worker. Many large offices that move out of cities to suburban areas find that although there is a readily available labor supply, there may be a severe shortage of young girls with clerical skills. Companies that want to hire large numbers of highly skilled tool and die makers must locate in areas where these tradesmen have established homes. Where fully trained workers are required, a new firm may have no choice but to locate near the plants of competitors. Auto stylists are most likely to be found in Detroit, and photographic engineers in Rochester, New York.

---

[2] See Daniel Bell, *Work and Its Discontents* (Boston: Beacon Press, 1956), p. 4.

[3] See Leonard Adams and Thomas MacKersey, *Commuting Patterns of Industrial Workers* (Ithaca, N.Y.: Cornell University, Housing Research Center, 1955).

Economic conditions. Economic conditions in the labor market itself affect recruitment. A new plant located in a depressed labor market may be swamped by unemployed workers. On the other hand, a firm trying to establish itself or to expand in an area where few qualified workers are out of work has quite a different recruiting problem.

Attractiveness of company. Potential employees find some organizations far more attractive than others. Company A is engaged in an expanding, profitable industry and can afford to pay high wages. It guarantees steady employment, high wages, rapid promotions, clean work, and attractive fringe benefits. This company may never really have to recruit, for a steady stream of prospective employees will come seeking work. When an opening does occur, the personnel department need only look through its files of applications and select the most likely candidates. Company B is in a highly competitive industry in which profit levels and wages are relatively low. The company has a reputation for unsteady work, and many of the jobs it offers involve dirty, dangerous work. This company has a difficult time recruiting employees, particularly in times of relatively full employment.

Companies that require relatively large numbers of a particular type of employee often have a severe recruitment problem. If a firm needs only a single bookkeeper, it usually has little trouble finding one—even though it pays less than competitors and has a poor reputation in the community. But in an insurance company, for example, which must hire hundreds of stenographers every year, relative wages and working conditions are critical.

Community attitudes. Communities differ in their appeal to new personnel, and many companies believe that communities also differ in their attitudes toward industry, work, and management—in what is sometimes called the prevailing "business climate." Some companies, for example, seek to avoid areas with a history of labor-management conflict.

The firm must also remember that unattractive communities will repel applications; locations with a good climate, attractive recreational facilities, plentiful housing, fine schools, and decent government will attract applicants from a wide radius. Increasingly, professional and managerial employees are demanding good living conditions as a job prerequisite.

Sources of Manpower

Once we have decided what workers we want and where we expect to get them, the next question is this: How can we induce qualified applicants to apply for employment? To answer this question, we must look at how workers seek employment.

The new worker taking his first job. An inexperienced employee has only a sketchy idea about job possibilities. He is likely to take several jobs during his first five or six years of employment (the "trial period," as it is called) in his search for the kind of job that is compatible with his expectations, ability, and personality. His final settling down is likely to be as much a result of growing family responsibilities and more realistic expectations as of his finding genuine job satisfaction. The job held by his father, the ambitions encouraged within his family, and his level of education all exert a major influence over what jobs he regards as acceptable.[4]

The already employed, but dissatisfied employee. Firms that require special skills often recruit employed workers who are looking for a better job. Every job has its disadvantages; we all rebel to some extent against authority, and are convinced that our talents are going unrecognized and uncompensated. Consequently, we might expect that most employees would constantly be on the look-out for a better job. The fact is, however, that most employees do not actively seek other jobs. Studies indicate that only a small percentage of employed workers actively compare their present job with any actual or potential alternatives.[5]

Family and friendship ties deter the worker from searching for opportunities outside his immediate neighborhood, and seniority and fringe benefits that are tied to length of service also reduce the motivation to look elsewhere. Furthermore, the early job-hunting experiences of a worker and his friends may have convinced him that good jobs are scarce, and that whatever its disadvantages a job in hand is worth innumerable possibilities in the bush. It is a striking observation that even employees who quit voluntarily do not usually have a specific alternative in mind.

There is one exception to this generalization, however. During periods of what has come to be called "over-full employment," when companies actively compete for labor and when jobs are remarkably easy to get, employees may begin to consider alternatives. Stories spread about how well Jim Jones did when he walked across the street to an employment office or answered an advertisement, and gradually other employees who are not completely tied by pension, insurance, or tenure guarantees begin to follow the same route.

> As a general rule, then, one can say that dissatisfaction with the present job does not make the worker search actively for a new job. It does make him more receptive to tips, rumors, and actual job offers which come to him. If none of these look promising enough and if his present job continues to be unsatisfactory, he will eventually (during a period of high employment) quit his job. *Active search for work usually does not begin until after he is unemployed.*[6]

---

[4] For a careful review of the influences on occupational choice, see Delbert Miller and William Form, *Industrial Sociology* (New York: Harper & Row, 1951), pp. 636-762.

[5] Reynolds, *op. cit.*

[6] Lloyd Reynolds and Joseph Shister, *Job Horizons* (New York: Harper & Row, 1949), p. 37. (Emphasis ours.) See also, Gladys Palmer and others, *The Reluctant Job Changer* (Philadelphia: University of Pennsylvania Press, 1963).

A small percentage of the labor force consists of perpetual malcontents, who, for one psychological reason or another, are never satisfied with their work and cannot tolerate the normal restrictions imposed by life in an organization. They move endlessly from one job to another. In a sense, these workers fit the economist's model: They do indeed try to maximize the net advantages they receive in return for their labor, and they actively compare the benefits offered by various employers. Personnel directors find such employees poor bets and are unlikely to hire them.

Another group of potential dissidents is made up of new employees. Longer-service employees have usually adjusted to their job and typically expect to stay with it for some time to come; the newly hired employee has made no such adjustment. He is still trying to accommodate himself to his fellow workers, to supervision, to the pace and work requirements of a specific job, and to the organizational "climate" of a particular company. Voluntary quits are highest by far during the first year or two of employment on a new job. (It is for this reason, it might be added, that turnover is particularly costly. In order to replace one long-service employee who quits, the company may have to hire two or three or even four new employees.)

Raiding. The practice of hiring employees from other companies raises the question of "raiding." The connotations of the term itself suggest that many employers consider this practice unethical. Some companies scrupulously refrain from recruiting employees from other firms in their community or industry. They may even require clearance from a potential recruit's present employer before they will accept his application. In actuality, however, so-called "no-raiding agreements" are honored more in theory than in practice. In order to avoid the stigma of "raiding," employers sometimes use intermediaries, such as executive recruiting and consulting firms, to make contacts for them. Significant legal liabilities, however, can be incurred when a company lures a key employee from a competitor in order to learn trade secrets or technical "know how" from him.[7]

There is modest evidence that executives as well as staff and technical specialists are becoming more profession-oriented. Identifying with their field as much or more than their employer, they are likely to "job hop" if their present post does not provide adequate psychological and financial returns. Although for an expanding firm with exciting promotional opportunities this situation may increase the supply of trained manpower available, for other employers it increases the costs of turnover. (Obviously, it should encourage greater efforts to diagnose the source of dissatisfaction and to provide countermeasures.)

The unemployed worker. Ordinarily, the unemployed worker is a man who has been laid off because of slack times, or because of an infraction of

---

[7] For some intriguing cases on this problem see "Who Owns What's In Your Head," *Fortune* (July 1964), pp. 175-178, 236-242.

company rules, or because of the permanent closing of his employer's business. If he has been laid off because of slack times, a company may hesitate to hire him for fear that he will return to his original employer as soon as possible in order to enjoy the seniority benefits he has accumulated there.[8] Of course, firms are suspicious of those who have been discharged from another job— this can cause the employee who has been inequitably discharged a great deal of grief.

The unemployed worker is no more systematic in his search for a job than the potential recruit who is currently employed and is under less economic pressure:

> Where the worker does not hear of a job through friends within a reasonable time [when seeking employment] he frequently resorts to direct application at a plant which is conspicuous because of its size, closeness to his home, or some other reason. In most cases, however, he knows little about conditions in the plant before applying for work.[9]

Eliminating Discrimination

When management surveys job applicants according to age, sex, and minority-group membership, long-standing patterns of discrimination often are disclosed.[10] As a nation we have come to recognize that this is a moral as well as economic problem. Significant segments of our population fail to share in rising standards of living and suffer needless poverty. Employers lose a valuable source of manpower. And now such discrimination my violate the law. The Civil Rights Act of 1964 (Title VII) forbids discrimination in employment practices because of race, color, religion, sex, or national origin. Further, many states have Fair Employment Practice laws which carry similar prohibitions.

Hiring older workers and women. Unfortunately, many companies will not hire employees over 40 years of age, and this creates enormous hardships for those who lose a job in the middle years.[11] Industry has been loath to employ older workers on the assumption that they are less energetic and flexible, accident- and grievance-prone, and more costly in terms of welfare payments. But evidence indicates that they compensate for some of their liabilities by virtue of their mature judgment, long experience, and steady application.

Women also have been discriminated against on many jobs because it has been felt that their family responsibilities would interfere with a work career. Yet women are becoming one of the most important sources of labor, since

---

[8] Reynolds found that 88 per cent of his sample of laid-off workers in New Haven, Connecticut, planned to return to their previous employer. (Reynolds, *op. cit.*, p. 88.)

[9] Reynolds and Shister, *op. cit.*, p. 106.

[10] It may be more important to get behind such records by analyzing hiring patterns as well as referral patterns, that is, which employment agencies fail to refer minority applicants.

[11] Somewhat less than half of the states have laws forbidding discrimination on the basis of age, but these are not well enforced.

their roles as wives and mothers no longer inhibit participation in the labor market:

> At the turn of the century, half of the women never worked outside the home and the average work life for all women was about eleven years. Today almost all women work at some time during their lives, and on the average a young girl can look forward to working at least twenty-five years.[12]

In fact, many companies find it useful, in trying to fill routine low-paid jobs, to direct their recruiting efforts toward groups that are not commonly regarded as constituting the work force in a given area. Labor economists refer to a "secondary labor force" consisting of people not now employed or actively seeking employment. Housewives, semiretired workers, and very young people will respond to attractive, close-at-hand jobs when they are brought to their attention.[13]

Minority-group members. Employers find that efforts to recruit members of minority groups that are discriminated against often fail. In part these individuals have never learned how to look for jobs. Also many are apprehensive or cynically realistic: "It's a waste of time to go to employment offices; the job is always filled." They have been discriminated against so long, they don't trust or believe advertisements that say "We are an Equal Opportunity Employer." Employers thus have to work through the high schools and colleges which have large enrollments of such groups, through The Urban League and civil rights organizations—all of which can communicate in terms that are more credible. Internally, the company may have to break down prejudice among its own managers and employees who resist the hiring of minority-group members, particularly if they are for jobs above the level of unskilled labor.[14] Collaboration with the union may be useful, since some unions have taken a strong stand against discrimination. For a case example in this area see Chapter 31.

The underqualified worker. Because of past discrimination and unsatisfactory educational backgrounds, many of these potential employees will have handicaps. They have not had the usual middle-class opportunities to grow up in an environment that would help them to realize their full potential. They may lack basic speaking and writing skills as well as arithmetic and clerical training. A number of companies have sought to bring these skill levels up to

---

[12] Eli Ginzberg, *Womanpower* (New York: Columbia University Press, 1957).

[13] See Richard C. Wilcox, "The Secondary Labor Force and the Measurement of Unemployment," in National Bureau of Economic Research, *The Measurement and Behavior of Unemployment* (Princeton, N.J.: Princeton University Press, 1957), pp. 167-210. For a good over-all review of company recruitment practices, see F. T. Malm, "Recruiting Patterns and the Functioning of Labor Markets," Paul Pigors, F. T. Myers, and Charles Malm (eds.), *Management of Human Resources* (New York: McGraw-Hill, 1964), pp. 242-256.

[14] For a summary of the experience of industry in widening employment opportunities for Negroes, see National Industrial Conference Board, *Company Experience with Negro Employment* (Studies in Personnel Policy #201) (New York: NICB, 1966).

that point at which they could qualify for available "entry" jobs in the community.[15] The sponsoring company itself may hire many of those underprivileged applicants who complete such programs; others will be in a much better position to compete in the wider labor market.

METHODS OF RECRUITMENT

The mere availability of jobs will not bring applicants into the employment office. True, a firm with an outstanding reputation in the community (for providing "good" jobs) may have a steady stream of applicants. But most companies must engage in active recruitment.

Word of mouth. Recommendations from satisfied friends and relatives are among the best sources of recruitment that a firm can have. Many companies conduct regular programs to encourage their employees to speak to friends about job openings in the company; some even give bonuses to employees who introduce applicants who are actually accepted for employment.

Word-of-mouth recruiting has a real disadvantage, however, for it may lead to nepotism, particularly in management positions. Such an emphasis may arouse resentment in the present staff and may impair morale and long-run efficiency.

Government employment agencies. State employment agencies are located in nearly every major city. In the past, many employers turned to these agencies only as a "source of last resort," or as a source of unskilled labor. Now, however, public employment agencies are seeking to win a reputation for carefully screening applicants for the needs of a particular job in a particular company, including a wide range of manual, technical, and professional occupations. They charge neither the employer nor the prospective employee for their services, for they have a public responsibility to serve both. In the past their reputation may have suffered because they also administer unemployment insurance benefits. At times, people getting benefits pretend to be interested in a job in order to continue their insurance payments; such applicants would disappoint the personnel departments to which they had been sent.

Private employment agencies. These tend to specialize in specific occupations and skills—clerical, manual, craft, or technical, for example. Sometimes the employer pays the fee, sometimes the employee; in either case, the fee may be quite substantial. Specialized executive-recruiting companies are utilized to find new managerial talent. They may scour the country looking for a man with highly specialized experience (such as directing a marketing pro-

---

[15] Recent federal legislation, The Manpower Development and Training Act, subsidizes such training programs.

gram in household detergents) and prescribed personality attributes. Most of the men they will look at will already be employed but will have indicated confidentially a willingness "to be considered." On the other hand, an unemployed executive may have difficulty getting himself considered seriously by these search firms.[16] He may be considered a failure.

Advertisements. Advertisements in daily newspapers, over local radio stations, in trade journals, and in the magazines of professional associations usually attract applicants in great numbers but of highly variable quality. A more homogeneous group will respond to an advertisement in the *Journal of the American Chemical Society*, for example, than to one in the community's local newspaper. Similarly, papers catering to a Negro readership will be useful in recruiting members of this minority group.

Although newspaper advertisements have no built-in screening mechanism, they do serve a useful purpose. When a company opens a new plant, for example, and requires a large work force, advertisements in the local papers provide an excellent means of announcing the fact that openings are available.

School recruiting. Many companies send representatives to interview seniors in high schools and colleges. This technique enables the company to paint an attractive picture of its employment opportunities and to do advanced screening of candidates. The better candidates are then invited to visit the company for further consideration. In addition, good contacts with school placement officials help in channeling suitable candidates to the company.[17]

Recently a major airline took a suite of rooms in a New York City hotel during the college holidays to display the advantages of an airline career. Students were shown films, given brochures, and interviewed by "career counselors." Airlines have also placed advertisements in student newspapers describing the very high lifetime earnings of a pilot, on the assumption that this is a career most students would not normally consider.

The union as recruiter. In certain occupations the worker feels a stronger attachment to the industry as a whole than he does to an individual firm. This is particularly true, for example, in the building trades and in the maritime industry. In these occupations, the union is the traditional clearing-house for jobs, and both employer and employee have come to accept the union hiring hall as a combination employment agency and recruiting office. To a lesser extent the union provides this service in the printing and entertainment industries, restaurants, and hotels (when union-organized), and sometimes in the

---

[16] For a good summary of the labor market techniques open to an executive seeking employment see Aurens Uris, *The Executive Job Market* (New York: McGraw-Hill, 1965).

[17] For recommendations on managing college recruiting, see George Odiorne and Arthur Hann, *Effective College Recruiting* (Ann Arbor, Michigan: Bureau of Industrial Relations, University of Michigan, 1964).

manufacture of men's and women's clothing. (The Taft-Hartley Act, in part, regulates these hiring halls.)

Notice that these are all industries in which there is instability of employment. Clearly it is to management's advantage to be able to tap a ready supply of skilled, experienced workers merely by lifting the phone and calling the union. This saves management the expense of recruiting and screening, and also means that management will be less hesitant to lay off an unneeded or incompetent worker. The union's stock-in-trade becomes its ability to maintain a full complement of readily available skilled employees.

Professional Contacts

As a work force becomes more professionalized, recruitment takes place through networks of personal relationship and small, specialized labor markets. Even in a country as large as the United States, many individuals sharing similar training and work experience get to know one another. Through trade association meetings, professional-society conventions, executive-development sessions sponsored by universities and management groups, and day-to-day business dealings—managers and technical specialists develop wide circles of friends. For example, although the stated purpose of professional societies for economists and electrical engineers is to exchange learned papers, much time is devoted to exchanging job information. When an opening occurs, a manager can telephone an acquaintance who might be interested in the job or who can recommend another personal friend. Thus, personal circles of acquaintanceship overlap and intersect to such an extent that a well-placed executive might locate the "two dozen people who know the most about solid state circuitry" in a matter of a few days.

SELECTION

Attracting qualified job applicants is only the first step in the process of acquiring new employees. Next, the firm must develop techniques for selecting, among these applicants, those to be accepted for employment. Management wishes to avoid hiring the employee who will quit because the job does not meet his expectations. Hiring and training costs are usually substantial. Several hundred dollars can be expended in placing a relatively unskilled employee on the payroll; several thousand dollars or more in the case of a professional or manager. Further, union standards and the expectations of employees and the community can serve to limit management's ability to discharge those who fall below performance standards. In many foreign countries, government regulations restrict such decisions more severely.

Such pressures sometimes encourage management to avoid permanent commitments. A firm can do so by using temporary workers supplied by agencies specialized in "lending" manpower.[18] (The hiring company usually pays a daily fee for each employee based on the skill required, but the employee remains on the payroll of the agency.) Also, the company thus gets to hire employees who know from the outset that they are temporary and cannot qualify for the security of the regular work force.

It should be noted, further, that most organizations use a probationary period as a check on their selection system. The newly hired worker does not become a regular employee until he has successfully completed a one- to three-month or even a one-year trial.

Alternative Selection Policies

Organizations tend to develop hiring methods that are consistent with their over-all philosophy of selection. These methods differ significantly from company to company.

Screening out applicants who don't fit. The primary objective of the selection procedure may be to screen out applicants who "obviously" don't qualify for the type of job typically available in the company. Such procedures endeavor to fit people to the organization as a whole rather than to specific jobs.

For some companies, "don't qualify" means that the applicant is in general unsuited to the company. Some of these criteria are based on the questionable assumption that there is a "right type" for the firm—that is, "right" in terms of physical appearance, background, age, degree of "drive," and similar characteristics. One researcher, for example, has found that banks try to maintain a very homogeneous group of employees, all of whom place security above advancement, lack aggressiveness, and prefer a job in which they are left alone.[19] Brokerage houses may favor applicants with an "ivy league" college background. Some companies seek handsome, white Protestants to fill most of their jobs.

There is evidence that even when the company sets up no formal restrictions, an informal self-selection process will operate. Certain types of people gravitate to and find working in certain kinds of organizations compatible with their own personalities. This pattern has been observed among operators in clothing manufacturing plants, retail store personnel, and government employees.[20] Thus, there may be some justification for attempting to avoid mismatching by

---

[18] For an analysis of this service, see Mack Moore, "The Temporary Help Service Industry: Historical Development, Operation and Scope," *Industrial and Labor Relations Review*, Vol. 18, No. 4 (July 1965) pp. 554-569.

[19] Robert McMurry, "Recruitment, Dependency and Morale in the Banking Industry," *Administrative Science Quarterly*, Vol. 3, No. 1 (June 1958), pp. 87-117.

[20] Margaret Chandler, *Labor Management Relations in Illinois City*, Case Study 3, Garment Manufacture (Champaign, Ill.: Institute of Labor and Industrial Relations, 1953). Eliot D. Chapple, "Contributions of Applied Anthropology to Institutional Psychiatry," *Human Organization*, Vol. 13, No. 2, p. 14.

weeding out those who will be uncomfortable in their new work environment. On the whole, however, most of these "right-type" criteria, which usually represent irrational discrimination, are ethically indefensible and now legally wrong.

There are other, more concrete, general selection criteria that may appropriately be utilized as screening variables. Where most jobs in the firm require technical ability, some minimal education requirement may be imposed on all entrants—for instance, completion of high school or college. (Of course, there is the real possibility that a good candidate may have achieved equal proficiency through less orthodox channels or the standard may be unrealistically high).

Fitting jobs to people.   Alternatively, management can go in the opposite direction and seek to adjust the jobs themselves to the people who are available to fill them. For example, during World War II, many male jobs were, with slight modifications, made suitable for women. Great progress has been made in recent years in modifying or redesigning jobs for those who are blind, infirm, or otherwise incapacitated. Experiments in adjusting working hours to permit housewives to be employed for split shifts have proved successful. Skilled craftsmen's jobs have been broken into components that could be learned by relatively untrained novices.

Psychologists in particular have been active in a field that has come to be called "human engineering." While industrial engineering has stressed fitting people to satisfy the time and motion requirements of machinery and production schedules, these psychologists have sought principles and methods to make equipment design better adapted to typical human characteristics.[21]

Fitting people to jobs.   The typical selection program tries to fit applicants to particular jobs—to match jobs and people. This selection philosophy assumes that the requirements of a given job, and the characteristics of a given applicant, are sufficiently unique and explicit to make possible an intelligent match between them. Most of the rest of this chapter will be devoted to discussing the problems involved in implementing this philosophy.

Selection Techniques

Obtaining job descriptions.   The first concrete step in carrying out any selection program is to develop adequate job descriptions for the positions that are to be filled. Job or occupational titles in themselves often give a misleading impression of the actual content of a job. A "milk deliveryman," in addition to being able to drive a truck, must also handle customer accounts and sell the company's products. An engineer may have to spend most of his time *selling* department heads on the importance of using standard parts. Many so-called

---

[21] See Ernest J. McCormack, *Human Engineering* (New York: McGraw-Hill, 1957).

"clerk" jobs embrace a range of duties that are unrelated to the simple tabulating or recording activities one might associate with the job title.

Particularly at managerial and staff levels, the personalities of the key people with whom the new person will be dealing (especially his boss) become an important element in any realistic job specification.[22]

> The buyer's job in a department store is very demanding because it includes day-to-day administrative responsibilities for the sales floor, for records and displays as well as the purchase of new merchandise. Buyers whose personality inclines them toward the details of stock work should be given assistants who enjoy interpersonal relationships and vice versa.

Care needs to be exercised that excessively broad and ambiguous requirements are not established like "intelligent worker" or "hard working" or "good personality." These encourage discriminatory hiring practices and should be replaced by specific duties. Also, needlessly high educational standards limit the number of applicants that can be considered, and where the job does not call for his full educational attainments, the new employee is likely to quit in discouragement.

The United States Government publishes a standard reference work, the *Dictionary of Occupational Titles* (3rd edition, 1966), which can be an important tool for personnel administrators in this connection. It contains descriptions and requirements for 22,000 jobs current in the U.S. labor market and the traits required of workers who must fill each of these.

Once there is a complete description of the duties that must be performed, a personnel requirement list for each job can be constructed. This would include the type of education and/or experience an applicant should have; what skills he must possess; what physical attributes he needs (stamina, height, and so forth); and what personality requirements are desirable. The list should also specify the types of relationship he will be expected to undertake and maintain with other people.

Careful descriptions produce certain valuable by-products. First, they give the applicant an accurate picture of the job and reduce the possibility that he will be unpleasantly surprised by the duties expected of him after he has started to work. Second, job descriptions are useful in setting wages and salaries through job evaluation, and as a check list against which to measure job performance (see Chapter 25).

When the company knows what it is looking for in a potential employee, it is ready to explore alternative methods of assessing the characteristics of candidates. Of the many techniques used, the following are some of the best known.

Application forms. The *application form* is a traditional, widely accepted device for recording information on such biographical items as: age; marital

---

[22] For a more complete description of "matching people to people" see Eliot Chapple and Leonard Sayles, *The Measure of Management* (New York: Macmillan, 1961), pp. 98-113.

status and number of dependents; previous education (subjects and grades) and training; previous work experience, including nature of duties, salary, length of time on the job, and reasons for leaving; and such personal items as association memberships, police records, if any, outstanding debts, and home ownership.[23] It also tests the candidate's ability to write, to organize his thoughts, and to present facts clearly and succinctly. The information recorded on the application blank provides interviewers with leads and points of departure for a formal job interview, and it provides the company with data for its permanent employee record. The application indicates, further, whether the applicant has consistently progressed to better jobs, and whether his education and occupational experience have been logically patterned.

The application blank can be used as a formal test, with the various questions weighted and scored according to their predictive value.[24] A statistical analysis is made of the relationship of various items on the application blank to the actual job success of candidates who have previously filled out these blanks. Weights are assigned to each of such factors as type of work experience, size of family, age, and sex, and these "scores" are compared to work records of those previously hired.[25] Scores are then computed from the applications of new people and matched against the scores of employees with good tenure and performance records.

Often references are to be listed in the application, though these may be of limited value because most people named will provide very favorable references, being loath to handicap the applicant in finding employment. There is a very low correlation between ratings given by references and observed job performance. Furthermore, when former employers are interviewed about candidates, there is almost no relationship between their full report and what they put on a short reference form.[26]

Interviews. The *interview*, unlike the application blank, is a selection technique that enables the person responsible for hiring to view the total individual and to appraise the person and his behavior directly. The objective

[23] The Fair Employment Practice laws adopted by many states make it illegal to ask questions about an applicant's religious affiliation, wife's maiden name, parents' names, race, and similar points, on the grounds that such questions constitute either direct or indirect attempts to ascertain race, religion, or nationality, and provide a basis for discrimination. See Theodore Kheel, *Guide to Fair Employment Practices* (Englewood Cliffs, N.J.: Prentice-Hall, Inc., 1964).

[24] Edwin Fleishman and Joseph Berniger, "Using the Application Blank to Reduce Office Turnover," in Edwin Fleishman, ed., *Studies in Personnel and Industrial Psychology* (Homewood, Illinois: Dorsey Press, 1961).

[25] A critical review of this type of testing procedure is provided by Harrison Trice, "The Weighted Application Blank—A Caution," *The Personnel Administrator* (May-June 1964), pp. 17-19.

[26] Howard Goheen and James Mosel, "Validity of the Employment Recommendation Questionnaire," *Personnel Psychology,* Vol. 12, No. 2 and Vol. 12, No. 3 (Summer and Fall 1959), pp. 297-301 and 469-477.

of the interview is to measure the applicant against the specific requirements of the job and to decide whether there will be a good "fit." It also permits the applicant to ask questions about the organization and the job.

The interview is a flexible tool; it can be used for many different types of job and with many different kinds of personality. It can emphasize the applicant's formal qualifications or seek to plumb the depths of his personality.

The interview is perhaps the most widely used selection technique. Does this mean that there are also widely accepted standards of what constitutes good and bad performance on the part of the interviewee? Not at all. Moreover, the practices and the competency of those who conduct interviews differ widely. Since interviewing is both expensive and time-consuming, it would be well for most organizations to take stock of how much benefit they are deriving from the practice.[27]

Ideally, the interview provides a valid sample of the applicant's behavior. Even though the applicant is "on guard," careful to present the best picture possible, the skilled interviewer can draw him out far more successfully than can an application blank. Furthermore, the interviewer can uncover clues to the applicant's motivation, to his attitudes toward himself and to the kinds of situation he finds troublesome and satisfying. Using the information recorded on the application blank as a springboard, the interviewer can guide the applicant into explaining why certain jobs appeal to him and others do not, and into speaking freely about the influence of family and educational experiences. By getting the applicant to talk about himself, the interviewer can gauge the candidate's level of aspiration (what he is "shooting for" in the long run as well as what types of job would be acceptable in the short run), his ability to deal with interpersonal situations, and his readiness to take the initiative in conversation and in dealing with strangers.

Nevertheless, even at its best, the interview is not a precise technique, and skillful interviewing is difficult to conduct. Candidates react very differently depending on who is interviewing them and how the interview is handled. Since there are no fixed criteria for success or failure, the prejudiced interviewer can easily evaluate the interviewee's performance in accordance with his own stereotypes. (If the applicant is interviewed by several people, it may be possible to cross-check observations.) Unfortunately, there are still people who believe that they can assess other people on the basis of the type of necktie they select, their tone of voice, or whether they "look you straight in the eye." The personality of the interviewer also has a major impact on the validity of the technique. It is easy for him to use this situation as a means of dominating or demeaning the dependent applicant or just as a vehicle to enable himself to talk, to have a captive listener.

---

[27] For a summary of research that endeavors to validate selection interviewing, see Eugene Mayfield, "The Selection Interview—A Re-evaluation of Published Research," *Personnel Psychology*, Vol. 17, No. 3 (Autumn 1964), pp. 239-260. For the most part, Mayfield is cautiously optimistic about structured interviewing.

Good interviewing requires great skill. Many supervisors find this out when they are required to interview an applicant only to find that the conversation lags, embarrassment grows and the procedure is stressful for both themselves and the other person.

In one sense the interview is a tug of war or battle of wits. The applicant, who wants to put his best foot forward, seeks both to cover up personal deficiencies and to provide answers that will please the interviewer. The latter tries to penetrate these defenses and catch a glimpse of the "real person" underneath. Opinion differs about how best to do so. Some favor putting the applicant at ease as much as possible and using nondirective methods (see Chapter 11). Others favor more structured or patterned interviewing.[28] It is also possible purposefully to introduce stressful elements into the interview to assess the interviewee's reaction to frustration and pressure.[29] Sometimes there is a division of labor in interviewing. Personnel seeks to assess personality and the line manager interviews for technical training and experience.

Physical examinations.   Many jobs require unusual stamina, strength, or tolerance of unpleasant working conditions. Physical examinations reveal whether or not a candidate possesses these qualities. Furthermore, the company's responsibility (both legal and ethical) for employee health and safety encourages widespread use of physical check-ups. Health insurance costs are increased when employees in poor health are hired. Thorough physical examinations also provide valuable records in the event of accidents.

FORMAL TESTS

To many people, tests are synonymous with selection methods, although many companies do not employ formal testing procedures in their selection programs. Tests have been developed in an effort to find more objective means of measuring the qualifications of job applicants, as well as for use with employees who are candidates for transfer or promotion. One of their major advantages is that they may uncover qualifications and talent that would not be detected by interviews or by listings of education and job experience. Tests seek to eliminate the possibility that the prejudice of interviewer or supervisor, instead of potential ability, will govern selection decisions. Because of their importance, we shall look closely at their design and their limitations, as well

---

[28] Milton Mandell, *Recruiting and Selecting Office Employees* (Research Report No. 27) (New York: American Management Association), 1956.

[29] Chapple and Sayles, *op. cit.*, pp. 114-141. The military has also experimented with efforts to standardize the interviewing procedure by means of a fixed format and the use of a panel of interviewers. The applicant is evaluated, not only in terms of the content of his answers, but also in terms of his reactions to the stress introduced by the situation. See also Arnold Judson, "New Approach to Executive Selection," *Harvard Business Review*, Vol. 32 (March-April 1954), pp. 127-136.

as at some of the policy problems involved in applying them to personnel selection and placement.[30]

Major Types

First we shall examine some of the more commonly used types of tests and the purposes for which they are designed. With this as background we shall consider the limitations of formal testing, stressing the extreme care that must be used in evaluating test results.

Performance tests. The simplest and perhaps most obvious type of testing procedure is the work-sample or performance test in which the applicant is asked to demonstrate his ability to do the job. For example, prospective typists are asked to type several pages and their speed and accuracy are then calculated. Or a prospective machinist is asked to interpret a blueprint and to make certain adjustments on the equipment he will be expected to operate.

But how about jobs like sales representative or control room attendant? Here the characteristics that make for success are less obvious, the requisite skills not so easy to test.

Intelligence tests. On the assumption that quick-learning, alert, bright people can learn almost any job more quickly than those who are less well endowed, many companies use general intelligence tests. On the other hand, for some simple, repetitive jobs management wishes to assure itself that intelligence is not *over* a certain level, to reduce employee dissatisfaction. The most accurate and reliable intelligence tests require many hours of careful professional administration, and they are expensive and cumbersome. Therefore most organizations make use of shorter paper-and-pencil tests which give a rough approximation of the I.Q. (Intelligence Quotient) of the applicant.

Psychologists are not unanimous in recommending the use of these abbreviated tests, nor is there general agreement on the concept of "intelligence" itself —that is, on what is being measured by the test. Clearly, rather than measuring potential to learn, many tests are biased in favor of applicants coming from backgrounds emphasizing verbal and numerical experience. Also some intelligence tests favor pedestrian ways of thinking over more creative and original solutions.[31]

---

[30] Three standard texts summarizing the testing field are: Ann Anastasi, *Psychological Testing*, 2nd ed. (New York: Macmillan, 1961). Lee Cronbach, *Essentials of Psychological Testing*, 2nd ed. (New York: Harper & Row, 1960). Donald Super, *Appraising Vocational Fitness by Means of Psychological Tests* (New York: Harper & Row, 1949). For a critique of tests in industry see Mason Haire, "Psychology in the Study of Business" in Robert Dahl, Mason Haire, and Paul Lazarsfeld, *Social Science Research on Business* (New York: Columbia University Press), pp. 49-69. A more popular and hortatory critique is Martin Gross, *The Brain Watchers* (New York: Random House, 1962).

[31] Banesh Hoffman, *The Tyranny of Testing* (New York: Crowell-Collier Press, 1962), p. 223.

Aptitude tests. In a sense, an intelligence test is a kind of aptitude test—measuring the *potential* ability of a candidate to learn a new job. However, psychologists have developed a large number of much more specialized aptitude tests which seek to predict the likelihood that an applicant can learn a certain type of job effectively. Individuals differ markedly, for example, in their ability to learn work involving precise eye-muscle coordination, such as the work done by the skilled shop craftsman or mechanic. It is difficult for some people to learn to do jobs that involve quantitative computations or that require the ability to visualize solid objects in space. There are tests of a person's potential to become a programer, just as there are examinations to predict the likely success a student will have in law, medical, or business schools.

A company undergoing technological change, seeking to retrain as many of its displaced employees as possible, will give aptitude tests to judge who will benefit most from the retraining program.

Personality tests. Many observers feel that more employees fail on the job because of personality defects than because of lack of aptitude or physical ability. A psychologically well-adjusted employee who is highly motivated to do a good job may be worth more to the company than a man with great potential who is emotionally upset or lazy. At times, personality affects job performance in the most unexpected ways, thus the value of good job analysis.

> During World War II, when great numbers of trained technicians were in demand, it was assumed that those who had mechanical aptitude would make good airplane mechanics. A careful analysis of this assumption proved otherwise. It turned out that a good shoe clerk in civilian life would become a better mechanic for military purposes than someone who had fixed cars most of his life and learned on a Model-T Ford. The critical trait was not mechanical aptitude but the ability of the trainee to follow instructions. The Army then worked out its instruction manuals so meticulously that the best recruit turned out to be a mildly obsessional person who could read and follow directions. The last thing they wanted was someone with his own ideas on how to fix equipment.[32]

In fact, for management jobs, personality tests may well be the equivalent of work-sample tests, since the most important component of many managerial jobs is the ability to deal effectively with people. As a result, many large companies now use personality tests, particularly at the executive level. There are hundreds of consulting firms that specialize in providing testing services as well as large numbers of full-time staff psychologists within personnel departments who conduct elaborate testing programs.

Personality tests seek to assess an individual's motivation, adjustment to the stresses of everyday life, capacity for interpersonal relations and self-image. These are expressed in terms of the relative significance of such traits within

---

[32] Edward T. Hall, *The Silent Language* (Garden City, N.Y.: Doubleday, 1959), p. 94.

the person as self-confidence, ambition, decisiveness, optimism, patience, fear, and distrust.

The most popular personality tests are also of the pencil-and-paper variety; [33] the applicant is given a test booklet in which he writes his answers. A standard key is provided with these tests to enable employment department technicians to process them easily with limited training and expense.

Here are some questions typical of those asked on paper-and-pencil personality tests:

   a. Do you ever feel that people are staring at you and laughing at your appearance? Yes ____ No ____
   b. Do you frequently wake up in a "cold sweat"? Yes ____ No ____
   c. Most people get into trouble because they have never been punished and don't know the meaning of discipline. Yes ____ No ____
   d. My mother was the greatest influence in my life. Yes ____ No ____
   e. I find it difficult to work when people are talking. Yes ____ No ____

Most of these paper-and-pencil tests claim to give a well-rounded picture of the applicant's personality, but many observers argue that they are superficial, easily faked, and misleading. Clinical psychologists favor depth interviews and projective tests that require many hours to administer and that must be interpreted individually by trained experts.[34] Originally, these tests were developed to analyze the abnormal or deviant personality. Only recently have they been used to assess the more "normal" personality.

Situational tests. Situational tests combine aspects of both performance and personality testing. They are designed to observe how job applicants react to stressful but realistic real-life situations.

During World War II, the Office of Strategic Services initiated a testing program that was a radical departure from traditional test forms and interviews.[35] Candidates for special assignments were placed in true-to-life situations and asked to work through actual problems. For example, a candidate might be told to complete a small construction project with the help of an assistant who had been carefully briefed in how *not* to cooperate without actually refusing to obey orders. The key measures in such tests were the applicant's reaction to the obstreperous assistant, his ability to undergo stress, and his demonstration of ingenuity under pressure. In industry, there has been some effort to apply this technique in "leaderless-group" situations. Several

---

[33] Some of the more widely used are: Minnesota Multiphasic Personality Inventory, Washburne Social Adjustment Inventory, Thurstone Temperament Schedule, Adams Personal Audit, Bernreuter Personality Inventory, Guilford and Martin Personal Inventory, Herman Wadsworth Temperament Schedule.

[34] Two well-known projective personality tests are the Rorschach "Ink Blot Test," and the Thematic Apperception Test. (These tests place little emphasis on measuring specific traits. Rather, they try to assess the dynamic relationships within the total personality. They are harder to fake, since there are no obvious "right" answers.)

[35] Strategic Services Assessment Staff, *Assessment of Men* (New York: Rinehart, 1948).

candidates for managerial positions are presented with a problem that requires group collaboration. Observers note which men are able to exercise and gain acceptance of their leadership skills.[36]

The "In-Box" situational test gives a whole series of realistic memos, telephone messages, and reports to potential managers, who must decide in what order and how to handle them. In addition, performance in simulated situations such as business games may be utilized to assess administrative skill.

EVALUATION OF TESTING PROGRAMS

It is not difficult to develop or purchase selection tests that will give numerical data concerning some of the characteristics of job applicants. However, management must assess the relative usefulness of this information, particularly in relation to its cost and in comparison to other selection methods. Numerical results, such as those provided by testing programs, often look deceivingly objective and valid to the casual observer. Given the inevitable uncertainties about picking the right candidate, many managers are tempted to "pass the buck" to the impersonal test. Let us look at some of the assumptions that lie behind formal tests, and the techniques employed in developing and using them in industry.

Underlying Assumptions of Testing Procedures

1. Testing procedures assume that there are significant differences in the extent to which individuals possess certain characteristics—such as intelligence, finger dexterity, knowledge of blueprint reading, and motivation.

2. Testing procedures also assume that there is a direct and important relationship between the possession of one or more of these characteristics and the individual's ability to do certain jobs. This relationship should enable the manager to predict the candidate's eventual job performance.

3. Finally, testing procedures assume that the organization can measure selected characteristics practically and evaluate the relationship between test results and job performance.

At first glance, all these assumptions seem perfectly reasonable. Actually, however, they often lead an unsuspecting management into trouble. For example, in some instances the degree of individual differences does not justify a testing program. As one psychologist points out, it would be wasteful to try to test differences in color discrimination among female applicants for inspection jobs, because "Color blindness in women is about as rare . . . as appear-

---

[36] Bernard Bass, "The Leadership Group as a Leadership Evaluation Instrument," *Personnel Psychology*, Vol. 7, No. 2 (Summer 1957), pp. 470-477. Milton Mandell, "The Group Oral Performance Test," in Paul Pigors, Charles Myers, and F. T. Malm (eds.) *The Management of Human Resources* (New York: McGraw-Hill, 1964), pp. 242-246.

1. Personnel specialist interviews current managers on characteristics that distinguish good from bad employees on particular job, or "what it takes to do well on this job."
2. Interview results are analyzed and consensus summarized in list form. These listed characteristics are sent back to managers to rank order.
3. Psychologist prepares test items that he believes will measure highly ranked characteristics in job applicants.
4. These questions are tried out on a random sample of potential applicants to see which do the best job of differentiating (that is, items which roughly half the test takers will get "right," half "wrong"). Also, intercorrelations are sought, often by factor analysis.
5. On the basis of these results, a tentative test is prepared from questions which differentiate among people.
6. Test is given to those now employed on this job and their scores are compared with job-performance ratings or production reports (often with the use of a scatter diagram).
7. If the test correlates—that is, if those who score "high" are also considered the most effective (and vice versa)—the test is introduced into employment procedure. Otherwise begin again at step 3.
8. Test is then given to all new applicants, but not used for selection. After 18 months, scores of those hired are compared to their work performance to see if test is validated. (Unfortunately, this last step is often omitted to save time.)

Test–Development Procedure.

ances of Halley's Comet." [37] Similarly, a self-selection process, by which people themselves decide whether or not to apply for a specific job in a particular company, may minimize differences among applicants to the point where they are hardly worth the expense of testing.

The fact that some jobs can be handled successfully by more than one type of person throws doubt on the assumption that there is a close relationship between certain employee characteristics and job performance. For example, the older worker, who is slower and less agile, may compensate for his liabilities by displaying greater attention, persistence, and energy.

The validity of the last two assumptions can be evaluated only after we have additional knowledge about how tests are actually developed for use in industry.

There are two traditional measures of the usefulness of a test: reliability and validity.

Reliability. This is a measure of the probability that a test will give stable, consistent results. A test is reliable if slightly different versions of a test

---

[37] Mason Haire, "Use of Tests in Employee Selection," *Harvard Business Review,* Vol. 28, No. 1 (January-February 1950), p. 44.

given to the same person at different times or the same test given to matched samples of people achieve approximately the same results.

Validity of a test.   But just as critical a question is *validity*: Does the test actually predict what it purports to predict? Does the test distinguish effectively between those who will be successful from those who will fail on a job? The best technique for validating a test is to administer a series (battery) of tests of different types to potential employees or candidates for a given position. The results of the tests are *not* used at this point to make hiring or placement decisions. Rather, the scores are filed, and then, after some extensive period of time has elapsed, the job-performance records of those who took the tests are examined. The test scores are then compared with the performance records to determine which, if any, of the tests helped predict who would be successful on the particular job. After this comparison has been made, and assuming that one or more of the test results did have a significant correlation with performance on the job, a new battery is developed using those tests or parts of tests that were shown to be useful predictors.

This appears to be a straightforward and reasonably simple procedure. Unfortunately, it is not. Most companies have neither the facilities nor the patience to undertake this type of program. As a result, they begin giving a test and use the results immediately to make selection decisions. This means that the evaluation data are "contaminated," for there is no way of knowing how those who were not hired, because of poor test scores, would have performed.

When the results of the testing program become generally available to supervisors before the test is validated, the test scores themselves may influence managerial decisions. Employees with relatively high scores may be given more personal encouragement and opportunities for promotion. Understandably, these high-scoring candidates are evaluated as being "superior" to those who came through with lower scores. Since, at best, supervisory evaluation of personnel performance is a subjective process, test results may introduce a strong biasing factor (what is called a self-confirming prophecy), and thus make it impossible for the organization to obtain any truly independent evaluation of the usefulness of the test.

Another short cut followed by some companies is to give present employees a new test to see how scores of "good" employees compare with the test scores of "poor" employees. However, this procedure may not give an accurate reflection of the population from which actual selections have to be made. Furthermore, employees who were hired years ago may have faced job and supervisory conditions very different from those that will be faced by employees hired now.

The use of any predictive method assumes that the organization can identify who is successful and who is not, distinguishing "good" from "poor." Actually, however, performance evaluation is one of the most frustrating elements in any personnel program (see Chapter 23). Most organizations rely on the judgments of supervisors, although these may be quite inaccurate. Fortunately, for some

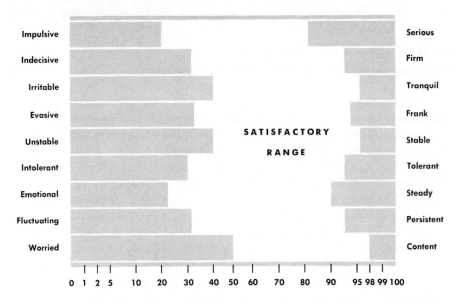

Impulsive																	Serious
Indecisive																	Firm
Irritable																	Tranquil
Evasive																	Frank
Unstable					**SATISFACTORY**											Stable
Intolerant					**RANGE**											Tolerant
Emotional																	Steady
Fluctuating																	Persistent
Worried																	Content

0   1   2   5   10   20   30   40   50   60   70   80   90   95 98 99 100

A Master Personality Profile for First-Line Supervisors in Company X. Some companies endeavor to match the personality-test results of applicants against a "master profile" based on tests given to all current job holders in a particular category. In this example an applicant's profile would have to be within the white area to be acceptable. Adapted from William H. Whyte, Jr., "The Fallacies of Personality Testing," Fortune (September 1954).

jobs it may be satisfactory to distinguish the employee who is still on the job from those who quit or were fired. Still, the questionable validity of most measures of employee performance seriously limits attempts to assess a testing program.[38] In addition, there is the inevitable temptation to look at immediate results rather than to wait for longer-term developments. Yet many outstanding employees will be slow starters and performance measures for them must be delayed for months or even years.[39]

Companies frequently rely on the reported success of other organizations with a particular test battery. But test adoptions of this sort may be based on fallacious reasoning, for the other companies may have quite different jobs to fill, even though they carry the same job title. A more serious shortcoming is that enthusiastic users of a test may have failed to undertake carefully controlled validating procedures. They may have used short cuts in deciding that the test was valid for them, and may have failed to apply objective criteria to ascertain whether or not the employees chosen by the testing procedure

[38] See S. Rains Wallace, "Contributions to Business and Industry," in American Institute for Research, *Planning for Progress* (Pittsburgh: A.I.R., 1956), pp. 13-19. Wallace deplores the lack of objective criteria for judging selection programs in the insurance industry.

[39] Edwin Ghiselli and Mason Haire, "The Validation of Selection Tests in the Light of the Dynamic Character of Criteria," *Personnel Psychology*, Vol. 13, No. 3 (Autumn 1960), pp. 225-231.

actually performed in a superior fashion to those who were rejected. In many companies, moreover, there is a strong tautological bias—that is, when a testing program succeeds in producing a number of candidates who bear a close resemblance to employees whom supervisors have previously judged to be "superior," everyone is pleased. No one knows whether or not the testing program is really able to select employees who will do better than those selected by other means. Used in this fashion, the tests simply confirm existing prejudices.

Thus, an organization that intends to use testing must be willing to go through the time-consuming and expensive routine of independently *validating* the tests. Surely the types of test to be tried out can be suggested by the experience of other organizations. However, to avoid the supervisory temptation of "seeing" improved selectivity that doesn't really exist, there is no substitute for rigorous validation.

Synthetic validities.   Since over-all performance, particularly in higher-level jobs, may be due to accidental or situational factors, an unusually good geographic location, or a sudden change in market forces and prices,[40] a test should often be validated by its ability to predict specific elements of a job rather than total results. Thus, if one were concerned with hiring parcel deliverymen, different tests (or parts of tests) might be used to try to predict their safe driving, flexibility, work output, ability to plan their routes, relations with customers, record-keeping ability, truck-repair record, honesty, and term of employment (how long they will stay on the job). A variety of mechanical, depth perception, hand-eye coordination aptitudes and personality and intelligence factors obviously interact here.

Unfairness to minorities.   Testing procedures assume that those being examined come from a population somewhat similar to the group on which the original tests were "standardized," that is for which the scoring system was developed.

It has been charged that some aptitude tests discriminate against minority-group applicants with "culturally deprived" backgrounds in favor of middle class applicants. Since such tests require knowledge about facets of everyday life that may not be equally common to the lives of all groups in our culture, it is possible to use the test to exclude such applicants. In a sense, this is ironic in that tests are often conceived as being more impersonal and therefore less open to bias than an interviewer. Employers who wish to violate neither the spirit nor the letter of Civil Rights legislation will have to take special pains to insure that their testing programs do not favor members of one group over another.

---

[40] *Cf.* Renato Tagiuri (ed.), *Research Needs in Executive Selection* (Boston: Harvard Graduate School of Business Administration, 1961). See also John Flanagan and Robert Krug, "Testing in Management Selection: State of the Art," *Personnel Administration*, Vol. 27, No. 2 (March 1964), p. 3.

Other Limitations of Tests

Statistical rather than individual predictions.   Test scores can never make firm predictions on what will happen if a specific individual, Mr. Jones, is hired. Rather, test scores simply tell management (assuming that the tests have been validated) that a greater proportion of the people who score above a certain point will be successful than those who score below that point.[41] However, test results can never predict precisely that Jones himself will succeed or fail. The testers tell management that, in general, people whose test results look like Jones' are successful or are not successful. The degree of accuracy of their prediction depends on how closely the test scores are correlated with job-performance evaluations, and these correlations are never perfect. Thus, some people who do poorly on the test will do well on the job, and some people who score well will fail on the job.[42]

Tests are more useful when many similar jobs must be filled. The military, for example, will derive more value from the use of testing procedures for pilots than will the XYZ Company that wants to hire one advertising manager.

Correlations not causes.   One must remember that a test does not tell you why someone succeeds or fails. Even if a testing program discloses that job success is associated with a particular personality characteristic, the trait does not necessarily contribute to performance. Individuals with that trait may simply have some other unmeasured and unknown characteristic that helps them on the job, or supervisors may respond favorably to it (even though it may have nothing to do with the work). Of course, this is the limitation of all correlations; they are not meant to indicate causality.

Labor market limitations.   The use of tests assumes that the supply of recruits is so large that management can afford to reject those who don't pass, even though some of them might have proved satisfactory employees. Unfortunately, this assumption conflicts with the conclusion that tests are more useful

---

[41] We are touching only superficially here on what is a complex problem of statistical analysis. During the test-development program, so-called "cut-off scores" are determined by correlation techniques. Hypothetically, after correlating test performance with job performance, the test-development group may say to line management, "If you insist that everyone hired for this job have a combined test score of 80, the validity of your hiring predictions will be improved 20 per cent over what they are now. If you raise the minimum required score to 85, you will improve the quality of hiring predictions by a factor of 30 per cent." That is, the test will be more selective and fewer employees will be hired who will fail. Of course, in the process of making the test more selective by raising the cut-off scores, management is increasing the costs of the testing program and requiring a larger number of candidates to be recruited, but more of this shortly.

[42] An exception to the statistical nature of testing results is found in the clinical personality tests referred to above as "projective" personality assessments. These endeavor to examine the single individual as a dynamic whole, interrelating the various drives, inhibitions, and values of his personality. However, the results are not directly relatable to job characteristics, nor can they be easily validated.

when many identical positions must be filled. The job of filling a great many such positions often taxes the recruiting skills of the organization. For example, large department stores must hire large numbers of salespeople. The problem is made more acute by the high turnover associated with jobs that attract young, unmarried women. The introduction of a new selection requirement— for example, all applicants must pass an employment test—may mean that the company will have to double or even treble the number of applicants recruited in order to find enough who can meet the new requirement. But conditions in the labor market may make this possible. Unfortunately, the amount of improvement that tests can generate is a function of the number of applicants that can be *rejected!* Of course, where the supply of applicants greatly exceeds the number of openings, test programs become more economical.

Insofar as tests reduce turnover, this variable becomes less important.

Costs. Testing is a specialized technical field that requires professional training, usually in psychology. If a company intends to develop, validate, and administer its own testing program, it must hire well-trained, high-salaried professionals. Moreover, most of the commercially available test batteries contain copyrighted elements, for which a fee must be paid each time they are used. Even companies that use outside consultants to administer and score tests incur substantial expenses. Simple paper-and-pencil tests cost only a few dollars to administer, but the information they provide is minimal; clinical psychological testing, including projective tests and other personality assessment techniques, may cost several hundred dollars per candidate. Also, as we have noted, additional recruiting costs may be incurred.

On jobs where training costs are high and the employee has considerable discretion in how to perform the job, the cost of testing programs is easier to justify than on jobs where these conditions do not prevail.

An important expense item that is frequently neglected because it is difficult to measure is the impact of testing on employee effectiveness, particularly where tests are used for promotion decisions.

PERSONNEL TESTING AND ORGANIZATION MEN

Given these limitations and costs associated with tests, particularly personality tests, we must assume that their use affects the organization.

Favoring conformity. Management sometimes becomes discouraged by the difficulty of proving that given personality attributes or aptitudes as revealed by test scores actually contribute to job success. Criteria for success in salaried positions, particularly managerial jobs, are very difficult to obtain. Consequently, there is a growing tendency to use personality tests to screen out people who look "different" from those now employed in similar jobs.

Lacking proof that the test scores are significantly related to job success, management simply assumes that unusual personality traits will probably be a handicap, and that people with these characteristics will be more difficult to absorb into the organization. Since white-collar jobs require people who can work closely with other people, management decides to look for "adaptable, conformist" personalities.[43]

There may be a measure of truth in this approach, particularly in selecting lower-level white-collar personnel. But there is an obvious danger inherent in this type of reasoning. Not only is there no proof that these attributes are desirable characteristics, but by emphasizing them management runs the risk of excluding creative, imaginative talent, including the type of people who can become strong top managers.

> Personality tests . . . are loaded with debatable assumptions and questions of value. The result . . . is a set of yardsticks that reward the conformist, the pedestrian, the unimaginative—at the expense of the exceptional individual whom management most needs to attract.[44]

Can tests be beaten?   Some have argued that many paper-and-pencil personality tests are really intelligence tests, and a bright applicant can "fake" the desired characteristics. A description of "How to Cheat on Personality Tests" suggests the test-takers should seek to project the following attitudes.[45]

    a. I loved my father and my mother, but my father a little more
    b. I like things pretty well the way they are
    c. I never worry much about anything
    d. I don't care for books or music much
    e. I love my wife and children
    f. I don't let them get in the way of company work

Some tests are more easily "faked" than others, of course. While psychologists have taken pains to build internal checks into many paper-and-pencil personality tests, individuals can usually vary their response to specific items in their desire to give answers the tester wants. Obviously such test results are of little value.

Low validities.   Personality tests in particular—and these are the tests which are most popular for staff and managerial positions—do not show encouragingly high predictive power:

---

[43] Consulting firms that specialize in evaluating candidates for managerial positions often concentrate on attempting to fit applicants to the over-all "climate" of the organization or to the personality of the top executive. It is assumed that they will "fit in" easily and not be troublemakers.

[44] William H. Whyte, Jr., "The Fallacies of Personality Testing," *Fortune* (September 1954), p. 118. Whyte's point of view is also presented in his book, *The Organization Man* (New York: Simon and Schuster, 1956), pp. 171-201. For a rebuttal of Whyte, see Saul Gellerman, "Personnel Testing: What the Critics Overlook," *Personnel* (May-June 1963).

[45] William H. Whyte, Jr., *op. cit.,* p. 405ff. Clinical psychologists dispute the "fakability" of the better tests.

> It must be concluded that, taken as a whole, there is no generalizable evidence that personality measures can be recommended as good or practical tools for employee selection.[46]

One reason for this defect may be that most of the major tests utilized have been designed to assist in the diagnosis and treatment of mentally ill people (such as the Bernreuter and the Minnesota Multi-Phasic Personality). They were not intended to predict on-the-job behavior.

Why then have personality tests been so popular? The uncertainties and potential cost of a mistake in the selection of key employees is certainly an important reason. Clearly, the motivation to work hard and the ability to collaborate with other people are crucial requirements in most of these jobs. Additionally, test-producing companies have used high-pressure selling tactics. Even though these have been decried by the psychological profession, many companies have succumbed to the unsubstantiated claims of the salesman. Many personnel people have been gullible and attracted by a test that they themselves "tried out" and which seemed to work.

> In one experiment, a reputable personality test was administered to 68 personnel managers attending a conference at the University of Illinois. The "scores" took the form of a fake personality analysis sheet containing 13 items collected from dream books and astrology charts, interspersed with fairly critical comments about the personality being tested. Each man's name was written in red pencil at the top of the sheet and the 13 items—"You have a great need for other people to like and admire you," "You pride yourself as an independent thinker," and so on—were circled in red. Thus, each identical sheet looked as though it had been specially prepared for the man concerned.
>
> The participants were then asked to rate the accuracy both of each item and of the over-all evaluation on a 5-point scale, ranging from "amazingly accurate" down to "almost entirely wrong." On only one item was there any substantial disagreement. Over-all, the analysis was rated "amazingly accurate" by 50 per cent of the group, and "rather good" by 40 per cent.[47]

Ethics.   Personality tests sometimes probe highly personal areas: unconscious sexual tendencies and family life, hidden fears and urges.[48] Unless a strong case can be made that these tests are highly predictive of future job performance, there can be serious ethical questions concerning the desirability of putting such information in the hands of supervisors and employers. In fact, the Civil Service Commission has recently restricted their use in the government on the grounds of invasion of privacy and potential misuse.[49] (In a some-

---

[46] Robert Guion and Richard Gottier, "Validity of Personality Measures in Personnel Selection," *Personnel Psychology*, Vol. 18, No. 2 (Summer 1965), pp. 135-164. The authors, two psychologists, painstakingly evaluate and summarize 133 validity studies and the literature of testing before coming to this discouraging conclusion.

[47] R. Stagner, "The Gullibility of Personnel Managers," *Personnel Psychology*, Vol. 11, No. 3 (Autumn 1958), pp. 347-352.

[48] *Cf.* George Strauss, "Organization Man: Prospect for the Future," *Industrial Relations* Vol. 6, No. 3 (Spring 1964), pp. 5-16.

[49] The pros and cons of this issue are well expressed in the "Special Issue: Testing and Public Policy," *American Psychologist*, Vol. 20, No. 11 (November 1965).

what similar vein trade unions have objected to the use of lie-detector tests designed to uncover deception in the pre-employment background information supplied by applicants.) [50]

SELECTION AND THE MANAGER

We have spoken before about the relative authority of staff and line executives. Since selection procedures contribute significantly to a manager's effectiveness, responsibility for decision-making must reside with the line. Personnel specialists can help the manager select his subordinates by recruiting and screening appropriately qualified candidates. But the final decision on whom to hire for a specific job must rest with the manager.

Unfortunately, the manager may try to shirk this responsibility. Selecting personnel is a difficult job in which the intangibles always seem to outweigh the tangibles, and the manager is tempted to pass the job along to some sort of testing procedure that provides numerical, apparently objective answers.

Understanding test limitations. The danger is that managers tend to ascribe more validity to test scores than test specialists do. When a test claims to measure the "impulsiveness" or "self-sufficiency" of an applicant, the manager may ignore the fact that these are just *labels* attached to test results, and that a given applicant who scores high in these categories may or may not demonstrate these characteristics on the job. The specialists readily admit that test results do not guarantee success or failure; they know that test scores are simply another set of data to be added to information about the applicant's previous experience, training, work evaluations, interview information, and the impressions of those who know him.

If the supervisor is to discharge his responsibility for making selection decisions, he must understand the use and limitations of testing procedures. For his own needs, as well as to reassure employees that personnel decisions are being made by line management, the manager should know how data of this sort are derived and what confidence can be placed in them.

Tests for Present Employees

So far, we have been talking about the selection of new employees. Some of the techniques we have mentioned, however, may be used to test existing personnel. Management often uses interviews, group rating, and tests in deciding whether to promote or transfer an employee to a position with different job responsibilities from those of his present post.

---

[50] Many employers are negligent in not undertaking a closer check of the personnel and credit references, police records, educational and past job experience listed on application blanks. They seek to short-circuit the process by such means as a lie detector.

The use of tests for such purposes may detract from the leadership position of the immediate supervisor. If good test performance is required for promotion in the organization, what happens to successful job performance as an incentive? As Whyte observes:

> The weight now being given test reports makes it clear that for those who aspire to be an executive the most critical day they may spend in their lives will be the one they spend taking tests.[51]

Employees often resent the great weight given to the results of tests that they do not understand and may even regard measures of validity as inaccurate. The problem is further aggravated by the statistical nature of test results. It is difficult to use test results to explain to an employee why he did not get a given promotion. At best, one can say that, "In general, those with scores like yours are less successful than those with higher scores."

Management also has to justify its decision to use specific tests. Many times the material covered by a personality or aptitude test bears little logical relationship to the job to which the employee aspires. And those who develop the tests are not much help here; as one expert remarked candidly:

> "All we look for are correlations between test items and our criterion of job success. We don't care whether it is the height of the applicant's grandfather or how much he likes fish. As long as it correlates, we will use it in the battery."

A company that bases its promotion decisions primarily on such test results must be prepared to inform employees how and why the tests are used. Otherwise it will be faced with serious morale problems, for employees will feel that they are subject to mystical forces and that hard work counts less than test-writing and interviewing skills. As many employees have said, "The headshrinkers decide which way you go in this company."

If the testing program has been carefully chosen and well administered, management can justify it to employees. Personality tests, for example, uncover talent that would otherwise go to waste. An immediate supervisor may overlook or be prejudiced against the abilities of a given subordinate, but an impersonal test may bring these abilities to the attention of higher management. Moreover, management can make it clear that test results are not the *sine qua non* for advancement, but only one type of evidence that is used. And the employee can be made to realize that tests are valuable for his own purposes, for they identify attributes that suggest types of jobs and training that he will find satisfying and rewarding.

Confidentiality of test results. The depth projective tests in particular probe into rather personal areas of the individual's life and psyche—his attitudes toward his parents and his family, for example, or toward sex, and life and

---

[51] Whyte, *op. cit.*, p. 174.

death. These responses are highly confidential and are subject to serious mis-interpretation except in the hands of a trained clinician; moreover, their very possession by a business organization, as we have seen, raises serious ethical and moral issues. Employees are justifiably disturbed when their test results fall into the hands of supervisors, and many companies have begun to question the practice of recording certain test findings in employee files. Where outside psychological consultants are employed to administer the testing, they may keep all the records and relay to management only their interpretation of them as they relate to specific job requirements.

Certainly management should assure employees that test results will not be made freely available to any curious party in the organization. Adequate safe-guards must be introduced to protect confidential information.

Self–Selection

There is some evidence that given the limitations of formal selection methods, it is often far better to let a man show what he can and is willing to do. Here is what one expert has to say on the subject:

> The individual with initiative will often smoke himself out. His own thrust will move him into a position where he is noticed. Moreover, most people have a fairly realistic view of themselves and will not overbid. . . . One of the larger chemical companies constantly creates conditions designed to discover the men willing to take on extra work loads . . . [to] differentiate between the great mass of people who are willing to do a good day's work . . . and the small minority who have both the prerequisites and the desire to push ahead—who are willing to offer suggestions about change and take the consequences if their suggestions don't pan out.[52]

In the same vein, actual observation of on-the-job performance can be a much better predictor of future performance than any test. In this vein, many companies de-emphasize precise selection in favor of minimal screening and close scrutiny after employment. However, this only works if the organization is able to offer adequate challenge and open-ended jobs that test the individ-ual's mettle.

SELECTION AND THE PERSONNEL DEPARTMENT

Personnel has responsibilities, too, particularly in the large and decentral-ized company. It is very easy for talented people to get lost. Either their own boss wants to hold on to them, their assignments do not make them visible to outsiders, or they are in a static part of the organization. Under these circum-stances a good person who does not feel he can find rewarding assignments

---

[52] Eli Ginzberg, "Identifying and Rewarding the Talented Individual" in Leonard Sayles (ed.), *Individualism and Big Business* (New York: McGraw-Hill, 1963), pp. 95, 98.

equal to his capacities may quit. Many times organizations are losing good people in one division while they are recruiting eagerly (and expensively) in another. Thus, Personnel must develop procedures for inventorying and updating the records on human resources in such a manner that all parts of the organization can use this as an internal labor market. Recent computer programs make it possible to "store" great quantities of information on each individual's background and performance so that a manager with an opening can receive "print outs" describing everyone in the company who meets the job specification.

Personnel should advise managers on hiring standards (see pp. 431-435, Chapter 18). For example, many managers may set standards too high, thus increasing recruiting costs and leading to serious morale problems, particularly when employees are overqualified by education for their jobs. By setting more realistic hiring standards many companies could enlarge their pool of potential recruits and provide opportunities for the underprivileged.

On the other hand, some automation decreases the number of menial jobs and raises hiring standards. Even shipping room personnel often have to read complicated instructions printed out by a computer, and many simple, repetitive jobs are now done by machine. Also, as we saw in Chapter 3, in automated plants, managers want to hire people who can be promoted through the ranks. All of these developments make it unlikely that anyone without a high school education can be hired.

In a large company, Personnel can perform invaluable work in validating existing selection procedures and in developing tailor-made tests that will do a much better job for the specific jobs and working conditions of their organization than can purchased, more general-purpose tests (often called "patent medicine tests"!).

Actually, Personnel's work in this area can help destroy a number of company-wide stereotypes. The assumptions that all salesmen have to be highly sociable or all managers have to be highly intelligent may not stand up under the scrutiny of a selection-research program. In one department store, Personnel's research on job requirements showed that very different personal characteristics were required to sell "big ticket" items from those needed for housewares and clothing.

Future research. Many companies are undertaking internal personnel research to see if they can improve their ability to identify future high-level executives. Examining with the aid of computers the employment records of their managers over a long period of time, they seek to identify "profiles" associated with rapid promotion to high levels. They are looking at factors like college grades and outside activities, length of time on each job, and internal appraisals. To date the results have not been conclusive, but it would appear that there is no one type of leader or successful executive.[53]

---

[53] *Cf. Business Week* (March 5, 1966).

In order to survive, every organization must attract an adequate supply of employees and must then assign them to the jobs for which they are best suited. In administering its recruitment program, the company must determine its personnel needs and the methods it will use in seeking to fill them. It must devise specific programs tailored to the numbers and skills to be recruited and to prevailing conditions in the labor market. Moreover, it must make a systematic evaluation of alternative selection techniques in light of their relative advantages and costs.

When psychologists first began to explore individual differences, the application of their research to selection promised to introduce a new era in employee relations. Theretofore, employee failures had been attributed to laziness or recalcitrance; now it could be argued that the real fault lay in trying to force square pegs into round holes. Testing enthusiasts claimed that careful appraisal of individual capabilities would solve most personnel problems. Placing the employee in the right job would assure a high level of performance and eliminate employee discontent.

These predictions have proved somewhat extravagant. The individual human being has shown himself to be more difficult to appraise and categorize than was anticipated. Frequently an employee with the requisite skills and learning potential has failed for lack of motivation. Personality attributes like motivation, although difficult to measure by simple tests, are often more important in explaining job success or failure than the more tangible characteristics of the individual.

There is a vast difference between selecting people for jobs that have very predictable and controlled behavior (a draftsman or machinist) and selecting people who will be "creative" or who will "innovate" or build up an organization from scratch. For many of these more complex jobs we are not even sure what abilities or behavior patterns will lead to success, so that it is naive to endeavor to use precise measuring instruments.

Nor are jobs themselves easy to classify, particularly the more complex managerial positions. As we mentioned in Chapter 16, different people will handle the same job in strikingly different ways. The requirements of a job may change radically when a new supervisor takes over, and there is no way of predicting organizational changes of this sort. Jones, who was selected to work in a department headed by Brown, finds himself unable to work effectively under the new head, Smith.[54]

At a more modest level we need to distinguish between hiring people for

---

[54] In spite of herculean efforts, in the vast and well-staffed U.S. Army, selection procedures had only limited success in World War II. A survey of this program notes that the performance of a soldier depends on (1) personal characteristics, (2) stresses he is subject to, and (3) special qualities of his immediate group and the larger organization of which he is a part. Tests only deal with (1). *Cf.* Eli Ginzberg, *The Ineffective Soldier* (New York: Columbia University Press, 1959).

specific jobs, for a range of interrelated jobs, or for a given organization. In many (but not all) instances, learning ability and the motivation to work may be much more important than more specific aptitudes or achievements.

Managers must not allow tests to become the sole basis of decision-making, for there is a variety of selection techniques available. And they should give more emphasis to the help tests provide in deciding where to put an applicant (placement) as distinct from deciding whether or not to hire him (screening).

Where selection techniques like interviewing and testing are unsuccessful, management is likely to endeavor to match "classes" of individuals to jobs. For example, the company may hire only graduates of "Ivy League" colleges, those with 5-10 years of relevant work experience, or applicants in the 22-30 year age bracket.

Many organizations concentrate on trying to fit jobs to people, rather than trying to fit people to jobs. This approach calls for the development of soundly based recruitment programs, techniques for screening out the obviously unqualified, and effective means of *finding* or *adapting* jobs within the organization for those who have been hired.

But we must not relegate all selection techniques to the dust bin just because they have serious limitations. Personnel programs are characteristically somewhat less than perfect, and the effective supervisor must learn to work within the limits set by his tools and techniques.

PROBLEM 1

HOW DO YOU SPOT A GOOD COPYWRITER?

Colton, Langenberg and Hartford is a large, successful advertising agency. One of the reasons for its success has been its ability to produce fresh, creative, eye-catching copy. The company employs about 60 copywriters working in 15 different departments.

The department heads, who are responsible for hiring, have different ideas on what makes a good copywriter. Their predilections are based pretty much on chance experience and ingrained stereotypes. One supervisor will tell you: "I can tell a good copywriter right away—all you have to do is to give him two minutes to come up with an original advertisement for something like condensed milk and see what he does." Others use this criterion: "I have him bring in all the ads he has ever written and ask him for his 10 favorites and 10 worst. Then I spend the next evening reading them all over and comparing my judgments to his."

The results of this haphazard approach to selection have not been good. At present the company needs five new copywriters, and one-third of the present staff have not worked out well. The agency's personnel department would like to use a more systematic procedure for evaluating applicants, including some technique for testing writing skill. The new program would be costly, however, and there would be little point in setting it up if the department heads ignored its findings.

1. If you were head of the agency, how would you set up an improved selection procedure that would not detract from the department heads' responsibility for turning out high-quality copy?
2. What information would you need before deciding on such a new policy?
3. How would you introduce and gain acceptance for the new approach?

NEW ENGINEERS

The Firstway Aircraft Company has just received a government contract to develop a new military transport plane. At least 175 additional engineers will be needed to initiate this program, although it is uncertain how long the contract will remain in effect. The funds will be cut off unless Congress increases the military budget at the end of the year.

Management is faced with several problems in recruiting the personnel required by this program:

1. Because of the recent cancellation of other projects by government cutbacks, the company has been left with a surplus of engineers. Unfortunately, however, they will not have completed their present assignment until one or two months after the new program is scheduled to get underway. Further, most of them are not experienced in designing transport planes. What criteria should management use in deciding whether or not to select engineers from the anticipated surplus to staff the new activity?

2. The new program may be short-lived. But if the company publicizes this fact, it will hamper its recruiting activities in a tight labor market. Is the company under any obligation to disclose that the work may be short-term? If so, how can it discharge that obligation?

DEAF—AND DISABLED?

Alfred Elkind had been with the Consolidated Electronics Company for seven years when he requested a six-month leave of absence to travel to Florida to visit his mother, who had an incurable disease. When Elkind returned, company policy required that he take a medical examination. The company doctor's examination disclosed what his fellow employees had known for more than two years. Elkind had become almost totally deaf as a result of a disease of the central nervous system. Hearing aids would do him no good.

Management refused to take Elkind back and placed him on an indefinite sick leave. The department supervisor and higher management felt that Elkind could not work efficiently and safely with such poor hearing.

Elkind appealed to the union, which filed a grievance including these arguments:

1. The supervisor had known for more than a year about this condition and had taken no action. A leave of absence is not supposed to prejudice a man's employment rights. It was taken with company approval for a pressing matter of justifiable family concern. A man should not be penalized for visiting his dying mother.

2. Elkind's job as an electronic tester does not require him to work closely with other people, and the supervisor can "find ways to communicate to him."

3. Elkind's personal doctor has given him a signed statement indicating that he is healthy enough to engage in all the work relating to his present job.

4. The company President, Mr. Vaughan, once signed a Chamber of Commerce policy statement indicating that "hiring the handicapped is good business."

486

5. The company has a moral and legal obligation to workers with seniority.

On reviewing the case, the general manager told the union that the company would try to find some job for Elkind but it would not guarantee to find one that required equal skill and that paid as well as his present job. "His present job, however, is too critical to the company's reputation as a producer of quality equipment. There are many instances when the supervisor and/or other employees have to discuss work problems centering on the workmanship and electronic characteristics of certain components and a man with a hearing problem cannot fill that part of the job description."

1. If you were the general manager, how would you evaluate the specific points raised in the union's grievance?
2. What steps would you have followed had the case been presented to you after the report of the company's medical director had been received?

PROBLEM 4

APPLICANT

The Phillips Paint Company trains the salesmen it hires to sell its product line to retail stores. The company seeks personable young men who have the energy and initiative to make the requisite calls on customers and the ability to speak enthusiastically and intelligently about the company's products. Flexibility and patience in meeting a wide variety of people, and accuracy in transferring orders to order forms, are also important requirements.

James Henry has applied for a sales job. The interviewer who is going to talk with him has noted the following entries on his application blank:

> Henry is 25 years old.
> He has completed one year of college, at a small teachers' college in the Midwest.
> He was divorced after three years of marriage, no children.
> He has held two jobs since leaving school; he had had no work experience prior to that time. The jobs were: laboratory assistant, Memorial Hospital (2 years), New York, and credit manager for collection agency (2 years), Buffalo.

No job is listed for one year. James notes on his application that he was recovering from an illness during that period.

1. If you were the interviewer, what objectives would you set for your interview with James?
2. How would you phrase your questions?

PROBLEM 5

WANTED: CUSTOM TAILORS

You are the executive vice president of a large "high-style" women's dress manufacturing organization. Your firm finds it increasingly difficult to find candidates for custom-tailoring positions. These craftsmen, in the past, at least, have been apprentice-trained in Europe, and most of the better American tailors have been immigrants.

1. What proposals would you make to your company concerning means of increasing the supply of custom-tailors available to your organization? (You employ about a hundred of them, many of whom are nearing retirement.)
2. In your proposal, consider the sources of information and the channels of communication you would explore in developing a proposal with reasonable chances of success. Remember that costs are a significant factor.

Promotions, Transfers, and Seniority

An employee does not stay on his job forever. Hopefully he will be promoted; transfers are always likely; and if conditions are unfavorable he may even be demoted or laid off. As we shall see in this chapter policies in these areas are difficult to formulate.

PROMOTIONS FROM WITHIN
VS. RECRUITMENT FROM WITHOUT

Every organization needs to decide which jobs are to be filled by promotion from within and which are to be filled by recruitment from outside. Let us briefly consider the arguments for these alternative approaches.

The Case for Promotion from Within

Providing better-qualified employees. No organization can rely on out-side recruitment to fill all its requirements. True, certain jobs are similar from one organization to another, but most jobs require specialized knowledge that can be obtained only within a particular firm. Even jobs that do not seem to be unique require familiarity with the people, procedures, policies, and special characteristics of the organization in which they are performed.[1] Thus, care-fully designed promotional ladders are needed to funnel upward those who have had broad experience within the various branches of the organization.

Internal recruitment is also a means of selection. We have already seen that most selection procedures, such as interviewing and testing, provide a far from perfect picture of a new applicant's potential worth. Seeing a man in action, however, over a period of years, enables management to make a realistic assess-ment of his skills.

---

[1] There is evidence that blue-collar jobs in the middle range of the promotional ladder are most likely to be unique to a particular company. Unskilled work and highly skilled jobs are more likely to be similar from one company to another.

Promotion also provides a process of "selective socialization." Over time, those whose personalities and skills enable them to fit into the organization's human relations tend to stay on; those whose personalities conflict tend to leave—either voluntarily or involuntarily.

Providing motivation.   People will work harder if they know this will lead to promotion. But employees have little motivation if the better jobs are reserved for outsiders. (Most managements want their employees to believe that promotions come automatically with hard work. But too many employees perceive this as a capricious process in which the instrumental factors are luck, being in the right place at the right time, and sponsorship by an executive who, himself, is rising rapidly.)

Providing job satisfaction.   Americans want to keep moving ahead. Being given additional responsibilities is not enough; people want the tangible recognition that a higher-ranking title provides. In addition, most workers look forward to unbroken, continuous service. They like to feel that they can get ahead in their own company without having to turn elsewhere.

The Case for Recruitment from Outside

Just as many organizations seek outsiders to sit on their boards of directors in order to introduce new perspectives, so they reserve certain lesser positions for newcomers. This infusion of "new blood" keeps the system from growing stagnant, repetitious, and overly conformist. This is probably of less importance in hourly-paid jobs than in staff and managerial jobs, however. (Actually, there needs to be an optimum "mix" of newcomers and oldtimers. Too many highly competitive, hard-driving executives can be almost as destructive as too many time-serving old fogies.)

Recruitment from outside the firm reduces the expense of training new employees, which can be very high, particularly for skilled tradesmen. In its more extreme forms, promotion from within can discourage the highly ambitious and well trained. For example, some advertising agencies insist that all new people, including some destined for administrative and creative responsibilities start at the very bottom in the mail room. How discouraging! Even the first jobs should be appropriate for and consistent with the employee's job competence.

A controversial policy followed in many companies is that of purposefully hiring a greater number of young, well-trained managers or specialists than ever can be promoted. It is hoped that the competitive atmosphere thus generated will serve to test the candidates' mettle and to weed out the less able and energetic. The competition can become destructive, however, and may lead to the loss of the best people rather than the worst.

People differ in what promotion means to them. Many managers tend to project their own feelings about promotion onto their employees, forgetting that not every employee wants to be promoted—at least not in the terms in which management typically conceives of promotion. Employees differ greatly in their "level of aspiration."

Some companies rely so heavily on the promotion-from-within policy that they cannot afford to keep people who do not qualify or are not desirous of moving ahead. Many universities similarly follow the practice of "up or out," which simply means that instructors and assistant professors must either earn a promotion or seek employment elsewhere.

Management sometimes makes the mistake of using a highly unpopular job as the required stepping-stone to higher positions. As a result, serious shortages may develop in these higher positions because few candidates are willing to spend time on the undesirable rung of the promotional ladder.

Similarly, when an employee enters into an apprenticeship program, he is often required to accept a reduction in pay for a number of years before he wins a craftsman's rating. Management officials assume that employees should be willing to make short-run sacrifices in return for long-run benefits, but they forget that their own time perspective may be quite different from that of their employees.

Thus, what management regards as a substantial promotion may not seem like a promotion at all to the employee himself. The nurse or salesman may not want to be an administrator. The additional responsibilities or travel requirements of some jobs may more than outweigh the status associated with the new salary and title.

Finally, there is always a group of employees who are quite content to stand still, who prefer the known to the unknown. Unwilling to risk what they have in hand, they want to stick close to the people they know and the responsibilities they are familiar with. To these people, *improvement* means regular wage increases, more security, and perhaps an easier job. Yet in some industries, technology has made it difficult to satisfy this last desire; the majority of jobs are fast-paced and demanding. This is more true of the automobile industry (mass production), for example, than of the chemical industry (process production).

Dual ladders. As noted in Chapter 25, technical personnel may be reluctant to give up their specialties to become administrators. In order to motivate and reward these professionals, many companies establish "dual ladders" which allow them to move up through a series of steps without assuming managerial positions.[2] Although this does alleviate some of the inequalities,

2 *Cf.* William Kornhauser, *Scientists in Industry* (Berkeley and Los Angeles: University of California Press, 1962), p. 137, 143-149.

it is doubtful that, given the present organization of industry, the same status and perquisites can be given to a "Principal Research Scientist" as to a "Divisional President." The promotion ladders are not really parallel.

To summarize: Management must provide realistic opportunities that will encourage promising employees to take the risks involved in moving upward. It must not discourage valuable employees from seeking advancement by making service in an unpopular job a prerequisite to promotion. It must provide for employees who do outstanding work but are unwilling to take on new and additional responsibilities. And it must provide alternatives for professionals who are reluctant to assume supervisory responsibilities.

SELECTING WHO IS TO BE PROMOTED

Having settled on a general promotion program, management must face the still more difficult task of deciding who to promote, since there are usually more candidates than openings. The choice usually revolves around evaluations of relative merit, ability, and length of service.

Merit and Ability

If promotion is to be an incentive, the best-performing employees ought to be advanced. However, since differences in merit may not be readily measurable, the fellow employees of a man who has made a step up can develop the demoralizing belief that favoritism rather than superior performance was a critical factor. As a further source of discontent, on many jobs results reflect the coordinated activities of many people or chance factors (for instance, selling a product that is in short supply)—thus making individual merit difficult to measure.

But there is also the question of *ability*—that is, potential performance on other jobs. Jones may be doing fine on his present job but lack the ability to do the work on a higher-ranked job. Smith, on the other hand, may be doing poorly at present because of inadequate supervision or the unchallenging nature of the work. Put him on more difficult work and he may blossom.

Long-term factors are also relevant. The individual best fitted for an immediate promotion may not have the greatest long-term potential. That is, the most deserving candidate at the moment may seem to be a senior employee who has the ability to move only one more step up the promotional ladder, but it may be better to promote a younger man who may eventually advance into higher management.

In addition, it will be remembered from our earlier discussion of testing that ability is as difficult to measure as merit. The specific traits, attitudes, personalities, and skills that make up ability are frequently ambiguous. For this reason companies often rely on objective measurements—years of education, for example.

To complicate matters further, some people may be given special opportunities to acquire valuable skills whereas others are not. Certain jobs give employees an opportunity to move about freely, bringing them into contact with high-level personnel whose opinions are crucial in promotion decisions. They "learn their way around the organization" and are on the spot when a promotional opportunity turns up.

What we are saying, then, is that the concept of ability is, like that of merit, surrounded by subjective elements that may create inequities. However, it is still important to make an effort to measure and reward merit and ability. Organizations that have failed to reward excellence in service, or that have relied too heavily on personal relationships or length of service, suffer in terms of both efficiency and morale.

Seniority

The extent to which promotions should be based on seniority is almost always an area of dispute between unions and management. Here are the arguments in favor of seniority.

Objectivity and equity. The use of such criteria as performance evaluation, selection tests, and supervisory opinions leads many employees to feel that promotions are not made fairly. And charges of favoritism and discrimination may lead to declines in morale and productivity. Unions object that as long as managers have the power to select the most suitable candidate for promotion, it is a simple matter for them to discourage ambitious employees from speaking out against company policy.

To avoid this difficulty, it is often suggested that promotions be based on some objective criterion, and that the only truly objective criterion is length of service. When management knows that it is going to promote the employee with the longest service, chances are that the company will give him the training he needs to move into the new job. Management will also tend to perfect its initial selection procedures, for once an individual gets into the organization his future will be relatively assured.

In certain societies, the older men invariably occupy the highest positions; although we do not follow this practice rigidly, we still feel that it is appropriate for the senior people within an organization to occupy higher positions than their juniors. True, we make a good many exceptions: the long-time employee who is clearly incompetent, and the young man who is a genius. However, ours is at least partially an "age-graded society" where age, position, and prestige are positively correlated.

Inequity through seniority. Excessive emphasis on seniority, however, may violate employee attitudes about the "right" way of getting ahead: Indeed, the promotion of incompetents solely on the basis of length of service clearly violates another strongly entrenched cultural attitude that rewards should be somehow commensurate with accomplishment.

> The top-skilled members of glass- and steel-making crews are typically men who have worked their way up through a lengthy, informal apprenticeship system. In the old days they worked long hours, often without pay, under the far-from-tolerant tutelage of a craftsman who would put up with his younger assistants only in return for numerous services. It was a long, hard, grueling road to the top, and those who have made it frequently resent the rather automatic manner in which men can now work themselves into similar positions primarily by accumulating seniority.

Even the employee who lacks the desire or the ability to advance, wants to know that others who are more able and more ambitious than himself are receiving appropriate recognition. Some cultures assume that advancement should be based on ties of family or friendship, but Americans tend to regard nepotism or other forms of favoritism as unethical or immoral. In part, this attitude reflects the relative absence of rigid class boundaries and strong restrictions on the individual in our national experience. We believe that an individual should be able to move ahead on his own merits, regardless of his family background and early life.

Contribution to ability. Up to some point, it seems likely that the longer an employee works at one job, the more qualified he becomes for promotion to the next-higher job. Research among production workers suggests that the employee with the longest service often is better prepared for promotion than management is initially willing to admit.[3] For many jobs, particularly those at the lower levels, differences in ability from one employee to another may be less important than management tends to think. Consequently, the gain in morale derived from promoting the most senior employee may more than offset any slight loss of efficiency.

But the correspondence between seniority and ability undoubtedly diminishes as length of service increases, and beyond a certain level, continued service brings very little gain. Indeed, after a point, increased length of service actually *reduces* an employee's ability to change jobs, producing in him what is often referred to as "a trained incapacity," that is, he becomes so imbued with the problems and procedures of his present job that he is unable to adjust to new circumstances and situations. The expert becomes simply too expert in what he is doing.

Reward for loyalty. In a sense, to grant promotions on the basis of seniority is to reward employees for loyalty. In an organization that wants to hold on to its employees and avoid costly turnover, a type of guaranteed promotion plan may be an effective personnel policy.

No one would deny that loyal service deserves reward. But the question is, how many loyal employees become discouraged about their future with the

---

[3] James J. Healy, "The Ability Factor in Labor Relations," *Arbitration Journal,* Vol. 10 (New Series), No. 1 (1955), pp. 3-11.

organization when they realize that they can be promoted only as fast as length of service permits? Also, the emphasis on longevity induces a "ritualistic devotion to duty" in which perfection in the small things, the job routines, and the avoidance of mistakes take precedence over imaginative and energetic pursuit of more challenging goals. Further, those characteristics that were most associated with job success at lower skill levels may not be as useful in higher level jobs. Balancing this, however, is the reduction in destructive interpersonal competition that can occur when there is too much uncertainty about who will be promoted.

Striking a Balance

Every organization must decide on the relative weights it will give to merit, ability, and seniority in making promotion decisions. Even when company policy or the union contract sets up merit and ability as the prime determinants, many an organization succumbs in time to the presumably more objective criterion of seniority. Supervisors in general believe that relations with their subordinates will be easier if they promote the most senior employee. Almost all companies give some weight to seniority in practice, although firms that are unionized give it greater weight than those that are not. See diagram.

Spectrum of merit-seniority criteria for making promotional decisions.

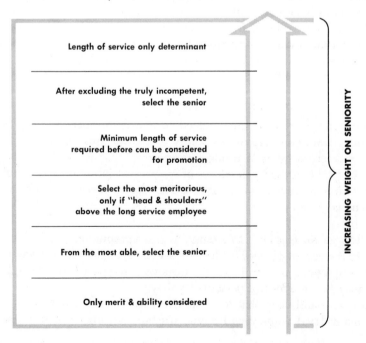

Dealing with the Individual

Handling employees who are unlikely to be promoted. A supervisor must be able to predict what members of his group will be the most likely candidates for promotion when openings occur. And he must try to keep those who are unlikely to be promoted from taking it for granted that they will soon be moving up the ladder. For example, an employee with seniority may think he is promotable even if he is not. If his supervisor allows that misapprehension to continue, the employee will be sadly disappointed when someone else gets the job. And if his buddies encourage him to think that he is wronged, he is likely to create a serious problem.

Problems of this sort can be avoided if the supervisor makes a point of discussing with the hopeful candidate the exact nature of the new responsibilities *long before the opening actually occurs.* Then, if the employee is clearly not qualified for the promotion, he may be brought around to accept his unsuitability. The supervisor may be able to suggest a way in which the employee can supplement his background or improve his performance so that he will eventually become eligible for a promotional opportunity. If he shows himself unwilling to make the extra effort required, the job of winning his assent to being "passed over" becomes much easier.

Handling employees who are likely to be promoted. When should an individual be notified that he is likely to be promoted? There is a middle ground between notifying likely prospects too early and waiting until the last minute to make the selection. A candidate will often be anxious to undertake additional training to prepare himself for the new job,[4] and tensions in the group may be reduced when the decision is reached. However, selection of likely candidates in advance, when the time period is too great, may appear unfair and discriminatory.

Dealing with the employee who doesn't want to be promoted. In our culture, anyone who does not want to advance is regarded as somehow queer or lazy. Many individuals take on higher-level jobs even when they are not suited for additional responsibility; but the cost is high to themselves and to the organization. In fact, people who really should not be promoted may come to feel that a failure to show interest in advancement is a black mark against their record. Actually, a clear recognition of each employee's psychological and intellectual limits is valuable both to the organization and to the individual.

The employee who has reached the limit of his ambitions or abilities still has a vital role to play. The armed services have discovered the value of the "old-line" master sergeants who stay with a particular unit, providing stability

---

[4] A good example of this procedure is described in the example in Chapter 21, in which older nurses were encouraged to take additional formal training to qualify for promotion.

and continuity, while its commissioned officers come and go. So, too, employees who have been in one department for a long time may help to break in newcomers, particularly new supervisors.

But nonmobile people must not be permitted to monopolize the training jobs in which more suitable candidates can be prepared for higher positions.

Helping the successful candidate. Serious problems are experienced by the man who does move up into a new position, particularly if it involves supervision. Unless he has been with the group for a long time, and unless the group has concurred in his promotion, he is bound to encounter some measure of fear and resistance. His new subordinates will be uncertain at first about what his new leadership will mean to their future. (This is sometimes called a "succession crisis." See Chapter 13.)

The employee who is promoted to a nonsupervisory position has his problems, too, for he may be facing new responsibilities for which he is not wholly prepared. Nothing is "automatic" in a strange job, and the new man is under great strain. In worrying about what he should do and how to avoid mistakes, he may become so tense that he performs clumsily or forgetfully. If his supervisor is aware of these strains, he can provide the understanding that will help the new man over the hump of the first days on the job.

Impact of Department Boundaries
on Promotion

The organization needs to guard against a situation in which pockets of promotable personnel build up in some areas where promotions are "sluggish" —and a dearth of promotable personnel builds up in other areas where promotional openings are more numerous.

Inequality in promotional opportunities. If opportunities for promotion differ greatly from one department to another, morale may be seriously impaired. Some departments are notorious for the lack of promotional opportunities they offer to employees. In one company, we found that participation in a new union was inversely correlated with promotional opportunities: The group that enjoyed the fewest opportunities for promotion was the most anxious to engage in union activities. Here, experienced, skilled men felt frustrated by their inability to move ahead.

In a sense, the opportunity for promotion is a function of the "width" of the promotional ladder. When management insures that, without sacrificing their accrued benefits, men can transfer easily from a unit in which they are blocked to a unit in which there are more openings, inequities are less likely to occur. One way of widening the ladder is to tie together "families" of jobs that call for common skills and common experience even though they are not related on the organizational chart. Such a policy also induces employees to see the problems of the organization from a less parochial point of view.

A seemingly innocent change in management policy within a given department sometimes wipes out the promotional opportunities of a whole group of workers. Whyte describes such a case:

> In view of the rapid scientific and technical development of the company [the Vice President of the department] decided that only college graduates should be appointed as foremen. The new ruling hit the HI-Test plant particularly hard, for some of these men had been singled out as especially able and promising. . . . They were at the top now with no place to go. . . . It was common to hear them say, "We're just bumping our heads against the ceiling here." [5]

When management finds that there are so-called "dead-end jobs" in the organization where promotions are unlikely, it should either try to open up these dead-ends or else fill them with employees who have neither the capability nor the desire to move ahead. Without promotional opportunities, organization effectiveness may suffer.

> A large English electrical manufacturing company noted that its small-appliance operations were very inefficient compared to its industrial-goods departments. A survey disclosed that promotions into top management always came from the latter area so that the highly motivated managers shifted out of appliances leaving that department with the less ambitious.[6]

It is more desirable to have "many roads to the top" so that no group is favored. Where technology is changing rapidly, this may be difficult to accomplish, and only a major retraining and development program can protect promotional opportunities.

> When the computer industry shifted from vacuum tubes to solid state components, a large number of traditionally trained electrical engineers who had been qualified to move to high-level positions found themselves "disqualified" because of their lack of knowledge about solid state physics, just as several years before that, the mechanical engineers had been displaced by the electricals!

The growing concern with equal opportunity and civil rights also affects the promotion area, and companies are recognizing that in the past, Negroes, for example, have not had the same chances of moving upward in the organization. The legislation described in the previous chapter applies to promotional opportunity as well as to initial selection.

Manpower hoarding. Departments sometimes try to hoard more employees than they need, particularly employees with scarce talents; for example, engineers were hoarded during the shortage of the 1950's. Understandably,

---

[5] William F. Whyte, "Engineers and Workers: A Case Study," *Human Organization,* Vol. 15, No. 4 (Winter 1956), p. 5.

[6] *Cf.* Kenn Rogers, *Managers—Personality and Performance* (London: Tavistock Publications, 1963), p. 68.

employees grow restless when they realize that the opportunity to advance is being blocked by the piling up of surplus manpower. Excess manpower can mean absence of job challenge; if there are too many people for too little work they get into one another's way.

Interdepartment competition may also be a factor in restricting promotional opportunities. For example, a department that was carrying on a full-scale training program for tool-makers refused to honor requests from employees who finished the course to accept a promotion to another department, claiming that the other department was "too cheap" to do its own training. On the other hand, there are situations in which everyone recognizes that certain departments will train workers for other departments. The important thing is to insure that the organization's control systems, such as cost accounting, reflect this contribution.

If some supervisors are reluctant to let their trained workers move on to higher-rated jobs in other departments, serious inequities are bound to develop.[7] Often the personnel department acts as a coordinator, encouraging "surplus" departments to send manpower to "deficit" departments. Personnel's effectiveness here depends in part on how centralized the organization is. In centralized companies, Personnel may *audit* manpower resources.

How Many Promotions?

The number of promotions possible is determined in part by the number of different wage or salary grades in existence. In an office employing 50 clericals, for example, it is possible to have, at the extremes, either 50 promotional steps or none. In practice, of course, neither would be likely. By de-emphasizing the differences in job duties, the company could place nearly all jobs in the same salary grade. Or, by carefully noting every conceivable difference between jobs, one could justify paying each employee a slightly different salary, thus making possible the 50 promotional steps.

What is the optimum number? Too few promotional steps may injure morale by eliminating the sense of personal progress and accomplishment. Too many promotional steps may mean that an excessive amount of time and effort must be spent in selecting candidates gaining acceptance for the choices, and shifting employees. The result may be chaos. In approaching this question of frequency of promotions, we must be careful to distinguish between promotion to a better job and periodic wage or salary *merit increases* (see Chapter 23).

There is a good bit of ambiguity, particularly on professional jobs, about when an employee has actually moved to a more important job, for job definitions are often quite elastic. An engineer, for example, may be required to work on a more difficult assignment for several months before the change in his job status is officially recognized by what we would call a promotion—that

---

[7] Some companies have even considered using the protests of a man's department when a promotion is in the offing as an important criterion of promotability!

is, a job title with more prestige and increased income. When a man is officially promoted to a more responsible position may be simply a matter of supervisory judgment.

There are two points at which crises are likely to develop in work careers: just after the transition from the school system, with its regular "promotions," to the job situation, where promotions are less assured; and after the employee has run through the course of easier, lower-level promotions and feels he is now on an endless plateau. These are the times when the employee begins to wonder whether he should look for a job where he can get ahead faster. The organization should be alert to the likelihood that these two transition points will give trouble, and should stand ready to help individuals adjust to both the anxieties and the realities of the situation.

TRANSFERS AND LAYOFFS

Life would be simpler if all movements of employees in an organization were upward, to higher-skilled and more responsible positions. In actuality, both because of the changing needs of the company and the shifting desires of employees, there is a great deal of horizontal movement (transfers between jobs paying approximately the same salaries) and downward movement (downgrading and layoffs).

Temporary Transfers

Rarely is work so smoothly and successfully scheduled that surpluses or shortages of personnel never develop. A Purchasing Department typist is ill; a sale of men's ties draws more customers than predicted; a machine breaks down, resulting in a surplus of machinists. What problems must be met in dealing with these short-run emergencies?

1. The typical employee resents being wrenched out of his normal work routines and assigned—even temporarily—to a new and unfamiliar job. In particular he may object to leaving his old job uncompleted. Thus, where possible, an employee should be allowed to come to a natural breaking point in his present job—to type to the end of the report or to fill the tote box with finished parts—before he is ordered elsewhere.

2. The employee may object to being transferred out of his old informal social group to another social group, which may well be hostile to all newcomers. To minimize this problem, the supervisor should carefully introduce the temporary employee to the group and explain why and for how long the transfer is to be made.

3. The employee may object that he is being discriminated against by being given more than his "fair share" of distasteful work. Here again the supervisor needs to remember that jobs with equal pay may not have equal social status,

and he may have to rotate undesirable assignments or resort to other techniques to make assignments seem fair.

4. The employee may be inadequately trained to handle the new job. For organizations that have frequent short-run transfers, the obvious solution is to train all employees to handle several jobs.

5. The employee may complain that he is being made to do work that is "out of his job description" (work that he did not expect to do on the basis of the original description of his duties)—that is, he may experience *craft-consciousness*. This problem is so serious that we shall devote a separate section to it.

Craft–Consciousness

Craft-consciousness—the feeling that no one should work outside his narrowly defined job duties—has traditionally been strong in the construction and maintenance trades. A carpenter will refuse to do any work but carpentry, and he will refuse to let other employees do carpentry work—even if this means that other employees must stand idle or be laid off.[8]

Other groups that lack the traditional craft status of the building trades try to erect barriers around their particular skills. The primary motivation seems to be job security, for workers feel that if they can prevent other men from doing their work, they will be able to make their own jobs more secure. Unions in general encourage craft-consciousness, because they look upon it as a means of restricting management's power to make transfers. And every time management gives in to a union demand to make craft boundaries more sacred, a "past practice" is established, which is in a sense "frozen" into the union contract.

> In one company, machinists were prohibited from picking up any material that had fallen on the floor. This was the janitors' work! Even valuable parts were sometimes swept away by the clean-up crews because the machinists refused to pick them up.

Management itself, by carrying specialization and division of labor to extremes, may be responsible for proliferating an unwieldy number of narrowly defined jobs. Where jobs are defined narrowly, each with a limited number of highly specific duties, the problem of shifting employees is accentuated. Employees, taking their cue from management, then proceed to erect artificial barriers that inhibit flexible transfers designed to expedite the flow of work and to even out work-load inequalities.

> "I am the only girl in the office who can run this mimeograph machine. It's not easy, let me tell you; it's old and has got lots of tricks to it that it takes years to learn. I don't want other girls using it; this way I know they really

---

[8] An unresolved problem, of course, is always this: What is the jurisdiction of the carpenter? He may want to include things that others claim as their rightful work or exclude tasks that management believes he ought to do.

need me around here. When we occasionally run out of work on the machine, I don't think it's fair for me to have to do other odd jobs. After all, this is what I am getting paid for."

Reducing craft-consciousness.   How can management deal with excessive craft-consciousness? First, by accepting as natural the work group's efforts to protect its members. Very little is accomplished by accusing employees of "feather-bedding," for employees are anxious to strengthen their "property right" in their jobs.

A second way of meeting this problem is to develop job descriptions that define jobs in terms of the work that needs to be done rather than in terms of abstract craft skills. In short, determine job duties by the requirements of the work process, not by traditional concepts of what a craftsman is. Of course, employees may resist such efforts, but this resistance may be minimized by skill in introducing change (see Chapter 13).

In inducting new employees, the supervisor should try to instill in them the broadest possible definition of their jobs. A good recruitment and training policy helps, for employees with diversified skills and good training are more easily transferred.

The impact of automation.   As we saw in Chapter 3, jobs in continuous-process automation are linked together in teams, with shared responsibilities and career ladders. Employees are expected to learn from their seniors about the higher-skilled jobs into which they will later move. The learning process frequently involves shared assignments and includes temporary transfers. Craft-consciousness is reduced by job enlargement, as reported in a study of an electrical generating plant:

> Each of [the new operators] is expected to have most of the skills and, especially, the knowledge and information previously held separately by the skilled boiler, turbine, and electrical operators. [These new operators] must be capable of running all of the major parts of the production system. The [lesser-skilled employees beneath their level are] . . . in the process of acquiring proficiency in all operations.[9]

Permanent Transfers

More permanent transfers may be used to solve longer-range problems.

Remedial transfer.   When an employee has trouble doing his work or develops personal friction with his boss or fellow employees, the answer may be to transfer him to another job. Remedial transfers, however, are often used as a means of glossing over serious problems. Where the supervisor is arbitrary, where inadequate training is provided to new hires, or where employees discriminate against members of minority groups, it is far better to resolve the

[9] Floyd C. Mann and L. R. Hoffman, "Individual and Organizational Correlates of Automation," *Journal of Social Issues*, Vol. 12, No. 2 (1956), pp. 12-13.

problem directly, rather than postpone it through a transfer. After all, the re-placement for the man who is transferred may face the same problems again.

Changing manpower needs.   When technological change is introduced or customer demands change, then the manpower needs of some departments may decline while the needs of other departments expand. To safeguard the jobs of long-service employees and to avoid losing the skills of trained personnel, most companies try to transfer employees to other jobs. Moreover, a company that follows a liberal transfer policy and provides retraining for employees who are transferred to new jobs has less difficulty in introducing changes.

SENIORITY AND LAYOFFS

In a free economy jobs cannot be absolutely guaranteed. When layoffs are necessary, some system is needed to determine who will lose his job first. Though many employers prefer to give major weight to *ability* in determining layoffs, *seniority* is the primary factor considered in unionized companies and to a considerable extent in nonunionized concerns as well. (Union contracts do sometimes permit small groups of employees—say, 10 per cent—who would otherwise be laid off, to keep their jobs during layoffs.)

Calculating Seniority

There are a number of alternate ways of calculating seniority.

1. Company-wide seniority: the length of time an employee has worked for the company.

2. Department seniority: the length of time an employee has worked in a particular department of the company.

3. Job seniority: the length of time an employee has held a specific job in a particular department of the company.

The method used obviously has a significant effect on the choice of which employee is laid off when, for example, there is a surplus of clerical help in the Accounts Receivable Department.

> The "youngest" employee (with least seniority) under formula 1 might be a recently hired stenographer in the Engineering Department. Then a girl from the Accounts Receivable Department would be transferred into the Engineering Department to take the job of the laid-off stenographer.
>
> The employee with least service under formula 2 might be a secretary who has been with the company for several years, but who recently transferred into the department when an opening occurred. (She will probably regret having shifted jobs!)
>
> Under formula 3, the company would be required to lay off the youngest employee doing the specific clerical job in the Accounts Receivable Depart-ment where the surplus existed.

Bumping.   Let us introduce another complication: *bumping.* The application of seniority may mean that a whole series of moves is generated when a single employee is laid off.

Let us look again at our earlier example. Under formula 2, the following would be a more typical sequence of events: The Accounts Receivable Department has too many stenographers. The stenographer with the least service in that position would lose her job. However, she would have the privilege of taking another job she could perform in the department, which is currently held by an employee with less department service than her own. Thus, the girl first displaced might "bump" a tabulating clerk with less service. In turn, the tabulating clerk may bump a file clerk with even less seniority than hers. And the process repeats itself as long as displaced employees can find other workers with less seniority than themselves occupying jobs that they are able to perform. Larger companies find that cutbacks in manpower may generate thousands of job shifts, which in turn create massive record-keeping and personnel problems. Shifts of this sort are bound to provoke countless grievances and complaints about alleged inequities in the demotions.

Selecting from among
Alternative Seniority Systems

Which seniority system is best from the point of view of the firm? Though there is no simple answer, the following criteria may help management in arriving at a solution.

Reducing frequency of movement.   One criterion to apply in evaluating a seniority system is whether it reduces the frequency of job-shifting. Shifts create grievances, and they also give rise to training and efficiency problems. Although management may require that an employee be able to perform the job for which he exercises his "bumping" privileges, it is hard to measure performance. Under the pressure of events, employee job shifts inevitably result in workers being displaced from jobs which they do efficiently and being placed on jobs for which their performance is marginal. "Bumping" works best when the movement takes place down a promotional ladder and where everyone in the department has worked his way up from the bottom jobs. In summary, to satisfy this criterion, management often favors a relatively "narrow" seniority unit, such as job or departmental.

Retaining valuable employees.   The use of "narrow" seniority units may be costly to the company, however. Assume that the need for machinists has declined temporarily. Under a system of job seniority, the company would be required to lay off machinists with long training and experience. Then, when the present period had passed, expensive recruiting and training would be required to acquire new machinists. Obviously, management would like to shift these employees to other jobs, and allow less valuable employees to be laid off. Many times some form of department seniority is a good compromise solution to a problem of this sort.

Encouraging requisite mobility.   "Narrow" seniority units discourage employees from accepting transfers, for they lose their seniority when they transfer from one unit to another. Thus, "wider" seniority units make it easier for the company to provide a flexible work force.

Swift return to normal production.   After the need for layoffs has passed, management seeks to return to normal production as quickly as possible. Naturally, key employees must be the first to be recalled. The seniority system usually specifies that those who were laid off last will be called back first.[10] Presumably the more senior workers will have held the more important positions. This correlation is not always a perfect one, however, and management may seek to recall junior employees whose skills are essential to the resumption of production.

Employees' desires.   Management also wants to be fair. But what is fair is not easy to determine.

In theory, employees and unions favor "wider" or more inclusive seniority units than does management. They argue that it is unfair to lay off employees with 15 years of seniority in one department, when there are employees with only one year of service in another department. Unions have sometimes sought corporation-wide seniority agreements to enable an employee whose job is terminated in one company location to shift to another; on occasion, they have even demanded that moving expenses be provided.

In actual practice, employees very often favor narrow units much as management does, only for quite different reasons. Because the employee tends to consider his job as a piece of "property," even though management has a very different interpretation, he seeks out the help of his fellow workers who share the same or nearby jobs to help him protect this valued possession.

The importance of seniority and the careful calculations of self-interest that go into employee decisions impinging on this area are revealed by the following case:

> In the ABC Chemical Company, John Jones was seriously injured in an explosion. After his recovery, the company sought to transfer him to a department where the resulting physical impairments would not be as much of a handicap to him as they were in his present job. The workers in the new department, even though they were aware of the reason for the transfer, filed a grievance. Since plant-wide, not departmental, seniority determined eligibility for layoffs, and this injured worker had very long service, each junior employee felt that his security would be worsened by this move.

---

[10] This last-out-first-back method means that newer employees are most directly exposed to the threat of unemployment—another reason why employees seek to build up seniority.

Either management or the union may seek modification in existing seniority regulations when changes in technology or in the company's business threaten widespread loss of their jobs.

> The Furst Corporation is eliminating its consumer product lines. Under the terms of the existing union-management agreement, even employees with 30 years of service expecting to retire in six months or a year will have to be laid off since the seniority clauses forbid interdepartment "bumping." Recently hired young men in adjacent departments will retain their jobs while these senior employees are separated.

These are very delicate problems of equity and contract. The union finds it difficult to decide what to ask the company, because inevitably some of its members will be injured and others will benefit.

Termination or Layoff?

Management has a responsibility to inform the employee when a layoff is assumed to be permanent. The union will scrutinize such layoffs carefully to insure that the company has not eliminated a job as a device to discharge an unsatisfactory employee whom it was reluctant to discipline through normal channels.

Most union-management agreements and company policies specify that an employee's right to be recalled, with a priority determined by his length of service, will not continue beyond one or two years. Thus, if the layoff persists for this length of time, the employee also loses his claim to other employment benefits associated with accrued service. If he is rehired, he will come back as a new employee.

Many companies pay a *severance* or *termination* allowance when an employee loses his job through no fault of his own. This allowance, usually based on a formula that increases with length of service, assists the employee during the period in which he is seeking new employment.

Reduced Hours or Layoffs?

Depending on the nature of the work process and the number of surplus workers, a company can sometimes choose between reducing the work-week for everyone or else laying off the least senior employees, keeping the remainder fully employed. Sharing work—which is what reduced working hours implies—means in effect that unemployment is distributed equally. Depending on circumstances, this may or may not be an advantage to the firm. Sometimes the exact procedure is specified in the union-management agreement, thus making discretion impossible.

What criteria does management use in deciding which procedure to favor? The nature of the industry itself is a critical factor in this decision. A department store could not arbitrarily reduce the hours it is open to the public without seriously damaging its business. Other firms have more flexibility in resorting to a reduced schedule when business warrants.

Naturally enough, longer-service employees are likely to press for the laying off of short-service personnel, in an effort to secure higher income for themselves. The availability and the magnitude of *unemployment insurance* benefits may also influence the choice between laying off employees and reducing work hours. At some point it becomes more desirable, from the employee point of view, to accept these insurance benefits and avoid the travel expenses, taxes, and effort associated with reporting to work for relatively brief periods.

REGULARIZATION OF EMPLOYMENT

Many state unemployment insurance plans, as well as company-sponsored supplementary benefit plans, are designed to penalize the employer with a record of unstable employment. (This is called "experience rating.") In addition, the process of laying off and rehiring is expensive to administer, and valuable employees may eventually be lost to other employers. Changes in employment levels involve expensive shifts of workers within and between departments. Just the fear of layoff may encourage employees to consider "stretching out the work" as they mark time, waiting to see "who will be the next to go." Disagreements over seniority criteria result in costly, time-consuming grievances, as do intergroup arguments over short work-weeks.

All these possibilities provide a stimulus for the firm to seek means of regularizing employment by using techniques such as the following:

1. Trying to develop a more flexible work force through careful selection and training, supplemented by contractual provisions that permit relatively free transfers between departments.

2. Using temporary employees in peak volume periods.

3. Taking on additional products or service lines whose variable demand will complement the demand for existing products—for example, if peak demand occurs in the summer, seeking products that are used primarily during the winter.

4. Exploring the possibility of warehousing goods during periods of slack demand, and offering new incentives for customers to stockpile during normally slow periods or order longer in advance.

5. Contracting-out work that would require the employment of new people who might not be needed when the job is completed—for example, maintenance or construction work.[11]

With effective administration of such programs, the company may find that it can shift an increasing number of employees from the "hourly" to the

---

[11] For a survey of the problems involved in using this method, see Margaret K. Chandler, *Management Rights and Union Interests* (New York: McGraw-Hill, 1964).

"salaried" payroll, thus guaranteeing full-time employment. This, in turn, may alleviate a number of personnel problems, such as restriction of output, resistance to technological change, and many union-management conflicts which stem from fear of layoffs. Further it reduces the blue-collar workers' jealousy of the white-collar employee who is hired on the basis of a monthly salary or an annual salary.

TURNOVERS: VOLUNTARY QUITS

Employees leave voluntarily, and when they do so in substantial numbers, it is often considered an indication of a failure in personnel procedures or a morale problem. Most companies make careful calculations of their rate of turnover [12] and compare these with comparable figures from other companies in their industry or with figures published by the U.S. Bureau of Labor Statistics in its *Monthly Labor Review.*

However, care must be exercised in interpreting these figures. Quit rates go up during periods of high prosperity. A high proportion of new employees or women workers will also result in higher turnover rates. Over-all raw figures can be misleading in other ways. It is many times more costly to lose a highly trained employee than a day laborer. Departments differ in the type of worker and job, and this leads to differential quit rates.

Turnover is not all bad. It is often preferable for some employees to leave, say, a dissatisfied worker or one for whom challenging work cannot be found; his staying may increase the total dissatisfaction within the work group. Turnover can reduce the cost of fringe benefits which reward long service.

In any case, an exit interview procedure, which encourages employees who have quit to express their reasons, can be a useful tool. At this point many are willing to be candid, and often organizational sore spots are thus revealed.

CONCLUSION

Each company needs to strike a balance between internal sources of personnel (through promotion) for higher-rated positions and external sources (through recruitment)—and between merit and ability as against length of service as criteria for promotability. Well-planned transfer and layoff procedures are necessary to deal with fluctuations in employment. The firm that fails to develop satisfactory procedures must be prepared to pay a severe penalty in terms of administrative costs, misallocation of personnel, low morale,

---

[12] Turnover can be divided into voluntary (quits) and involuntary (retirement, death, layoff, military service, etc.). Rates are usually calculated in terms of monthly terminations per hundred employees in the work force. Thus a 3% rate would mean that there was a turnover of 36% a year. A large share of this might be accounted for by a volatile segment of the work force (e.g., new and youthful employees).

and ineffectual performance, among both nonmanagerial employees and their supervisors.

All these policies must undergo constant revision in light of shifts in the company's business and manpower demands. Finally, as we noted particularly in the case of seniority policies, few rules or systems provide automatic answers to specific employee grievances or specific managerial decisions. Only through careful, intelligent investigation and assessment can management cope with the ambiguities inherent in matters of promotion, transfer, and layoff.

PROBLEM 1

SENIORITY

When Bill Jones, with six years' seniority, was promoted to the position of straw boss, Al Smith complained. Smith, with fourteen years in the department, argued that he could do the job himself, and furthermore the company in the past has promoted the senior man to such jobs.

As divisional superintendent, you are notified by the Industrial Relations Department that a union grievance is pending. Here are the two sides of the case:

Supervisor's argument: The job of straw boss requires good judgment in making work assignments. Jones has held the job temporarily several times and has demonstrated this competence. Smith, on the other hand, some years ago in another department, failed when he was promoted to a foreman's position. His records were always "mixed up"; he used poor judgment in requesting repair help, assignment of men, and so forth. Furthermore, Smith is not a good "leader" from the point of view of his own colleagues. He was appointed to fill a vacancy as a union steward, but was not elected when he ran at the next regular election.

Smith's argument: He has never been given a chance to try out as a leader—Jones always was given these chances. His "failure" took place ten years ago when he was young and less mature. The supervisor has never criticized his work; the company and the supervisor are discriminating against him because of his union record. While he was steward, he fought through many difficult grievances that embarrassed management. He lost the election because he was Polish and a majority of the department are of Italian descent. In general, it is company practice to promote by seniority unless there are overwhelming reasons favoring the less senior man, although the contract states that management will give substantial weight to merit and ability and will use seniority as a criterion only when there are no significant differences in ability.

1. How would you investigate this case?
2. What further information would you need? How would you assess the facts you now have?
3. What responsibilities does the supervisor have in this case?
4. What criteria would you use in making your decision?

While you are evaluating this situation, the Industrial Relations Department reports the following comments to you—from another company supervisor in a different department:

"Sure, our union contract says that management can promote the employee with the most ability, and only when there are no substantial differences do we have to take the most senior. But try and do it! I have tried it. The men get together and almost force the oldest guy to file a grievance, and then the union opens up on you. As a supervisor, you are put into the position of having to come up with solid-gold proof that the senior man isn't as good as the man you selected, and believe me, it is hard to get such proof. Sure there are no problems when the older man has been constantly absent, drunk, or a troublemaker. But if he has 'kept his nose clean,' the union can put up an awfully good case that you are discriminating against him for something he did 15 years ago. Then during the grievance procedure your relations with the rest of the men in the department are strained; it's like a cold war. In the end, the Industrial Relations Department may reverse your decision anyhow because they feel that they can't win the case in arbitration or for some other reason. Then you swallow your pride and take the man off the better job whom you promoted (and is he upset!), and put the other guy on the job whom you first turned down—and his feelings toward you are nothing to write home about either. Your reward for following the contract out to the letter of the law is poor morale and a lot of lost time for yourself in grievance meetings, and in the Industrial Relations Department. Do you blame me for taking the easy way out?"

1. Does this statement alter your evaluation of the case?
2. As the divisional superintendent in this company, how concerned would you be if these sentiments were prevalent in the organization?
3. If you wanted to change the situation, what steps would you take?
4. Does the prevailing situation mean that the union-management contract is not really a contract?

PROBLEM 2

INFORMAL PROMOTION

Myers was a mechanical engineer himself before being promoted to supervise a department of engineers. The new job provided a great deal of challenge. Time, however, was always a problem. While Myers believed in delegation, he couldn't resist getting involved in the technical problems of the work in his department, and this took time away from the daily round of administrative questions that came to him, largely on personnel and scheduling problems. Therefore, when Myers found that one of his subordinates, a young engineer by the name of Thompson, was eager to take on new responsibilities and handled them well, he began assigning certain administrative detail work to him. Thompson filled the job of assistant supervisor, which appeared nowhere on the department's organization chart, and he handled many of the work-assignment decisions and relationships with other departments.

After four months, in which this informal arrangement had worked well in relieving the pressures on Myers, the supervisor requested a formal promotion for Thompson to a managerial job classification. While Myers' superiors were willing to add an additional manager to the division, they turned down Thompson as being too inexperienced and lacking in adequate formal education (Thompson did not have a college degree).

Myers was left with a difficult problem. He could not get a salary increase or change in status for Thompson, although he had pressured for this. Should he take away the additional duties from Thompson, although his subordinate did not request him to do so, or should he encourage him to seek a job in another division of the company that would recognize his managerial capacities and not discriminate against him for his lack of a college degree?

1. What should Myers' decision be?
2. Did Myers handle the informal upgrading of Thompson appropriately? (Remember that Thompson liked his administrative work, wanted additional responsibility, and was, in fact, receiving good training.)
3. Are there circumstances that justify a "promotion" without a commensurate increase in income and status?

THE SKILLED AND THE UNSKILLED

The Frank Home Oil Service has had a long-standing tradition of promotion from within, largely on the basis of length of service. Men were hired as laborers and moved up through several promotional ladders to higher-paying positions, including maintenance work. Older workers typically "bid" on the mechanics' jobs when there were openings, because this work was easier than delivery and pumping jobs. Recently the company became concerned that its maintenance mechanics were less skilled than those of its competitors. As new and more complicated equipment was purchased, the company found itself without adequate maintenance personnel.

The company was finally able to negotiate an agreement with the union permitting it to use aptitude tests in selecting new mechanics. The steady stream of older workers bidding on these jobs was now halted. To fill openings as they occurred, the company for the first time was able to go outside the organization and hire young trade-school graduates who quickly learned the requisite skills. Over time the older mechanics who had come into their jobs "unscreened" were shifted to the less-skilled work in the department—largely building-maintenance work.

The immediate problem is that declining business is forcing a cutback in the size of the maintenance department. Normally, department seniority is used to determine who will be laid off. The result in this case will be that nearly all of the relatively new and more able younger mechanics will be laid off, except those who have enough seniority to "bump" the few unskilled laborers in the department. The company fears that its maintenance work will be crippled, and that a good share of the mechanics will leave the company permanently to take jobs elsewhere.

1. How would you analyze the company's problem? What mistakes have been made that other organizations can profit from?
2. What are the alternative solutions, and how would you go about trying to put any of them into effect?

THE WRONG JOB

Bill Allen accepted a new promotion with mixed feelings. He was proud of having his work recognized, but he had some doubts about how he would like the new work. His former job had involved regular contacts with salesmen—trouble-shooting, helping them with special customer problems, and so on. His new job in market research was essentially a research job, working with population data, industry marketing reports, and the like.

Bill missed the routine of his old office and the men he had worked with. He had a private office now, but he felt he really did not have the educational background for the job. When he submitted his first report, the division head was nice enough—suggesting some changes that in fact meant that Bill had really used the wrong approach. His boss said not to worry, "We all have to learn a new job." The more Bill thought about it, the more he wanted to go back to the old job. But he hesitated for fear that he would be considered a failure by management and thus disqualified for any further promotion.

1. If you were Bill's boss, what could you do to correct this situation?
2. What would your objectives be?
3. Could this situation have been avoided altogether? How?

Technical Training

The efficiency of any organization depends directly on how well its members are trained. Newly hired employees almost always need some training before they can take up their work, while older employees require training both to keep them alert to the demands of their present job and to fit them for transfers and promotions.

Training also motivates employees to work harder. Employees who understand their jobs are likely to have higher morale. And the very fact that management is confident enough of their abilities to invest in training provides a sense of assurance that they are valued members of the organization. This is particularly important in dynamic companies undergoing changes in technology and methods. Such changes as automation are resisted when workers fear that they will not be competent to assume the new jobs that are being created.

For these reasons, American companies spend enormous amounts on training.[1] In this chapter we shall be concerned with technical training, and in Chapter 24 with management training.

Training vs. recruitment. Training complements selection. If the personnel department can recruit well-qualified candidates, there will be less need for training inside the organization; if it can recruit only poorly qualified candidates, then training must try to fill the gap.

> For example, until recently the commercial airlines relied on their ability to recruit almost fully trained ex-military pilots. As the supply of these has waned relative to the demand, the airlines have had to develop training programs to assure themselves an adequate supply. Needless to say, this is much more costly than having the government do the training!

And yet training cannot do everything, for some candidates may be so poorly qualified that they lack the ability to learn.

---

[1] Next to public schools and the military, industry is the third major educational factor in the U.S. It is variously estimated that expenditures in these programs amount to billions of dollars annually.

At one extreme, training consists of a few hours (or only a few minutes) of induction by the supervisor, who gives the new employee a skeleton outline of company policies, the location of the locker room, and a summary of work rules. At the other extreme, training consists of formal courses designed to develop qualified specialists over a period of years. In between these extremes are countless programs tailored to fit the needs of particular organizations: short courses on local safety hazards, or on customer uses of company products or services; instruction in writing sales slips or insurance policies; and courses in sales techniques, automobile repair, mechanical drawing, or internal auditing.

But it is misleading to think of job training purely in terms of formal courses and programs. Almost everything that happens to an employee after he joins a company serves as a training experience. That is to say, the worker learns what is expected of him in a new situation through the experiences he undergoes. Those elements in an employee's repertoire of behavior that are rewarded and thus provide him with satisfaction tend to be repeated; those that are punished tend to be abandoned.

There are many people within the organization who provide these rewards and punishments in addition to those who are formally assigned to train employees. The informal work group, with its clearly defined codes of behavior, has a potent influence on its members; formal groups like the union also exert a strong effect. Many times the supervisor may be training his subordinates without even being aware of it. The acts that provoke discipline or that fail to provoke discipline tell an employee what is expected of him and what he can do with impunity. Good housekeeping practices that are praised and slovenly workmanship that goes uncriticized both serve as a source of training. Similarly, the methods, short cuts, and routines practiced by fellow employees all carry important meanings that are assimilated by the novice as he learns his way in a new job situation.

The training derived from all of these varied sources may be in sharp conflict with the prescribed ways of doing things. But it is those sources of information and advice that prove most consistent which will surely have the most profound effect on the employee. So management must be careful to see that the impact of casual, day-to-day experiences does not nullify the practices stressed in the more formal training sessions.

WHO SHOULD TRAIN?

In many companies training is very informal. It consists of assigning new employees as helpers to old employees, or telling an old employee to "show this fellow what he should do." At times the results are excellent, but often the old-timer fails to train adequately. Sometimes the failure reflects the old-timer's indifference or even hostility to "breaking in a new employee," a job he feels he isn't being paid to do or that may create a competitor for his own job. More often, the old-timer fails because he is unable to communicate and lacks systematic knowledge of learning principles.

Most managements today make formal provision for training, either through holding line management directly responsible or by hiring training specialists, and sometimes both. Sometimes these training specialists report directly to line management; more frequently, a special training section is established in the personnel department.

As a staff expert, of course, the training specialist faces the problems of staff men everywhere: Line management may resent his efforts as interference; he may try to teach employees methods that conflict with those their boss wants them to use (either because standard company procedures are not being followed, or because the trainer has not kept pace with developments "out on the floor"). Conflicts often arise when the training specialist insists on telling employees who are under the direction of line supervisors how they should do their job. Equally unfortunate, once a training specialist has been appointed, the line supervisor may decide to pass the buck and give up all responsibility for training. Some companies have tried to create an amicable division of responsibilities by having the staff trainer conduct classes off the work floor and advising the line supervisor on how to do better training on the floor (in a sense the staff trains the trainers), and by holding the line supervisor responsible for all training in production areas.

TYPES OF TRAINING PROGRAMS

Induction

Sometimes, the busy, hard-pressed supervisor tends to neglect what he considers the mere formalities of induction training and concentrates exclusively on the immediate job assignment. Haste and lack of sensitivity at this early stage, however, will spawn unnecessary personnel problems later on—for example, an employee refusing to do a task claiming it's not part of his job, having never received a complete explanation of his duties.

Progressive companies have long recognized the need for properly introducing a new employee to his job. Not only do they familiarize him with the tasks he will be expected to perform, but they also provide him with information about company rules and personnel policies, introduce him to his fellow workers, and give him an idea of where his job fits into the total operation. A carefully planned orientation-induction program helps the new employee to identify with the organization and its procedures and gives him some feeling for the significance of the work he will be doing and thus helps him overcome the fears and anxieties that are bound to arise on a new job.

Where employee duties are clearly described at the outset, misunderstandings are less likely to develop. Furthermore, proper induction training makes it unnecessary for the employee to unlearn methods and procedures that prove unacceptable. Unlearning is both difficult and time-consuming.

Realistically, of course, no supervisor can expect to communicate everything about a new job at the outset. And some of the information he presents is bound to seem meaningless and confusing to the inexperienced subordinate, who simply has not had enough experience to appreciate the significance of what is being told him.

> Cashier trainees in department stores report that they found much of their induction training meaningless because, never having been on the job, they knew nothing of the situations to which the information would apply. Once they had gone out on the job, however, and started receiving mutilated, faulty sales slips, they felt a need for the training they had once felt was worthless.

Vestibule Training

Management must decide whether training is to take place in the normal work location or off the job.

Where the job is difficult, where mistakes or slowness will materially impair production schedules or methods, and where very special coaching is required, off-the-job, or *vestibule training* is called for. On certain jobs, placing the new employee in the work situation immediately would endanger his own safety and the welfare of others, and would risk damage to costly equipment.

"Simulation devices" are an invaluable form of vestibule training. For instance, computers make it possible to simulate the operations of an entire refinery, enabling employees to learn to cope with emergencies and to make the proper responses at minimal cost. In this way, the learner is shielded from the pressure of the actual job situation and the demands of supervisors who are primarily interested in getting out production.

Off-the-job training does have certain disadvantages. Many skills simply cannot be learned in "slow motion." In effect, doing a task slowly may transform it into an entirely different kind of task; this is particularly true of certain difficult muscular-sensory coordination jobs. Also, the noise and other distractions of the real work-place may be factors that the trainee must learn to accommodate, just as he must also master specific body motions and intellectual responses. Finally, vestibule training is expensive, and the employee is being taught by instructors who will not work with him and evaluate his performance when he moves on to the actual job.

Remedial Training

When an employee fails to measure up to established standards, his performance may signal the need for additional training. Over time, an employee may forget procedures he learned during induction, or he may develop slipshod short cuts that require less energy and thought. Or management itself may introduce new procedures and equipment that alter the employee's job. Thus training is not a one-step process; it is a continuing managerial responsibility.

Training employees with some experience on the job may be a more difficult task than giving them induction training, however. Oldtimers may resent being told that they can't do their job, or may suspect that the training is an attempt to "show them up," perhaps for disciplinary reasons, or to step up output—all at their expense. Telling an employee that he needs remedial training may embarrass him before his colleagues, for it is a threat to his status as an intelligent, competent workman.

As an alternative to remedial training for individuals, some companies use regular refresher courses in such areas as safety, job methods, and housekeeping. This practice avoids spotlighting the poor performers and may head off the tendency to slip into short cuts. Periodic training also permits the regular introduction of new methods and techniques. New accounting practices, new company products or engineering standards, new equipment—all require explanation. If these explanations are presented regularly, the possibility that important changes will be overlooked is substantially reduced.[2]

Training for Advancement

Effective training may help individuals to climb promotional ladders to more responsible and better jobs. (Of course, this is the function of all education in a free society: to permit individuals to advance on the basis of merit and ability.) Careful ordering of jobs in promotional ladders also permits individuals to learn, primarily through observation, some of the skills of higher-ranked positions while doing their present job. Filling-in for higher-ranked colleagues during vacations or absences also provides a type of informal on-the-job training.

Many companies have developed their own school program. Organizations that employ skilled tradesmen like machinists, construction workers, or printers, for example, may conduct formal apprenticeship programs. Here, on-the-job training, directed by skilled journeymen, is supplemented by classroom instruction. Smaller companies that cannot afford programs of their own often join together to sponsor community-wide training programs, usually in collaboration with unions and the public-school system.

Trade unions that represent skilled craftsmen have a strong interest in these. Above all, they want to keep down the number of men trained, so that excessive competition for job opportunities can be avoided. In fact, many agreements specify a definite ratio between the number of journeymen and apprentices, thus limiting the number of trainees.

---

[2] For a review of methods of training hourly employees, see William McGhee and Paul Thayer, *Training in Business and Industry* (New York: Wiley, 1961).

The typical apprenticeship takes two to five years to produce a journeyman. The school portion of a typical program for an electrician might include among other subjects shop math, blue-print reading, basic physical science, and local building codes. This material is "sandwiched" into more practical on-the-job training. The best programs provide for rotation among jobs and even among employers so that the apprentice learns all aspects of his trade.

Such programs are more common in Europe, where a much wider variety of jobs (such as hotel and office work) have formal apprenticeships, and one boy out of five participates. Apprentice-like programs extend to other jobs in this country as well. For example, the distributive trades (retailing) are often taught in cooperative training programs involving technical institutes and department stores. Traditionally, would-be accountants and lawyers apprenticed themselves to fully qualified professionals who taught them the "trade." After a given number of years of supervised practice they were allowed to take the examination to qualify for *certification*. It is possible that as more occupational groups seek to professionalize (see Chapter 3) and establish experience and examination requirements for their members, the apprenticeship type of training program will become more widespread.[3] (*Cf.* real estate and stock brokers.)

Training to handle new techniques.   Most fields of knowledge are changing at a rapid pace—an engineering or nursing degree just a few years old may already be obsolete. Further, technical skills not used regularly on the job are quickly lost; refresher training is needed. A major policy question is, how much should the organization do to keep employee knowledge and skills updated, and how much should the individual do for himself? Here are not untypical problems:

> Carters was the chief engineer on the Pluto project. For more than 3 years he worked 50-plus hours a week to deal with a never-ending series of technical and managerial problems. It was an exhausting pace. Two years later Carters was bypassed for promotion because he did not have up-to-date knowledge in the laser field which was the current major thrust of the division. In conjunction with a nearby university the company regularly sponsored a variety of math and physics courses, but Carters never enrolled.

> The X Corporation at one time hired large numbers of technically trained sales personnel to service a product line that has now been abandoned. To earn comparable salaries, these people would have to develop a great deal of new skill in manufacturing, including production engineering. A two-year combined university and on-the-job program would be required.

---

[3] For a survey of the scope of both apprenticeship training in the United States and other industrial training programs, see *Training of Workers in American Industry* (Washington, D.C.: U.S. Department of Labor, Manpower Administration, 1962). This discloses (p. 24) that skilled-trades training was the most prominent type—having twice the number of programs (58,000) as the nearest competitor, supervisory training (29,000).

For the view that apprenticeship is likely to decline, see George Strauss, "Apprenticeship: An Evaluation of the Need," in Arthur Ross, ed., *Employment Policy and the Labor Market* (Berkeley: University of California Press, 1965), pp. 299-332.

A study committee made up of engineers, educators, and administrators in a major corporation recently made the following recommendation:

> The professional must have the means to keep up with his field: the time and the facilities. If the company will establish a carefully planned program of continuing voluntary education, the conscientious professional will supply his own motivation, which will be the most fruitful. Management, however, must recognize the ensuing basic conflicts between immediate job demands and continuing professional growth.

Among other things this policy can require tuition rebates and time off at company expense to attend courses, some of which the company itself must staff and finance; generous leaves of absence (for instance, to acquire advanced degrees); and the inclusion of course attendance as a part of performance evaluation. It may even require the company to help in the establishment of a branch of a college or university where the community lacks adequate educational resources.

How much training? Policy questions arise when a company utilizes these types of advancement training. Perhaps the most obvious has to do with the economics of training. How much can a company afford to spend on developing employees who may leave at any time, permitting another firm to harvest the fruits of the effort? Some companies have no choice in this matter: Their needs are so acute and the supply of trained personnel so meager that training programs are an absolute necessity. These firms must insure that their wage and salary levels, the quality of their supervision, and their working conditions are sufficiently attractive to hold trained personnel. They cannot assume that their employees' gratitude for the training received will outbalance genuine disadvantages. In fact, those employees who are most ambitious and most eager to grasp educational opportunities are the very ones who will be most alert to other job offers.

Another policy decision has to do with the amount of "credit" the company will assign to an employee who has successfully completed a training program, particularly if the training has been taken during uncompensated time. Should those who undertake extra training be guaranteed advancement in preference to those who do not elect to do so? If so, all employees should be made aware of the policy and its implications. In one organization, we observed that certain technical courses were designated as "voluntary" and "optional," although attendance was a prerequisite to promotion.

Resolving questions like these require that Personnel be able to measure the contribution of any training effort. On some routine jobs this may be simple; productivity before and after can be calculated. On many more jobs it is difficult to measure the performance or contribution of the employee since many people jointly contribute and other factors are changing at the same time training is proceeding. As we shall see in Chapter 23, performance evaluation is an imperfect technique. Thus, it is difficult to show that helping an engineer obtain a master's degree improves his work; but management in this, as in other personnel programs, wants the evidence that dollar expenditures are providing comparable improvements in operations.

Aiding Displaced Employees

Increasingly, farsighted management takes the view that if an employee is displaced by new technology, management has a responsibility to endeavor to retrain him so that he will be able to maintain comparable earnings and status. Guarantees also serve to decrease worker and union resistance to change. Federal legislation also provides funds to pay unemployed displaced workers who are taking retraining programs sponsored by companies and schools.[4]

Among the special problems faced in such programs are the age and previous education of the displaced employees. Particularly in companies where automated equipment is replacing unskilled and semiskilled labor, the employee may be handicapped by inadequate basic training in arithmetic, English, and so on. He may not even be literate. Thus pretraining preparation may be necessary.

Further, the older employee is likely to lack confidence in his own flexibility and to be upset by the threatened elimination of long-established work customs, social groups, and job skills. Matching this may be supervisory bias against the older worker and doubts concerning his ability to develop new skills. However, there is increasing evidence that, properly handled, the over-40 employee is capable of very substantial retraining.[5]

Here are two examples of such retraining programs: [6]

INDEPENDENT TELEPHONE CO.

Telephone messages are now transmitted by microwave and the cable splicer has been replaced by the expert in microwave transmission. The company coped with this problem largely by retraining existing personnel and training new people as they are hired. The company arranged with a state industrial education agency to give courses in electricity and related mathematics, telephone equipment and circuits, plant construction principles, and basic technical writing.

Classes were held four hours a night for 10 weeks. Employees paid a $2 registration fee and the company furnished textbooks and materials. Employees with practical experience were used as instructors.

The company makes use of suppliers' educational offerings as well. For intensive training in the use of new telephone equipment it sends selected employees to a supplier's school in Chicago.

---

[4] Cf. *Report of the Secretary of Labor on Research and Training Activities Under the Manpower Development and Training Act* (Washington: U.S. Government Printing Office, 1966). See also Ida R. Hoos, "Retraining in the United States: Programs and Progress," *International Labor Review*, Vol. 92, No. 5, pp. 410-425.

[5] Cf. A. T. Welford, *Aging and Human Skill* (London: Oxford University Press, 1963).

[6] *Personnel Management Bulletin*, Report No. 147, December 15, 1961, pp. 2-3.

Installation of automatic reservation machinery made retraining of clerical employees a must. The new machinery, specially developed electronic data-processing devices, did the posting work of 75 pairs of reservation clerks. However, a large number of clerks were still required to answer telephones and to operate the "Reservisor," as it is called.

The airline set up a special classroom program during working hours for both reservation clerks and supervisors. The first step was training instructors and preparing an instructor's manual. Classes were begun while the new equipment was being installed. About 40 supervisors and lead agents received a week's intensive instruction from the company's research engineer.

LEARNING PRINCIPLES IN TRAINING

Whatever type of training management decides to provide, some attention to the principles of learning is worthwhile. Most of these have been formulated by psychologists.[7]

Motivation

The indifferent, reluctant student will learn little, even from a brilliant instructor. For an employee to benefit from training, he must be anxious to improve his abilities and job performance and thus enhance his opportunities for advancement. Clearly, the return the company receives from its investment in training will depend upon the over-all level of morale in the organization.

On the other hand, overly intense motivation may actually inhibit learning. If an individual becomes too tense (too fearful) or if he sets goals for himself that are greater than his ability to attain them, the results may be acute disappointment and loss of motivation.

Reinforcement

Related to motivation is the need for *reinforcement*—that is, for learning to take place, the individual must receive some encouragement or reward. The reward need not be tangible. All the individual needs is to experience some feeling of progress, either through the teacher's comments or through his own observation that he has done well.

Such positive rewards for progress appear to have a much better effect than

---

[7] Additional references to the field of learning are: Ernest Hilgard (ed.), *Theories of Learning; NSSE 63rd Yearbook* (Chicago: University of Chicago Press, 1964). B. F. Skinner, *Science and Human Behavior* (New York: Macmillan, 1953), a basic work on conditioning that also provides the theoretical background for concepts of programmed instruction and teaching machines. Harold Leavitt, *Managerial Psychology* (Chicago: University of Chicago Press, 1964), pp. 73-98.

punishment or the threat of punishment when mistakes are made. Most people have only a limited tolerance for failure. If punishment for failure is excessive, the phenomenon of "fixation" may develop, in which the same unsuccessful response is repeated over and over again.

Obviously, the trainee will not always be successful in his attempts to learn. But his ability to tolerate failure will still be a function of the success he has achieved and the degree to which his correct behavior has been reinforced.

Feedback

For reinforcement to be effective in improving performance, there must be feedback, or *knowledge of results*. Imagine how difficult it would be to improve one's marksmanship without being able to see the target. If self-correction is to take place, the trainee must know the relationship between his behavior and the impact, or result, of his behavior. Unless he knows how close his achievement is to the desired standard of good performance, he will not be able to improve his performance, no matter how hard and how frequently he tries. This means that the supervisor should resist the temptation to contact the subordinate *only* when he has made a mistake. The learner also needs to know when he has made the right decision. And when he has made a mistake, he needs to recognize *why* and *how* he went wrong and how close he came to doing the work properly. Feedback of results should be provided as quickly as possible after the trainee's performance.

Here are two examples of the effective use of feedback in improving job performance: [8]

> Previously, furnace crews had no measure of the effectiveness of their work. When gauges were installed to indicate the efficiency of individual boilers graphically, it was estimated that $333,000 was saved in fuel costs.
>
> A recording device was invented to show employees their cutting patterns on a foot-operated abrasive wheel used to cut tungsten discs. The device revealed learner errors so dramatically that training time was cut almost in half.

Finally, feedback should be presented in a nonthreatening environment; the learner should be made to realize that mistakes will not cost him too dearly and that difficulties in learning are natural and expected. It is the supervisor's responsibility to provide this feedback, not just during the so-called training period, but on a continuing basis.

Learning by Doing

Learning is most efficient when the learner is actively involved in the learning process, rather than merely listening to a description of it. Motor

---

[8] Both examples are adapted from James N. Mosel, "How to Feed Back Performance Results to Trainees," *Journal of American Society of Training Directors* (February 1958).

activity (muscular movement) directly stimulates the higher mental processes, such as learning.[9] In fact, the greater the number of senses involved, the more effective the learning. To learn a poem quickly and accurately, it is much more efficient to recite it aloud than to read and reread it silently. Doing rather than just seeing or hearing also means that the individual is more likely to devote more of himself to the task; he becomes more *involved* in the learning process.

This principle has obvious implications for the supervisor's role in training. Instead of relying exclusively on lectures, or on training films and manuals, he should encourage the employee to try out new jobs, to ask questions, and to go through all the requisite motions. Of course, he watches for mistakes and insures that they are corrected, but he reinforces the correction by having the trainee repeat the activity properly. Active repetition is useful only when the training situation permits the trainee to try out alternative approaches in the full assurance that he can make mistakes and learn from them.

Spaced Repetition

Training need not be continuous, however. Many experiments have shown that *spaced repetition*—that is, learning periods distributed through time—are more efficient than attempts to learn "all at once." Apprenticeship programs, in which the trainee learns by repeated doing, are an excellent example of this approach. Another obvious value of repetition is that it serves to inhibit forgetting. Without practice, learned skills gradually disappear.

Learning by Parts

Learning is expedited when the total process or skill to be mastered is broken down into small, "digestible" segments. Thus, the trainee can obtain satisfaction from reaching each one of the subgoals, and these, in turn, help him to reach his objective of learning the whole job. Whether or not this type of training is possible depends in part on what is to be learned. For example, the electrician can learn simple wiring and the associated arithmetic and then gradually move in logical steps to more complex circuitry.

On other jobs, this progression is hampered by the indivisibility of the work. Student nurses in medical wards occupied chiefly by chronically ill patients complain that they are always doing unimportant jobs that teach them nothing: custodial duties like bed-making and water-carrying. On the surgical floors, however, where each patient requires one or more of the "nursing arts," every student and assistant gets assignments commensurate with her growing ability.[10]

---

[9] See Gordon Allport, "The Psychology of Participation," *Psychological Review*, Vol. 53 (May 1945).

[10] T. Burling, E. Lentz and R. Wilson, *The Give and Take in Hospitals* (New York: Putnam, 1956), pp. 252-253.

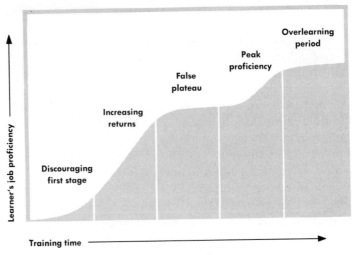

Hypothetical learning curve.

Learning by Mastering Large Segments

Learning is inhibited if the segments to be mastered are too small, however. Anyone who has learned to swim knows how difficult it is to combine leg movements with arm movements. If a job is broken into fragments, each of which must be mastered by itself, the problem of learning to integrate them into a whole activity, as a smooth, continuous process, becomes extremely difficult.

But how "small" a part of the job is "too small"? Wherever possible, the learner should try to master as a single unit all those activities that must be performed in a smooth, continuous sequence. In this way, each subpart becomes an internalized "cue" that stimulates the next part of the sequence. The trainer may have to encourage the learner to try out what seems at the outset to be an impossibly large segment. But it is more efficient in the long run for him to make many mistakes in trying to master a logically constituted unit, to fumble badly because of the number of coordinations required, than to concentrate on learning the parts as if each were to be performed in a vacuum.

In addition, emphasis on these larger segments of the job may de-emphasize the trainer's tendency to assume there is only "one best way." When arm, hand, finger, and body motions are taught individually, in violation of what is easiest and most natural for the trainee, the training degenerates into an artificial, stilted ritual. Further, when these theoretically correct motions are combined, the resulting behavior pattern may be unsuited to the idiosyncrasies of the individual worker's nervous and muscular system (see Chapter 26).

Providing Theory

One of the more controversial training questions concerns the amount of *theory* or *background* the trainee needs to learn most effectively. Obviously the electrician has no need to go back to quantum mechanics. However, the effectiveness with which he learns repair or maintenance methods will be materially enhanced if he has some knowledge of electrical theory. The theory itself may not be essential to the specific tasks he will be performing, but it will help him to *transfer* his knowledge to new jobs, equipment, and processes. If the employee is to develop insight into new problems that arise during the course of his work, he must achieve more basic understanding of his activities than that provided by the "this-is-how-you-do-it" type of training. "Logical" training is always more effective than "rote" training—at least for jobs that call for any degree of sophisticated performance. As we noted in our discussions of management, the manager explains *why* when he gives directions, to insure that the employee will be able to handle unusual, unanticipated situations that may occur.

TYPICAL LEARNING PATTERNS

Managers need some understanding of the pattern in which new skills are learned—of what are called "learning curves" (see figure opposite). When the employee first begins to learn a new skill, he is likely to find himself unusually clumsy or inept—"all thumbs." This can be very discouraging, particularly to a man who prides himself on his agility and ability; and so, during this early stage, the learner needs the supervisor's encouragement. (This, of course, is one justification for conducting certain kinds of training off-the-job.) The duration of this first stage is a function of the complexity and newness of the skill being learned—it may be only a few minutes or a few weeks.

After this period, the typical learning rate is rapid. This is the stage of increasing returns, in which small additional amounts of practice by the trainee produce substantial increases in job-proficiency. During this second period, the employee's confidence and satisfaction rise.

After more training time has elapsed, a "plateau" develops. Now additional training time does not result in very significant increases in proficiency, and both the supervisor and the learner may be deceived into thinking that the maximum proficiency has been attained.

These plateaus seem to be the result of two factors: (1) a loss of motivation as early surges of progress are dissipated and as further progress becomes more difficult, and (2) the trainee's need for substantial blocks of time to develop new and improved skills. Initially the employee may be forced to learn a new job in segments, thinking consciously about each part of the job. A great deal of practice is required before a real "break-through" takes place that permits these separate parts to become merged and the motions to be joined into a single, coordinated sequence of actions. Ghiselli and Brown describe this stage as follows:

> Through practice, certain phases of the action patterns are automatized, superfluous activities are dropped out, precision of movement and smoothness of coordination are effected, excess tension is eliminated, the energy require-

ments of the total performance are greatly reduced, and the trainee develops self-assurance and confidence in his performance.[11]

The supervisor must also be wary of assuming that the employee's training has been completed once he has achieved a peak skill. Continued repetition needs to be encouraged so that *overlearning* will take place. An experienced automobile driver can refrain from driving for six months or even six years, and still be able to drive when the occasion demands. This is largely the result of overlearning, which diminishes the likelihood that forgetting will take place. Apparently, the reflex sequences that relate muscular responses and sensory stimuli become more deeply ingrained when the individual continues to practice even after he has reached top performance.

One note of caution: The learning curve of all employees is not the same. On the contrary, there are profound differences in native ability to synchronize muscular movements, to effect eye-hand coordinations, and to sense subtle differences in tactile and muscular responses. When these individual differences are added to differences in motivation and morale, they result in wide disparities in learning rates.

These differences pose serious problems for the supervisor. Should the same or greater rewards go to the highly motivated employee with lesser ability who achieves the same level of performance as the less highly motivated employee with greater ability? Would your answer be the same if you knew that the more gifted employee was working less hard and performing at a lower level of accomplishment than he would if he were to exert himself? (Professors face such questions every day!)

SOME TRAINING TECHNIQUES

Teaching Machines and Programed Instruction

In-company training, along with education in general, is being drastically changed by teaching machines and programed instruction. Computers, projectors, and even closed circuit TV are often utilized. For example, in learning a complicated new assembly operation, each employee is placed in a booth where visual and auditory stimuli are presented in a carefully designed step fashion. Questions or challenges are posed which enable the trainee to assess whether or not progress is being made (and to receive regular reinforcement). Mistakes cause material to be repeated or remedial "branches" of the program to be displayed. Each learns at his own pace with very little need of external instruction and since the student is actively participating and having to make constant responses, learning is facilitated.[12]

---

[11] E. E. Ghiselli and C. W. Brown, *Personnel and Industrial Psychology*, 2nd ed. (New York: McGraw-Hill, 1955), p. 384.

[12] *Cf.* National Foremen's Institute, *What You Should Know About Programmed Instruction* (Waterford, Connecticut: Bureau of Business Practice, Inc., 1964). Gabriel Ofiesh, *Programmed Instruction* (New York: American Management Association, 1965).

Each programed instruction manual consists of hundreds of questions called frames. The answer to each question helps the trainee to answer those that come after.

For example, the first frame in a sequence could be:

> A fire can keep us warm because it gives off energy in the form
> of _____. The sun also gives off _____ in the form of
> _____.

When the student completes the three responses, he exposes the preprinted answers: "heat," "energy," and "heat," and checks them against his written answers. He then proceeds to the next frame:

> Heat is one form of _____. Physicists call it thermal energy.
> A quart of boiling water has more energy than a quart of cold water.

Having checked his answers again, the student goes on to next frame:

> As a warm object grows cooler, it loses heat, that is, it loses
> _____ energy. When a cool object gets warmer, it gains
> _____, that is, it gains _____.

Note how small and simple are each of the steps and how the answer is almost self evident, but this builds confidence and increases motivation.

Programed learning works best when there are specific answers. For example, it is easier to program a production scheduling technique than supervisory skills. While there has been a rush to employ the equipment associated with these new techniques, one should remember that most programed learning does not require the use of teaching machines or other gadgetry. Of course, more complex programs (like the business game discussed in Chapter 24) may be facilitated by computers. Further substantial student interest is generated, at least initially, by equipment that directly feeds back results and/or displays the questions and illustrations. Some of the equipment, the closed circuit TV, for example, also is useful with more traditional teaching methods like lectures and discussions.

Job Instruction Training

Job Instruction Training (J.I.T.) represents a much older technique. It was developed in World War II to provide a simple, quick training method that could be easily applied by new supervisors. This method embodied many of the learning principles we have just been discussing. Here are the main stages in a J.I.T. training program:

1. A job description is worked out that breaks the job down into a series of motion sequences that can be described. The trainer identifies the special techniques required, the special precautions that need to be taken, the criteria that indicate whether the job is being performed correctly, the quality and safety levels required, and so forth. These are the *key points* of the job.
2. At the beginning of the training session, the equipment and supplies are arranged in the way in which the worker is expected to keep them.
3. The trainer puts the learner at ease, finds out what he already knows, explains the relationship of his job to other jobs in the organization, and shows him the correct working position.
4. The trainer describes the job completely, stresses the key points, and then performs the job, describing "what" and "why" at each step. The learner is encouraged to ask questions.
5. The learner then tells the trainer how the job is to be done and the trainer follows his instructions.
6. The learner does the job, explaining to the trainer at each step "what" he is doing and "why."
7. The trainer follows up with periodic checks and tells the trainee where he can go for help if he runs into difficulty.

CONCLUSION

Training means changing behavior patterns, and this is always a difficult task. An individual's method of doing a job, the skills he employs, the energy and thought he applies, the checking and coordinating with other people he undertakes—all partly reflect his own personality structure. The supervisor must assume that the employee's old pattern of behavior brought certain satisfactions—else he would have abandoned it. Since a change in work methods will be a threat to these satisfactions, the employee will resist new learning (see Chapter 13). This resistance may be bolstered by his desire for the approbation of his work group and by his psychological needs for security and a sense of accomplishment. Efforts to increase productivity through teaching better work habits may run counter to group-enforced production "bogeys" based on a fear that increased output will lead to layoffs and demotions (see Chapter 27).

The success of any training program is a direct function of the success of other aspects of the personnel program. Where employees are already highly motivated and closely identified with the goals of the organization, well-conceived training programs will lead to better performance. On the contrary, where morale is low and employees are suspicious and resentful of management, training will be ineffective. For example, in one company a course in work-simplification was seriously handicapped because it was associated in the workers' minds with the widely disliked time-study department. If the trainees fail to see how they will benefit by adopting the techniques being taught, no amount of good teaching will change their behavior.

Nevertheless, the satisfactions an employee derives from his work experience depend on his knowing what to do and how to do it. The employee who lacks confidence in his ability to perform successfully can never do his job well, no matter how vigorously management pursues the other aspects of its personnel program. And training can influence attitudes toward the personnel program. Employees develop more favorable sentiments for an employer who invests in their development. Education and training have become central values in American life. There is wide recognition that one cannot "cantilever" an entire career from the base of pre-employment, formal school education. Periodic infusions of new knowledge are essential.

Just how much is dependent, in part, on the recruitment and selection program for, as we have seen, problems in finding the correct skills in the labor market can be solved by internal training.

PROBLEM 1

WHAT REWARD FOR DILIGENCE?

John Adams with 10 years of service was eager to take courses to improve himself and to get an advanced degree. He was a purchasing invoice clerk with the Draper Equipment Company and was never considered outstanding as an employee. Starting with a night school degree in business, he began taking graduate courses when the company adopted a tuition-rebate plan. He also participated in several of the company's voluntary, after-hours training programs and computer courses taught by faculty members from a nearby college. After 7 years he qualified for a master's degree in accounting at the City University. However, when recently he discussed promotional opportunities with his supervisor, he was told that his work record was just average and there were no openings coming up for which he would qualify.

1. Does the company owe Adams something for his diligent pursuit of an advanced degree?
2. How should this kind of problem be dealt with to avoid the disappointment and frustration associated with being overqualified for a job?

PROBLEM 2

HANDLING UNSATISFACTORY PERFORMANCE

Wilma Granger works in the accounts receivable section of a large department-store billing department. Her supervisor has found a large number of mistakes in a random check of the accounts she is responsible for, and her over-all output of work is lower than the department standard.

1. What "checks" should the supervisor make in evaluating whether this poor work is due to inadequate training or other causes?
2. If this investigation discloses inadequate training, how should he introduce remedial training?
3. How should the training be carried out?

WHEN TRAINING FAILS

The packaging department was the most troublesome department in the U.S. Auto Parts Company. The employees' job in this department was to watch high-speed, semi-automatic packaging machines and make adjustments and compensations for unexpected operating difficulties. Though the work was simple and easily learned, productivity was low. Employees frequently neglected obvious danger signals and failed to make the proper adjustments.

Management tried all sorts of solutions to this problem: employees were disciplined for making mistakes (they objected violently); supervisors were sent through a training program; a new incentive system was introduced. When all these efforts failed, management decided to experiment with a retraining program. Some of the employees may have forgotten their initial training, or perhaps it had been inadequate. In any event, many employees were using clearly inefficient, fatiguing motions on the job, and improved job performance would actually make the work easier.

Management had another reason for introducing training: It was contemplating discharging some of the worst offenders, but felt that it should give these men every opportunity to improve before it took such drastic action. Systematic training would head off union charges that the men had not been properly instructed.

The department head, in collaboration with the Industrial Engineering Department, prepared a training manual that outlined all the steps required in doing this particular job. One of the first-line supervisors was chosen to administer the training during the regular work routine of the department. He spent several hours with each employee, going over the procedures step by step in good J.I.T. fashion.

The results were discouraging. No improvements in productivity were forthcoming. The operators claimed that the trainer was a spy seeking evidence that they were malingering rather than trying to train them. Furthermore, "He knows less about the job than we do—we should be training him."

1. What mistakes, if any, were made in this training situation?
2. Describe completely how you would handle these problems, including the selection of the trainer.

GRADUATES VS. NONGRADUATES

The Bayworth Pharmaceutical Company has had a long-established training program for laboratory technicians. Women employees in lower-paying jobs who wish to become technicians are taken into a three-year training program. Under the direction of senior technicians, trainees rotate through all the jobs in the laboratory involving technicians. In addition, the company gives a series of supplementary courses in mathematics, introduction to organic chemistry, and methods of quantitative and qualitative analysis on a six-hour-per-week basis. (Half of this time is not compensated for, since the class meets after working hours.) Successful completion of the course program and a recommendation from the department supervisor entitle an employee to be promoted to laboratory technician, with a starting salary of $135 per week. The beginning trainee salary of $95 is increased by $10 at the end of each year.

Eight years ago, during the development of a new vaccine, huge government orders necessitated a rapid expansion of several of the company's laboratories. Lacking adequate manpower, the management of the laboratories sought a shortcut solution for this personnel problem. In consultation with lower levels of supervision, new job descriptions were developed reflecting a change in the division of labor. Rather than relying on fully trained, all-around technicians, management trained employees to do individual laboratory jobs, such as specimen analysis, preparation, and equipment testing. An alert employee could be trained in three months to do one of these "laboratory assistants' " jobs.

In recent years a number of these assistants, who, through careful observation and informal trial have learned most of the other jobs in the laboratory, have been promoted to the job and salary of technician. Out of the original group of 18, in fact, nine have been so promoted.

At present the laboratory employs a total of 30 technicians. However, a sharp dip in the demand for this type of company product has necessitated a 30 per cent reduction in the number of technicians. (All the assistants who had not been promoted already have been transferred to other divisions.)

The 21 technicians who have completed the formal training program have signed a petition requesting that the laboratory adopt a policy of transferring first all employees who have not graduated from the training program. The petition argues that the training-program graduates have made financial and other sacrifices to attain their present position, and that by implication the company has guaranteed them a special status which is superior to that of any technician not so trained.

If this request were honored, several excellent technicians who came up through this informal program and have been on the job for more than seven years would have to leave the laboratory, while other technicians who were hired less than four years ago would remain. These women argue that such a policy would represent arbitrary discrimination against them, since they have been formally promoted to their present position by management. The immediate supervisors want to retain the long-service employees because of their knowledge and skill. Furthermore, the self-trained group includes several of the best employees.

1. Could this intergroup struggle have been foreseen?
2. What steps could have been taken to prevent this problem from occurring?
3. What effect may this dispute have on the future of the training program?
4. As a member of management, how would you evaluate the variables in this situation?
5. What policy decision can provide a reasonable solution to the present problem and a basis for future laboratory development?

Management Development

Management development, the subject of our next three chapters, is one of the fastest-developing areas in personnel, for there is a growing realization that an effective management team may be as important to the survival of an organization as any tangible item on the balance sheet. Investment in management development may pay off as well as investment in capital equipment. This chapter will be concerned with some of the general problems of providing people with experience that will enable them to develop their fullest potentialities. The next two chapters will handle two specific areas: performance evaluation and management training.

Interest in management development is great partly because of a shortage of well-trained managers. The number of managerial jobs is rising much faster than the size of the work force generally. This growth in the number of managers may foreshadow a completely automated world in which everyone will be a supervisor. The shortage in business is rendered more acute by competition for high-talent manpower from education, the professions, and the government.[1] And yet the size of the male labor force 35-54 years of age (the age level from which most executives are selected) is likely to increase very slowly over the next ten years.

In addition, there is a growing feeling that management is a *profession* for which special training is required. Professionalism implies the need for special skills and for formal training and apprenticeship. As a General Electric vice-president put it, "Perhaps the most provocative—and important—idea on which we are proceeding is that managing should be regarded as a distinct type of work, with its own disciplines, its own criteria for achievement; something which is both learnable and teachable."[2] Evidence of this emphasis is the growth of business schools and professional organizations, such as the American Management Association.

---

[1] Frank H. Cassell, "Corporate Manpower Planning," *Stanford Graduate School Bulletin,* Vol. 34, No. 1 (Summer 1965), p. 30.

[2] Harold E. Smiddy, cited in Herbert Harris, "How Managers Are Made," *Nation's Business,* Vol. 44, No. 3 (March 1956), p. 91.

In part, too, this growing professionalism reflects the widening gap between the ownership and control of American corporations. This is a broad issue, but briefly, control over corporate destinies is falling more and more into the hands of hired or "professional" managers, whose reward, in addition to salary, resides in the sense of personal satisfaction that comes with having done a good job and with having one's achievements recognized by other managers. Getting ahead has come to mean rising within the "management profession," rather than going into business for one's self.

Thus, management development as a program has received impetus both from the increased demand for managers and from their own growing sense of professionalism.

SOME BASIC ISSUES

Before we look at the details of management development, it may be useful to introduce some basic controversial questions which will underlie our discussion in the next three chapters.

Special Programs
or Good Environment?

The first controversy relates to the effectiveness of special developmental programs, such as planned rotation, performance evaluation, and training classes. On one side are those who argue that such programs develop proper attitudes and skills. But those on the other side claim that attitudes and skills (at least in the management area) can't be changed directly; the most that can be done is to create a challenging and permissive environment in which people can develop themselves. In a sense this is a question of strategy: Should our first emphasis be on changing people or on changing the organization? If we change people first, then hopefully they will make the organization work better. But if we change the organization first (through changing elements such as organization structure, work-flow, and methods of reward), then hopefully this changed environment may produce, if not better people, at least a situation to which people can adapt more successfully.

To take a specific example (to which we shall return more fully in Chapter 24), development or training programs accomplish little if they aim to produce in subordinate managers behavior which their own bosses disapprove of; a man is more likely to be concerned with what his boss thinks than what he learns in class. This may suggest that it is best to have each manager train his own subordinates. But the boss' behavior itself may be far from ideal. Even if it were exemplary, he may not have the ability to engage in training, and organizational pressures may not give him the time to do so. So special development programs may be needed, if only to provide the manager with some "ideals" which he may aspire to practice on the job.

Conformity or Diversity?

Should the purpose of development be to instill certain common values in managers, or should it be to encourage each individual to develop his own style of behavior, one which seems best to fit his own personality and the requirements of his job?

Many development programs are, in effect, forms of indoctrination. As we have seen, indoctrination, through providing a uniform way of thinking and a standardized approach to problems, permits a substantial amount of innovative behavior within a common frame of reference, without the need for close supervision.

Yet some observers are concerned lest developmental procedures, as used in many companies, create too many "organization men," conformists who are mainly concerned with pleasing the boss, and fail to produce enough of the nonconformists who are needed at the top.[3] Indoctrination has been attacked on practical grounds as stultifying individual growth and on moral grounds as a form of brain-washing inconsistent with individual dignity.

"The basic assumption [of those who support indoctrination] is that the institution knows better than the individual what kind of man it needs or wants in its higher levels of management." [4] Indoctrination's opponents argue that development should foster personal growth and help managers work out problems by themselves.

It should be recognized that there is strong trend toward conformity even without a formal management development program. The smart, aspiring young manager soon learns the values and behavior which are necessary to get ahead. He engages in what sociologists call "anticipatory socialization," that is, he copies those on higher levels.[5]

A subsidiary question is whether companies should develop all-purpose *generalists* with broad points of view or more narrow *specialists* who think in terms of their own particular functions. With the development of specialists, organization-man conformity is reduced, but perhaps a new conformity to the specific viewpoint of the given specialty is encouraged. A man trained as a computer programer, for instance, is likely to think in terms of problems which can be expressed in computer language. There is a dilemma here. Each boss wants to hire specialists and reward specialization at the lower level, yet each company wants generalists at higher levels. Where are the generalists to come from?

---

[3] William H. Whyte, Jr., *The Organization Man* (New York: Simon and Schuster, 1956).

[4] Edgar Schein, "Management Development as a Process of Influence," in Harold Leavitt and Louis Pondy, eds., *Readings in Managerial Psychology* (Chicago: University of Chicago Press, 1964), p. 334.

[5] Research also suggests that the typical fast-moving young executive often has a "sponsor," someone from higher management who is impressed with his abilities, finds him useful to have around, and who looks after his interests.

Open Systems or Closed Systems? [6]

Related to the conformity issue is the question of the degree to which an individual should be free to choose his own career path. In many companies the individual has little choice in the kind of job he does or the kinds of training or developmental opportunities he receives. For example, when caught in an unrewarding, seemingly dead-end job, he is not allowed to apply to fill a job opening elsewhere in the company which seems more promising. In effect, this is a "closed system" in which the individual's freedom is greatly restricted.

Other companies have more "open" systems. They publicize job openings or training opportunities and let managers "bid" on them. They let individuals who wish take risky assignments, even though there is a good possibility they may fail. Rather than train personnel for specific jobs, they provide opportunities for self-development and then let people go where they can. Both the boss who has a job to fill and the subordinate who bids for the job have a wider range of options than under the closed system. And the individual is less dependent on his own particular boss.

Decision–Making or Human Relations?

What is the main job of the manager: to make decisions or to deal with people? As we shall see, the two most stylish forms of training today, the T-group and the business game, involve these two radically different concepts of the nature of the manager's job.

The T-group technique (see pp. 580-582) assumes that the manager's main function is to deal with people. The T-group is designed to help executives develop greater sensitivity to their own behavior and in their perceptions of others. By contrast, business games, particularly those which involve a computer, generally require analytical ability and little or no human-relations skills. They assume that all relevant problems of decision-making can be quantified. Once a decision has been reached there is little problem of implementation; [7] all the participant need do is write his answer and the computer obeys without question.

Naturally the arguments can be overstated. We need better decisions and better means of implementing them. As we shall see, training programs have

---

[6] We are indebted to Theodore M. Alford for this concept.

[7] True, if teams are involved in the game, then there is a human-relations problem of getting team members to agree to a decision. Interestingly, advocates of T-groups and business games both claim that their techniques improve decision-making abilities, but they use the term decision-making in different ways. One group is concerned with the social process by which the group makes a decision, the other with the intellectual process by which the individual makes one. See, for an example of the first view, Robert R. Blake and Jane S. Moulton, *Group Dynamics—Key to Decision-Making* (Houston, Texas: Gulf Publishing Company, 1961).

been developed which provide experience with both aspects of decision-making. And yet the question is related to those we have already discussed. What kinds of executives should we develop? Executives who make risk-taking decisions and set the general tone and direction of the firm in ways that are difficult to program? High-level executives who work toward goals in a rational fashion, evaluating alternative goals, appraising and re-appraising results? Organization men, skilled in carrying out orders and reducing human frictions? Or technicians with specialized interests in narrow areas? [8]

Crown Princes or All Employees?

Who should be developed—just those with special promise or everyone? Because of the critical shortage of manpower after World War II, the early emphasis was on crash programs to discover individuals (both inside and outside the company) who would be capable of moving to top-management jobs. In the effort to ferret out such exceptional men, there arose a widespread use of tests (see pp. 469-470) and evaluation forms designed to identify traits that might point to *future* ability rather than to *present* performance. The men thus singled out (the "crown princes") were given special training away from the job (often at universities) and were marked for rapid promotion.

As might be expected, this program led to a wave of resentment among those who had not been selected and to a feeling that it was unfair to base promotions on vague character traits instead of on proved performance. Also, since the selection process tended to emphasize the safe, conformist, all-round man, there seemed to be a prejudice against the unusual individual who was able to get things done in spite of "character deficiencies." In other words, observers began to suspect that, by weeding out deviationists, management might also be weeding out the very men who would produce the original ideas of the future.

Recent Trends

On the whole, the emphasis in recent years has switched from the hunt for the ideal "organization man" to more routine, continuing programs of training, designed to help *all* managers perform more adequately on their present job. After all, opportunities for promotion are limited.[9] Companies are trying less hard to mold their managers into a single form; instead there is greater interest in providing conditions which permit self-development, thus creating a more "open system."

Evaluation forms are being used as a tool to enable the manager to discuss with his subordinates how they can improve their performance, rather than as

---

[8] See John G. Hutchins, "Education for Business Administration," *Administrative Science Quarterly*, Vol. 5, No. 2 (September 1960), p. 279.

[9] A study in one not untypical company disclosed that only one-third of the managers had any likelihood of being promoted again during their career, and only one-tenth were likely to be promoted twice. Earl Brooks, "An Experimental Program for Executive Development," *ILR Research*, Vol. 1. No. 2 (March 1955), p. 11.

a means of selection. There have been other changes as well: personality traits (which cannot be changed easily) are receiving less emphasis than performance (which can); training is coming to be regarded as an essential management function rather than a peripheral frill; hence the primary responsibility for training is being shifted away from staff to line management.

With this background let us look at management development programs in practice. The first step involves planning.

PLANNING FOR DEVELOPMENT

In planning for management development, the company must predict its long-range managerial manpower needs and decide how to meet them; it must also schedule the shorter-range movements of individuals from one job to another. The values of careful planning are many:

> It insures an orderly flow of people, trained and available to fill vacancies as they occur.
>
> It helps forecast and spotlight areas where training or even outside recruiting is necessary.
>
> It insures that everyone has a chance to be considered and that nobody gets lost in the shuffle.
>
> It makes it possible to bring people up from the ranks rather than having to recruit from outside.

Long-range Planning

Ideally, management should try to predict the company's supervisory and executive needs for as far into the future as possible.

> Of all economic resources, high-level manpower takes the longest time to develop, and thus it demands the most careful consideration in planning for the future. . . . For the most part, companies are preoccupied with their immediate requirements and with short-run development projects. In long-range manpower planning, most companies really don't know where they are or whither they are going.[10]

Most organizations fill the majority of their management needs through promotion from within. This means that plans must be made for 30 or 40 years into the future, for the newly hired college graduates of the 1960's may well provide the top management of the 1990's. If too few potential managers are hired at the bottom, management may get caught short in the future. On the other hand, it is almost as dangerous to bring in too many bright young people. When this happens, channels of advancement clog up, promotional opportunities are slow, and morale declines—with a result that men with good potential go elsewhere. (Paradoxically, managerial turnover is very high in some well-known companies with excellent development programs, largely because men

---

[10] Samuel E. Hill and Frederick Harbison, *Manpower and Innovation in American Industry* (Princeton, N.J.: Industrial Relations Section, 1956), p. 66.

trained by these companies can command excellent salaries elsewhere and advancement in their own company is relatively slow.)

In any case, long-range planning must be highly tentative. In the shorter-range development of individual managers, far more precise planning is possible.

Scheduling of Promotions and Transfers

Many large companies keep careful track of the progress of each of their managers and tentatively schedule their future movements from job to job in order to insure that they will get optimum training and experience. Individual

Replacement chart.

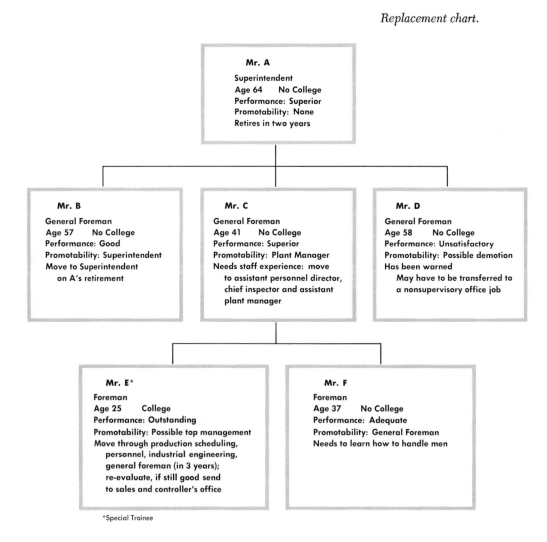

Mr. A

Superintendent
Age 64   No College
Performance: Superior
Promotability: None
Retires in two years

Mr. B

General Foreman
Age 57   No College
Performance: Good
Promotability: Superintendent
Move to Superintendent
    on A's retirement

Mr. C

General Foreman
Age 41   No College
Performance: Superior
Promotability: Plant Manager
Needs staff experience: move
    to assistant personnel director,
    chief inspector and assistant
    plant manager

Mr. D

General Foreman
Age 58   No College
Performance: Unsatisfactory
Promotability: Possible demotion
Has been warned
    May have to be transferred to
    a nonsupervisory office job

Mr. E*

Foreman
Age 25   College
Performance: Outstanding
Promotability: Possible top management
Move through production scheduling,
    personnel, industrial engineering,
    general foreman (in 3 years);
    re-evaluate, if still good send
    to sales and controller's office

Mr. F

Foreman
Age 37   No College
Performance: Adequate
Promotability: General Foreman
Needs to learn how to handle men

*Special Trainee

careers are closely meshed with company growth and development. Normally, policy in this area is the responsibility of a top-level management committee, while the administrative work is handled by the personnel director or a special coordinator of management development who reports directly to the president.

The key tools in scheduling programs of this sort are *executive inventories* and *replacement charts*. An executive inventory consists of a file card for each executive with such information as: age, length of service, education, positions held within the company and with other companies, results on psychological tests, hobbies, membership in outside organizations, and so forth. More important are evaluations by superiors of his work since he first came with the company, a statement by his present boss about the type of experience he still needs, and an estimate of how far he might go in the future.

Frequently these data are computerized. When a new job opens up, all management need do is to set the standards as to the type of man best qualified. The machine does the rest. There are those who claim that once the standards are properly set, only a minimum of human judgment is required.

Many companies like to look several jumps ahead. They are interested in more than just finding who is most qualified at the moment. Some try to schedule moments five or ten years in advance. Here's where replacement charts are useful. The accompanying chart is typical, though it somewhat exaggerates the range of possibilities among six men.

From individual file cards and replacement charts it is possible to plan many years in advance. For instance:

Mr. A

| Jan. | 1968 | Superintendent |
| Jan. | 1970 | Retires (to be replaced by Mr. B) |

Mr. B

Jan.	1968	General Foreman
Summer	1969	Executive Development Program at X University
Jan.	1970	Superintendent (to be replaced by Mr. F)

Mr. C

Jan.	1968	General Foreman
June	1968	Assistant Personnel Director (to be replaced by Mr. E)
Jan.	1969	Chief Inspector
June	1969	Assistant Plant Manager (position to be created)
Jan.	1970	Plant Manager

Mr. E

Jan.	1968	Foreman
June	1968	Assistant Chief, Production Scheduling
Jan.	1969	Assistant Personnel Director
Jan.	1970	Assistant Director, Industrial Engineering
Jan.	1971	General Foreman
Jan.	1972	Plans and Scheduling Department, Corporate Headquarters

Note that Mr. B is to receive special training to prepare him for Mr. A's job. Mr. C is to move three different jobs to gain breadth of experience. Mr. C, whose performance is superior, will jump the Superintendent's post altogether and eventually become Plant Manager, though not until he has served in inspection and personnel and then gained six months experience as an understudy to the man he will succeed. Mr. E, the only college man in the lot, may have a still more brilliant future ahead. After short tours in three staff departments, he will serve a year as General Foreman (at age 28) and then move on to broader horizons in corporate headquarters. (He is lucky to stay in this one plant so long; in many companies, promising young executives move more frequently than once in four years.)

Note, too, that all these plans must be extremely tentative. If Mr. E fails to develop as anticipated, the schedule must be changed. Yet the very existence of such forecasts may lead to what some observers call a "self-fulfilling prophecy." The very fact that Mr. E is tagged as a "comer" means that he receives special opportunities and so is likely to become a good manager because everyone expects him to. Those who are less favored get less attention and so tend to lose hope. Furthermore, the system we are illustrating is "closed": Managers are rarely consulted about their future moves; indeed, not uncommonly they are kept completely in the dark.

The purpose of all this planning is to insure that the right man is available with the right experience at the right time. Naturally there is no absolute agreement on the best way of providing men with the experience they need. For instance, how long should a man stay on a given job before he moves on? How much variety of experience should he get? How much special attention should be given to the unusual "comer"? Although answers to these questions vary widely, we shall consider four typical kinds of programs which provide "guided experience": understudies, systematic rotation, "jet" trainees, and special "broadening" assignments. Many companies use a combination of these programs.

Understudies

In some companies before an executive can be moved to a higher position, he is required to train a replacement. The understudy program is the least ambitious form of development program and requires the least-centralized control and use of replacement tables. And yet, modest though it is, it raises many problems. Should there be a single understudy or several? If there is only one, those who have not been chosen may give up all hope of getting ahead. If there are several, intense rivalry will spring up among them.

When should understudies be selected? Some companies require a new manager to select a successor-elect almost as soon as he moves to his desk,[11]

---

[11] Often the selection is made by the management-development committee and the manager has relatively little to say about the choice.

on the grounds that early selection gives maximum opportunity for the under-study to gain experience, while insuring that someone is immediately prepared to take over in case of an emergency. On the other hand, the appointment of an understudy at too early a stage may impair the morale of other men who feel themselves qualified for the job.

Systematic Rotation

In many companies the rising executive regularly moves from one job and location to another once every two to five years. These movements are usually accompanied by promotions or salary increases. Normally rotation is regarded as a sign of progress; to stay frozen in one job for too long often signifies failure. Rarely is a man *forced* to move. But if he declines an opportunity for transfer, he knows his chances for advancement will be severely limited.

Companies that practice systematic rotation often maintain tightly central-ized programs and make extensive use of replacement charts and schedules. The decision on who is to be moved, and where and when he is to be moved, must be made on a coordinated, company-wide basis.

Such programs are expensive. Besides the company's out-of-pocket expenses for administering the program and defraying the costs when managers move their residence from one location to another, there is a substantial loss in ex-ecutive time when a man gives up an old job and sets about learning a new one. Why, then, are so many companies willing to undergo this expense?

1. A systematic rotation program develops, not specialists, but generalists—men who can take a broad, company-wide point of view, men whose chief ability is handling people and making decisions.

2. The outsider who comes into a department often brings with him new ideas and fresh points of view. Having no vested interest in the old ways of doing things, he can make changes quickly. In contrast, a man who has been in the department for many years has many personal ties and must always be careful not to step on his friends' toes.

3. Rotation makes it possible to compare one man against another, and so it tends to give everyone an equal chance. With a program of understudies, by contrast, no man can advance till his boss dies, retires, quits, or moves up, and, in departments where there are lots of good men, some talent is bound to be wasted. Rotation also protects a man from being frozen in a job merely because his department is expanding less rapidly than the rest. And it gives him a chance to make a good showing in the line of work for which he is best suited.

4. Rotation fosters organizational flexibility. In case of sudden expansion of one line of work, there will always be a number of people around who have had some experience in it.

5. Rotation also avoids the problems which arise when a newly promoted manager is required to supervise his former peers.

But in spite of the obvious advantages of systematic rotation as a program of management development, it does give rise to certain problems.

1. Rotation often means that the manager must pull up stakes and move to another location. This is particularly hard on children who must constantly readapt to new schools and new friends; after a while they learn not to make close friendships and to withdraw into themselves.

Beyond the time and emotional strain involved in packing, unpacking, and finding a new house, constant movement makes it difficult for managers to sink their roots into the community, and it disrupts their ties with relatives and friends.[12] Particularly to the adult who has poured love and energy into creating a garden or fixing up a house, giving up one's home is a painful experience.

Sooner or later most people who are obliged to move around a good bit learn to adjust. They learn not to make close friends, not to become closely involved in community affairs, not to develop long-term ties of any sort. By ruthlessly rooting out all other ties, rotation may develop the Organization Man who identifies only with the company for whom he works. Of course this company-centered manager may not be the all-around well-adjusted individual some companies purport to desire. Dedicated individuals are rarely "well rounded." But the question arises whether men who are so largely dependent on their job for satisfaction are really mature.

Many outstanding managers have simply refused to continue in the "rat race" (these are the heroes of many contemporary novels). Fully aware that to refuse a transfer may kill all chance of further advancement, they still insist on staying put. Clearly, men are not being used to the best advantage when top managers are picked on the basis of their willingness to be rotated rather than just innate capability.

2. Just as moving around discourages the executive from undertaking long-range projects at home, so it makes him reluctant to take a long-range approach to his job. If a man knows he will be transferred in two years' time, he will concentrate on short-range projects with a quick pay-off—immediate cost reduction, for instance, rather than personnel development. He knows that he will have none of the satisfaction of completing long-range projects and, when they are completed, the credit will go to his successor. Understandably, he is tempted to make changes that *look* good, since there rarely is time to test how they will work out in practice.

Rotation penalizes the slow starter who never has enough time on a given job to prove his ability. Yet the man who takes a long time to adjust to the people he works with and to learn his way around may at times be the best man.

3. The rotation system is like a highly competitive game of musical chairs. Every time there is another round of promotions and transfers, some people

---

[12] See Elsa Gidlow, "Promotion? No Thanks—Not If I Have to Move Again," *Sales Management*, Vol. 81, No. 3 (July 18, 1958), p. 35.

are left behind. And the system, as practiced by most companies, puts a high premium on conformity. As long as you do *adequately* you are retained. An *outstanding* job may help you somewhat, but a *mistake* will knock you completely out of the running. As a consequence, the smart rising young executive plays it safe; he avoids taking risks. Knowing that he may be judged more by whether he sticks to the rules than by long-term accomplishments, he learns not to raise a fuss or rock the boat.[13]

4. Rotation means that a man spends a large part of his time learning the job. Since the purpose of rotation is training, the new manager is assigned to the job not because he is the best man for it (that person might be an underling with years of experience in the department), but because the job is the best for him (that is, it provides him with the most training).

It may take a new manager months or years to learn both the technology and social geography of his department. At first, all he knows are the formal rules, so he enforces these even when they are inappropriate.

If he is wise, he lets his subordinates train him for the job. His lack of knowledge may force him to delegate responsibility (yet there are some managers who insist on making decisions without proper knowledge). In the early months, in most instances, it is the subordinates who help the manager, rather than the manager who helps the subordinates. Eventually the new manager begins to institute a policy of his own. Often, just after the department and the manager become accustomed to each other's idiosyncrasies the manager is transferred, a new man comes in, and the process begins all over again.

If carried too far, the policy of regular rotation may throw the affected departments into almost constant turmoil. The employees, knowing that their boss won't be with them for long, never develop respect for him. They learn to resist the supervisor's attempts to introduce change (which are often inept due to his lack of knowledge) and to develop strong group standards, which the supervisor of the moment finds almost impossible to modify. (Often the old-time working supervisor or an informal leader becomes the real head of the department.) As a long-service clerk in one office put it:

> "Bosses come and go. Each one has his pet peeves. We pretend to go along; but to tell you the truth we run things our own way."

5. Rotation sometimes leads to subtle class distinctions. The men who are not rotated tend to develop defensive reactions and identify with their own

---

[13] See Jack A. Hill, "Undetected Employee Incompetence," *Training Directors Journal,* Vol. 19, No. 7 (July 1965), pp. 46-48. Actually this point may be exaggerated. It may well be that the really successful rising young executive is the man who can be either conformist or nonconformist as the situation demands. In terms of social behavior and attitudes, he conforms; but in his own area of job competence he takes the initiative *at the proper time.* Perhaps the sense of when is "the proper time" is among the necessary requirements for a good executive. See George Strauss, "Organization Man: Prospect for the Future," *California Management Review,* Vol. 6, No. 3 (Spring 1964), p. 15, and William R. Dill, Thomas L. Hilton, and Walter R. Reitman, *The New Managers* (Englewood Cliffs, New Jersey: Prentice-Hall, 1962).

department against the "carpetbaggers" from without. This cleavage leads to misunderstanding and poor communications, with top management exerting pressure to get the local "stick-in-the-muds" to accept change and with local management strongly resisting every effort.

In an earlier chapter we pointed out that the manager is a man in the middle. His job is to represent his subordinates to his superiors and his superiors to his subordinates. He must try to maintain a balance, and if he favors anybody it should be the subordinates. The rotation system swings the balance sharply the other way. The man who is being rotated cannot afford to take the time and energy to develop relations downward; he must always look ahead to that next promotional shift.

6. The rotation system may easily become overcentralized, inflexible, and "closed." The plant manager, for instance, may have little to say about who is moved into his plant, and may be forced to accept as an assistant someone whom he has never seen before. A manager who is promoted under these circumstances is less likely to show loyalty to his boss than he would if the boss had been personally responsible for the promotion.

Long-run replacement schedules often look better on paper than in practice. People quit or die; business recessions dictate cut-backs in operations; products fail to develop as expected; men turn "sour." In short, there are too many variables to make planning for very far in the future much more reliable than crystal-gazing.

In conclusion, rotation has both advantages and disadvantages. Some managers find it challenging and exciting. Others find it frustrating, for both themselves and their families. Some departments would benefit from being shaken up by outsiders, but others would suffer in morale and efficiency in the hands of an outside supervisor unfamiliar with the special human and technical problems of the situation.

In spite of its personal and financial cost, rotation provides useful training for the potential executive, particularly if the rotations are not too frequent.[14] But management should rotate only those men who are genuinely anxious to move and should not discriminate against those who prefer to stay put (thus making the system more "open"). Furthermore, management should insure that the rotated executive does not disrupt the departments to which he is assigned.

Junior Trainee Programs

Many companies conduct special training programs for recent college graduates. Trainees in these programs, which run for as long as two years, are often known as "jets" (junior executive trainees). The purpose of "jet" pro-

---

[14] Yet one eminent authority concludes that rapidly promoted managers learn no faster than nonrotated managers. Moorehead Wright, "Individual Growth: The Basic Problems," *Personnel*, Vol. 37, No. 5 (September 1960), pp. 8-17.

grams [15] is to provide the trainee with a general orientation to the company and its policies, and to provide the company with an opportunity to observe and evaluate the trainee intensively.

Typically, "jets" are rotated from department to department every few months, holding such jobs as that of salesman or junior foreman. Often, on-the-job training is interspersed with formal classes, seminars, and discussion groups. Every month or two the trainees are carefully evaluated by their supervisor of the moment and by the over-all program coordinator. Trainees who completely fail to measure up to expectations are dropped; others are counseled on how to do a better job. At the end of the formal training period, each trainee is assigned to the department to which he seems best suited.

The advantages of such programs to both the company and the trainee are considerable. They provide the recent college graduate with an easy transition from the campus to the very different atmosphere of business. Further, they give him a breadth of experience and insight that he never would obtain were he to stay in a single department. Indeed, the whole process is designed to help trainee and company pick the job for which the trainee is best qualified.

But these programs have disadvantages as well. The "experience" of the "jets" in any one department often consists of little more than superficial observation. And the trainees are never evaluated under natural conditions; everyone knows that they are special individuals and treats them accordingly. Also, the noncollege men in an organization sometimes display intense antagonism toward these so-called "crown princes." [16] The fact that the company is hiring college men and training them specifically for management positions means that promotional opportunities for noncollege men are reduced. As one foreman commented:

> "Look at that kid there. His dad had money enough to send him to college and so he is a big shot. Right now he's assistant foreman and he don't know one per cent of what the men he bosses know. Five years from now he'll be my boss and he still won't know anything. So I got to watch how I treat him. Look how he struts around. The men hate him."

Because of this antagonism, many companies avoid according special treatment to newly hired college men. And if they do conduct a special training program, they try to include a few noncollege men who have come up from the ranks.[17]

---

[15] These programs go by various names: executive trainee program, cadet program, management development program, college trainee program, and so forth. Though there may be no confusion in the particular company, an outsider may confuse these programs with some broader aspect of management development.

[16] See "The Crown Princes of Business," *Fortune*, Vol. 48, No. 4 (October 1953), p. 151.

[17] As one substitute for a "jet" program, a company at first may assign recent college graduates to supervisors who know how to teach, are familiar with the emotional problems of late adolescence, and are willing to provide the new man with challenging problems where the penalty for failure is not great. See Edgar Schein, "How To Break In the College Graduate," *Harvard Business Review*, Vol. 42, No. 6 (November 1964), pp. 68-76.

Special "Broadening" Assignments

Although rotation and "jet training" give trainees a broad experience, this experience is all at a relatively low level. Yet different kinds of skills are required at various levels of the organization. At the lower levels perhaps technical ability, a willingness to obey orders, and skill in dealing with people are the chief requirements. At higher levels the ability to innovate and to make bold, long-range decisions becomes more important.[18] The men who do outstanding jobs at lower and middle levels of management may be totally ineffective at the top; on the other hand, the brilliant innovator might seem very inadequate in a subordinate post.

Since, at the lower levels, getting ahead depends on the recommendations of one's immediate boss, some men get no chance to advance because the boss is too unimaginative to appreciate their abilities (or even feels threatened by them). Thus, the "organization man" conformist will be favored rather than the kind of daring innovator needed at the top. In addition outstanding men sometimes lose their spark as they work their way slowly upward.

As a means of distinguishing the men who are outstandingly qualified for high positions, some companies are giving their promising junior executives special assignments which permit them to sample top-level responsibilities. The nature of these assignments varies greatly. Normally they are devised on a temporary or part-time basis—in addition to the executive's regular job. Some organizations have "junior boards of directors" or "management cabinets" [19] to which the senior board of directors may refer special problems (or the junior board may consider substantially the same agenda as the senior board). More frequently, trainees are assigned to capital budgeting, product development, or long-range planning committees where they work in the company of more senior executives. At times a trainee may be assigned to study a problem area, prepare recommendations, and present and defend them in person before a top-management committee.[20] Or he may be assigned as an "assistant to" a member of top management and work as his personal aide.

If such special assignments are to be successful as development tools, three requirements must be met:

1. The problems assigned must be genuinely "broadening"—that is, they must cut across departmental lines and involve long-range planning.

[18] See, for instance, Norman H. Martin, "Differential Decisions in the Management of a Business Firm," *Journal of Business*, Vol. 29, No. 4 (October 1956), pp. 249-260; and Basil S. Georgoplous and Floyd C. Mann, *The Community General Hospital* (New York: Macmillan, 1962), p. 238. In addition, there is considerable evidence that, while managers prefer originality and decisiveness on the part of their peers and their bosses, they prefer their subordinates to be passive, loyal, and reliable. Thus, initiative may not be rewarded in making promotions. See Raymond C. Miles, "Human Relations or Human Resources?" *Harvard Business Review*, Vol. 34, No. 4 (July 1965), pp. 148-183.

[19] John R. Cref, *Junior Board of Directors: A Management Training Device* (New York: Harper & Row, 1958).

[20] See Arjay Miller, "Reporting to Top Management at Ford," *California Management Review*, Vol. 1, No. 1 (Fall 1958), pp. 30-37.

2. The trainees must operate under the direct observation of top executives who are personally responsible for evaluating the trainees' performance.

3. The problems must be *tough*, challenging ones—tough enough so that the merely adequate answer appears unsatisfactory and so that the truly outstanding man can show his real merits.

Special assignments should be designed to give the rising junior executive top-level experience both in operating on his own and in serving as a committee member.

> There must be evaluation of the results not only by the senior committee members but also by the juniors themselves. The juniors' evaluations must be evaluated. There must be a chance for juniors (anonymously?) to indicate those of their colleagues whom they judge to show superior intelligence, ability to accomplish, leadership, etc.[21]

In general, programs of this sort permit the junior to be observed and evaluated by a group of top executives and reduce his dependence on a single boss. The junior is judged on his ability to handle a top-level job, not just on his ability to cope with lower-level jobs. The "crown-prince" problem is minimized since the trainee performs his special assignments in the presence of higher management rather than in the presence of subordinates. The program may bring a wealth of useful suggestions to the attention of top management, as well as provide the junior men with invaluable experience.

The Average Manager

The above programs are primarily designed to select and develop *top* managers. Yet organizational survival depends as directly on strong middle and lower management as it does on strong top management. How about the average supervisor whose promotional opportunities are quite limited? He has little opportunity to make major innovations or long-range decisions and is likely to function primarily as a specialist in one aspect of the organization rather than as a generalist. Still, special broadening assignments and training programs will be quite useful for him too, both to prevent obsolescence and to keep him from slowing down. Opportunities to grow should be provided for every man at every level.

Even the man who will never be promoted can improve his performance on his present job. Often it is necessary to move such men laterally so as not to block promotional opportunities for younger, promising men. For managers whose ability is actually declining, it may be useful to "kick them upstairs" in a way which is not obviously a demotion, or to cut down discreetly on the responsibilities of their present jobs.

Particular attention must be given to men who are likely to feel passed over when promotions are made. As soon as it becomes known that there is a

---

[21] Thomas L. Whisler, "Performance Appraisal and the Organization Man," *The Journal of Business,* Vol. 31, No. 1 (January 1958), p. 26.

vacancy in higher management, great hopes are kindled at lower levels. Unless management handles the situation with great care, many people will be so disappointed when the final decision is announced that they will lose their desire to cooperate. The grounds for making promotions should be made clear, particularly to those who are apparently passed over. In the long run, an explanation of a promotion makes it easier for subordinates to accept the legitimacy of the man who is moved up.

A regular program of appraisal interviews (see Chapter 23) may help each employee achieve a realistic attitude toward his prospects and give him a clear indication of how he stands. Such interviews tend to counteract overoptimism and provide

> ladders of escape which will insure [subordinates'] being able to accept adverse decisions and still maintain a normal self-respect . . . Also-rans are happier in their organization when they feel the race has been fairly run; when they have positive evidence of thought being given to them; and when they know that some recognizable procedure—not favoritism—has been used.[22]

There is much that a company can do to reduce the feeling that a supervisor is a failure merely because he has stopped advancing.[23] If salary schedules make allowance for years of service on the job, for example, the supervisor who has been bypassed can still look forward to increased earnings. As mentioned, he can be given broadening assignments and training courses to help him improve his performance on his present job. And his boss can show that he values the man's opinion by asking for his suggestions on matters of importance. Indeed, the more intimately a man participates in the organization, the less importance he attaches to the formal status of his job.

DEVELOPMENT AS A MANAGEMENT RESPONSIBILITY

A basic question is this: Are managers at all levels held responsible for providing opportunities for subordinate growth? Superiors can't develop subordinates; they must develop themselves. Nevertheless, superiors can provide the atmosphere in which subordinates can experiment and grow, or they can stifle any attempt at self-development. For a development program to be effective, every manager must assume personal responsibility (1) for helping his immediate subordinates develop, and (2) for insisting that these subordinates in turn contribute to the development of those under him.

Thus we ask: What importance does management place on development? Are managers ever rewarded for doing an outstanding job of training subordinates? Or do the chief rewards always go to the manager who keeps

---

[22] Virgil K. Rowland, "They Also Ran . . . ," *Executive Selection, Development and Inventory,* Personnel Series, No. 171 (New York: American Management Association, 1957), pp. 55 and 58.
[23] For a good discussion, see W. R. G. Bender, "No Room at the Top," *Management Review,* Vol. 48, No. 7 (July 1959), pp. 9-14.

immediate costs low and gets production out? Does the reward system encourage the manager to think that developing subordinates is a waste of time?

> One unpublished study made within a gigantic corporation indicated that those who had reached the highest positions were not remembered by anyone in the company as having done anything significant in developing men, while those who had achieved the reputation of being wise and effective counselors invariably reached only modest levels.[24]

Often managers learn that their only reward for training a subordinate is to have him leave and be replaced by someone with less experience. Knowing that a good subordinate is hard to find, the manager is tempted to recommend his poorer subordinates for special training programs in order to get rid of them. Too often, units that do a good job of training find themselves raided by other units.

The most effective development occurs in an atmosphere where management permits self-development. "Is management willing to take a chance on its men, greeting an occasional failure as the price of taking risks?"[25] Does the manager feel free to make suggestions? Is he encouraged to contribute his ideas? How much responsibility does he have? Does he take part in making management decisions? Is there supervision by results rather than in detail? Does the manager feel that he has to cover up when he makes mistakes, or can he talk his problems over with his boss without fear of being blamed?

Further, the formal organization of the company itself affects the manner in which men behave. Flat organization and organization by product (instead of by function) make it easier for a man to develop new ways of doing things and to be his own boss.

"All this may be summed up in the statement that executives develop best in those organizations which are already well managed by recognized standards of good management."[26] A permissive atmosphere in the organization at large helps stimulate individual growth.

CONCLUSION

The strength of any organization depends largely on its management. If the organization is to remain strong, it must provide opportunities for the continuing development of competent replacements for those who die or retire.

Development is a matter of demand and supply. It is important to predict future needs for management manpower and to establish programs designed to supply competent men to fill vacancies as they occur. However, since it is impossible to look to the future with certainty, any development program

---

[24] Whisler, *op. cit.*, p. 22.

[25] Robert K. Stolz, "Getting Back to Fundamentals in Executive Development," *Personnel*, Vol. 30, No. 6 (May 1954), p. 456. This is an excellent article.

[26] Paul Pigors and Charles A. Myers, *Personnel Administration*, 3rd ed. (New York: McGraw-Hill, 1956), p. 118.

must be flexible. Clearly it is desirable to have an orderly system that gives everyone an equal opportunity (dependent on real ability) for training, experience, and consideration for promotion. But an over-rigid rotation or promotional system can put the company into a strait jacket.

Further, special programs are not enough. Overemphasis on a few select "crown princes" may be harmful to the morale and efficiency of the whole organization. Development should not be confined to a select few, though it may be desirable to give the most promising candidates special opportunities (and challenges).

The most effective development program is the one that involves every member of management, both as a trainer and a trainee. Management must give to the development of human assets the same priority it gives to the development of physical assets.

In the next two chapters we shall discuss two important developmental tools: performance evaluation and training.

PROBLEM

BEMUS COMPANY

The Bemus Company was founded in the basement of its president, Andrew Bemus, about ten years ago. Mr. Bemus had developed a highly sensitive instrument which immediately found use both in defense and civilian production fields. As a consequence, the firm grew very rapidly. It had seven employees nine years ago, 200 employees five years ago, and over a thousand today.

As of today, most of the company's top management consists of Mr. Bemus' earliest associates, many of whom are under the age of 45. They are a highly self-confident group who have worked together closely over the years.

And yet trouble seems to lie ahead. Sharp competition from other companies has developed for the first time and profit margins have fallen. Labor costs are obviously too high and there is much confusion and divided responsibility in management. Most decisions are made by the top-management group and there is little delegation of authority. Many of the more recently hired engineers complain that their ideas are given very little consideration by the inner clique—and that there is little or no chance for promotion since all the top jobs are handled by younger men. As a consequence, three of the more brilliant recent hirees have resigned after spending only a short time with the company.

1. What sort of management development program does this company need?
2. Assuming that you were recently hired from the outside as personnel director, what steps would you take to win acceptance for this program?

Performance Appraisal

In the typical large company every executive and supervisor is subject to a periodic appraisal of his performance. As with other aspects of management development, the primary purpose of these appraisals has shifted in recent years. Originally a device to provide guidance to management in selecting supervisors for promotions or salary increases, they are now also used as a training and coaching device to help men on all levels of management to improve their performance.

> The armed forces pioneered the development of evaluation procedures as a means of making a systematic comparison of large numbers of officers. Suppose, for example, that the army is faced with the problem of picking 1,000 men for promotion to first lieutenant from a group of 20,000 second lieutenants. Since no one individual knows all 20,000 men personally, some rating technique must be used to provide an objective basis of comparison. Each officer is rated by his superior (or in some cases by committees), and, though other factors may be taken into account, those with the highest ratings are considered first for promotion.

In industry, an effective performance-appraisal program provides management a rational basis for determining who should be promoted or receive salary increases. It permits each man to be considered on the same basis as everyone else. Thus, hopefully, fewer charges of favoritism are made and better men are selected for promotion. In addition, subordinates are motivated to work harder in order to win a favorable rating. Long-range personnel planning is also facilitated, since it becomes easier to determine who should be promoted now, who should be ready after further experience and training, and who, while satisfactory on his present job, is not a likely prospect for a more difficult one. Further, transfers can be more easily custom-tailored to meet the needs of individuals, while managers who need special training can be identified. Finally, appraisals are useful in helping a company to make an evaluation of the over-all effectiveness of its program for management development and selection.

Performance-appraisal techniques can be used for more than just pinpointing those who should be promoted, receive pay increases, or obtain special attention. They can also be used as a springboard for coaching and for helping individuals set goals for their own development. Unfortunately, the procedures which are most useful for selection purposes are less useful for self-development. As a consequence, many companies have abandoned their *traditional* procedures, which often emphasized the rating of an employee's personality traits by his boss, for newer, hopefully less biased methods. And some companies have abandoned ratings as such for *results-oriented* evaluation procedures, which frequently involve the setting of goals by superiors and subordinates working together.

We shall look first at traditional procedures and then at various newer ones. Before doing this, let us point out that performance appraisal is often conducted at the hourly-paid level as well as at the management level; in the former case it is often called "merit rating" (see pp. 621-625). Although we shall emphasize management appraisals in our discussion, most of what we say applies to merit rating as well.

TRADITIONAL PERFORMANCE RATING

Stripped to its essentials, traditional performance rating is a matter of thoughtfully filling out a rating form (see illustration opposite). Normally the form is completed by the immediate supervisor of the man being rated, then checked by the supervisor's boss. Sometimes the rating is made by a committee consisting of the direct supervisor, the supervisor's boss, and one or two others who are in a position to judge the man who is being rated. Committee ratings have one great advantage: By bringing several viewpoints to bear on the rating, they offset the immediate supervisor's special bias. The committee meetings themselves, however, may be extremely time-consuming. In some companies, the forms are filled out by the immediate supervisor in collaboration with the personnel director, who takes advantage of the rating session to help the supervisor think through ways of doing a better job of developing the subordinate in question.

Rating Scales

A conventional rating form of the check-the-box type is sometimes called a "graphic rating" or a "rating scale." The important part here is the over-all summary rating or score, which makes it possible to compare large numbers of managers. The ratings on specific factors do serve a purpose, however, in helping to pin-point areas in which a subordinate needs further development.

In one variety of rating scale, the over-all score is determined by adding up the scores given to specific factors (as in the upper portion of the form illustrated). In spite of its deceptive simplicity, this approach has severe limitations. Note, for example, some of the basic assumptions lying behind it: One is

Conventional rating form.

Name _Wilson Olcott_   Position _Asst. Director Marketing Research_   Date rated _6/25/67_

Date hired _Apr. 12, 1955_   On position since _Aug 8, 1963_

	Unsatisfactory	Fair	Good	Very good	Exceptional	
Job knowledge Extent of theoretical knowledge and practical know-how as related to present job.	1	2	3	4	(5)	5
Judgment Ability to obtain and analyze facts and apply sound judgment.	1	2	3	(4)	5	4
Organizing ability Effectiveness in planning own work and that of subordinates.	1	2	(3)	4	5	3
Attitude Enthusiasm shown for job; loyalty to company and superiors; ability to accept criticism and changes in company policy.	1	2	(3)	4	5	3
Dependability Reliability in carrying out assignments conscientiously and with effectiveness.	1	2	3	(4)	5	4
Creativity Ability to apply imagination to job, to develop new plans, cut costs, etc.	1	2	3	4	(5)	5
Dealing with people Ability to get along with others; tact, diplomacy; ability to command and influence people	1	(2)	3	4	5	2
Delegation Ability to assign work to others and to coordinate others through distribution of workload and responsibility.	1	2	(3)	4	5	3
Leadership Ability to stimulate subordinates to perform their jobs effectively	1	(2)	3	4	5	2
Personal efficiency Speed and effectiveness in carrying out duties not assigned to subordinates.	1	2	3	(4)	5	4

Total Points _35_

In order of importance, state *three* performance characteristics which need improvement with respect to his present condition.

1. _Emotional stability_
2. _Dealings with subordinates_
3. _Cost control_

What might he do to improve his job performance?

Try harder to get along with other people. Don't blow his stack all the time. Be more practical.

Are there any factors in the health, personal life or other outside influences which may have affected his performance during this appraisal period?

Divorced wife last month

Comments

A very able researcher who finds it hard to get out of the clouds. His subordinates respect his ability though many are irritated by his moodiness. Possibly he may settle down when he solves his family problems.

Evaluated by: _Burt New fane_

Title: _Director Marketing Research_

Approved by: _Gerry Falconer_

Title: _Marketing Manager_

Unsatisfactory: 10-16 points
Fair: 16-25 points
Good: 26-35 points
Very good: 35-44 points
Excellent: 45-50 points

that each of the factors (cost control, judgment, and so forth) is of *equal* importance and that this holds true on all jobs. Yet clearly, on some jobs creativity is more important than effectiveness in dealing with people, and on others just the reverse is true. Another assumption is that these qualities are "additive"—for instance, strength in job knowledge will offset lack of leadership.

Unwilling to accept these assumptions, some companies permit their managers to give their subordinates an over-all rating directly, without the necessity of adding up separate factor scores. This summary rating of over-all ability may be given either in numerical terms, from one to one hundred, or in descriptive terms, from "unsatisfactory" to "outstanding."

Both forms of rating are often supplemented by open-ended, essay-type questions such as those illustrated on the bottom of the form on p. 551. In fact, in some companies the essay portion of the evaluation form takes considerably more space than does the quantitative portion. These subjective, qualitative evaluations tend to give a fuller picture than is presented by numerical ratings alone.[1] They are also more useful for coaching, but they are of little help in comparing large numbers of people for purposes of pay increases or promotion.

Human Errors in Rating

Both forms of numerical rating are subject to certain human evaluative errors. (Incidentally, these same errors distort merit rating and job evaluation, to which we will return in Chapter 25.)

Clarity in standards.   Unless all raters agree on what terms such as "good" or "excellent" mean, their final ratings simply cannot be compared. To cite an extreme example, the rating scale in one hospital included Excellent, Very Good, Fair, Satisfactory, and Unsatisfactory. Several head nurses objected to using the term "satisfactory" on the grounds that "no nurse is ever really satisfactory." To them "satisfactory" meant "better than excellent."

Differing perceptions.   People differ in their standards of judgment. Even where there is no conscious prejudice, unconscious factors may bias a superior's evaluation of his subordinates. Even the fairest of people find it difficult to be impartial when judging the actions of individuals who differ greatly from themselves in terms of background, values, and style of behavior. More than obvious factors, such as racial discrimination, are involved here. The man who is accustomed to making quick decisions may be antagonized by the man who moves ponderously and deliberately—and vice versa. And "appraisal also requires that we ask people who are perhaps not themselves good managers to

---

[1] But a real problem arises because bosses with writing skills are able to get bigger promotions and salary increases for their subordinates than are bosses who write less persuasively.

rate the managerial competence of others who may have more managerial competence than their bosses." [2]

Excessive leniency or strictness. As every student knows, there is a big difference between hard and easy graders. Supervisors in industry often hesitate to give low ratings for fear of antagonizing their subordinates and making them less cooperative.[3] Furthermore, the supervisor may be afraid that low ratings will reflect on his own ability. There is always a chance that his boss will say, "If your subordinate is as bad as all this, why don't you do something about it?" Some executives regularly rate new employees very low, then gradually raise them—thus making the employee feel good and displaying to their superiors their excellence as trainers.

In many organizations there is a tendency for average ratings to rise over time. Thus, during World War II practically every enlisted man got the highest rating. To get the next-to-highest rating was evidence of downright incompetence.

The halo effect. There is a natural tendency (sometimes called the "blending tendency") for the rater to be influenced in rating one factor by the kind of rating he gives on another. In fact, the individual rater tends to give each man approximately the same rating on all factors. If a supervisor has a general feeling that a man is good, he will rate him high on all factors—and vice versa.[4] Or his rating on the first factor listed or on the factor he thinks most important may "contaminate" his ratings on all others.

Influence of a man's job. Performance rating is designed to evaluate how well a man does on a particular job. Although in theory it is vastly different from job evaluation (which rates the job, not the man), in practice there is a common tendency to give a man on a higher-paid job a higher rating just because of his position.

All these human errors in rating can be at least partially counteracted by insuring that the managers who do the rating are properly trained.[5]

---

[2] George S. Odiorne, *Personnel Policy: Issues and Practices* (Columbus, Ohio: Merrill, 1963), p. 310.

[3] One study showed that supervisors in a government department gave much higher ratings if they expected to have to show them to the men they had rated than if they expected the ratings to remain confidential. Fred Massarik, Irving R. Weschler, and Robert Tannenbaum, "Evaluating Efficiency Rating Systems through Experiment," *Personnel Administration*, Vol. 14, No. 1 (January 1951), pp. 42-47.

[4] The supervisor can reduce this halo effect by rating all his men on a single item before going on to the next, rather than rating one man at a time.

[5] Group discussion of the natural tendencies toward bias in rating seems to be more effective that straight lectures. Jacob Levine and John Butler, "Lecture vs. Group Discussion in Changing Behavior," in Dorwin Cartwright and Alvin Zander, eds., *Group Dynamics* (Evanston, Ill.: Harper and Row, 1953), pp. 280-286.

Traits or Performance?

A more fundamental criticism of the traditional rating scale is that excessive emphasis is placed on personality traits as opposed to measurable objective performance. Management development was originally introduced into many companies as a crash program designed to reveal executives who were promotable to top positions. Actual performance on the job was often considered secondary, in part because the emphasis was all on *potential* for development.

In any event, many organizations ask raters to evaluate subordinates on factors such as optimism, drive, and ability to learn. Among the armed forces, for instance, ratings are required of qualities such as "initiative," "force," "moral courage," and "loyalty." [6]

What has proved wrong with this emphasis on traits? In the first place, the ratings secured are of little use in helping an employee do a better job. For instance, it is hard for a man to make a real change in his "personality," though he might put up a false front and pretend to be, in the words of one typical form, "radiant, confident, cheerful, courteous."

In trait-rating, standards are often unclear. Although there may be considerable agreement among managers about what constitutes acceptable standards of output in a given department, degrees of "loyalty" and "moral courage" are particularly subject to personal bias. In fact, judgments in these areas are often difficult for anyone not trained as a psychologist.

Trait-rating shares with some forms of personality testing the assumption that there is one psychological configuration that makes the best executive. Yet jobs do differ in their psychological requirements: Sales managers, for example, may require more aggressiveness than do laboratory managers. And even where jobs are alike, people with vastly different personalities may perform equally well.

More important, an emphasis on traits gives the advantage to the conformist, "the individual who has nothing wrong with him. More particularly, [the] emphasis on human relations favors the individual who always gets along with other people and never rubs anybody the wrong way." [7] A large chemical company, for example, offers the following choices for the single trait "co-operation": [8]

1. Concedes nothing. Obstructive, antagonistic.
2. Poor mixer. Tries to run with the ball. Occasionally indulges in obstructive argument.
3. Generally adapts self to person and situations. Responsive to leadership and reasonably tactful.

---

[6] Herold L. Jones, James L. Keating, and George Postich, "Officer Appraisal in the Armed Forces," *United States Naval Institute Proceedings*, Vol. 91, No. 4 (April 1965), p. 80.

[7] Robert K. Stoltz, "Is Executive Development Coming of Age?" *The Journal of Business*, Vol. 28, No. 1 (January 1955), p. 50.

[8] Ernest Dale and Alice Smith, "Now Report Cards for Bosses," *New York Times Magazine* (March 31, 1958), p. 56.

4. Willing and eager to please. Works in complete harmony with group. Adaptable and courteous.
5. Adapts self very well without sacrificing standards. Goes out of his way to promote common end.

Note that by favoring the man who is "willing and eager to please" over the one who "tries to run with the ball," this company is in effect molding its own character. It is giving first priority to good human relations as opposed to decisive decision-making.[9] Yet those at the very top often are 100 per cent rugged individualists. How many of the great tycoons of industry have been "radiant, confident, poised, courteous"? "Charles E. Wilson guided the vast General Motors organization to outstanding success despite his admitted susceptibility to foot-in-mouth disease. Henry Ford, Sr., got along pretty well without too much sense of humor. And Abraham Lincoln would never have been given a passing mark if his contemporaries had thought to grade him."[10] As Stoltz puts it, "realistically speaking, most executives are curious combinations of strengths and weaknesses."[11]

NEWER RATING METHODS

As a consequence of these criticisms of traditional rating scales, personnel researchers have tried to develop new rating procedures that are less affected by raters' personal biases and less concerned with imponderables such as traits. Among the best known of these new forms of rating are *forced distribution*, *forced choice*, and the *critical incident* technique.

Forced distribution. This method is familiar to many students as the old principle of "grading on the curve." The manager who uses this system of rating is expected to rank subordinates by class, instead of ascribing a set of rating points to each individual.[12] "Ranking" and "paired comparisons" are two other techniques which are somewhat analogous to forced distribution. Ranking involves listing all those being rated in strict numerical order of merit; "paired comparisons" involve rating each member of the group being compared against each other member of the group, comparing each set of two in turn. In a typical system the top 10 per cent of the men are placed in the highest class, 20 per cent in the next, 40 per cent in the middle bracket, 20 per cent in the next-to-lowest, and 10 per cent in the very bottom class. Ordinarily, only one over-all rating of ability is given, rather than a series of ratings on separate factors.

---

[9] This is not so much the fault of rating traits as of the frequent emphasis on the wrong traits. A company could just as easily use trait-rating to pick nonconformists. See Stanley Stark, "Executive Personality and Psychological Testing," *Current Economic Comment*, Vol. 20, No. 2 (May 1958), pp. 15-32.

[10] Dale and Smith, *op. cit.*, p. 58.

[11] Stoltz, *op. cit.*, p. 51.

[12] See Joseph Tiffin, "Merit Rating: Its Validity and Techniques," *Rating Employee and Supervisory Performance* (New York: American Management Association, 1950), pp. 17-19.

This system obviously eliminates any danger that the manager will be over-lenient or the possibility that the standards will be interpreted in different ways by different managers. Moreover, the system is easy to explain and administer. Yet this scheme has distinct drawbacks: In effect, it assumes that all groups have the same proportion of average, poor, and outstanding men. But this is not likely to be true, particularly where there are only a few men on a given job.

Forced choice.   This radically different approach was developed by a distinguished group of psychologists at the end of World War II for use in rating army officers. Its purpose is to reduce human bias by setting up a system in which the rater is presented with four possible statements about a person, such as:

	MOST	LEAST
Doesn't try to pull rank	_____	_____
Knows his men, their capabilities and limitations	_____	_____
Low efficiency	_____	_____
Uses a steady monotone in his voice	_____	_____

The rater is expected to check two items, one of which is the *most* and the other the *least* characteristic of the person being rated. Two of these are apparently favorable and two apparently unfavorable. However, only one of the favorable items gives a plus credit; the other, if checked, gives no credit at all. Similarly, only one of the two negative items affects the final result. The zero-credit items (in this case, possibly, "Doesn't try to pull rank" and "Uses a steady monotone") are ones that have been shown by tests to have significantly less correlation with military efficiency than the two that give a score.[13] The important thing is that the rater doesn't know which items are the ones that count. His own prejudices and biases are minimized, since his only function is to give an objective description of the subordinate's performance by checking the blanks.

Following the war, the forced-choice technique was adopted by many industrial firms. It has the advantage of reducing such forms of bias as leniency and the halo effect; no training is required to prepare a supervisor to use it; and there is some evidence that it does a better job of pin-pointing the best men than do simpler forms of rating—that is, it correlates more highly with ratings by fellow employees and with objective factors such as productivity.

Though from many points of view forced choice seems clearly the best system of rating, its use has not spread widely. In the first place the system is

---

[13] For a description of how these tests were constructed, see Donald Sisson, "Forced Choice—The New Army Rating," *Personnel Psychology*, Vol. 1, No. 3 (Autumn, 1948). For a more general description of the forced-choice technique, see Marion W. Richardson, "Forced Choice Performance Reports," in M. Joseph Dooher and Vivienne Marquis, eds., *Rating Employee and Supervisory Performance* (New York: American Management Association, 1950), pp. 35-46.

expensive to install, for the items must be custom-tailored to the demands of the particular job and company. (Suppose a set of four items contained these two favorable items: "Has a constant flow of new ideas" and "Shows careful judgment." The first choice might represent a good mark for an advertising executive and the second one for a banker.)

Forced choice is often resented by both raters and ratees. The implicit assumption behind the system is that supervisors cannot be trusted to rate fairly, an assumption that naturally prejudices them against its use. A department manager summarized the common attitude: "I try to reward my good men by giving them good ratings—but you just have to guess what those psychology boys [who set up the items] want. No one understands how it works. Some of the men call it promotion by Ouija Board." (Actually there is some evidence that raters can figure out which items count, and so give the kinds of ratings they want.) [14] A final objection is that forced choice makes it difficult or impossible to use ratings for the purpose of counseling employees.

Critical incidents. The critical-incident technique of rating is also known as the "critical requirement system" and the "performance-record program." [15]

The first step is to draw up for each job a list of *critical job requirements.* For a foreman, for instance, these requirements might include "improving equipment," "getting along with staff," "meeting schedules," and so forth. Typical job requirements for a sales manager might be "developing new customers" and "avoiding losses."

Once the critical job requirements have been determined, the next step is to train supervisors to be on the lookout for *critical incidents* or outstanding examples of success or failure on the part of the subordinate in meeting the requirements. The manager lists the incidents as he observes them and gradually builds up a record for each subordinate, with the "debits" on one side and the "credits" on the other:

Dealing with Unions

9/21	Failed to consult with steward before making transfer.	8/6	Persuaded steward to withdraw grievance in regard to employee discharged for excessive absenteeism.
11/7	Made transfer in violation of sect. 39 (c) of contract.	12/3	Gave excellent answer to union grievance.

---

[14] H. Maher, "Studies of Transparency in Forced-Choice Scales: I Evidence of Transparency," *Journal of Applied Psychology,* Vol. 43, No. 4 (August 1959), pp. 275-278.

[15] This system has been adopted rather widely by the government. See John C. Flanagan, "A New Approach to Evaluating Personnel," *Personnel,* Vol. 26, No. 1 (July 1949), pp. 35-42; John C. Flannagan and Robert K. Burns, "The Employee Performance Record," *Harvard Business Review,* Vol. 33, No. 5 (September 1955), pp. 95-102.

Normally, no attempt is made to balance the "debits" and the "credits." And yet the critical-incident method does provide the raw materials for the more conventional rating-scale appraisal previously discussed.

The great advantage of this approach is that all ratings are based on objective evidence rather than on a subjective evaluation of traits. It is no longer enough for the boss to say, "Joe has trouble in dealing with people." The boss must cite specific incidents to prove his contention. To insure objectivity, the manager is requested to record each incident immediately instead of trying to think back over, say, the last six months before making a rating. This requirement improves his ability as an observer and also reduces the common tendency to rate a man chiefly on what he has done most recently.

On the other hand, care must be taken to insure that the manager's record-keeping does not degenerate into supervision in detail. He should emphasize *what* is accomplished, not *how* it is accomplished. Further, keeping a "little black book" in which all mistakes are recorded conflicts with the philosophy that supervision should not overemphasize blame-finding. When a supervisor records an unfavorable incident, he should be careful to tell the subordinate about it at the time and give him every chance to tell his side of the story.

THE EVALUATION INTERVIEW

Many companies now require each supervisor to sit down periodically with each of his subordinates to discuss his performance with him. The evaluation report is ordinarily used as a springboard for the discussion. Evaluation interviews serve two purposes: (1) They enable the evaluation to serve as a form of feedback, which helps the individual know his progress and where he stands in the eyes of his boss, and (2) they provide an opportunity for the manager to counsel the subordinate on how to improve his performance.

In some companies the managers are never told how they have been rated; [16] they don't know where they stand, which may be bad for morale. In other organizations, however, management feels that it is only fair to inform men of the results of ratings. As one junior executive commented, "Before this evaluation system was installed, the only time the boss would tell you how you were doing was when you were really in trouble. If he'd say 'I'd like to talk to you about your future' that meant you were really going to get chewed out."

Yet too often managers recoil at the thought of having to tell another man how he stands or what he needs to do to improve himself. "They fool themselves into believing that the subordinate knows all this from day-to-day contacts on the job, and they are often shocked to learn that the boss 'never told me how I was doing.'" [17] Actually, the evaluation interview may reduce misunderstanding between manager and subordinate.

---

[16] Officers in the Navy, Air Force and Marine Corps are not shown their appraisal report unless the report indicates their performance is below minimum standards. Jones, Keating, and Postich, *op. cit.*, p. 79.

[17] Paul Pigors and Charles A. Myers, *Personnel Administration*, 3rd ed. (New York: McGraw-Hill, 1956), p. 124.

Evaluation interviews are not easy. Poorly handled they may lead to hostility and greater misunderstanding. Consequently, many companies have spent a great deal of time and effort on training their managers to handle evaluation interviews, giving particular emphasis to skill in the use of nondirective techniques. To insure that no essential part of the interview is left out, managers are often encouraged to follow a standardized outline. For example: [18]

1. The superior tells the subordinate the purpose of the interview, and that it is designed to help him do a better job.

2. The superior then presents the evaluation, giving the strong points first and then the weak points. (There is no reason why the superior has to show the entire evaluation to the subordinate, nor, as we shall mention later, does he have to be 100 per cent frank about the subordinate's prospects.)

3. Next the superior asks for general comments on the evaluation. He anticipates that the subordinate may show some hostility to negative evaluations and allows him to blow off steam.

4. The superior then tries to encourage the subordinate to give his own picture of his progress, the problems he is meeting, and how these can be solved.

5. The interview ends with a discussion of what the subordinate can do by himself to overcome his weak points and what the superior can do to help. The superior tries to accept any criticism or aggression on the part of the subordinate without argument or contradiction. He helps the subordinate save face and does not expose his unjustified alibis. (Note: No matter how the interview is handled, more time will be spent on the bad points than on the good ones.)

Some supervisors start the interview by asking the subordinate, "Tell me, how do *you* think you are doing?" Then they show the subordinate the evaluation. This approach has the advantage of letting the subordinate tell his side of the story first; it is often easier for a man to criticize himself than to accept criticism from others. Were it not for the fact that the subordinate knows that he is about to receive an evaluation from his boss, this would be an excellent form of training. Under the circumstances, however, the subordinate may look upon this as a cat-and-mouse affair and wonder what the boss wants him to say and how much it is safe to reveal.

Difficulties in Conducting Evaluation Interviews

In recent years many companies have become discouraged with the type of evaluation program just described. The rating period often turns out to be a time of apprehension and discomfort for managers and subordinates alike.

---

[18] See Bernard J. Corner, "The Communication of Merit Rating," *Personnel*, Vol. 30, No. 2 (September 1953), p. 88; Earl G. Planty and C. A. Efferson, "Counseling Executives after Merit Rating or Evaluation," *Personnel*, Vol. 27, No. 5 (March 1951), pp. 384-396; Norman R. F. Maier, *Psychology in Industry*, 2d ed. (Boston: Houghton Mifflin, 1955), pp. 623-629; Benjamin Balinsky and Ruth Berger, *The Executive Interview* (New York: Harper & Row, 1959), Chapter 9.

True, most managers endorse performance appraisal as a matter of principle: They believe that people should know where they stand.

> In actual practice, however, it is the extremely rare operating manager who will employ such a program on his own initiative. Personnel specialists report that most managers carry out performance appraisal interviews only when strong control procedures are established to ensure that they do.[19]

Many managers just go through the motions of conducting interviews and some "forget" about them altogether. It is not uncommon for managers to hand subordinates their rating without comment, or to explain the rating in a rather embarrassed fashion without giving the subordinate a chance to comment or reply.

Why are managers generally so unenthusiastic about the evaluation program? Many have little skill in nondirective interviewing procedure; others, feeling that their primary function is "to get production out," have very little interest in taking time from their "main job" to develop subordinates. As one executive put it, "This is personnel's idea, personnel ought to carry the ball. I think it's a bunch of nonsense."

Yet even managers who are sympathetic to the principles of supervisory development feel uncomfortable when they have to criticize subordinates. As one manager said, "I dread the time when I have to give ratings. Nobody appreciates them and I get into an endless series of arguments which make it just that much tougher to get the work out." This reluctance is particularly evident when the rating plan requires the supervisor to discuss the subordinate's personality traits. It is reflected by the tendency to avoid, if possible, giving anyone a low rating. Douglas McGregor concludes: [20]

> The conventional approach, unless handled with consummate skill and delicacy, constitutes something dangerously close to a violation of the integrity of the personality. Managers are uncomfortable when they are placed in the position of "playing God." The respect we hold for the inherent value of the individual leaves us distressed when we must take responsibility for judging the personal worth of a fellow man. Yet the conventional approach to appraisal forces us, not only to make such judgments and to see them acted upon, but also to communicate them to those we have judged. No wonder we resist.

Or, as other observers put it, "Only in rare instances is a business executive properly qualified to assess the personality of an individual and, more important, to try to get the individual to change aspects of his personality." [21]

Subordinates also tend to react to performance evaluation with defensive-

---

[19] Herbert H. Meyer, Emanuel Kay, and John R. P. French, Jr., "Split Roles in Performance Appraisal," *Harvard Business Review*, Vol. 23, No. 1 (January 1965), p. 123. For a somewhat different view, see Harold Mayfield, "In Defense of Performance Appraisal," *Harvard Business Review*, Vol. 38, No. 2 (March 1960), pp. 81-87.

[20] "An Uneasy Look at Performance Appraisal," *Harvard Business Review*, Vol. 35, No. 3 (May 1957), p. 90. See also Spencer J. Hayden, "Getting Better Results from Post-Appraisal Interviews," *Personnel*, Vol. 31, No. 6 (May 1955), p. 542.

[21] Alvin F. Kindall and James Gatza, "Positive Program for Performance Appraisal," *Harvard Business Review*, Vol. 41, No. 6 (November 1963), p. 154.

ness, suspicion, and hostility.[22] They hope that the boss will recognize their merits, but fear that he will criticize them unfairly. Since many are primarily concerned with defending themselves, they resist the boss's criticisms and suggestions. Subordinates in this state of mind are hardly in a mood to "learn" from the interview. In fact, evidence suggests that subordinates tend to rate their own performance higher than do their bosses; as a consequence the interview turns out to be a deflating experience.[23] Criticism may result in lower performance not higher, particularly in the areas most criticized.[24]

Thus, the interview may seriously impair the supervisor-subordinate relationship by creating animosity and misunderstanding. To prevent ill-feeling many managers avoid unpleasant truths. And "evaluation often becomes a ritual devoid of real meaning. Executives report that they never know what their bosses want them to do," [25] where they really stand or what is required of them to get a promotion or salary increase.

Another explanation for the widespread resistance to conventional forms of evaluation interviews lies in certain assumptions that lie behind them: (1) People want to be told where they stand, and (2) if they are told, they can change for the better. Neither assumption is universally valid. Let us look at two examples:

> A liberal-arts college decided to rate all faculty members on a scale from 1 (drop from faculty) to 5 (deserves immediate promotion) and to reveal the results to each faculty member. The rating program was conducted by a joint faculty-student committee. A 65-year-old professor was given a 2 grade on the grounds that his teaching lacked luster and he was hard to understand. Thus, the professor's grade for a lifetime of devoted service to his college was a D! He was too old to change his ways, and in any event the college had not the slightest intention of dropping him a few years before his retirement. Still, the shock contributed to a heart attack he suffered shortly afterward. Some people don't really want to know where they stand, nor will the knowledge help them.

> The second case involves a laboratory division head who was brilliant technically, but suffered from shyness and insecurity in dealing with people. Would telling him of his failing improve his dealings with people? Of course not. Certainly it would not help him gain self-confidence. The only thing that might help him would be a form of psychotherapy much deeper than his superior could offer.

---

[22] For an interesting study of such reactions, see Kenneth E. Richards, "A New Concept of Performance Appraisal," *The Journal of Business,* Vol. 32, No. 3 (July 1959), pp. 229-243.

[23] Meyer, Kay, and French, *op. cit.,* p. 126; James W. Parker and others, "Rating Scale Content: III. Relationship Between Supervisory and Self-Ratings," *Personnel Psychology,* Vol. 12, No. 1 (Spring 1959), pp. 49-63.

[24] Meyer, Kay, and French, *op. cit.,* p. 126.

[25] William R. Dill, Thomas L. Hilton, and Walter R. Reitman, "How Aspiring Executives Promote Their Careers," *California Management Review,* Vol. 2, No. 4 (Summer 1960), p. 12. This point can be exaggerated, however. The evidence suggests that some appraisal is better than no appraisal. Where managers engage in regular appraisal interviews with their subordinates, the subordinates report they know better where they stand and superior-subordinate relations are significantly better. Walter R. Mahler, "Improving Coaching Skills," *Personnel Administration,* Vol. 27, No. 1 (January 1964), p. 28; and Kenneth E. Richards, "Performance Rating as a Supervisory Tool," *The Personnel Administrator* (January 1965), p. 7.

Obviously there is no simple answer to the question of whether an evaluation interview will be useful or what sort of interview should be used in a given situation. The choice depends directly on the personality of both the supervisor and the subordinate. Moreover, the supervisor should use the form of interview that he finds most comfortable. For instance, the supervisor who tries to use the nondirective interview with no understanding of the approach will simply give the subordinate the impression that he is two-faced, particularly if the nondirective approach is totally inconsistent with his normal pattern of supervision. In any event, the manager should recognize that the objectives of the interview vary from one person to another. For example:

1. Where the fault is difficult or impossible to correct, as in the two cases described above, there is no point in discussing it at all (unless the subordinate demands to know why he hasn't been promoted).

2. If a man has faults that are correctable, it may be better to let him bring them up himself when he sees fit. Since evaluation interviews are held periodically, there is no need for the supervisor to be disappointed if the subordinate doesn't give a perfect self-analysis during the first session. The important thing is that the subordinate make gradual progress in correcting his limitations where he can, and in accepting his limitations where he cannot overcome them.

3. In some cases an individual's performance may be so poor as to raise the possibility of his being discharged. Under such circumstances it is only fair that he be given warning, even though there is little chance of changing his behavior.

The appraisal interview is actually a form of coaching. So why formalize the process? After all the good manager recognizes that coaching should occur more frequently than once every six months; he holds the equivalent of an evaluation interview whenever he thinks a subordinate will profit from it, and he does not need to be prodded into conducting interviews at a special time. On the other hand, the poor manager will probably only go through the motions of a proper evaluation interview (which may do more harm than good) or perhaps ignore it altogether.

Thus, a company-wide policy requiring periodic evaluation interviews is most useful for the *average* supervisor, for it forces him to take time off from his duties, to think through how each of his subordinates has been progressing, and then to sit down with each man to talk over their long-range relationships.

Still, one fundamental objection remains: The conventional appraisal interview demands that the supervisor be a part-time psychiatrist. As the management development chief at Standard Oil of Ohio once asked: "Are we in the business of changing people or are we running a business? Are we interested in personalities or are we interested in on-the-job results?" [26]

---

[26] O. A. Ohmann, "Executive Appraisal and Counseling," *Michigan Business Review*, Vol. 9, No. 6 (November 1957), p. 21.

Designed to overcome the limitations of more traditional systems, *results-oriented appraisals* have been widely adopted by a number of companies. This new approach to appraisal is based on (1) quantitative, measurable (or at least concrete) performance goals (2) which are often set jointly by superior and subordinates. Instead of requiring the supervisor to rate his subordinates, under this approach each subordinate is requested to establish, for himself, short-term performance goals or targets, ways in which he can improve his own efficiency and that of his department. For example, cut idle machine time by 5 per cent, reduce scrap by 3 per cent, or install a new production line by January 30. Together the superior and the subordinate talk over what is required to meet these goals and to adjust them to make them consistent with goals of other subordinates or the organization as a whole. At the end of a set period (say, six months) they meet again to evaluate how well these goals have been met, to discuss what could be done better, and to set goals for the next period.

> This procedure gives the subordinate an opportunity to make his own evaluation of the operating results. When he is discussing results he is actually appraising himself and probably gaining some insight on how he might improve his own attitudes, methods, or behavior.[27]

Of course, there is always the possibility that the subordinate may set his targets too low or rate himself too highly. However, "most subordinates normally have an understandable wish to please their bosses and quite willingly adjust their targets or appraisals if the superior thinks they are unrealistic."[28]

The advantages of results-oriented appraisal over conventional appraisal are many.[29] Results-oriented appraisal provides each man a custom-made standard of evaluation based on the special characteristics of his own particular job. It emphasizes the *future*, which can be changed, rather than the *past*, which cannot. Though emphasizing forward planning it helps clarify responsibilities, organize the job, and iron out problems in advance. The job of the supervisor shifts from that of criticizing the subordinate to that of helping him improve his record.

Results-oriented appraisal is consistent with the psychological principle that people work better when they have definite goals which they must meet in specified periods. By providing feedback, it helps subordinates know where they stand and thus enhances learning.

---

[27] Ohmann, *op. cit.*, p. 24.

[28] McGregor, *op. cit.*, p. 91.

[29] For two studies which suggest that results-oriented appraisal may give superior results in practice than conventional appraisal, see Philip G. Hanson, Robert Merton, and Paul Rothaus, "The Fate of Role Stereotypes in Two Performance Appraisal Situations," *Personnel Psychology*, Vol. 16, No. 3 (Fall 1963), p. 269; and Meyer, Kay, and French, *op. cit.*

The emphasis on specific performance, rather than character traits, permits recognition for the nonconformist who obtains results by nonconventional means. In contrast to the "closed system" implied by traditional ratings according to which the subordinate is rated in terms of the supervisor's value system, results-oriented appraisal permits the subordinate to participate in setting his own goals. It gives him a more active role, increases his sense of control over his environment, and reduces his dependence on his boss.

Limitations

Despite the initial enthusiasm with which this new approach was greeted by a number of companies, experience suggests that results-oriented appraisals have a number of limitations and drawbacks.[30]

In the first place the theory that the subordinate sets goals by himself (or jointly with his boss) may in practice turn out to be illusory. It all depends on whether the nondirective approach, which is required for goal-setting by the subordinate, is consistent with the boss' ordinary management style. The boss who regularly consults with his subordinates finds this new approach to appraisal quite easy. Not so the boss who is decisive and directive and never takes time to listen.[31]

In any case, knowing that his boss is the one who hands out rewards, the typical subordinate may look anxiously for some indication of what the boss thinks are proper goals and once these become clear, quickly adopt them with "enthusiasm." Indeed, some subordinates might prefer that their boss indicate his wishes frankly from the start, instead of make them go through guessing games. Even at best any one subordinate can be given only limited freedom to set his own goals. After all, the various goals should be consistent with each other and it would make little sense were the sales department to try to raise sales by 10 per cent if manufacturing planned to increase its efforts by only half as much.

Results-oriented appraisals place heavy stress on measurable performance, and this may lead to all the problems which we previously discussed under "statistical controls" (see pp. 357-365). It leads subordinates to emphasize the measurable, such as production, at the expense of the unmeasurable, such as morale. For example, creative work, such as in engineering, personnel, or advertising, is often difficult to quantify, as is indeed most staff work. Because of this difficulty, quality may be sacrificed for sheer quantity.

> An engineering director set as a goal the enhancement of his laboratory's professional prestige, but since prestige is difficult to measure, he set as a performance target a certain number of papers to be read at professional meetings. And to fill this quota he "encouraged" individual subordinates to accept the writing of papers as goals for themselves. The result, as might be expected, was

---

[30] See, for example, Charles Coleman, "Avoid the Pitfalls of Results Oriented Appraisals," *Personnel*, Vol. 42, No. 6 (November 1965), pp. 34-38.

[31] Meyer, Kay, and French, *op. cit.*, p. 126.

that the required number of papers were read, but they were of such poor quality as to lower rather than raise the laboratory's prestige. (The story might have been less tragic, however, if the director's subordinates had felt really free to reject their assignments.)

Overemphasis on measurable factors may also encourage the covering up of poor performance, actual falsification of data, or the setting of low goals. Since each individual is anxious to make himself look good, cooperation is discouraged. In addition, to the extent a manager's over-all performance is evaluated on the basis of a relatively few measures, there is always the risk that accidental factors may distort the picture. A good manager with bad luck may well look worse than a bad manager with good luck.

In any case, a manager's apparent "performance" is a function of his initial goals. If his goals are set low it is easy to look good. And so the trick (where results appraisal is working poorly) is to set a low initial goal and sell one's boss that this goal is really very hard.

We can conclude, then, that results-oriented appraisals are a useful management tool, but if too much emphasis is placed on measurable results, the technique may boomerang. Used with discretion, goal-setting provides a framework within which subordinates are better motivated and receive more specific cues about how they stand and what they should do to improve themselves. Goal-setting by subordinates is more effective than goal-setting by the boss, but only if the boss uses participative techniques on a day-to-day basis. Goal-setting by the boss may be useful even in the absence of participation.

For Promotions
and Salary Increases?

Should results-oriented appraisals be used as a means for determining who should get promotions or salary increases? Here the experts disagree. It can be argued that, even at best, results-oriented appraisal measures only how a man has done on a specific job. It provides little indication of how he might do on other jobs. For example, a man who does well under close supervision may do poorly under general supervision. In addition, managers shouldn't be promoted to higher-level jobs purely on the basis of performance at lower levels. As a consequence, some companies isolate any evaluation of a man's potential almost completely from an evaluation of performance on his present job. They use different forms for each purpose, with the form used to measure potential putting greater emphasis on traits. Often the evaluation of potential is not even shown the subordinate. Hopefully, this separation of the two forms of evaluation reduces the unsatisfactory compromise which results when evaluation is used for a variety of purposes. And it avoids "undue emphasis ... on 'upward-and-onward' possibilities to the neglect of improvement in present responsibilities." [32]

---

[32] Earl Brooks, "An Experimental Program for Executive Development," *ILR Research,* Vol. 1, No. 2 (March 1955), p. 12; see also Richards, *op. cit.,* p. 529.

Results-oriented appraisals may not be appropriate for determining who should get a salary increase either, for they make it difficult to compare one man against another. Yet any salary program which seeks to pay higher salaries to men who do better work must make such comparisons. And so a separate procedure may have to be established for salary purposes. Thus, a company may have as many as three appraisal programs, each for a different purpose: for training, for promotions, and for salary increases.

But, having three different procedures may lead to chaos, particularly if the ratings are inconsistent with each other. "Often men find themselves appraised for development by one method and for rewards by a second. The most meaningful appraisal, the one that will prove most effective in inducing developmental action, is the one that 'pays off.'" [33]

The dilemma is not an easy one to solve. Certainly salary increases should be consistent with appraisals, whether or not the latter are based on subordinate-set goals. How well these goals are met should be a major consideration in determining whether a subordinate should get a salary increase, though other factors such as seniority, the company's financial position, and salaries paid by competitors might also be taken into account.

Promotion to a different position involves another matter. A man's past performance on his present job may be only an imperfect indicator of his potential for a new job. Other factors, such as test results and even personality traits, are also relevant.

CONCLUSION

Performance evaluation serves two important purposes in the management-development program: (1) It provides a systematic, objective means for selecting those who should be promoted, and (2) it provides a tool to help managers train subordinates (as well as to help subordinates to improve themselves). In addition, it can play an important role in a salary-administration program. Yet, as we have seen, objectives often conflict. It is largely because of this conflict that the whole field of performance appraisal has become so controversial and has given rise to so many clashing schools of thought.

In theory, selection, salary administration, and training can be combined into one attractive management-development package. Ratings can be used by higher management for selection purposes and also as a form of feedback, through the evaluation interview, to inform subordinates on where they stand and to suggest ways in which they can do better. Unfortunately, the information management receives from an evaluation program designed primarily to permit an objective comparison of a large group of employees is seldom useful in the coaching of individuals. Many observers feel it wise to separate the selection and training aspects of evaluation altogether.

---

[33] Walter Mahler and Guyot Frazier, "Appraisal of Executive Performance: The 'Achiles Heel' of Managerial Development," *Personnel*, Vol. 31, No. 5 (March 1955), p. 432.

Both superior and subordinate, in many organizations, have come to dread the day when evaluation interviews must be held: The subordinate is afraid of being criticized unjustly and the superior is apprehensive about provoking the subordinate's antagonism. Because of the general inadequacy of traditional appraisals many companies have switched to results-oriented appraisals. Results-oriented appraisals are hardly the perfect solution to the problem, yet their emphasis on specific goals makes evaluation more objective, and subordinate involvement in goal-setting tends to make "goals more realistic and more palatable to the individual. . . . No small accomplishment." [34]

But other objectives besides development must be considered. The organization also needs some information which will help in determining promotions. "The vital test of appraisal is whether or not it allows the right men to rise and prevents others from doing so." [35] Certainly no one approach can answer all the problems, and the wise organization will proceed flexibly, without becoming wed too closely to any one method.

As far as development itself is concerned, appraisals are only part of the picture. We now turn to management training.

PROBLEM

ROBERT JACKSON

Robert Jackson, age 25, has been with the advertising department, of which you are manager, for three years as a copywriter. His job is to design advertisements for use in newspapers and magazines. He must work closely with the girls in the art department, with the members of the sales department, and with the Vice President, Sales and Promotion, who is in charge of the whole division.

Bob is an extremely enthusiastic worker with lots of good ideas. When you hired him you had great hopes that he would advance rapidly. He still can, but he has considerable trouble in dealing with people. He is too impatient with the girls in the art department, seems to fidget whenever he notices one of them taking a break, and is constantly pushing them to finish his work. In dealing with the people in the sales department, he makes it perfectly clear that his ideas are always best. During a recent conference, when the Vice President was thinking out loud, Bob shouted out his own answer, and cut the VP off. It was a good answer, and the VP didn't mind, but some of the other people thought Bob had behaved badly. You are quite concerned about the animosity he is creating in your department.

A new company policy requires that each employee have an evaluation interview every six months. There are no performance-rating forms. This is Jackson's first evaluation under the new policy.

1. What should your strategy be in handling the evaluation interview with Jackson?
2. Role-play this interview. Jackson is quite sure that his ideas are good and will press for a substantial pay increase.

---

[34] William G. Rothstein, "Executive Appraisal Programs," *ILR Research,* Vol. 8, No. 2 (1962), p. 17.
[35] Odiorne, *op. cit.,* p. 307.

Management Training

Management training, an essential part of management development, supplements other developmental techniques such as job rotation and performance evaluation. Training is necessary to help promotable managers prepare for advancement, to assist managers having difficulties with their present job, to prevent managerial obsolescence, and to build morale in lower-level managers by demonstrating top management's interest in them.

Although formal management training is generally conducted by the personnel department or a special training unit, every leader engages in informal training, whether he knows it or not. The people who participate in management training range from a top executive studying Plato at an Ivy League college to a general foreman explaining to a new foreman how to fill in a time sheet. There are tremendous differences in the subject matter, materials, and teaching personnel used in these training programs. Among the most common types of formal training today are the following (these types may easily overlap):

1. Technical training regarding the specific technology of the firm.
2. Functional training, such as how to sell or how to engage in production control.
3. Education regarding environmental background to give an understanding of the economic, political, legal, and social trends in society which have an impact on business.
4. Indoctrination: providing managers with a common attitude, approach, or spirit (the kind of training which makes a good Marine) as well as disseminating rules and standard operating procedures.
5. Human-relations training: how to improve interpersonal relations within the organization (in the past the emphasis has usually been placed on how to deal with one's subordinates, but today such training is increasingly concerned with dealing with one's peers and bosses as well).
6. Decision-making training (often involving so-called business games): how to assess complex variables and to draw implications for action from them.

In practice many good training programs combine several forms of training. And yet, some programs are weak because management has not given sufficient thought to deciding what objectives it seeks to accomplish.

This chapter will be concerned primarily with training designed to develop general management attitudes and skills. We shall say relatively little about technical, environmental, or functional training, though our discussion in Chapter 21 is highly relevant to these. We shall first seek to provide some insights into how training may go wrong by discussing forms of *ineffective* training and organizational barriers to training. With this background we will proceed to look at the general conditions for effective training, then at some specific training techniques and at who should engage in training; finally we will consider how a company can evaluate whether its training program is worth the time and money spent on it.

ORGANIZATIONAL BARRIERS TO EFFECTIVE TRAINING

The influence of the organization—in particular, the attitude of top management—is crucial to the success of a training program. In many companies management regards training as of only marginal importance and consequently gives it only token support. Many managers feel that training is purely a staff function for which line has no responsibility, or they institute training programs merely because it is the fashionable thing to do. Yet attitudes of this sort are quickly discerned by the trainees themselves, who may begin to feel that training is a waste of time and resent being held as a captive audience in a training class. As long as management thinks of the training process as something apart from everyday activities on the job, the chances that training will affect behavior are slim indeed.

Few rigorous attempts have been made to evaluate the effectiveness of training (later, we shall discover why such evaluation is so difficult). However, two studies stand out.[1] In each case, just before the managers entered training, their subordinates were asked questions on how well they thought their bosses did their job. After the managers had finished their training, the subordinates were asked the same question again. The purpose, of course, was to discover whether the training had made any difference in behavior that was observable by the subordinates.

The results? Very disappointing. In one case, the subordinates reported that their bosses' behavior had changed for the better immediately after training was completed, but that within two years it had reverted to its pretraining

---

[1] Edwin A. Fleishman, Edwin F. Harris, and Harold E. Burtt, *Leadership and Supervision in Industry: An Evaluation of a Supervisory Training Program* (Columbus: Bureau of Educational Research, the Ohio State University, Monograph No. 33, 1955); T. Hariton, *Conditions Influencing the Effects of Training Foremen in Human Relations Principles*, reported in Norman R. F. Maier, *Principles of Human Relations* (New York: Wiley, 1952), pp. 184-192.

level. The second case involved two divisions of the Detroit Edison Company. One division showed a gain, the other a loss.

How can we explain these ambiguous results? The training programs themselves may have been at fault, but a better explanation is probably that what the trainees learned in class just wasn't useful on the job. Instead, it conflicted with the behavior expected of them by their bosses and even by their subordinates. If training is to be worthwhile, trainees must feel free to apply what they learn and to change their behavior if they wish. When the organizational climate denies this freedom, subordinates are more likely to imitate their boss than to follow what they have learned in class.

Where higher management does not *in practice* support the objectives of training, managers feel uncertain about whether to follow the theory of the course or the example of their boss. As a result, they appear vacillating and inconsistent. For instance, subordinates might well become confused if their hard-as-nails supervisor started to listen to them before bawling them out. Naturally, subordinates, uncertain of whether their boss is going to be "tough" or practice "human relations," find this unpredictability highly frustrating. Under the circumstances, it may be a blessing that so many supervisors leave their training in the classroom and never let it interfere with their daily behavior.

In the establishment of a training course, there is often little effort to find out why managers behave as they do or to consider whether company policy or top management behavior may be the cause of whatever seems wrong; instead training is viewed as a magic cure for all ills. Managers often talk as though it were only their subordinates' behavior that needed changing, not their own. They fail to recognize that their own behavior affects that of their subordinates, and that it is difficult to change one without changing the other.[2] No wonder many a student has told us after a training class, "I wish my boss would take this stuff. He is the one who needs it."

Too often, training programs are concerned only with dealing with subordinates; yet to the trainee his biggest problem may be dealing with the boss. Foreman training, for example, may "increase the foreman's internal tension, his feelings of hostility toward management, and his sense of separateness in the organization, because it never comes to grips with his true predicament—the fact of his being a man in the middle."[3]

Only limited results can be obtained by training lower management alone, particularly if the training is of the typical classroom variety. Possibly the best way to train a foreman is to train his general foreman first; but it is difficult to train the general foreman until the superintendent has been trained, or at

---

[2] For an excellent discussion of this point, see Mason Haire, "Some Issues of Industrial Training," *The Journal of Social Issues,* Vol. 4, No. 3 (Summer 1948), pp. 44-45.

[3] Chris Argyris, "Employee Apathy and Non-Involvement—the House that Management Built," *Personnel,* Vol. 38, No. 2 (July 1961), p. 11. For a good example, see A. J. M. Sykes, "The Effects of a Supervisory Training Course in Changing Supervisors' Perceptions and Expectations of the Role of Management," *Human Relations,* Vol. 15, No. 3 (August 1962), pp. 227-243.

least induced, to behave in a manner that permits those on lower levels to try out new techniques.

Does this mean that the only way to start is with the Board of Directors? Perhaps. The Board of Directors of one of the nation's largest companies established a Human Relations Committee, whose job, in effect, is to train top management. Top management then trained the next lower level of management and so on down the line in a carefully planned program until finally the general foreman trained the foremen.

As we shall see, there are very definite advantages in having every boss train the people he supervises. Yet there are managers, otherwise competent, who are just poor trainers. Further, if all training is done by the boss there is a real danger that the organization will perpetuate its past mistakes and allow little room for new ideas. Training conducted by line personnel is not the complete solution to the problem.

More important than the person who conducts the training is the organizational atmosphere in which it occurs. For training to be effective this atmosphere must permit the manager to experiment with new patterns of behavior and to learn through making mistakes.

FORMS OF INEFFECTIVE TRAINING

As an illustration of what not to do in the training field we shall describe five typical forms of poorly conceived training programs. These forms are not meant to be mutually exclusive. In fact, any given program may include several or even all of them. As you read the next few pages, ask yourself: (1) Why does management offer such programs? And (2) what impact are they likely to have on trainees?

Gimmicks and froth. Training in some companies is on the level of the after-dinner speech and the booster talk. "It substitutes good intentions and wheezes for intelligent reflection about experience."[4] Instructors come armed with attention-getting jokes, cute parlor tricks, and gadgets, and look upon training as a form of salesmanship. They regard their lectures as the equivalent of the inspirational sermon or the coach's last-minute spiel before sending the boys out onto the field.

As for content, programs of this sort often consist of folksy platitudes ("You can catch more flies with honey than you can with vinegar"), oversimplified psychology ("The single, most important thing a worker wants is recognition"), and a list of desirable traits ("A supervisor should be loyal, ambitious," etc.).

Frequently the organization itself is responsible for the superficiality of the training. If top management tolerates training only as a frill, the training staff tends to stick to safe, inspirational, noncontroversial generalities.

---

[4] Fritz Roethlisberger, "Training Supervisors in Human Relations," *Harvard Business Review*, Vol. 29, No. 5 (October 1951), p. 51.

"Bringing the boys into line." Sometimes top management really expects training to improve supervisory behavior. One of the authors was once asked by a personnel director to set up a training program because:

> We know that front-line supervision isn't giving us the loyalty and enthusiasm it should. We want them to feel part of the organization. We know that lots of times they get policy from our level which they only go through the motions of carrying out, or they tell their men, "That's what top management wants." We want them to understand that they are part of the team.[5]

Note that the trainer was expected to build up enthusiasm and loyalty. There was no suggestion that top management had any responsibility for the existing situation or that perhaps top management itself should change.

Abstract theory. A third form of ineffective training is devoted to abstract theories and rules of behavior, often dressed up in psychological garb. Yet supervisors tend to think in terms of their own problems rather than in terms of generalized theories. Indeed, if the training is to be effective, the primary emphasis should be on the trainees' own problems. Often the theories presented seem to the trainees as oversimplified or difficult to apply. As one supervisor put it, "It's all theory—bookstuff. It has nothing to do with supervision."

There is evidence that when managers are asked how they handle subordinates, it is the poor ones who answer in terms of general principles like "treat everyone equal." The good manager usually gives specific examples from his own experience. The poor manager talks a good game; the good one plays it.

The charm school. Many a training course preaches that the secret of supervisory success lies in dressing up one's personality, in "making friends and influencing people." Yet the formula "be nice—show interest in the other person" is too superficial to be of much help in industrial life. A veneer of "niceness" may actually do more harm than good, since most employees easily see through it.

The pat program. Some instructors follow a rigid outline which they refuse to vary to meet the particular needs of the trainee. Their communication is mainly one-way: *to* the group. To capture class interest, they use a host of audio-visual aids, such as movies, slides, and other gimmicks. They invite participation only for the purpose of extracting the "right answer." They are careful to keep the class "in control," for if it wandered off the carefully prepared path, they would be lost. Some trainers are not permitted to draw up their own program, but must follow a "canned" outline prepared by an outside consultant or by top management.

These five forms of training are much alike. Their common failing is that they emphasize generalities and praiseworthy maxims but fail to help trainees

---

[5] As it developed the real reason for the foremen's lack of loyalty was fear of a substantial cut-back in production which would lead to many of them being laid off.

to handle their daily problems. Any effective program of training must start from the felt needs of the trainees themselves.

With the foregoing introduction, let us ask what are the positive conditions that are required so that training results in behavior changes?

1. The training program must be addressed to the trainees' own problems and must be realistically adapted to their own needs. There is little point in discussing union grievance procedure with managers who never have any contact with a union. One way to insure that a training program is built about problems as the trainees see them is to invite them to participate in setting up the program (or at least to survey their felt needs before launching the program).

2. The people who take part in the program must feel a need for training; they must be dissatisfied with their old ways and willing to unfreeze their attitudes (see p. 298).[6] A wise personnel director once told us that he never starts a training program until the people to be trained (as well as their superiors) are anxious for the program and sure of the problems they want to discuss. If the men are forced into a training program against their will, they may well resent and sabotage it.

There is some evidence that newly promoted men react better to training programs than those who have been on the job for a long time. The oldtimers feel that they know all the answers—after all they have had lots of experience. But the new men are hunting desperately for help. With oldtimers it is sometimes desirable to utilize feedback techniques as a form of "shock treatment" to make them aware of their inadequacies and instill in them a "conviction of sin."[7]

3. A training program should provide a moratorium from the pressures of immediate problems. It should get participants away from their regular environment and give them time to reassess their present behavior and to examine alternatives. For this reason full-time training away from the job is often more effective than training which takes place an hour or two at a time.

4. Trainees must be encouraged to work through to their own conclusions. The only way they can understand a problem is to think it out for themselves. They suspect the fast talker who tries to trick them into accepting ready-made

---

[6] There is a danger, however, that the program may become *too* realistic and, through taking up the immediate, short-run problems, become bogged down in detail.

[7] John M. Pfiffner, *The Supervision of Personnel*, 2d ed. (Englewood Cliffs: Prentice-Hall, 1958), pp. 462-463. Some companies start their training program with an employee attitude survey (see p. 354). Using the survey findings as a springboard for discussion, they seek to induce managers to look for ways of correcting the inadequacies which the survey has disclosed. For a good example of how this technique may be used, see Floyd C. Mann, "Studying and Creating Change," in Conrad M. Arensberg, *et al.*, eds., *Research in Industrial Human Relations* (New York: Harper & Row, 1957), pp. 146-167.

solutions. As Robert Burns warns, "He who is convinced against his will, remains of the same opinion still."

A trainee can memorize what the instructor thinks is right, but this does not make it his own. Particularly in the area of emotional (as distinct from conceptual) learning, people learn primarily through experience, not through passive listening. Real learning is "gut" learning. If there is to be a carryover from the classroom to the office or shop, it is essential that the trainee *feel* through the problem, experiencing and overcoming its difficulties as he works toward a solution. We emphasize the word *feel* because many of the problems in this area are emotional, involving the ways managers see, and feel about, the people and events that affect them deeply.

5. Human-relations training is often more effective when it is conducted in groups, for most attitudes in this area are group-conditioned. For instance, a foreman will be less likely to consult with his steward if his fellow foremen feel that to do so is being soft.

We have already discovered that group discussion at times provides an effective means of changing attitudes. When group norms are involved, it is easier to change members as a group than it is to change individuals. When a group of managers with common problems decides to change together, no individual has the unsettling feeling of being a pioneer, of being different. The group provides its members with emotional support and they learn from each other.

Typically, attitudes and behavior begin to change only when the trainees recognize that they all have problems in common that they have not been able to handle satisfactorily (for instance, handling an unreasonable steward and living under a tight budget). It helps if they can work off their resentment—let off steam—a bit before moving on to the next step. The opportunity to share one another's burdens reduces frustration and makes them more willing to consider new approaches.

6. A training program is more effective if it makes allowances for the difficulties of giving up old ways of doing things. Understandably, people feel more secure with old patterns of behavior that have proven reasonably satisfactory in the past. And they resent suggestions that their performance is unsatisfactory. Similarly, they object to outsiders telling them what to do; they feel that their long experience makes them more qualified than any trainer.

One approach to handling this problem is to encourage trainees to consider new practices without attacking the old ways directly—that is, to ask them to consider a range of alternatives without committing themselves to any particular one. They should be encouraged to try new ways tentatively. Only after they have tested the new procedures on an experimental basis can they be expected to change their behavior permanently.

Even after the training program has been completed it is often useful to reconvene the training group to permit participants to discuss the problems they have faced in trying to implement new ideas on the job. Otherwise trainees may try these new ideas out for a while but abandon them just as soon as the going gets difficult. The reconvened training group provides the trainee support in carrying change into practice.

7. For training to mean anything it must move from the intellectual to the practical level. It must provide skills that are useful to the manager in solving what he sees as his own problems on his job—and skills that higher management will permit him to practice.

To summarize much of the above: Effective training which changes attitudes should run through three stages.[8] In the *unfreezing* stage trainees learn to be dissatisfied with their old patterns of behavior. In the *change* stage they experiment with new patterns in a safe environment away from everyday pressures. And in the *refreezing* stage they adopt these forms for practical use and carry them out on the job.

TRAINING TECHNIQUES

Now let us examine some of the more common training techniques. These techniques are designed for many purposes and few, if any, completely satisfy the criteria listed above. And yet, because of the wide variety of training objectives and the great range of sophistication among trainers and trainees, no one form of training is uniformly superior to another. The most we can do is try to find the situations for which each form is most appropriate.

Lectures

Lecturing, the traditional form of teaching, gives the trainer the greatest degree of control over the training situation. It enables him to present the material exactly as he wants to, with little danger that anyone will talk back.

But lecturing has obvious limitations as a training technique. As every student realizes, many lecturers are boring and some are entertaining without being instructive. The instructor who can keep his class constantly stimulated through the sheer force of his ideas—and who is powerful enough to effect a change in the behavior of those who listen to him—is rare indeed. A lecture is unlikely to change fixed attitudes and certainly is of little help in developing skills. It is useful chiefly in presenting background facts—for example, the meaning of a new contract.

Guided Conferences

In order to escape the limitations of straight lecturing, many companies have turned to the "guided-discussion" type of conference in their training programs. In a guided conference the instructor knows in advance what infor-

---

[8] Indeed, the problems connected with human-relations training have much in common with those involved in introducing change generally (see Chapter 13).

mation or procedures he wants to bring out. The training sessions are similar to small, discussion-type university classes.

These conferences have certain limitations, however. Unless the discussion is directed to the felt needs of the participants, they may well feel that the whole session is useless. In a university class, the professor is assumed to be an expert. Not so in the office or plant.

> Practically never do the trainers have more experience at being foremen than the trainees. The contrary is usually true, to the extent that very few trainers have ever been foremen. I think we can say that the world's foremost experts on the problems of being foremen are foremen.[9]

The conference leader should be careful not to cram things down people's throats, things that they may regurgitate in class but won't take back to work. Too often, training directors deserve such criticisms as these:

> They do not accomplish what they are supposed to do, that is, to help supervisors with the human aspects of their jobs. Many of them raise "loaded" questions, give facile answers that cannot be applied to concrete situations, and discuss unreal situations, situations that have never existed except in someone's imagination. In many of these the conference leader is armed with points the trainees are supposed to make. He is allowed so much time to draw these points out, and should the trainees fail to respond, he is instructed to draw them out himself. . . . What so often astonishes me is how docilely supervisors go through these verbal hoops and how readily they learn the proper verbal response to please the instructor.[10]

There is a constant danger in a guided conference that the group will become overdependent on the leader. Expecting him to give *the* answer to their problems, the trainees are reluctant to go through the hard work of puzzling out their own answers. The conference may easily degenerate into a session in which the leader asks questions and the trainees give pat answers. In short, guided conferences can induce genuine learning only when the leader concentrates on asking questions and lets the group provide its own answers.

The Case Method

This technique, which has been popularized by the Harvard Business School,[11] is one of the commonest forms of training. (Many of the cases that we present at the end of chapters are typical of those used in this method.)

The success of the case method depends directly on the ability of the instructor. Under an unskilled instructor, the trainees tend to look upon the case as a puzzle that can be solved by finding the right answer. They make value judgments about each character and try to identify the "villain." Often, too,

---

[9] James R. Surface, "Resistance to Training," *Harvard Business Review,* Vol. 32, No. 2 (March 1954), p. 301.

[10] Roethlisberger, *op. cit.*, p. 47. One training director told us, "Training makes the students accomplished actors. They sound great in class, but don't change on the job."

[11] See Kenneth R. Andrews, *The Case Method of Teaching Human Relations and Administration* (Cambridge: Harvard University Press, 1953).

a poorly conducted discussion will degenerate into a rambling session from which the participants derive no learning. Or else the leader may mastermind the session, leading participants to accept his own conclusions or even ramming the lessons down their throats.

A skillful instructor, on the other hand, emphasizes useful ways of thinking about human relations rather than ways of reaching specific conclusions.[12] He puts his stress on:

1. Increasing the trainee's power of observation, helping him to ask better questions and to look for a broader range of problems (for instance, not "Who is to blame?" but "Why did it happen?").
2. Encouraging the group to look for more and more implications in each solution, keeping them away from pat analyses and oversimplified solutions.
3. Helping the student to discard vague principles, such as "Be tactful" or "Apply the golden rule," and urging him to consider not only *what* to do but *how* to do it.
4. Encouraging the trainees to test their solutions against reality.

In the university classroom the case method introduces a note of realism that is absent from abstract, theoretical discussions. For management trainees in industry, however, cases are always less realistic than the actual problems that arise on the job. A well-chosen case may promote *objective* discussion, but the lack of *emotional* involvement may make it difficult to effect any basic change in the behavior and attitudes of the trainees. After all, human-relations training is more concerned with developing skills and self-insight than with providing intellectually satisfying solutions.

> Executives have been observed to analyze beautifully and verbally solve a case that focuses on "understanding the other person" and five minutes later show little or no ability to use this knowledge in a hot argument with the man across the table.[13]

Simulation

By simulation is meant a broad range of techniques in which trainees act out samples of real business behavior in order to get practice in making decisions, or in working together as a group, or both. It involves learning through doing rather than through memorizing principles. In effect, it is a form of vestibule training. Since it is more realistic than the case method it may lead to greater involvement.

The *management game* is one form of simulation now popular with many

---

[12] For a description of how a case might be presented to a group of foremen, see A. Zaleznik, *Foreman Training in a Growing Enterprise* (Boston: Harvard University, Graduate School of Business Administration, 1951), pp. 227-30. Andrews, ed., *op. cit.*, gives several examples of the case method in the university classroom.

[13] Chris Argyris, *Personality and Organization* (New York: Harper & Row, 1957), p. 221.

companies.[14] Typically it involves several teams, each of which is given a "firm" to operate for a number of "periods." In each period each team must make decisions on such matters as what prices to set, how much to produce, how much to spend on advertising and on development, how much to invest, how much of an inventory to maintain, and so forth. Since the teams are competing with each other, each firm's decisions will affect the results of all the other firms. All the firms' decisions are fed into a computer which is programed to behave somewhat like a real market. At the end of each period the computer reports back how well each firm has done. This report provides the data needed for the next period of play. The winner, of course, is the firm which has accumulated the largest profit by the end of the game. Often the game ends in a postmortem in which the participants analyze their mistakes and attempt to generalize from their experience.

What do participants learn from such games? Primarily how to make better decisions, to select and analyze relevant data, and to choose from among alternatives. Most management games are concerned with the external environment of business, particularly marketing, and the aspects of it which can be quantified. Though participants gain some experience in working together making decisions, such games provide training chiefly in the making of quantitative decisions rather than in the implementing of them. They provide little insight into problems connected with organizational structure or personnel management.

Such games often generate a great deal of player enthusiasm. There is still a good deal of doubt, however, about the extent of carryover from the game to the job.

The *in-basket* technique is a form of simulation which permits emphasis on internal as well as external problems.[15] A typical in-basket exercise might be as follows:

> An "executive" (the trainee) is catapulted into a new job on the sudden death of predecessor. His secretary presents him with an in-basket containing a number of letters, memos, and notes of phone conversations—all accumulated over the last few days. A host of urgent problems face him, such as a union grievance (as well as poorly written proposed reply drafted by a subordinate line manager), a complaint from an important customer, and a sudden supervisory vacancy for which there are three obvious candidates.

The trainee is given a short period of time to deal with these problems, either by drafting a reply at once or getting further information. Once each trainee has handled his own in-basket, he meets with other trainees who have handled identical in-baskets to discuss the logic behind how they handled them.

---

[14] See Joel M. Kibbee, and others, *Management Games: A New Technique for Management Development* (New York: Reinhold, 1961); G. R. Adlinger, "Business Games—Play One," *Harvard Business Review*, Vol. 36, No. 2 (March 1958), pp. 115-125; and Alfred G. Dale and Charles G. Klasson, "Executive Development in Small Business," *California Management Review*, Vol. 6, No. 2 (Winter 1963), pp. 55-61.

[15] For a good example of how the in-basket technique may be used, see Lewis B. Ward, "The Use of Simulation in Business Problems," *Management Record*, Vol. 22 (June 1960), pp. 30-33.

This technique provides experience both in making decisions and in implementing them. It differs from the business game in that there is no feedback on how well the decision "worked."

Role-playing is a form of simulation which emphasizes human-relations problems. Parts are assigned to students to act out as they would in real life.[16] It differs from ordinary drama in that the actors are given no lines to memorize; rather, they must improvise as they go along. (For examples of cases susceptible to role-playing, see pp. 394, 396, 567.)

Among the advantages of role-playing are these:

1. It helps participants to appreciate other points of view, as, for example, when a foreman plays the role of a union steward.

2. It helps trainees to experience a situation emotionally.

3. It makes trainees more self-conscious and analytical of their behavior than they would be in real life.

4. It permits trainees to show imagination and daring in devising solutions, since they are not playing for "keeps." No harm is done if they make a mistake.

Even the trainees who merely observe a role-playing session profit from observing the mistakes of others. Certainly this is a highly dramatic technique for arousing interest and stimulating class participation.

Role-playing is far more fruitful when it is followed by class discussion. Before the session starts, the trainer may suggest crucial areas for the students to observe and then use these areas as a framework for the subsequent discussion.

Other forms of simulation may also be utilized. Individuals may be given roles, such as plant manager, sales manager, purchasing agent, and comptroller—and information about their jobs which these individuals might normally have. Then several emergencies are assumed to occur—for instance, a large rush order and a major equipment breakdown—and the trainees are required to solve the problems. Such simulation provides training in both decision-making and human relations, and after each "period" the participants can profitably hold a postmortem about how they handled their problems.[17]

---

[16] This technique was first popularized by J. L. Moreno, *Who Shall Survive* (New York: Beacon House, 1953), as a technique for inducing mentally ill patients to act out their emotional problems. An outstanding guide to the use of role-playing in industry is Norman R. F. Maier, Allen R. Solem, and Ayesha A. Maier, *Supervisory and Executive Development: A Manual for Role Playing* (New York: Wiley, 1957). See also Raymond J. Corsini, Malcolm E. Shaw, and Robert W. Blake, *Role Playing in Business and Industry* (Glencoe: Free Press, 1961). A variant of role-playing is the skit, in which a few participants present a situation to the class, which then discusses it as in the case method.

[17] See for example, P. Hesseling, "Using a Communication Exercise for Training Managers," *British Journal of Industrial Relations,* Vol. 3, No. 1 (March 1965), p. 76. For programs of this sort used to train prospective top management of a new plant, see John H. Wakeley and Malcolm E. Shaw, "Management Training—An Integrated Approach," *Training Directors Journal,* Vol. 19, No. 7 (July 1965), pp. 2-14.

T-Group Training

T-group training (the "T" stands for training) is also known as sensitivity training, laboratory training, and executive action.[18] Regardless of the name it goes by, the technique has its strong supporters and strong detractors. For some it is almost a religion; others see it as a quack nostrum. Though dating back to the 1940's, this form of training has been used widely in industry only recently. By now it has been utilized for top management training by such corporate giants as AT&T, General Motors, Esso Standard, and Westinghouse—and extensively by the federal government and the American Management Association.

T-group training differs from the kinds of training previously discussed in that it is concerned with the real, not simulated, problems existing within the training group itself, not in the organization outside or in some hypothetical case. Rather than just provide skills and intellectual understanding, it seeks to change underlying attitudes and thus behavior on the job.

Although individual trainers may differ in emphasis, T-group training can be used to help participants:

1. learn more about themselves, especially their own weaknesses and emotions,
2. develop insights into how they react to others and also how others react to them,
3. discover how groups work and how to diagnose human-relations problems,
4. find out how to behave more effectively in interpersonal relations and, in particular, how to manage people through means other than power, and finally,
5. develop more open, "authentic" relations among people in which feelings are discussed openly.

T-group training is often called "laboratory training" because T-groups are, in effect, laboratories in which people experiment on themselves and generate data for their own discussions. T-groups are really small discussion groups with no set leader. (The trainer merely raises questions and provides occasional comments.) Usually the groups are totally unstructured; they have no set task or agenda except for a strong focus on the feelings and mutual impact of the participants.[19] Learning takes place through analyzing one's emotions rather than intellectually through logic. The group talks about what seems important at the moment. It is felt that the lack of structure will motivate peo-

---

[18] For a popular review, see Spencer Klaw, "Two Weeks in a T-Group," *Fortune*, Vol. 64, No. 2 (August 1961), pp. 114-117. For more extensive reports, see Leland P. Bradford, Jack R. Gibb, and Kenneth Benne, *T-Group Theory and Laboratory Method: Innovation in Re-education* (New York: Wiley, 1964); Warren G. Bennis and Edgar Schein, eds., *Human Relations Laboratory Training: Theory and Practice* (New York: Wiley, 1965); and Warren G. Bennis and Edgar Schein, *Personnel and Organizational Change through Group Methods: The Laboratory Approach* (New York: Wiley, 1965).

[19] Most forms of T-group training are supplemented by lectures, which provide participants with suggestions for what to look for in their own groups, as well as, often, by simulated problems to provide further material for discussion.

ple to bring their feelings out in the open where they can be analyzed and dealt with in a more rational fashion. An example may illustrate how such groups operate.

> At one early meeting, in a recent workshop, one executive got up from his chair and remarked to the stunned group: "I don't think this discussion is getting anywhere! I move that we appoint a committee to set up an agenda and report back their recommendations. Maybe this way we'll get something done. Are there any *serious* objections?" No one said anything. "All right, then, who would like to be part of this committee?" Four men raised their hands. The five left for an adjacent room.
>
> During their absence, those remaining seemed infuriated. Their displeasure toward the five who had left was obvious. When someone asked why no one had objected, he was told there was no point "in getting killed by a steam roller."
>
> The "secessionists" returned after a few minutes. When asked how they thought the group would respond to their recommendations, they felt sure there would be great interest in what they had to say. The trainer asked for a show of hands. The overwhelming majority was interested in neither the report nor its recommendations.
>
> The rest of the session was spent in helping the five see what had happened. Much was said about authoritarian attitudes, "talking down," lack of respect for the integrity of the group, and aggressive, irritating mannerisms. A rude shock was followed by a slow awakening.[20]

In a well-conducted T-group, the trainees in effect train one another, though the trainer helps by asking a few skillful questions that the group may purposely (but perhaps unconsciously) have been ignoring. The few instances in which he intervenes in the discussion may make the crucial difference between a rambling bull session and a genuine learning experience.[21]

T-groups go through periods of shock, frustration, and hostility, but hopefully all these stages lead to understanding. Indeed, T-groups make much use of feedback techniques, such as evaluation forms filled out by participants, process observers, and playbacks of tape recordings of critical sessions. All this is to help the participants learn more about their own behavior and to test out new forms of behavior.

Effective T-groups go through the three stages discussed in the early part of this chapter: unfreezing, in which the participant develops, often through shock, a sense of dissatisfaction with his present behavior; change, in which he experiments with new behavior; and refreezing, in which he develops an internalized commitment to a new approach.

Though all T-group training generally takes the same over-all form, T-group

---

[20] Robert Tannenbaum, Verne Kallejian, and Irving R. Weschler, "Training Managers for Leadership," *Personnel*, Vol. 30, No. 4 (January 1954), pp. 257-258. Reprinted by permission of the American Management Association.

[21] Some T-groups function without the presence of a trainer. Self-rating scales, which the participants use to evaluate their group effectiveness, take the place of the trainer in providing feedback.

trainers differ somewhat in their emphasis. One school places its greatest emphasis on individual emotions (and the training this group offers is often called "sensitivity training"); the other is more concerned with externally observable trends within the group. Sensitivity training is in a sense the deeper form of training and is somewhat akin to group psychotherapy.

As mentioned previously, T-group training in general is highly controversial.[22] The critics of the technique argue as follows: T-group trainers create stress situations for their own sake. These stress situations may go out of control and often do. There is a danger that training of this sort may do a better job of tearing people apart than of bringing them together. It may trigger hidden psychological instabilities, leading to mental breakdown. At worst, T-group training creates higher levels of tension than some people can handle, and at best, it is a highly frustrating series of unproductive conferences. In particular, it leads to enmity and bad feeling rather than to insight and improved relations.

Defenders counter that businessmen are usually pretty stable and that there is little prospect of danger, provided the trainer keeps on his toes. To these arguments critics reply that many companies in fact send to T-group training only those who "need" it most—and often these are the men who are most unstable. And too often, groups are started by unqualified trainers who lack the skill to keep pressures at tolerable levels.

Indeed, the impartial observer cannot help but be impressed by the number of cases in which T-group training has been misused. But this may be an argument chiefly for greater care in selecting trainers and trainees, particularly when the "deeper," more individual-centered type of training is used.

It is also argued that any personality change induced by training may be for the worse, since what is needed in management is not more sensitivity, but more decisiveness [23] (though the two are not necessarily incompatible). In addition, it is suggested that little is accomplished if the behavior of a single individual is changed and the rest of the organization is unchanged. To counter this last point, there seems to be increasing emphasis on training together groups of people who work together.

How valuable is T-group training? As we shall discuss, all training is difficult to evaluate. Though some participants leave T-group training feeling very hostile, a majority feel it a "worthwhile experience" (though they are not always sure in what sense it is useful), and many are extremely favorable. The "hard" research to date suggests that T-group training improves job perform-

---

[22] See the debate on the subject between Chris Argyris and George Odiorne, "Twenty Years of Management Development," *Training Directors Journal*, Vol. 17, No. 10 (October 1963). See also William F. Whyte, *Leadership and Group Participation* (Ithaca: New York State School of Industrial Relations, Bull. No. 24, 1953), pp. 9-15, 17-26.

[23] It is suggested, however, that since T-group training teaches people to behave more openly, with less defensiveness, it also teaches them not to fear to act in a forceful fashion if the situation requires. For a stimulating discussion of this point, see Abraham Maslow, *Eupsychian Psychology* (Homewood, Ill.: Dorsey, 1965), p. 186.

ance (at least as measured by reports from fellow employees) for some people, but not all. Whether trainees benefit seems to be related to (1) how well they react during training—the extent to which they engage in "unfrozen" participation in class and their willingness to accept feedback reports (and these, in turn, seem related to basic personality variables, such as ego strength and flexibility), and (2) the trainee's security, power, and autonomy on the job.[24]

Mixed Programs

Naturally it is possible to combine several forms of training, and this course seems to be becoming increasingly common.[25] A not uncommon sequence is the following:

1. The program starts with some sort of problem, perhaps a simulation (such as an in-basket game), a psychological exercise designed to show the extent of stereotyped thinking, or even a questionnaire designed to show managerial styles.

2. The group uses this as a springboard for self-analysis, perhaps along T-group lines, but often with greater emphasis on the styles of interpersonal relations revealed in stage 1 than on personal introspection. The group learns about its own effectiveness as a team and also seeks to develop a human-relations philosophy.

3. The discussion then switches back to home problems. Using these as exercises, the group tries to apply the philosophy and insights developed in previous sessions.

WHO DOES THE TRAINING?

In exploring the question of who does the actual training, we shall start with the form of training most remote from the trainee's day-to-day contacts: university executive development. Then we shall look in turn at training in company institutes, training by outsiders, training by line personnel, and, finally, training by staff personnel or the training department.

---

[24] Mathew B. Miles, "Change During and Following Laboratory Training: A Clinical-Experimental Study," *Journal of Applied Behavioral Science*, Vol. 1, No. 3 (July 1965), pp. 215-242. See also Douglas R. Bunker, "Individual Applications of Laboratory Training," *Journal of Applied Behavioral Science*, Vol. 1, No. 2 (April 1965), pp. 131-148; William J. Underwood, "Evaluation of Laboratory Training Method," *Training Directors Journal*, Vol. 19, No. 5 (May 1965), pp. 34-40.

[25] The "Managerial Grid" is a recently common form of mixed training. For a brief discussion of the "Grid" and a case in which this form of training "was responsible for at least several million dollars of controllable cost savings . . . , a sizable increase in employee productivity . . . and improved boss-subordinate, group, and inter-group relations," see Robert R. Blake and others, "Breakthrough in Organization Development," *Harvard Business Review*, Vol. 42, No. 6 (November 1964), p. 135.

University "Executive
Development Programs"

On many campuses it is a common sight to see middle-aged, balding busi-nessmen going back to school for advanced training. Specialized programs for members of middle and top management who live on campus are now well accepted in American colleges. Many of these courses focus on case-method discussion of typical management problems. They are usually designed to broaden perspective and to create a greater tolerance and sensitivity toward other points of view. Some schools, however, offer instruction in specialized skills, such as accounting, rapid reading, public speaking, and creative thinking.

What advantages does the typical university executive-development program have over the usual in-company training? [26] In the first place, the executives are isolated from their jobs and their families, perhaps for the first time in years. This "moratorium" from daily pressures gives them an opportunity to re-evaluate themselves and their performance on the job. [27] In a sense, the pro-gram is a secular equivalent of the religious retreat. The executives learn fresh points of view both from their classes and from their association with counter-parts in other companies. The authors' experience is that management trainees work considerably harder than the typical undergraduate and derive tremen-dous stimulation from dealing with difficult intellectual problems.

But university training is not a cure-all. Some companies have genuinely unique problems, and the patterns of behavior that the executive learns at college may not be consistent with management policy. Consequently, the trainee may come home dissatisfied and upset because he knows that he will be unable to put into practice what he has learned.

Evidence suggests that university training is more valuable for men who have just been promoted or are about to be promoted, since these are the ones who are most in need of an expanded viewpoint; confronted by a new job, they are anxious to develop new skills and willing to discard old points of view. This enthusiasm for learning is especially strong among staff specialists, such as accountants or engineers, who are being promoted into line positions where they will be faced with an entirely new set of problems. [28]

Since only a limited number of executives can be sent to university programs, management must exercise great care in making selections. The man who is picked may feel that he is slated for rapid advancement and so may alter his expectations and behavior accordingly; [29] if he fails to get promoted soon after

---

[26] Winston Oberg, "Top Management Assesses University Executive Programs," *Business Topics*, Vol. 11, No. 2 (Spring 1963).

[27] Kamla Chowdry, "Management Development Programs: Moratorium for Executives," *Human Organization*, Vol. 23, No. 3 (Fall 1964), pp. 254-59.

[28] Kenneth R. Andrews, "Reaction to University Development Programs," *Harvard Business Review*, Vol. 39, No. 3 (June 1961), pp. 116-134.

[29] "Among the more significant reasons" for managers' enthusiasm in taking part in such a program "were the implications which program participation had relative to advancement and greater prestige within the organization." Reed M. Powell, "Business Looks at University Executive Programs," *Business Topics*, Vol. 10, No. 4 (Fall 1962), p. 64.

he returns, he is likely to feel cheated and demoralized. On the other hand, those who are not selected may consider their being passed over as almost a demotion. Sending a man to a special school often makes him a "crown prince."

University-run programs are not the only opportunities available to executives to develop a broader, fresher point of view through exchange of ideas with executives from other institutions, or to acquire special training away from the job. The American Management Association offers a number of seminars similar to the university development programs but shorter ones. Various professional associations and conventions also give executives a chance to make intercompany contacts and compare experiences. In addition, many concerns pay part of the expenses of employees who take special courses. In few of these instances, however, is there the feeling of retreat that marks the longer, on-campus course in which the executive is isolated from his daily routine. The lack of isolation makes it difficult to engage in "unfreezing," the essential first step for behavior change.

Company-run Institutes

A few large companies have set up their own management-training programs. Those chosen are sent to some isolated, attractive location for a training program of a week or more. These firms feel that company training provides the same benefits as university programs, and, in addition, may increase company loyalty and inculcate a common company point of view. The function of company schools in indoctrinating managers has been described by IBM President Thomas J. Watson as follows: [30]

> These schools were not only to teach general management but—most important—they were to give our managers a feeling for IBM's outlooks and beliefs. After a time we found that the schools tended to place too much emphasis on management, not enough on beliefs. This, we felt, was putting the cart before the horse. We felt it vital that our managers be well grounded in beliefs. Otherwise, we might get management views at odds with the company's outlook.

The danger of such an approach, as of all forms of indoctrination, is that it may lead to excessive uniformity of thinking and behavior. Of course, if students are taken from all the branches of an organization as big as General Electric or AT&T, a very wide range of experience and viewpoint will be represented. And yet, though the jobs of these men differ greatly, they all work under the same management philosophy; as a consequence, there may be fewer novel approaches to problems than when the students came from many different companies.

Outsiders

A good many companies hire outsiders, often at high fees, to run their training programs. These men—members of consulting firms, college professors,

---

[30] *A Business and Its Beliefs* (New York: McGraw-Hill, 1963), p. 91.

or free-lancers with experience in training—may vary greatly in their sophistication and ability.

Why do companies hire outsiders? For the company without any other training program it may be the easiest solution; now it can have training without burdening top management with the chore. Further, there is the feeling that an outsider, particularly if he is from a university, will command more respect. "They've heard us before. You are a new face and a college professor. They'll listen to you."

Outsiders generally work under heavy handicaps, however, for they know very little about the company, its problems, or its policies. More important, even if managers listen to what the outsider has to say, they will continue to behave on the job in the way their boss wants them to behave.

But outsiders often make a real contribution in teaching content courses such as engineering or public speaking, as consultants in helping companies think through and set up their own training, and in participating in programs where they confine themselves purely to the role of moderator or observer— as in T-group training or the case method.

Line Personnel

Many types of training may be lumped together under the general category of line-run training. Every manager, for instance, trains by example, and individual coaching is an important form of training. Similarly, every time a manager talks to a group, he is in effect conducting an informal class. There is little point in making a sharp distinction between training and management, for each partakes of the other. Perhaps the best training program of all is the supervisory conference called to discuss current production problems.

There are many strong arguments for having line management conduct formal training programs as well as informal training:

1. Often the teacher learns more than his pupils. The very fact that a manager must teach may make him more conscious of his own human-relations practices. Indeed, he may carry over to the job the pattern of listening to others in class.

2. When the manager does his own training there is less chance that the subordinate will learn one form of behavior in class and another on the job. Since coaching, instruction, and order-giving are all coordinated, subordinates experience a consistent policy of supervision.

3. The classroom setting affords managers and subordinates an opportunity to talk over long-range problems that they may have been too busy to consider on the job.

In setting up a class, is it better to have students come from many departments or just from one? In favor of having all students come from the same department are these arguments: (1) They will talk about common problems; (2) when individuals who have been trained alone return back from training they often find their peers unsympathetic to their newly learned skill; [31] thus it is more efficient to train a group as a whole than to work separately with individuals; (3) if the boss is present in the class, he can give his approval to new ideas on the spot; and (4) the mere process of discussing problems together in class may stimulate similar behavior on the job and thus improve the team's performance.

On the other hand, many companies prefer to hold "interdepartmental conferences" in which a few representatives from every department meet together. These conferences make it possible to meet people from other departments, to become familiar with their problems, and to compare points of view.

Coaching

Perhaps the most valuable form of training is coaching by one's superior right on the job.

> Leadership is not something that is learned by reading about it, by listening to somebody talk about it, or even by discussing it in a conference. Leadership is learned by *doing*, under the watchful eye of somebody who has learned the art and is willing to take the time to give constructive criticism.[32]

Like other forms of teaching, coaching is most effective when it encourages the trainee to learn by himself. What does this mean in terms of day-to-day activities?

1. The coach should provide for enough delegation of authority to enable the trainee to learn from his own mistakes.

2. The coach should set goals and standards of performance toward which the trainee can work.

3. The coach should adopt a relatively nonpunitive approach to the trainee's mistakes—and remember that the functions of judge and coach don't mix well. (But the coach, as boss, can't sit idly by while mistakes are repeated too often.)

4. The coach should require the trainee to be very explicit about the steps he takes in handling a problem, asking such questions as, "How much authority did you delegate to subordinates? What standards did you set up? How did you communicate to those below?" [33]

5. The trainee should be given "special assignments" which require him to develop new experiences outside his normal routine.

6. The supervisor should provide constructive criticism, encourage the trainee to talk through his problems, and help him discover for himself how and why he has made mistakes.

---

[31] Indeed, whenever individuals are trained apart from their work group, considerable attention should be devoted to possible reaction to new techniques by the "folks back home."

[32] J. W. Miller, "Foreman Selection and Development: Key to Efficient Operation," *Assuring Adequate Reserves of Key Personnel*, Personnel Series No. 169 (New York: American Management Association, 1956), p. 9.

[33] See Louis A. Allen, "Does Management Development Develop Managers?" *Personnel*, Vol. 34, No. 2 (September 1957), pp. 18-25.

Above all, the supervisor must practice good human relations himself. Since his subordinates copy him, they learn his bad traits as well as his good.

Training through coaching is successful on a company-wide basis only if each level of management holds the next level responsible for training results —in other words, only if the supervisor's boss starts asking questions when the supervisor's subordinates are inadequately trained. Unfortunately, many otherwise good executives are very poor at developing those under them. In some instances a supervisor's training ability can be improved through classroom instruction in training techniques or through coaching by his own boss. However, since there are many "hard-core" managers who do not respond to this sort of training, there will always be a place for the other forms of training we have discussed.

There is a further danger that coaching will turn the subordinate into a carbon copy of his boss. Slavish copying of the boss's behavior is desirable only when (1) boss and subordinate have identical personalities, so that what is good for one is good for the other; (2) the boss is already an ideal supervisor; and (3) there is no need to experiment with new approaches. Since these three conditions are never met in practice, coaching should be supplemented with other forms of training.

The Role of Staff Personnel
in Management Training

What is the role of staff personnel in management training? Ideally, for all the reasons we have already mentioned, it would be better for line personnel to conduct these training programs themselves. Why, then, is it so common for training to be considered primarily as a function of the personnel department? Many well-meaning executives, who believe that training is peripheral to line's primary job of production, feel that training is a simple matter of teaching, and that teaching, like dentistry or surgery, is best left to specialists. Further, many highly competent executives fear that they will become tongue-tied in class. They would rather slough off the job to the experts and concentrate on what they regard as more essential activities. And it is true that many line supervisors are poorly qualified to act as teachers.

In any case, many personnel departments are more than anxious to assume the responsibility for management training. Every personnel director is interested in building up a record of accomplishments—and a successful training program is just that. It is usually easier for the personnel department itself to run classes than it is to go through all the work of patiently prodding reluctant line managers to set these courses up. Yet staff-run classes have many limitations, particularly if they are met with only grudging support from line.

What role *should* the personnel department play in management training? The answer depends on such factors as higher management's general philosophy of human relations and supervision, its understanding of the importance of training as a line function, and the ability of line personnel, both as supervisors and as trainers.

Ideally, the functions of staff should be:

1. To train the trainers—to equip them with skill in using such techniques as role-playing and conferences.
2. To act as coach or consultant to line managers who desire such help.
3. To provide teaching materials, such as cases or incidents.
4. To coordinate and arrange classes and to handle housekeeping details.
5. To provide some sort of feedback in an effort to evaluate the effectiveness of the program both for the trainers themselves and for higher management.

The personnel department should also seek to involve higher management more directly in the training program. The training director may, for example, interview members of higher management in an effort to identify specific needs and to pinpoint specific areas of weakness. Even better, he can organize a top-management committee to review the abilities and deficiencies of subordinates (perhaps using individual evaluation data as a springboard) and to suggest ways of correcting deficiencies. These committee deliberations are themselves a valuable form of training for the participants. Indeed, the personnel director's job will be much easier if he can start his training program (however camouflaged) at the highest possible level.

EVALUATING TRAINING

The field of management training is still in its infancy. Many of its proponents, flushed with enthusiasm, have made extravagant claims and have relied excessively on gadgets that promise wonderful results with a minimum of effort. Only recently has there been much effort to evaluate the effectiveness of training. The results so far are inconclusive, in part because it is so difficult to isolate the impact of training from the other variables which also affect management behavior.[34]

One way of evaluating training is to ask the students themselves to evaluate the program and to make suggestions for improving it. The value of such "customer reactions" is doubtful, however, since the participants try to be polite and usually give a kind answer. Moreover, real learning is often painful and frustrating, and the shot-in-the-arm inspiration peddler may win the popularity contest over the teacher who poses difficult questions and refuses to give pat answers.

A second evaluation technique is to measure the change in student attitudes (or perhaps the change in approach to handling cases) that takes place during

---

[34] For a listing of some of the major research in this field, see Theodore J. Carron, "Human Relations Training and Attitude Change," *Personnel Psychology*, Vol. 17, No. 4 (Winter 1964), p. 403.

the course, perhaps by the use of before-and-after tests.[35] Unfortunately, a change of attitude expressed on a paper-and-pencil test or in class discussion may not carry over into change in behavior on the job. Even if a new technique is tried on the job, it may not persist for long if the boss or fellow managers are hostile to it.

A third but more difficult test is to measure change in on-the-job behavior. A series of tests may be administered to the trainees' supervisors and subordinates just before training, immediately after training, and finally well after training (the last series to measure whether change has persisted).[36] Or else performance-evaluation forms may be used as an index of change.

To many members of management the most crucial test is this: Does training cut costs? Does it make managers more efficient? Yet in practice it is extremely difficult to prove that training reduces costs, because so many other factors may be responsible, such as better materials or longer production runs. The ideal method of evaluating training is to take a number of groups doing the same work under identical conditions and then to train the managers of some of these groups and leave the others as controls.[37] Yet in a live organization (in contrast to a research lab) it is difficult to find exactly identical work groups which will remain identical (except for the characteristics under study) during the period of study.

The truth is that we have very little real proof of the effectiveness of management training or indeed of any sort of education. We know that college graduates earn more than nongraduates, for instance, but don't know whether this is due chiefly to what is actually learned in college, or the status which a college degree provides, or to the supposed fact that graduates possess greater innate intelligence than nongraduates. Management invests a good deal of money in training courses with very little evaluation of their worth. Much more research can be done in this area, but for the immediate future it seems that, as with education generally, the value of training courses must be taken pretty much on faith.

---

[35] For examples of studies indicating a positive impact of training, see Antoine Papaloizuz, "Personality and Success of Training in Human Relations," *Personnel Psychology,* Vol. 15, No. 4 (Winter 1964), pp. 423-428; Morris S. Viteles, " 'Human Relations' and 'Humanities' in the Education of Business Leaders: Evaluation of a Program of Humanistic Studies for Executives," *Personnel Psychology,* Vol. 12, No. 1 (Spring 1959), pp. 1-28.

[36] Before-and-after tests were used in Harold Guetzkow, Garlie A. Forehand, and Bernard J. James, "An Evaluation of Educational Influence on Administrative Judgment," *Administrative Science Quarterly,* Vol. 6, No. 4 (March 1962), pp. 483-500, and also in Daniel M. Goodacre, "Stimulating Improve Man Management," *Personnel Psychology,* Vol. 12, No. 2 (Summer 1963), pp. 133-143.

[37] In one such study supervisors in two departments were trained in "democratic techniques" and those in two others were placed under close supervision (itself a form of training). After a year's experience, the department placed under close supervision had better cost records; however, their morale was lower and their turnover higher. The researchers predicted that in the long run the democratically trained supervisors would have better cost records because they did not waste human resources. Rensis Likert, "Measuring Organizational Performance," *Harvard Business Review,* Vol. 36, No. 2 (March 1958), pp. 41-50.

Perhaps the question of how to *measure* the effectiveness of executive training may be less important than the question of deciding on *goals*. Instead of emphasizing methods, perhaps those who are responsible for evaluation should concern themselves with such hard-headed questions as, "What are we trying to accomplish? What kind of organization are we trying to build? In what ways do we want supervisors to change?" Until these questions are answered realistically, it may be premature for management to try to refine its methods.

CONCLUSION

People learn chiefly from their jobs, their fellow workers, and (particularly in the case of managers who seek promotion) from their bosses. Indeed, whether he intends to or not, the boss is always training his subordinate through the demands he makes, the behavior he rewards, and the behavior he punishes. Training can be a means by which a superior can induce a subordinate to do a better job without having to supervise him in detail. The good superior provides an atmosphere in which subordinates can constantly learn new skills and develop their highest capabilities. In the end, the most effective development is self-development. But, as suggested in Chapter 22, unless the job environment is conducive to self-development, classroom training will lead to frustration, confusion, and wasted effort. Little can be expected of training if management regards it as a peripheral staff function or a quick cure-all for basic problems.

Classroom training can be a useful supplement to on-the-job training if it is designed to improve the manager's ability to observe and think about his problems rather than provide him with pat answers. Classroom training can help the executive digest his experiences on the job, to develop more realistic solutions to his job problems, and perhaps to discuss these in the safe atmosphere of the class. At best it can help him function more effectively in his environment.

Forms of training vary. More or less stress can be placed on indoctrination, human relations, and decision-making. As suggested earlier, this depends in part on management's concept of the role of the manager. But the purpose of most forms of management training (aside from training for skills or broad cultural education) is to induce change in behavior and attitudes. Since behaviors and attitudes are ingrown, change is difficult (even if the job environment encourages it) and emotional resistance is often encountered. In designing a training program all sorts of subtle psychological factors must be considered. Above all, if the program is to succeed it must be seen as providing a payoff in terms of greater success on the job.

TRAINING PROGRAM

The Stockton Company had 15 plants scattered through the country. As a professor and training consultant, I was involved in only one plant, where I worked with Otto Fitch, the plant training director. After I had known him for a while, Otto told me that the training program had started at a meeting of the 15 plant managers. Allen Higgins had just been put in as company-wide training director.

> "He sold the president on the idea there ought to be a development program in every plant; it was the modern, progressive thing. Higgins is a great salesman. So the president brought him to the meeting and said, 'We've been thinking about a supervisory development program and Higgins will tell you about it.' I doubt if any of the plant managers knew the slightest bit about training before Higgins spoke and I doubt if they knew much more after. One man spoke against it. He said, 'My foremen are pretty good as they are. I don't want anyone changing them.' The rest were quiet."

So the program was initiated. Each plant manager was asked to pick a training director from among his men. Otto's manager asked Otto, his safety director, to take on the job. The program got off to a flying start; all the new training directors spent three weeks learning their job at a resort hotel.

> "We really got the works; how to run movies, buzz sessions, role-playing, conference leadership, just about everything except how to handle management back home. There were outside speakers, a big banquet every week. We figured the company put out $2,000 on each of us—companies don't spend money like that unless they are serious. I went home in a blaze of enthusiasm.
> "Only there were no brass bands to meet me. Now I was safety *and* training director. That was a blow. I figured someone else would take over safety. But I was going to get a training program somehow. The plant manager said he would back me up on anything. However, when I tried to get the foremen released for classes, the production superintendent said he needed them on the job. I took that to the plant manager; he felt maybe we ought to hold the classes after work on their own time. I asked for suggestions on what to cover. He said anything I said went; I was 100 per cent in charge.
> "I waited till Higgins came in town. He sized things up quickly and soon it was settled that foremen would get overtime for coming to class. So I started my classes. We had sessions on first aid, safety, job evaluation, and conference leadership. But this wasn't going so well—not enough interest—so that's why we went to the University for help."

Of course, I didn't know all this background when Otto and Humphrey Cadiz, the personnel director, called on me to ask if I would conduct an eight-week course for their foremen. I asked, "What do you want? What do your foremen need?" Cadiz replied, "Well, we came to you because you are an expert. I understand you have done a good deal of this before. We'd like our foremen to get all the latest information on human relations. We've got a pretty old group, most of them have been with the company for 25 or 30 years and all they know is production."

We talked a while. I suggested that it might be desirable for me to work with the superintendents and general foremen to get their ideas on what should be done with the foremen. Even some of the general foremen might be trained as instructors so they could teach the foremen themselves.

"No," said Cadiz, "our top management is just too busy and frankly I don't think one of them has the temperament to be a teacher. We want the best. That's why we picked you."

The job was going to be a tough one, but I agreed to take it on. The first class was not too bad. I lectured on what workers want from their jobs. Cadiz was there and so was the plant superintendent. Next session the superintendent was absent (he never returned). I switched the subject and tried to get discussion on day-to-day problems of supervision. Cadiz took part and it seemed that when the other men talked, they were looking to him for approval. After the session was over, Cadiz told me he thought it would be better if I lectured, since the men were really interested in hearing my ideas, not their own.

For the next few weeks I plunged into interview techniques, starting out with a lecture on why it pays to listen. Soon I had the class broken down into pairs, each pair enacting an interview. The group seemed to do reasonably well, but I sensed a certain hostility toward me—and each session it got worse. Getting discussion was like pulling teeth. When I got what I thought were good answers, I had the feeling that the people didn't believe what they said.

On the sixth session Cadiz was out of town. I decided to take advantage of his absence by bringing the problem out in the open. I said, "I have the feeling that a lot of you think this kind of approach, listening and all, might be fine for a professor, but just doesn't have any practical value, that it is a waste of time." I stopped and paused for a reply. Over a minute rolled by until somebody was brave enough to say, "You tell us we should listen to our employees' problems. But how are we going to get them to talk to us in the first place? They take their problems to their stewards."

I wrote his objection on the blackboard and waited for some more.

"Also, you say we should consult with the steward before we make any changes. I agree. But if we do that the personnel department will be on our neck for instigating grievances. Anyway the stewards get information from management before we do."

"Why do we have to listen politely to worker grievances when management won't listen to ours?"

Now it was my turn. "All right," I said. "Why do workers go to see the stewards instead of you? What can you do to get them to see you?"

Everyone had an answer to that. I've rarely seen so enthusiastic a group. "They see the steward because management listens to them and not us. In fact the only way we foremen can get a needed improvement in the department or get a man a raise is to see the steward. . . ." And so on.

Things died down for a second. Then a hand popped up. "I have a question for you, Professor. The men in my department all stop work about fifteen minutes before quitting time and gather around the time clock. How can you get them to stay on the job?"

(A wonderful question for discussion, I thought, but I suspected it was loaded.) "What have you tried so far?" I asked.

"Well I tried asking them not to congregate, but they laughed at me. I gave one a warning slip, but management tore it up. Unless I get some backing, I can't do a thing. What do *you* think?" I ducked the question, and tried to explore some more positive approaches without much luck. The group was too interested in telling me their troubles. And I was worried what management would think when they found I was running a session like that.

It was probably fortunate that Cadiz attended the rest of the sessions. I suggested it might be useful for him to spend a little time explaining the company's interpretation of the union contract. He felt not: The foremen were too close to the union as it was, and if he were to discuss company strategy it would soon leak back to the union.

A year later, Otto, the training director, and I were reminiscing. Otto had been sounding out the foremen on their reactions to the program, asking questions like, "How did you like it? Did you get anything from it?" His conclusions:

> Well, they enjoyed it. It was something very new. And they would like another course like it. But, if by "get anything from it" you mean a change in behavior— no, I'm afraid there is no change. They still think the only thing the company wants is production and that is what they try to get. I doubt if the course changed anyone at all. There was one fellow who was rather disappointed. He told me, "When the program started I thought there would be great changes. At last the company has found the foremen and we will be in on things. But I guess it doesn't mean anything at all."

1. What was wrong with this training program?
2. If you were Otto Fitch, the training director, and had to work under the conditions described here, what kind of program would you set up? How would you go about winning acceptance for it?

INCENTIVES FOR EFFECTIVE PERFORMANCE

Having the right people in the right jobs at the right time is only one part of management's responsibility to develop and maintain personnel policies. Employees and managers alike—and the organization in which they work—are also vitally interested in the conditions of employment. These affect every working hour.

No one is surprised to find that employees expect payment for the services they render. The problem arises when the organization has to determine *how much* money each employee is to receive for the work he or she performs. Each firm must make a number of interrelated decisions concerning the relative magnitude of its wages and salaries (as compared with those in other organizations) and the relative rates for different jobs within the firm. Chapter 25, "Wage and Salary Administration," presents criteria for both kinds of management decisions.

Employees receive income from the firm in exchange for work performed, but how much work constitutes a "fair day's work" or the effort that management can reasonably expect? "Work Measurement Techniques," described in Chapter 26, illustrate some of the methods that have been developed by the industrial engineers who have been struggling for many years to answer this question. Unfortunately, the unresolved problems in this area are still substantial. The techniques that have been developed do not provide precise, incontrovertible results. Nevertheless, the student of personnel should be familiar with the application of these techniques to the setting of work loads.

Moreover, time studies frequently serve as the basis for financial incentive plans covering production workers. Increasingly, management has turned to wage-payment systems that emphasize work accomplished rather than just the number of hours spent on company premises. But even incentive plans that seem to be logically defensible and psychologically sound may produce a wide variety of complex personnel problems. These problems are analyzed in Chapter 27, "Individual Incentive Systems."

The incentive programs discussed in Chapter 27 have been developed for individual employees. The shortcomings of these programs have motivated a search for other means of rewarding employee productivity, ingenuity, and group effort. A variety of techniques have been tried, and their relative advantages are summarized in Chapter 28, "Incentives for Organization-wide Participation."

Although unsafe work procedures and accidents are not a direct wage cost to the firm, they may have a substantial effect on both operating profits and productivity, not to mention their cost in human terms. "Safety," Chapter 29, reviews the areas in which effective managerial action can reduce or eliminate the hazards of work.

The cost of employee compensation is not limited exclusively to wages and salaries. Another source of employee remuneration—and one that is continuously increasing in importance—is discussed in Chapter 30, "Service and Benefit Programs." Popularly known as "fringe benefits," these programs are now an established component of nearly every organization's personnel program. Much more is involved in their administration than mere agreement to pay for vacations and insurance. In fact, some of the most perplexing questions in personnel arise in this area. Whether or not the benefit programs serve as an incentive for increasing productivity depends on how successfully management answers these questions.

Wage and Salary Administration

Ask a man why he works and chances are he will say to make money. True, men and women want more from their jobs than just a wage or salary—yet this is a basic need. Even teachers and ministers, who may willingly accept less take-home pay for more on-the-job satisfaction, regard *relative* pay as highly important. A professor may be unconcerned about the fact that he earns less than a bricklayer, but still he may become enraged if Professor X across the the hall, with six less publications than he, gets a salary increase while he does not. Alleged wage and salary inequities are among the most dangerous sources of friction and low morale in an organization.

Without a sound policy of *wage administration*, wages are often determined on the basis of "personalized," arbitrary decisions without regard for the over-all wage structure. (For the sake of brevity, we will talk of "wage administration" rather than "wage and salary administration," since roughly the same problems are involved.) Wage administration is a *systematic procedure* for establishing a sound compensation structure. By reducing inequities between employees' earnings, a good wage-administration program raises individual morale and reduces intergroup friction. It also sets wages high enough to permit the company to recruit satisfactory employees (but not so high as to cause unnecessary expense), motivates people to work for pay increases and promotions, reduces union and employee grievances, and enables management to exercise centralized control over the largest single item of cost: wages and salaries. But, as we shall see, some of these objectives are in conflict.

ASPECTS OF WAGE AND SALARY ADMINISTRATION

There are four closely related aspects of wage administration: wage and salary surveys, job evaluation, merit rating, and incentives. *Wage and salary surveys* are designed to determine the general pay level in the community and industry, thus giving a company a base for setting its own rates. *Job evaluation*

597

establishes the relationships between wages on various jobs within the company. Together, wage surveys and job evaluation set the "base" or minimum rates for each job.

Instead of setting one rate for each job, many companies establish a series of rates or *steps*. A new employee normally starts at the *base rate* for the job; then, as he gains proficiency and seniority, he advances through *merit rating* to higher steps. (Merit rating on one job should not be confused with *promotion* from one job to another.)

Companies with *incentive* plans pay the base rate only for a "normal" amount of production, as determined by time study. If a worker produces more than normal, he receives an extra incentive bonus. Similarly, salaried personnel may qualify for bonus earnings of one kind or another.

The personnel department is normally responsible for the administration of the wage and salary program and often has a special division that concentrates on this function. Top management, however, has a continuing responsibility to review wage and salary policies, and every level of management may become involved in merit rating and in introducing a new job-evaluation program.

In this chapter we shall review the factors that must be taken into account in setting the over-all wage level through wage and salary surveys, then we shall look at job evaluation and merit rating, and finally we shall consider some of the special problems involved in salary administration for executives and engineers. (Incentives will be considered in Chapter 26.)

DETERMINING THE OVER-ALL WAGE AND SALARY LEVEL

Determining the over-all wage and salary policy—whether to pay wages and salaries that are high, average, or below-average as compared with standards elsewhere—is one of management's most difficult decisions.[1] What factors must management take into account in making this decision?

1. The company wage policy is related to its recruitment and selection policy, for high wages attract more job applicants and permit management to choose employees from a wider reservoir of talents. Moreover, they help maintain morale and make employees more reluctant to quit their jobs. And yet high wages in themselves do not guarantee motivation for high production, as we saw in Chapter 6. (But a sound merit-rating and promotional policy may provide such motivation.)

2. Employment conditions in the area naturally affect wage policy. When there is a great deal of unemployment, a nonunionized company may be able to hire all the men it needs at little more than the minimum wage set by law.[2]

---

[1] For a classic discussion of this problem, see Richard A. Lester, *Company Wage Policies* (Princeton, New Jersey: Princeton University Press, 1948).

[2] The minimum wage in interstate industry was set by the Fair Labor Standards Act at $1.40 an hour for 1967 and $1.60 for 1968 and thereafter. The Walsh-Healey Act requires firms which sell to the government to pay somewhat higher wages.

When the labor market is tight, an employer may have to pay more than the going rate if he is to recruit qualified new employees.

3. If a company is anxious to gain a reputation in the community as a good employer and a good citizen—as are many public utilities—it may decide to pay high wages to insure good public relations. Small companies not in the public spotlight are not under compulsion to follow suit.

4. Unionized companies may be forced to pay high wages as a result of union pressure. Nonunionized companies may pay equally high wages to keep the union out. Yet if wages are too high, other employers may object that the company is "unstabilizing the market" and may exert subtle pressures to bring the company into line.

5. A company's profitability sets limits on its wage policy. The company that is losing money finds it hard to pay more than the minimum; the company that is known to be profitable is expected by the community and its employees to pay liberally.

6. Wage policies may be influenced by other factors too. Companies which are known for their stability of employment need not pay as high wages as those in which layoffs are frequent. Substantial fringe benefits may also reduce the need for high wages. And pay levels in unionized companies are inevitably affected by collective bargaining agreements providing for wage increases based on changes in productivity or the cost of living.

Once the company has decided on its over-all wage policy, the next question it must answer is this: What are other companies paying on *comparable* jobs? This information is useful in determining whether the company is meeting community standards and also in bargaining with the union. The U.S. Bureau of Labor Statistics collects data for many jobs in large cities, and local chambers of commerce and employers' and trade associations often make available more detailed data. There are times, however, when a company is obliged to conduct a *wage survey* itself.

This is not an easy task. What are "comparable" jobs in other companies? It is simple enough to call another company and ask, "What are you paying your machine operators?" The other company answers $3.20 an hour; that makes you feel good, since you pay $3.30. But the other company failed to mention that their operators also earn incentive bonuses and do easier work than yours. To insure getting data that are really comparable, the survey should be made in person by means of oral interviews.

Rarely are two jobs performed in exactly the same way in different firms. Consideration must also be given to fringe benefits and continuity of employment. It is traditional, for instance, for maintenance men in factories to get lower pay than maintenance men who work for construction firms, because the latter are less assured of steady employment and receive fewer paid holidays, vacations, or other fringe benefits.

What companies should you use as the basis of your comparison—companies in the same community regardless of industry, or companies throughout the country in your industry? The management of nation-wide firms faces the problem of whether to pay uniform wages throughout all their plants or to adjust to the local wage patterns in each community. At times it is far from clear in what industry a firm should be classified. For instance, is a firm that makes rubber soles in the shoe industry or the rubber industry? Unionized firms are under pressure to pay the wages equivalent to those paid by other firms that have contracts with the same unions, even though these firms may be in other industries.

After the wage-survey figures have been gathered, great caution must be exercised in interpreting them, particularly if, as often happens, there is no central tendency or clear "going rate." The survey itself, however, does provide a series of bench-marks against which the company can compare its present wage and salary rates and decide whether adjustments are necessary to make them consistent with its over-all wage policy. Surveys are meaningful chiefly in regard to "key" jobs which are common to many firms. Wages for jobs which are unique to a given firm cannot be set by wage surveys alone.

The company should keep its rates under constant review—if the workers are unionized, of course, management will have little chance to forget this need. New wage surveys should be made periodically to determine whether the company's rates are getting out of line. Wage rates undergo constant change—in recent years, in an almost steadily upward direction. Adjustments may also be dictated by changes in the cost of living or in company profitability or productivity.

Once the over-all wage level has been set, the company can turn to a consideration of individual rates. Here job evaluation is widely used.

JOB EVALUATION

Strictly speaking, job evaluation is a method of determining the *relationship between* wage rates, not the rates themselves. In practice it is hard to consider these two questions separately. In theory, for instance, the completion of a job-evaluation program need not lead to any increase in the total wage bill: Some people will get increases, others decreases. In practice, however, some increase in the wage bill is necessary if the program is to be accepted by the employees; normally no one gets his wage cut. Furthermore, if the rates that are finally set for any job are out of line with prevailing rates for that job in the community, the job-evaluation program may have to be adjusted.

Job evaluation is a systematic way of applying judgment, but it does not eliminate the need for exercising judgment. It is not an automatic process, for it is administered by people and is subject to all the human frailties.

In this section we will first present a very general picture of how a job-evaluation program is conducted. This background will make it easier for you to understand the problems involved in applying job evaluation to a particular situation. Our purpose is not to transform you into a job-evaluation expert, but simply to present some of the policy questions that job evaluation raises.

There are many methods of job evaluation, some of which are quite simple, but many of which are extremely complicated. In essence, however, all forms of job evaluation are designed to enable management to determine how much one job should pay relative to others. Most companies use one variation or another of the *point system* of job evaluation, though the *factor-comparison, ranking,* and *job-classification methods* are also quite common.[3]

THE POINT SYSTEM

The point system involves four steps, which we will first describe briefly and then discuss at some length:

Step 1: A manual or yardstick is drawn up (for an example, look at pp. 632-633), which provides a set of standards against which each job can be compared. Notice that the manual lists a number of *factors* on which each job is to be rated and then breaks each factor down into a number of *degrees.* Each degree is worth a certain number of *points.*

Step 2: The requirements of each job are described and listed in a standardized fashion in what is called a *job specification* (see p. 605 for an example).

Step 3: Each job—as described in the job specification—is rated, one factor at a time, in accordance with the manual. A point value is assigned to each factor. Then the points are added up.

Step 4: Each job is slotted into a *job classification* in accordance with its evaluated point total. A wage rate is then assigned to the job.

Step 1: Setting Up the Manual

It is very difficult to draw up a job-evaluation manual that is consistent and free from ambiguity, and that will give a fair evaluation of the relative worth of each job. Because of this difficulty many companies adopt standardized, ready-to-use plans prepared by such organizations as the National Metal Trades Association or the National Office Management Association. Yet other

---

[3] The standard method of factor comparison is described in Eugene J. Benge, Samuel L. Burk, and Edward N. Hay, *Manual for Job Evaluation* (New York: Harper & Row, 1941). For variations, see Edward N. Hay, "Four Methods of Establishing Factor Scales in Factor Comparison Job Evaluation," *The AMA Handbook of Wage and Salary Administration* (New York: American Management Association, 1950).

Two somewhat simplified job evaluation techniques are *ranking* and *job classification.* Ranking, as its name implies, involves listing a given set of jobs in order of importance, from highest to lowest, taking into account the characteristics of each job as a whole (though sometimes specific factors, such as job difficulty, are given special attention). The job classification system, used by many government agencies, is also somewhat self-descriptive. First, a set of job classifications or grades are established (say from Grade 1 to Grade 12); then the level of difficulty of each classification is carefully described; and finally individual jobs are fitted into what seems their most appropriate classification. All this is done without the elaborate analysis which occurs in the factor comparison or point systems.

companies, particularly those that have jobs with unique characteristics, prefer to draft their own custom-made manual. In either case, management should be aware of some of the problems involved in preparing job-evaluation manuals. (For an example of a poorly drawn manual, see pp. 632-633.)

Selecting factors. What are the factors or dimensions on which the jobs are to be evaluated? Each factor represents a certain characteristic of the job that management feels is worth compensating. Two of the best-known plans, those of the National Metal Trades Association and the National Electrical Manufacturers Association, use the following factors, with the weights indicated:

Skill (total 50%)	*Responsibility (total 20%)*
Education 14%	Equipment, process 5%
Experience 22%	Material or product 5%
Initiative and ingenuity 14%	Safety of others 5%
	Work of others 5%

Effort (total 15%)	*Job Conditions (total 15%)*
Physical demand 10%	Working conditions 10%
Mental or visual 5%	Hazards 5%

Naturally, different factors are used evaluating supervisory jobs than in evaluating, say, production or clerical jobs. A job-evaluation manual for supervisory jobs might list such factors as public contacts, staff contacts, complexity of duties, responsibility for money, and number of employees supervised—factors that would be largely irrelevant on hourly-paid jobs.

Some plans have used as many as 40 factors, but the trend has been to use considerably fewer. A plan with fewer factors is simpler and easier to understand, and statistical studies have shown that almost the same results are obtained when only two or three factors are used.[4] There are two reasons:

> The first is the *halo effect* (see p. 553), the tendency of evaluators who rate a job high on one factor to rate it high on others, particularly if the factors are closely related.
>
> The second is that in practice some factors are more *effective* than others. An example may help clarify this concept of effectiveness: Suppose an examination has only two questions, each worth 50 points. The instructor grades each paper exactly 30 points for Question I, but disperses his grades on Question II from zero to 50. Since all students receive exactly the same grade on Question I, obviously Question II has the crucial "effectiveness" in determining differences between a high and low total grade on the over-all examination. Similarly in industry, the majority of jobs in a given situation may be pretty much alike, with differences concentrated on a few effective factors.

Thus, increasing the number of factors may not result in a more "accurate" job evaluation. Still, it may be desirable to have a reasonably large number of

---

[4] For a list of such studies, see David Belcher, "Employee and Executive Compensation," in Herbert G. Heneman and others, eds., *Employee Relations Research* (New York: Harper & Row, 1960), pp. 118-119.

factors to help "sell" the program to employees and to reduce complaints that important factors are not being considered.

A novel and highly controversial approach to job evaluation takes account of only one factor, "the time span of discretion," or the length of time which may elapse between the time an employee performs an act or makes a decision and the time it is reviewed by his superior.[5] (Thus, an unskilled worker might have his work checked once an hour, a skilled craftsman once every three days, while an executive might go for six months before his work is reviewed.) Presumably the time-span of discretion measures the weight of responsibility, a factor which is common to all jobs since the activities at higher levels of responsibility take longer to complete and are therefore more difficult to review. Indeed, it has been argued that the wide-spread adoption of this single standard might permit a nation-wide system of job evaluation which would eliminate much of the cause for industrial strife.

Selecting degrees.   Just as inches are a basic unit in determining length, so degrees are the basic unit in measuring the importance of any one factor in a given job. There is no set rule governing the number of degrees into which a factor should be broken down. If the scope of the jobs to be evaluated covers a wide range, from unskilled through highly skilled, there will be a large number of degrees. However, if there are too many degrees it may be hard to distinguish one from another.

It is helpful to define the degrees as closely as possible (for example, see manual, pp. 632-633). "Lifts weights in excess of 50 lbs." is more specific than "Lifts heavy weights." But there is a danger in being *too* specific. For instance, physical effort is more than a matter of pure weight-lifting; constantly carrying a number of small bulky objects may be more tiring than infrequently lifting an easily grasped heavy object.

Assigning weights to factors and degrees.   Next, point values must be assigned to each degree of each factor. The table below summarizes the point values that have been assigned by the manual on pp. 632-633.

Points assigned to factors

FACTORS	DEGREES						
	1	2	3	4	5	6	7
Education	20	40	60	80	100	120	140
Training	20	40	60	80	100	120	140
Physical effort	25	50	75	100			
Dexterity	60	120	180	240			
Mental effort	20	40	60	80			
Responsibility	25	50	75	100			
Working conditions	20	40	60	80	100		
Safety	20	40	60	80	100		

---

[5] See Elliott Jaques, *Equitable Payment: A General Theory of Work, Differential Payment and Industrial Progress* (New York: Wiley, 1961).

At best, this process must be completely arbitrary. One must, for example, decide whether a requirement of "two years of college or equivalent" is worth more or less points than "hard work with constant physical strain."

The number of points may total 500 or 1000 or even more. The reason is purely psychological: It is easier to justify not putting a man into a higher rate range if he is 10 points off out of 1000 than if he is 1 point off of 100. Similarly, the lowest degree is never fixed at zero. Presumably to give a man a zero on any factor would be insulting. Note that since the relative standing of the jobs is the thing that counts, it makes no difference if point values are added or multiplied, provided each factor is treated in the same way.

Step 2: Drawing Up Job Specifications

Although many knotty problems of judgment are involved in drawing up the job-evaluation manual, in practice the really difficult disputes start when job evaluation moves from the general to the specific—that is, with the drawing up of job specifications when specific individuals become first involved.

Job titles.   The first question is one that we discussed in an earlier context (pp. 500-501): What does a particular job consist of? How should one draw the boundaries around a specific job title? Particularly in the clerical and technical fields, this decision may not be easy to make. It may be that every secretary does work that is somewhat different from that of every other secretary. Should all secretarial work be classified under one job title? Or should there be a separate job title (and a separate pay rate) for each secretary's job? The Vice President for Sales is out of town a great deal, so his secretary must make many decisions for herself. Should this added responsibility give her more pay than the secretary to the Executive Vice President? Bob Jones is in charge of the Red Feather drive this year. Does this mean that he should receive higher pay? And so forth.

Similar problems arise on production jobs. For instance, material-handling may be considered as one job or several. In a company where the men insisted on higher pay for handling heavier material, management ended up with a separate job title for each material handled—over 100 job titles! Excessive elaboration of job titles may "deprive management of flexibility of assignment, restrict the workers' training and competence to the narrowest of fields, make seniority systems burdensome and impractical, and turn each job into a narrow caste to which a worker clings because outside it he is untrained and insecure." [6] Companies engaging in rapid automation find narrow job titles particularly restricting since they find it difficult to combine jobs or to induce employees to accept additional duties.

---

[6] Clark Kerr and Lloyd H. Fisher, "Effect of Environment and Administration on Job Evaluation," in Paul Pigors and Charles A. Myers, eds., *Readings in Personnel Administration* (New York: McGraw-Hill, 1952), p. 390.

Job Title_____ Grinder - Rough (Castings)_____

Department_____ 49 - Grinding_____ Section _Foundry_____

Factor	Rating	Basis of Rating
1 General Knowledge	1 (5)	Requires the ability to understand English, understand and carry out specific oral instructions and recognize signs.
2 Experience	4 (48)	Requires 6 to 9 months experience to perform routine semi-skilled work of grinding fins, burrs, gates, etc., from a wide variety of Blanko attachments and castings using various sizes and types of grinding wheels on stand grinder and hand air grinder.
3 Judgement	3 (21)	Some judgement required on standardized rough grinding operations where variations in location of burrs, fins, gates, etc., on a wide variety of Blanko attachments and castings. Involves making decisions such as correct grinding wheel to use, distance between wheel and rest and type of rest best suited for job and maximum production.
4 Initiative & Ingenuity	2 (14)	Performs work of grinding gates, fins, burrs, etc., off castings, according to limited detailed instructions in following standard grinding methods but makes occasional changes in grinding rests and set-ups to grind castings in more efficient manner.
5 Manual Dexterity	4 (24)	Considerable manual skill and speed in the use of fingers, hands, and arms on repetitive operations of holding castings between rest and grinding wheel and manipulating part in most efficient manner and against wheel without use of grinding rest and burring of Blanko attachment where burrs are ground off by rapid touching of head and open end on side of wheel.
6 Accuracy	2 (16)	Moderate accuracy required in performance of rough grinding duties involving removal of fins, burrs, gates, etc., from a wide variety of castings where care must be taken to insure removal of the proper amount of metal.
7 Physical Activity	4 (28)	Sustained repetitive physical activity in manipulating Blanko attachments and castings between rest and wheel and burring of Blanko attachments and castings on wheel when rest is not used. Requires manual pressure for all types of grinding.
8 Strength	5 (25)	Requires the strength and physical activity to constantly handle castings weighing up to 5 lb and lift 30 to 50 lb

Total Points	281	
Date	1/20/67	

Source: L. C. Pigage and J. L. Tucker, *Job Evaluation* (Urbana, Illinois: Institute of Labor and Industrial Relations, University of Illinois, 1955), pp. 28-29. Reprinted by permission.

Job specification with points assigned.

The common union insistence that a man should not work outside his classification has important ramifications here (see p. 500). Questions of status are also involved. A highly skilled maintenance man might object to the same job title as someone with no skill at all. A man who is proud of being "in charge of incoming vouchers" may be very unhappy to have his title changed to "Clerk II."

Job description.   Next, each job must be described—that is, a list must be compiled of its duties and responsibilities (see figure on p. 634 for an example).[7] Particularly in unionized plants the job description must be prepared with great care, since many union members refuse to work outside their job description.

Management faces a dilemma here. If it includes only a few of a man's duties in a job description, he may well refuse to perform others. Yet every additional requirement in the description tends to inflate the number of points given to the job and therefore improves the union's case for getting more pay.

Job description cannot be performed in a vacuum, for it impinges on many areas of status and informal organization. An impressive job description builds up one's prestige. Purely as a matter of pride, everyone wants his job description to sound difficult. Companies that have tried to base their job descriptions on questionnaires filled out by the employees themselves have discovered that there is a strong tendency to puff up one's job beyond recognition.

Job specification.   The next procedure is to formulate the job specification itself, which involves breaking the general job description down into specific categories, one for each factor. Here, for each job, one must decide such questions as how many years of schooling are required, how much noise is involved, and so forth. (An example of a job specification is illustrated on p. 605.) A careful job specification is useful in selection and training as well as in actual job evaluation.

Step 3: Assigning Points

Now we come to the critical point: rating each job by assigning a certain number of degrees to each factor. The points are then computed and added together. The total is the *evaluated point score* for the given job (in the example on p. 605, 281 total points).

Though job specifications and the job-evaluation manual may make rating easier and more systematic, rating is still entirely a matter of judgment. As such, it is subject to all sorts of human bias, including:

The halo effect.   (See our discussion, p. 553.)

---

[7] Especially in evaluating management posts, some companies use "functional job descriptions" which avoid ambiguous terms such as "have general responsibility for sales" and instead specifies the employees' functions in great detail, such as, "...2. (a) Receives daily machine-load charts from each of his departments. Analyzes to see what machines were down and for how long. (b) If he was not notified by foreman as to the reason on the preceding day, goes to him to find out the cause. (c) If he and the foreman agree that faulty material caused the down-time, gets a sample and takes it to the superintendent of the responsible department to request corrective action. (d) If the cause is mechanical, goes to the chief mechanic to determine whether the cause is routine maintenance, operating or machine construction..." Eliot D. Chapple and Leonard Sayles, *The Measurement of Management* (New York: Macmillan, 1961), p. 49.

Leniency.   Often raters tend to be overly generous in handing out points. There is no harm in this provided they are equally generous with all jobs, since job evaluation is a matter of *relative* standing.

Consistency.   Regardless of how carefully the manual has been written, there will be countless questions of interpretation. The problem is to achieve consistency in interpretation. Seemingly irrational decisions which are consistent with each other may be better than more rational decisions that are inconsistent.

> One plan assigned 100 points for constant noise and 80 points for intermittent noise. One machine on which many of the employees worked made a great deal of noise 300 times a minute, but this job was classified as having intermittent noise. When a new job was established in this shop, the union insisted that it should be evaluated as being subject to "constant noise." Management objected on the ground that this noise had been rated as intermittent for years, that if 20 points were added to this new job for constant noise, then 20 points should be added to all other jobs in the shop and that doing this would amount to giving a general wage increase to 30 per cent of the employees. The company argued that the union should wait until the contract expired to demand a change.
>
> Eventually the matter went to arbitration. Though the arbitrator agreed that the noise sounded pretty constant to him, he still ruled for the company. He pointed out that the purpose of job evaluation was to establish *relative* wage rates, and that to give this one job an additional 20 points would disturb the traditional relationship between jobs.

Step 4: Determining the Wage Rate

From this point on, evaluation schemes vary a great deal. We will describe one common variety.

Once the point scores for each job have been calculated, they are plotted on a graph with point scores on one axis and present wage rates on the other. Notice that on p. 608 the utility assembler is evaluated at 300 points and now makes $3.10 an hour.

Next a trend line is drawn through the data, either freehand or in accordance with some mathematical formula. Jobs that lie above the trend line presumably are overpaid; those that lie below are underpaid. In the example given, the assembler is overpaid by 10 cents an hour, the tool and die man is underpaid by 20 cents.

If the trend line has been properly drawn, the cost of bringing the underpaid jobs *up* to the trend line is just balanced by the savings achieved by bringing those that are overpaid *down* to the line. If the rates are adjusted in this way, roughly half the employees will get wage increases and half will get wage cuts. However, such widespread wage cuts will make it extremely difficult to win acceptance of the plan (since the man who is about to get a cut will normally react much more violently than the man who is about to get a raise). Management can adopt two approaches to make the change more palatable:

Figure labels:
- 6, 5, 4, 3, 2, 1, 0 (y-axis)
- Pay in dollars (y-axis title)
- Trend line resulting in no cost to company
- Trend line with 20¢ "sweetener"
- "Red circle" Screw machine operation
- Tool and die man
- Utility assembler
- 0, 200, 400, 600, 800, 1000 (x-axis)
- Evaluated point score

Determining the wage rate.

1. *"Sweeteners."* Management may decide to offer a "sweetener"—that is, a wage adjustment that will make the plan more acceptable. For example, it may draw the trend line 20 cents above the present mid-point, causing fewer workers to suffer wage cuts. The utility assembler, for instance, would get a 10-cent raise instead of a 10-cent cut, while the tool and die man would get a 30-cent raise. This sweetener is sometimes called an "adjustment for inequities." Note that it costs the company as much as an across-the-board wage increase. (Normally the size of the "sweetener" is determined by reference to collective bargaining or wage surveys.)

2. *"Red-circle rates."*   Management may also guarantee the men who are now overpaid that as long as they *personally* are on this job the rate will not be cut. However, anyone who takes their place will receive only the rate set by job evaluation. This is traditionally called "red-circling" the job. Often, too, where there is a general wage increase, the men on red-circle jobs get no increase, or only a partial increase, until the evaluated rate catches up with the red-circle rate.

Job classification chart.

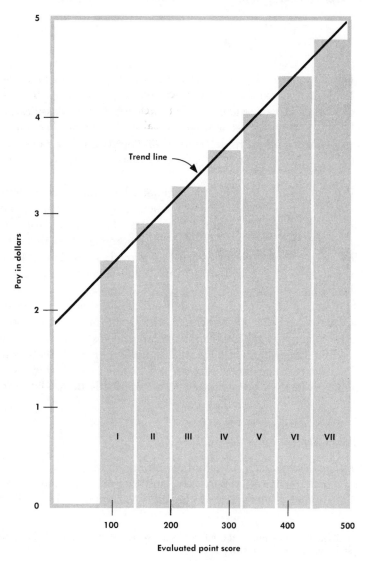

Job classifications. Actually, instead of separate wage rates for each job, it is common under job evaluation to bracket jobs with roughly similar point totals into *job classifications* (sometimes called labor grades), each of which will receive the same rate of pay (see chart on p. 609).

Since moving from one job classification to another constitutes a promotion, management should give careful thought to the number of job classifications it establishes (see pp. 498-499). If there are too few classifications, it will be hard to promote employees and give them the feeling that they are moving ahead. On the other hand, if there are too many grades, every time a man changes his work slightly, he may move into a different classification with a different rate of pay. Too many changes create expense and confusion.

POLICY PROBLEMS

There is far more to job evaluation than merely going through the mechanical procedures that we have just described. True, by following these procedures management can tentatively slot each job into a classification and for each classification it can set a wage or salary rate. However, job evaluation cannot provide scientifically determined or objectively fair rates. As we have seen, it is a highly subjective process and there is much room for judgment and human error.

But it is not enough to strive for complete, laboratory-like objectivity.[8] The crucial question is not whether management has followed the job-evaluation procedures with scrupulous care, but whether the resulting wage and salary structure meets the objectives of sound wage administration that we discussed on p. 597. In particular, does the structure provide rates that (1) seem fair to those concerned and (2) will attract and retain enough competent employees to do the job?

In short, an effective program of job evaluation should be concerned with employee values on the one hand and with going market rates on the other. These criteria are sometimes called "internal" and "external" standards. A technically sound job-evaluation plan that ignores either of these standards is bound to lead to tremendous friction and to fail in achieving its objectives. To complicate matters even further, these standards themselves are often in conflict.

Internal Standards

Who gets compared. Usually there are separate job-evaluation programs for production, technical, supervisory, and clerical personnel. Perhaps from a theoretical point of view it would be fairer to compare jobs in all these cate-

---

[8] For a discussion of some of the efforts to improve the statistical reliability and validity of the system, see Belcher, *op. cit.*, p. 91.

gories against each other, but the practical difficulties would be enormous. The less jobs have in common, the more difficult it is to compare them.

> Indeed one theory of wage determination suggests there are "clusters" of jobs which are related to each other by technology, organization, and custom.[9] Each cluster has one or more "key" jobs to which major attention is devoted during the wage-determination process. The relationship of wages paid to other jobs within the cluster to the "key" rate is well determined by custom. Wage-making forces are concentrated on the position of the key rates in each cluster relative to the position of key rates of other clusters both within and without the firm. Thus, individuals compare their wages with the key rate in their own cluster and, to a lesser degree, they compare key rates with each other.

The job requirements of nurse, sales engineer, and riveter, for example, have so little in common that it would be almost impossible to get agreement on which factors are the relevant ones to compare. How is one to compare the skill or responsibility required by these very different jobs? Fortunately, there is little need to do so. People tend to compare their jobs only with those "close by" them. A clerical worker is unlikely to compare her wage with that paid for any specific production job (though she may feel that all production workers earn too much). Consequently, it is possible to establish separate programs for each group and to exercise a separate set of criteria for each program.

It has even been suggested that there should be separate job-evaluation programs for automated and nonautomated jobs.[10] On automated jobs, responsibility is the most important factor; on nonautomated jobs, skills are most important. A program that gives equal weight to both factors might not be fair to either kind of job.

Rates should seem fair. In Chapter 4 we discussed the determinants of status and suggested that a major cause of employee discontent is the *status inconsistency* that develops when various measures of status, such as job title and size of office, get out of line. Two of the major determinants of status are the nature of a man's work and the size of his paycheck. Great dissatisfaction arises when the *people concerned* decide that these determinants are out of line. The individual is unhappy if he thinks his pay is too little, relative to what others get for the same work. The others are unhappy if they think his pay is too high. One purpose of job evaluation, therefore, is to realign the status ladder so as to reduce the perceived inconsistencies between pay and job requirements.

Employees in most situations have a pretty good idea of what various jobs are worth.[11] In part this is a matter of tradition. Job A has always paid more

---

[9] John T. Dunlop, "The Task of Contemporary Wage Theory," in George W. Taylor and Frank Pierson, eds., *New Concepts in Wage Determination* (New York: McGraw-Hill, 1957), pp. 127-139.

[10] John R. Bright, "Does Automation Raise Skill Requirements?" *Harvard Business Review*, Vol. 36, No. 4 (July 1958), p. 98.

[11] See Martin Patchen, *The Choice of Wage Comparisons* (Englewood Cliffs, New Jersey: Prentice-Hall, 1961).

than Job B. Yet the "accepted" wage structure varies widely from one situation to another.

> A number of specific examples come to mind: (1) In one company all the major maintenance crafts are in the same labor grade and rate range. The evaluated result follows the previous custom of equal payment. In a neighboring plant these same craft skills carry historical differentials. In each instance they are accepted as correct. (2) Within one industry several different skilled jobs are at the top of the pay ladder in different companies. Where Job A is at the top it appears to be regarded as the most skilled by management and employees alike. The same holds true where Job B is most highly paid.[12]

For this reason job evaluation may be most readily accepted—and most acutely needed—in new plants where there are no traditional rates and in old plants where technological change has thrown all the old job responsibilities and wage relationships into a state of flux.

In any case, care must be taken not to disturb established status hierarchies. If employees are generally satisfied with current pay relationships, why upset the applecart to achieve the theoretical equity afforded by job evaluation? If Job A has always paid more than Job B, in the eyes of the employees Job A is a better job. An "A" man has always had a tendency to look down on a "B" man. Now suppose job evaluation leads to higher pay for Job B than for Job A. The pay on Job A has not been cut, but status is a relative thing and Job A now has lower status than Job B. The "A" men consider themselves demoted; they are frustrated, lose interest in their work, and may even quit or take a militant antimanagement position in the union.

Job evaluation can also unwittingly upset promotional sequences. Let us assume that Jobs A and B are in the same "seniority district"—that is, when there is a vacancy in either job, men from the entire "district" may bid for it. Naturally if Job A originally paid more than Job B, the senior men would tend to move to Job A and turn down Job B. Moving to Job A would be considered a promotion. Now job evaluation reverses this relationship: Job B becomes the better job. The men who had previously chosen Job A over Job B are understandably bitter. Then senior men on Job A will be getting less than the junior men on Job B. Of course, management may permit the senior men on Job A to "bump" the junior men from Job B, but the bumping period will be one of confusion and expense to management and of great ill-feeling on the part of employees.

Another problem arises in evaluating hard, dirty jobs. According to worker logic, clean jobs are better than dirty ones. A new man should start at the bottom, at the hardest, dirtiest, least desirable job. Then, as he acquires seniority, he should move up to better, easier, higher-paying jobs. But this is contradictory to the logic of job evaluation, which says that more points should be given for hard work and dirty conditions. Yet people will resist being "pro-

---

12 E. Robert Livernash, "Wage Administration and Production Standards," Arthur Kornhauser, Robert Dubin, and Arthur Ross, eds., *Industrial Conflict* (New York: McGraw-Hill, 1954), p. 336.

moted" into a higher-paying job that has lower status. In practice, this problem is solved by giving very low point values to the factors of physical effort and job conditions [13]—or by socially separating the two kinds of job so that there will be little invidious comparison. At times management disregards the logic of job evaluation almost completely; dirty jobs are paid less than clean jobs. But the dirty job is a starting job through which all employees must move. As a man gets promoted, he moves by the ordinary process of seniority from a dirty, low-paid, low-status job to a cleaner, higher-paid, higher-status job.

Similar problems arise when job evaluation fails to take into account such job characteristics as opportunities for overtime or promotion. For instance, Job X pays 2 cents more an hour than Job Y, but Job Y is generally considered a better job because it presents greater opportunities for overtime. If evaluation raises Job X's differential to, say, 15 cents an hour, the men who had previously picked Y over X will feel cheated. On the other hand, if Y's hourly pay is increased still further, others may say that this is unfair, since Y's weekly pay may now exceed that of Z, a job that everyone agrees is more demanding than Y.

Similarly, a man who has a so-called dead-end job, on which there is little opportunity for promotion, feels that he should be somehow recompensed for this disadvantage. So does the man whose job has been automatized. Perhaps his work requires less skill and effort than before, but his output has vastly increased and he feels that some of the benefits should go to him. Yet strict job evaluation would say that since less skill and effort are required, the wage for the job should be cut.

Under strict job evaluation, too, it makes no difference whether the work is performed by a man, a woman, or a member of a minority group. Morally this is just. Yet both management and union should recognize that many workers feel that so-called "women's" jobs, or jobs that are typically performed by minority groups, should pay less, despite the fact that such discrimination violates federal law. We do not suggest that concessions should be made to undemocratic prejudices, but that both union and management should be aware that there will be resistance to change if an attempt is made to eliminate or ignore this discrimination.

Another question concerns the differentials between skilled and unskilled workers (in effect, the slope of the trend line mentioned on p. 607). All through the 1940's and early 1950's wage increases were given generally on an "across the board" basis (so much per hour for all employees), thus reducing the differential. Since then pressures by skilled employees have tended to restore the previous balance by increasing differentials.

Thus, there are many factors that wage administration must take into account other than the abstract requirements of the job as determined by job evaluation. It should be emphasized again that the objective is to obtain wage stand-

---

[13] And yet several authorities have argued that too little emphasis is given to physical effort. Solomon Barkin, "Wage Determination: Trick or Technique," *Labor and Nation,* Vol. 1, No. 6 (June 1946), p. 25; Kerr and Fisher, *op. cit.*

ards which *seem fair* to the people involved. The outsider should not substitute his frame of reference for that of the people involved (except possibly on moral and legal grounds to prevent sex or ethnic discrimination).

External Factors

It is not enough for wage administration to achieve internal consistency, however, for employees and their unions compare their wages with those paid on comparable jobs in other companies. If wages lag behind those paid for similar work elsewhere, some employees may quit, the rest may grow dissatisfied, and it will be harder to hire new men. External comparisons are more likely to be made in some situations than in others.

1. Skilled maintenance men and unskilled common laborers are more likely to make such comparisons than are workers who hold jobs in the middle range of the spectrum. Maintenance jobs are pretty much alike throughout the community; the carpenter, for instance, knows what he can earn elsewhere. To a lesser extent the same is true of unskilled laborers' jobs, the starting jobs at which new employees are hired.

There is less market pressure on semiskilled jobs. These are not hiring jobs; instead, one must have considerable seniority to earn them. A semiskilled employee may become dissatisfied with low pay but he is less willing to quit because he will lose his seniority, pension rights, and so forth. In any case, most semiskilled jobs are relatively specialized; there are fewer comparable jobs, so fewer comparisons are made.

2. Comparisons are more likely to be made in times of full employment when a new worker can choose among employers and when older employees can transfer to jobs elsewhere. We repeat, however, that few workers make systematic comparisons before accepting a job (see p. 455), and most employees are reluctant to quit a job on which they are reasonably happy just to make higher pay elsewhere.

3. Workers are less likely to make comparisons if the plant is geographically isolated or if the type of work is so highly specialized that there are few comparable jobs.

Thus, the pressure to meet comparable rates is higher in times of full employment and in certain job ranges. Many companies use wage surveys in order to keep their wages from getting inadvertently out of line, either in terms of over-all wage levels or of specific jobs which are common to many enterprises.

Reconciling Internal
and External Standards

What should a company do when internal and external standards conflict, when the rates set by job evaluation are lower than those set by the market? High-wage companies need not worry too much about this problem, since most of their evaluated rates are well above those of the market. However, the lower the company's average pay, the more likely there is to be "conflict between the disorderly operation of the labor market and the orderly operation of the internal wage system." [14]

Job evaluation frequently favors different groups from those favored by the market.

> The jobs which tend to rate high as compared with the market are those of janitor, nurse, and typist; while craft rates are comparatively low. Weaker groups are better served by an evaluation plan than by the market; the former places the emphasis not on force but on equity. Ideally, for a system of factors to accurately reflect the market, it should give heavy weight to those considerations to which the market most responds: skill, job conditions and bargaining power.[15]

Some sort of adjustment is required when the market rate on a specific job is higher than the evaluated rate. Many companies pay an "out-of-line" rate. Other companies engage in trial-and-error adjustments to make their job-evaluation scheme conform more closely to market forces. For instance, if some rates are well above the market and others below, the job-evaluation manual may be giving the wrong weights to the various factors, and these weights should be corrected. "If working conditions were given the major weight and skill a minor weight, there would be no correlation with the realities of the market place." [16] In some job-evaluation plans, "balancing points" are added to the point totals produced by ordinary job evaluation in an effort to make the results accord more closely with prevailing rates.

The greater the difference between evaluated rates and market rates, and the lower the company's average pay, the more point-juggling and factor-balancing will be required to devise an acceptable wage structure. Finally, there comes a point where job evaluation simply isn't worth the trouble. A really low-wage employer in a highly competitive industry, for instance, will have little use for job evaluation. He will just pay the lowest rate he can to recruit or retain employees for each job.

Many companies follow market rates exclusively for skilled jobs and use job evaluation only for semiskilled jobs on which it is difficult to make comparisons with other companies. Or a company may pay prevailing rates on jobs where such rates exist, and then use job evaluation to interpolate other job rates between those set by the market.

Thus, if job evaluation is flexible enough, there need be little conflict between the rates it establishes and the external standards set by the market.

---

[14] Frank H. Cassell, "Corporate Manpower Planning," *Stanford Graduate School of Business Bulletin*, Vol. 34, No. 1 (Summer 1965), p. 31.

[15] Kerr and Fisher, *op. cit.*, p. 392.

[16] Edward Robert Livernash, "Wage Administration and Production Standards," Arthur Kornhauser, Robert Dubin, and Arthur Ross, eds., *Industrial Conflict* (New York: McGraw-Hill, 1954), p. 336.

But this very flexibility may lead to dissatisfaction with internal standards. According to job evaluation, Jobs Q and R are equally difficult, and for years they have been paid the same rate. Then a tremendous demand arises in the community for workers to do Job R. So on the principle of adjusting to market rates, R's pay is raised while Q's remains the same. The man on Q protests, "My job is as hard as his. Why shouldn't I get an increase too?" Wage administration must constantly face dilemmas of this sort. Whether satisfactory adjustments can be made, however, depends at least as much on how the plan is administered as on the rates that are set.

Automation

Automation raises difficult job-evaluation questions. Automation reduces physical effort and dilutes job skills. Thus, by some standards the worth of the job declines. But workers (and their unions) insist vehemently that pay should be increased, since readjustment to new work is difficult and the new equipment involves vastly greater responsibility and mental fatigue (a factor often not measured by job-evaluation plans). In addition, since the new systems are more productive, workers whose jobs have changed argue that they should share the "fruits of progress." And, understandably, workers on adjacent jobs claim that productivity gains should not be hoarded by one group but divided among all those in the bargaining units. To alleviate problems such as these, some companies, such as Kaiser Steel, have introduced group incentive plans (see pp. 673-675).

ADMINISTRATION [17]

Any system of job evaluation is doomed to failure unless it is accepted as fair by all parties concerned. Introducing a job-evaluation plan involves all the problems of introducing change discussed in Chapter 13. Employees fear that job evaluation will upset the old structure of social relations; supervisors fear that it will deprive them of their traditional prerogative to set the wages of those who work for them; the union fears that it will reduce the scope of collective bargaining. All may well look on job evaluation as an impersonal, impossible-to-understand system which threatens their old established ways of doing things.

One way of reducing these fears is to make the plan easier to understand; indeed, there is a strong trend toward greater and greater simplicity. Another is to involve the maximum number of people in administering the plan. In general, the larger the number of people who take part, the more likely the plan is to be accepted—though there is always danger that if too many people

---

[17] For an excellent discussion, see Kerr and Fisher, *op. cit.*

are involved in the early stages, so much time will be spent in discussion that the plan will never be put into effect at all.

In a nonunionized organization the job-evaluation program is usually administered by a committee representing a broad range of departments and levels of management, possibly with rotating membership to broaden participation as much as possible. The line supervisors involved are consulted at every stage, and their approval is required before a job specification is made final. Moreover, the individual workers are consulted when the job specifications are drawn up.

Usually the personnel department acts as general coordinator for the program, though a few companies assign this task to the industrial engineering department. (It can be argued that job evaluation is more properly the personnel department's function, since above all the program demands flexibility and skill in dealing with people.) Sometimes the personnel department writes the job specifications; sometimes this is done by the committee itself. In almost every case the final rating is performed by the committee. After the new rates are tentatively decided upon, the committee must give ample opportunity for objections to be heard and must be willing to make changes where necessary.

One of the problems of administration is deciding on the proper degree of centralization: Should job evaluation be conducted on an office-wide, a plant-wide, or a company-wide basis? To what extent should the individual supervisor be permitted to make exceptions in special cases (*e.g.*, to grant a salary increase to avoid losing an exceptionally good man)? Too much centralization severely limits the freedom of the individual supervisor or plant manager; too little makes it possible for an individual supervisor to be exceptionally liberal, thus adding unnecessary expense and raising the danger that others will feel discriminated against. The trend is toward allowing supervisors to make exceptions, but only with the approval of the personnel department.

Once a plan has been set up, constant "maintenance" is needed to keep inequities from arising. Changes may occur either in wage rates elsewhere or in the job requirements of particular jobs. New jobs are created and must be evaluated. Suppose, after a plan has been put into effect, that one group is still very much upset over the wage rate it has received. Neither wage rates elsewhere nor job requirements within the company have changed. Should the job-evaluation committees give this group another hearing and perhaps yield to their pressure? Many authorities suggest that the committee should be quite willing to make adjustments *before* the plan is finally adopted, but that it should strongly resist pressure for change *after* the plan has been adopted. If the committee does not stand fast, every discontented group in the plant will continue to make trouble and unrest will persist indefinitely.[18]

Some companies make use of outside consultants in installing job-evaluation

---

[18] For an example, see *ibid.*, p. 390.

programs. The consultants may actually do the whole task, from writing the job description through rating the jobs and setting the rates. The more reputable consultants, however, recognize that if the plan is to win acceptance, those who will be affected by it must participate in making the evaluation; consequently, they insist on confining their activities to training and troubleshooting. Job evaluation is a responsibility that management cannot easily delegate to an outsider.

The Role of the Union

Union attitudes toward job evaluation vary greatly, more in response to the over-all quality of union-management relations than to union policy toward job evaluation as such. Union objections center around the charge that job evaluation is a management tool used to restrict or eliminate collective bargaining. By its very nature, some union leaders argue, job evaluation prevents a realistic consideration of market forces or bargaining strength, and makes it impossible to work out adjustments suited to individual needs. It is "just hocus-pocus which prevents workers from understanding the pay system under which they work . . . a cumbersome calculus in which nothing seems to add up." [19]

Nevertheless job evaluation is often introduced in the first place in response to the union's insistence that something be done to eliminate wage inequities. Union proponents of job evaluation argue that "the basic concepts of job evaluation were used by trade unionists long before these ideas were formalized into a systematic body of thought. . . . As soon as negotiators recognized that a tool and die worker warranted a different scale than a broom sweeper, then job evaluation had been introduced into collective bargaining. Like Molière's famous character, many trade unionists may be surprised to find that they have been talking prose all their life." [20] Job evaluation, they would argue, is merely a systematic framework for negotiation.

In practice, the role of the union varies from outright opposition to complete participation. The UAW, for instance, is firmly opposed to evaluation. As a consequence, some automobile manufacturers engage in informal evaluation for their own purposes, but make no use of it in negotiations.

In contrast, some of the unions that believe in complete participation appoint specially trained international representatives to assist in the process.[21] Local unions often select members, who are then trained by management, to sit on

---

19 Boris Shiskin, "Job Evaluation: What It Is and How It Works," *American Federationist* (July, August, September, 1947), as cited in Edward N. Hay, "The Attitude of the American Federation of Labor on Job Evaluation," *Personnel Journal,* Vol. 26, No. 5 (November 1947), pp. 168-169.

20 William Gomberg, "A Collective Bargaining Approach to Job Evaluation," *Labor and Nation* (November 1946).

21 For a study of a program in which a union took a very active part, see Jack Steiber, *The Steel Industry Wage Structure: A Study of the Joint Union-Management Job Evaluation Program in the Basic Steel Industry* (Cambridge: Harvard University Press, 1959).

joint union-management evaluation committees. These committee members participate equally with management in writing job descriptions, rating jobs, and setting rates. In some cases the members may take an active part only in rating jobs and setting rates, though they have the right to protest and review job descriptions.

A different approach is for the company to conduct the entire evaluation, but to secure union approval at every stage, or to guarantee the union the right to object only to the end-product.

One reason for the union's reluctance to take an active part in the evaluation procedure is its realization that job evaluation is a dirty job. Many of the questions that arise concern disputes between union members over who should have higher status. Regardless of how impartial the union officers try to be, some members will accuse them of favoritism. Rather than make themselves the butt of complaints, many officers would prefer to let management take the responsibility and reserve for themselves the freedom to criticize from the sideline. For this same reason, management is often glad to pass the buck to the union, if it will accept it.

Regardless of the union's role, disputes over rates play a large part in union politics.

> To take a typical example, a public utility union included, among other members, DC and AC operators. At one time the president was a DC operator who, through his activities on the evaluation committee, was able to get for his group an extra 5 cents an hour, on the ground that their job required extra physical effort. Resentment against this apparent favoritism helped contribute to his defeat at the next election. The AC group, which gained power, was able to win a 5-cent advantage for itself on the grounds that its equipment, being more modern, required more responsibility. In retaliation, the DC group tried to lead the local into an affiliation with a new international union.

Job evaluation is more difficult to administer if the company is obliged to deal with several unions, for each will be concerned with how it makes out relative to the others, and each will be reluctant to make concessions in its relative position. For that matter, job evaluation is also difficult to administer if there are internal disputes within one union.

Management has good reason to encourage the union to take an active role in job evaluation and not just to force it to accept partial responsibility for the final result. To repeat the theme of this chapter, one of the primary objectives of job evaluation is to devise a wage structure that workers regard as fair. And the union is in an ideal position to sample and present worker opinions. A personnel director once told us that the first time he regretted not having a union in his office was when he started a job-evaluation program there. He selected a committee of employees as a sounding board, but he felt that they were far less willing to express their true opinions than an equivalent union committee would have been. For this reason many of the inequities felt by the employees at large were never expressed.

Whether job evaluation is desirable depends directly on the state of union-management relations. Certainly a joint committee will turn into a battle-ground if a cold war is in progress between the parties. In any case, it is almost impossible to devise a successful plan in the face of strong union opposition. On the other hand, if management is flexible in its attitude toward job evaluation and if the union is favorable to it, there may be very little distinction between bargained and evaluated rates.

There seems to be some evidence that acceptance will be easier to achieve if the parties first agree on the amount of the wage increase or "sweetener" to be provided before they proceed to establish relative job ranks. Once boundaries have been set to the amount to be distributed, consensus comes more readily than when the sky is the limit.

WHEN SHOULD MANAGEMENT ENGAGE IN JOB EVALUATION?

Job evaluation has been adopted in many companies just because it is the "proper" thing to do. Those responsible for its administration are often more concerned with developing a technically perfect product than in measuring its impact on people or in finding out whether it is accomplishing what it is designed to do. As two observers have commented:

> The tendency is to . . . plug loopholes, to ferret out imprecision and make it precise, to define jobs more and more exactly . . . to substitute means for ends, to forget that the objective is simply the acceptable determination of wages for a group of employees and to lavish more and more care on the production of a systematic end result which will be logical, polished, and final.[22]

And yet management should be aware that job evaluation is always expensive to administer and to keep up to date, and that it almost invariably leads to headaches for management and to friction with workers and unions. By altering relative wage rates, job evaluation disrupts established social and psychological relationships and opens a Pandora's box of troubles. Once management starts handing out wage increases, everybody expects something—and most people are likely to be at least partially disappointed. Even though management institutes evaluation in response to the union's demands for fairer wage rates, friction with the union over the administration of the program is almost inevitable.

As a consequence, many personnel directors feel that job evaluation, like appendectomies, should be avoided unless they are really necessary. So long as problems are not too serious, job evaluation may be postponed by patching things up here and there or by pragmatic negotiations with the union. The real question is whether evaluation will improve matters enough to be worth the trouble—or whether it will actually make matters worse. Job evaluation may

---

[22] Kerr and Fisher, *op. cit.*, p. 394.

be desirable if wage rates are far out of line with what employees feel are fair, or if the union is constantly complaining of inequities. But if the employees and the union are not too unhappy with the existing wage structure, it would seem foolish to create unnecessary friction. On the other hand, resistance to evaluation programs tends to drop over time, once they have been installed.

We shall conclude this section with a list of some of the circumstances under which job evaluation has the best chance of success:

1. When it does not cause undue disruption of either traditional wage patterns or established promotional ladders.

2. When the company's over-all wage level is relatively high, so that not too many adjustments or exceptions must be made to meet market pressures, *or* when the company is so isolated from other firms (either in terms of geography or job requirements) that comparisons with wages elsewhere are difficult to make.

3. When relations with the union are generally good, when the union accepts an active role in administering the program, and when there is little internal conflict within the union.

4. When there is broad participation in administering the program throughout all levels of management.

5. When the company is willing to pay a "sweetener" to encourage acceptance.

MERIT RATING

Merit rating is used by many companies to determine which employees should receive *merit increases* that will lift their wages or salaries above the minimum rate set by job evaluation. These companies hope to reward outstanding performance and provide motivation for all employees to work harder.[23] Indeed, even a smoothly functioning job-evaluation system will operate primarily as a "hygienic" factor (see pp. 136-137) preventing employee *dis*satisfaction. A merit-rating system provides positive motivation for hard work.

Instead of a single wage or salary rate for each job, companies that practice merit rating normally have a *rate range*. For instance, the rate range of Job Class III might be from \$2.20 to \$2.60 (see chart p. 621). Typically, each range is divided into a series of intervals or *steps* (the steps are \$.10 apart in the chart). A new employee starts at the bottom step and is subject to periodic *merit reviews,* usually conducted by his supervisor. These reviews determine whether the employee should receive a raise that will carry him up one or more steps. They are made at regular intervals, possibly every four, six, or twelve months. In conducting the review, the supervisor often makes use of a

---

[23] Merit rating is useful in deciding who will be promoted from one job to another as well as in deciding who will get raises (see Chapter 23).

Job classification and merit progression chart.

merit-rating form (see p. 624), which provides a convenient means of summarizing the employee's weaknesses and strong points. After the review has been completed, the supervisor at times sits down with the employee to communicate the results in a *merit-rating interview,* which is analogous to the appraisal interview at the management level.

Merit rating gives rise to several special problems, each of which we will discuss in turn.

Rate Ranges

Rate ranges normally overlap—that is, the highest step in one job classification may pay more than the lowest step in the next job classification. In the following chart, for example, the top step of Job Class III pays $.20 more than the lowest step of Job Class IV. What happens if an employee is at the top step of one job classification—must he take a cut in pay in order to move into a higher job classification? Normally he does not; he carries his old rate of pay with him and starts from the equivalent step in his new classification.

Not uncommonly, the rate ranges for higher job classifications are wider than those for lower job classifications. In our example, Job Class I has a range of only $.30 while Job Class VI has a range of $.50. Wider ranges are customary on higher-paid jobs to provide employees with more opportunity to display unusual skills on more difficult work. Also, as jobs become more difficult and important, it is more worthwhile to give employees a substantial financial incentive to contribute outstanding work.

Merit Reviews
and Merit Interviews

Merit rating of hourly-paid and lower-ranking salaried employees involves many of the problems of performance rating that we discussed in Chapter 23. There are numerous types of rating forms, though the check-the-box type illustrated on the following page is the most typical. As in performance rating, numerous sources of bias such as the halo effect and over-leniency serve to reduce the effectiveness of the rating process.

In theory, the merit-rating interview gives the supervisor a chance to discuss each subordinate's problems with him and to coach him to do a better job. In practice, supervisors show little sympathy for the interview process and tend to conduct their interviews in a mechanical and insensitive manner; it is possible, of course, to improve their proficiency through careful training.

Union Attitudes
Toward Merit Reviews

Unions in general oppose merit rating, insisting that it opens the door to rivalry and bad feeling between employees and to favoritism on the part of supervisors. They would prefer that all employees receive the same rate, and feel that if there is to be a rate range, employees should move up from step to step purely by seniority. (Of course, unions prefer a formalized system of merit rating over giving the employer complete freedom to set wage rates as he wishes.)

When merit-rating systems are established in unionized plants, the union tends to pressure management into giving each employee an increase every time a rating period comes around. If an employee is skipped over, the union files a grievance and requires management to explain why he did not receive an increase. Understandably, grievances of this sort often lead to recriminations and bad feelings between supervisor and subordinates. Yet where management yields to such pressures, wage increases from one step to another become completely automatic and depend exclusively on seniority rather than performance. Sometimes a compromise is worked out whereby employees automatically move up one step each review period until they reach the "mid-step" halfway between the top and bottom of the range. Pay increases above the mid-step are given purely at the discretion of management. (In government service, however, it is quite common for increases to be based entirely on seniority.)

When Should Merit Rating Be Used?

In theory, merit rating should relax the rigidity of job evaluation (which emphasizes the job, not the man who performs it) and should provide recognition for performance. It should also raise both productivity and morale, since employees who do a good job are rewarded. In practice, however, employees often come to expect that raises will be given automatically, instead of as a reward for good work. Indeed, for an employee to be denied an increase is sometimes regarded as a form of discipline, and is sharply resented unless it is clearly justified. Moreover, a poorly administered merit-rating program may

Merit rating form.

NAME *Howard Bowman*   JOB *Tool crib attendant*

DATE *7/16/67*   FOREMAN *David Thatcher*

If on job less than six months state time   —

Supervision Required	4
Job Knowledge	2
Attitude, Conduct, Cooperation	4
Safety	3
Housekeeping	2
Absenteeism and Tardiness	4
Adaptability	2
Judgment	1
Quantity	4
Quality	2
Rating	28

Remarks: *An able employee who shows a tendency to be lazy. He knows his job well but is frequently late to work and uncooperative with other employees.*

Reviewed by Board ☑   Rating Code: 1. Top
Total   3   2. Above average
                                            3. Average
                                            4. Below average
                                            5. Unsatisfactory

lead to constant tension and ill feeling between supervisors and subordinates (and between management and union).

In general, merit rating should not be introduced unless the employees themselves accept the principle that there may be a legitimate difference in compensation among employees who hold the same job title. If employees think such distinctions are unfair, they are bound to resist any attempt to create them. Such distinctions are most likely to be accepted by highly skilled workers and by white-collar workers. On highly skilled production jobs there is a significant difference between outstanding performance and merely adequate performance, while white-collar workers are particularly anxious to advance in their work. For this reason, and because of blue-collar union opposition, rate ranges are considerably more common among white-collar than among blue-collar employees.

Finally, merit rating should not be attempted unless subordinates have confidence that the rating will be fair. Ratings do more harm than good if employees assume that there is any arbitrariness or favoritism in the way they are made. Thus, a company would be wise to forego merit rating unless its supervisory practices are generally sound and it enjoys good union-management relations.

SALARY ADMINISTRATION FOR EXECUTIVES

Salary administration for executives involves most of the problems that apply to clerical and production employees, but it also involves certain peculiar problems of its own. Indeed, some argue that principles of wage administration, developed at the factory level, are completely inappropriate for management. In evaluating executive performance, many companies use a modified version of the standard job-evaluation procedure—that is, they go through the normal steps of job description, point rating, and establishing salary grades and salary ranges. And yet executive jobs are particularly hard to describe. They are more complex than lower-level jobs, and many of them are unique. For instance, the manager of Plant A, which concentrates on experimental work, has a different set of responsibilities from those of the manager of Plant B, which specializes in routine, mass-production work. Yet both executives have the same title: "Plant Manager."

> Job descriptions for managers not only are more important than for clerical or hourly workers; they are also more difficult to prepare, because the supervisor is given "areas of responsibility" rather than specific work assignments, and the procedures he follows in accompanying these objectives are not officially proscribed.[24]

---

[24] Robert E. Sibson, "Plan for Management Salary Administration," *Harvard Business Review*, Vol. 34, No. 6 (November 1956), p. 104. For a job-description plan designed primarily for executives, see John K. Hemphill, "Job Descriptions of Executives," *Harvard Business Review*, Vol. 37, No. 5 (September 1959), pp. 55-67.

Obviously most of the factors used to evaluate subordinates' jobs (such as skill or working conditions) are not appropriate to an evaluation of executive responsibility. Executive jobs, after all, require a great deal of decision-making, planning, and supervision of others. Yet these special executive skills are often difficult to define, measure, or reduce to the "degrees" that are required by most forms of job evaluation.

Moreover, since there is usually a great difference between the efficiency with which two men perform the same job at the executive level, executive jobs are usually assigned salary ranges (for instance, $18,000 to $25,000) rather than a specific salary ($20,135).

> The width of salary grades—the within-grade progression or percentage by which the salary of the man classified at the top of the grade exceeds that of the men at the bottom of the grade—should depend theoretically on the extent to which the performance of the individual job holder can determine the value of the job. In other words, how much can man-worth affect job worth? [25]

The progress of each executive, from the bottom of his salary grade to the top, can be determined by periodic salary reviews, perhaps every six months or every year. This is the equivalent of merit rating at lower levels. In such a salary review, how large a salary increase an executive receives is largely determined on the basis of an evaluation by his direct superior (see Chapter 23). Since individual differences are so significant at the executive level, performance evaluation may be more important than job evaluation. The two programs must be closely coordinated, however, to prevent inequities from arising (for instance, to prevent executives of equal merit from being paid more in Division A, which has a generous division manager, than they are in Division B, whose manager is more cost-conscious). Many companies permit a certain amount of flexibility in their evaluation system to provide for individual bargaining—that is, to make it possible to grant a special raise to keep a good man who has had a better offer from another company.

Keeping Costs in Line

Excessive flexibility can cause trouble. In being overgenerous in granting salary increases to his subordinates, the executive can both jeopardize his company's profit position and create inequities between departments. Expectations arise in some departments that all employees will receive merit increases annually. When this happens the "merit" increase becomes the equivalent of an across-the-board increase and those who fail to get increases feel very much discriminated against. To prevent inequities and preserve merit rating as a means of rewarding good performance, some sorts of guidelines are necessary to keep departments in line. Often, departments are given "quotas" which they

---

[25] Sibson, *op. cit.*, p. 112. Since the individual is so much more important than the job at these levels, it has been suggested that job evaluation should never be applied to top management.

cannot exceed without special authorization. For example, the average increase may not exceed 5 per cent, or not more than half the employees may receive increases in any one year. Typically, even in companies which do not follow programs as rigid as this, higher management, the personnel department and the accounting department all police the salary structure pretty closely. An executive whose structure gets out of all proportion may well have to give some careful explanations to his boss.

Communicating Salary Positions

The details of the executive salary program are often kept secret—either by design or because of poor communications. Top management fears that all sorts of rivalry and bad feeling will develop if each executive knows what his colleagues are getting. But there is little justification for keeping an executive from knowing how he himself stands. At times, for example, in companies with managerial rate ranges, an executive who receives $25,000 a year has no idea whether he is already at the top of his salary grade, or whether he can reasonably expect to receive several thousand dollars more in salary increases without having to go to a higher-ranking job. Typically, executives are in the dark about the basis upon which their work is judged or what they are required to do to increase their earnings. Uncertainty of this sort leads to the suspicion that raises are distributed in an arbitrary manner or purely on the basis of favoritism. Nothing is more harmful to morale and motivation than the fear that one is being cheated on his salary.

Extra Compensation

As one goes higher in the management hierarchy, one finds that base salaries are supplemented more and more heavily with extra compensation in the form of bonuses (often based on the profitability or effectiveness of the executive's own department or of the company as a whole) and fringe benefits, ranging from free life insurance and liberal retirement benefits to company-paid membership in the country club.[26] Stock options provide another form of extra-salary compensation, particularly for top management. Stock options permit a participating executive to purchase a specified number of shares of company stock during some future period, but at a price close to that prevailing when the options are issued. Thus, if the price of the company stock goes up in the future the executive can buy below market and so stand to make a profit (taxed at the low rate for capital gains), whereas if the price falls he loses nothing.

It is estimated that the value of all forms of "extra compensation typically averages from 10% to 15% of the base compensation for middle management,

---

[26] For an excellent description of the forms of extra compensation, see J. Grant Macdonnell, "A Struggle to Reward Good Executives," *California Management Review*, Vol. 2, No. 3 (Spring 1960), pp. 25-33.

and as much as 100% or more at the top." [27] Indeed, in recent years extra compensation seems to have grown much more rapidly than base compensation, again particularly at the highest management levels.[28] The income tax laws have been largely responsible for this development. Deferred income, such as retirement benefits, is subject to tax only when it is received (when presumably the recipient will be in a lower tax bracket), while benefits such as country-club memberships and liberal expense accounts do not count as income at all (provided some showing can be made that these have a relationship to company business). The United States 1964 tax law placed certain restrictions on the use of stock options and limited tax-free company-paid life insurance to $50,000. But the tax advantages of extra-salary forms of compensation are still quite substantial.

Supporters of fringe benefits argue that these tend to reduce turnover and provide incentives for harder work. But a number of recent critics have warned that benefits can be carried too far.[29] They claim, first, that in the case of deferred benefits, such as life insurance and retirement, the period between performance and reward is so long that it does not provide effective incentive, and second, that such benefits in any case, serve primarily to keep the barely competent from leaving rather than to motivate the really dynamic.

Tax advantages are an attraction chiefly for the older, higher-paid executives, and this same group places greatest importance on pensions. Junior executives with growing families and large mortgages seem to be interested primarily in take-home income. Indeed, one psychological study indicates that executives as a whole want only a small proportion of their income in the form of benefits.[30] By in effect imposing a ceiling on their own income, top executives have squeezed salary levels below them and have imposed their own scale of compensation preferences upon those who have different needs and interests. Recently some companies have begun to experiment by permitting each executive to decide for himself how he will divide his compensation among take-home pay and various fringe benefits.

Bonuses and stock options can provide substantial incentives, but only to the extent that executives feel there is a relationship between their own efforts and over-all company success. Yet these are often given automatically to

27 Sibson, *op. cit.*, p. 103.

28 The average pay of very top management, those in the highest-paid one-hundredth of one per cent group, increased from $136,000 to $138,400 or only 1.7 per cent during the eight-year period 1956-1963, according to a study of 84 large corporations. Arch Patton, "Current Trends in Managerial Compensation," in Robert Andrews, ed., *Managerial Compensation* (Ann Arbor, Mich.: Foundation for Research in Human Behavior, 1965), pp. 7-12. Obviously these executives did receive substantial increases in total compensation during this period, but almost all of it was obtained as extra-salary benefits.

29 For example, Arch Patton, "Executives Compensation by 1970," *Harvard Business Review*, Vol. 42, No. 2 (September 1964), pp. 137-146; David W. Belcher, "Ominous Trends in Wage and Salary Administration," *Personnel*, Vol. 41, No. 5 (September 1964), pp. 42-50.

30 Thomas A. Mahoney, "Compensation Preferences of Managers," *Industrial Relations*, Vol. 3, No. 3 (May 1964), pp. 135-144.

everyone who reaches a certain managerial level, rather than on the basis of specific performance.

Salaries as Motivators

Some critics argue that the whole concept of salary administration, which has grown up in the factory, is inappropriate on the executive level. "The primary goal of executive compensation should be to motivate the manager to maximum effort rather than simply to pay him for his work." [31] Pay and particularly benefits should be based on "contributions to the decision-making process," risk-taking, and innovative activity, rather than just on seniority and job title. Stock options should be restricted to those at the very top who are able to influence over-all company policy. Bonuses should be given not so regularly as to become expected, but instead reserved for a few individuals who do spectacularly. Similarly, it is argued that salaries should be designed to reward outstanding performance far more than routine job holding, and should be tied in closely to performance appraisals. (And yet, as we have seen, performance appraisal is never easy; furthermore, in a period when technological change requires an increasing emphasis on teamwork, it is becoming increasingly difficult to isolate individual performance and the fostering of competition among managers may do more harm than good.)

A somewhat different view is that both salaries and fringe benefits have been overemphasized as means of attracting, holding, and motivating high-level executive and professional personnel. Instead, it is argued that companies should improve their work surroundings through moving their offices and laboratories away from grimy industrial centers to areas which offer a "university environment, good schools for the children, and pleasant living conditions." [32] Even if this is impractical, offices and office buildings can be made more attractive, working conditions can be improved, and organizational structure and policies can be changed to make executive work less frustrating. Though this approach may seem to involve hygienic rather than motivating factors, it is undoubtedly true that, in today's tight labor market, executives (and their wives) prefer to work and live in a pleasant environment.

SALARY ADMINISTRATION FOR ENGINEERS AND SCIENTISTS

The application of standard job-evaluation techniques is even more difficult with engineers and scientists than it is with executives. In professional work there is even ambiguity about when an employee has moved from one job to another, for job definitions here are quite elastic. An engineer, for ex-

---

[31] George S. Odiorne, "Company Growth and Personnel Administration," *Personnel,* Vol. 37, No. 1 (January 1960), p. 37.
[32] Cassell, *op. cit.*

ample, may be required to work on a more difficult assignment for several months before the change in his job status is officially recognized by a formal promotion. And the distinction between an engineer doing "more responsible" work and an engineer doing "less responsible" work is often vague. The jobs of both may change over time as new projects come in and old ones are completed.

In any case, it should be clear from the above that job classification means relatively little in engineering and scientific work. An engineer's salary may increase year by year, through merit rating. In many companies, when he reaches the top step of one job classification, he is almost automatically advanced to the next higher classification. But this promotion may mean relatively little change in work.

As a consequence, the emphasis in salary administration for engineers is usually on the individual worth of the particular engineer rather than on the job he is doing at the present. Yet engineering supervisors often claim that it is hard to measure individual professional ability. Since engineers normally work on projects that have never been attempted before, it is difficult to predict in advance how long a given project should take. Two engineers may be assigned to what seem to be equally time-consuming projects. Yet Engineer A finishes long before Engineer B. Is this because Engineer A is better? Or because his solution is slipshod? Or because the two projects were not really of equal difficulty?

Engineering supervisors may tend to exaggerate the difficulty of making judgments on the quality and quantity of professional output.[33] In any case, the trend is toward setting engineering and scientific salary rates largely on the basis of a man's education and seniority. Thus, two engineers, both with a master's degree and ten years' experience, will get roughly the same salary unless one is clearly outstanding. Many national scientific and engineering societies publish statistics on the salaries received by men with various degrees and various years of experience following graduation. Depending on the company's over-all wage policy (pp. 598-600), it can decide to base its salaries on the median, above the median, or below the median shown by these "career curves." Unfortunately, the rigid use of career curves as the sole basis of setting salaries leaves little opportunity to reward individual excellence. Most companies use such curves merely as guidelines. They permit larger-than-average

---

[33] It has been suggested that "standard times" be established for engineering research projects, and that incentive bonuses be given to those who take less than standard time to complete their project. James L. Wyatt, "Are Creative People 'Different'?: Developing Incentives in Scientists and Engineers," *The Management Review*, Vol. 48, No. 7 (July 1959), pp. 20-24, 82-85. We see enormous difficulties in such an undertaking. Nor are bonuses a particularly effective means of motivating engineers. See Albert B. Chalupsky, "Incentive Factors as Viewed by Engineers and Managers of Pharmaceutical Laboratories," *Personnel Psychology*, Vol. 17, No. 4 (Winter 1964), p. 385; and Edward Hartshorne, "The Effect of a Bonus System on Patentable Inventions on Research Productivity," in R. T. Livingston and S. H. Milberg, *Human Relations and the Industrial Research Manager* (New York: Columbia University Press, 1957).

salary increases for those who have done exceptionally well and withholding of increases from those whose work has been poor.

During the 1950's the starting salary for newly graduated engineers tended to rise faster than the salary paid to more experienced men. In some firms engineers with five or ten years' experience were paid little more than recent graduates. Consequently, many engineers felt that the only way to get a salary increase was to take a job with another company. The discontent provoked by inept salary administration even led some engineers to form their own unions. But by the early 1960's the traditional differentials were gradually being restored.

A salary increase is one way of rewarding good work, but public recognition of competence is usually given through change of title or promotion. During the early stages of an engineer's or scientist's career, it is possible to reward merit by promoting him through several nonsupervisory ranks—junior engineer, engineer, senior engineer—but in most companies the only way to reward continued excellence is by promotion into management. But many outstanding engineers and scientists are poor administrators. Promoting such an individual may merely make the company lose a good engineer and gain a poor administrator.

Some companies try to get around this dilemma through the use of "dual ladders of promotion." In addition to the first, purely administrative ladder, there is a second ladder which is used to reward technically competent individuals with titles such as engineering consultant and senior engineering consultant. Engineers and scientists on the technical ladder receive salaries equivalent to those of their administrative counterparts. (Thus, a senior engineering consultant may receive as much as a laboratory manager.) Also, they are given greater freedom to choose their own research topics, and, in addition, receive status privileges such as private offices or labs and admission to the executive parking lots and dining rooms. But dual ladders are rarely perceived as an ideal solution to the problem, if for no other reason than the fact that positions on the technical ladder are seen as "booby prizes" for those who fail to make the more prestigious administrative ladder. The dual ladder seems to work better with research scientists than with engineers. For most engineers, success seems to consist of winning a place in management.

CONCLUSION

Monetary reward is the primary motivation for most employees, and yet many are more concerned about how their earnings compare *relatively* to the earnings of other employees than they are about their absolute take-home pay. Without a sound wage and salary administration program, it is almost impossible for management to recruit or maintain a work force motivated to strive for the company's long-range objectives.

Wage administration is a particularly delicate activity, since it deals with one of our most sensitive areas, our pocketbook. And, since it results in the comparison of one man with another, it cannot help but lead to emotionally fraught rivalries and resentments. The struggle for a salary increase often shows human behavior at its very worst.

There are some managers who feel that the way to avoid all these problems is to retreat to the Olympian heights of "scientific objectivity." But, as we have seen, such aloofness requires that they ignore many of the most troublesome economic and human relationships in our society.

At best, wage and salary administration can only channel conflict and provide for a systematic review of difficult problems.

PROBLEM 1

JOB EVALUATION MANUAL

The following is a simplified example of a *poorly designed* job-evaluation manual. Read it carefully and try to find the bugs, the areas of inconsistency, and the areas of ambiguity.

DEGREES	POINTS

Education

1. None required.	20
2. Ability to speak English.	40
3. Four years school or equivalent.	60
4. Grade school or equivalent.	80
5. Graduate of high school or equivalent.	100
6. Two years college or equivalent.	120
7. College degree or equivalent.	140

Training required

1. Less than one week.	20
2. One week to four weeks.	40
3. Four weeks to six months.	60
4. Six months to a year.	80
5. A year to two years.	100
6. Two years to four years.	120
7. More than four years.	140

Physical Effort

1. No significant amount required.	25
2. Frequent handling of lightweight material. Must lift or handle objects of less than five pounds	50
3. Repetitive or sustained physical effort. Usually handling light or average weight material or occasionally working with heavyweight material. Lifting not over 30 pounds.	75
4. Hard work with constant physical strain or immediate severe strain. Lifting over 75 pounds required.	100

DEGREES	POINTS

Dexterity

1. None required. — 60
2. Low degree of dexterity required. — 120
3. Considerable skill and craftsmanship required. — 180
4. Very high order of skill. — 240

Mental effort

1. Flow of work is intermittent. No pressure of work. Attention required only at intervals. — 20
2. Operation requires frequent but not continuous attention. Inspection work where flaw is easily detected. — 40
3. Close attention is required at all times. Eye-hand coordination needed. — 60
4. High degree of concentration. Very close, exacting use of eyes — 80

Responsibility

1. Little possibility for mistakes. — 25
2. Small losses might occur but mistakes are easily caught. Errors might go up to $15 a week. — 50
3. Substantial loss possible before errors are discovered. Worker must exert care. Losses might be very great but normally shall not exceed $50 a week. — 75
4. Responsible for an important operation. Errors could cause substantial damage to equipment or material. — 100

Working conditions

1. Works regularly under desirable working conditions. — 20
2. Works regularly under poorer than average working conditions; illumination and ventilation are considered only adequate (as in enclosed vault or work-room space). — 40
3. Works under conditions which entail some sacrifice of personal comfort. Subject to heat, noise, dirt, and cold. — 60
4. Works under difficult conditions such as high, though not continuous noise, heat, cold (such as work in refrigerator), and so forth. — 80
5. Works under highly hazardous or difficult conditions, such as continual high noise, constant movement from refrigerator or hot room, constant dust. — 100

Safety

1. Almost no hazards. — 20
2. Some chance of personal injury such as scratches and bruises. — 40
3. May be subject to moderately serious injury if proper precautions are not taken. — 60
4. Exposure to health hazard which might result in incapacitation if proper precautions are not observed. Minor accidents are common. — 80
5. Must be constantly on guard against serious accidents which often occur in spite of precautions. — 100

JOB DESCRIPTION

Using the above job-evaluation manual and the following job description, evaluate the job of a press and liner operator. Notice that this job description is also inadequate. Observe the areas of ambiguity that develop as you try to apply the manual.

<u>Job Description of Press and Liner Operator</u>

This girl works in a can-making factory. She stamps out ends for the cans on a machine which makes 200 ends a minute.

The girl works in front of the machine. Sheets of metal are put into the rear by men. Circular ends are punched out by a metal punch which resembles a cookie-cutter. These ends pass through several complicated operations and drop onto a rack.

The girls take piles of ends and put them in crates. Each pile includes about 40 ends and weighs about 3 lbs. A good deal of dexterity is required, otherwise the ends will slither all over the floor. Lift-truck operators take filled crates to storage until needed.

The girls also watch the machine closely, stop it when something goes wrong and make minor repairs. Major repairs are made by mechanics.

Usually the girls can tell if something is going wrong by changes in the noise. The punch makes a very loud staccato sound.

When ends are coming through poorly, each one can be inspected separately. Otherwise a girl can talk to the girl next to her. Girls must stand all day except for short rest periods.

Girls can and do cut their fingers on ends, although they are encouraged to wear gloves. Also, if they don't shut the machine down when making repairs (they are instructed to do so), they can seriously injure their fingers.

If they fail to pay attention to their work, a lot of bad ends can go past them. These must be re-inspected by inspectors and discarded. Such inattention rarely lasts more than 20 minutes. Ends are worth perhaps 1/4 cent.

About three weeks are required to train a girl. There are no education requirements other than the ability to speak English. However, the company believes that girls with low intelligence are not aware when the machine is operating improperly.

FOUNDRY WAGES

The foundry has always been regarded as one of the worst places to work in the Pushem Manufacturing Co. The work is hot, dirty, and heavy. Brawn rather than brains is considered the chief requirement to get the job done.

Yet according to the job evaluation plan, "physical ability" and "working conditions" are weighted relatively lower than "responsibility," "training," and "skill." As a consequence, most of the foundry jobs are rated at the bottom of the wage scale.

In recent years it has been increasingly difficult to get foundry help. Management has had to take men who could not get jobs elsewhere—thus further lowering the already low social status of the foundry in the eyes of the other men in the plant. The whole matter has now reached a crisis. There are now 17 vacancies in the foundry and it is impossible to hire new men at the evaluated rate.

1. How should this problem be handled? Should management completely revise its job-evaluation program? Should it make foundry jobs an exception to job evaluation?
2. How should management deal with the reactions of other workers if it decides to increase foundry wages but not other wages?

BANK WAGES AT BEMUS BAY

The Busti National Bank has just decided to open a branch in Bemus Bay, an exclusive resort located about 20 miles from Arkwright, a large city. There is no bank there at present.

Busti is anxious to determine the appropriate wage for the clerical staff it expects to hire. Clerks in the bank's offices in Arkwright receive a starting wage of $85 a week, but through promotions they can work up to $115. As a matter of company policy, these wage rates have been set at the midpoint of the range for other banks in Arkwright.

A survey of the local businesses at Bemus Bay, primarily realty and insurance offices and offices for local stores, indicates that the "going rate" for qualified clerical personnel is $110-125 a week. The higher rates in Bemus Bay may be attributed in part to the substantially higher cost of living in this resort town, the limited number of young women seeking employment, and the fact that there are no other banks in Bemus Bay. Banks in Arkwright have traditionally paid lower wages than other businesses, on the grounds that banks offer better working conditions and higher prestige.

1. What should the Busti Bank establish as its hiring rate for clerical personnel? What factors should be considered in making the decision?
2. Could the bank justify to its Arkwright employees the fact that it was paying higher wages in Bemus Bay?

Work-Measurement Techniques

The purpose of work measurement is to help management establish standards for the amount of work an employee should turn out within a given period. These standards have many uses: They help the supervisor allocate work fairly and judge whether a man is performing satisfactorily; they help management predict the labor requirements and the probable costs of new products and techniques; and, most important, they serve as the basis for piece-work and incentive plans (see Chapter 27).

Supervisors or personnel administrators rarely conduct work-measurement studies themselves—normally this responsibility is assigned to industrial engineers. In this chapter we will briefly outline some work-measurement techniques and phraseology for the benefit of the nonengineer.[1] Our chief emphasis, however, will be on the difficulties that such measurements sometimes create for supervisors and personnel administrators. And we will be concerned primarily with time study, the most widely used of the work-measurement techniques.

ORIGINS OF TIME STUDY

Time study is a relatively new technique. It first achieved popularity as a means of determining the "standard output" on which the piece rates used in incentive plans could be based.[2]

---

[1] For a general description of this area, see Phil Carroll, *Time Study for Cost Control* (New York: McGraw-Hill, 1943). An excellent pamphlet is L. C. Pigage and J. L. Tucker, *Motion and Time Study*, Bulletin 24 (Urbana: Institute of Labor and Industrial Relations, University of Illinois, 1954). Work-measurement techniques are most usually applied to manufacturing operations, but they may also be applied to the office. For example, see Kenneth W. Olm, "A System for Measuring Office Work Performance," *California Management Review*, Vol. 2, No. 2 (Spring 1960), pp. 80-89.

[2] Time study was an important part of the Taylor System and the scientific management movement. Taylor first used it at the Midvale Steel Company in the 1890's. See Frederick W. Taylor, *The Principles of Scientific Management* (New York: Harper & Row, 1911). This book is a "must" for all serious students of industrial relations.

Early forms of incentives were not based on time study at all, however. A typical approach was that of the Halsey Gain Sharing Plan, which was first presented to the American Society of Mechanical Engineers in 1891.[3] Under this plan, management in effect offered to share with workers any savings in labor costs brought about through increased production. Suppose a 50 per cent gain-sharing plan were put into effect in a plant where a group of workers had been producing 100 pieces an hour at $1.00 an hour. Now, if they could produce 150 pieces in an hour (that is, if they could do an hour and a half's work in one hour), they would get half the time savings, or $.25, as bonus.

Although such plans were once common, they have been largely abandoned for plans based on time study in which the worker enjoys a 100 per cent reward from increased production. For instance, if he increases production by 10 per cent, his earnings go up 10 per cent too. There have been a number of reasons for this shift:

1. Workers—and later, unions—insisted that any less than a proportional 100 per cent reward was a form of stealing. Indeed, during World War II one union demanded a 110 per cent bonus for extra work, on the grounds that the extra work was more than proportionally hard.

2. Since bonuses were based on the existing rate of production, employees who had been taking life easy found it simple to increase their production (and thus their earnings) considerably, while those who had been working hard right along made very little more. Moreover, some groups decided to peg their production low while waiting for piece rates to be set.

3. In theory, the piece rates set up under gain-sharing plans were not to be altered when management introduced new and better ways of production. Rather, the workers would continue to share in the increased savings in labor costs. But this created serious inequities, for employees who benefited from technological improvements received higher wages than those who did not. In actual practice, management found it difficult to resist the temptation to cut rates.

For all these and other reasons, most present-day incentive systems are based on standards developed through time study.[4] (Both time and motion study are expensive techniques: They require large industrial engineering staffs and, as we shall discuss in Chapter 27, they may cause substantial human-relations frictions. As a consequence, these procedures are not profitable on operations that are infrequently performed. So-called "work sampling" techniques are

---

[3] Among other gain-sharing plans which were once quite popular are the Rowan, Barth Variable Savings, Taylor, Merrick, Gantt, and Emerson Plans. For a description of the whole family, see David Belcher, *Wage and Salary Administration*, 2nd ed. (Englewood Cliffs, N.J.: Prentice-Hall, Inc., 1962), pp. 394-403.

[4] One study of over 200 plants disclosed that only 16 per cent of all employees who did incentive work were still paid under a gain-sharing plan that gave them less than 100 per cent reward; in these plants only 6 per cent of time standards were still set by historical data. "The Truth About Wage Incentives and Work Measurement Today," *Factory*, Vol. 117, No. 4 (April 1959), p. 77.

somewhat cheaper, but they tell management only how much time an operation takes *at the moment,* not how much time it *should* take.) [5]

Time study makes it possible to determine the *normal* time required to do a particular job. But industrial engineers insist that before time study can be undertaken the *one best way* must be determined through *motion study.*

Considered broadly, motion study (often called "work simplification") encompasses the entire field of industrial engineering—namely, the determination of the most efficient method of production. It is related to plant design and materials-handling as well as to operator techniques. Here, however, we shall look at only those techniques of motion study that affect individual workers.[6]

Essentially, motion study involves: (1) analyzing how the job is currently being done, (2) questioning whether steps can be eliminated or combined, and (3) setting up a quicker, easier way of doing the job. In Taylor's words, the objective is to "eliminate all false movements, slow movements, and useless movements . . . collect into one series the quickest and best movements." [7] To help in the systematic framing of questions, the industrial engineer makes use of flow and process charts, operations charts, and micromotion charts.

Flow charts plot the progress of a product through the plant from raw material to finished product. *Process charts* analyze the steps taken, using special symbols to highlight the various steps, such as:

Through the use of these charts the industrial engineer can raise such questions as: Can the parts be made more accessible to the worker? Can conveyors be used? Are certain steps duplicated?

Operations charts plot the manner in which a given operator performs his task, usually by indicating separately what he does with each hand. Here too the purpose is to question existing procedures and to suggest easier ways of

---

[5] For a sensible discussion of when time study should and should not be used, see R. C. Horne, "What Kind of Work Measurement Program?" *Personnel,* Vol. 36, No. 6 (November 1959), pp. 25-34.

[6] Ralph M. Barnes, *Motion and Time Study,* 2nd ed. (New York: Wiley, 1940), is an extremely useful introduction to this field.

[7] Taylor, *op. cit.,* pp. 117-118.

OPERATION CHART

Present METHOD

Scale – each square about 1 ft.

Page 1 of 1
Operation Straighten Welded "T" Bracket
Operation No. 25   Dept. 13
Parts Bracket   Weld "T"   Part No. 1040
Machine Bench   Mach. No. None
Specif. No. None   Draw. No. None
Operator & No. U. Doit   Fixt. No. None
Charted by Jon Doe   Date Any time

Left hand			Right hand
Reach for part	○	▽	Wait for left hand
Grasp part	○		
Carry to vise	○	○	Reach for vise handle
Position in vise	○	○	Grasp handle
Hold for tightening vise	▽	○	Tighten vise
Release part	○	○	Release handle
		○	Reach for hammer
		○	Grasp hammer
Idle	▽	○	Carry hammer to vise
		○	Hit part to straighten
		○	Carry hammer aside
		○	Release hammer
Reach for part		○	Reach for vise handle
Grasp part	○	○	Grasp vice handle
Hold part	▽	○	Open vise
Remove part from vise	○	○	Release vise handle
Carry part to level block	○		
Sight part for straightness	○	▽	Idle
Aside part	○		
Release part	○		

SUMMARY

L.H.		R.H.
7	Operations	9
5	Movements	5
3	Holds & delays	2

LCP-52-Form 3

OPERATION CHART

Suggested METHOD

Scale – each square about 1 ft.

Page 1 of 1
Operation Straighten Welded "T" Bracket
Operation No. 25   Dept. 13
Parts Bracket   Weld "T"   Part No. 1040
Machine Bench   Mach. No. None
Specif. No. None   Draw. No. None
Operator & No. U. Doit   Fixt. No. S101
Charted by Jon Doe   Date Any time

Left hand			Right hand
Reach for part	○	○	Reach for hammer
Grasp part	○	○	Grasp hammer
Carry part to block	○	○	Carry hammer to block
Position part in hole in block	○	▽	Wait
Release part	○	○	Strike part
Reach for gage bar	○	○	Aside hammer
Grasp gage bar	○	○	Release hammer
Carry gage bar to part	○	○	Reach for part
Gage part for straightness	○	○	Grasp part
Aside gage bar	○	○	Aside part
Release gage bar	○	○	Release part

SUMMARY

L.H.		R.H.
6	Operations	5
5	Movements	5
—	Holds & Delays	1

COMPARISON

Original Method	Operations	Suggested Method
16	Operations	11
10	Movements	10
5	Holds & Delays	1

LCP-52-Form 3

These are operation charts. According to the present method, above, the operator must reach for the part and place it in the vise with his left hand. He then uses his right hand to hit it with a hammer. Both hands are required to take it out of the vise and finally the left hand alone is used to test it for straightness on the leveling block. Neither hand is used continuously. The suggested system, below, uses two new pieces of equipment: a straightening board, which is much more convenient than the vise for fitting the bracket, and a gage bar to take the place of the leveling block. These two new pieces of equipment make it possible for both hands to be used simultaneously, thus saving 5 operations and 4 holds and delays. Source: L. C. Pigage and J. L. Tucker, Motion and Time Study (Urban, Illinois: Institute of Labor and Industrial Relations, University of Illinois, 1954), pp. 20-21. Reprinted by permission.

performing the task. What motions can be eliminated? Can "gross," simple movements be substituted for "fine," more complicated movements which require greater dexterity? Can the sequence of operations be rearranged so that both hands will be kept busy where before one was idle? Can symmetrical, rhythmic, or circular motions be substituted for straight-line, jerky, or uncoordinated motions?

Micromotion charts (sometimes called simo charts) are the product of the fertile imaginations of the Gilbreth husband-and-wife team. Far more precise than operations charts, micromotion charts are based on motion pictures which provide a slow-motion analysis of each motion. The Gilbreths broke down all body motions into 17 basic motions or therbligs (Gilbreth spelled backwards), each with its own symbol. Some of these are:

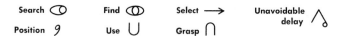

Micromotion studies eliminate the need for a stop watch (which is used in other forms of time study) since the speed of an operation can be computed from the number of frames of film required to picture it. Further, micromotion charts help minimize debates over the accuracy of a study. Still the system is not very commonly used, largely because of the cost of preparing the films and making the extremely fine analyses required.[8]

Limitations of "One Best Way"

The industrial engineer uses all these motion-study techniques in an effort to determine the *"one best way"* for a worker to do a particular job. Behind this effort, of course, lies the assumption that there actually is one best way. What are the limitations of this assumption?

First, it tends to force everybody to work in the same way; it seems to ignore the fact that people are different. The best method for a right-hander, for instance, might be different from that for a "leftie." Moreover, it disregards the fact that, over a long period of time, varying one's work method may be less fatiguing than constantly doing the same thing.

Motion study often pays little attention to the sequence in which motions are taken or to the value of pauses. Carried to its logical extreme, this insistence on the "one best way" would eliminate the windup from the baseball pitch. The tendency in motion study is to consider each motion separately, rather

---

[8] Some psychologists have challenged the entire psychological and physiological basis of motion-study units such as therbligs and have suggested other, presumably more meaningful ways of classifying human activity. See Mason Haire, "Psychology and the Study of Business," in Robert Dahl, Mason Haire, and Paul Lazarsfeld, *Social Science Research on Business* (New York: Columbia University Press, 1959), p. 55.

than to determine whether it contributes to *over-all* efficiency. Considered by itself, the windup is clearly an unnecessary motion.

More important, behind this assumption lurks an implication that the seasoned worker's years of experience on the job are useless and that an engineer with a few hours' observation can find the one best method. To be sure, the engineer with his trained and questioning mind can spot mistakes that the worker on the job has always overlooked. Yet it is not safe to ignore the worker's experience altogether.

Further, even if the method that the engineer finally devises is clearly better than the existing method, there may be trouble in getting workers to accept it. Certainly if they are skeptical of the engineer's method and enthusiastic about their own, chances are they will turn out higher production by sticking with the less efficient method.

> One of the authors was observing a worker in a shop. As the foreman approached, the worker quickly hid a small brace and began to work in an obviously less efficient way. When asked why he did so, he answered, "When the foreman's around I do it his way. My way is better but I took my idea to engineering and they said the stop watch said their idea was quicker. But I know I make more money on piece work my way."

The point is not that the worker's method was more efficient—perhaps it wasn't—but that the worker *thought* it was better and refused to accept anyone else's.

A final criticism is summed up in Taylor's suggestion that those assigned to work under the "one best way" should be as phlegmatic as an ox, for, to the extent that work is reduced to one fixed routine, it may well become dull and boring. Certainly, adherence to the "one best way" is inconsistent with the philosophy of job enlargement.

Acting on the principles of motion study, a group of British engineers are supposed to have submitted the following report after attending a symphony.[9]

> For considerable periods the four oboe players had nothing to do. The number should be reduced and the work spread more evenly over the whole of the concert, thus eliminating peaks of activity.
>
> All the twelve violins were playing identical notes; this seems unnecessary duplication. The staff of this section should be drastically cut. If a larger volume of sound is required, it should be obtained by electronic apparatus.
>
> Much effort was absorbed in the playing of demi-semi-quavers; this seems to be unnecessary refinement. It is recommended that all notes should be rounded up to the nearest semi-quaver. If this were done it would be possible to use trainees and lower-grade operatives more extensively.
>
> There seems to be too much repetition of some musical passages. Scores should be drastically pruned. No useful purpose is served by repeating on the horns a passage which has already been handled by the strings. It is estimated that if all redundant passages were eliminated the whole concert time of two hours could be reduced to twenty minutes and there would be no need for intermission.

---

[9] *Council Compass,* Vol. 13, No. 3 (July 1957), p. 16.

The above tongue-in-cheek "report" was printed in an engineering journal, an indication that engineers themselves are aware of the limitations of too simplified an approach to motion study. In fact, industrial engineers today are increasingly taking into account the factors that we have discussed, such as individual differences and the need to introduce variety into work.[10] In co-operation with industrial psychologists, they are making increased use of carefully controlled psychological and physiological experimentation. Indeed, the field of human engineering (which is concerned with designing such apparatus as aircraft control panels) is simply an extension of motion study. Many industrial engineers have become aware of the problems and limitations of their staff role, and are spending more time advising managers and workers on ways of working out their own solutions—rather than dictating solutions to them.

In spite of these encouraging signs, there are still many industrial engineers who insist that the "one best method" approach is *the* only scientific and proper way to determine how men should do their job. The unyielding insistence of these men often intensifies the human-relations frictions that grow up when time-study and incentive systems are introduced.

TIME-STUDY PROCEDURE

Once the proper way of doing a job has been determined by motion study, it is possible to begin time study. Time study is a procedure for determining the *standard time* required to do a job. Usually it consists of four steps:

1. Selecting the employee and describing the job.
2. Determining the *observed* time.
3. Applying a correction factor.
4. Introducing *allowances* for fatigue, personal time, and contingencies.

Selecting the Employee and Describing the Job

A typical union contract includes the following provision:

> The time standards shall be based on the time required by a qualified normal employee working at a normal pace under normal conditions, using the proper method with normal material at normal machine speeds.

Notice how often the word "normal" is used: What are the normal machine speed, normal material, and normal conditions? Usually these are prescribed by the industrial engineer and all the details are listed on the time-study form. It is essential that these details be listed accurately, for if, some months later,

---

[10] See, for example, Louis E. Davis, "The Effects of Automation on Job Design," *Industrial Relations,* Vol. 2, No. 1 (October 1962), pp. 53-72.

a worker feels that, say, the sheet of metal on which he is now working is thicker than that which was used when the original time study was made, he can always claim higher piece-rate earnings than originally allowed.

What is the "proper method"? That is the one best way, of course, which we have already mentioned.

What is meant by "normal" worker, "normal" work pace? Behind these questions lies a major area of contention between management and union. In most cases the industrial engineer makes no effort to find a "normal" employee. Instead, he times a more or less typical employee, and, then, if the man seems to be working at a pace which is slower or faster than the engineer's preconception of "normal," he applies certain corrections (as we shall discuss) to bring the employee's observed speed in line with that conception of "normal."

Timing the Job

Once the worker has been selected and the job conditions thoroughly described, the engineer is almost ready to start timing. But first he must break the job down into *elements*, each of which will usually be timed separately. An element is a clearly distinguishable motion, such as "place piece in jig." It should have a definite starting and stopping point, and it should last long enough (at least three seconds) to make accurate timing possible.[11] The engineer is interested not only in the total time for the entire *cycle*, but also in the time for each element. Close examination of "elemental" times enables him to determine exactly in what parts of the job there are needless operator, machine, or materials delays.

How long a time should the study cover? Practice varies, but it is usual to time enough job cycles to insure that an adequate sample is obtained. Unless the whole operation is unusually long, at least 10 or 20 cycles are ordinarily observed.[12]

---

[11] Short elements are difficult to measure. One study found that a group of experienced time-study men, observing an operation taking .10 minutes (6 seconds), made a mean observation of .09674 minutes (off 3.5 per cent) while their standard deviation was .0107. This means that a majority of observations were at least 15 per cent off. William Gomberg, *A Trade Union Analysis of Time Study*, 2nd ed. (Englewood Cliffs, N.J.: Prentice-Hall, 1955), pp. 73-76.

[12] The typical procedure at this point has been attacked as statistically unsound, or at least as reflecting few of the more recent developments in sampling theory. It has been argued that the time-study man rarely gets a statistically adequate sample, nor is he sure that his readings are representative or that his data show what statisticians call "stability." See Gomberg, *op. cit.*, and Adam Abruzzi, *Work, Workers and Measurement* (New York: Columbia University Press, 1956). To these criticisms the time-study man may answer that he "collects data to familiarize himself more intimately with the job and to perceive the distortions, abnormalities and variations. . . . These are to help him reach a sound *personal* evaluation of the proper time value. The results cannot and are not designed to be checked by statistical criteria." Solomon Barkin, "Diversity in Time Study Practice," *Industrial and Labor Relations Review*, Vol. 7, No. 4 (July 1954), p. 452.

The engineer usually works with a stop watch,[13] and a form on which to record the time measured for each element. Once the timing has been completed and the necessary calculations made, the observer is left with a number of readings for each element. If he has observed 20 cycles, he will have 20 readings for each element. Doubtless these readings will vary. The usual practice is to throw out all "abnormal" values—those that are too high or too low. But it is not easy to determine which readings are *too* high or *too* low. Naturally the union will want to throw out the low values, and management will challenge the high ones. One compromise is to throw out only those values for which the observer has indicated either that part of the element was omitted (too low) or that extraneous motions were introduced (too high).

Next the time-study man selects some sort of "average." There are four sorts of "average" in use: the mean, the median, the mode, and "good time" (in the strict sense, the last is not an average at all). Let us assume that the observations on a given element, listed in order of magnitude, came to: 10, 10, 11, 11, 11, 12, 12, 12, 12, 13, 13, 13, 14, 14, 15, 16, 17, 18, 22. Here the mode, or the *most frequent* time would be 12, and the median, or the *half-way* point, 13. If the 22 were struck out as being abnormal, the mean, or garden-variety *average*, would be 13. Probably the most common average used is the mean. Occasionally the study will be based on *good time*, which is flexibly defined as the fastest time that an operator can maintain with some consistency. In our example this would probably be 11.

Applying a Correction Factor

The next step is to apply a correction factor to adjust for the fact that the worker observed may be working at a pace slower or faster than "normal." Correction factors are applied frequently, through effort-rating.[14]

Effort-rating means merely that the time-study man estimates at what percentage of normal the operator is working.[15] (He can make an effort-rating for the job as a whole or separately for each element.) If he estimates that the operator is working at only 90 per cent of normal pace, then the observed time is obviously too long. The normal time can be obtained by multiplying the observed time by .90.

Effort-rating assumes that the observer has in the back of his head some

---

[13] The "marstochron," an electric timing device, is more accurate, yet more cumbersome than the stop watch.

[14] "Leveling," another method of applying corrections, takes into account not only effort, but also skill, consistency, and working conditions. For a description of this method, see S. M. Lowry, H. B. Maynard, and G. J. Stegemerten, *Time and Motion Study*, 3rd ed. (New York: McGraw-Hill, 1940), Chapters 16-19.

[15] Ralph Presgrave, *The Dynamics of Time Study* (Toronto: University of Toronto Press, 1940), pp. 76-107.

NOTES	CYCLE	1	2	3	4	5	6	7	8	9	10	11	12	13	14
A FUMBLE	1	7	14	31 A	14	23	35								
	2	6	15	21	16	22	36								
B WIPED NOSE	3	7	13	21	22	21	39 B								
	4	8	14	23	17	23	36								
Z MISSED READING	5	6	15	21	15	22	Z								
	6	7	13	20	16	21	36								
	7	9	15	19	16	22	35								
	8														
	9														
	10														
	11														
	12														
OBSERVED TIME		.07	.15	.21	.16	.22	.36								
RATING		.75	.75	.75	.75	.75	.80								
CORRECTED TIME		.05	.11	.16	.12	.17	.29								

ALLOWANCES

PERSONAL	5 %
FATIGUE	5 %
CONTINGENCIES	10 %
	20 %

TOTAL CORRECTED TIME ___.90___

ALLOWANCES AT 20 % ___.18___

ALLOWED TIME ___1.08___

In this time study, the average used is the mode and elements have been timed in accordance with the snap-back method. The number of readings is illustrative only. There are not enough values shown here to determine a standard time for a job.

standard of what constitutes normal pace. Taylor and his followers felt that normal pace could be determined objectively and *scientifically*, but today it is pretty generally conceded to be purely a matter of judgment. What one man considers normal performance, another may consider soldiering.

How is the standard to be determined? Basically this is the age-old question of what constitutes a "fair day's work," the subject of frequent union-management negotiation. Sometimes the parties can agree on standards for a few bench-mark jobs. The 1946 contract between United States Steel and the Steelworkers Union defined a "fair day's work" as "that amount of work that can be produced by a qualified employee when working at a normal pace. . . .

A normal pace is equivalent to a man walking without load, on smooth, level ground at a rate of three miles per hour." [16] Or, another example:

SHOVELING SAND

Material: River sand, moisture 5.5% approx.; weight per cu. ft. 100-110 pounds.

Equipment: Materials handling box (steel); effective height above floor 32"; shovel, no. 2 furnace.

Working conditions: under roof; smooth concrete floor; all other conditions normal.

Production rate for shoveling sand from pile to box, average weight sand on shovel 15 lbs.; 12.5 shovelsful per minute.[17]

Such mutually agreed-upon standards provide bench-marks against which the time-study man can compare the normal pace for other jobs. For instance, when rating a man shoveling gravel, the time-study man may ask himself, "How fast does he seem to be working compared with a man shoveling sand 12.5 shovelsful per minute?" (A most difficult comparison to make!)

Nonunion plants (and many unionized plants as well) normally follow bench-mark standards set by leading industrial engineers. One such standard calls for typing 50 words a minute or dealing a deck of cards in 30 seconds [18] (but one engineer insists that only 27 seconds are required [19]).

Often, movies are taken showing employees working at standard pace.

The Society for Advancement of Management used essentially this approach. Films were prepared for 24 operations at five different work paces. These 120 separate performances were viewed by 1,800 engineers in over 200 industrial companies, and the resulting 150,000 ratings constitute the basis of the final standards.[20]

Films of this sort may be prepared jointly by union and management, although more often they are prepared by management engineers alone. When run at the speed that has been negotiated as "normal," they provide criteria by which to judge the pace of men on new jobs. Such films are also used in training time-study men to judge "normal" pace.

In spite of its seeming simplicity, effort-rating has been attacked as being arbitrary and imprecise. Why?

1. Time-study men rarely claim to be more than 95 per cent accurate; yet if the time-study man makes a 5 or 10 per cent error in computing the proper time for a job, the worker's piece-work earnings may be affected by as much as

---

[16] Cited in Daniel Bell, "Work in the Life of an American," *Manpower in the United States,* William Haber and others, eds. (New York: Harper & Row, 1954), p. 10.

[17] *Ibid.*

[18] Presgrave, *op. cit.,* pp. 140-153.

[19] Frederick W. Shumard, *A Primer of Time Study* (New York: McGraw-Hill, 1940), pp. 64-73.

[20] Belcher, *op. cit.,* p. 353, citing V. A. Flynn, "A Word on the Rating Films," *Advanced Management,* Vol. 18, No. 4 (April 1953), p. 29.

$.20 to $.30 an hour. Long strikes have occurred over wage disputes involving smaller amounts than this.

2. In following the effort-rating approach, the time-study man assumes that by observing a worker he can tell how hard he is working. For instance, he assumes that by knowing what the normal pace is for shoveling sand he can also judge the normal pace for shoveling gravel.[21] Yet a pace that is normal for one job may be very hard to maintain on another.

3. At best, all the time-study man can do is be *consistent*—that is, he can compare one man against the standard and say whether this man is working faster or slower than the standard, and by how much. But since all the bench-mark standards are matters of controversy and judgment, one can never really tell whether the time-study man is *accurate*. For example, there are experi-mental studies which show that trained time-study men are likely to rate a given worker as slower than does a man without training.[22] (In other words, a time-study man may be more pro-management in his ratings than the man in the street.) But who is to say that the time-study man is more or less accurate in his judgment of what is "normal pace" or a "fair day's work" than an un-trained individual?

Consistency is a very important objective in itself, however. If standards are inconsistent, a man on a "loose" standard can do his day's work (or make "base-rate" pay) with less effort than can a man who is on a "tight" standard. In fact, one of the greatest causes for dissatisfaction over incentives is the fact that some rates are "tighter" than others. If all rates are equally tight or equally loose, everyone may be getting paid too much or too little but there are no perceived inequalities between rates.

4. Unfortunately there is considerable evidence that time-study men often do not achieve a high level of consistency. The real test of consistency is whether or not several time-study men, each timing and rating a different worker (all of whom are doing the *same* job) will arrive at the same conclu-sions on the proper time to allow. A number of experimental studies have been made of this question, each using experienced time-study men as subjects. These studies conclude: [23]

(a) Two time-study men may differ in their ratings of the same job by as much as 2 to 1. Differences of 25 per cent to 50 per cent are common.

(b) Time-study men tend to underestimate differences in performance. For instance, if the same movie is run at 1000 frames per minute and then at 500, the time-study man will recognize that the new speed is slower, but not by 50 per cent—perhaps only by 35 per cent.

---

[21] Taylor himself recognized this problem and made careful studies to determine optimum shovel sizes and work paces for various types of material. Time-study men today are not always this careful.

[22] See Abruzzi, *op. cit.*, Chapter 4.

[23] For a discussion of these studies, see Abruzzi, *op. cit.*, Chapters 3 and 4. Roughly the same criticisms were made much earlier by Robert F. Hoxie, *Scientific Management and Labor* (New York: Appleton, 1916).

5. Perhaps one of the biggest drawbacks of effort-rating was expressed to us by a time-study man:

> Unless you have had a great deal of experience, you are always deceived by the man who has been on the job for a long time. His efforts are so smooth that he looks like he is doing very little work—while a new man might look totally exhausted putting out the same amount.

Predetermined time systems.   Because of the obvious disadvantages of traditional forms of time study, industrial engineers are turning increasingly to predetermined time systems (sometimes known as synthetic data).[24] The use of standard data completely eliminates the need for timing each individual job. How?

First, the one best method for each job is determined, as discussed above, and waste motions are eliminated. Then the basic motions for each hand are carefully listed. Once this is done, reference is made to the "standard times" which have been developed by enginering firms for each basic motion.[25] In the example circled in the table on p. 650, moving a ten-pound part from skid to machine is allowed .08 minutes. The standard times allowed for each motion are merely added together to get the equivalent of "corrected time."

The advantages of this technique are many. By side-stepping time study and the rating problem, it eliminates endless union-management wrangles (that is, if the union accepts the standard data and, what is more unlikely, if its members accept the results). A worker can no longer fool the time-study man by pretending to work fast, nor does the time-study man (now better called an industrial engineer) have to worry about being outsmarted. Nor is there any problem of consistency. Predetermined data make the whole rate-setting process quicker, cheaper, more mechanical, and less subject to personal discretion. Indeed, computers can be used to calculate piece-rates.

But if the predetermined time method is so advantageous, why isn't it used universally? There are many objections to it.[26]

The method assumes that the time for each motion can be determined independently of how it fits into the overall sequence—in other words, that the time required to perform one motion in an operation is independent of the time required to perform another. But this would be true only if each movement started at rest and ended at rest. Numerous studies have disproved this assump-

---

[24] One study of 302 plants disclosed that 30 per cent of all plant standards were set by predetermined systems, as contrasted to 49 per cent by time study, and 21 per cent by other methods. "The Truth About Wage Incentives and Work Measurement Today," *Factory*, Vol. 117, No. 4 (April 1959), p. 77.

[25] Some systems provide times for fairly lengthy motions the size of elements, while others break the job down into finer parts roughly the size of therbligs. One author even provides times for "nerve reactions—eye to brain—or reverse—.0003" minutes and "eye focus—get image clear—.0020 to .0040" minutes. Walter G. Holmes, *Applied Time and Motion Study* (New York: Ronald, 1938), p. 244, cited in Gomberg, *op. cit.*, p. 225.

[26] See Abruzzi, *op. cit.*, Chapters 13-15; Gomberg, *op. cit.*, Chapter 15.

tion of *independence*.[27] In fact, the over-all time for an operation can rarely be determined by adding up the independently determined times of the parts. An efficient worker develops a rhythm in his work, and his speed in any one part of the job depends in part on what he has just done and what he intends to do next.[28] (Some predetermined-time systems distinguish between the time required to lift an object when the hand starts from rest and when it is already in motion. Few go further than this and most do not go that far.)

Moreover, although it is probably true that most motions can be broken down into a fairly small number of categories, no motion will fit any category perfectly. And some motions are unique (for example, those of a go-go girl)— to force them into a category would be highly arbitrary.

Any firm that uses predetermined times accepts the prescribed times as the normal pace for the basic motions. But there are various competing predetermined-time systems, each with its own set of synthetic data, and each sold by different firms of industrial engineering consultants. This means that for the same set of motions there may well be several sets of times—and why not, since there is no generally accepted definition of what constitutes normal pace? Unions are even more suspicious of standard-data schemes than they are of regular time-study systems. As one international representative expressed it:

> MTM [29] is management's idea of the right time. We have ours and we settle the matter by collective bargaining. The trouble is that some managements think that MTM is the answer and won't bargain at all. Naturally we can't accept that. MTM is an effort to take something which is really a matter for joint judgment out of collective bargaining and tries to give management the right to give the final answer.

In spite of these criticisms, standard-data systems do provide a rough check on the times obtained through direct observation. And when such a system is applied to a number of roughly similar jobs, such as using a drill press in a standardized fashion, it may result in considerably greater consistency between standards than does time study. Indeed, one union, the International Ladies Garment Workers', has developed its own standard data for use in setting piece-rates for dresses. As the union's Director of Management Engineering once said, "The secret of its success is that it is viewed as a completely pragmatic method. It introduces a greater degree of consistency into the settlement of piece-rates than would be available without it." [30]

---

[27] See, for example, an exhaustive German study, Heinz Schmidtke and Fritz Steir, "An Experimental Evaluation of the Validity of Pre-determined Elemental Time Systems," *Journal of Industrial Engineering*, Vol. 12, No. 3 (May 1961), pp. 182-204.

[28] The speed at which a baseball player can run from home plate to first base depends on (a) whether he has just bunted or driven a line drive, and (b) whether he intends to stop at first or go on to second. It might also depend on whether he is first man up and still slightly tired from running in from center field at the end of the previous inning.

[29] Method-Time Measurement, a form of standard data.

[30] Gomberg, *op. cit.*, p. 217.

1.	HANDLING ELEMENTS	WEIGHT IN PART ONLY						UNIT TIME	O R C C K T	EXT. TIME
		0-.5	.5-5	5-15	15-30	30-40	40 UP			
	A. PARTS FROM SKID TO MACHINE	.010	.050	.080	.100	.120	.140			
	REPLACE TO SKID									
	B. PLACE IN JIG – REMOVE	.036	.040	.050	.060	.080	.120			
	C. PLACE & REMOVE JIG SECTION	.032	.035	.044	.055	.075	.110			
2.	JIGGING ELEMENTS	WEIGHT OF PART AND FIXTURE								
		0-10	10-40	40-50	50-60	60-70	70 UP			
	A. BLOW CLEAR OF CHIPS	.040	.060	.080	.100	.120	.120			
	B. WIPE BEARING POINTS @	.030	.030	.030	.030	.030	.030			
	C. CLOSE AND OPEN LEAF	.033	.033	.048	.052	.060	.060			
	D. ¼ TURN SCREW	.040	.040	.040	.040	.040	.040			
	E. SCREW, NUT, KNOB, JACK BY HAND	.065	.080	.090	.090	.090	.090			
	F. SOCKET HEAD SCREW	.081	.081	.081	.081	.081	.081			
	G. CAM LOCK OR QUICK CLAMP	.036	.036	.036	.036	.036	.036			
	H. NUT OR BOLT BY O. E. WRENCH	.123	.123	.130	.150	.162	.162			
	I. FIXTURE CLAMP – UNFASTENED	.047	.057	.070	.080	.090	.098			
	J. PLACE AND REMOVE PIN	.070	.108	.108	.108	.108	.108			
	K. HOLD CLAMP OR "C" WASHER	.047	.047	.049	.052	.052	.052			
	L. PREPOSITION JIG BEFORE ATC	–	.012	.020	.030	.038	.046			
	M. JIG ON AND OFF ANGLE PLATE	.030	.030	.040	.060	.080	.100			
	N. INDEX JIG OR PART PER INDEX	.004	.029	.035	.044	.060	.076			
	O.									

* FOR TAPPING ON 707 ALLOW DOUBLE ATC AND WD *

3.	MOVEMENT ELEMENTS	SMALL	MEDIUM	LARGE	LARGE SINGLE SPINDLE	NATCO 701 707*	NATCO 735 737			
	A. ADVANCE & WITHDRAW TOOL	.025	.033	.043	.054	.022	.170			
	B. INDEX JIG ON TRUNNIONS	.045	.056	.070	.083	.056	.090			
	C. MOVE JIG ON ROLLER TABLE	–	–	.059	.059	–	.080			

4.	HANDLE TOOLS AND BUSHINGS	MAGIC CHUCK			WIZARD CHUCK	SINGLE SPINDLE				
		#1	#2	#2						
	SIZE TOOL	SMALL	MED.	LARGE	LARGE	LARGE				
	A. CHUCK TOOL	.030	.040	.055	.055	.065				
	B. UNCHUCK TOOL	.020	.030	.045	.045	.050				
	C. PLACE BUSHING IN JIG	.030	.040	.055	.055	.065				
	D. REMOVE BUSHING FROM JIG	.030	.040	.055	.055	.057				
	E. CHUCK TOOL AND PLACE BUSHING	.040	.052	.075	.075	.095				
	F. UNCHUCK TOOL – REMOVE BUSHING	.030	.042	.056	.056	.058				
	G. MOVE BUSHING TO ADJACENT HOLE	.040	.050	.065	.065	.065				
	H. REPLACE TOOL OR BUSHING ONLY	.040	.052	.075	.075	.095				

5.	GAGE PART (÷ BY # BETWEEN GAGINGS)									
	A. MICROMETERS	.150	D. PLUG	.210	G. FLUSH PIN		.120			
	B. DEPTH MICS.	.180	E. SNAP	.060	H. TEMPLATE		.190			
	C. RING GAGE	.210	F. THREAD	.350	I. SCALE		.080			

6.	MISCELLANEOUS ELEMENTS									
	A. RAP WITH MALLET – FIRST RAP		.030	ADDED RAPS	@	.008				
	B. BRUSH OIL ON TOOL – FIRST TOOL		.044	ADDED TOOLS	@	.006				
	C. START AND STOP MACHINE	.048	D. CHANGE SPEED			.030				
	E. MOVE SKID OF PARTS (+ BY # PCS. ON SKID)					1.500				
	F. PLACE SKID RING (+ BY # PCS. RETAINED BY RING)					.300				
	G. BLOW OUT BLIND HOLE	.080	ADDITIONAL HOLES	@		.010				
				TOTAL HANDLING TIME						

Typical standard data table.

Allowances

Once the time for a particular job has been determined, either by corrected time study or on the basis of standard data, the time-study man adds a certain percentage *allowance* to this time to account for what the worker may lose during the day for personal time, fatigue, or unexpected contingencies.

Normally, the *personal* allowance is set arbitrarily at 5 per cent. The purpose of this allowance is to permit the worker to attend to his personal affairs, such as going to the washroom or to the drinking fountain.

The *fatigue* allowance is designed to compensate for the worker's increasing tiredness as he does the job. Fatigue allowances are often set uniformly for all jobs; it is obvious, however, that some jobs are more tiring than others, and larger allowances are sometimes made for heavier jobs. Attempts have been made to measure fatigue scientifically on different jobs, but these have not been fruitful.[31] As we have seen, fatigue is partly a psychological factor that is influenced by the worker's home life, his relations with his fellow workers and his foreman, and his attitudes toward his job. Theoretically it might be possible for a worker to claim a higher fatigue allowance because he has a poor foreman. In practice, no such nonsense is allowed.

Allowance for contingency is a general catch-all category that may include setup time, delay for materials, delay for minor breakdowns, time for oiling, and other stoppages beyond the operator's control. Sometimes an arbitrary allowance is made to cover all such contingencies. More often, a contingency allowance is computed on the basis of a rough time study made over a period of several days.

Downtime

Downtime refers to the pay a worker receives when he is unable to earn his regular incentive pay. Downtime may be incurred as a result of a major breakdown in machinery (minor breakdowns are included under contingencies), or because a worker is performing a "daywork job"—for instance, training a new employee, doing a special assignment on which no incentive standard has been developed, or handling a union grievance (where the company pays for this). Whenever management sets up an incentive system, it must answer two questions in deciding downtime policy: (1) When is downtime to be paid? (2) How much is to be paid for downtime?

Some contracts provide that downtime be paid for all delays of over ten minutes (sometimes 12, 15, or 20 minutes). A provision of this sort, however, encourages a worker who has already undergone an eight-minute delay to make it last two minutes more. Consequently, many contracts now provide that no downtime will be paid for the first ten minutes (or whatever figure is used) of each downtime period.

Naturally there is some question about whether a given delay will be included under downtime (and paid separately each time it occurs) or under contingencies (and paid on an incentive basis). Take oiling a machine as an example. If this delay is covered by downtime, the worker may be excessively

---

[31] See A. T. Welford, "The Psychologist's Problem in Measuring Fatigue," *Symposium on Fatigue*, W. F. Floyd and A. T. Welford, eds. (London: Lewis, 1953), pp. 183-191; Lucien A. Brouha, "Fatigue—Measuring and Reducing It," *Eighth Annual Time Study and Methods Conference Proceedings* (New York: Society for the Advancement of Management, 1953), pp. 57-66.

slow in oiling. But if it is included under contingencies, the worker will be motivated to spend as little time as possible on oiling and may do permanent damage to his equipment.

Custom and union contracts vary a great deal on how much a worker should be paid when he is on downtime. Often he is paid the base rate, as set by job evaluation. At other times he is paid the "average earnings" which he normally receives while on piece-work. Sometimes downtime is paid at a stated percentage, say 110 per cent of the base rate (often this is called the "scale").[32]

Under certain circumstances "average earnings" may be abused. In one factory it was discovered that workers were spending as little as 10 per cent of their time on incentive work and the rest of the time on special activities which paid downtime. Since their rate of speed on incentive work determined their earnings for the rest of the year, naturally there was strong motivation to work exceptionally hard then and to take things easy the rest of the year. On the other hand—as might be expected—workers greatly resent being put on downtime if all they receive is the base rate.

CONCLUSION

Time study represents an attempt by management to introduce objectivity into the process of determining how hard a man should work or, if he is on piece-work, how much he should earn. And yet, though the intentions of management in introducing time study are often the best, time study is highly controversial and frequently unpopular among both unionized and nonunionized workers. Why should this be?

Probably the chief reason for its unpopularity is that management often disregards the fact that *though time study is a systematic method of exercising judgment, it does not do away with the need for judgment.* Results reached by time study are neither "scientific" nor beyond dispute. Indeed, many subjective decisions must still be made: in the choice of work methods (since there is probably no *one* best method), in the timing and averaging of observed times, in the making of corrections through effort-rating, and in the determining of allowances.

On the other hand, used intelligently, with judgment and discretion, work-measurement techniques can narrow areas of ambiguity and provide the evidence on which managements and unions can make intelligent decisions. In many companies such techniques are well accepted. Even where not used as a basis for setting incentives, work measurement provides a vital tool in helping management keep track of how efficiently its operations are being run. After all, standards of some sort are essential to financial control, accurate

---

[32] One study of 245 plants disclosed that 47 per cent paid the base rate for trial work on new products, 34 per cent paid average earnings, and 19 per cent paid according to some other plan, often the "scale." "The Truth About Wage Incentives and Work Measurement Today," *Factory, op. cit.,* p. 81.

scheduling, and capital budgeting. The most common use of work measurement, however, is in setting incentives and measured day work—as we shall discuss in our next chapter.

SOME PRACTICE CALCULATIONS

Using the following time-study data (timed in hundredths of a minute), calculate the time that should be allowed on this job by means of the effort-rating approach.

CYCLE	ELEMENT			
	1	*2*	*3*	*4*
1	17	22	26	29
2	17	22	27	34
3	16	21	28	39
4	18	21	29	29
5	19	20	30	36
6	25	22	31	31
7	17	23	29	33

ALLOWANCES

fatigue	5%
personal	5%
contingencies	10%

The employee was estimated to be working at 130% of normal speed through all cycles. To compute the first element, use the mode; for the second, "good time"; for the third, the median; and for the fourth, the mean. (In practice, of course, but one system would be used.)

(For answer, see bottom of p. 689.)

Individual Incentive

Systems

Now that we have explored the role of time and motion study in setting work standards, let us look at incentive plans based on these and synthetic data. The basic principle underlying these plans is very simple: Employees will be more productive if their income is tied to the amount of work they turn out rather than just to the amount of time they spend on the job.

Most incentive systems are based on piece-work—that is, individuals or groups are paid on the basis of the number of units they produce. Such plans are most common in mass-production industries, where the conditions essential to incentive systems are most likely to prevail:

1. Standardized work and working conditions with relatively continuous processing.
2. Measurable units of output assignable to individuals or small groups.
3. Quantity of output proportional to employee effort and attention, and quality of secondary concern.

Where these conditions are not present—for example, in automated plants or on assembly lines—piece-work plans are less useful.

There are other "payment by result" plans that do not make use of time-and-motion-study standards or their equivalents. These plans call for salesmen's commissions, or for efficiency bonuses paid to supervisors and nonproduction workers when certain quotas are exceeded. Although this chapter will concentrate on piece-work plans in mass-production industry, some mention will be made of these other incentive systems.

WHY USE INCENTIVES?

Built-in Motivation

Ideally, incentive plans are superimposed upon a carefully constructed wage structure determined by job evaluation. The time-study engineer usually attempts to set the production standard at a level that will permit the average employee who applies himself to the job to make additional earnings of from 20 to 25 per cent above the evaluated base rate. In contrast to other employee benefits which are granted almost automatically to all workers or which are proportional to length of service, incentive plans, presumably, establish a direct relationship between performance and reward. In diverse cultures, even in countries in early stages of industrialization, piece rates hold appeal.[1] They may permit employees with different skill and motivation levels to work together with some equity; that is, those deserving more will earn more. And many employers find incentives consistent with free enterprise: A man gets what he earns for himself.

Worker autonomy. On the other hand, there will be employees who prefer an easier job to increased earnings and who will trade leisure for income. Even they, however, may favor incentives if they gain the option of working less hard while their colleagues earn more money! For either group, incentives help protect the employee in his strong desire to control his own work pace: "No man yields easily to another control over the amount of effort he must exert daily." [2]

Added Job Interest

The possibility of making extra money, of racing the clock, of pitting one's abilities against "normal" performance—all add an extra dash of interest to jobs that are inherently monotonous and tedious. This opportunity to set goals, and the chance to improve one's "score," provide the employee with a sense of accomplishment (see Chapter 1).

> "When I am going hell bent for election on a good piece-work job, the evening passes very swiftly and I do not realize that I am tired until it is all over. On these daywork jobs I get so bored I could stand in the aisle and yell. . . ." [3]

Less Worker-Management Conflict

Ideally, incentive plans provide the sense of common interest between workers and management. They emphasize the fact that both will benefit from higher production and from improvements in supporting services, such as scheduling and quality of materials. The supervisor has less need to push for higher output, and the employees feel that they can vary their pace to suit their moods without antagonizing the supervisor. In a very real sense, these plans increase the opportunity to apply what we have called "general supervision."

---

[1] *Cf.* Clark Kerr, John Dunlop, Frederick Harbison, and Charles Myers, *Industrialism and Industrial Man* (Cambridge, Mass.: Harvard University Press, 1960) p. 252.

[2] Everett Hughes, *Men and Their Work* (New York: Free Press, 1958), p. 47.

[3] William F. Whyte, *et al.*, *Money and Motivation* (New York: Harper & Row, 1955), p. 32.

Increased Control over Labor Costs

Incentive plans also help the firm to control its labor costs. After all, it is argued, most wage contracts are ambiguous when it comes to stipulating how much work an employee is expected to do for a given wage, yet the amount of work is just as important to management as the rate of pay. By insuring that employees will be paid on the basis of production, rather than on the number of hours they work, piece-rate systems enable the firm to predict its labor costs in advance. Particularly in highly competitive industries like textiles and clothing, this ability to look ahead is highly important. Piece rates also make it possible for management to develop more accurate cost-accounting estimates in establishing budgets and in preparing bids on new contracts.

This is a rosy picture we have painted. Surely it would seem that incentive systems should eliminate many of the sources of industrial conflict and employee-relations problems—after all, they encourage delegation of responsibility, increase worker motivation, and strengthen management's control. Unfortunately, the results have proved disappointing, for incentive plans have been the source of serious friction between labor and management. In fact, many observers attribute the rapid growth of unions in certain companies directly to the existence of incentive payment systems. How can we explain this paradox? Why should a program that is theoretically sound prove so deficient in practice?

PROBLEMS WITH INCENTIVES

To understand why incentive plans tend to generate conflict, we must first assess the impact of these wage-payment systems on employees: how employees react to incentives.

The Work Group Imposes a Ceiling

It is unrealistic for management to assume that individual employees will respond to the opportunity for additional earnings by producing as much as they can. The members of certain inexperienced work groups may react that way, but most employees are quick to learn that such behavior is *dangerous*. Why do they feel it is dangerous?

Employees fear that if they begin to pull down earnings that are "too high" under a particular piece rate, management, particularly the time-study department, will decide that the rate is too generous. As we saw in the preceding chapter, time study is not an exact science. When employees begin to earn incentive premiums of 30 or 40 per cent above the base rate on the job, chances are that management will begin to question its time-study findings.

Management usually promises it will not "cut rates" except when changes are made in working conditions or in the methods by which the job is done. Employees, however, believe that management will always be able to find an excuse to restudy a job on which incentive earnings are obviously very high.

Further, many workers fear that if they increase their production markedly they will work themselves out of a job—that is, that management won't be able to sell the increased output.

Moreover, incentive plans may threaten the status hierarchy within the group, since older workers—who customarily have the highest status—may be unable to match the pace of their younger colleagues and thus find that their relative earnings have declined. Naturally, to protect their social position the older workers put pressure on the younger ones to "take things easy."

In response to all these factors, the work group begins to establish norms ("bogies") of what is the proper or safe level of output; the employee who overproduces is belittled as a "rate-buster." New employees are indoctrinated into the group's standard almost as soon as they enter the department:

> This was my first job. The foreman told me I was on piece work and to make just as much as I could. I was scared and anxious to make a good impression so I tried pretty hard.
>
> About an hour had passed when several guys told me "Take it easy, guy—don't knock yourself out." I thought they were showing kindness, so I thanked them and kept plugging ahead.
>
> Then an older man came to me and said, "Let me give you a piece of advice. The most we ever make on that piece is sixty an hour, and a new man doesn't make that much. If you want to make any friends here, I'd watch your count pretty closely."
>
> "How come?" I asked.
>
> "Because if we put out more than that, they'll cut our rates. We will have to work that much harder for the same amount of money."

Those men, who do not rely on group acceptance as a source of job satisfaction, ignore the group's norms and produce at a level substantially above the agreed-on ceiling.[4] They trade their social acceptability in return for higher income. The friction that develops between rate-busters and the other group members may explode into severe supervisory problems. Efforts of the group to get the rate-buster to conform may show themselves in the sabotage of equipment as well as in ostracism—neither of which is conducive to harmonious working relationships.

As a result of these pressures, a relatively "straight-line" production curve is established for each employee and for the group as a whole. There will be certain variations from this curve because of factors beyond the workers' control, of course; but in general everyone will try to maintain and report approximately the same "safe" output. If the group inadvertently overproduces, this excess is concealed and reported on a day when the group falls short of

---

[4] *Ibid.*, pp. 39–52.

its normal production. And in this respect the group's efforts to control output actually work to management's advantage. Individual workers are reluctant to be considered excessively lazy or unskillful; therefore the ability to "make out" —to earn a reasonable incentive bonus—becomes a mark of prestige. Furthermore, very low output would attract the attention of engineers and supervisors, who might eventually make undesirable changes in methods or standards.

Struggling for "Better" Rates

Employees under an incentive plan do not restrict themselves to manipulating the output level, however. They also struggle with management and the time-study department to obtain more desirable or "looser" rates. They believe that the time-study engineer cannot evaluate precisely how many pieces per day or per hour each worker should be able to complete; they know that he must resort to certain subjective judgments (what we called "leveling" in the preceding chapter). Consequently they suspect that management will try to make them work harder than they should to obtain a reasonable bonus, or even that management will establish such "tight" rates that it will be impossible to make satisfactory earnings.

This distrust shows itself most dramatically when the time-study engineer appears in the shop to study a job that requires a new rate. What happens is aptly described in the following verbatim account:

> (Starkey is advising Tennessee, a relatively inexperienced worker, in the ways of dealing with time-study men.)
> "If you expect to get any kind of a price, you got to outwit that——You got to use your noodle while you're working, and think your work out ahead as you go along! You got to add in movements you know you ain't going to make when you're running the job! Remember, if you don't——them, they're going to—— you! . . . Every movement counts!
> ". . . You were running that job too damn fast before they timed you on it! I was watching you yesterday. If you don't run a job slow before you get timed, you won't get a good price. They'll look at the record of what you do before they come around and compare it with the timing speed. Those time-study men are sharp! . . ."
> (Later Starkey describes Ray Ward, one of the "heroes" of the department.)
> "Ray knew his drills," said Starkey. "He'd burn up a drill every four or five pieces when they were timing him, and say the speed was too high for the tough stuff he was running. Tough stuff, nuts! They'd lower the speed and feed to where he wasn't burning up the drills, then afterwards he'd speed up and cut through that tough stuff like cheese."
> "What I want to know," said Tennessee, "is how in hell could Ward burn up the drills like that? You can't just burn up a drill when you feel like it."
> "It's in the way you grind the drill," said Starkey. "Ray used to grind his own drills, and he'd touch them up before they timed him. The wrong kind of a grind will burn up a drill at a lower speed than the drill can take if it's ground right for the job." [5]

---

[5] *Ibid.,* pp. 15-17.

One study of management's problems in administering incentive programs gives additional examples of the deceptions engaged in by employees during time-study checks:

> [The employee] had succeeded in obtaining a standard of 120 coils per hour for a job on which the workers could easily produce 300 coils per hour. He did this by distorting the tension on the steel. When the time-study men requested that the mill be speeded up, the uneven tension on the steel would cause a breakdown.
>
> [Other deceptions involved] oiling belts on machines to decrease friction and thus to reduce actual machine speeds; saving up defective materials to be used during time studies; using slow drive gears; and surrepetitiously cutting yarn to increase down time.[6]

Arguments over Allowances

Both sides may legitimately disagree over the frequency and importance of equipment failures, material shortages, or imperfections that delay and hamper the employee in his production. Obviously the employees want to insure that the allowances are ample; management wants to insure that they are kept within reasonable limits.

Time-study engineers come to see the employees as tricksters who feign difficulties when jobs are being timed, are dishonest about their ability to do the job within the time allotted, and are always pressuring for looser standards, whether legitimate or not. Time-study engineers may even overcompensate for the expected bluffs and shenanigans of employees. They fear being tricked into setting too "loose" a rate, and consequent embarrassment. Expecting the worst, they take extra pains when first setting a rate to make sure it is reasonably tight. Employees recognize this tendency and try to make sure that they don't have to accept the rate the company first establishes for a new job.

The Negotiation Process

Thus, the introduction of new jobs often marks the outbreak of an extended cold war between employees and management. Employees may have learned by experience that if they object vigorously to the rates set by management's industrial engineering department, and if they fail repeatedly to meet the standard output set by the time-study engineer, eventually they may be able to win a slight loosening of the rates. Management recognizes that by giving in to such pressures it may only encourage further slowdowns, grievances, and similar protests; they insist the workers aren't giving it a "fair trial." The war rages until the employees are convinced that they can do no better and management is satisfied that it has won something approximating a reason-

---

[6] William B. Wolf, *Wage Incentives as a Managerial Tool* (New York: Columbia University Press, 1957), p. 26.

able standard. The ultimate result is a "negotiated" rate that may depart significantly from the time-study data. Particularly when a situation involves only a small group of workers who control a critical step, a | potential | bottleneck in the work flow, management is tempted to concede rather than suffer a prolonged loss of output.

Here is a colorful description of this cold war.

> The setting of rates and the reaction by the operators is a routine you have to go over again and again, forever and ever apparently, as long as there shall be garment rates, and broken needles. You study carefully and set the rate, say 49½ cents a dozen for hemming. You post the rate and then the operator has a fit. She says she "can't make nothing on that rate." She says she's been here on the line for 23 years and no young squirt time-study man is going to push her around. You tell her there's a lot of factors involved (what would we do without those involved factors?), and that management wants to meet the operators half way and continue to enjoy mutual confidence for the highest production, Sleep Tite quality, and high earnings based on output and ability. The operator says she "can't buy no groceries on mutual confidence" and is going to go to work at the Packing Plant unless something is done about the rate. The other girls in the unit glare at management and exchange significant looks and talk so much about it all day that production goes off 12 dozen. You promise to analyze the situation and make an "eight-hour study" to check for any factors that might have been overlooked (or involved)....
>
> You agree to raise the rate from 49½ cents per dozen to 50¼ cents. Two weeks later the operator is running away with the rate and making $1.33 an hour, within 17 cents of the machinist, who is the best machinist in the area and knows more about a Singer machine than the Singer people.[7]

Living with the Rate: Rising Costs

While they are being observed by the time-study man, employees try to prove that they have to work very slowly indeed. Then, after the rate has been set, they do just the opposite. They try to find short cuts: devising ways of running the machine faster, using special jigs or fixtures, leaving out some of the required operations. To avoid punishment for using unapproved short cuts, and to avoid retiming of the job, all these tricks must be kept secret.

Thus employees may earn large incentive bonuses but productivity may not increase proportionately. Sometimes management is deceived into thinking its rates are "in line" because the incentive earnings do not appear abnormally high. Of course, as we have seen, this in part merely reflects the adroitness of the work group in establishing output ceilings. "Loose rates" are hidden by carefully controlled output restriction, and the benefits from these rates are taken in the form of increased leisure on the job rather than increased earnings.

Even after the battle seems to be over and the employees begin to work under an established rate, management's problems are still not solved. On some

---

[7] Richard Bissell, *7½ Cents* (Boston: Little, Brown, 1953) pp. 132-134.

jobs, employees are able to take advantage of the "product mix." When they have a number of tasks to do, each with its own time-study rate, they can build up their incentive earnings by working hard on the jobs with looser rates, and coast on the jobs with tighter rates, producing just enough to avoid trouble. This device, of course, upsets the production schedule.[8]

In their efforts to earn high bonuses, employees may pressure management for higher-quality materials, more assistance in handling materials and tools, and better maintenance. They are also likely to neglect work that does not help them increase their earnings—for example, keeping their work area clean, oiling equipment, and caring for tools. As a result, management is confronted with higher overhead costs that detract from the direct improvements in output provided by the incentive plan.

Frequently, too, these plans provide that employees will receive "average earnings" during delays that are beyond their control. This provision, in turn, motivates employees on occasion to seek delays and to fail to take adequate care of their own equipment. By pressuring job-setters, maintenance men, tool-room personnel, and even supervisors to "adjust" the time records and to report incorrectly the time when an employee began a particular job or the time when a breakdown occurs, employees can inflate the amount of time their machines were idle due to factors "beyond" their control, and can understate the time they were actually able to devote to their job. Thus employees can earn more money without working harder.[9] The emphasis on quantity may induce employees to pay only perfunctory attention to quality. As a result inspection costs rise significantly.

In administering incentive plans it is assumed that job changes which make the employee's work easier or faster will be reflected in changes in the incentive rate for the job—that is, as improvements are made in the process, new rates will be established calling for higher production. In practice, however, management is often reluctant to begin the long tedious struggle over rate-setting, and therefore does not insist that a new rate be set every time a minor change is made on the job. Cohesive, aggressive work groups benefit most in such circumstances.

Thus, these minor job changes have a cumulative effect, causing piece rates to loosen more and more. The result is unjustifiably high earnings in relation to employee effort, and failure of the company to benefit from the investments it makes in improved technology, scheduling, and supervision.[10] Actually these "creeping rates" may nullify most of management's potential gains from the incentive plan.

---

[8] Donald Roy, "Efficiency and 'The Fix,'" *American Journal of Sociology,* Vol. 60, No. 3 (November 1954).

[9] Donald Roy, "Work Satisfaction and Social Rewards in Quota Achievements," *American Sociology Review,* Vol. 18, No. 5 (October 1953).

[10] For an excellent discussion of these problems, see Herbert R. Northrup, "The Other Side of Incentives," *Personnel,* Vol. 36, No. 1 (January-February 1959), pp. 32-41.

Coercive Intergroup Comparisons

To make matters worse, when one group succeeds in gradually loosening its rate, others then demand the same improvements, particularly when there is a union that is supposed to provide equal benefits for all:

> Taking advantage of the continuous technological changes that characterize the industry, the local unions seize opportunities to press home a wage gain for a particular job. A few such changes in incentive earnings, flowing out of changes in technology and job content, lead to inequities in relationships between jobs and this affords additional negotiating opportunities for the union.[11]

Because incentive plans may affect relative earnings, potentially they can upset long-established status relationships between groups. Certain groups do work that has traditionally been considered as relatively low-paying and undesirable. Under a loose incentive rate, these groups may begin to earn substantially more than do workers on higher-status jobs. Almost invariably, intergroup bickering and dissatisfaction will arise, leading eventually to pressures on management to re-establish the traditional relationship between rates.

Thus, a slight concession made by management in order to avoid serious disagreement may mushroom over time into substantially higher labor costs. And once this process has been initiated, it is almost impossible to reverse. A work group that has grown accustomed to relatively lucrative piece rates is understandably reluctant to accept a cut-back, even though the company's market position becomes unfavorable.

At best, rate-setting is a tedious process and work groups resist retiming even more strongly than they resist the original time study. Moreover, employees fear that management may resort to engineering changes on the job just as an excuse to "get another crack" at a piece rate that has proved too loose.

In fact, management cannot really live by the maxim, "We never cut a rate." When, for whatever reason, one group of workers begins to earn bonuses so large that their relative position in the earnings hierarchy is altered, the unstabilizing affect on other groups may force management to take action—sometimes a contrived engineering change that will justify retiming. In any case, reducing a rate is a painful process for all concerned. The lesson it teaches employees with high earnings is to exercise greater restraint—that is, greater control over output—next time.

Other groups in the plant are often affected by incentive systems, even though they themselves do not share in them. Workers who transport materials, for example, or who do maintenance or tool-room work, may be pressured into increasing their efforts to help incentive workers earn a greater bonus. These so-called "indirect employees" work harder and harder, plant production in-

---

[11] N. Goldfinger and E. M. Kassalow, "Trade Union Behavior in Wage Bargaining," in George W. Taylor and Frank C. Pierson, *New Concepts in Wage Determination* (New York: McGraw-Hill, 1957), p. 78.

creases, and yet their earnings remain unchanged. In fact, their relative position in the earnings hierarchy may deteriorate. Understandably, these workers demand special wage concessions to restore them to their former position.

Impact on the Union

The local union is often torn by differences of opinion over the value of incentives. Some groups, particularly younger employees, welcome incentive rates. Older and less fortunately situated employees, particularly "day workers," may fight for higher hourly rates that will counterbalance the incentive earnings of other employees. The fact that certain groups are making higher earnings than others may actually embarrass the union, particularly in deciding whether or not to accept management's efforts to "retime" the very lucrative jobs. The over-all result is political instability for the union leader, who must choose whether to concentrate the union's bargaining strength on defending the "lucky" groups or on fighting for those less fortunately situated.

Because incentives do create intergroup problems, many unions have policies prohibiting their use, and to craft unions they are an anathema. However, many industrial unions that in theory are opposed, accept incentives because the membership insists. In any case union-management relations are probably less amicable with incentives. Evidence suggests that a significant proportion (over 20 per cent) of arbitration concerns incentive problems.

IMPROVING
THE SUPERVISOR-EMPLOYEE RELATIONSHIP

One of the most rewarding starting points in meeting incentive problems is the supervisor-employee relationship. Research suggests that employees are more likely to respond positively to incentives if they believe that their supervisor has some influence over the rate-setting process.[12] We have seen that the effective supervisor must be willing and able to *represent* his subordinates, to respond to suggestions from them, and to bring their problems to the attention of higher management (see Chapter 15). Where the supervisor has no voice in the incentive system and no specialized knowledge of how it works, or where he feels that the whole process is "out of his hands," it is highly unlikely that the system will function successfully. Thus the successful administration of an incentive plan requires the active and intelligent participation of the first-line supervisor.

Unfortunately, however, the supervisor is often left out of the rate-setting and administrative processes. Because of the technical complexities of the plan, management ordinarily engages industrial engineers as special staff personnel to handle the whole plan. Also, fearing that concessions in one department will cause the mushrooming effect that we have already described, management

---

[12] See Donald Pelz, "Influence: A Key to Effective Leadership in the First Line Supervisor," *Personnel*, Vol. 29 (1952), pp. 209-217.

often deprives the supervisor of the right to suggest that rates be raised, lest he succumb too readily to employee pressure.

Thus, the supervisor is tempted to respond to an employee question about his standard by saying, "Look, I don't understand it either; those engineers in time study work these things out, not me. If you're dissatisfied, they're the ones to argue with; I can't help you."

But this attitude undermines the whole system. Once the employees realize that their supervisor is isolated from the rate-setting process, they fear that they will be taken advantage of. The supervisor soon communicates his disrespect for or lack of understanding of the system to his subordinates, and they, in turn, are encouraged to help themselves by resorting to trickery and trumped-up records. The supervisor must be trained in the administration of the incentive plan and made to feel that it is part of his job. His skills in handling rate grievances must be cultivated. When employees find that he is informed and willing to "go to bat" for them when they are right, and unwilling to collude with them when they are wrong, the whole tenor of the system is likely to improve.

Improving
the Supervisor/Time-study Relationship

Before this improvement can be achieved, however, the relationship between time-study personnel and the supervisor must be put on a sound basis. This is one of the stabilization relationships that we described in Chapter 16, and as such it is well stocked with problems. There is also the natural antipathy between the production man, who is likely to have been promoted through the ranks, toward the smart specialist who may be a relative newcomer to the organization. This antipathy is aggravated by the fact that time study is so often a source of difficulty to the supervisor.

Actually, the foreman has a strong incentive to support his work group in its struggle with management. Loose rates leave employees happy and eliminate the "cold war" type of grievances, slowdowns, and the like. Employees working under loose rates have energy left over to pitch in during an emergency when the supervisor needs their help. In addition, his own production record is likely to look better when employees have easy rates and always make a 20 or 30 per cent bonus.

To the time-study man, such supervisory attitudes are anathema, for he knows that even slight concessions on rates quickly grow to major proportions as other groups demand the same "loose" rates. Intraplant pay distortions spring up when easy rates make it possible for some employees to make disproportionately high earnings, and the time-study men are embarrassed when evidence suggests that they have been unable to set good tight rates. As a result they feel that the supervisor is too weak, too willing to concede to employee and union pressure, and unsympathetic toward the need for "scientifically correct" standards and frequent retiming.

The following hypothetical dialogue between a supervisor and a time-study man illustrates their different points of view.

> *Supervisor:* "It looks to me as if that rate is pretty tight and we are going to get a lot of gripes from the operators."
>
> *Time-study Man:* (To himself) "How does he know; he hasn't even looked over the study—in fact, he probably doesn't even understand time study; he just wants to avoid any personal troubles with the men."
> (To Supervisor) "Well, I've done a careful job, and I think it is a good standard."
>
> *Supervisor:* (To himself) "Here is another one of those know-it-all kids who thinks he has learned in a couple of days what it took me 15 years to learn. There's no use trying to reason with them."
> (To Time-study Man) "I've already heard a number of complaints from the men that they can never make out under this new standard. I wonder whether there might not be some factor that was overlooked in the study."
>
> *Time-study Man:* (To himself) "Just as I thought, he doesn't have the ability to get his people to accept the new standard; they are so used to only doing half a job that tightening up seems unfair."
> (To Supervisor) "If they would only give it a chance and really try it out, I know they could make it, but they prefer to gripe rather than work."
>
> *Supervisor:* (To himself) "There is not much use even talking to him; he doesn't care about what happens *after* he sets the rate. In fact, he probably gets a pat on the back from his boss for the amount he increases the standard on the job; the greater the increase the more likely he is to get a raise himself. I'm left holding the bag as far as dealing with the men is concerned and with the new quality problems that are going to come up when they try to beat it and with more tooling breakdowns and costs which those guys never figure on."
> (To Time-study Man) "O.K. We'll see what happens but I can tell you right now we are in for trouble on this."
>
> *Time-study Man:* (To himself) "Sure, if that's the way the supervisor feels about the standard already, what can you expect from the men? We'll have trouble from them."
> (To Supervisor) "If they'll only give it a fair trial I know it's going to work out."
>
> *Supervisor:* (To himself) "They think they can never make a mistake! Everything was fine here until he came in."
> (To Time-study Man) "We'll see. . . ."

The solution of such conflicts of interest demands both organizational change and training. William F. Whyte, generalizing from a study of the Inland Steel Container Company, has described the type of reorganization that will eliminate many of the problems we have described:

> No longer was he [the time-study man] to be a free-wheeling, apparently autonomous agent who carried the threat of change with him wherever he went in the plant. Instead, management decided that he should not enter a department for purposes of making a study unless he had written approval by one of two production management officials. Furthermore, he had to present this clearance to the foreman in whose department he was to work, and the foreman then took the initiative in bringing in the union steward so that the three of them could discuss the work that was to be done. Then, before the

work was started, the foreman and steward would accompany the time-study man to the worker or workers whose jobs were to be studied so that the next steps could be explained to them.[13]

Notice that this approach shifts the time-study man in the direction of an advisory relationship. The next step is for management to provide the kind of training in industrial engineering techniques that will enable the supervisor to deal intelligently with the problems and grievances raised by time and motion study.

Effective handling of incentive problems at lower levels also requires the use of simple formulas for converting production into earnings. Many companies develop unnecessary complex formulas that neither supervisors nor employees understand; neither can calculate the effect of a particular day's production or a particular breakdown on earnings. A simple though necessary step in improving receptivity to incentives is the use of simple, direct plans that do not give the impression of deception on the part of management.

AUXILIARY INCENTIVE PLANS

In addition to the immediate supervisors themselves, hourly employees who transport materials, maintain equipment, make and distribute tools, and do inspection work are in a position to influence the pace and efficiency with which incentive employees work. These so-called nonproductive, auxiliary workers, who "service" the production workers, are not on incentive. And, as might be expected, these nonproductive workers resent this "discrimination." They complain with justice that their efforts are essential to the incentive employees' earnings, and whenever the incentive employees work harder, they must work harder, too—without compensation.

Many companies have simply tried to provide extra compensation for auxiliary employees in proportion to the piece-work earnings of the incentive workers, on the assumption that their work increases roughly in the same ratio as the size of the bonus earnings. Thus, supervisors get a monthly bonus that is tied to the bonus earned by their subordinates, and other indirect workers get a supplement based on the incentive earnings or the total production of the employees they service. In the case of a tool-room worker, the formula might be based on total plant production; the bonus of material-handlers might be based on the production of the department or departments they service.

However, the manager must be careful not to encourage undesirable practices by providing auxiliary bonuses. An inspector who is paid a bonus in proportion to the incentive earnings of the group as a whole may decide to be less diligent in looking for rejects. Extra precautions need to be taken to check his work (and this means extra costs). A supervisor, similarly, who is rewarded in proportion to the incentive earnings of his subordinates may be motivated

---

[13] Whyte, *et al.*, *op. cit.*, p. 229.

to agitate for looser rates for his men and to be careless in his administration of the incentive plan.

Many companies have become disillusioned with incentives.[14] In part this results from the extravagant claims made by the management literature and industrial engineering consulting firms.[15] In fact, many firms continue using incentives as an act of faith, ignoring the extra inspection, accounting, negotiation, and engineering costs (to name but a few).[16] But even when unrealistic expectations cannot be attained, adequate personnel planning can improve the administration of these programs.[17]

Piece work has a long history; workers in agriculture and textiles traditionally received such payments. However, modern technology, particularly automation, reduces the close connection between individual effort and output. Also, as we saw in Chapter 3, service and white-collar jobs are increasing in numbers, and these do not readily lend themselves to piece-work.[18]

Both as a means of increasing supervisory control and to provide an explicit target for the employee, management now often turns to *measured day work*. Although there are a number of varieties of this technique, most consist of using systematic measurement methods to establish explicit objective output goals. Many organizations believe that output is as high under such systems, assuming good supervision, as under incentives, and that administrative costs are less. Further, such systems may facilitate the introduction of technological change. Since these changes help workers to meet production goals, they are not seen as a speed-up device or a technique for cutting the piece rate as is technological change under traditional incentive plans.

---

[14] For critical reviews of the status of the incentives field see Garth Mangum, "Are Wage Incentives Becoming Obsolete," *Industrial Relations*, Vol. 2, No. 1 (October 1962), pp. 73-96; R. Marriott, *Incentive Payment Systems: A Review of Research and Opinion*, 2nd ed. (London: Staples Press, 1961); Hilde Behrend, "The Effort Bargain," *Industrial and Labor Relations Review*, Vol. 10, No. 4 (July 1957), pp. 503-515.

[15] *Cf.* "Increase Productivity 50% in One Year with Sound Wage Incentives," *Management Methods*, Vol. 15 (February 1959), pp. 38-43.

[16] *Cf.* Hilde Behrend, "Financial Incentives as the Expression of a System of Belief," *British Journal of Sociology*, Vol. 10, No. 2 (June 1959), pp. 137-147. Dr. Behrend is one of Europe's foremost experts on incentives. In this study of 250 British firms, she finds no evidence that piece work improves productivity.

[17] As of 1960 it was estimated that 27% of manufacturing employees were covered by incentives: L. Earle Lewis, "Extent of Incentive Pay in Manufacturing," *Monthly Labor Review*, Vol. 45, No. 45 (May 1960), pp. 461-463. There is some disagreement over whether this number is decreasing. Also see *Monthly Labor Review*, Vol. 87, No. 3 (March 1964), pp. 271-276.

[18] There have been many efforts to use incentives in the office, but these have not become popular. However, piece-work has invaded the bank: Those who prepare cancelled checks for the computer process which handles customer balances are sometimes on incentive. This is an example of the early stages of automation which causes clerical operations to resemble "white-collar factories" (see Chapter 3).

Measured daywork is no panacea, however. When these rates are used as a stick (through threats of discipline for those who fall below the stated rate) or as a carrot (with merit increases or promotions for those who meet or exceed the rate), many of the problems associated with traditional incentive plans come to the fore, although perhaps not with the same severity.

Another system is used with automatic or semi-automatic machinery: Standards for equipment utilization are established. The employee's job is to be alert to the needs of the machinery and, by minor adjustments, to keep it going during as much of the work shift as possible. He may be paid a bonus according to the percentage of utilization above a certain level.

Both measured-daywork and equipment-utilization bonuses highlight a flaw in traditional piece-work plans. As we have seen, under these arrangements, employees are rewarded for extra *effort*, not for productivity. Management therefore puts itself in the position of bargaining over how much effort should be expended.[19] Although industrial engineers assume that there is a direct connection between the two, this is not always the case. (For instance, employees may be rewarded for complicating their job and causing more breakdowns and be penalized for finding shortcuts.) In fact, technological changes which increase productivity are often accompanied by retiming and rate cuts! In the next chapter, we shall look at some other incentive plans which encourage employees to increase productivity and give them financial rewards even when their effort may be less.

CONCLUSION

It is not unusual for management to regard financial incentive plans as a cure-all. Faced with weak and ineffective supervision, difficulties and delays in work flow, low morale, and unsatisfactory output levels, management decides that all these problems can be solved by incentives. Also, shortsighted managements may neglect nonmonetary incentives, which can be powerful motivators, in favor of too exclusive reliance on monetary rewards.

Actually, an incentive plan neither eliminates nor reduces the need for good supervision; it requires alert, skilled supervisors who can facilitate the rate-setting process and handle the difficulties inherent in any plan. Worker confidence and good relationships with employees and union are essential if the plan is not to become bogged down in constant bickering. Each management must weigh the costs involved and decide for itself whether or not incentives will produce a net gain. Careful administration and vigilance may produce a gain, but the gain does not come automatically. Just installing incentives does not guarantee lower costs.

Management, in instituting an incentive plan, must be willing to pay the price of administering it. It must be willing to struggle with grievances, and

[19] Behrend, *op. cit.*, p. 505.

to correct inequities and imbalances in the wage structure resulting from differences in the relative "tightness" or "looseness" of incentive rates in various parts of the organization. It must also avoid the temptation to establish a looser rate when critical production is at stake or to offer incentive pay as "extra remuneration" to gain acceptance of technological changes. Concessions made during good times will cause trouble when profit levels decline. Otherwise there is the strong tendency for rates to become looser and looser over time, for more money to be paid for less productivity. But with good administration, it is reasonable to expect that productivity will be improved under an incentive plan:

> It is also true, of course, that although wage incentive payment plans and related techniques do not release all the worker's productivity capacity, they do by and large liberate a greater share of it than comes from time work systems.[20]

Over time, incentives become accepted by those who work under them and any threat of removal generates substantial resistance.

Also, certain healthful pressures may be generated in the work group itself by incentive plans. Employees under incentives become concerned over unnecessary work delays or material shortages, equipment problems, and scheduling. They urge management to expedite the flow of work because they now have a stake in the effectiveness of the organization. Thus, any incentive plan depends upon a well-engineered work flow: materials coming in and leaving as scheduled, equipment and tools in good condition, and working conditions maintained at prearranged levels.

In short, incentive systems cannot compensate for managerial ineptness. Rather, they demand managerial excellence. They are wasteful when they are used to bring production levels *up to* reasonable standards; they should be used only to compensate employees for performance *above* reasonable standards. Then they are a genuinely useful managerial tool.

PROBLEM 1

WHITE-COLLAR PIECE-WORK

The Office Manager for your company's executive offices has called you in to discuss his labor-cost problems. He is seeking help from the personnel department in halting the steady rise in office costs and what he feels is a trend toward lower individual productivity. Specifically, he wants to know whether the experience of companies with incentive plans in manufacturing operations would have any applicability in his office environment. He thinks he may want to develop a type of "production standard" for the more routine jobs: IBM card-punch operator, stenographer, file clerk, mimeograph-machine operator, collator, and similar positions.

---

[20] William Gomberg, "Union Interest in Engineering Techniques," *Harvard Business Review*, Vol. 24, No. 3 (Spring 1946), p. 365.

1. In discussing this matter with him, what knowledge about the operation of incentive plans would you use in framing questions and making comments?
2. What criteria would you apply in deciding whether or not formal incentive plans would be useful in the office?
3. How would you decide whether any or all of these jobs were suitable for such plans?
4. What problems would you envision in administering an incentive plan in such an office?

PROBLEM 2

WHEN CAN INCENTIVES BE IGNORED?

A group of production employees is refusing to work any faster than "base rate" in protest against the elimination of a soft-drink machine near their work area. Top management is pressuring supervision "to do something" quickly, for scheduling throughout the plant is being affected by the decreased output here. The foreman is reluctant to succumb to employee pressure, both because of the bad precedent that would be set and because the machine itself was a nuisance—cups, bottle caps, and bottles were strewn about the area, and the dispenser encouraged loitering. Disciplinary measures are being considered against the ringleaders for organizing a "slowdown." Some members of management are urging caution, claiming, as the men themselves do, that the employees do not have to work at an *incentive pace*. The company provides the opportunity for workers to earn a bonus if they wish to work more intensively than a *daywork pace*, but this decision is up to the employees. Other members of management take the opposite point of view—in accepting work on a job with an incentive rate attached, the worker obligates himself to try for such additional earnings, and this is a concerted effort to hold back production.

1. Comment on the merits of the divergent opinions within management on the employees' obligation to seek incentive earnings.
2. Discuss what management's approach should be to the workers' protest action. (There is no union in the organization.)

PROBLEM 3

WHO GETS THE "TIGHT" AND "LOOSE" JOBS?

Machine-shop employees are constantly wrangling among themselves and with their supervisor over work assignments. Several senior employees have filed grievances claiming that their foreman is discriminating against them. Here is a typical case:

Waljack claims that his incentive earnings were cut 40 per cent the previous week because the supervisor assigned him several jobs that had very "tight" rates. During the same period most of the other employees, nearly all of whom had less seniority than Waljack, received highly desirable jobs with "looser" rates. Waljack further claims that the supervisor did all this on purpose to punish him, because he dislikes him.

When the superintendent reviewed this particular grievance he was told by the departmental foreman that it was not serious. "This is just another effort by the older men to get all the good jobs and leave the dregs for the younger employees. What they want me to do is to spend hours analyzing every job that comes into the department and figure out just how much bonus the operator is going to get on it. Then I am supposed to plan out the work so that the senior workers get only the high-paying ones and when they finish one good one, I will have another choice job to give them. This way I would spend my whole day working out earnings schedules rather than planning the most efficient way to schedule production in my department."

The superintendent also spoke to the union chief steward about the problem. The steward said that the union felt that the company's incentive system provided an easy means for the foreman to reward his friends and punish those whom he didn't like (and who might be vigorous union supporters). The union wanted management to come up with a proposal to take this power away from their foremen.

The superintendent learned that the department itself was divided on this issue. Some of the men were afraid that the union would set up a system whereby the good work was distributed according to length of service, which would mean that the newer employees might take a real wage cut. At the same time they were not happy about the supervisor holding these assignments over their heads "as a club."

The personnel department cautioned that any management decision here might have far-reaching implications. The supervisor's right to make work assignments was a crucial element in management's ability to run the plant efficiently. The union would be in a good position to limit this vital prerogative if it got a foot in the door in a case like this one.

1. As the superintendent, how would you evaluate the case? Assuming that Waljack had some grounds for making his complaint, how would you deal with it in such a way as to avoid other problems?
2. Can the right to make work assignments be separated from other aspects of incentive-plan administration?

PROBLEM 4

SALES QUOTAS

The Superior Floor Covering Company has an incentive program for its salesmen. Incentive earnings are based on the amount of sales in relation to an assigned quota. The quota is computed each year by management, taking into account the number and type of customers in each salesman's territory and the previous year's sales records for the company and for its competitors. In the administration of this incentive program, the following problems have arisen. Suggest the type of analysis you would undertake to provide data that might lead to a solution and the alternative plans you would consider in eliminating these difficulties. Note also the parallels between the problems here and those involving blue-collar, manufacturing incentive plans.

1. Some of the best salesmen now have too many accounts in the area assigned to them. From the company's point of view it would be advantageous to reduce the size of the districts covered by each of these men and to add several new salesmen who could give more thorough coverage. However, the outstanding salesmen resent this proposal, claiming that it would penalize them for their success. Furthermore, they argue that while their sales records are high now, some of their good accounts may go to competitors and then they will be worse off than other salesmen who have not had their districts "trimmed."

2. The top-earning salesmen also complain that their base quotas increase each year, reflecting their previous success. This, too, they feel is discrimination for success.

3. Management believes that the company is not acquiring as many new accounts as it should. So-called "missionary work," trying to induce a store that has not previously purchased Superior products to become a customer, takes more time and energy than selling old customers. Also, the results of this missionary work may not show up for several years. The present incentive plan gives no credit for this type of work. Should extra allowances be given for new accounts? How will this affect the over-all sales effort of the company?

4. When business is booming within a salesman's territory, he may receive high bonus earnings even without great effort on his part. When there is a great deal of unemployment in his territory or when competition decides to lower prices to penetrate this new market, his bonus earnings may decline even though his sales efforts are at a maximum. How can these factors be taken into account so that the incentive plan will motivate and reward effort rather than reflect fortuitous circumstances?

Incentives for Organization-Wide Participation

In this chapter we shall discuss some of the approaches that have been devised to provide broader employee motivation than is furnished by individual incentive plans. These approaches serve a dual purpose: (1) to increase productivity and (2) to improve morale by giving employees a feeling of participation in and identification with their company.

As we discussed in the last chapter, individual incentive plans often do not provide adequate motivation. Even when they are successful in inducing employees to work harder, their value as an incentive is reduced by output restriction, conflicts over rate-setting, and intergroup conflict. Nor are high wages, fringe benefits, and good working conditions in themselves a complete answer to the problem of motivation. These inducements may be effective aids in recruiting and retaining good employees, but they provide little help in motivating them to work harder.

We will make a critical examination of five techniques that are being used by management to provide greater motivation: (1) group piece-work, (2) profit-sharing, (3) suggestion systems, (4) employee-management and union-management consultative committees, and (5) the Scanlon Plan. Let us look at each in turn.

GROUP PIECE-WORK

In group piece-work, each member of the group receives a bonus based on the output of the group as a whole, unlike individual piece-work, in which each employee receives a bonus based on his individual output. The "group" may include the entire plant or company. More frequently it consists of a single department or the men who work on a single process or product. In these smaller groups, output standards are usually set by time study, just as they are in individual piece-work.

Group piece-work is particularly useful when the job assignments of members of the group are so interrelated that it is difficult to measure the contribution of any single employee to total production. For example, where eight girls work together on a small assembly line packaging pharmaceuticals, the speed of any one employee is governed by what the others are doing. Group piece-work makes it possible to reward workers who provide essential services to production workers, yet who under individual piece-work are usually paid only the regular day rates. Since all the members of the group share in the same bonus, conflict is reduced between workers on "tight" rates and workers on "loose" rates. Moreover, in theory at least, since everyone's earnings are dependent on everyone's efforts, the group may put pressure on the laggard individual to work harder. Certainly, as the spread of automation makes individual piece-work less appropriate, companies that wish to retain some form of incentive may turn increasingly to group piece-work.

Group piece-work encourages cooperation among employees, whereas individual piece-work militates against cooperation. Rather than struggling with one another over choice work locations, materials, and job assignments—the sources of much friction under individual piece-work—the employees work out their own allocation problems, knowing that everyone will share in the final result. For example, waitresses who pool tips are often eager to help each other out of jams.

On the other hand, group piece-work shares many of the disadvantages of individual-incentive plans. The workers still fear that if they produce too much management will cut the rates. Many of the intergroup differences that we discussed in the previous chapter remain. Also, since each individual may feel that his own efforts have very little effect on the over-all output of the group, he may experience less motivation to work harder than he would under individual piece-work.

Group piece-work systems that include an entire company or plant are less common than those that include only a single department. These broader systems are usually based not on time study but on some general measure of production, such as pounds produced or value of goods produced. For example, it was proposed in one union-management negotiation session in the automobile industry that the company put aside $10 for every car produced and that the whole fund be divided among all the employees. Company-wide systems often call for less than 100 per cent gain-sharing—that is, a 10 per cent increase in production results in a less than 10 per cent increase in earnings.

Company-wide plans naturally eliminate the intergroup incentive problems and fights over time study that we discussed in the previous chapter. Most important, they make employees less fearful of the introduction of new equipment, since all gains in productivity are usually shared by all employees (in contrast to individual piece-work, where the gains can be taken away through a new time study).

Both of these factors contribute to Kaiser Steel's decision to introduce its highly successful group-incentive, or gain-sharing, plan.[1] Rewards under this plan are based not only on gains in output but also on reductions in material costs. When set up, the plan also provided for substantial lump-sum payments to "buy out" workers who had been enjoying unusually high earnings from "loose" piece rates under the old individual-incentive plan.

In smaller plants, company-wide piece-work systems may provide some incentive for the average employee to work harder. However, in larger plants where hundreds or even thousands of employees share in the bonus, the employee may feel there is little relationship between his own effort and the ultimate reward, and consequently may feel little motivation to increase production.[2] Moreover, the union may oppose the scheme unless the amount of the bonus and the method of computing it are determined through collective bargaining.

PROFIT-SHARING

In profit-sharing plans, the employees receive a bonus that is normally based on some percentage (often 10 per cent to 30 per cent) of the company's profits beyond some fixed minimum. For example, employees might receive 25 per cent of all profits in excess of 6 per cent on the company's net worth. In some corporations (for instance, Eastman Kodak) the amount of bonus is dependent on the size of the dividend paid to stockholders.

In some profit-sharing plans the bonus is paid directly to the employees, usually at the end of each year. In other plans the bonus is deposited in a welfare or pension fund. These are often called *deferred* plans, because payment of the benefits is "deferred" until the employee retires or makes use of the welfare fund. With such deferred plans, the company hopes to obtain the advantages of both profit-sharing and fringe-benefit programs.

Profit-sharing has had a long history, but for various reasons it has not been very widely adopted in this country. One of the best-known plans is that of the Lincoln Electric Company, which in some years pays a bonus that doubles employees' pay. Sears Roebuck, Procter and Gamble, American Motors and Eastman Kodak also have profit-sharing plans of one type or another.[3] Profit-sharing plans, however, are more common in smaller companies, particularly those in which the workers are not unionized.

The advocates of profit-sharing claim many advantages for it as a means of

---

[1] Robert A. Bedolis, "The Kaiser Sharing Plan's First Year," *Conference Board Record* (July 1964).

[2] Thus, although bonuses and savings mounted rapidly during the first months of the Kaiser plan, it proved difficult to maintain the rate of increase.

[3] Portions of the Sears Roebuck savings have been reinvested in Sears stock, thus multiplying employees' returns.

strengthening the sense of involvement that employees feel toward the company: It makes them feel like partners in the enterprise, it motivates them to work harder, cut waste, push sales, and so forth. And, under the deferred plans, profit-sharing makes it possible for the company to provide pensions and fringe benefits without increasing fixed costs, for the company makes contributions only in profitable years.[4]

Yet profit-sharing has severe limitations, which may explain its failure to be more widely adopted. For one thing, it provides even less relationship between individual effort and ultimate reward than do group piece-work plans. After all, profits depend on a great many factors other than individual performance: for example, the state of the market, sales efficiency, technological development, and so forth. Moreover, the fact that the bonus is paid only once a year means that there is a long delay between effort and reward, and this delay tends to impair the worker's feeling that he is working toward a goal. To complicate matters even further, many workers find it hard to understand how profits are computed, and, particularly where labor-management relations are bad, they may suspect that a good deal of sleight of hand is involved in the calculations.[5]

What actually happens is that employees tend to regard profit-sharing as just another fringe benefit ("added gravy"). Naturally they are happy to get a bonus once a year, but they recognize little concrete relationship between how hard they work and how much they get. Further, once they begin to count on their profit-sharing bonus to maintain their standard of living, they may become extremely resentful in years when no bonus is paid. Under deferred profit-sharing plans, pensions and welfare benefits are put on a rather insecure basis, for they depend not on how long an employee has been with the company but on whether the company has made a profit during that time. Still, in companies that can afford no other form of pension plan, even this is probably better than nothing.

Although profit-sharing has been extremely successful in some companies, many have tried it for a few years and then abandoned it. Its success seems to depend to a large extent on the company's over-all personnel policy and on the state of union-management relations. Although it may provide motivation for employees to work harder, particularly in smaller companies, its chief merits would seem to lie in raising morale, in keeping the union out (if this is indeed a merit), and perhaps in reducing pressure for wage increases.

---

[4] Many companies provide a form of profit-sharing for their top management through the device of stock options. In addition, many companies encourage their employees at all levels to purchase company stock; in some cases companies may contribute part of the purchase cost. (See Chapter 30.)

[5] The president of one company with a "profit-sharing" plan once told us, "I don't think my profit figures are any of my employees' business. I give them a bonus each year which is fair. They trust me." But do they? And do they really feel that they are *involved* in a profit-sharing plan?

Suggestion systems are quite common in American industry. Their purpose is twofold:

1. To give management the benefit of employee suggestions on how to improve company efficiency. The average worker may have countless ideas on how to cut waste, eliminate unnecessary motions, prevent safety hazards, and so forth. Unless there is some systematic way of bringing these ideas to management's attention, a reservoir of ingenuity and experience may be overlooked.

2. To raise employee morale through giving them a chance to express their ideas on how the job should be done, to display their creative talents, and to take pride in seeing their ideas accepted—in other words, to reduce the employee's feeling that "as far the company is concerned I'm just a machine. Nobody wants my ideas."

In the typical suggestion system a worker writes his idea out on a special form and drops the form into a special box. All suggestions go directly to the suggestion director or to a suggestion committee. The practicability of each suggestion is then explored and evaluated, usually in consultation with the supervisors who might be affected. If the suggestion is accepted, the employee receives a reward, often 10 to 25 per cent of the savings produced by the suggestion during the first year. For suggestions whose savings cannot be measured, token awards of from $3 to $25 are paid. If the suggestion is rejected, most companies insist that the employee be given a detailed explanation of why it was turned down, along with encouragement to make more suggestions in the future. It is customary to promote suggestion plans by means of active publicity programs, posters, articles in plant newspapers, award presentations, and so forth.

A reasonably successful plan may elicit 25 to 50 suggestions from every hundred employees each year, 25 to 35 per cent of which will be acceptable. Frequently, however, results are a good bit less impressive than that. One explanation for poor employee response to a given suggestion plan may be that it is ineptly administered, with inadequate publicity or explanation of how the program is run. Moreover, delay in evaluating suggestions may give employees the impression that their ideas are not being given serious consideration. If the suggestion needs considerable time to be evaluated, progress reports should be issued to the employee to let him know that his idea has not been forgotten.

Since normally a majority of suggestions are rejected, the way in which suggestions are turned down is of crucial significance to the success of the plan. One authority recommends that "the turndown letter should be delivered to the employee in person by the investigator and/or the employee's immediate supervisor, so that the matter can be discussed and further questions answered." [6]

Even with good administration, suggestion plans often have only limited success. Employees may feel that the rewards are too meager, particularly when they amount to only 10 per cent of the first year's savings. This means that management keeps the remaining 90 per cent the first year and 100 per cent of the savings in future years. Of course, even when awards are small on a percentage basis, it is not unusual for an employee to earn several thousand dollars for an especially good suggestion.

Employees may fear that their suggestions will backfire—that in effect they may be suggesting themselves out of a job. The man who makes a labor-saving suggestion is not likely to be very popular with his fellow employees, even though no one loses his job right away. The reward for the suggestion goes to the individual, but the suggestion may have disastrous effects on the entire group. Understandably, a group attitude may develop that discourages employees from making suggestions.

The very fact that suggestions are submitted and rewarded on an individual basis may generate serious resentment within the group. On the worker level especially, many of the best ideas grow out of long-term group discussions. If one man turns in an idea as his own suggestion, the rest may accuse him of larceny. In a sense, the suggestion system discourages teamwork in working out ideas and encourages individual workers to keep their ideas to themselves.

In addition, all suggestions must be submitted in writing, even though the average worker can do a much better job explaining himself orally, particularly if he can demonstrate his idea and answer questions directly.

In most instances the suggestion system by-passes the foreman. Yet many suggestions point up areas where the foreman has fallen down on the job or suggest ideas that the foreman should have thought of by himself. Understandably, employees fear that the foreman may retaliate if his failures are exposed, and as a consequence they hesitate to make suggestions at all. Some companies try to get around this problem by giving the foreman credit for all suggestions made in his department, by having his employees submit their suggestions directly to him instead of to the suggestion committee, and by involving the foreman in evaluating suggestions and handing out rewards.[7]

Suggestion systems sometimes arouse union opposition because, as a form of upward communication, they usurp what the union regards as one of its rightful functions. Consequently, many companies permit union representatives to sit in on the suggestion committee, in an effort to win union cooperation in implementing the plan and to alleviate workers' fears that their ideas are not being fairly evaluated.

---

[6] Herman W. Seinwerth, "Suggestion Plans—Their Value to the Personnel Relations Program," in *Getting and Using Employees Ideas,* Production Series No. 165 (New York: American Management Association, 1946).

[7] In Russia foremen are given bonuses when their subordinates submit award-winning suggestions. David Granick, *The Red Executive* (Garden City: Doubleday, 1960), p. 16.

In general, the success of the suggestion system depends largely on the quality of the over-all personnel and labor-relations atmosphere. If the union suspects management's every move, and if supervisors discourage subordinates from doing things on their own—then employees will keep new ideas to themselves.

To sum up: a well-run suggestion system may yield a never-ending stream of ideas which cut costs and increase the employees' feeling of accomplishment and participation. Yet many plans are often poorly administered. And even when well administered, they often by-pass both foreman and union, and place primary emphasis on the individual, though most problems involve the entire group.

CONSULTATIVE COMMITTEES

In an attempt to avoid the suggestion system's exclusive emphasis on individual workers, many companies have tried to elicit broader group participation by setting up consultative committees. The purpose of these committees is to improve two-way communication with lower levels of the organization. They give lower-ranking supervisors or employees a chance to express their points of view directly to top management, thus by-passing intermediate levels.[8] For example, the first-line supervisors may elect representatives to meet weekly or monthly with the general manager to present and discuss current problems, ask about the rumors, pose questions, and ventilate gripes.

Management may institute similar committees for consultations with hourly-paid employees or their union. Joint worker-management or union-management consultative committees are involved in many activities such as solving production problems, cutting waste, reducing accidents, planning recreational programs, and soliciting for the Community Chest.

Union-management committees normally work in three areas:

1. *Collective bargaining.* Consultative committees have proved extremely useful in facilitating collective bargaining on such matters as job evaluation, incentive rates, and job transfers. These committees permit the orderly, systematic consideration of problems that would otherwise be handled piecemeal through the grievance procedure. An example of a consultative committee on a wider scale was the so-called Human Relations Committee which was established in the steel industry to explore means of handling joint problems on a continuing basis without the pressure of a contract deadline. Although this committee no longer functions, in two instances it was successful in negotiating new contracts without the threat of a strike and well before the expiration of the existing contract.

---

[8] For a description of how one company makes use of consultative committees that blanket the entire organization, see Elliott Jaques, *The Changing Culture of the Plant* (New York: Holt, Rinehart & Winston, 1952).

2. *Welfare activities.* Often joint committees assist in running athletic programs, handling welfare funds (perhaps derived from the profit from coffee machines), and so forth. These are areas in which the company has no special interest so long as workers are satisfied, and is glad to let the union share responsibility.

3. *Production problems.* In some industries consultative committees have been established to explore persistent production problems, such as scrap, productivity, and safety. Committees of this sort are common only in companies that enjoy good labor-management relations, however, since production decisions are traditionally conceded to be management prerogatives.

In unionized companies, consultative committees give the union leadership an opportunity to make a positive contribution toward running the company rather than merely sitting on the sidelines or filing grievances. Often they provide management with a valuable source of information on worker and union problems, and provide union officials with a better understanding of management's problems. Thus, they have a potential ability to improve the general tenor of labor-management relations. Sometimes nonunionized companies set up consultative committees composed of representatives who are elected directly by the workers or appointed by the foremen.

When consultative committees, either union-management or worker-management, work effectively, they improve the quality of both upward and downward communication within the company. They give the workers a chance to by-pass middle management and bring their suggestions, problems, and gripes directly to the men who actually make the decisions. Management may use these committees as a sounding board by releasing information on sales trends, safety problems, and so forth, in the hope that it will be passed along to workers at lower levels.

In short, consultative committees provide many of the same advantages that are derived from face-to-face conferences between subordinates and their immediate supervisor (see Chapter 10)—such advantages as lowered resistance to change, greater feeling of autonomy, better understanding of why orders are issued, and more effective implementation of instructions.

Nevertheless, joint committees labor under several disadvantages which sometimes limit their effectiveness:

1. Committee members may not communicate effectively with the workers back in the shop. Indeed, as they learn more and more about management's point of view, they may become more and more removed from the other workers. They may become extremely aware of production or safety problems, but they may fail to pass their enthusiasm on to the rest of the shop. Production committees, for example, are rarely successful unless the committee members energetically canvass their constituents for ideas.

The now-defunct Human Relations Committee in the basic steel industry suffered from the disadvantages of isolation from the rank-and-file membership.

Consisting of top-level representatives of union and management, it operated largely without verbal fireworks and in secrecy—thus giving the average member little feeling of participation in collective bargaining and even leading some to suspect that their officers were in collusion with management against their best interests. This suspicion may have contributed to the defeat of union president David McDonald by I. W. Abel, a man committed to more conventional collective bargaining techniques.

2. Consultative committees run the risk of impairing the morale and status of the middle managers whom they by-pass.

3. The success of these committees depends pretty much on the over-all quality of labor-management relations. If committee meetings are looked upon primarily as battlefields in a continuous war between union and management, then little will be accomplished.

4. Finally, consultation in itself does not provide a specific incentive for individual employees to work harder. True, employees do gain personal satisfaction from influencing company policy and seeing their ideas adopted, but in our society we require a more specific goal toward which we can work, most often in the form of an economic reward. Thus the consultative committees that have proved most fruitful have been those with some highly specific incentive for cooperation: to win the war, to save the company from going out of business,[9] to earn more pay, or to remove accident hazards.[10]

If consultative committees are to be successful in solving production problems there must be participation throughout all levels of the organization as well as a definite incentive or goal to unite everyone's efforts. On the other hand, such complete participation is not required if the committee's efforts are restricted to handling collective-bargaining problems or fringe areas. Probably this explains why consultative committees have been most useful in solving specific, limited problems. They do not, in themselves, provide motivation for higher production or a general sense of participation.

THE SCANLON PLAN

The Scanlon Plan is one of the most promising approaches yet suggested to securing widespread employee participation and obtaining industrial peace and higher productivity as well.[11] Although the plan is not widely accepted,

---

[9] One of the earliest plans involved the attempts of the Amalgamated Clothing Workers to help financially embarrassed clothing firms to stay in business. See Sumner H. Slichter, *Union Policies and Industrial Management* (Washington, D.C.: The Brookings Institution, 1941).

[10] For a penetrating analysis of a plan which failed, see William F. Whyte and others, *Money and Motivation* (New York: Harper & Row, 1955), Chapter 13.

[11] The late Joseph Scanlon, author of this plan, rose from an ordinary worker in a steel plant to be a top officer of the United Steelworkers of America and later a Lecturer at the Massachusetts Institute of Technology. For fuller discussion of the plan see William F. Whyte and others, "The Scanlon Plan," *Money and Motivation* (New York: Harper & Row, 1955), Chapter 14; Frederick G. Lesieur, ed., *The Scanlon Plan: A Frontier in Labor-*

we shall discuss it in some detail because it seems to avoid many of the problems raised by other plans. The plan consists of two basic parts: (1) a wage formula or incentive, and (2) a new form of suggestion system.

The *wage formula* is designed to distribute the gains of increased productivity proportionally among all employees involved. Although each formula is tailor-made to the needs of the particular company, wages are typically tied to the sales value of goods produced, so that, for example, for every 1 per cent increase in productivity there is a 1 per cent increase in wages and salaries. In contrast to usual incentive plans, bonuses are paid to the clerical force, salesmen, supervisors, and sometimes even to top management.

Notice that this is really a form of group piece-work covering the entire plant. As we have seen, a bonus of this sort is valuable not only as an incentive to productivity, but also as a form of feedback or yardstick by which the plan's success can be measured by the participants themselves.

The mechanics of the *suggestion system* are simple: In each department a union *production committeeman* is elected or appointed by union officers. The production committeeman and the foreman constitute a departmental *production committee*, which meets periodically to discuss suggestions from individual employees and to formulate general plans for the improvement of productivity. Rejected suggestions or suggestions that affect the plant as a whole are referred to a plant-wide *screening committee*, which includes top management as well as the union leadership.

This suggestion system may be likened to an enlarged version of the typical union-management grievance procedure. The written suggestion is in many ways similar to the written grievance, the production committeeman corresponds roughly to the steward, and the meetings of the screening committee are somewhat equivalent to third-stage negotiations between management and the union grievance committee. However, the suggestions relate to every phase of production, not just to complaints about contract violation—and the purpose is to improve company efficiency, not just to protect individual rights.

Note how the Scanlon Plan differs from the typical suggestion system: Instead of individual rewards for accepted suggestions, the group gains as a whole through a higher bonus whenever productivity is increased. The union takes an active part instead of worrying whether suggestions will result in a speedup. Individuals cooperate with each other in developing suggestions instead of keeping their ideas to themselves. Further, under a suggestion system management normally waits passively for workers to submit suggestions; frequently under the Scanlon Plan management itself suggests problems for mutual discussion.

Management Cooperation (New York and Cambridge: Wiley and The Technology Press, 1958); George Strauss and Leonard R. Sayles, "The Scanlon Plan: Some Organizational Problems," *Human Organization*, Vol. 16, No. 3 (Fall 1957), pp. 15-22; *Group Work Incentives: Experience with the Scanlon Plan* (New York: Industrial Relations Counselors, 1962).

Before the Scanlon Plan was put into operation in a particular printing plant, management had tried to introduce a conveyor system. The plans had been developed exclusively by the engineers, without consulting the employees. The system immediately ran into trouble and the employees showed little interest in making it work.

After the Scanlon Plan was accepted management decided to try another conveyor system, but to introduce it in a different manner. Employees were shown a small scale model of the proposed layout and encouraged to make criticisms and suggestions for improvements. On the basis of these comments the joint production committee made modifications to eliminate "bugs" that the engineers had not foreseen. The new system was enthusiastically accepted by the employees.[12]

Both the quantity and quality of suggestions seem to be higher under the Scanlon Plan. An annual rate of one suggestion for every three workers is considered quite satisfactory under the usual suggestion system.[13] Under the Scanlon Plan the rate may be more than doubled. More important, with the usual system, normally only one suggestion out of four can be used.[14] With the Scanlon Plan the acceptance rate has risen to 80 per cent.[15]

As a means of increasing productivity, the Scanlon Plan has met with varied success. For example, take the experience of the LaPointe Machine Tool Company over a period of 58 months. Here the monthly bonus ranged from 0 to 52.1 per cent, with no bonus at all during 16 months and bonuses in excess of 20 per cent during another 20 months. Gains of over 40 per cent are not uncommon, however.[16]

In summary, there are gains for everybody under a successful Scanlon Plan: (1) more and better suggestions, (2) higher productivity and profits, (3) decreased resistance to change, (4) better union-management relations, (5) greater cooperation among work groups and between individuals and their supervisors, and (6) increased motivation to work. Because of these advantages, use of the plan has spread rapidly in recent years.

And yet the Scanlon Plan, promising though it seems, is not a cure-all for every industrial ill.[17]

1. If the plan is to be successful, management must be willing to make substantial changes in its attitudes. Traditional company prerogatives must be forgotten. Foremen, superintendents, and even the company president must learn to consult with subordinates and be willing to listen to sharp criticism.

---

[12] Adopted from George Shultz, "Worker Participation in Production Problems," *Personnel,* Vol. 28, No. 3 (November 1951), pp. 201-211.

[13] Paul Pigors and Charles A. Myers, *Personnel Administration,* 3rd ed. (New York: McGraw-Hill, 1956), p. 370.

[14] Seinwerth, *op. cit.*

[15] George Shultz and Robert P. Crisera, "The LaPointe Machine Tool Company and the United Steelworkers of America," *Causes of Industrial Peace Under Collective Bargaining, Case Study No. 10* (Washington, D.C.: National Planning Association, 1952), p. 55.

[16] Shultz and Crisera, *op. cit.*, p. 58.

[17] *Ibid.*, p. 55; Strauss and Sayles, *op. cit.*

Many managers find this adjustment too hard to make, and the thin-skinned individual or the confirmed autocrat must either be restrained or else removed from positions of authority.

In companies that already practice general supervision and enjoy a good system of upward and downward communication, the transition of the Scanlon Plan may be relatively easy. Others may find that the plan requires adjustments that they are unwilling to make.

2. The Scanlon Plan presents the union with a real dilemma. In fact, the plan is bound to fail unless the union officers give up the militant view that the "member is always right." But there is also a danger that the officers may become too concerned with jacking up production. If they refuse to handle individual grievances and concentrate too much on pushing their members to work harder, the members may become resentful, give the plan only passive support, and even reject their officers at the next election. Indeed, as the officers become more and more closely identified with management's point of view, they tend to become alienated from the average member. This dilemma may be partly resolved if the officers are careful to explain new developments to the rank-and-file and to listen carefully to their reactions. Still, the plan blurs the union's primary function of providing representation for its members.

3. As we have seen, one of the disadvantages of traditional incentive plans is that they engender ill-feeling among groups—both where technology makes one group's earnings dependent on the production of another group, or where groups suspect each other of having "loose" rates. The Scanlon Plan presumably eliminates this problem by establishing plant-wide incentives. But a plant-wide incentive means that each individual's earnings are dependent on the effort of the entire plant. Harder work by any one individual will bring him only negligibly higher monetary return. Hopefully, self-satisfaction, the desire for praise from fellow workers, and interest in the group as a whole will be sufficient to elicit high productivity. But for this to happen there must be a high degree of cohesion and employee identification with the plant as a whole.

How likely is this to occur? The answer depends on a number of factors, including the size, homogeneity, and history of the work group. One thing is certain: There are bound to be some rivalries among groups, and skill in human relations is constantly required of all parties to prevent these rivalries from reaching serious proportions. All the evidence is that loyalty to the face-to-face group is greater than to the plant as a whole. It is too much to expect the traditional differences between the office and the shop and among various departments to cease the moment the plan is introduced.

In fact, the plan may actually generate greater interdepartmental antagonism. No longer is it possible to unite against a common enemy—management. Now it is easy to pass the blame for poor production along to another group—for Department X to say, "Why should we work so hard when Department Y has fallen so far behind?" The larger the plant, the greater are the possibilities for dissension, and the more difficult it becomes to maintain support for plant-wide production goals.

4. The Scanlon Plan has been successful both in very depressed companies, where the employees have cooperated to save their jobs, and in prosperous companies, where the employees realized that there were big bonuses to be won. The plan may well be less successful in industries where the market conditions make it difficult to sell increased output and where greater productivity may in fact mean fewer jobs (in economic terms, where demand is inelastic). Nor do we know what happens when a successful plan goes through a long period of poor earnings (some have weathered short periods).

In short, the Scanlon Plan seems to be most successful where both union and management are able to make substantial changes in their patterns of behavior, where good internal communications exist within and between both groups, and probably only in smaller organizations.

CONCLUSION

We have looked at five different plans designed to raise employee morale, develop teamwork, and promote a sense of identification with the entire organization. All these plans imply a more sophisticated approach to motivation than do the philosophies of "be strong," "be good," bargaining, or competition (see Chapter 6). All seek to provide on-the-job satisfaction for doing a better job.

And notice, too, that all seek to reach these goals through changing human relationships. Group piece-work and profit-sharing aim for greater cooperation among individuals. Suggestion systems and consultative committees seek to improve communications between individual employees and higher management. The Scanlon Plan seeks to attain both objectives.

Each of these plans has been adopted by management as a panacea for a whole range of industrial-relations ills. Yet none of them will work well except in an atmosphere of good labor-management relations and sound supervisory, organizational, and personnel practices. In our opinion, the *basic relationships* among the members of the organization must be sound before any one of these plans can be put to effective use.

PROBLEM

THE CONSULTANT'S STORY

It all started when Harry Beard phoned and asked me to "come out to the plant and give us a little advice on our suggestion system." I readily agreed, though I told him I was dubious about what I could do in a single visit. However, before hanging up I asked him how he was involved and what was the problem. He said, "My job is chiefly trouble-shooting and right now I'm up to my ears on a new product line we're installing—almost completely automatic. But the Plant Manager wants me to do something about suggestions. We have a plan but it isn't working. We get a fair number of piddling ideas on safety and housekeeping—but almost nothing which saves us any money. We have a new plant here and there must be lots of ideas around—lots of things need improvement and the workers must see them—but we have the worst record in the company—and you know how the Head Office watches these things."

I arrived at the plant at noon. Harry had invited me for lunch and I had visions of the nearby Country Club. Instead we went to the plant cafeteria with the Plant Manager, the Industrial Engineer, and the Personnel Man. Table talk was dull and the food worse. I decided to let them broach the subject at hand. I did notice that everyone deferred to the Manager's ideas—even on sports. Then to the conference room—attractive but noisy. Plant Manager opened up, "Harry brought you here because he said you had some ideas on suggestion systems."

"He wants his answer wrapped up 1-2-3 in cellophane," I thought, and countered. "Well, first I'd like to get a little idea of your problem."

The Plant Manager did most of the talking, though the others broke in at times to underscore his words. There was plenty of opportunity for suggestions, he felt, but no good ones were forthcoming. With a plant of 2,000 employees, last year they had 750 suggestions, but of these only 300 were acceptable—and of these on 230 the savings were unmeasurable, so only the minimum $3 reward was given. Total awards last year came to $1,940. The largest: $55.

I asked what determined the size of the award. "We pay 10 per cent of the first year's savings." He must have seen my inward shudder, for he asked, "Is that low?"

"Not very," I added tactfully. "Awards seem to vary from 10 to 25 per cent. Have you thought of raising it?"

"We can't. It's set by corporation policy. For a while we paid $5 as the minimum reward, but then we heard the company policy was $3. Of course it made us seem rather cheap to cut it down."

My questioning then turned to the mechanics of the program. "Suggestions are made on this form," he said as he handed it to me. "You see, the suggestor's name goes on a special tab which the Suggestion Director tears off, so that no one but he knows who made the suggestion. That way we eliminate favoritism."

"Are you the Suggestion Director?" I asked the industrial engineer.

"Oh, no," said the Plant Manager. "We have a full-time man. Possibly you might like to meet him—you might give him a few pointers." I nodded. He continued, "To get back to our system. The Suggestion Director refers each suggestion to the man in whose area of responsibility it lies—to the foreman, the maintenance department, and so forth. They investigate the suggestion. If they think it is good, they pass their recommendation back to the Suggestion Director, along with their estimate of likely savings. The suggestion committee takes up the accepted suggestions and decides how much the award should be."

"Has the union shown any interest?" I asked—hopeful that this question might lead to pay dirt.

"Oh, yes, the union president sits in on every meeting," he said.

Just then the Personnel Director interrupted: "I never got a chance to tell you that at the last meeting the International Representative showed up. The union wanted to have three men sit in on meetings in the future. I told the Representative that he could attend this meeting, but in the future we'd let only one man in. After all, it's purely a company committee."

"That's right," said the Manager. "We can't let the union run away with this."

"Do you have any idea how the union feels about this?" I asked. I knew the answer, but hoped to stimulate them to do a little thinking.

There was a slight pause, then the Industrial Engineer answered, "They take the position that these suggestions shouldn't force anybody out of a job. I think they're scared that just that will happen. Frankly, I think maybe the union is sabotaging it."

"Do you think there is any justification for their fears?" I asked, trying not to sound argumentative.

"I suppose there is," he replied. "Seventy per cent of our costs are in labor. You can't save anything in material. We're in a highly competitive industry and we're going to have to save on labor costs."

There was a pause. I said nothing, hoping for further discussion. There being none, I asked, perhaps a little gruffly, "Well, where do you think the weak points of the program are?"

They paused. Then the Plant Manager spoke up, "I've been wondering whether our form (on which the suggestions are made) is adequate. I wish you would look it over."

This set me back. I tried another tack. "How do the foremen feel about it? Is there any chance they think these suggestions threaten them—point out things they should have noticed themselves?"

"Not that I've heard," said the Industrial Engineer. "After all, good suggestions would improve the efficiency of their department—and they will do better on their EIP."

"What's that?" I asked.

"EIP—that's our Efficiency Improvement Plan. Every member of management is rated monthly on a number of factors such as cost control, production, scrap, and so forth."

"Are foremen rewarded under EIP for the number of suggestions made in their department?" I asked. The Industrial Engineer shook his head.

There was some more discussion, along the same vein. Finally, the Plant Manager said, "Well, I have another meeting. Harry will take you around the plant, answer any questions, and I will be anxious to get your recommendations."

After he left, Harry gave me the "Grand Tour." It was a beautiful plant—most of the operations involved assembling—almost all routine—a great deal of finger work.

Finally Harry pointed: "There's the Suggestion Director's office." He was in a glass cubicle, right off the main assembly line, with two other men, both industrial engineers.

Bill Dongle obviously had been waiting for us. He seemed a little nervous as he shook my hand. Harry was fairly tactful: "Bill, as you know, we've been talking a bit about suggestions among other things and we were sure he [me, the consultant] wanted to get the real picture from you."

"That's right, I do. I gather your program sounds pretty much like the normal—that is, you're having the normal number of headaches."

Bill looked a little relieved. I felt sorry for him as he started telling his problems. Among others they were:

"I don't get much cooperation from the foremen. They don't seem to talk it up among their men. When I do refer suggestions to them, they always seem to be negative. Lots of times they turn down ideas which I think are pretty good—in fact, sometimes they put them in later on—and do I catch hell from the men. Also they take so long to make a report. Sometimes it is six months till a man gets an acknowledgment that we have accepted his ideas—he may even see it being put into effect, but the procedure is, we don't tell a man his suggestion is accepted until the award committee figures out how much it is worth. Sometimes, of course, if the suggestion is not written up too well, I call the man in to talk about it—and that lets him know we're thinking about it. You know—maybe I should talk to every man who has a suggestion—that lets him know we're interested. It would be better than our usual short note saying that we have accepted it or rejected it."

"Harry, what do you think?" I asked.

Harry said, "It might be a good idea, but I don't know about taking all the men off their jobs."

"Maybe I could see them on the job," Bill volunteered. It was agreed he might do this—though Harry wondered whether Bill's presence might make the other workers think that the man who made the suggestion was a "company man."

I then asked, "I gather you feel that foremen turn down some good ideas. I wonder if anything can be done about this?"

(We discussed this for a while, but you can figure out for yourself what Harry and Bill decided.)

Near the end of the discussion Bill said, "What we've got to do is get the foremen to show more interest."

I asked, "To what extent does supervision indicate to the foremen that they are backing the suggestion plans?"

"Well," said Harry, "it's mentioned all the time in the company magazine and the plant newspaper."

To myself I asked, "Who writes these newspapers? Staff."

To them I asked, "Do you know of any situation where a foreman has been praised by his superior for getting good suggestions or questioned when he got none?"

Both shook their heads, but perhaps the import of my question slipped by them.

Later Bill returned to the original theme. "All the suggestions we get are trifles. Perhaps if we could get a few good ideas and give some really big awards, it would get the ball rolling. You know we have scrap and safety contests between departments. The record of all the departments are posted monthly as well as their improvement over previous months. Perhaps we could do this with suggestions."

We discussed this for a while. Then I had a bright idea. I asked to go over some typical suggestions. We took two from the file that seemed more complicated than most.

The first involved a change in the carrier that held the product as it passed through the assembly line. I noticed the company had spent $800 to make the change, but the suggestion was classed as "housekeeping—no measurable savings," and got the minimum $3.

"Why put it in," I asked, "if there are no savings?"

"Well," Bill said, "before we made the change there was always the chance that a piece might fall off. This would cause a great deal of damage—but you just can't estimate the chance of its falling off or how great would be the damage."

Another accepted suggestion involved a minor change in an operation. Harry said, "It did make the job easier to do and a little faster. But since the union wouldn't let us retime the job, there were no savings. So we paid just $3."

The phone rang and I had a short pause to collect my thoughts. I had a lot of questions to answer—and quick:

Why were so few suggestions made?

I hadn't talked to any workers, but what did they *probably* feel about the whole scheme?

How did the union officers feel?

How did the foremen feel?

Assuming I were plant manager (nice to daydream), what would I do to solve the problem?

Ah, I'm just a consultant and there are definite limits to the ideas they are willing to accept—no point in suggesting things they won't carry out. But what has my brief experience with this company taught me about the way they handle problems? How good is the union-management relationship, for instance? Why was the Suggestion Director so tense?

Are there any suggestions I could make that would be *likely to be accepted* and that would also change the attitude of the workers, of the union, of the foremen?

The Plant Manager wanted ideas on how to improve the application blank. What does this indicate?

Above all, what next? How should I go about putting my ideas across? Should I make a written report? Should I give my ideas to the Suggestion Director, to Harry, or to the Plant Manager? Or do I need to do further research? If so, what questions should I seek to answer?

More fundamentally, I wondered whether the whole situation might have some implications for staff-line relations.

How's my interview technique? What am I trying to accomplish? Should I have followed some of these points more deeply?

(*Answer to problem on p. 653: 1.56 minutes.*)

Safety

Accident prevention is an area in which American industry has just cause for pride. Since 1926 our industrial injury frequency rate has dropped from 24.2 to 12.9, a truly remarkable victory that deserves to be ranked with the development of Salk vaccine and the "miracle drugs." [1] And yet there is still much to do. In a single year as many as two million people may be the victims of disabling work injuries, and the total monetary cost of these injuries has been estimated as high as four or five billion dollars.

We shall discuss safety in this chapter both because it is an important problem in itself and because it provides a useful case example of how a specific personnel problem can be handled. Our discussion will necessarily deal with questions of motivation, group standards, leadership, and control. We will illustrate the dilemmas of the staff-line relationship as well as the limitations of the mechanical, gimmicky approaches to personnel. Hopefully, too, our discussions will suggest approaches to problems similar to safety, such as absenteeism and turnover.

WORKMEN'S COMPENSATION

Widespread interest in safety dates back roughly to 1910, with the passage of workmen's compensation laws in many states. Prior to that time the tendency in industry was to look upon manpower as expendable and to weep few tears when an employee was injured or killed. (There were pioneering companies

---

[1] United States Bureau of Labor Statistics, *Handbook of Labor Statistics*, Bulletin 1016 (1950); "Injury Rates in Manufacturing, 1st Quarter 1966," News Release, U.S. Department of Labor, July 15, 1966. The rate reached an all-time annual low of 11.4 in 1958 and has climbed slightly since then, in part in response to higher rates of employment and overtime work.

The term "injury frequency rate" refers to the number of lost-time accidents per million man hours worked. Thus, if a company with a thousand workers on a forty hour week had one lost-time accident per week, it would have a frequency rate of 25. Notice that minor accidents which do not involve loss of time are not included in computing this rate.

strongly motivated by humanitarian impulses, but these unfortunately were in the minority.) This attitude was the target of social reformers who contended that management should be assessed at least part of the cost of the medical expenses and lost wages incurred by those who were injured in its service. Only then, argued the reformers, would industry take steps to reduce the appalling number of cripples, widows, and orphans being created each year.

Prior to the passage of workmen's compensation laws, a man injured at work could sue his company for damages, but this was not an easy task. In the first place he had to hire a lawyer and sue through the courts, an expensive and time-consuming process. Even then, the company could avoid incurring liability in a number of ways: through the *fellow-servant doctrine,* if it could prove that another worker was responsible; through the *contributory-negligence doctrine,* if it could prove that the worker himself was at least partly to blame; and through the *assumed-risk doctrine,* if it could show that the work was inherently dangerous and the worker knew this when he took the job.

Now, instead of going to the courts, all a worker need do is file a claim with the compensation board. Although the board's proceedings are often time-consuming and technical, they are far less so than the usual legal proceedings. A lawyer is not necessary, although sometimes desirable. More important, management is directly responsible for all accidents *arising out of and in the course* of a worker's employment. A few examples may indicate what this phrase means. Management may be responsible if: [2]

> Two workers engage in rough-house in the company cafeteria at lunch hour and one knocks out another's tooth.
> After work is over, an employee stubs his toe in the company parking lot.
> A painter with a heart condition gets a heart attack and falls off a ladder.
> A salesman in the field away from home is injured in an auto accident while driving to a movie at 10 P.M., after his sales calls.
> A 50-year-old maintenance man works 72 hours without a break and two days later dies of a heart attack.
> A man gets a slight bruise. Six months later cancer develops on the site and evidence indicates it was caused by the bruise.

In most states if an employee is injured under circumstances such as the above he receives free medical expenses plus a proportion of the income he loses for all the weeks he cannot work. In New York, for instance, he would get two-thirds of his previous weekly pay—but no more than $60. Since average weekly manufacturing earnings in New York in 1965 were over $105, the vast majority of injured workers receive the maximum, $60. There are many who consider this compensation inadequate, particularly if a man and his family must live on it for the rest of his life. In addition to this basic compensation, if a worker suffers so called "scheduled injuries" to specified portions

---

[2] The laws vary considerably from state to state. Under the circumstances listed, however, the company would be liable in many states.

of the body he receives additional payments for a specified number of weeks. Among the typical payments in New York are these:

Loss of arm	312 weeks	*Loss of eye*	160 weeks
Loss of leg	288 weeks	*Loss of 4th finger*	15 weeks

In most states, industrial diseases (for example, silicosis, which is common in mines) are also covered.

Most employers take out insurance to meet these risks, either through a state insurance fund, or through private companies, though some large firms are self-insured. In any case, the company's insurance cost depends on its "experience." By keeping its accidents low a company can reduce its costs substantially; a poor safety record can be enormously expensive.

Naturally the desire to keep insurance costs down affords a powerful incentive for companies to reduce accidents. However, the direct cost of insurance is not the only cost the company must pay. It must also cover the cost of loss of production caused by the accident, the cost of training a new man to take the injured one's place, the cost of dislocations created by the sudden loss of a skilled man, and so forth. In addition, it is often difficult to find people to work in dangerous departments. Some authorities estimate that for every dollar of direct compensation cost there are four dollars of indirect cost, plus, in the case of a serious accident, intangible costs in loss of morale and community reputation.

For these reasons almost every large company carries on an elaborate safety program with a full-time safety staff. Even small concerns find it worth while to have some sort of safety activity. However, these programs differ widely in techniques and in effectiveness.

ALTERNATE APPROACHES TO THE SAFETY PROBLEM

Students and practitioners in the field of safety have approached the problem from a number of points of view. At the extremes have been: (1) the engineering approach, which assumes that accidents can be avoided by constructing a "safe" plant, free from potential hazards, and (2) the selection approach, which assumes that accidents can be avoided by refusing to hire workers whose personality characteristics or physical make-up would suggest that they are "accident-prone." The first approach emphasizes physical environment, the second emphasizes individual personality. Although both have considerable validity, there has been a growing realization that both are over-simplifications of the problem, and that a major cause of accidents is the *relationship* of the individual to his environment—or, to put it in simpler terms, poor working habits.

In an effort to eliminate poor working habits, management's first reaction has been to work through a staff safety department whose function is to make and police safety regulations, to analyze accident causes, and to conduct a safety-education program. Increasingly, however, companies are beginning to see that this too is a rather limited approach, and are coming to regard safety as a line responsibility that should be handled by the supervisor in each de-partment—with the help of a differently oriented staff safety department, one whose function is to motivate people to accept more responsibility and to seek additional training.

There are, then, four main approaches to safety: (1) engineering, (2) selec-tion, (3) staff, and (4) line. Let us examine each of them in turn.

THE ENGINEERING APPROACH:
THE PHYSICAL ENVIRONMENT

Because of differences in technology and physical environment, some in-dustries are more hazardous than others. As the following table indicates, logging is thirty times as dangerous as communications. Furthermore, within an industry some jobs are more likely to lead to accidents. Thus a clerk in a lumber mill may well be safer than a buzz-saw operator.

*Injury Frequency Rates
in Representative Industries* *

All manufacturing	12.9
Ammunition, except small arms	1.9
Communications	1.2
Logging camps and contractors	42.5
Leather tanning and finishing	41.3
Construction	28.4
Mining, underground coal	36.7
Blast furnaces and steel mills	5.3
Broad woolen textile	19.8
Federal civilian employees	7.7

* Sources: Communications, construction, coal min-ing and federal civilian employees from *Accident Facts* (Chicago: National Safety Council, 1966), p. 28; other data from "Injury Rates in Manufacturing, 1st Quarter 1966," News Release, U.S. Department of Labor, July 15, 1966. It should be noted that National Safety Council data is collected chiefly from larger firms with better developed safety programs and con-sequently data reported by it tend to be lower than are data reported for comparable manufacturing in-dustries by the U.S. Department of Labor.

Each of these accident rates is a function of (1) how inherently dangerous the industry is, and (2) what management has done to eliminate accident causes. For instance, the low rate in communications is in part due to the Bell System's strenuous safety program. The explosives industry is the safest of all manufacturing industries precisely because safety is so clearly of overriding importance. Worsted textile's relatively poor showing may reflect the less progressive personnel policies and impoverished state of many textile mills.

The engineering approach concentrates on reducing technological hazards by redesigning machinery, equipment, and working procedures. To date, this approach has been extremely fruitful. Indeed a very large part of the credit for the substantial reduction in accidents over the last 30 years must go to safety engineers for introducing safeguards ranging from Geiger counters in radioactive work, additional "props" in mines, mirrors positioned at sharp corners, to rounded corners on office desks.[3]

Certain human-relations problems arise in trying to gain acceptance of safer work methods, for even if the new way is no harder than the old, it is different. It breaks established ways of doing things, and, where piece-work is involved, learning the new way may even result in loss of income. All the problems of resistance to change discussed in Chapter 13 are involved.

> One company installed a device consisting of a steel-cored cable to pull workers' hands out of the way when they got too close to the press. No notice of the change was given either to the union or the workers. When the president of the union heard of the new device he objected strongly to the workers being "chained" to their machines. The men refused to work with it.[4]

These workers may have felt that this device, though safer, was just one step along the road to transforming workers into machines. Had they been consulted in advance about whether they were willing to try the device, probably much less resistance would have arisen.

> In another plant, the safety man had great difficulty persuading young girls to wear safety nets on their heads. "They're too ugly," the girls complained. When he provided more stylishly designed net-caps and gave each girl her choice of color, the problem disappeared. The same thing happened with safety shoes once the men were allowed to choose from among different models.

Safety devices are also resented if they require extra motions or cut down incentive earnings. The safety man must consider normal human motions and, if possible, design a technique that makes the work easier or at least does not require special effort. For instance, on some processes the standard procedure is (1) position piece in machine, (2) put up guard, (3) operate machine, (4) take down guard, and (5) remove piece. Here the worker is strongly tempted to save two steps by operating without a guard. A fixed guard would eliminate this problem.

Employees often make a game of trying to avoid the use of safety devices—they regard evasion as a chance to show their independence. The workers in one plant told gleefully of the heroic figure who had deceived management

---

[3] Credit also must be given to improvements in lighting, ventilation, and heating, all of which tend to reduce the accident rate.

[4] Almost identical versions of this case appear in Paul Pigors and Charles A. Myers, *Personnel Administration* (New York: McGraw-Hill, 1948), pp. 464-475, and in Michael J. Jucius, *Personnel Management* (Homewood, Ill.: Irwin, 1955), pp. 705-707.

for years by wearing goggles with the glass taken out. Sabotage of this sort is particularly prevalent if the worker can make higher earnings by dodging time-consuming safety measures.

> Many injuries are caused when workers position material under a press and leave their fingers there too long. Some companies have installed controls which require that the worker push a button with each hand some distance from the press before the press will operate. Since this takes time and effort, and results in loss of incentive earnings, however, workers devise a way of pushing the two buttons at the same time with a stick.

Even when workers show no particular resistance to safety devices, they sometimes forget to use them. For this reason engineers try to design equipment that simply cannot be operated if safety measures are ignored. In general, it seems wiser not just to add attachments to the machine to make it safer, but to redesign it from the beginning.

The human factor is not simple to analyze. Safety measures that reduce part of a hazard, for example, may actually increase the number of accidents, since they encourage workers to become less careful.

> In electrical installation work, it was found that accidents occurred because inspectors sometimes pressed high tension bars with their flashlights. Exchanging the fiber-barreled flashlights with metal ones overcame this source of accident. Since the metal ones obviously were conductors, the men adjusted to this properly and avoided making contacts with their flashlights. The fiber-barreled flashlights were not conductors for low voltage, but conductors for high voltage, and the men did not adjust themselves to the limited degree to which these fiber cases were safe.[5]

Safety engineers have been quick to recognize that exclusive emphasis on mechanical safety measures has reached a point of diminishing returns. They have achieved such great success in devising safer equipment and devices that today the vast majority of accidents are caused by human rather than mechanical failure. Machinery has in many cases been made almost as safe as technology will permit.

The causes of accidents may be divided into *unsafe conditions* (that is, technology and physical environment) and *unsafe acts*. Progress has been so rapid in eliminating unsafe conditions that it has been estimated that almost 90 per cent of all accidents are now caused by unsafe acts—that is, in most cases it is the worker who is unsafe, not the machine.

THE SELECTION APPROACH:
ACCIDENT-PRONENESS

When we study a group of workers who are all doing the same job and are all subject to the same physical environment, we usually discover that a

---

[5] Norman R. F. Maier, *Psychology in Industry*, 2nd ed. (Boston: Houghton Mifflin, 1955), p. 508.

few workers have substantially more accidents than the rest. In the following table, which gives the distribution of accidents among 648 employees of a British shell factory,[6] notice that about 10 per cent of the women had over half the accidents.

NUMBER OF ACCIDENTS	NUMBER OF WOMEN
0	448
1	132
2	42
3	21
4	3
5	2
Total	648

Other evidence of the same phenomenon lies in the fact that those who have more than the average number of accidents in any one given period of time are sometimes likely to have more than the average number later on. We all know people who are always stumbling and dropping things. Regardless of whether they are driving a car, pouring milk, or counting change, they make mistakes. Evidence of this sort has led some researchers to try to identify the innate physical and psychological characteristics that make an individual "accident-prone."

Other researchers claim that true accident-proneness can be exaggerated. They point out that just by the laws of chance we would expect accidents to be unevenly distributed among the work force. Thus, if 200 employees were to have accidents we would expect, on the basis of statistical probability, that 121 will have no accidents at all, 61 will have one accident, 15 will have two, and three will have three or more. Thus, 9 per cent of the group will have 39 per cent of the accidents.[7]

Even if the above caution is kept in mind, still some evidence points to the role of psychological factors in accident incidence.[8] Just as many illnesses (such as ulcers and high blood pressure) spring in part from psychological causes, so there are individuals whose high accident rate seems related to psychological disturbances. Either they are so concerned with their own problems that they forget to take proper safeguards, or else it seems almost as if they unconsciously want to be injured in order to punish themselves or avoid a difficult situation. Workers who are unusually impulsive or have aggressions to work off on the job may have the most accidents.[9] Many accidents occur on no-attention jobs when something unexpected happens that interrupts the

---

[6] Cited in Maier, *op. cit.*, p. 520.

[7] Wayne K. Kirchner, "The Fallacy of Accident Proneness," *Personnel*, Vol. 38, No. 6 (November 1961), pp. 34-37; Alexander Mintz and Milton L. Blum, "A Re-examination of the Accident Proneness Concept," *Journal of Applied Psychology*, Vol. 33, No. 3 (June 1949), pp. 195-211.

[8] Much of the pioneering work in this area was done by Flanders Dunbar. See her *Psychosomatic Diagnosis* (New York: Harper, 1943).

[9] For a strong statement, see Alexander M. Hirshfield, "Some Workers Want To Have Accidents," *Occupational Hazards*, Vol. 26, No. 8 (August 1964), pp. 35-36.

worker's usual rhythm. Instead of smoothly adapting to the interruption, accident-prone individuals "manifest a sort of disorder in their defense reaction mechanism. They panic easily and feel this inner shock as a 'moment of terror.'" [10]

Evidence suggests that workers who have an unusually high number of accidents are generally those who have made poor adjustments to work: They make a higher number of short trips to the dispensary, they have a higher number of unexcused absences,[11] they are less efficient on the job,[12] and they have a higher spoilage rate.[13]

Authorities disagree on whether it is possible to screen out individuals who are likely to have accidents. One author states that "accident-prevention is largely a by-product of proper selection and placement, professionally planned and carried out." [14] Among the tests which have been used to spot the accident-prone worker before he is hired are those which measure manual dexterity, rhythm, reaction time, and short-distance vision. Tests that measure the degree of an individual's emotional reaction (in terms of glandular changes) to unexpected occurrences show some relationship to accidents, particularly if an individual is tested under stress.[15] Personality tests have been used to measure such factors as compulsion, aggressiveness, and social orientation, though there is considerable doubt about their effectiveness.[16]

Accident experts are becoming more and more convinced that accident proneness is not an innate personality characteristic. Instead, an individual's susceptibility to accidents may vary over time, depending in part on the conditions under which he works. For example, accidents are more frequent among younger workers, those who are just learning their jobs,[17] and in general those who are making difficult adjustments. Many individuals seem to be accident-prone for a while and then stop having accidents. Accidents are often related to contemporary emotional stress.

---

[10] George Friedmann, *Industrial Society* (Glencoe, Ill.: Free Press, 1955), p. 114, citing *Journal de Psychologie* (1937), pp. 290-294.

[11] J. M. M. Hill and E. L. Trist, "A Consideration of Industrial Accidents as a Means of Withdrawal from the Work Situation," *Human Relations*, Vol. 4, No. 4 (1953), pp. 357-380. It is interesting that the Caspar Milquetoast type who asked for permission before being absent had a better safety record than those who were never absent at all.

[12] Friedmann, *op. cit.*, p. 114.

[13] T. T. Patterson, *Glasgow, Ltd.* (Cambridge: Cambridge University Press, 1960), p. 95. Patterson points out that roughly the same factors which lead men to quit their work also lead them to have accidents. Hill and Trist, *op. cit.*, suggests that having an accident is an acceptable way of withdrawing from the work situation.

[14] Alfred J. Cardall, "Psychological Factors in Accident Prevention," *The Personnel Journal*, Vol. 26, No. 8 (February 1948), p. 290.

[15] E. Farmer and E. G. Chambers, *A Study of Personality Qualities in Accident Proneness and Proficiency*, Industrial Fatigue Research Board, Report No. 55 (1929).

[16] F. J. Harris, "Can Personality Tests Identify Accident-Prone Employees?" *Personnel Psychology*, Vol. 3, No. 4 (Winter 1950), pp. 455-459. For the opposite position, see Thomas N. Jenkins, "Identifying the Accident-Prone Employee," *Personnel*, Vol. 38, No. 4 (July 1961), pp. 56-62.

[17] R. H. Van Zelst, "The Effect of Age and Experience upon Accident Rate," *Journal of Applied Psychology*, Vol. 38, No. 5 (October 1954), pp. 313-17.

An example is the case of a mechanic with a long record of being accident free. Unexpectedly, within a period of six months, this man developed what appeared to be an accident habit, with four major and six minor injuries to himself and considerable damage to company equipment. It took very little investigation to discover feelings of guilt concerning an extramarital affair, which started before the first injury.[18]

A man's likelihood to have accidents seems to be related both to his personality and to his environment. One expert concludes: [19]

... the-time honored approach of the psychologist and the psychiatrist which emphasizes identification of subtle personality conditions which predispose to accidents by some employees seems to be a less promising approach than that which emphasizes study of the total psychological climate in which the typical employee works. If proneness (or liability) to accidents exists such tendency may be a group psychological phenomenon as well as an individual psychological phenomenon.

It is probably safe to say that in American industry, with the exception of the transportation industry (truck and bus drivers, and airplane pilots), little apparent effort is being made to identify the accident-prone at the hiring stage. There seems to be considerable doubt among operating personnel about the accuracy of any of the tests so far developed in discriminating between safe and accident-prone workers. Furthermore, particularly during periods of expanding employment, the personnel department has little opportunity to pick and choose among otherwise qualified applicants. (See our discussion on pp. 476-477.)

It seems clear that work conditions and individual accident-proneness are only two of the many determinants of accidents. Accidents are partly the fault of individuals, partly the fault of technology, and partly the fault of such factors as group attitudes and improper supervision. Management has begun to realize that neither industrial engineering departments nor employment departments can alone or in conjunction stop accidents completely, and the emphasis has shifted toward involving all levels of management and the work force.

THE STAFF APPROACH: THE SAFETY DEPARTMENT

The safety director is a staff man who usually reports to the personnel director or the industrial engineer, although in some organizations he is directly responsible to the plant manager. His functions normally include the

---

[18] Alan McLean, "Accidents and the Human Factor," *The Personnel Journal*, Vol. 34, No. 9 (February 1956), pp. 423-24. See also Rexford B. Hershey, "Emotional Factors in Accidents," *The Personnel Journal*, Vol. 15, No. 2 (June 1936), p. 60.

[19] William A. Kerr, "Accident Proneness in Factory Departments," *Journal of Applied Psychology*, Vol. 34, No. 3 (June 1950), p. 167. See also Leon Broady, "The Accident Phenomenon," *Personnel Administration*, Vol. 26, No. 6 (November 1963), pp. 11-14.

general promotion of safety education (through posters and safety campaigns, for example), analyzing the causes of accidents, preparing accident statistics and records, purchasing safety equipment, and so forth.

But these activities are only incidental to the safety director's main responsibility for devising and administering a plant-wide safety program. He is usually given a grant of power that reads somewhat like this: "To inspect the plant for unsafe conditions, to promote sound safety practices, to make safety rules, and to report, when necessary, violations to the plant manager." Powers as broad as these, of course, may well lead to conflict with line supervisors.

> The safety man sees a grinder working without the required goggles. Should he speak to the grinder, the foreman, or the plant manager? Whatever he does will make someone feel as though he has been bypassed.
>
> The safety man decides that the drop-hammer mechanism is unsafe. He feels that the worker should be required to push a button every time he wants the hammer to operate. This would be safer but would cut production. To whom should he speak first? How should he handle the expected opposition?

Problems such as these are almost inevitable once a staff man assumes responsibility for making and enforcing rules (see Chapter 18). How are the line supervisors likely to respond to such an extension of staff activities?

1. If the safety director pre-empts too much authority, the supervisors may decide that safety is the safety man's responsibility and forget about it altogether.

2. The supervisors may sabotage or ignore safety regulations that they have had no part in making. Often they feel (sometimes with justice) that a particular rule should not apply to their particular situation.

3. The supervisors and the safety director may just pass the buck back and forth. Whenever an accident occurs, each may put the blame on the other. If production costs rise too high, supervisors can always say that the safety man is at fault (this is particularly true where the safety man has the authority to order new equipment).

4. In most cases, accidents are caused by a worker doing his job in a dangerous fashion. Yet if the safety director instructs a man on how to do his job, he is usurping one of the supervisor's primary responsibilities. Sometimes the supervisor tells the worker what he *should* do and the safety director tells him what he *should not* do. This too can often lead to conflict.

5. Both the supervisors and the workers may begin to resent the safety man's efforts to implement his program. One safety man complained:

> "I feel like a cop. Everybody suspects me. When I come around everybody covers up, especially the men. All I am trying to do is help them. Yet I never get cooperation from anyone. I got to fight every inch of the way."

No wonder safety men often retreat from their efforts to enforce safety rules and try to achieve the same results through "educational" activities. As long as the safety director sticks to posters, propaganda, and contests, he is unlikely to get into anyone's hair.

Publicity

Such publicity devices as posters, slogans, and contests form the backbone of many safety programs. Most posters and jingles are punchy and amusing. But, apart from giving workers a slight chuckle, how much can these devices be expected to accomplish? For an answer to this question we must turn to psychologists who have studied how attitudes and behavior can be changed.

In general, psychologists agree that posters and jingles are reasonably effective in making consumers think of a particular brand when buying commercial products such as cigarettes—or even in creating new needs for such appliances as color TV. But these devices seem to be less effective in changing basic attitudes. "Dogmatic methods are not satisfactory for conveying emotionally-powerful ideas which are inherent in personal, physical safety." [20]

Workers soon come to regard posters as part of the scenery. They glance at them from time to time, but are unlikely to remember the tricky safety message at the crucial moment when they are in a hurry and about to take a risk. Most safety posters in effect say, "Work safely." Yet no one gets injured on purpose. Like exhortations not to sin, constant repetition of the dire consequences of taking risks seems to have little effect.

Many organizations insist that all employees attend periodic safety meetings, often run by the safety department. These meetings are quite valuable if they provide for group discussion of problems that are actually faced by the employees. Ordinarily, however, the participants simply sit and listen to canned programs couched in fairly unsophisticated terms. A head nurse told of the experience in her hospital:

> "We are supposed to attend a safety meeting once a month. You can always predict what will happen: one month they show you how to use a fire extinguisher, another month they tell you not to leave mops where people can trip over them and to make sure that the floors aren't waxed too heavily. Every six months they show us a movie—the same one—I know it by heart. I got better things to do; I have patients to take care of."

Many safety directors sponsor contests between departments in the hope that they can make a dramatic reduction in the accident rate by means of group pressure and competitive spirit. They post elaborate charts to mark the contestants' standings, and present small prizes such as pens or cigarette lighters to all the workers in the winning department. Observations suggest, however, that the safety director is usually far more enthusiastic about the contest than are any of the so-called contestants. Normally the participants are not asked whether they want to engage in a contest, and the prizes are rarely large enough to provide much motivation.

---

[20] McLean, *op. cit.*, p. 344.

Records and Analysis

Normally, whenever an accident occurs the supervisor is required to fill out a form including such information as the time, place, and cause of the accident, the extent of the injury, and a statement of what can be done to prevent such accidents in the future. Some of these forms are so complicated that the supervisor feels they have been designed as punishment for permitting an accident to occur.

Records of this sort serve several purposes: (1) They are useful if litigation arises involving workman's compensation, (2) they serve a control function, since, like cost and turnover figures, they indicate to higher management areas of supervisory inefficiency, and (3) they help management diagnose the causes of accidents, and thus provide a springboard for corrective measures.

It is the responsibility of the safety department to review, classify, and tabulate these reports. In fact, the safety program sometimes degenerates into a "whodunit" as the safety director tries to assign each accident to its proper category. Often responsibility is extremely difficult to fix. For instance, because the maintenance department has failed to keep a machine in proper order, oil drips out on the floor; the janitor fails to sweep it up; and a worker from another department runs through the department, slips, and hurts himself. Which department should be assigned the blame? The maintenance department, the department in which the fall occurs, or the department whose man is hurt?

Carefully recorded statistics do provide higher management with a useful control in putting pressure on lower levels of supervision. And they serve as valuable case materials in safety-committee meetings which may lead to corrective action by supervisors.

The Staff Role: an Evaluation

A young man was appointed as the first personnel director of a small company that had a particularly bad safety record. One of his first official acts was to cancel the company's contract with an agency that supplied safety posters. Why did he take such an unorthodox step? His answer was very revealing: "I wanted everyone to know that just because we had safety posters didn't mean that we had a safety campaign."

There is a regrettable tendency in the safety field, as in other areas of personnel administration, to rely on gadgets to provide easy solutions to hard problems. The process is a familiar one. Management recognizes that accidents are a serious expense. "Something must be done about it!" Line management is too busy, so an expert is hired, a specialist who can handle the problem for them. This done, line management breathes a sigh of relief: "That problem is solved."

The safety man realizes that he can achieve results only by eliciting the cooperation of the supervisors and workers. Yet to them safety is *his* job, not theirs—they are too busy. So in frustration he resorts to "gadgets," easy answers, measures that require little cooperation from line management. Perhaps he concentrates on posters, snappy slogans, elaborate statistical analyses of accidents and accident causes, safety contests between departments. Or, if he feels courageous enough to take a more direct approach, he insists that foolproof gadgets be placed on machines, rather than attempt to change worker attitudes. Or else he devises elaborate tests to eliminate the accident-prone at the gate before they are hired.

But a safety program of this sort is sometimes worse than none at all, for it lulls management into assuming that all its problems have been solved. As long as safety is primarily a staff function, the foreman will not give it high priority. Too often the safety man receives only lip service from a management that is much more interested in its "primary responsibility" of production. A safety program can be made effective only if the line supervisors and the workers are determined to make it work. A safety director by himself cannot make a plant safe.

The safety man does have a vital function to perform, however: He must be an adviser and counselor, an expert on both human relations and engineering, a man who helps but does not supplant the foreman. For instance, if during his rounds the safety man observes a worker who is operating unsafely, he should neither instruct the worker (except in emergency) nor report it to top management. Instead, he should discuss the matter with the foreman. Together they should try to figure out why the worker is motivated to take risks and how he can be motivated to avoid them. Even more important, the safety man should help coordinate line management's safety activities—activities in which the union and individual workers also participate. Let us look at these activities for a moment.

THE LINE APPROACH: SAFETY AS A SUPERVISORY RESPONSIBILITY

The following story illustrates the advantages to be gained when safety is made a line responsibility.

> In 1949 the Thatcher plant of a nation-wide company had an injury frequency rate of 21. Two years later its rate was 5, the lowest in the company.
>
> Even in 1949 the Thatcher plant had been conducting an active safety program in accordance with the directives issued by the national office. Safety posters were prominently displayed on every bulletin board. Over the main entrance to the plant was a sign that read: "——— days since the last accident." Every month information was posted on all the bulletin boards comparing the accident rate by departments. Safety guards had been placed on all machines. Mirrors had been installed at every sharp turn in the hallways and on the stairways.
>
> And yet the plant was cursed with an abnormally high number of accidents, most of them caused by unsafe acts, not unsafe conditions. A lift truck careening around a corner scooped up an unwary worker. Girls cut their fingers on

sharp edges because they failed to wear the gloves provided them. A mechanic positioned his ladder carelessly and fell off it while inspecting some high machinery. Two 18-year-old boys were roughhousing in the locker room; one stumbled over a bench and broke a rib. And so forth.

At last top management notified the plant manager that his job depended on his reducing the accident rate immediately. He was instructed to appoint a full-time safety director. The new safety director intensified the plant's publicity program and carried on constant safety checks through the plant in an effort to discover unsafe conditions and unsafe work habits.

More important, he began to enlist employee participation by working through the union. In consultation with the union, a plant-wide safety committee was established consisting of the safety director, personnel director, and several general foremen, together with one representative selected by the union from each department. The union committeemen were limited to a one-year term, in order to give as many workers as possible a chance to participate in the program.

Before each monthly meeting, the committee made a plant-wide safety inspection, with the assistance of the foreman and the union steward in each department. As the members went through the plant, they noted such hazards as slippery floors, mushroomed hammers, and improper guards. At the meeting, these hazards were discussed, along with suggestions submitted by rank-and-file workers. After the committee members had agreed on what should be done in each case, they relayed instructions to the proper supervisor, who was required to report at the next meeting on whether or not he had carried them out. The committee also analyzed all the accidents that had occurred during the preceding month.

The union took a direct interest both in checking up on management and in keeping its own members in line. The safety committeemen wore a special button and were authorized to stop unsafe acts committed by union members. At the meetings, committeemen often reported on how "I stopped Bill Smith from running across the hall. I told him, he'd be sure to kill himself." Or "There was a new man just in who didn't know how to lift things properly. I showed him how to do it."

Line management was quick to recognize that the plant manager meant business with the new program. In addition to preparing the usual written reports on accidents, each foreman now had to give the plant manager a personal report. As one foreman said: "I never want to go through an experience like *that* again. I never felt so small in all my life. I know one thing, there will be no more accidents in my department."

Gradually, the foremen began to realize that preventing accidents was just as important as keeping up production. They became extremely receptive to suggestions from the safety committee. (On occasion, too, they tried to evade assuming responsibility for accidents. As one foreman said: "See that man. He's doing me a great favor. He strained his arm yesterday but I asked him to come in and just pretend to work. I don't want to have any accidents on my record.")

The net result of this many-pronged program was an outstanding improvement in safety performance.

This case highlights the fact that safety is essentially a line problem. There is little difference in the managerial problems involved in cutting accidents and raising production. Both involve questions of motivation, enforcement of standards, and working through groups.

Group Factors

There are, as we have seen, accident-prone individuals. But safety is to a considerable extent a function of group attitudes. In a gang of teenagers it may be smart to take risks; in a group of mature businessmen irresponsibility is frowned on. To miners as a group, safety is of tremendous importance. (In one gypsum plant the "prop" man, who installed wooden props to hold up the roof, was found to enjoy high social status even though his job required little skill.[21]) United States corporations operating plants in certain Latin-American countries have found that accident rates are difficult to reduce there because of the widespread feeling that using a safety device is inconsistent with being a red-blooded man.

Clearly, the establishment of proper group attitudes is one of the most important requirements of an effective safety program. This is particularly true when the safety rules make the workers' jobs harder or more unpleasant, or are regarded as an unjustified restriction on freedom. Hairnets are unattractive; goggles and safety belts are uncomfortable; pushing a safety button often requires an extra motion.

If management can get the group to participate in the safety program, safe work habits may become accepted as a group norm that will be enforced by the group just as rigorously as any production "bogey." The group itself may punish the man who takes chances or fails to use proper equipment. In many plants no-smoking rules are consistently ignored in spite of constant attempts to enforce them. Not so in oil refineries. Here the legitimacy of the rule is well accepted. One employee reported that "regardless of who you are in the plant, if you see someone smoking you can stop him. I know. The first day I was there I absentmindedly reached for a butt and was practically lynched. The boys have special fun catching visitors, especially big shots." Here we have a group-enforced pattern of behavior.

Group meetings provide a unique opportunity to ferret out possible accident hazards and to elicit suggestions that would not have occurred to line super-vision or the safety department. After all, the men on the spot know more about their jobs than anyone else. Furthermore, most safety rules are easy to ignore and difficult to enforce. Rules are much easier to enforce if those who must obey them also have a voice in drawing them up.

The Union

In contrast to wage determination and discipline, safety is an area in which the interests of labor and management are identical. Everyone gains by keeping accidents at a minimum, and no safety program can be conducted

---

[21] Alvin Gouldner, *Patterns of Industrial Bureaucracy* (Glencoe, Ill.: Free Press, 1954), p. 12.

effectively without joint effort. Ironically, however, unions and management often use the question of safety as a pawn in the struggle for power.[22]

Many members of management take the position that the union has no right to be consulted on matters of safety. As one personnel director explained, "Safety is so important in our industry that we cannot share responsibility. We have worker safety committees in each department, but we keep these sharply separate from the union."[23] Unions frequently resist management's efforts to install safety equipment or to enforce safety rules. On the other hand, many wild-cat and legally called strikes have been caused by management's insistence that men work under conditions they regard as unsafe.

There are a few encouraging signs of cooperation in safety matters, however. Joint union-management safety committees, like the one in the Thatcher plant, are becoming increasingly common. In fact, they are perhaps the most successful of the various sorts of joint union-management committee that have been tried.

For these committees to be genuinely successful, the rank-and-file members must feel they are playing a real part in the safety program. Rules negotiated with top union officials alone are less likely to be accepted than rules to which a large number of individual employees have contributed. Too many joint safety committees consist only of top local officers who may have less knowledge of conditions in a given department than does management. Yet if union cooperation is to be obtained, the top officers should participate in setting up the committee and in selecting its members.

Supervision

To a large extent the attitude of the rank-and-file workers toward safety is a reflection of the attitude of their immediate supervisor. A worker in a railway freight yard once told the following story:

> There's a company rule that you aren't supposed to cut between cars. If the safety man sees you he will give you three days off. But the supervisor doesn't care. In fact, when you have to get the numbers of some cars, that's the only way to get them. If you don't get the numbers, he'll give you time off. And he is more likely to catch you than the safety man.

In safety, as in other areas of supervision, the attitudes of the foremen in turn reflect the attitudes of higher management. To the foreman operating

---

[22] Actually, union-management cooperation in safety may serve as a starting point for cooperation in other fields. As Herbert Hoover put it years ago, "Good-will and cooperation with respect to safety—which is a noncontroversial subject as between employer and employee—lead to good-will and cooperation in other more delicate problems of shop management, such as hours of work and wages." Quoted in Friedmann, *op. cit.,* p. 118.

[23] The union president told us: "These committees are a waste of time. Management pays no attention to what they bring up. If it was a union committee, we could force management to clean things up. They really are more interested in production than safety here. As for us, it's safety first."

under the pressure typical of modern industry, maximum production and maximum safety are simply incompatible. One can be achieved only at the expense of the other. (Perhaps this is a short-sighted point of view, but it is sometimes difficult for the foreman to take any other.) If top management really wants "Safety First," it must clearly indicate that it is willing to pay the possible cost in terms of lower production. It must get tough with supervisors who permit unsafe practices to continue. It must show that it consults the safety records in deciding who should get promoted. If management talks loud about safety but permits a dangerous condition to persist for "just another few days" so that no production will be lost, it must expect only lip service from everyone down the line.

Companies that have the best safety records customarily use accident reports as one of the control statistics by which supervisory efficiency is judged.[24] As we discovered in Chapter 15, however, overemphasis on such records may induce supervisors to bend all their efforts toward *looking* good. They may fall into the habit of buck-passing, and may even try to persuade injured workers to report to work in order to avoid being charged with a "lost-time accident." [25]

What, specifically, can the supervisor do to promote safety?

1. He can train new employees. The foreman should do more than merely exhort the new employee to work safely. He should point out to him the possible causes of accidents and should help him develop work habits and motions that will keep him out of danger.

> "Such actions as assuming a posture which allows a man to lose his balance if a wrench slips, holding a finger in line with the cutting edge so a finger injury occurs if there is a moment's inattention or if an error is made ... and holding the face so close to a grinding wheel that particles of steel may injure the face, are examples of behavior elements which should be eliminated from the work pattern." [26]

2. He can make it clear that, though he wants high production, he won't insist on workers working so fast that they run risks.[27]

3. He can listen to and consult with employees. Often the foreman gets his best safety ideas by keeping his ears open and making it clear that he is interested in suggestions.

---

[24] For an excellent example, see Chadwick J. Haberstroh, "Control as an Organizational Process," *Management Science*, Vol. 6, No. 2 (January 1960).

[25] For an example, see Melville Dalton, *Men Who Manage* (New York: Wiley, 1959), p. 80.

[26] Maier, *op. cit.*, p. 513.

[27] There is some evidence that the accident rate is higher when the job pace is too fast for workers to maintain. (Friedmann, *op. cit.*, p. 117.) A conflicting study made at the Camden RCA works, however, showed that departments on incentive had approximately the same accident rate as those on day work, even though other factors (such as monotonous work, low job prestige) would lead one to expect accidents to be higher. As an explanation of this unexpected finding, the author suggests that incentive systems "appear to make [the worker] more alert to make a reasonable production goal and this alertness apparently makes him safer in his operations." (Kerr, *op. cit.*, p. 170.)

4. He can engage in constructive discipline. He can tactfully point out to employees when they are working unsafely, and he can be firm in imposing punishment when lesser measures fail.

5. Finally, he can make a habit of checking on unsafe conditions and unsafe behavior as part of his daily routine. In some General Motors plants each foreman is expected to speak to at least two of his employees each day about safety. The foreman should be on the lookout for employees who seem emotionally upset; if necessary, he should either counsel them or transfer them to a safer job. In some companies, supervisors are required to make a daily "morale check" of all employees engaged in dangerous work.

In addition, there is evidence that just having an over-all atmosphere of relaxed human relations is one of the best ways to promote safety. Clearly, a high accident rate is a symptom of more serious personnel problems which cannot be solved by a safety campaign alone.[28]

CONCLUSION

There is no one sure-fire approach to safety. The engineering approach has paid off remarkably well, but it seems to be rapidly reaching the limits of its effectiveness. The most safely engineered car in the world is a murderous weapon in the hands of an unsafe driver—and the same is true of industrial equipment.

There is less unanimity about the selection approach to safety. Debate still continues about the value of interviews and tests in eliminating accident-prone workers. Certainly such screening cannot eliminate the carelessness and accidents that spring from temporary emotional disturbances. Further, evidence suggests that risk-taking is largely a group phenomenon. In a situation where there is heavy pressure for production or where fellow employees encourage one another to take chances, almost everyone begins to take the hazardous short cuts that lead to injury.

So long as management regarded accident prevention as a problem that could be solved exclusively through an engineering approach, or exclusively through a selection approach, there was some justification in considering safety as a separate, special program. Safety engineers could be expected to install safe equipment; proper psychological tests could be expected to eliminate the accident-prone. But once management realized that safety was intimately related to *the way people work*, it became clear that only line supervision could handle the problem.

Safety demands the support of every level of management. Workers must participate as well as supervisors, for workers often spot danger areas and

---

[28] See Willard Kerr, "Complementary Theories of Safety Psychology," *Journal of Social Psychology*, Vol. 45, No. 1 (February 1957), pp. 3-9.

devise effective solutions. But when they fail to perceive safety as something vital to their welfare, they will resist the most carefully devised safety program. Safety must be considered as a responsibility for the whole organization; any attempt to departmentalize it inevitably leads to confusion and inefficiency.

PROBLEM 1

RESPONSIBILITY FOR SAFETY

Personnel Director: "We've got to constantly watch our production people [on safety]. Our safety man must go over all orders for tools. A lot of our departments have high explosion dangers and we've got to use spark-proof hammers. But a spark-proof hammer costs three times as much and only lasts a third as long, so the foremen are always trying to get steel ones."

Question: "If the safety man objects to what the foremen want to buy, who has the final say?"

Personnel Director: "The safety man all the time. We want to build up a good record."

1. Discuss the impact of this point of view on line-staff relations.
2. What would be a better approach?

PROBLEM 2

SAFETY MANUALS

The following quotations are taken from various safety manuals. Comment on each in turn.

"Every worker should be given a safety handbook and made to familiarize himself with it."

"In order to keep workers on the alert, those in charge of safety education should make use of posters prominently displayed and frequently changed."

"The competitive spirit does wonders. Build up competition between departments."

"The key to effective safety is to build up interests. Always have something new, a new gimmick, a new gadget, a new way to rouse a chuckle."

PROBLEM 3

INVESTIGATING SAFETY PROBLEMS

You are Vice President in charge of Industrial Relations for a large company with many plants scattered throughout the nation. In going over your monthly report from the Jonesville plant, you notice a significant increase in the accident rate. You had planned to go to Jonesville some time this month in any case, and you now resolve to look into the problem.

1. What are the possible explanations for this increase in accidents?
2. Bearing in mind that you are a staff man, describe in a step-by-step fashion how you plan to deal with this problem.

Service and Benefit Programs

Fringe benefits—insurance, holidays, pensions, overtime pay, and other benefits —now make up a significant part of employee remuneration.[1] Perhaps one third of a firm's labor costs may go to cover these items, and it is likely that the proportion will continue to increase. In this chapter we will examine the reasons for the growth of fringe benefits and the special problems involved in administering them.

WHAT ARE FRINGE BENEFITS?

There is no rigid, all-inclusive definition of fringe benefits, but the following list suggests some of the items that are commonly included under this term: [2]

> *Paid vacations, paid holidays, and Christmas bonuses.*
> *Paid rest periods, lunch periods, wash-up time, supplements for military duty, jury duty.*
> *Overtime pay* for hours worked beyond the "regular" work period. The Fair Labor Standards Act requires a 50 per cent premium to be paid for all hours worked in excess of 40 per week for firms engaged in interstate commerce. Many companies also pay premiums for work on holidays, weekends, and beyond eight hours in a single day.

---

[1] The term "fringe benefit" became popular during the 1940's as a means of referring to the whole bevy of employee benefits provided by the employer in addition to traditional direct-wage payments.

[2] For basic data concerning types of benefits offered and their costs, see the following three references:

1. Chamber of Commerce of the United States, *Fringe Benefits, 1963* (Washington, 1964).

2. "Employee-benefit plans: developments, 1954-63," *Social Security Bulletin* (Washington: Government Printing Office, April, 1965).

3. U.S. Bureau of Labor Statistics, *Employer expenditures for selected supplementary compensation practices for production and related workers in manufacturing industries, 1962*, Bulletin No. 1428, 1965.

Hospitalization and *medical benefits.*

Sickness and accident benefits for the continuance of part or all of an employee's regular wage or salary while he is ill.

Old Age and Survivors' Insurance Benefits (popularly called Social Security). These are paid directly by the federal government but to finance them the company must pay a tax on the employee's annual earnings.

Pension plans to supplement federal benefits.

Thrift and saving plans by which the company supplements any savings put aside by employees (within specified limits). Sometimes the supplement is in the form of savings bonds or company stock.

Unemployment benefits paid by state governments but financed by taxes on the employer's payroll.

Supplemental unemployment benefits beyond those paid by the state.

Workmen's Compensation to pay for medical and hospital bills and provide partial payment for lost earnings while an employee is disabled due to an industrial accident or illness.

Disability insurance to provide income for those unable to work.

Severance pay given to employees whose jobs are permanently eliminated.

Recreation programs, including company-financed social, athletic, and recreational clubs.

Subsidies to reduce employee expenses for cafeteria food, work clothing, and tools.

Discounts on company products, company securities.

Tuition rebates for education and special training.

Medical, legal and personal counseling.

Post-retirement insurance benefits.

Omitted from the above list are certain items that might properly be considered as fringe benefits: Isolated company locations, for example, often require that the company carry a major share of the cost of housing, community schooling, and recreation programs, and so forth. In many firms, sales personnel and executives consider liberal expense allowances and trips to exotic resorts (for conventions or customer good will) and overseas junkets as fringe benefits.[3]

The magnitude of these benefits may encourage some employers to utilize overtime work and temporary employees rather than hiring additional personnel.[4] However, industries traditionally have differed in the relative proportion of labor costs devoted to fringe benefits. Financial institutions and insurance companies have been on the "high" side, for example, over 30 per cent, whereas hotels have been on the other side of the distribution.

Some rough guide to the relative cost of various "fringes" is provided by the table on page 711.

The cost of benefit programs conducted by United States firms in overseas plants are still higher. In Latin America, for example, estimates give the figure as 150 per cent of direct labor costs. In Western Europe, the figures are some-

---

[3] The Internal Revenue Service may rule to the contrary, of course.

[4] This is a controversial issue. See Joseph Garbarino, "Fringe Benefits and Overtime as Barriers to Expanding Employment," *Industrial and Labor Relations Review,* Vol. 17, No. 3 (April 1964), pp. 426-442.

where between those for the United States and Latin America. In addition to those benefits granted in the U.S., in other countries a firm may be required to provide family allowances and other social insurance benefits.

Hourly Fringe Costs for Steelworkers *
(Average Hourly Rate of Pay—$3.19)

Pensions, Insurance,	
Unemployment Benefits and Social Security	$ .50
Vacation pay	.20
Sunday premium pay	.05
Shift differential	.05
Holiday premium pay	.04
Holiday pay (not worked)	.06
Total	$ .90

* American Iron and Steel Institute, 1962. Note, amounts have been rounded off, but these fringes amount to almost 30 per cent of the wage rate.

WHY FRINGE BENEFITS HAVE EXPANDED

Why has the amount of money devoted to these programs risen so rapidly in recent years? In theory at least, all these benefits could be purchased by employees from increased direct wages. Why then has management chosen to provide them in addition to wages?

Employee Demands

Paradoxically, as our country has become richer and more self-assured, the desire to eliminate risk and increase personal security has grown stronger.[5] And the prevalence of fringe benefits reflects a strong urge on the part of employees to eliminate insecurity from every conceivable source.

Besides more security, employees are also demanding more leisure, and leisure has become a significant component of our high standard of living.[6] Employees want paid holidays and paid vacations so that they will have both the time and the money to pursue recreation. (Of course, some demands for increased leisure are really efforts to spread work by requiring the firm to hire or retain more employees to fill in for those on vacation or on shorter hours.)

[5] For an interesting analysis of the almost universal American desire to eliminate risk and insecurity, see John K. Galbraith, *The Affluent Society* (Boston: Houghton Mifflin, 1958), Chapter 8. See also our discussion in Chapter 1.

[6] The steel industry now provides a 13-week "sabbatical with pay" every five years for senior workers. The Steelworkers union sought this both to provide leisure *and* to spread employment. In one study, when a company offered employees a choice between the extended vacation and work at extra pay, 80 per cent chose the pay, not the leisure! *Nation's Business* (June 1964), p. 37. This finding contradicts the generalization.

Further, many employees find it more convenient to have their contributions for benefits deducted from their paychecks than to pay them by themselves. If this money never appears in their paychecks and is never available for them to spend, the whole process becomes less painful. Thus, many of these programs provide *forced savings* without demanding habits of thrift. For example, under one company's saving plan an employee may elect to have up to 6 per cent of his earnings deducted from his paycheck and deposited in a company savings account. (The company matches half of this amount, provided the employee leaves his savings in for at least three years.)

Employees have other compelling reasons for favoring benefit programs. Many of these benefits, like extended paid vacations and sickness pay, give hourly workers increased status in the organization and in the community, placing them on a level closer to that of salaried employees. Other benefits, like premiums for certain types of overtime and irregularly scheduled work hours and call-in pay, serve to discourage the employer from taking advantage of workers. Americans have also become more health-conscious and are increasingly anxious to enjoy preventative and remedial treatment through health-insurance programs. For executives, "expense account living" sometimes provides a much higher standard of (untaxed) living than their salaries would allow. Many of the privileges and benefits provided by these programs cannot be won by individual employees; they must be procured on a company-wide basis.

Union Demands

The special conditions prevailing during and just after World War II also help explain the expansion of company-paid benefits. During the war, when union-management negotiations became deadlocked, both the union and management learned that the offer of or the demand for some special concession like an extra holiday with pay or pay for jury duty would resolve the stalemate. Over a period of time, these concessions increased in number and importance far beyond the expectations of the original negotiators. By the end of World War II, unions had shifted their position dramatically: Instead of opposing company welfare programs as paternalistic, they had come to insist on them as the worker's proper due.

Unions also became increasingly skillful in parlaying a fringe benefit offered by one company in lieu of greater wages into similar grants elsewhere. Non-union firms found they had to follow suit if they were to attract labor during periods of labor shortage. A great impetus was given to these efforts by a Supreme Court ruling in 1949 that pensions were a bargainable issue. Previously, there had been some doubt that a union could require management to negotiate over pensions. Once granted, these special provisions became firmly rooted among the normal conditions of employment.

Management sometimes has tried to check the expanding role of govern-ment by providing private security programs for employees either as a supple-ment to or as a substitute for the type of public social-security programs established by other countries of the world.

There are very real pressures on management to grant fringe benefits com-parable to other firms in the industry or the community, and many such health and welfare plans merely reflect a "follow-the-leader" pattern of adoption. Many personnel and labor-relations reporting services now publish regular surveys of fringe-benefit practices, thus, in effect, throwing the spotlight on an organization that is not offering a full complement. In some instances, both government tax policy and the principle of spreading risk over a large group make it more economical for companies to pay health and welfare benefit costs than for employees to pay them out of their earnings, which are taxable. Many fringe benefits are either not taxed (because they are paid for directly by the employer) or else the tax payment is deferred until a much later period, when the individual's liability may be less (say, after retirement).

Morale Improvement

Clearly, it is to management's advantage to maintain a sound health and welfare program. Employees seek security as well as leisure, and deprivations in either area may lead to paralyzing unrest that reflects itself in decreased effectiveness. Furthermore, employees do make coercive comparisons between organizations, and even though the direct wages paid by Company A may be a good bit higher than those paid by Company B—enough higher, in fact, for employees to pay for their own private annuities—Company A employees may still be resentful that they do not have a company-paid pension program like the one offered by Company B.

Many companies establish recreation programs for a more immediate reason. They view company-sponsored bowling teams, resort facilities, and social clubs as a means of bringing together various levels of the organization in an infor-mal, pleasant environment. When supervisors share common team membership with their subordinates, it is hoped that human relations will improve.

But many observers are critical of this approach. Free time, they argue, should give employees an opportunity to express a diversity of interests—going to the theater, attending a ball game, sitting at home and reading, or tending the garden. Especially when conformity is required on the job, free time should enable individuals to strike out on their own, unencumbered by company in-fluence. The American tradition of pluralism—with its emphasis on varied groups competing for the interests and affiliations of citizens—is endangered when companies, or unions for that matter, try to exercise control over the leisure-time activities of individual workers.[7]

Organized recreational activities are based on the assumption that most employees have the same interests and motivations. Sometimes company-sponsored activities strike a note of compulsion, even though management intends them to be voluntary.[8] Many employees resent being forced to attend after-hours social events.

Further, some programs go so far in their effort to provide employees with security and welfare benefits that they smother the individual. By providing lavish health, recreational, and educational benefits, the firm may foster a sense of overdependence among some employees and a destructive resentment against excessive paternalism among others. Company programs also may weaken the community's efforts to stimulate citizen participation in its own programs.

Sooner or later, each company must decide how much is "enough" and how much is "too much." It must decide where the line should be drawn between services and programs that ought to be provided by the family, the community, and church and political organizations, and services that ought to be provided by the firm. The simple criterion of "satisfying employee needs" is not adequate. Human wants are multitudinous, and dissatisfaction that will affect job performance may come from many sources beyond the reach of management. Few companies would want to involve themselves in marital or religious problems, for example.

Services designed to build employee morale may backfire with disastrous effect, as some companies that operate plants overseas or in company towns have discovered. Service programs that provide housing, food, schools, and the like often develop into rich sources of worker grievances. When is it "fair" for the company to raise house rentals or the price of food in the company restaurant? How often should hash be served? Even when the company funnels substantial amounts of money into such programs, they persist as sources of discontent and petty grousing. Understandably, many firms are eager to cede responsibility for them to the employees themselves or to outside contractors in order to save time, energy, and morale.

Identification
with the Firm's Profitability

Over many years profit-sharing plans have been popular as a means of rewarding employees for their contribution to increased profits. Sometimes

---

[7] For an elegant statement of this point of view, see Clark Kerr, "What Became of the Independent Spirit?" in *Fortune*, Vol. 48, No. 1 (July 1953), pp. 110-111, 134-136.

[8] See Conrad Arensberg, "Work and the Changing American Scene," in *Research in Industrial Human Relations*, C. Arensberg, *et al.*, eds. (New York: Harper & Row, 1957), pp. 57-68.

these plans provide for annual bonus payments (related to net income of the firm), but often the payout is deferred to a later period or even to retirement. In the latter instance, of course, long tenure is rewarded and quits are penalized. It is hoped that employees will begin to feel somewhat like owners and identify with and serve the cause of expanding profit levels.[9]

A problem can occur when employee effort is maintained, but forces out of their control serve to lower income. Indeed, profit is often a function of many forces over which most employees have little direct control. Sudden decrements in what have become anticipated bonus earnings can be costly in morale terms.

Similarly stock options at the executive level, as noted in Chapter 25, can be a significant source of executive earnings and interest. These provide that over a period of years an executive can purchase company shares at the market price prevailing at the time the options were issued. If the stock rises in price, the executive exercises his option, purchases the shares and may later resell them as a long-term capital gain.[10]

The major difficulty inherent in stock option plans as a means of getting key managers to seek greater profits for the firm is that they will become overly engrossed in the stock market. As with profits, share prices are influenced by a variety of forces, and excessive interest in the gyrations of the market can detract time and energy from the manager's job.

Employee Rehabilitation

A somewhat narrower objective of many service and benefit programs is to help employees meet personal problems that may affect their job performance. Adequate insurance programs, for example, will alleviate fears about being able to meet high medical expenses.

Many companies also provide a limited amount of health, legal, and personal counseling in an effort to help employees with minor problems. In effect, the company serves as a detection station, and genuinely troubled employees are urged to get professional help. It is thus hoped that lingering unattended-to personal problems will be avoided and employees will maintain a healthier personal outlook. Medical, legal, and social-work groups in the community at large are not enthusiastic about company programs that threaten to usurp their functions, however, and enlightened companies are careful not to invade professional preserves.

Our own attitude is that services of this type should be kept at a minimum except in situations where employees cannot procure them for themselves. In

---

[9] *Cf.* B. L. Metzger, *Profit Sharing In Perspective* (Evanston, Illinois: Profit Sharing Research Foundation, 2nd ed., 1966).

[10] The Internal Revenue Service has precise regulations surrounding the terms under which options may be issued, and they are now a less attractive source of gain than before they were so restricted. However, they still can increase income very substantially since the tax rate on long-term capital gains is typically far below what the executive pays on current income.

isolated locations, for example, where the work involves unusual health or legal hazards, in-company service programs may be almost obligatory. It seems regrettable, however, to discourage employees from taking responsibility for their own affairs. They are not dependent children, and they need not be protected from *every* hazard. Some employees who fail to take care of themselves may turn out to be inefficient workers, but the cost of assuming full responsibility for their welfare may prove far in excess of the benefits enjoyed either by them or by the company.

Benefits as a Reward for Service

Many fringe benefits are weighted to favor the senior employee. The length of vacations and the amount of pension benefits, for example, increase with length of service. In fact, some plans specify that employees will lose all their pension and profit-sharing credits if they leave before reaching retirement age. These programs, it is felt, reward long service and discourage turnover, and are a necessary concomitant to sound policies of management development and promotion from within.

Yet fringe benefits too heavily weighted in favor of long-service employees have certain drawbacks: They may discourage employees from leaving who ought to leave, and they may make it embarrassing for the company to discharge unsatisfactory employees who have accumulated rights to substantial benefits.

Management can escape these disadvantages by easing the rigid relationship between length of service and benefits received. For example, it can extend to employees the privilege of taking with them company contributions to the pension plan if they decide to leave for another job. This practice, which is called "vesting," provides for employee equity in pension contributions *before* retirement age. Vesting privileges increase company pension costs substantially, perhaps as much as 40 per cent over the cost of nonvested pension plans. The reason for this is quite simple: Many employees normally leave the firm before retirement and their pension costs are returned to the company.

Vesting is used at executive levels as well as at lower levels in the hierarchy:

> [Some executives] see liberal vesting as a way of easing out executives who don't make the grade. The president of a billion dollar oil company which has adopted liberal vesting puts it in these terms: Take a 50-year old vice-president who has been with the company 20 years but isn't pulling his weight in his new post. If the company fired him, the officer wouldn't get a dime's pension; few other companies would take him on because he represents too large a pension cost.
>
> But with liberal vesting, the officer could retire right now on a tidy pension or go into the job market and tell prospective employers that his retirement was already taken care of.[11]

---

[11] *Business Week* (January 31, 1959), pp. 102-103. Most vesting schedules provide for gradual acquisition of a 100% status—say 25% after five years' service, 50% after 10.

In some industries there is a great deal of employee mobility—for example, in construction, clothing manufacture, and entertainment. Here the unions have negotiated industry-wide pension agreements which provide that an employee will retain all his pension credits as he moves from employer to employer within a given industry. Most pension plans, however, provide that an employee will receive benefits only if he stays on with the company to the age of retirement.[12]

Unfortunately, rewards based on length of service sometimes displace more important incentives. Fringe benefits that are bestowed equally upon all employees, regardless of merit (e.g., company-paid hospitalization), or are given in proportion to length of service (e.g., vacations), fail to reflect the difference between the good and the mediocre employee. And the dramatic growth in the value of savings-pension funds may even encourage employees to look forward to retirement benefits as their major compensation.[13] Programs of this sort clearly do little to motivate superior performance.

Facilitating Transition Periods

Management may also use benefit programs as a device for easing the employee's transition from one status to another.[14] Unemployment may be softened by severance pay plans, supplementary unemployment benefits, and loan programs. Similarly, a pension plan will safeguard the welfare of employees who are obliged to retire at some specified age (typically at 65).

Another forced transition for employees occurs when a company closes a plant. In fact, some companies procrastinate in making this decision, even though it is ultimately unavoidable, because of the dire effect it will have on the community and on its own reputation. Early retirement and severance-pay plans that provide for lump-sum payments to permanently discharged employees help to reduce this shock considerably. Management can pay the costs of moving and re-establishing homes.

As noted in Chapter 21, many companies absorb the cost of retraining employees in an effort to encourage them to improve their abilities on their present job or to prepare themselves for a shift to a more responsible post.

Kaiser Steel Corporation, for instance, guarantees its regular employees that they will not lose their jobs because of technological change. They are assured their regular income for at least a year while they are assigned to a reserve pool, even if they do not work. (After a year, however, their pay can be reduced if they are assigned to a lower-rated job.)

---

[12] Of course, many plans do make provision for early retirement for health reasons after a minimum number of years of service or voluntary early retirement with reduced benefits.

[13] A newspaper account reported that a truck driver with 44 years of service with Sears Roebuck retired with accrued profit sharing-pension benefits of $289,000 (including contributions of $5,928 from his own wages).

[14] This philosophy contrasts sharply with the earlier attitude that people should prepare themselves for any and all contingencies by exercizing thrift and frugality.

Benefit programs also make many difficult management decisions easier. For example, a pension plan with compulsory retirement has these advantages:

1. Management does not have to make the difficult and controversial decision of when each employee is no longer able to work effectively or when his health would be endangered by continued employment.

2. The approximate costs for retirement benefits can be estimated and budgeted in advance for the total organization.

3. Promotion steps are opened up automatically, as senior employees retire, thus providing "new blood" for the organization and an incentive for younger employees.

There has been growing criticism of mandatory retirement. Not everyone grows old at the same rate, and chronological age may be a poor measure of vigor and effectiveness. A man who is forced to retire at an age when he is still active undergoes a severe shock, and may find it impossible to compensate for the loss of the social and egoistic satisfactions that come from regular work. Moreover, the economic costs of premature retirement are high, both for the company and for the economy.[15] The valuable skills of a highly experienced employee are lost, and the long-range costs of his pension are proportionately higher. If a man is able and willing to work beyond the normal retirement age, it would seem unwise to cut off his employment arbitrarily.

It seems likely that the practice of mandatory retirement will be significantly modified in the years ahead. For example, an employee may be permitted to retire at 65 with full benefits, but may be permitted to stay on to 70 if he passes an annual physical examination. Or he may be required to take a longer vacation each year after he reaches a certain age.

There is also a growing trend toward special *early* retirement programs in which employees who have aged prematurely or whose jobs have been changed may retire on benefits that approximate those they would receive at the normal retirement age.

Avoiding Individual Discrimination

Prior to the widespread adoption of the various plans we have been discussing, a good many benefits were provided voluntarily by charitably disposed companies. Conscientious owners and managers lent money to long-service employees who found themselves in economic straits as a result of illness, injury, or layoff. And many firms extended pension benefits and regular holidays as a matter of company largess. But, since employees had no established rights to these benefits, they were susceptible to gross discrimination. The regularized company policies and contractual obligations of recent years have served to eliminate the possibility of such discrimination.

---

[15] Richard A. Beaumont and James W. Tower, *Executive Retirement and Effective Management* (New York: Industrial Relations Counselors, 1961).

Unfortunately, however, even formal, contractual programs give rise to charges of inequity, for not everyone benefits equally from them. Some employees are far more interested in present income than in future benefits, and they feel that they are being penalized by the growing emphasis on pension and savings programs. In addition, differences in age, health, length of service, size of family, and sex have a significant effect on the amount of benefit individual workers derive from such programs. For example, the introduction of supplemental unemployment benefits which cost about 5 cents per employee hour has caused dissension among many senior employees. Why? Because it is the less-senior employees who are most likely to become unemployed and thus derive benefit from these programs.

There is some danger that most fringe benefits accent the impersonality of the large company since everyone in a particular category receives the same amount. There is a trend toward more tailor-made benefit programs that consider the needs of the individual. In his earlier years an employee may want to invest more in insurance; in later years vacations can be more significant. One recent union-management agreement provides a credit of 1.6 weeks' pay each year for every 5 years of service. This credit can be taken in company stock, cash or as vacation (or in any combination).

Improving Public Relations

Generous fringe benefits help create a more favorable "image" of the company in the eyes of the public, thus making it easier for management to recruit high-caliber employees and to maintain amicable relationships with the entire community. Like fair wages and salaries, adequate health and welfare programs impress the community with the value of the firm, particularly as these programs become more widely identified with what constitutes a "good company." [16]

PROBLEMS OF ADMINISTRATION

Fringe benefits give rise to many complex administrative problems. Here we can suggest only a few of the types of problem that administrators of benefit programs must face.

Employee Participation

Where possible, employees should participate in these programs. The management of recreation programs, in particular, should be taken over by

---

[16] Some unions compete with management in developing benefit programs that will attract employee and community interest. Union-sponsored hospitals and clinics which provide health services at substantial reductions, or at no cost at all, to union members, and even subsidized vacation resorts, are not unusual.

employees *on their own time.* If they show themselves unwilling to spend the necessary time and effort to put a program across, this should be a clear sign that the program has not elicited enough interest to warrant its continuance.

The fact that employees have accepted responsibility spares the company many time-consuming and embarrassing decisions. Should Bill Jones be replaced by Sam Smith as first baseman on the company ball team? Should the bowling uniforms be financed by the welfare fund, or should this fund be reserved for activities that benefit all employees? Similarly, an employee-managed credit union saves the company from having to make difficult decisions in extending and collecting emergency loans.

Finally, most people are far more appreciative of what they have done for themselves than of what has been done for them. Employee control tempers the resentment against paternalism that is directed toward many fringe-benefit activities.

Employee Financing

Should employees make any contribution to the expense of the firm's benefit programs? If they do not share in the costs, they tend to forget how expensive the programs are. Free programs are often "taken for granted," and, since the employees carry none of the financial burden, their demands become more and more unrealistic. As we have already suggested, employees should be made to realize that the money going into these plans is an alternative to higher wages and salaries. Having employees share the costs also makes it possible to adjust assessments to the benefits received—thus eliminating some of the discriminatory features of benefit plans.

On the other hand, most unions and employees are strongly opposed to "contributory" programs. Of course, we have already mentioned the tax advantage—company contributions are usually not taxable as income to the employee (except after pensions are received as income). Moreover, since many employees feel that they have earned the benefits that are granted, they cannot understand why they should pay part of the cost any more than they pay part of their own wages.[17]

In attempts to dramatize to employees the expense of fringe benefits, many companies issue an annual report to each employee summarizing the total amount contributed in his name to various benefit funds, as well as the current status of his pension accumulation, insurance protection, vacation allowance, and so on. Some of these reports seek to highlight how much of the company's total expenditure for each employee never appears on his paycheck. Others

---

[17] These sentiments are strengthened by the union practice of announcing welfare gains at the same time as, or in place of, wage gains: "We got 15 cents in direct wage improvement and another 15 cents to be applied to our insurance and pension plan or a "total package" of 30 cents.

are designed to provide a simple accounting of the employee's current status in the programs and to summarize the company's contributions.

Of course, in all these efforts the hope is that employee demands will be moderated by the realization that benefit programs are an *alternative* to higher wages and salaries. It is unlikely, however, that techniques of this sort will diminish employee pressure for increased contributions to these programs. As we noted in Chapter 1, more generous fringe benefits may simply be regarded as a substitute for other forms of advancement.

Eligibility

In almost every type of company benefit program, the answer to the question "Who is eligible to receive these benefits?" will have a major impact on its cost. The answer to this question has a profound effect on the cost of the programs. The more liberal the eligibility rules, the higher the cost. For example, companies usually try to restrict pay for a particular holiday to employees who were in attendance both before and after the holiday. Otherwise employees might be tempted to convert the holiday into a vacation by taking several days off. Similarly, sickness benefits must be carefully controlled in order to keep employees from treating these as vacation days due them. Some companies do not pay for the first day or even the first week of illness. Others require that the company nurse visit the employee's home to make sure that he is not malingering.

Attempts by employees to discover loopholes in benefit plans also contribute substantially to their cost. The company may find itself paying out benefits that are not deserved, and it may also have to spend extra money for "control" purposes—that is, checking holiday-pay records, administering sick pay, and so on. Conflicts over eligibility sometimes lead to bad feelings, complaints, and union grievances—all of which are threats to morale.

How would you decide such cases as these:

1. Jones claims holiday pay for the Fourth of July, even though he failed to report for work on the third. Reason: his car broke down in isolated location.
2. Smith claims sickness pay, although when the nurse dropped in to see him he was not at home. His explanation: sick as he was, he had to take his wife to visit her invalid mother.

Checking up in order to test the validity of such excuses is an extremely unpleasant and time-consuming task.

Claims for overtime allowances are also a source of trouble. There are hundreds of claims that cannot be predicted in the formal agreement setting forth the conditions under which such premiums should be paid. For example, Brown is asked to come in an hour early to do some work before the start of his regular shift, but he is permitted to leave an hour early at the close of the day. Is he entitled to "overtime"?

Management must recognize that when it introduces a benefit plan it commits some part of the firm's future economic resources. Even where there is no legal obligation to do so, employees often feel that management has made a moral commitment to continue the program indefinitely. Before entering into a program, then, management should make a thorough, realistic evaluation of its cost, both short-term and long-term. For example, what happens to employees on pension after a plant is closed?

Difficulty of Computing Costs

It is extremely difficult for management to make accurate cost predictions for fringe-benefit programs. Before deciding to grant a 5-cent per hour wage increase, management can estimate quite accurately the resulting additional labor costs it will incur. But this is not true when it is contemplating benefit programs. For example:

1. The cost of a pension plan is directly influenced by the rate of turnover. If a great many employees leave the company before they are eligible for their pensions, and if the plan does not provide for vesting, the costs will be relatively low. But if most employees stay with the company until pension benefits become due, the costs will be relatively high.

2. Similarly, the cost of sick-pay benefits depends on the incidence of illness; the cost of severance pay on the number of employees dropped from the employment rolls.

3. Many states review the turnover record of a given company in determining how much the company should be assessed for the unemployment insurance fund. Employers with low turnover pay relatively less than employers with high turnover.

4. Many pension plans used to, and some still do, provide for a certain monthly payment at retirement *less* any social security payments to which the retired worker is entitled. Consequently, as federal law governing social security payments was progressively liberalized, employer contributions to company pension funds were progressively reduced while their OASI tax went up.

5. Changing interest rates in the economy affect the premiums that companies have to pay for privately financed insurance programs.

6. From the extra costs of early retirement must be subtracted the possible savings attributable to higher productivity (from a somewhat younger work force with less resistance to technological change) and lower costs of supplementary unemployment benefits. In addition, costs often go down, assuming some surplus of employees, when a firm retires older workers rather than laying off younger workers. Similarly, extra relief time might increase productivity (see Chapter 2).

7. A company may choose from among many alternative means of financing the more expensive types of benefit programs. Pensions, for example, may be financed on a pay-as-you-go basis, which means that the company incurs a direct cost only as each employee retires and begins to receive pension payments. Other companies "fund" their plans—that is, they make regular payments to a pension account during the working life of each employee (typically, a certain percentage of his income or so many cents per hour). These funds are administered either by the company or jointly by the company and the union. Still other companies engage a bank or an insurance company to serve as trustee of the fund or to sell policies (annuities) with regular premiums, as a means of accumulating the reserves from which payments to retired employees will eventually be made.

These alternative means of financing involve very different costs, produce very different tax benefits, and have very different effects on the capital and liquidity of the organization. Understandably, the difficult decisions that must be made in instituting a coherent benefit program are commonly entrusted to experts.[18]

Management has made some effort to stabilize its financial position vis-à-vis benefit programs by specifying fixed costs at the outset, particularly in plans negotiated with a union. Rather than guarantee certain health and welfare benefits, for example, management promises to contribute 5 cents an hour to a health and welfare fund. The sum thus accumulated is invested at going market rates, and the income is used to defray the cost of the benefits. Unions prefer benefit guarantees, however, for reasons that are listed below.

Creeping Costs

One reason for the difficulty in making accurate predictions of the cost of benefit programs is their tendency to grow more and more expensive over time. Pressures from employees who observe "fringe" rewards in other companies, plus the post-World War II inflation, have led to a rapid increase in the cost of pension and insurance plans. Medical services, like most personal services, have risen in cost rapidly, to such an extent that some unions have accused the medical profession of using every increase in medical insurance as the basis for higher fees. There is also a tendency for all benefits to become liberalized over time: vacations, pensions, insurance, and the rest. One recent example is the spread of early retirement provisions which substantially raise the cost of pensions.[19] Furthermore the cost of many benefits goes up auto-

---

[18] See, for example: "Corporate Retirement Policy and Practices," *Studies in Personnel Policy No. 190,* National Industrial Conference Board; Robert Tilove, "Employee Benefit Plans," in *A Decade of Industrial Relations Research,* N. Chamberlain, *et al.,* eds. (New York: Harper & Row, 1958), pp. 146-173 (Tilove's footnotes at the end of this article provide an excellent bibliography of materials in this field); "Computing the Cost of Fringe Benefits," *Studies in Personnel Policy No. 128,* National Industrial Conference Board.

[19] It is estimated that costs of pensions can easily triple under these circumstances. See "The Drift to Early Retirement," *Fortune* (May 1965), pp. 112 ff.

matically as wages and salaries rise. For instance, overtime payments and vacation benefits calculated on the basis of the employee's regular salary increase in direct proportion to increases in his salary level. One company estimates that each 1-cent hourly wage increase brings with it a 0.3-cent increase in fringe benefits.

NEED FOR CONSTANT REVIEW

If management is to insure that its benefit programs are working out in practice as originally planned, it must subject them to constant review.

> A company introduces 10-minute rest periods to reduce worker fatigue. Checks must be made to determine whether these rest periods are being maintained at 10 minutes or are being gradually lengthened, and whether the time chosen is most appropriate for combating fatigue. (In one company, employees were able to convince their supervisor that they should take their rest period as an end-of-the-day wash-up break; here the break no longer served its original purpose.)
>
> A company broadens its health program to include psychotherapy. After the new program has been put into effect, the company should review its records to determine how many employees are using the program and whether it seems to be worth the expense as compared to other benefits that might be obtained at the same cost.
>
> A company that provides extensive out-patient services may decide to alter its insurance plan in order to discourage the use of expensive hospital facilities and encourage the use of clinics.

Periodic surveys of employee opinion might disclose quite different orders of preference among various fringe benefits and between "fringes" and direct pay than management has been assuming. For example, in one recent survey sick leave was preferred over more costly pension and pay raise options. Life insurance ranked quite low while pension improvements were preferred about as much as pay raises.[20]

Impact on Employee Incentives

We have already noted that fringe benefits may shift the balance of incentives away from concern with present performance toward an exaggerated interest in tenure and even in retirement. And these programs contain other "built-in" incentives.

In reviewing its experience with benefit programs, management may discover that they are actually working against other company objectives. For example, the provision of fully paid sick leaves may encourage employees to take time off even when they are not ill. This practice impairs production,

---

[20] Stanley Nealey, "Pay and Benefit Preference," *Industrial Relations*, Vol. 3, No. 1 (October 1963), pp. 17-28.

saddles supervision with the continuing problem of finding temporary replacements, and creates a double cost: sick pay plus lost time. Consequently, management may decide to experiment with ways of changing the direction of this built-in incentive. Some companies, for example, have found that by permitting employees to convert unused sick leave into additional holiday pay, costs are reduced and absenteeism discouraged.

Companies in the glass industry have experimented with a scheme whereby individual employee accounts are set up to cover supplementary unemployment benefits. Any money that is not needed for this purpose may be used by the employee to improve his pension payments or even to augment his savings. This arrangement provides employees with an incentive to help management in its efforts to stabilize employment and to perform more effectively in a competitive market.

Steel industry negotiations have introduced another innovation. As we have seen, the costs of company welfare plans are highly uncertain, since they depend on the incidence of illness, accidents, and so forth. Under an agreement worked out between the steel companies and the Steelworkers' Union, increases in certain welfare benefits beyond a specified cents-an-hour amount are to be paid by employees as an alternative to raises in hourly wages stemming from increases in the cost of living.

Sometimes a relatively small group of employees receives much more than their proper share of a benefit plan, to the disadvantage of others. For example, readily available compensation benefits for injuries may actually induce a few workers to injure themselves or to fake accidents. The company should make clear to the entire work force just how the costs of these unnecessary benefits penalize more honest employees. Hopefully, group pressure will be exerted on the offending employees, and management will be supported in its attempts to discourage malingering through disciplinary action.

RELATIONSHIP TO THE OVER-ALL PERSONNEL PROGRAM

Benefit programs are an integral part of the over-all personnel program; they cannot be considered in isolation. As an example, let us look at some of the programs that have been developed to deal with the problem of alcoholism in industry.[21]

Some companies take the position that alcoholism is strictly a private matter, at least until it becomes chronic. When it does become chronic, even a long-service, loyal employee must be discharged, because his problem now affects his job performance.

---

[21] Our discussion here has benefited from the work of Harrison Trice, particularly his informative study, *The Problem Drinker on the Job*, Bulletin No. 40 (Ithaca, N.Y.: New York State School of Industrial and Labor Relations, 1959).

As an alternative to this highly "laissez-faire" approach, other companies now treat alcoholics as *both* a medical *and* a disciplinary problem.

1. They train supervisors to detect incipient cases and to report them to the personnel department.

2. They require the supervisor to discuss the problem with the offending employee, pointing out that his unsatisfactory performance and excessive absenteeism will lead to penalties and eventually to discharge. They have trained counselors or members of the medical staff to encourage the employee to undertake appropriate treatment, making it clear that the company is willing to help but that it is also the responsibility of the employee to help himself.

3. They help the employee arrange for treatment either from trained personnel within the organization (usually medical personnel with special training in problems of alcoholism) or in the community (clinics, groups like A.A., and so forth).

4. They involve the union as an ally in detecting alcoholics and in rehabilitating them. Stewards are sometimes able to convince the employee that he will lose his job unless he gets his problem under control. Early involvement of the union may help forestall grievances later on.

5. They establish clear policies specifying who is responsible for counseling alcoholics and what benefit programs (such as health insurance and leave of absence) are available to afflicted employees.

We have used alcoholism simply as an example of the close relationship that exists between any specific area of employee services and the entire range of company service and personnel programs. Notice that this one example has impinged on a whole range of policies and activities: discipline, supervisory training, union-management relations, the role of staff groups like the employee-relations and medical departments, and the availability of company insurance and leaves of absence. Many policy decisions need to be made concerning who is going to take initiative and responsibility for conducting all the various parts of any service program. In addition, it should be clear that these programs very quickly require significant company expenditures, not only for executive time consumed in their administration, but for record-keeping, special facilities.

CONCLUSION

Managers wise in the ways of personnel relations will undertake a variety of programs to insure that the working environment is conducive to superior job performance. Working conditions, quality of supervision, selection, training, and promotion programs—all are designed to develop a quality of human relationships within the organization that will motivate workers and provide need satisfaction.

But why should management want to do more than simply provide adequate wages and salaries in return for satisfactory job performance? Isn't management's primary role to produce goods or services for some body of consumers? True, employees must be recruited and encouraged to stay with the firm. But isn't it enough just to pay them a fair day's wage for a fair day's work? In this chapter we have tried to present the answers to questions of this sort.[22]

And yet a sound, realistic personnel program cannot be based on the simple prescription: We shall satisfy our employees. Human wants and problems are multitudinous and diverse. The family, the community, and social, religious, and political organizations provide services and assistance that no company could or would want to provide. Child-rearing, religious, and legal problems, for example, are in general outside the province of the firm. Management often observes, however, that there is no sharp dividing line between the job and home, for domestic fears about illness and security have a direct impact on the employee's ability to work effectively.

But management must draw the line somewhere. At what point should it say, "This is an employee problem that we will have nothing to do with?" This is a question that every organization must answer for itself.

Few observers doubt that employee benefit and service programs will continue to grow in importance. A minority says, "I would ask business to revert to the view that labor is a factor of production . . . to buy the labor power of the worker and to leave his psyche alone." [23] Whether or not this attitude seems realistic to you will depend on your attitude toward the whole area of personnel administration. In any case, it seems clear that the problems of administering employee benefit and service programs are among the most difficult personnel problems confronting management.

PROBLEM 1

HIRE THE HANDICAPPED

The ABC Company decides that it will cooperate with a community-wide program to "hire the handicapped." The company agrees to seek out jobs that can be done by workers with eye-and-limb handicaps and to try to recruit suitable candidates from the community.

1. What jobs should be selected? Who decides? According to what criteria?
2. How should pay rates be determined for these jobs? Who decides? According to what criteria?
3. Who makes the hiring decisions? According to what criteria?
4. What additional safety and insurance provisions will be required?
5. What impact will the program have on present employees? On their seniority? On their promotional opportunities?
6. What role, if any, should the union have in implementing the program?

---

[22] For an historical summary of the evolution of fringe benefits see Donna Allen, *Fringe Benefits: Wages or Social Obligation* (Ithaca, New York: New York State School of Industrial and Labor Relations, 1964).

[23] Kerr, *op. cit.*

ANYONE FOR GOLF?

The Wilton Plastic Company is located in a community of 20,000 and employs 500 people. The only golf club in the community is about to go bankrupt and can be purchased at a "sacrifice price."

1. What criteria should the company use in deciding whether to buy the club for its employees?

RELIGIOUS VALUES AND THE COMPANY

Your plant is located in a medium-size midwestern city. It employs 800 workers. You have recently received a petition signed by 200 employees requesting that an annual Catholic holiday be observed as a company-wide paid holiday. At the present time you have six paid holidays. You have only a modest allowance for fringe benefits. Two smaller companies in the area observe this day as a paid holiday, but other large firms in the community do not recognize it as such. About 50 per cent of your employees are Catholics, and half of them have children in parochial schools that give the day off.

1. Should the company grant this request?
2. What additional information would you want before making a decision?
3. What criteria would you use in making the decision?
4. If you granted the day as a holiday, would you be willing to give compensating time off for workers who do not celebrate it? (Christmas is a paid holiday, although 10 per cent of the employees are of Jewish origin.)
5. If the union had made a formal request on this issue during negotiations, would your decision be any different?
6. What difference would it make if this were a branch of a multi-unit company, with other plants in communities in which there were few Catholics?

CREEPING COSTS

The Faraday Insurance Company undertook a blood-bank program in response to what seemed to be an important employee need. When a company employee or a member of his family was ill and required a transfusion, one or more other employees who had voluntarily signed up would be called by the company personnel office to report to one of the local hospitals. Recently, the personnel department has noted that the costs of this program are greater than originally anticipated. Often a great many telephone calls have to be made before a donor can be located. This task requires almost the full-time services of one clerk. Moreover, some donors do not return to work until the next day, even though the transfusion has been given in the morning, and overtime replacements have to be brought in.

1. How would you weigh the cost of this program against the benefits it provides?
2. Is there any way of cutting costs without nullifying the advantages of the program and without damaging the company's reputation?

728

MANAGEMENT'S RESPONSIBILITIES

It may seem strange to elevate a single chapter to the level of a "part" of our book. But it seemed appropriate to us to "step back" from the pressures of day-to-day human-relations problems to ask some broader questions. Although it would be presumptuous of us to refer to this last chapter as a philosophical treatment of "management's responsibilities in dealing with people," we have at least tried to suggest some of the long-range implications of these responsibilities. At some point the administrator has to ask himself what *values* he will observe in making human-relations decisions. How should he weigh "human" against "profit" considerations? Should he even try to weigh them? What is the meaning of "social responsibility" and what are the organizational problems of giving effect to these responsibilities? These are not easy questions to answer, although many critics of business, and many businessmen themselves, are quick to criticize contemporary trends in the personnel and human-relations field. Many of these criticisms are reviewed here.

Management's Responsibilities in Dealing with People

Unlike such specialties as electrical engineering or finance, management involves *human beings*. The engineer, for instance, need never give a thought to the impact his maintenance program will have on the "personality" of his equipment. The accountant busies himself with tractable, obedient figures. But the manager must keep himself constantly alert to the impact of his personnel administration on the employee as an individual and as a citizen. And he must understand the subtle relationships that prevail between corporate efficiency and employee satisfaction.

HISTORICAL PERSPECTIVE

Private Charity

For hundreds of years, managers have been aware of their special obligations to employees. The early New England textile manufacturer, for example, often provided elaborate opportunities for his "charges" (typically young girls) to worship and to gain an education. Some owners, of course, were flagrantly paternalistic—eager to extend benefits in order to receive praise for their generosity. Rockefeller and Carnegie are today better known for their philanthropy than for their often ruthless business practices. Even the worst of the "robber barons" might provide housing facilities, grant Christmas gifts, and distribute other forms of largess to those who worked for him. Yet much of this philanthropy was personal (rather than corporate) charity, and benefits were given as gifts, not rights. By the 1920's many companies had institutionalized these obligations by establishing a special department—the personnel department—to deal with the legitimate needs of their employees. ("Legitimate" needs, as we have seen, can be defined in many different ways.)

The personnel department was sometimes regarded as a buffer between management and workers, as the workers' "representative" that could be counted on to intervene on their behalf. Although management often encouraged this attitude simply to keep the unions out, there was also a sincere feeling that every organization needed a "conscience," someone who could speak for employees and who would be responsible for their welfare. Many managers genuinely believed that their decisions should be guided by concern for human beings as well as by a desire for profit maximization. In making layoffs, companies often gave special consideration to men with families or with long service, even though they might be less efficient than the men actually dismissed.

Gestures of good will and efforts to be just were haphazard and erratic. John Jones, whose needs happened to come to the attention of top management, received excellent treatment; Gus Smith, who was not quite so lucky, lost his job, even though his claim for consideration was as valid as Jones's. Some personnel directors proved effective spokesmen for employees; others had neither the interest nor the ability to do so.

Cynics argued that these humanitarian policies were only a reflection of management's deep-seated opposition to unions, or evidence of a selfish desire to raise morale in order to boost productivity. Clearly, however, many managers went beyond dollars-and-cents considerations and were genuinely altruistic.

How Contemporary Managers View Their Role

Management attitudes have become more complex in recent years. Top managements of many corporations have become self-perpetuating groups who own relatively few shares of stock in the corporations they control. Since management's control can no longer be legitimatized purely on the basis of ownership, many managers are now seeking other bases on which to justify their powerful economic role. Increasingly managers look upon themselves as professionals, and as we saw in Chapter 3, professionals traditionally concern themselves with ethical bases for their actions.

Corporate objectives are less clear than they once were. Growth, share of the market, company (and managerial) prestige are partially supplanting the goal of maximizing profits, and some managers claim that their function is to act as trustees for a number of interests (some of which admittedly conflict). It is not uncommon for managers to talk of being mediators among stockholders, employees, customers, and the community rather than solely representatives of the stockholders.[1]

On the other hand, many sincere businessmen feel that business should not pose as the guardian of the general welfare. They, too, argue on practical and moral grounds.[2]

---

[1] Earl F. Cheit, "The New Place of Business: Why Managers Cultivate Social Responsibility," in Earl F. Cheit, ed., *The Business Establishment* (New York: Wiley, 1964), pp. 152, 156.

[2] In a letter to *The New York Times* (Western Edition, Nov. 8, 1963, p. 8), Roger Blough, Chairman of the Board of U.S. Steel, explained his attitude towards the suggestion that his company should play a positive role in solving racial problems in Birmingham, Alabama:

"As individuals we can exercise what influence we may have as citizens, but for a corporation to attempt to exert any kind of economic compulsion to achieve a particular end in the social area seems to

First, they claim that management cannot mediate among the competing claims of stockholders, employees, suppliers, and the community. The business-man owes his first responsibility to the owners of the business, which means that he must devote primary attention to profits and efficiency. When he takes other interests into account, he abdicates that responsibility. In fact, only by concentrating on profits and efficiency can he bestow the greatest benefits on the community as a whole. These observers argue that only then will he make economic use of the company's personnel and material resources, with maxi-mum production and minimum costs.

Yet the close interrelationship between business and society seems more clearly recognized by businessmen today than it was before the Great De-pression and World War II—and this is true even in industries not closely affected by government purchasing and government regulatory commissions. Many businessmen—more commonly in some circles than in others—are be-ginning to develop a sense of having, as a class, a special responsibility (call it *noblesse oblige* if you like) to behave in the interests of the national welfare, to function as good citizens.

There is also a more practical motivation. With improved and widespread public education and effective mass communication media, public opinion is a more potent pressure on business. The alert business leader recognizes that if he is to maintain reasonable autonomy in decision-making, he must maintain public good will. As the Celanese Corporation announced:

> The company proudly cherishes its freedom to innovate and considers that corporate self-discipline, like personal self-discipline, is the chief condition of retaining that freedom.[3]

Ever since Taylor's scientific management, executives also have been en-deavoring to increase their rationality. Objectivity is also another hallmark of professionalism. For example, it is felt that promotion and salary increases ought to be awarded on the basis of merit, not friendship,[4] since this policy is rational in terms of the welfare of the business. The emphasis on behavioral sciences as a guide to solving human-relations problems is, in fact, an emphasis on what is presumed to be an orderly, scientific way of approaching problems in contrast to an emotional, personal-preference mode of solution.

Another aspect of this rationality is the greater use of rules and general policies. Both devices avoid the complexities of deciding each individual case by itself and the difficulty of justifying such decisions. In the broadest sense, it is a shift towards the rule of law. Leaves of absence and vacations tend to be granted in terms of general rules rather than managerial whim. Of course,

---

me to be quite beyond what a corporation should do, and quite beyond what any corporation can do . . . I believe that any attempt by a private corporation like U.S. Steel to impose its views, its beliefs and its will upon the community by resorting to economic compulsion or coercion would be repugnant to our American constitutional concepts, and that appropriate steps to correct this abuse of corporate power would be universally demanded by public opinion and by Government."

[3] As cited in Cheit, *op. cit.*, p. 188.

[4] The sociologists call this shift from personal to impersonal decision-making a move from *particularism* to *universalism*.

union and government pressure for written contracts and better record-keeping have both been spurs in this direction.

Finally, professional managers tend to take a longer-run point of view. Although good human relations may not show up immediately in lower costs and higher profits, it is asserted that over the long run, investments in a more satisfied work force will show a return, just as do capital investments in any other area.

Unfortunately, these various sources of increased managerial awareness of human-relations responsibilities may not always provide mutually consistent answers. Decisions that could be justified by asserting that management has certain *social* responsibilities as a good citizen may not be justifiable in terms of long-run profitability. But such problems will be less abstract if we look at some actual cases. We shall see in the two cases following, therefore, a more professional concept of the managerial role does not provide any automatic solutions to the complex problems of human relations in the modern organization.

Here are two examples of the problems of applying the concepts of management's responsibility for human relations. In the first, larger problem, the field of race relations, we shall view some of the organizational realities that make difficult the translation of broad policy into practice. In the second, the Duffy Case, we shall see that decision-making in what first appears to be a small problem is made difficult by the large number of tough questions that have to be answered (questions on which data and behavioral principles are not easy to find).

MANAGEMENT'S RESPONSIBILITIES IN THE FIELD OF RACE RELATIONS [5]

What is management's responsibility in the area of race relations? Does management in a free enterprise system have any responsibility other than to stay within the law and to maximize profits? And if management does have an added responsibility, is it enough to be scrupulously color-blind and always to select and promote the best man? Or should management go further, actively seek Negro applicants, and offset the previous discrimination against Negroes with reverse discrimination which favors them? If so, by how much?

Most managers will tell you that the company policy is to treat people *objectively,* not to allow race (or religion or national origin) to be a determinant of how individuals are treated by the organization. Further, many have a sense of *social responsibility* to do something in the race relations field to further the public good. Although these beliefs have existed for a number of

---

[5] The material in this section is drawn from a research project conducted by George Strauss in the San Francisco Bay area in 1964. It is adapted from an article by George Strauss, "How Management Views Its Race Relation Responsibilities," to appear in Arthur Ross and Herbert Hill, eds., *Employment, Race and Poverty* (New York: Harcourt, Brace & World, 1967).

years in many organizations, there is rather impressive evidence that Negroes have been widely discriminated against. To explain this gap between ideology (belief) and practice, we must apply some of our knowledge of how organizations function. We shall also review some of the problems of implementing policy decisions in this area.

Why the Discrepancy?

At least three reasons can be given for management's failure to translate its feelings into action.

1. Obligations towards Negroes are relatively low on management's perceived list of obligations.
2. Few managers see themselves as discriminating or treating Negroes unfairly.
3. In some cases top management's policy is not translated into action at lower levels.

Low priority of obligation.   Though management does recognize moral and social obligations, purely business obligations usually come first. Until recently, management tended to keep its obligations toward Negroes primarily on the eleemosynary level (for example, grants to Negro colleges), and to compartmentalize these obligations from purely business ones. Though many managers—particularly in personnel departments—may have felt a moral obligation to hire Negroes, they also felt a practical obligation not to stir up present employees or customers. And in this case the practical obligation came first, since there were real fears (some justified) that introducing Negroes would lead to "trouble."

Modern organization theory has rediscovered the old saw that it is the squeaking wheel which gets the grease. Though management may try to solve problems on a rational basis, it doesn't attempt to solve all problems at once; instead, it tends to go from crisis to crisis and the span of attention given to any one problem may be fairly short. Obtaining acceptance of Negro employees requires that management give up some of its limited supply of time and energy; in the past other problems seemed more urgent.

Management's concept of social responsibility is strongly influenced by its perception of what the public wants. Management would like to be socially responsible, but normally only to the extent that its actions are noncontroversial. Managers want to be considered good citizens, but being a good citizen is often viewed as adjusting to the community's values rather than trying to change them. Until recently, managers believed that, on the whole, the community wanted discrimination.

No perception of discrimination.   Few managers perceived themselves as being discriminatory or irrational and nonobjective in their selection policy. Many were surprised to discover that their firms hired no Negroes. Management just did not see the Negro applicant as a potential skilled tradesman, salesman, or executive. Stereotypes (see Chapter 10) such as these were easy to maintain because in many cases very few qualified Negroes would apply for such jobs—both because there were in fact very few qualified Negroes and because those qualified realized there would be little point in applying.

Poor communications. In some cases, discrimination has occurred because a sincerely felt top-management policy not to discriminate has not been implemented at operating levels. In a hierarchy, certainly, such policies are not self-enforcing. In most cases they represent sharp contrasts with past practices and many employees will tend to resist them if they can. Since there is such a sharp conflict between creed and deed in this area and pious platitudes are frequently uttered, it is understandable that many employees are uncertain about what is being communicated, about whether these new policies are to be taken seriously.

Lower management is subject to a great deal of pressure: to maximize production, to minimize labor expense, to maintain quality, to eliminate grievances, to prevent accidents, and so forth. Many of these pressures exerted by various staff groups as well as upper management are mutually inconsistent: For example, an increase in production is usually attained at the cost of higher labor expense, more accidents, and so forth. The smart subordinate learns what is really important, emphasizes these matters, and tries to "get by" in other areas. In a sense every executive is like a juggler, tossing balls so fast that he cannot stop. Some of these balls are heavy balls and if he drops them it really hurts his toes. Other balls are light and it doesn't matter what happens to them. The supervisor learns that if he drops the ball marked "production" or "costs" he quickly gets into trouble. But in the past no one really cared if he dropped the ball marked "equal employment."

Thus, when management really wants to get something accomplished, it must do more than issue a policy statement or make a token gesture. It must adjust the rewards and punishments, the pressures within management, to be consistent with these goals. It must change *controls.* (*Cf.* Chapter 15.)

The Impact of Recent
Civil-Rights Pressures

The foregoing should help us understand the impact of recent pressures from Negro action groups and the government.

These pressures have brought the problem to the forefront of management's attention, for it is hard to ignore a chorus of chanting pickets at your front door. Pressures help translate moral obligations into practical necessities and raise the Negro question quite a few notches higher in management's scale of priorities.

These pressures and associated governmental actions have spelled out in much greater detail the social and moral obligations of businessmen. Those businessmen who believe that their only obligation is to stay within the law, now know that the law outlaws discrimination. Those who wish to remain "good citizens" now know that the obligation set for them by the more articulate representatives of society calls for them to hire an appreciable number of Negroes at all levels of the organization.

In addition, there is a certain tendency to follow the leader among management groups. Once the pattern is set by leading firms, other companies may follow because it is the thing to do.

The requirement of government-contract agencies (and Negro action groups) that employers take a periodic census of the number of Negroes employed, by level and occupation provides management with "statistical control data." Executives can no longer plead lack of knowledge of what is happening in their own organization. And management always pays greater attention to a problem once it can be stated in terms of numbers, as we saw in Chapter 15.

There is also considerable feeling that business should not botch up the Negro question the way it did the union question in the 1930's. It is felt that if business does not take the lead in this area, then the government and civil-rights groups will be able to place restrictions on business policy which business will never be able to remove. A top executive was blunt: "If we don't take the responsibility here and handle it our way, we will create a monster which we won't be able to handle in the future."

Thus, we have seen how a sense of responsibility does not translate itself automatically into organizational change. But even when resistance to change is breached, a number of difficult policy questions remained to be solved. These pose dilemmas for which there are no easy answers.

Color Blindness
or Affirmative Action?

Let's look more closely at the problem of translating nondiscrimination into management action. Management can be neutral and "color-blind" in its policies. It can step up efforts to recruit Negroes without lowering hiring standards. It can pick Negroes for job vacancies even though they are not the *best*-qualified applicants, just as long as they meet minimum standards. It can provide special training for those who don't meet minimum standards at the moment, but might eventually be qualified. And it can lower its present minimum standards to accommodate those who will never meet them.

Generally speaking, the argument focuses on two alternatives. Some believe that it is enough to be color-blind and scrupulously impartial. Others feel their companies should take affirmative steps to recruit and hire Negroes.

Color blindness. Those who believe in color blindness, or neutrality, recognize the legitimacy of the nondiscrimination argument (and some will admit that perhaps they had been inadvertently discriminating in the past), but they feel that reverse discrimination in favor of Negroes is just as unfair as discrimination against them.

Affirmative action.   Affirmative action is demanded because color blindness rarely results in integration. "You can post an equal-employment sign for a hundred years," the director of an employers' association remarked, "and a hundred years from now, there will still be no change in the work force."

The traditional recruitment channels—word of mouth, relatives of present employees, union hiring halls, better (that is, white) schools and colleges—rarely reach Negroes. Even when Negroes hear of vacancies they seldom apply for jobs which past history has taught are not open to them.

For a number of jobs now opening up for Negroes, there are few, if any, trained, qualified candidates. If Negroes have never had the opportunity to gain experience or training, obviously there will be no experienced or trained Negroes available. Educational requirements tend to preserve racial imbalance because of the relatively low proportion of Negro high school and college graduates. Even so-called objective intelligence and aptitude tests may contain built-in cultural bias which tends to reduce their effectiveness as a predictor of Negro ability.

Thus, if a company is to hire any Negroes at all for some jobs, it must lower or drop its requirements of experience, education, or training, revamp or eliminate its testing procedures, and—if qualified Negroes still cannot be found—provide training so that Negroes can obtain these qualifications.

Does affirmative action mean reverse discrimination? This is largely a semantic question. Those who are committed to the principle of integration normally use the euphemism "affirmative action" in public, but in private admit that this involves reverse discrimination, at least in the sense that opportunities are granted to Negroes which are not made available to whites and that where two candidates are equally qualified, the Negro will get the job.

Which is the socially responsible, the long-run profit-maximizing course?

SATISFACTION VS. PROFITABILITY

Rules, contract clauses, and even behavioral science findings often do not furnish a ready answer to two critically important questions: What are the legitimate needs of employees, and when is it justifiable to put those needs aside in favor of the profit needs of the company? Unfortunately, most personnel problems still cannot be resolved simply by reading the company manual or the union contract. And the most important problems of all have a dismaying tendency to crop up between the rules, in the uncharted territory where there are no clear precedents, no obvious "right" or "wrong" answers.

The Duffy Case

Bill Duffy is the head of a clerical department in a large brokerage office. Most of the work is relatively routine though of considerable importance to the company. Duffy's department has always been known for its high morale and for its ability to maintain work schedules.

Duffy started with the company right after finishing high school. Although he is just celebrating his 50th birthday, he has already accumulated about 30 years of seniority. In many ways, he seems much older than his years. He lacks stamina and his thinking processes are slower than those of many of his older colleagues.

Over the past year, the responsibilities of managing the department have been pretty much taken over by the assistant department head, Joe Jenkins. When a difficult problem comes up, the clerks now turn to Joe for an answer. Duffy continues to sign papers that need the signature of the department head, and he is consulted as a matter of form on all major policy questions. But Jenkins has become the real head of the department.

Top management considered Duffy's case at a recent meeting. A couple of the men present thought that the company should encourage him to accept early retirement, although they recognized that this would be a serious psychological and financial blow to him. His retirement benefits would be less than half of what they would be if he continued to work until 65. It might be possible to demote him to a less responsible position, but there were no jobs open that would fit his capacities. After reconsidering the matter, management decided to retain Duffy in his present position, feeling that too "harsh" an approach to the problem would prompt substantial dissatisfaction in the organization.

Nagging Questions

The Duffy Case presents us with a number of more explicit questions than did the question of employment policies in the racial area. These are questions involving all sorts of intangibles, conjectures, and risks.

Equity Considerations and Individual Satisfaction.

1. How much does the company "owe" an employee who has given 30 years of loyal service? What obligation does it have to him?

2. Can this obligation be met in financial terms? What is the relationship between Duffy's dissatisfaction, on the one hand, with being only a "figure head" and his satisfaction, on the other hand, with maintaining his salary and title?

3. Should management adopt a more liberal policy toward early retirement for long-service employees who become "disabled"?

4. Is it fair to Jenkins, whose salary is approximately 30 per cent lower than Duffy's, to let him assume the responsibilities of a managerial job without granting him both the prestige and the economic rewards that normally go with it?

Organization and Profit Considerations.

1. What effect would Duffy's forced retirement have on the morale and performance of other long-service employees? Would it be more harmful than their realization that inefficiency and ineptness are protected by the fiction of having a formal department head and a real one? What impact will management's decision have on employees' attitudes toward opportunities for promotion?

2. What would be the long-run costs of establishing more liberal early-retirement benefits? How would these costs compare with the apparent savings offered by the present policy?

3. What is the effect on department efficiency of having two managers? Can Duffy's salary be justified in terms of the contribution he is making?

4. Will management's decision have any effect on the company's ability to recruit highly motivated young men?

These are only a few of the highly complex short- and long-run questions raised by this case. There are two fundamental problems: (1) How much importance should management ascribe to efficiency as against human satisfaction, and where does one draw the line? And (2), assuming that management can resolve this first problem, what are the best ways of achieving optimal efficiency and human satisfaction?

What at first glance appears to be a single organization problem is normally intertwined with a whole host of other policy problems. This case, for example, is tied in with the company's promotion policy as well as with its policies on fringe benefits (pensions and severance pay). Also involved are job evaluation, recruitment, organizational structure, individual needs and motivations, and the attitudes of the work group.

The manager must constantly seek to resolve the diverse and conflicting claims of individuals and groups both in the short run and in the long run. And yet, since he cannot ascribe exact weights to each factor, or predict the future with any real accuracy, he must rely heavily on intuition, personal judgment, and probability.

Nor do employee needs and company needs fit into neat, separate compartments. There is no simple answer to what course of action is "equitable" or what decisions will improve "efficiency," for the two objectives are intimately associated. There are very few decisions that affect employee satisfaction which do not also have a direct bearing on work efficiency.

Management in recent years undoubtedly has begun to show greater concern for the welfare of its employees. True, strong unions, government regulations, and labor shortages have contributed heavily to this shift in attitude, but enlightened executives are sincere in their acceptance of human relationships as a vital part of managerial responsibility. In fact, the human-relations movement has profoundly altered the qualities that have traditionally been associated with the successful business leader. No longer is he judged solely on his drive, ambition, decisiveness, or ability to make money. Now he is also expected to develop cooperative, satisfying relationships within the organization.

Both the economic position and the psychological position of subordinates have improved tremendously over the last generation. The emphasis on human relations has tended to take the bite out of authority and the harshness out of arbitrary rules; it has promoted compassion and dignity at the work place. There is less likelihood of arbitrary discharge, less discrimination in handing out rewards. Work loads are easier and supervision is fairer. At least in larger companies, employees have considerable opportunity to protest inequities through union or company grievance procedures. No one would pretend that we have achieved Utopia, but tremendous progress has been made.

In recent years, however, the human-relations approach to management has been subjected to a sustained and unexpectedly strong attack from observers who stress efficiency and productivity above all other management objectives. These criticisms, which have come from many sources, reduce themselves to the following charges:

1. The human-relations approach tends to complicate what are essentially very simple problems. All that is required in dealing with people is honest common sense and the application of the golden rule.

2. Computers will solve the problems, not managers.

3. The human-relations approach leads management to interfere in the personal life of employees, to take over community functions, and to encroach on areas that are outside the province of the business organization. It manipulates people and dupes them into accepting changes that really are against their best interests.

4. By overemphasizing people at the expense of productivity, the human-relations approach may prove disastrous to the organization.

Let us look briefly at each of these charges. Since they are so commonly leveled, the student of management—whether in the university or the business firm—must expect to run across them in one form or another.

Does the Human-Relations Approach
Complicate Simple Problems?

Recently in a talk before a group of businessmen, one of the authors tried to explain how complicated human relations really are; he emphasized all the factors that the manager should take into account before making a decision involving people. He felt reasonably proud of the presentation, but complacency was shattered during the discussion period by the following comment from the floor: "Professor, doesn't everything you say boil down to the golden rule? I've had 40 years' experience in industry and I've found that the important thing is to be honest and sincere with people. Show an interest in them and you'll never have any human-relations problems."

But are sincerity and good will and even common sense enough? We think not.

The findings of modern psychology suggest that applying the golden rule is just too simple an approach, mainly because it assumes that everyone has identical needs. In the Duffy case, for example, a great deal of insight into the total organizational situation would be required before management could make a truly ethical decision. Is it more ethical to transfer an older employee to a lower-paying job, or to terminate his employment and give him early-retirement benefits? What does common sense tell you?

Unless management is aware of the impact of each decision on the individual and on the group, it cannot know whether it is acting to the advantage or to the detriment of the members of the organization. It is not enough to apply the golden rule or to ask, "How would I want to be treated in a similar situation?" This projection of oneself into the position of the other person may lead to unwise and highly unjust actions.

Many disastrous mistakes are made with the best of intentions. A kind-hearted supervisor decides not to penalize an employee who has family troubles even though he is persistently late and fails to meet production standards. The situation grows worse and worse until finally the employee is discharged. Were the supervisor's intentions good? Of course they were. But they led him to injure both the individual and the organization. No businessman really lets concern for others control everything he does. Were he completely motivated by charity and altruism, he would never try to take business away from a competitor and he would never discipline a subordinate. What the ethically motivated businessman *does* believe is that he should take into account the welfare of others *along with* other factors.

Won't Computers
Solve These Problems?

With recent developments in the management sciences and computer technology, it is widely believed that many subjects which now take managerial resources and time will be handled in routine fashion by data-processing and operations-analysis techniques.[6] It has even been argued that many human-relations problems are complicated needlessly by unthinking managers or those seeking to make work for themselves to justify larger staffs.

However, in reviewing the previous two cases, it does not appear that these problems lend themselves to the decision-making techniques that are useful in deciding what size batch of a variety of components to manufacture or where to locate a warehouse. There were such a multiplicity of considerations, each of which is laden with value judgments, and such heavy requirements for personal skill in the execution of any decision reached (or even in securing adequate data) that it is unlikely machines will ever do the job. In fact, in the future, because computers will handle effectively some other technical aspects of the managerial job, it is likely that an increasing proportion of the managerial work load will be in the human-relations area.

Does the Human-Relations Approach
Involve Manipulation and Interference?

Managers are often charged with trying to manipulate their employees.

> In many cases human relations has been used or is intended to be used, to manipulate, to adjust people to what the boss thinks is reality, to make them conform to a pattern that seems logical from the top down, to make them accept unquestioningly what we tell them.[7]
>
> The ... evil of the "human relations" fad is its repeated violation of the dignity of the individual. It becomes a technique for manipulating people. There are certain areas that should be free of the boss's review and his standards of performance. Today, we stick our noses into other people's business, analyzing their motives and judging their lives. We should be able to take a man at face value and not always fret about what he really means. Too many of us are trying to be little tin Freuds ... consciously trying to be a gentleman. If it doesn't come from the heart, it is phony.[8]

It is claimed that such techniques as nondirective interviewing and group decision-making are designed to get employees to do things they don't want to do, or at least that they don't realize they are doing. A familiar example is the supervisor who pretends to be interested in his subordinates and to consult with them, but only in order to disguise his essentially authoritarian approach (see Chapter 8).

Also, these critics insist, excessive concern over the individual usually leads to paternalism, with all its attendant evils. Attempts to plumb the employee's personal feelings and attitudes thrust the company into areas that are properly the province of the individual, the family, and the community. (The union adds

---

[6] For a sophisticated view of the impact of these new techniques on the managerial job see Herbert Simon, *The New Science of Management Decision Making* (New York: Harper and Row, 1960).

[7] Peter F. Drucker, "Human Relations: How Far Do We Have to Go?" *Management Record* (March 1959).

[8] Malcolm P. McNair, "Too Much 'Human Relations'?" *Look* (October 28, 1958).

that only an organization which is directly responsible to workers—that is, the union itself—can protect the individual's welfare consistently and vigorously.)

Fortunately, most employees are quick to spot insincerity. Gimmicks and deceit are soon exposed, as some companies have learned to their sorrow. The only group that is duped is management itself, which has underestimated the intelligence of its employees.

We see little danger that brainwashing, mass persuasion, or subliminal suggestion will win much acceptance in organization administration. The power of suggestion may be quite effective in persuading a customer to buy one brand of cigarettes rather than another—but this is because cigarette brands are not very different and because most customers have no vested interest in which brand they smoke. Brainwashing may change basic attitudes in prisoner-of-war camps where the individual is isolated from alternative sources of information. In the typical work situation, however, personnel decisions are of immediate importance to the people involved; employees do have a vested interest in what happens to them on the job. Further, few companies can isolate their employees from other points of view. Whatever the company or the individual supervisor says and does is discussed and criticized by the employees on the job, by the union, and by other groups in the community. Management's pronouncements can always be checked against the viewpoints of others. Clearly, the employee is not likely to succumb to propaganda; indeed, his suspicion is often so great that it is hard for management to get the truth across to him (see Chapter 10), let alone falsehood.

Some critics argue that the supervisor is resorting to manipulation whenever he tries to minimize conflict and gain acceptance for a point of view or for some change. But is there anything objectionable about efforts to weigh alternative courses of action and to select the one that avoids personnel problems? Is it not, rather, highly desirable for management to enlarge its perspective to include rational solutions to its human-relations problems? In short, are not human relations deserving of as much careful attention as engineering and finance?

Do Human Relations
Impair Managerial Efficiency?

"Management has been sold a bill of goods by human relations. In the process of coddling people it has lost sight of its major objective—getting work accomplished profitably. Management's job is to get the work done and to let employees worry about themselves."

This is the considered view of many critics of the human-relations movement in management.[9]

---

[9] Many criticisms of this sort have appeared in the *Harvard Business Review*; for instance: Malcolm McNair, "Thinking Ahead: What Price Human Relations?" Vol. 35, No. 2 (March-April 1957), pp. 15-39; Robert N. McMurry, "The Case for Benevolent Autocracy," Vol. 36, No. 1 (January-February 1958), pp. 82-90.

To assess the validity of this charge, we must place the problem in historical perspective. Only a short time ago business was being accused of neglecting personnel problems. Now it is being accused of ignoring business objectives in its attempts to "coddle" people. Why this remarkable shift?

Many companies discovered only quite recently that they had "people" problems. Years ago, when businesses were much smaller, most managers (who were also the owners) knew their employees personally and were able to handle problems informally. Turnover was not particularly worrisome, for good replacements were readily available. Unions were weak. Perhaps most important, there was no professional concern with the job of management— certainly not with personnel administration. Businessmen busied themselves with buying and selling in the marketplace and gave little thought to organizational problems. No manager considered himself inept or ineffective simply because he had high turnover or labor strife—this was the fault of weak foremen or troublemakers in the work force.

Today, businesses are large and impersonal. Trained employees are harder to replace, and alert unions are ready to transmute management's mistakes into costly grievances. It is generally accepted that all levels of management have a continuing responsibility for solving human-relations problems—that these are not just transitory phenomena or the result of bad luck.

In the course of this rapid transformation of the executive into a professional, and this rapid acceptance of personnel administration as a general management responsibility, it is not surprising that many mistakes have been made. Naive managers seeking quick and easy solutions have been victimized by charlatans. Companies have purchased expensive suggestion systems, engaged enthusiastic speakers, prepared expensive give-away brochures, and have footed the bill for whole kits of supervisory gimmicks in the mistaken belief that there were simple, quasi-mechanical techniques for solving employee-relations problems. Rather than try to understand the functioning of organizations, the nature of groups, and the importance of individual differences, some companies have gone overboard in embracing such cure-alls as "participative management" or "public speaking for everyone." There has been a regrettable follow-the-leader fashion-conscious acceptance of anything called "human relations."

Some managers have simplified human relations to the point of absurdity. They insist that good management is just a matter of liking people and inducing them to like you. "Getting to know your people" is the sure guarantee of success, perhaps tempered by this warning: "Don't get pushy about production; it annoys people."

The principle of two-way communication has been particularly abused. Some authorities seem to assume that all trouble within the organization is purely and simply the result of "misunderstanding." Jones misinterprets Brown's motives and Brown fails to realize that Jones is operating within a different frame of reference. The moment the communication dam is broken, understanding will flood through the organization.

Given this simple definition of the management problem, one might well ask why improvement has been so long in forthcoming. A ready answer is that the human being is recalcitrant, hard to change. Some ardent "human-relationists" throw the whole problem right onto the psychiatrist's couch. There has been a mushrooming of quasi-therapeutic cures for insensitive, uncommunicative people: role-playing, group therapy of one kind or another, sensitivity training, nondirective counseling. Apparently the hope is to change the manager's personality, to make him show more "consideration," to induce him to be less autocratic.

Many of these techniques have a useful role to play, but they may be over-emphasized. What is wrong with this approach? At least three things, in our opinion:

1. True, some problems are created and others are magnified by poor communications. But many problems cannot be solved by better understanding alone. They can be solved only by carefully wrought changes in technology, work procedure, organizational structure, or personnel policies.

2. True, counseling and training may improve communications and may even help people develop skills—and that is all to the good. But changing personality itself is an expensive, arduous job, with a poor prognosis.

3. Human relations is not an end in itself. The purpose of business is not to make people happy (though some have argued otherwise) but to achieve its over-all goals of productivity and profitability. And the purpose of *human relations* is to help management elicit the cooperation of people in working toward those goals.

Although we decry the uncritical acceptance of human relations as a magic cure, we feel that it is a mistake to go to the opposite extreme. The manager cannot be concerned about getting work done without also being concerned about people. Even in the fully automated factory or office, important jobs must still be done by human beings. Their willingness to coordinate their efforts with those of other people and with the system and equipment developed by engineers is an essential component of a successful organization.

In his efforts to conquer disease, man has resorted to charms, incantations, and witch doctors. But no one would suggest that just because he put his faith in gimmicks and myths in the past he would be better off today to ignore the problems of illness and concentrate on "living."

The manager cannot ignore the human-relations problems of his organization and concentrate exclusively on getting the work out. Getting the work out depends on getting cooperation out of people both inside and outside the formal boundaries of the organization. The future will see increasing, not decreasing, attention paid to the human-relations problems of the organization.

We hope you have not been discouraged by our survey of the human problems inherent in the organization. As most managers have learned, there are no perfect, final solutions to these problems. Every area we have explored is rich in challenges to the decision-making skill of the executive.

Only when we place these problems in the larger context of American life does their full significance become apparent. The individual human being, and his opportunities for development and satisfaction, have a high value in our culture. We expect our institutions to provide him with a chance to express and satisfy his needs and to fulfill his capabilities. The evolution of private organizations that are consistent with and complementary to our democratic political institutions is a high achievement in itself. Throughout the ages, man has struggled to achieve individual freedom without jeopardizing the safety and welfare of others, and to engage in productive work that will satisfy the economic and physical needs of himself and society. Not unexpectedly, severe conflicts arise between the needs of the individual and the needs of the groups and organizations that make up society. As the administrator makes choices between organizational efficiency and the satisfaction of individual needs, he is acting as a mediator in this inevitable, and, we believe, socially useful, divergence of interests.

PROBLEM 1

MARY'S AILMENTS

The Ames Department Store prides itself on the excellence of its Medical Department. All new employees are required to take a rigid pre-employment physical. Because of an error, Mary Fillipi came to work as a salesgirl several days before completing her physical exam. She was a charming person and immediately made fast friends among everyone in her department including the buyer and assistant buyer.

Thus, everyone was disturbed when Mary received a notice from the Personnel Department that she could not be hired because the medical examination had disclosed two rather serious internal ailments.

The buyer represented the department in requesting that Personnel make an exception in this case because (1) the girl had already been working a week and (2) she promised to become, not only one of the most well-liked employees, but also an excellent salesgirl. Further, the employees, whose sympathies had been aroused, felt that Mary was being discriminated against because of a health problem when, in fact, Ames should help people with problems.

Personnel turned down the request on the grounds that the hiring requirement of passing the medical examination was a fixed, long-established company policy. Also, as the Director of Personnel put it,

"The employees should be told that the store's ability to pay unusually generous fringe benefits, including the best sickness plan in the city, is due to our selectivity in hiring. Should these standards be eroded, over time, the employees will receive less favorable fringe benefits."

Evaluate the decision of Personnel in this case and its implementation.

747

INADEQUATE PERFORMANCE

Bill Carter had been hired by a former general manager as an administrative clerk, originally at a salary of $40 per week. His work had never been good, and several times during the past thirteen years his immediate managers had considered discharging him. But Bill was a pleasant, mild-mannered person who never committed any serious errors, although he lacked energy, perseverance, and intelligence. Also, he had a big family, was often heavily in debt, and aroused the sympathies of many who knew him. His assignments, however, were performed perfunctorily and often had to be redone by others. Although his work had been criticized, no serious penalties had ever been assessed. His case recently came up for review since his annual salary was now $15,000 and his present boss refused to continue him on his budget. During the course of the discussion among the top management group, the following points were made:

1. There was no way to justify his present salary. The work of the department had become more complex over the years at the same time that Carter's work had become more slovenly. He was not even suited for any lower-level positions, and such a demotion would be likely to aggravate his already marginal performance.

2. On the other hand, Carter was now 49; other jobs at his age and with his record would not be easy to find, and management was at fault for sustaining him over years of inadequate performance.

What should be done in the Bill Carter case? Consider, among others, the following two positions:

    a. Why should present management be penalized for the errors of omission and commission of an earlier management?

    b. At least some, if not all, of Carter's behavior is the product of what he learned in the company, namely, that marginal effort is quite enough and that one can get by with little accomplishment. His former supervisors taught him this.

SCANDAL

Hollis Corfu's name appeared in the local paper in connection with a rather scandalous event. Corfu was a young man in his early twenties who had been working in a modest clerical position for the Carp Insurance Agency for several years. His work had been considered very satisfactory, and he was a pleasant person, so everyone was shocked to see his name in print.

Some weeks later it was learned that Corfu had pleaded guilty and received a suspended sentence. By this time the manager of the Agency had received a large number of telephone calls from parents of other young people who worked for the firm. All indicated they were surprised that Carp employed people of questionable moral character, and many said they would urge their sons or daughters to resign unless Corfu was discharged. In one case, a job applicant turned down a position when it was offered, mentioning the case as her reason.

When the manager interviewed Corfu, he learned that the case was by no means clear-cut. There were real doubts that the lad had been involved in the incident, but he had received poor advice from his attorney and had pleaded guilty simply to avoid the cost and embarrassment of a court case. Of course, to the community at large he now *was* guilty.

1. How would you weigh the equities in this case?
2. What responsibilities does the firm have in this case?
3. If there is additional information you believe is required, make your own assumptions and consider the impact of these on your decision.

PROBLEM 4

HOW GOOD SHOULD A NEIGHBOR BE?

The Foremost Aluminum Company has a clear antidiscrimination employment policy. However, the company also subscribes to what it calls its "good neighbor" policy. It endeavors to behave in a way consistent with local mores and customs and to "fit" into each community in which it operates.

Thus, in plants located in Southern communities, Foremost has been less forceful in recruiting Negroes than it has at plants in other locations.

1. How do you evaluate these somewhat contradictory policies?
2. Would your assessment vary if you knew that the local union in a specific location (a) agreed with management's position or (b) disagreed?

Index

Name Index

Page number indicates footnote reference, unless accompanied by *t*.

Abegglen, James, 170
Abrams, Frank, 207
Abruzzi, Adam, 643, 647, 648
Adams, Leonard, 453
Adlinger, G. R., 578
Agnew, Paul C., 292
Alford, Theodore M., 533
Allen, Donna, 727
Allen, Louis A., 587
Allport, Gordon, 521
Anastasi, Ann, 468
Andrews, Kenneth R., 576, 577, 584
Andrews, Robert, 628
Arensberg, Conrad M., 40, 135, 144, 166, 191, 331, 573, 714
Argyl, Michael, 166, 185
Argyris, Chris, 22, 23, 44, 129, 203, 294, 319, 339, 363, 364, 570, 577, 582
Arrow, Kenneth, 359
Äs, Dagfin, 298
Asch, Solomon, 88

Back, Kurt, 81
Bailey, Joseph, 71
Bakke, E. Wight, 22
Baldamus, W., 14
Bales, R. F., 265, 272, 278, 280
Balinsky, Benjamin, 559
Barkin, Solomon, 613, 643
Barnard, Chester, 193
Barnes, Louis, 93
Barnes, Ralph, M., 638
Bass, Bernard, 471

Beaumont, Richard A., 718
Beane, Kenneth, 237, 268
Bedolis, Robert A., 675
Beem, H. P., 338
Behrend, Hilde, 667, 668
Belcher, David W., 602, 610, 628, 637, 646
Bell, Daniel, 41, 453, 646
Bellows, Roger M., 354
Bender, W. R. G., 546
Bendix, Reinhard, 9, 389
Benge, Eugene J., 601
Benne, Kenneth, 580
Bennett, James T., 51
Bennis, Warren G., 173, 580
Berg, Ivar, 91*t*, 98
Berger, Bennett M., 10
Berger, Ruth, 559
Berman, Hyman, 31
Berniger, Joseph, 465
Berry, Paul, 206
Bissell, Richard, 660
Blake, Robert R., 533, 583
Blake, Robert W., 579
Blau, Peter M., 48, 79, 156, 258, 338, 362
Blauner, Robert, 4, 12, 16, 21, 24, 29, 30, 32, 56, 57, 157, 166, 293
Block, Clifford H., 206
Bloomberg, Warner, Jr., 40
Blough, Roger, 732
Blum, Milton L., 696
Boggs, Stephen T., 21
Bradford, Leland P., 237, 265, 580
Brayfield, Arthur H., 135
Bright, James, 54
Bright, John R., 611
Broady, Leon, 698
Brooks, Earl, 534, 565

Brouha, Lucien A., 651
Brown, C. W., 524
Brown, J. A. C., 4
Brown, Wilfred, 206
Bunker, Douglas R., 583
Burger, Chester, 69
Burgess, Eugene, 170
Burk, Samuel L., 601
Burling, Temple, 19, 77, 85, 159, 160, 191, 345
Burns, Robert K., 557
Burtt, Harold E., 569
Butler, John, 553

Cannell, Charles E., 253
Caplow, Theodore, 348
Capwell, Dora, 17, 135
Cardall, Alfred J., 697
Carroll, Phil, 636
Cartwright, Dorwin, 93, 160, 185, 198, 298, 335
Cassell, Frank H., 530, 615, 629
Caulkins, D. Douglas, 170
Centers, Richard, 61
Chalupsky, Albert B., 630
Chamberlain, N., 723
Chambers, E. G., 697
Chandler, Margaret, 228, 442, 462, 506
Chapple, Eliot D., 235, 403, 416, 462, 464, 467, 606
Cheit, Earl F., 732, 733
Cherry, Colin, 232, 241
Chinoy, Ely, 9, 10, 37, 38
Chowdry, Kamla, 584
Christensen, C. R., 80, 91
Cioffi, Frank, 166, 185
Coates, Charles H., 63
Coch, Lester, 298
Coghill, Mary, 424

Subject Index